Introduction to Character Animation

PEARSON
Custom
Publishing

Printed in the United States of America

10 9 8 7 6 5 4 3

ISBN 0-536-90412-X

2004200353

AP/JS

Please visit our web site at *www.pearsoncustom.com*

PEARSON Custom Publishing

PEARSON CUSTOM PUBLISHING
75 Arlington Street, Suite 300, Boston, MA 02116
A Pearson Education Company

TABLE OF CONTENTS

Introduction

About the Book ix
Conventions Used in the Book x

Chapter 1—Basics of Animation

1.1 Introduction to Animation **1.3**
1.1.1 Animation Types 1.3
1.1.2 Animation Methods 1.6
1.1.3 Storyboarding 1.10
1.1.4 Principles of Animation 1.13
1.2 Animating with 3ds max 6 .... **1.20**
1.2.1 Animation Tools and Controls 1.20
1.2.2 Time Configuration 1.22
1.2.3 Using Transforms for Animation 1.25
Summary **1.31**
References **1.32**
Assignments **1.33**
Lab Exercises **1.35**
Exercise 1 .... 1.35
Exercise 2 .... 1.40
Exercise 3 .... 1.47
Project **1.52**
Scenario 1.52
Activities 1.52

Chapter 2—Using Track View

2.1 Introducing Track View **2.3**
2.2 Controlling Animation Using Track View **2.11**
2.2.1 Track View Curve Editor 2.11
2.2.2 Track View Dope Sheet 2.32
2.2.3 Optimizing Performance of Track View 2.40
Summary **2.46**
References **2.47**
Assignments **2.48**
Lab Exercise **2.49**
Exercise 1 .... 2.49
Project **2.63**
Activities 2.63

Chapter 3—Controllers and Constraints

3.1 Animation Controllers **3.3**
3.1.1 Types of Animation Controllers 3.3
3.1.2 Applying Controllers 3.4
Practice Questions **3.33**
3.2 Animation Constraints **3.34**
3.2.1 Types of Constraints 3.34
3.2.2 Animating with the Path Constraints 3.45
3.2.3 Animating with the Surface Constraint 3.49
Summary **3.53**
References **3.55**
Assignments **3.56**
Lab Exercises **3.57**
Exercise 1 .... 3.57
Exercise 2 .... 3.58
Exercise 3 .... 3.59
Exercise 4 .... 3.63
Exercise 5 .... 3.68
Exercise 6 .... 3.74
Exercise 7 .... 3.77
Exercise 8 .... 3.85
Project **3.90**
Activities 3.90

Chapter 4—Structuring for Animation

4.1 Hierarchies 4.3
4.1.1 Components of a Hierarchy 4.3
4.1.2 Kinematics 4.5
4.1.3 Animating Hierarchies 4.7
4.2 Standard Helper Objects 4.28
4.2.1 Dummy Helper Object 4.28
4.2.2 Grid Helper Object 4.30
4.2.3 Point Helper Object 4.32
4.2.4 Tape Helper Object 4.35
4.2.5 Compass Helper Object 4.37
4.2.6 Protractor Helper Object 4.38
4.3 Advanced Helper Objects 4.42
4.3.1 Manipulator Helper Objects 4.42
4.3.2 Atmospheric Effects 4.47
4.3.3 Creating an Animation with the Dummy Helper 4.63
Summary 4.67
References 4.69
Assignments 4.70
Lab Exercises 4.71
Exercise 1 .... 4.71
Exercise 2 .... 4.77
Project 4.82

Chapter 5—Character Animation

5.1 Character Model 5.3
5.1.1 Modeling Techniques 5.3
5.1.2 Creating a Suitable Model for Animation 5.5
5.1.3 Modifiers Used in Character Modeling 5.46
5.1.4 Types of Characters 5.58
5.2 Introducing Bones 5.61
5.2.1 Creating a Bone System 5.62
5.2.2 Object as a Bone 5.65
Summary 5.68
References 5.69
Assignments 5.70
Lab Exercises 5.71
Exercise 1 .... 5.71
Exercise 2 .... 5.77
Exercise 3 .... 5.88
Exercise 4 .... 5.100
Project 5.111
Activities 5.111

Chapter 6—Forward and Inverse Kinematics

6.1 Introducing Forward Kinematics **6.3**
6.1.1 Defining Forward Kinematics 6.3
6.2 Introducing Inverse Kinematics **6.8**
6.2.1 Applying Inverse Kinematics 6.8
6.2.2 Displaying IK Controls 6.10
6.2.3 End Effectors 6.12
6.2.4 Manipulator Helpers 6.13
6.2.5 Joint Constraints 6.19
6.3 Types of IK Solvers **6.24**
6.3.1 History-Dependent IK Solver 6.24
6.3.2 History-Independent IK Solver 6.26
6.3.3 IK Limb Solver 6.26
6.3.4 Spline IK Solver 6.27
6.4 Walk Cycle **6.31**
6.4.1 Walking Mechanism 6.31
6.4.2 Animating a Simple Walk Cycle 6.31
Summary **6.46**
References **6.48**
Assignments **6.49**
Lab Exercises **6.51**
Exercise 1 .... 6.51
Exercise 2 .... 6.58
Project **6.70**
Activities 6.70

Chapter 7—Skinning a Model

7.1 Introduction to the Skin Modifier **7.3**
7.1.1 Applying the Skin Modifier 7.3
7.1.2 Weighing the Skin Modifier 7.16
7.2 Deformations **7.21**
7.2.1 Modifying the Skin Object 7.22
7.2.2 Deformers 7.28
Summary **7.35**
References **7.37**
Assignments **7.38**
Lab Exercises **7.39**
Exercise 1 .... 7.39
Exercise 2 .... 7.43
Exercise 3 .... 7.45
Project **7.47**
Activities 7.47

Chapter 8—Animating Expressions

8.1 Characters in Motion **8.3**
8.1.1 Character Acting 8.3
8.1.2 Character Expressions 8.5
8.2 Animating the Eyes and Mouth **8.10**
8.2.1 Animating Eyes 8.10
8.2.2 Morpher Modifier 8.17
8.2.3 Lip-Sync 8.32
Summary **8.35**
References **8.37**
Assignments **8.38**
Lab Exercise **8.39**
Exercise 1 .... 8.39
Project **8.49**
Activities 8.49

Glossary

Glossary **G.1**

Bibliography

Bibliography **B.1**

Index

Index **I.1**

About the Book

This book discusses the process of creating character animations using the various tools offered by 3ds max.

Chapter 1 describes the types of animation and the ways of creating the same. The chapter also discusses the criticality of a storyboard for a character animation and the principles of animation.

Chapter 2 details the use of Track View to control animations. In addition, the chapter demonstrates controlling animation using the Curve Editor and Dope Sheet.

Chapter 3 describes how to define the path and direction for an animation using constraints and controllers.

Chapter 4 discusses the role of hierarchies in managing and rearranging various parts of an animation. It also defines helper objects that are useful in positioning objects and measuring dimensions.

Chapter 5 describes how to model and animate a character.

Chapter 6 explains how to apply bones and kinematics.

Chapter 7 describes how to apply skin modifiers and understand the uses of joint, bulge, and morph angles.

Finally, Chapter 8 of the book covers the various aspects of facial expressions such as the eyes and the mouth.

The treatment of concepts is simple yet comprehensive. The book presents fundamental concepts with illustrative examples and offers several opportunities to practice the knowledge and skills gained through lab exercises and assignments. These help verify that the learning objectives have been achieved. In addition, the practice questions and homework exercises enable students to attempt research exercises outside class.

Conventions Used in the Book

This book contains features, such as notes, tips, warnings, and references, identified by various icons. Each of these icons presents a different type of information. Following is the list of icons that will be used in the book.

A note provides information about the topic in context. This is additional information related to the topic.

A tip provides an alternative method for performing a task. It can also contain a simplified, although unconventional, method of doing a task.

Just-a-Minute presents nice-to-know information or a quick question that checks the learners' understanding of the current topic.

A warning informs you about the dire effects of an action. Focusing on these warnings reduces the likelihood that learners will make the same errors.

A reference provides links to Web sites or relevant books and white papers for further study on a particular topic.

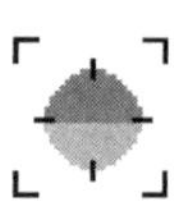

Each topic begins with objectives that inform learners about the learning outcome of a topic.

In addition, you will come across *italicized text* that represents newly introduced terms.

Basics of Animation

1

Improvement in technologies in the IT and the entertainment industry has led to an increase in demand for computer-created moving images. You can create these images using various methods, such as 3D and 2D computer graphics.

At the end of this chapter, you will be able to:

- Describe the various types of animation.
- Identify the methods of creating animation.
- Identify the need for storyboarding in the animation process.
- Explain the differences between the Autokey and Setkey modes of animation.

1.1 Introduction to Animation

1.2 Animating with 3ds max 6

1.1 Introduction to Animation

An animation is created when a series of images move in quick succession. Animation creation is based on the concept of persistence of vision, which means that an illusion of movement is created by a series of images. The retina of the human eye retains an image for one-tenth of a second and then picks up the next image. If a sequence of images moves past the vision in one-tenth of a second or less, the eye fails to keep pace with the quick changes and the images appear in a continuous sequence. You can create animation using computer graphics or images.

The history of animation can be dated back to the days when silent films were introduced. The first cartoon was created with an animated system of 12 images and films of about 500 to 600 images. In this section, you will learn about the various types of animation.

1.1.1 Animation Types

Identify the various types of animation.

Animation enables you to add effects to various objects, such as games, cartoons, and movies. The types of animation styles are:

- 2D
- 3D
- Stop frame
- Motion capture

2D Animation

2D animation uses hand-drawn drawings or 2D computer graphics. These graphics are created on the x-axis and the y-axis denoting length and breadth, respectively. The animator defines the keyframes of the animation, and the tween artist creates the necessary tweens.

Figure 1.1 displays a 2D hand-drawn animation of a boy removing his sweater. This animation was created on the x-axis and the y-axis.

Figure 1.1: Boy Removing His Sweater

Courtesy of Dorling Kindersley, by permission of Silver Fox Films Ltd.

3D Animation

In 3D animation, graphics are drawn on three axes: x, y, and z, which denote height, width, and depth, respectively. This makes 3D graphics look more real-life than 2D graphics.

Figure 1.2 shows the sequential frames of a 3D hand animation in the Max environment.

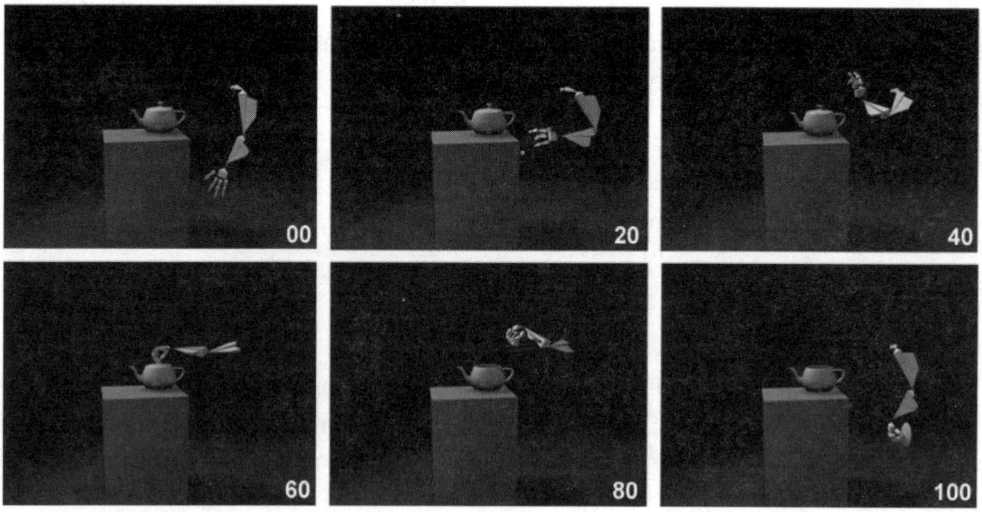

Figure 1.2: 3D Hand Animation in the Max Environment

Stop Frame

Stop frame is a technique that makes static objects appear as if they are moving. A film camera or a video camera shoots one frame at a time. The subject is moved a little and another shot is taken, and so on. Claymation and Wallace and Gromit are popular examples of Stop frame animation. Figure 1.3 shows a still of Wallace and Gromit.

Figure 1.3: Wallace and Gromit

Wallace & Gromit © Aardman/W&G Ltd 1989

Motion Capture

In motion capture, you capture the movement of a real object and map it to a computer-generated object. You can create simulated actors by capturing the motions of real actors. In this process, special markers are placed over the joints of actors. Then, a special hardware device samples the position or orientation of those markers in time and generates a set of motion data. This data is also known as motion curves. Motion capture has been used to produce incredibly realistic animation in many big movies, such as *Terminator 2* and *Star Wars.*

1.1.2 Animation Methods

Identify the various methods of creating animation.

Earlier, graphics were manually drawn to create animation. Today, many types of animation are created and generated on the computer. Some methods used to create animation are:

- Cel animation
- Keyframe animation
- Path animation
- Inverse kinematics (IK)
- Sprite animation

Cel Animation

Cel animation is a manual method. The term cel is derived from celluloid, which is a piece of transparent plastic. In this method, animated characters are drawn and colored on separate celluloid sheets. One or more background scenes are drawn on opaque sheets, and each character is placed on its background and photographed.

Figure 1.4 shows a background, a cel, and a combined graphic.

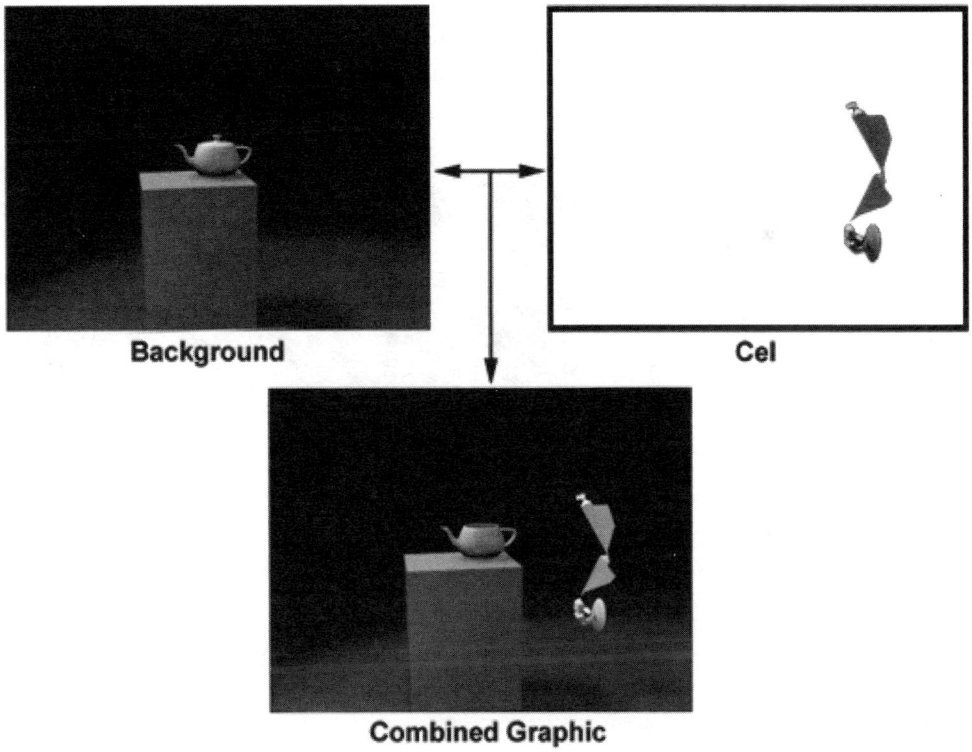

Figure 1.4: Background, a Cel, and a Combined Graphic

Although commonly used, cel animation is expensive and time-consuming. Only movie production houses such as Warner Bothers and Walt Disney can invest a lot of money to use cel animation. The movie *The Prince of Egypt* was created using cel animation.

Keyframe Animation

Keyframe animation is similar to cel animation. You can use keyframe animation method to create 3D animation. In this technique, the frames that show the start and end of a movement are known as keyframes. One artist, known as the key or master animator, draws the important stages or keyframes. The remaining intermediate stages of the animation are drawn by other artists called tween artists or are generated by using software. This applies to both 2D and 3D animation. In keyframe animation, the time taken to create an animation is reduced because many persons work simultaneously. Keyframe animation has been effectively used by computerized applications. Most applications allow you to specify the start and end keyframes and then automatically create the in-between stages. This technique is known as tweening.

In Figure 1.5, the images of a hand rising from below and picking up the lid are the keyframes. One is the start keyframe and the other is the end keyframe. The rest of the frames, or in-betweens, are generated by the software.

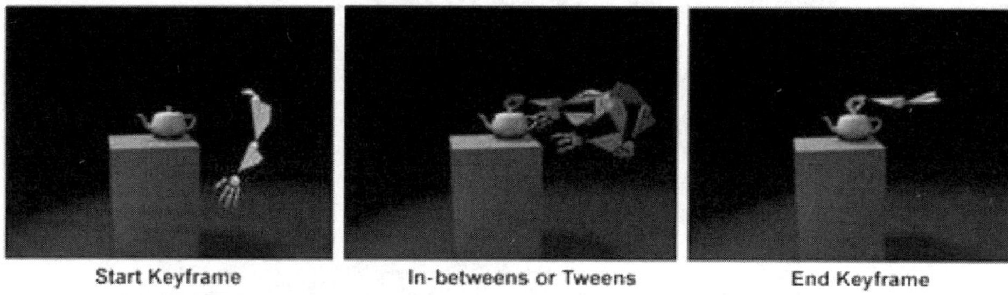

Figure 1.5: Start, Tweens, and End Keyframes

In 3ds max 6, you can create animation using the keyframe animation technique.

Path Animation

Path animation is another computer-based method used to create 2D and 3D animation. In this method, an object travels on a predefined path of straight lines, curves, or both. The shape of objects or figures can change.

Figure 1.6 displays a ball traveling on the dotted line path.

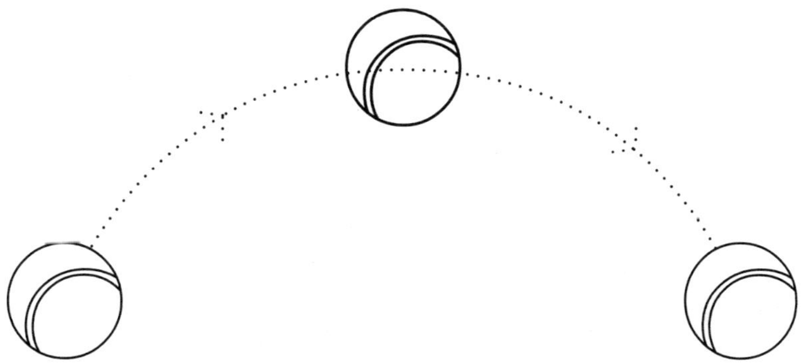

Figure 1.6: Ball Traveling on a Dotted Line Path

Inverse Kinematics

To understand inverse kinematics (IK), you must first understand forward kinematics (FK). Consider animating the rotation of a human arm. To create such an animation, you need to perform the following steps:

- Rotate the upper arm.
- Rotate the forearm.
- Rotate the wrist.

In FK, a top-to-bottom approach integrates the preceding actions. However, creating a human body or a skeleton in motion is a complex procedure because it involves the need to break and align the various parts at appropriate angles. To align a part, all the related parts of the body need to be aligned appropriately. For example, to align the wrist, the shoulder also needs to be aligned.

IK, unlike FK, follows a bottom-to-top approach. For example, to align the wrist, you need to specify the position of the various body parts. The angles of the related parts of the body, such as the forearm, the upper arm, and the shoulder, are determined automatically by the application. In other words, you need to specify the position for the body part that is lowest in the level of hierarchy.

Sprite Animation

Sprite animation is used in gaming and interfaced animation. Sprites are small files that control objects such as graphics, buttons, or text, and render them on a screen in real time. A sprite may contain the object, such as a hero who runs jumps, throws, and punches, or it may contain the moving background of a game. The graphics are all pre-rendered, but the animation is rendered in real time when you play the game. This type of animation is interactive.

While using sprite animation, it is difficult to make objects partially transparent or make them fade in and fade out of the screen. The quality and pace depends on the configuration of the computer because this animation is rendered in real time.

Table 1.1 lists the methods used to create 2D and 3D animation.

2D Animation	3D Animation
Cel animation	Keyframe animation
Keyframe animation	Path animation
Path animation	Inverse kinematics
	Sprite animation

Table 1.1: Methods Used to Create 2D and 3D Animation

1.1.3 Storyboarding

Identify the role of storyboarding in creating an animation.

The goal of any animation is to tell a story and capture the attention of a viewer. To tell the story, you need to create a storyboard, which is a pictorial outline that helps you visualize the animation by mapping the movement in each scene. The storyboard organizes your thoughts and ideas before you actually create the elements of an animation. In addition, it helps create a common understanding between the members of the production team. You can show the storyboard to a client for approval, before the actual production, to avoid rework.

The storyboard can be as simple as a few quick sketches on paper, or as detailed as an annotated drawing of every step in every scene. You can create storyboards for various types of animation. In this chapter, you will learn how to create storyboards for 3D animation.

Creating Detailed Storyboards for 3D Animation

If you want to create a detailed storyboard, you need to draw panels similar to those in comic books. In the panel, you need to include the following points:

- Storyboarding ensures that your animation models are realistic. For example, you can model a car using a rectangular box.
- After you sketch the basic form, divide it into animate and inanimate parts. Apply color, texture, and movement to each part. For example, the car might have black rubber tires that move in circles.

A storyboard enables you to plan for other animation components, such as:

- Character roles
- Scene changes
- Sequence design
- Sequence length
- Camera moves
- Light positions

To create a detailed storyboard, draw panels similar to those in comic books. In the panel, include:

- Clear markings, arrows, instructions, and a description about the activity in a scene.
- A caption stating the changes to occur in a scene and the scene's role and placement.

Figure 1.7 shows panels of a storyboard.

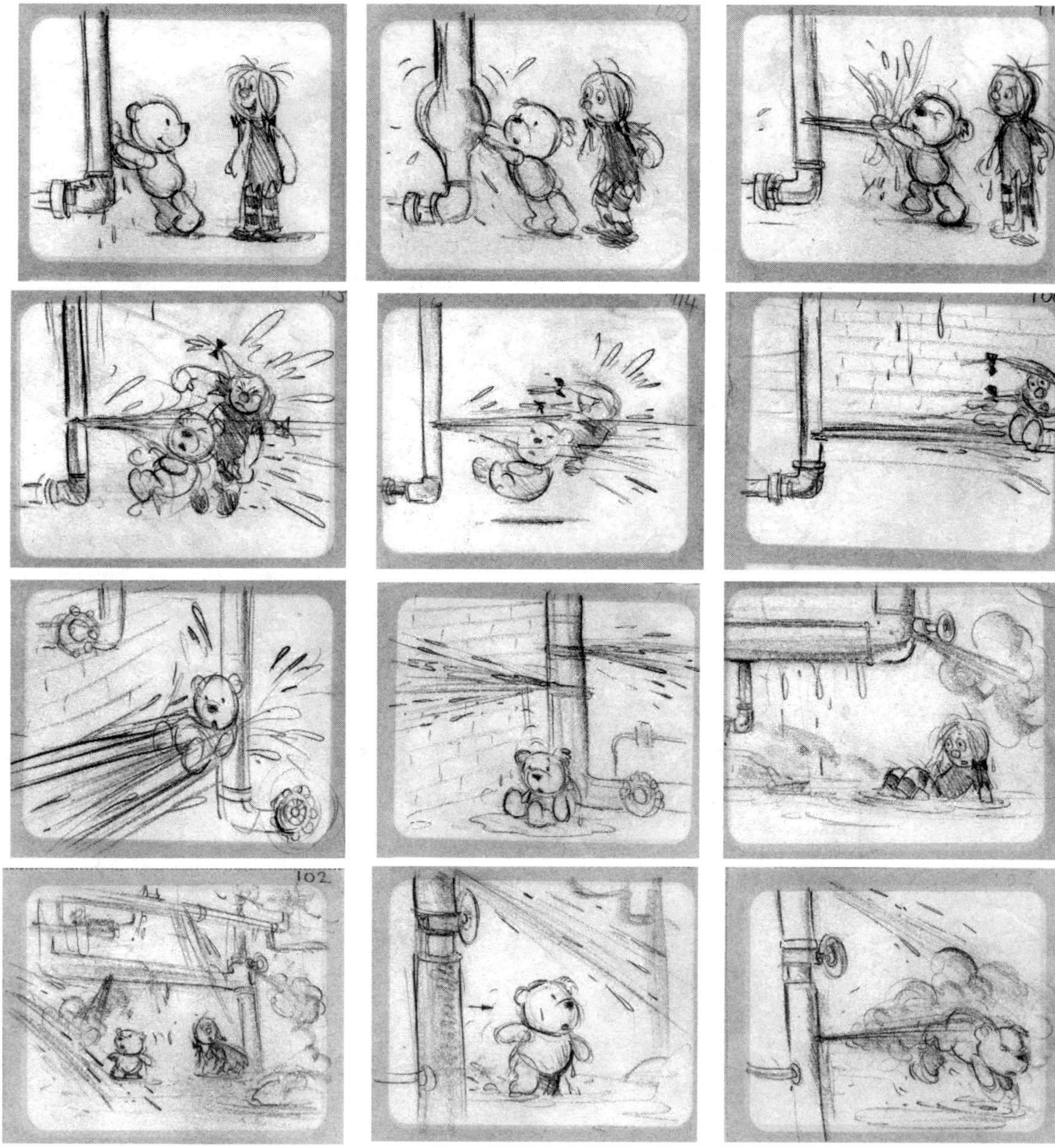

Figure 1.7: Storyboard

A finished storyboard looks similar to a well-illustrated story. It clearly communicates how the animation will be created and the effect it will generate.

1.1.4 Principles of Animation

Identify the principles of animation applied in a given situation.

You need to apply certain principles to an animation depending upon the script, the characters, and the action. The principles that govern believable animation are classified as:

- Principles related to an action
- Principles related to an overall animation

Principles Related to an Action

The principles related to an action define how an animation should behave when an action is performed. Some of the principles are:

- Squash and stretch
- Exaggeration
- Slow in and slow out
- Anticipation
- Follow through and Overlapping action
- Secondary motion
- Timing
- Arcs

Squash and Stretch

Squash and stretch helps you demonstrate a character's rigidity or elasticity by deforming its shape during an action. You need to always maintain a character's volume, or the animation will appear unrealistic. To retain a character's volume, a stretch in one direction (Y-axis) must be accompanied by a squash in the other (X-axis). For example, when a character flexes its forearm, the muscles in its upper arm get squashed and a bulge (bicep) appears. This bulge disappears when you straighten the arm because the muscles stretch. Figure 1.8 depicts squash and stretch of a character's muscles.

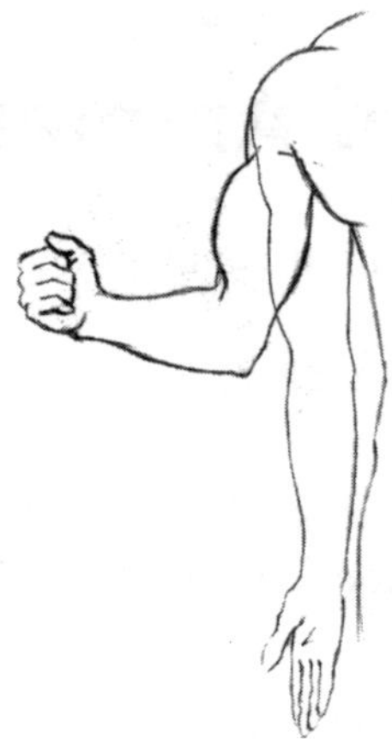

Figure 1.8: Squash and Stretch of a Character's Muscles

Exaggeration

To entertain the audience, you can occasionally show them what they do not see in real life. This is the principle of exaggeration, usually used to present an element of humor. While you can use your imagination and experiment with exaggeration, you need to be very careful. Too much exaggeration may destroy the believability of the scene. An example of exaggeration is a dog rolling out its tongue on seeing a bone and the tongue touching the ground as the dog salivates. Figure 1.9 shows an exaggerated example of a dog with a long face.

Courtesy of Photodisc/Getty Images

Figure 1.9: Example of Exaggeration.

Slow In and Slow Out

Slow in refers to the gradual deceleration of the action of a character and slow out refers to the acceleration of an action performed by a character. You cannot have an object, a character, or part of a character's body such as a limb, move with the same speed throughout an animation. The object picks up speed gradually until it gains momentum and then gradually comes to a stop.

Figure 1.10 shows the slow in (ease in) and the slow out (ease out) process in a paper plane flying action.

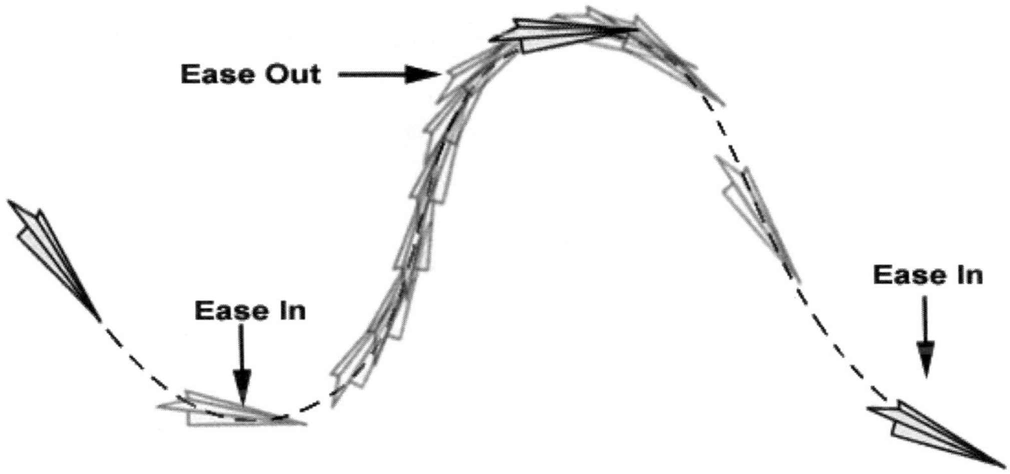

Figure 1.10: Showing Slow In (Ease In) and Slow Out (Ease Out)

Anticipation

Most actions in an animation occur in three parts: preparing for the main action, the main action, and the end of the action. The lead-in to the main action is called anticipation. Figure 1.11 shows the anticipation before hitting a ball.

Figure 1.11: Player Anticipating the Ball

Follow Through and Overlapping Action

Follow through is the movement beyond the point of the end of the main action. For example, after a character throws a ball, the arm swings backward before coming to a halt next to the body.

After a follow-through action, when a body part or the character finally comes to a stop, some other body part or object unrelated to the main action may still be in motion. This is called the overlapping action.

While throwing a ball, the character's arm comes to a halt next to the body. Here, the character's clothes continue to move and their movement overlaps that of the hand coming to a halt.

Secondary Action

In most animation, characters perform additional actions to support the main action or to create interest and realism. These are called secondary actions. For example, a character, while reading a book, scratches its head or adjusts its glasses. In this example, the main action is reading the book, and the secondary actions are scratching the head and adjusting the glasses.

The main action and the secondary action may not be directly related to each other, but the secondary action helps create interest and realism. The secondary action should not distract the audience from viewing the main action.

Timing

The time taken to perform a certain action gives meaning to the action. For example, a tired character can be shown as walking slowly. On the other hand, if you want to animate an excited character, you can make the character walk fast.

Timing is also related to the weight of a character because heavy characters take longer to accelerate and decelerate than the characters that are not heavy. For example, an overweight character takes longer to gain speed or to slow down while running than a lean character.

Arcs

In real life, almost all actions follow a curved path or an arc, not a straight line. For an animation to be believable, characters need to follow an arc, or else the movements might appear unbelievable. For example, when a character picks up a glass from a table, its arm follows a curved path and not a straight line.

Figure 1.12 shows a formation of an arc while lifting a glass.

Figure 1.12: Formation of an Arc While Lifting a Glass

Principles Related to an Overall Animation

The principles related to an overall animation define how you should prepare and present an animation for effective communication. The principles in this category are:

- Staging
- Appeal

Staging

Staging defines the presentation of an idea, an action, a character, or an object in such a way that the audience understands it clearly. If this principle is not followed, an animation may lose its impact and appeal. For example, if you animate an old character walking with a stick, showing the character's profile is preferred to showing its front view. The walking stick appears as a separate entity in the profile and the action is clearer to the audience.

Figure 1.13 shows an old man with a walking stick.

Figure 1.13: Old Man with a Walking Stick

Appeal

Appeal defines the charm and attraction of a character. This does not imply that only good characters have appeal and bad characters have none. In fact, every character in a scene should be appealing so that the audience finds the animation interesting.

Practice Questions

1. List the various types of animation used to create different objects.
2. What is cel animation?
3. What are the three things that you need to include while writing a storyboard?
4. List the two principles related to an action of a computer animation.
5. List the principles related to overall animation.

1.2 Animating with 3ds max 6

With the growth of technology, various GUI-based software packages are available for creating 3D animations. These packages enable you to provide real-life effects, such as different types of lighting, color, and texture while providing tools and techniques to simplify character animation. 3ds max 6 is an animation software package developed by Discreet. It provides tools and options to create real-life 3D characters. This section introduces 3ds max 6 and identifies the parts and the features in its interface that enable you to create animation.

1.2.1 Animation Tools and Controls

Identify the various tools and controls available in 3ds max 6.

3ds max 6 enables you to create animation using various objects, such as models, materials, lights, and cameras. The tools and controls that help create animation in 3ds max 6 are:

- Time slider and current frame field
- Track bar and keys
- Playback controls

Time Slider and Current Frame Field

The time slider control is a movable rectangular tab with arrows, as shown in Figure 1.14.

Figure 1.14: Time Slider Control

The time slider moves forward to the selected frame while you view the animation in 3ds max 6. You need to drag the time slider forward or backward to move to a particular frame. The time slider also displays the total number of frames. In Figure 1.14, the number 50 represents the current frame and the number 100 represents the total number of frames.

Track Bar and Keys

The track bar displays a timeline of frames. As you make changes to an object in a frame in 3ds max 6, a key indicates the keyframe created in the track bar. The track bar's frame indicator is colored light blue to indicate the current frame. The Track bar consists of keys or keyframes of multiple animated objects. You need to click, and then drag the keys on the track bar to select, reposition, or delete keys.

Playback Controls

The lower bar in the 3ds max 6 window displays playback controls to view the objects animated in the scene in different viewports in 3ds max 6. Figure 1.15 shows the playback controls.

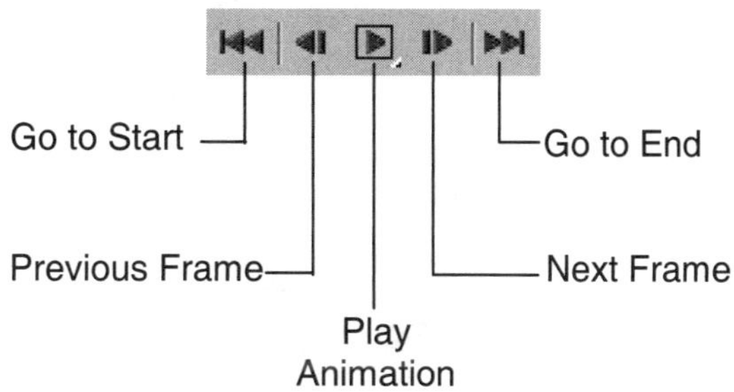

Figure 1.15: Playback Controls

Table 1.2 describes the various functions of playback controls.

Name of the Button	Icon	Description
Go to Start	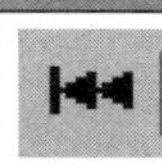	Enables you to move to the first frame in the animation sequence.
Previous Frame		Enables you to move to the previous frame in the animation sequence.
Play Animation		Plays the animation from the current frame onwards in the selected viewport. When clicked, it changes into a stop button to stop the animation.
Next Frame		Enables you to move the next frame in the animation sequence.
Go to End	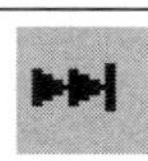	Enables you to move to the last frame in the animation sequence.

Table 1.2: Playback Controls

1.2.2 Time Configuration

Identify the various time configuration settings possible in 3ds max 6.

3ds max 6 enables you to modify time configurations using the Time Configuration dialog box, which provides the settings for Frame Rate, Time Display, Playback, and Animation. You can use this dialog box to perform various actions, such as changing, stretching, or rescaling the length of your animation. In addition, this dialog box enables you to set the start and end frames of the active time segment animation. You can access this dialog box using the Time Configuration button, which is located on the lower-right corner of the status bar.

When you click the  Time Configuration button, the Time Configuration dialog box appears, as shown in Figure 1.16.

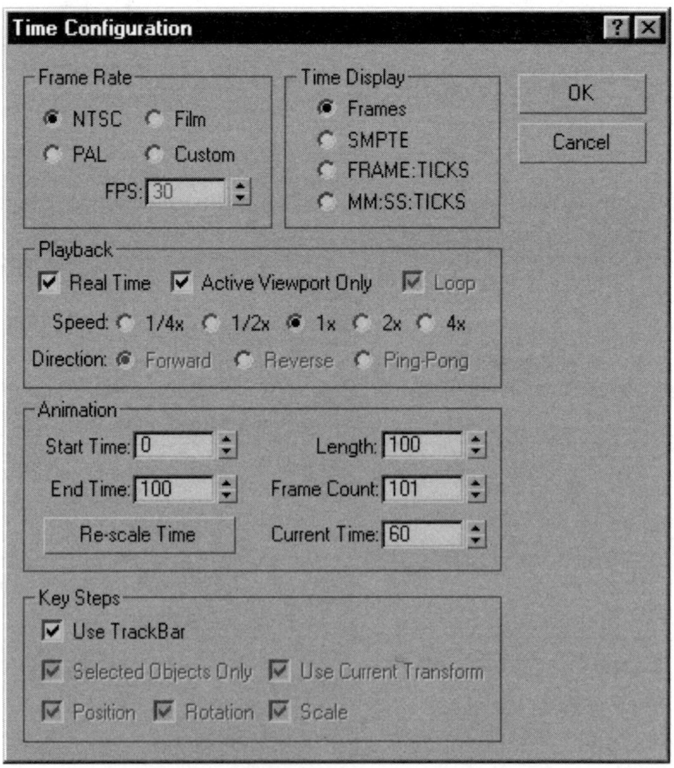

Figure 1.16: Time Configuration Dialog Box

The Time Configuration dialog box provides the following sections for selecting the appropriate settings:

- Frame Rate
- Time Display
- Playback
- Animation
- Key Steps

Frame Rate

The frame rate of an animation is expressed in frames per second (FPS). This refers to the number of frames the software displays and renders for every second of real time. The Frame Rate section consists of four option buttons that enable you to set the frame rate. This section provides you the flexibility to either choose from the standard FPS or specify your own FPS by adjusting the spinner. It consists of the following options:

- National Television Standards Committee (NTSC): Enables you to set the frame rate used for television (approximately 30 frames per second). This video standard is used in North America, Central and South America, and Japan.
- Film: Enables you to set the frame rate used in movies (approximately 24 frames per second).
- Phase Alternate Line (PAL): Enables you to set the frame rate used in Europe and Asia (approximately 25 frames per second).
- Custom: Enables you to set your own frame rate using the adjoining text box.

Time Display

The Time Display section enables you to specify the method for displaying time in the time slider and throughout the program. It enables you to set the duration of the animation. This section provides the following options:

- Frames: Enables you to display the number of frames in an animation in 3ds max 6.
- Society of Motion Picture Technical Engineers (SMPTE): Enables you to display time in minutes: seconds: frames.
- FRAME: TICKS: Enables you to display frame numbers and ticks elapsed in the current frame. In one second, there are a maximum of 4800 ticks. The number of ticks depends on the number of frames per second.
- MM: SS: TICKS: Enables you to display minutes: seconds: ticks.

Playback

3ds max 6 enables you to play your animation at a specified rate that depends on various items, including the complexity of the scene, the number of objects moving in the scene, and the geometry display mode. For example, the worst case is a camera move in shaded mode, in which the viewport is filled with detailed geometry. In these cases, you need to simplify the viewport display using either the wireframe display or, in extreme cases, the box display mode. The Playback section consists of the following options:

- Real time: Enables you to play the animation according to the frame rate and sets the missing frames.
- Active Viewport Only: Enables you to play the animation in the selected or the active viewport.
- Loop: Enables you to loop the animation but works only when the Real Time checkbox is not selected.
- Speed: Enables you to set the speed of the animation in the viewport.
- Direction: Enables you to set the animation to play forward, backward, or ping-pong.

Animation

The Animation section of the Time Configuration dialog box allows you to determine the time span of the animation. This option provides the following options:

- Start Time/End Time: Enables you to set the number of active frames. The Start Time, the End Time, or the frame numbers are displayed on the time slider.
- Length: Enables you to set the number count in the actively used frames decided by the Start Time and End Time fields.
- Frame Count: Enables you to set the number of frames to be rendered. The number of frames is always one more than the actual length.
- Current Time: Enables you to display the current frame of the animation in the field.

Key Steps

The Key Steps section enables you to determine the method through which the Key Mode button works. It consists of the following options:

- Use Track Bar: Enables the Key Mode to use all the keys in the track bar.
- Selected Objects Only: Enables the Key Mode to consider the transform values of only the selected objects.
- Use Current Transform: Enables the Key Mode to work only in the current selected type of the transform key.
- Position: Enables the Key Mode to work only in the position transform key type.
- Rotation: Enables the Key Mode to work only in the rotation transform key type.
- Scale: Enables you to specify the Key Mode in the scale transform type.

1.2.3 Using Transforms for Animation

Identify the features of the various types of transform animation.

3ds max 6 enables you to transform your object with respect to the position, the rotation, and the length of the object. You can transform the object by turning on the Auto Key button and then by performing the transform at any frame other than Frame 0. For example, consider a scenario where you want to animate an object between three points in 3ds max 6. To do this, perform the following steps:

1. Click the **Auto Key** button in the 3ds max 6 window. The Auto Key button and the highlight border around the active viewport turn red in color.
2. Drag the time slider to Frame 25, and move the object from point A to point B.
3. Drag the time slider to Frame 50, and move the object from point B to point C.
4. Click the **Auto Key** button to stop recording.
5. Click the **Play** button. The object moves from point A to point B over frames 0 to 25 and then proceeds to point C over Frames 26 to 50.

3ds max 6 enables you to combine several transforms in a single animation sequence so that an object appears to move as it rotates and changes in size. To transform an object, you need to select an object, and then click any transform button on the main toolbar to display the Transform gizmo icon of the object. Transform gizmos are viewport icons that enable you to quickly select one or two axes when transforming a selection with a mouse. Select axes by placing the mouse over any axes of the icon, and then drag the mouse to transform the selection along the axes. In addition, when moving or scaling an object, you can use other areas of the gizmo to perform transforms along any two axes simultaneously. 3ds max 6 provides the following types of transform gizmos:

- Move transforms
- Rotate transforms
- Scale transforms
- Squash transforms

Using the Move Transform Gizmo

The Move Transform gizmo includes plane handles and the option to use a center box handle. You can select any of the axes handles to constrain movement to those axes. In addition, plane handles enables you to constrain movement to the XY, YZ, or XZ planes. The selection hotspot is within the square formed by the plane handles.

To apply move transform, perform the following steps:

1. Select the  **Move Transform** button.
2. Click the object to select it.
3. Drag the mouse on any of the three axes to apply the move transform. Figure 1.17 shows the effect of move transform.

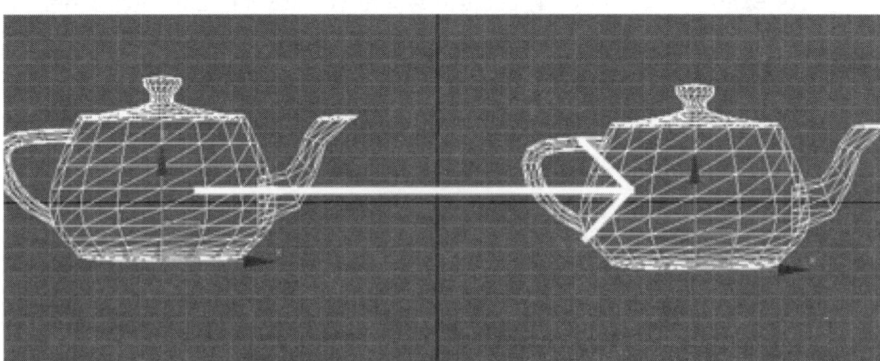

Figure 1.17: Effect of Move Transform

Using the Rotate Transform Gizmo

3ds max 6 provides the Rotate Transform gizmo, built around the concept of a virtual trackball. This type of gizmo enables you to rotate an object along the X-, Y-, or Z-axes using free rotation. You can also rotate the object on a plane perpendicular to the viewport. Axes handles are circles around the trackball. You can drag axes handles, and you can rotate the object along those axes. As you rotate along the X-, Y-, or Z-axes, a transparent slice provides a visual representation of the direction and amount of rotation. In addition to XYZ rotation, you can also use free rotation or the viewport handle to rotate objects.

To apply rotate transform, perform the following steps:

1. Select the  **Rotate Transform** button.
2. Click the object to select it.
3. Drag the mouse on any of the three axes to apply the move transform. Figure 1.18 shows the effect of rotate transform.

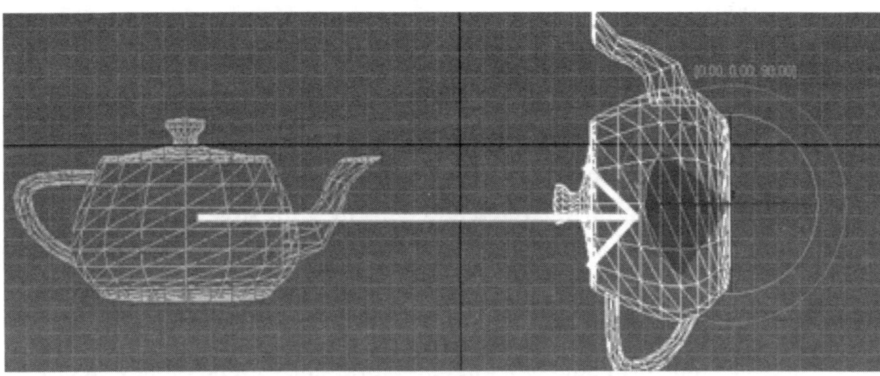

Figure 1.18: Effect of Applying Rotate Transform

Using the Scale Transform Gizmo

The Scale Transform gizmo enables you to perform uniform and non-uniform scaling without changing the selection on the main toolbar. To perform uniform scaling, drag the object to the center of the gizmo. To perform non-uniform scaling, drag the object on a single axis or a plane handle.

To apply scale transform, perform the following steps:

1. Select the  **Scale Transform** button.
2. Click the object to select it.

3. Drag the mouse to the center of the gizmo of the object to apply the Uniform Scale transform.

   Figure 1.19 shows the effect of applying scale transform.

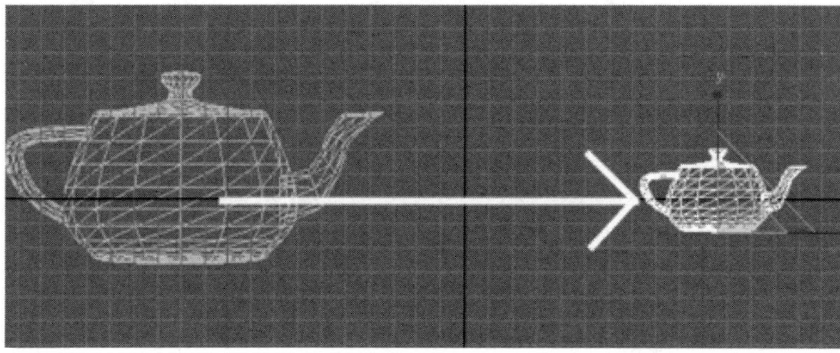

Figure 1.19: Effect of Applying Scale Transform

TIP: To perform a squash operation, you must click Select and Squash on the main toolbar.

The scale transform gizmo provides the feedback by changing its size and shape. In the case of a uniform scale, it will grow or shrink as the mouse moves. During non-uniform scaling, the gizmo will stretch and deform while dragging. However, the gizmo will return to its original size and shape after the mouse button is released.

Using the Squash Transform Gizmo

Squash Transform helps maintain the original volume of an object while scaling the two axes in different directions. You can restrict object scaling about the X-, Y-, or Z-axes, or to any two axes. You can select the squash tool from the main toolbar, as shown in Figure 1.20.

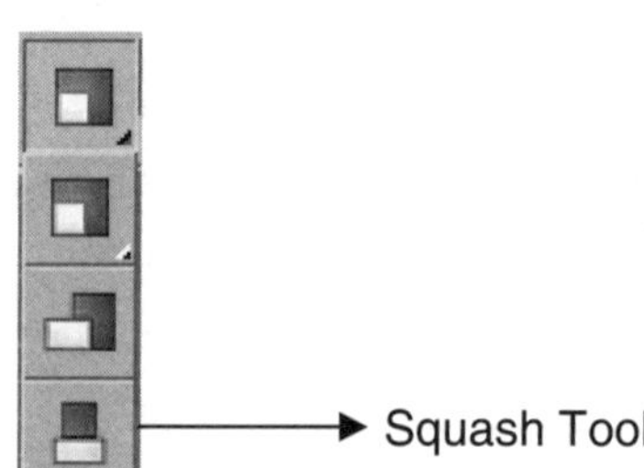

Figure 1.20: Squash Tool

You can select an object by clicking on it and scale it by dragging the mouse. In Figure 1.21, you can see the effect of the squash tool. It deforms the object in a particular axes keeping the volume the same.

Figure 1.21: Effect of Squash on an Object

To apply squash transform, perform the following steps:

1. Select the  **Squash Transform** button.
2. Click the object to select it.
3. Drag the mouse to the center of the gizmo of the object to apply the Squash Transform, as shown in Figure 1.22.

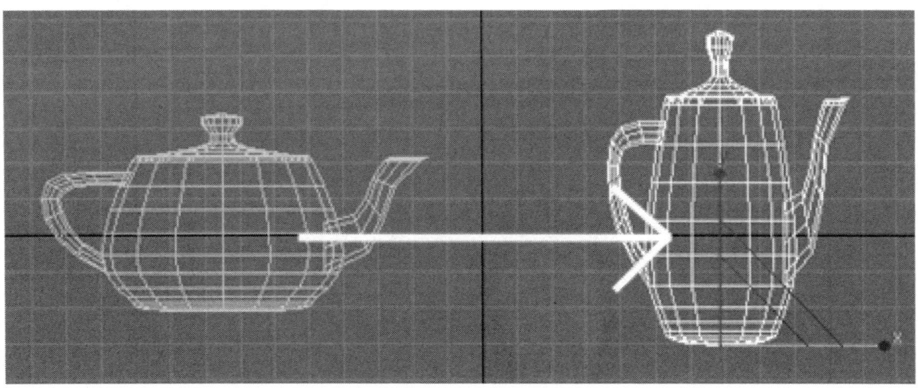

Figure 1.22: Effect of Applying Squash Transform

Always use uniform scaling for objects because it affects the attributes of other objects. In addition, uniform scaling can be used to make changes in the axes for scaling the objects.

Practice Questions

1. Define NTSC.
2. List the time configuration settings.
3. What are the various transform gizmos used in 3ds max 6?

Summary

- An animation is created when a sequence of images moves in quick succession. Animations are based on the concept of persistence of vision.
- Movies, cartoons, and games use the following types of animation:
  - Two-dimensional (2D)
  - Three-dimensional (3D)
  - Stop frame
  - Motion capture
- The methods used to create animation are:
  - Cel animation
  - Keyframe animation
  - Path animation
  - Inverse Kinematics
  - Sprite animation
- A storyboard is a pictorial outline that enables you to visualize the animation by mapping the movement in each scene.
- You need to apply certain principles to an animation in varying combinations depending upon the script, the characters, and the action.
- 3ds max 6 provides a toolbar for providing shortcut methods to the functionality available in the menus.
- 3ds max 6 enables you to create animation using various objects, such as models, materials, lights, and cameras.
- 3ds max 6 enables you to modify time configurations using the Time Configuration dialog box, which provides settings for frame rate, time display, playback, and animation.
- You can use the Time Configuration dialog box to perform various actions, such as changing, stretching, or rescaling the length of your animation.

References

- http://www.discreet.com/docs/products/3dsmax/3dsmax6_techspec.pdf (February 10, 2004)
- http://www.siggraph.org/education/materials/HyperGraph/animation/character_animation/principles/prin_trad_anim.html (February 10, 2004)
- http://www.evl.uic.edu/ralph/508S99/contents.html (February 10, 2004)
- http://home.comcast.net/~harrymott/principles.html (February 10, 2004)
- http://www.animationarena.com/principles-of-animation.html (February 10, 2004)
- http://ali.apple.com/ali_media/Users/1000313/files/others/animationprinciples.pdf (February 10, 2004)
- http://www.toon3d.com/help/animating.html (February 10, 2004)
- http://www.miralab.unige.ch/5teaching/assdb/htmls/StudentFiles/Cours_3DSMax/A02_TimeConfig.pdf (February 10, 2004)
- http://www.codecolony.de/opengl.htm#Trans1Ani (February 10, 2004)

Assignments

1. Describe the various types of animation.
2. What is the function of cel animation?
3. What is the function of keyframe animation?
4. How does a storyboard help in the process of animation?
5. List some of the principles related to overall animation.
6. What is the difference between NTSC and PAL frame rates?
7. What is a transform gizmo?
8. List the sections that you need to include in a storyboard in the process of animation.

Lab Exercises

Exercise 1

Objective

- Create an animation using the move and rotate transforms.

Problem Statement

Health Life, a pharmaceutical company, wishes to produce a commercial to promote its new health drink Energy Plus. You are working for an animation company that has been approached by the agency representing the firm to produce a 10-second animated spot. The short commercial consists of two shots: the first short is a pan of the basketball court as the animated character Beano slam-dunks the basketball. In the second shot, Beano delivers the punch line of the commercial to the camera. Create an appropriate 10-second animated spot.

Lab Setup

- 3ds max 6

Procedure

To create an animated spot, perform the following steps:

1. Create a primitive object and place it at –90, 0, and 70 at the x-, y-, and z-coordinates in the front viewport, as shown in Figure 1.23.

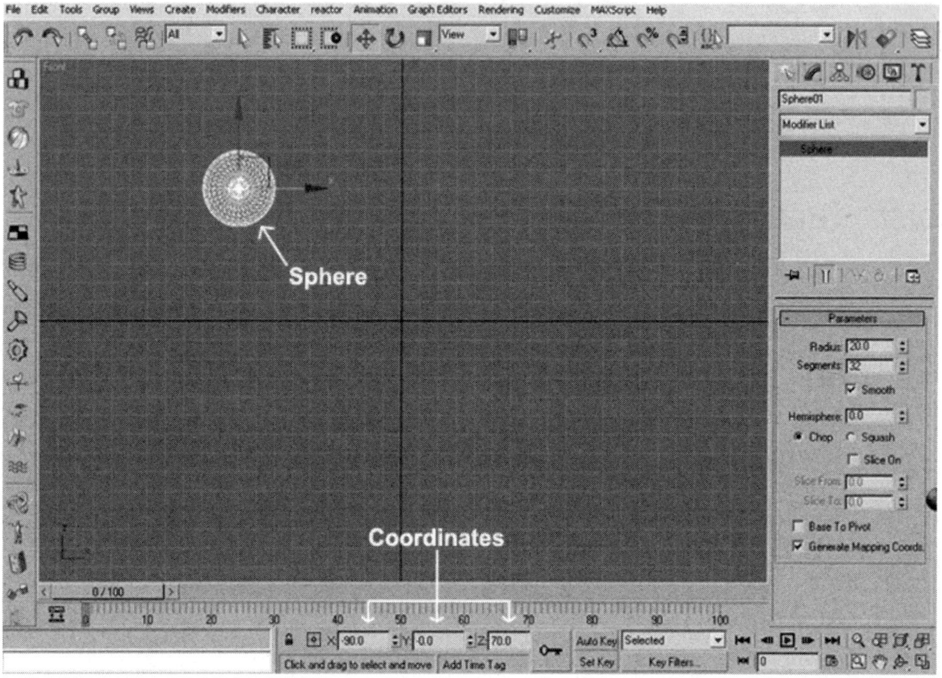

Figure 1.23: Ball Placed in the Front Viewport

2. Move the Time Slider to 100 and switch to the Auto Key mode, as shown in Figure 1.24.

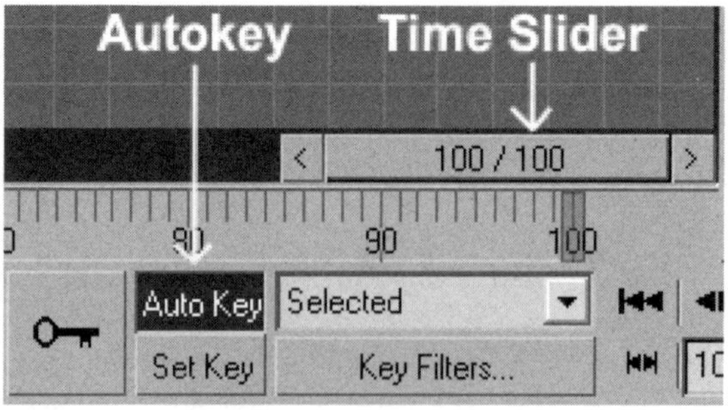

Figure 1.24: Auto Key Mode

3. With the help of the Move Transform button, relocate the object in space, as shown in Figure 1.25. Here, the new coordinates of the object are 130, 0, and -80.

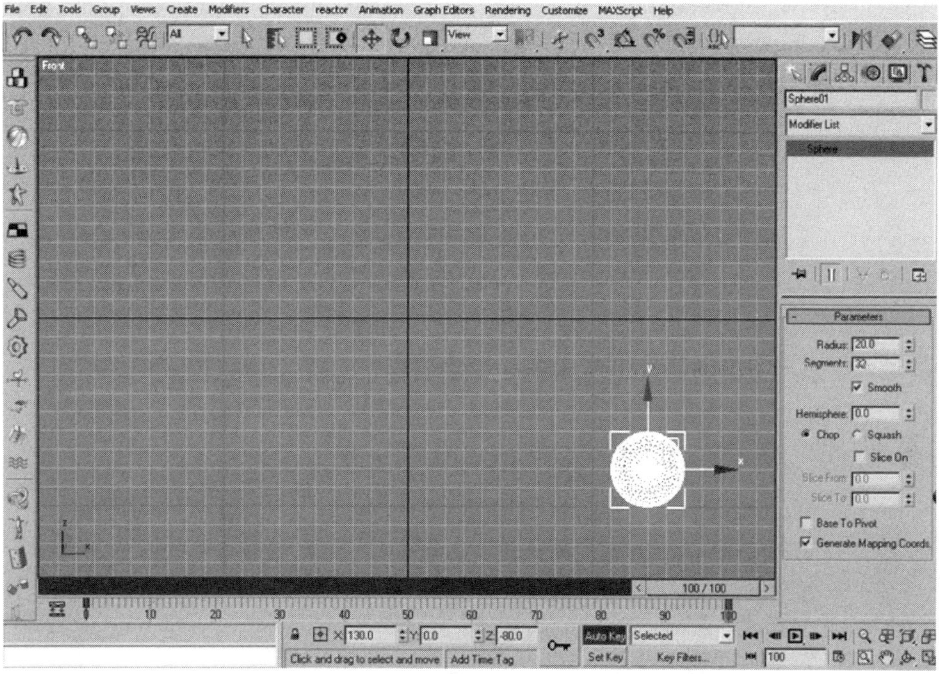

Figure 1.25: Object Relocated

4. With the help of the **Rotate Transform** button, rotate the sphere by 359° manually around the y-axis, as shown in Figure 1.26.

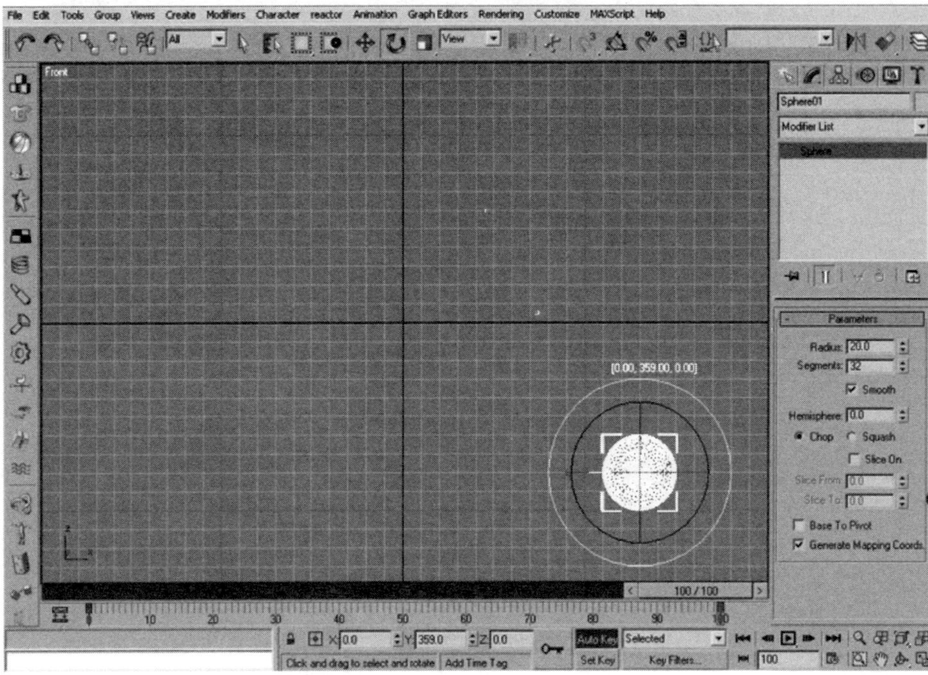

Figure 1.26: Object Rotated

5. Switch off the Auto Key button. Select the Perspective viewport, and click the 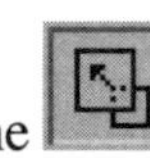 **Maximize Toggle** button.
6. Play the animation.
7. Save the file as **ch01_lab_ex1_sol.max**.

Figure 1.27 shows the resulting animation in different frames.

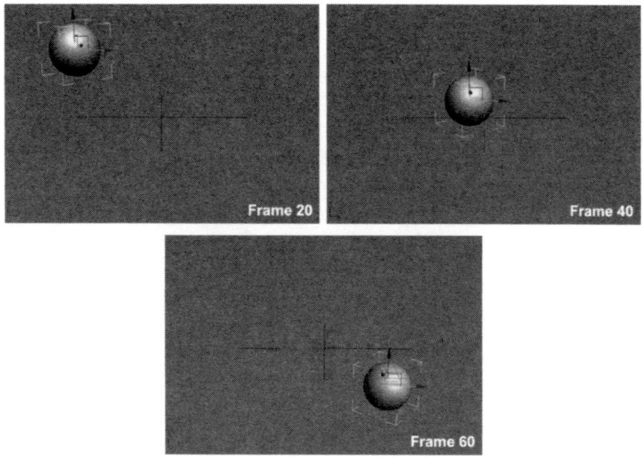

Figure 1.27: Final Animation

Lab Activity Checklist

S. No.	Tasks	Completed	
		Yes	No
1.	Created the primitive object		
2.	Animated the primitive		
3.	Applied the Move and Rotate Transform		

Exercise 2

Objective

- Create a simple animation.

Problem Statement

Create an animation of a ball jumping on the steps. The max file ch01_lab_ex2_model.max is available in Student CD.

Lab Setup

- 3ds max 6

Procedure

To create a simple animation of a ball jumping on the steps:

1. Click **File** on the menu bar to load the objects of the ball and the steps.
2. Click **Open**. The Open File dialog box appears.

3. Select the file **ch01_animatedball.max** file, and click **Open**. A ball and the steps appear in the viewport. Figure 1.28 displays the ball and the steps.

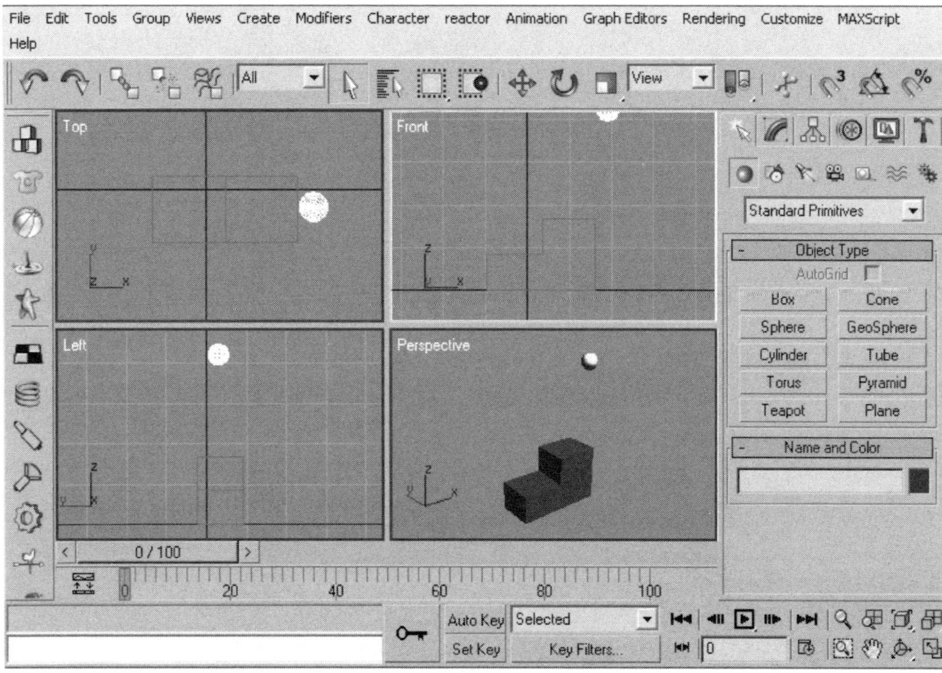

Figure 1.28: Ball and Steps

4. Click **Auto Key**. Note that the button and the time slider turn red to indicate the animate mode.
5. Move the time slider to **Frame 20**.
6. Select the ball using **Select and Move**.
7. Click and drag the ball to the top of the steps.

As you move the ball, a key is created in the track bar. The first key of the animation also generates a key at the start of Frame 0.

Figure 1.29 displays the ball placed on top of the steps.

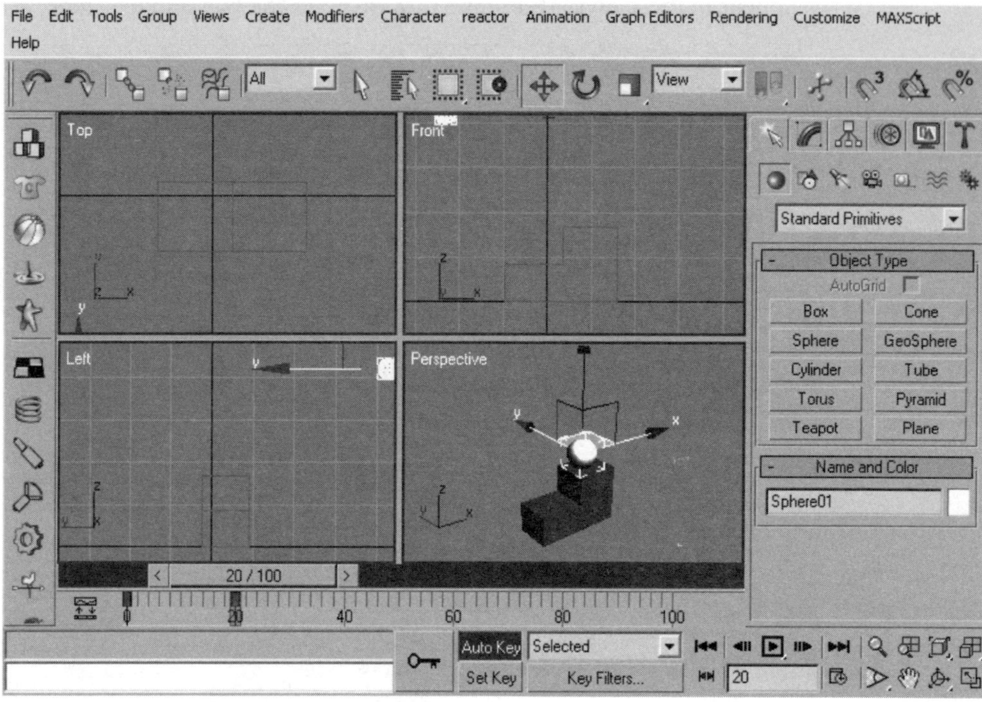

Figure 1.29: Ball Placed on Top of the Steps

8. Move the time slider to **Frame 40**.

9. Move the ball upward in the front viewport. A key is created at Frame 40 on the track bar. Observe the x and y dimensions corresponding to the change in the x and y fields in the lower bar. Figure 1.30 displays the upward movement of the ball.

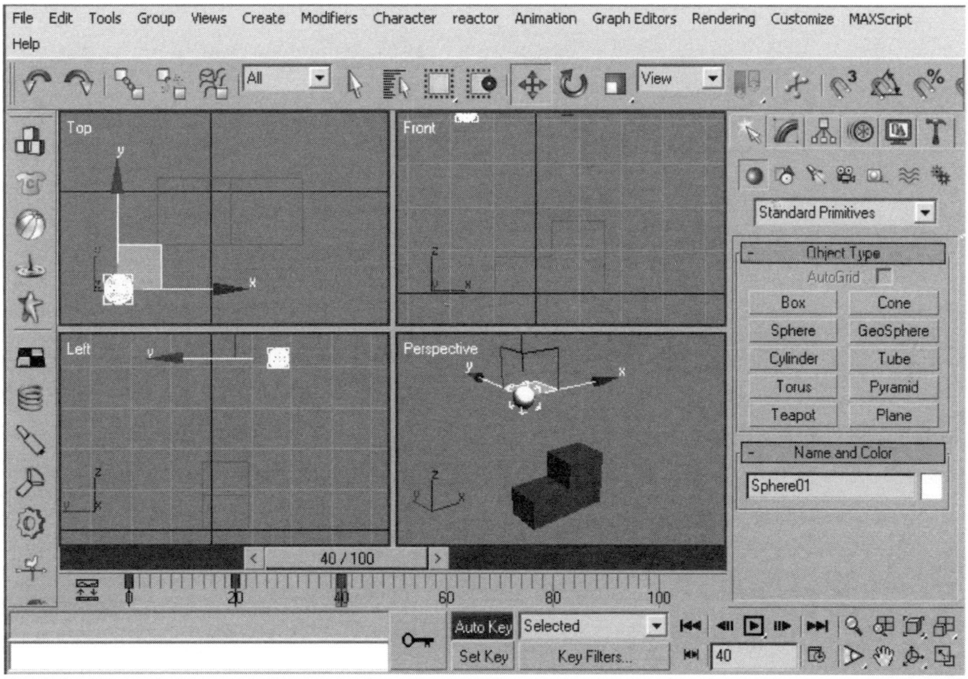

Figure 1.30: Upward Movement of the Ball

10. Move the time slider to **Frame 60**.

11. Move the ball to the lower step in the front viewport. A key is created at Frame 60 in the track bar. Figure 1.31 displays the ball on the lower step.

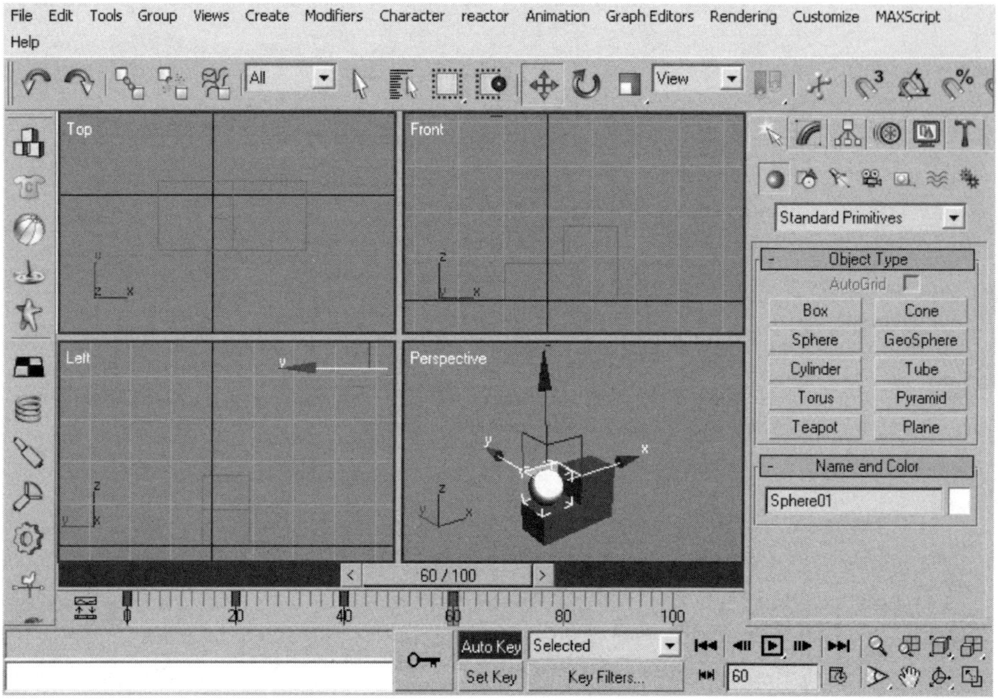

Figure 1.31: Ball on the Lower Step

12. Move the time slider to **Frame 80**.

13. Move the ball upwards in the front viewport.

    A key is created at Frame 80 in the track bar. Figure 1.32 displays the ball movement from the lower step to the front viewport.

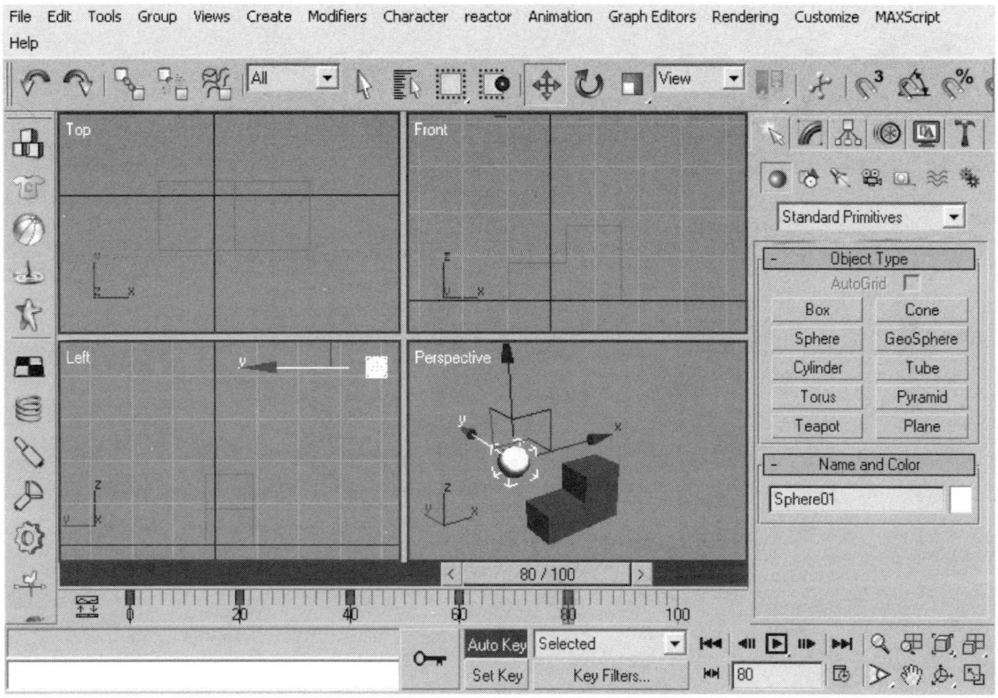

Figure 1.32: Ball Moves Upwards from the Lower Step

14. Move the time slider to **Frame 100**.

15. Place the ball on the ground at the bottom of the steps.
    A key is created at Frame 100 in the track bar. Figure 1.33 displays the ball placed at the bottom of the steps.

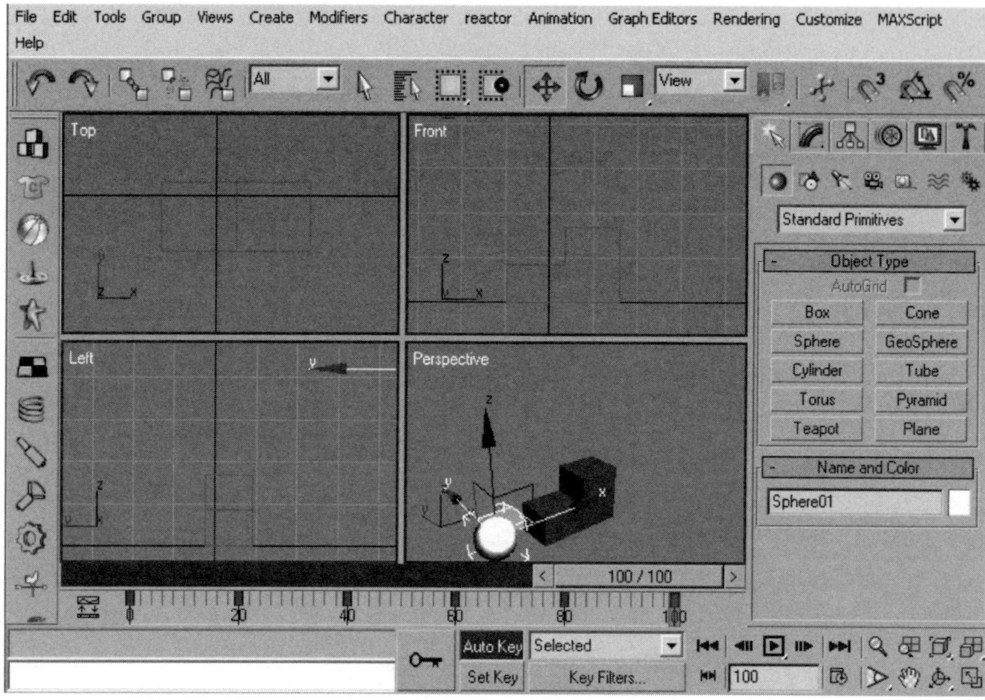

Figure 1.33: Ball at the Bottom of the Steps

16. Click **Auto Key** to deactivate it.
17. Click **Play** to play the animation. Observe the ball jump on the steps.
18. Save the file as **ch01_lab_ex2_sol.max**.

Lab Activity Checklist

S. No.	Tasks	Completed	
		Yes	No
1.	Opened the ch01_animateball.max file		
2.	Placed and locked the ball at various positions		
3.	Played the animation		

Exercise 3

Objective

- Animate an object, such as a Sphere or a Torus ring.

Problem Statement

Create a simple animation of two spheres colliding with each other, showing the effect of squash on impact.

Lab Setup

3ds max 6.0

Procedure

1. Select **File → Reset**.
2. At the front of the viewport, make a Sphere of radius 50 units, a Torus ring of approximately 80 units in radius 1 and 12 units in radius 2. You can make changes to the dimensions in the Create panel or in the Modify panel → Parameters rollout.

3. Place both the objects at the center of the world, at XYZ coordinates (0,0,0), as shown in Figure 1.34.

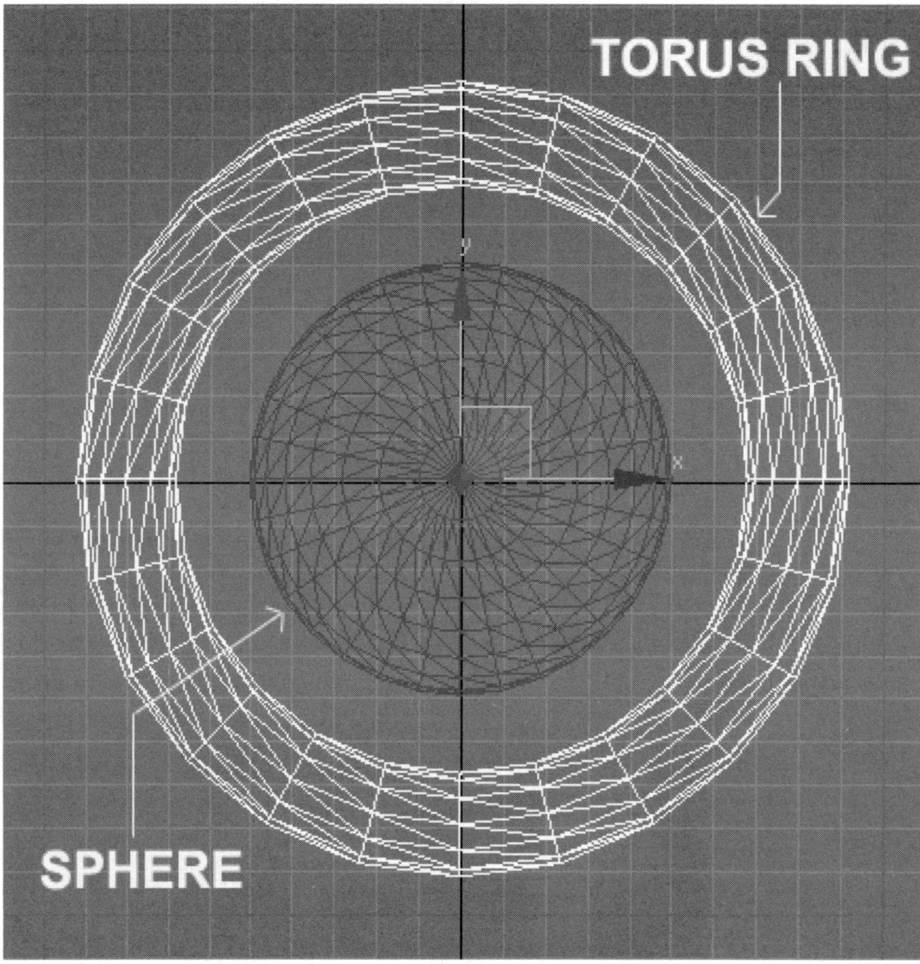

Figure 1.34: Sphere and Torus Ring Placed at the Center of the Coordinate Space

4. Move the time slider to frame 100 or enter the frame number **100** in the current frame field in the time controls, and press **Enter**.
5. Activate the **Auto Key** button for animating the first object, as shown in Figure 1.35.

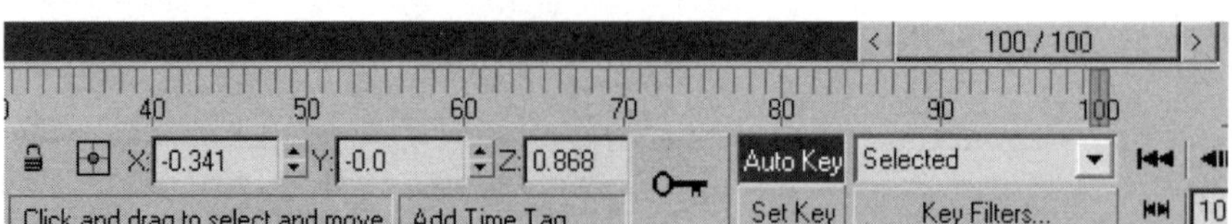

Figure 1.35: Auto Key Button Activated

6. At the top of the viewport, activate the **Select and Rotate** button, as shown in Figure 1.36. Rotate the Torus 180 degrees in the z-axis or enter the value 180 in the z-axis coordinate, then press **Enter**.

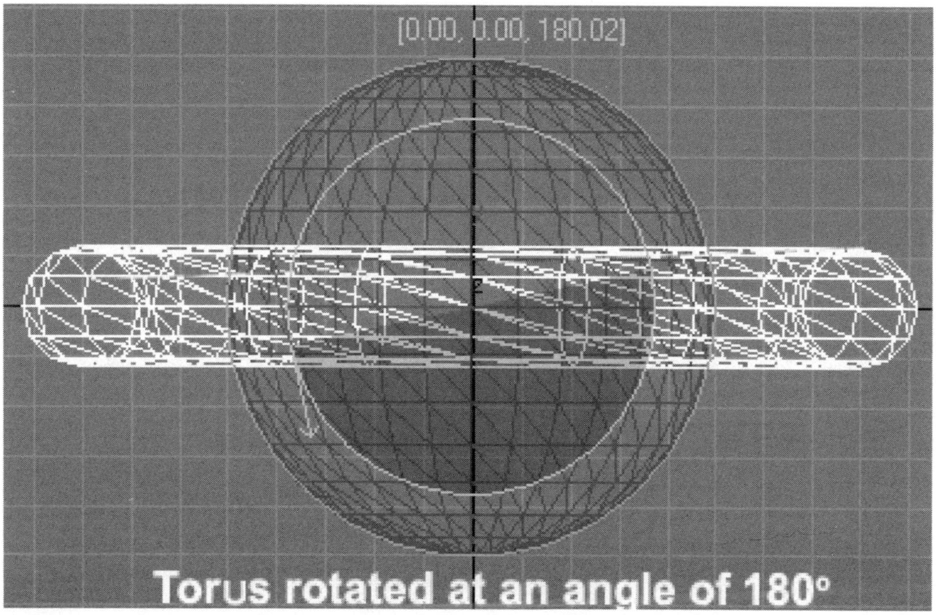

Figure 1.36: Torus Rotated

7. At the top of the viewport, activate the **Select and Rotate** button. Rotate the sphere –180 degrees in the z-axis or enter the value –180 in the z-axis coordinate, as shown in Figure 1.37. Press **Enter**.

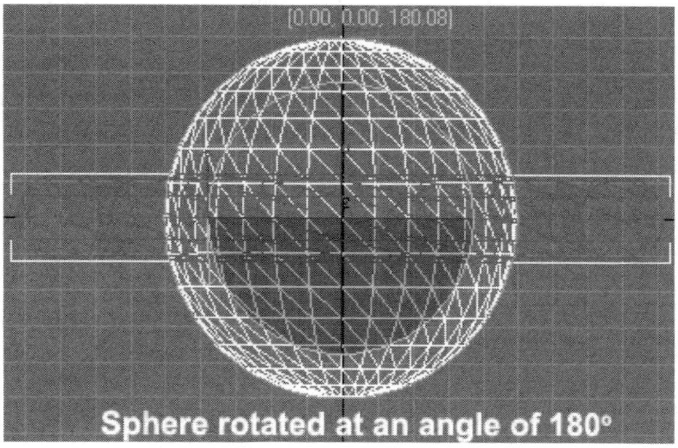

Figure 1.37: Sphere Rotated at an Angle of 180°

8. Deactivate the **Auto Key** button, as shown in Figure 1.38.

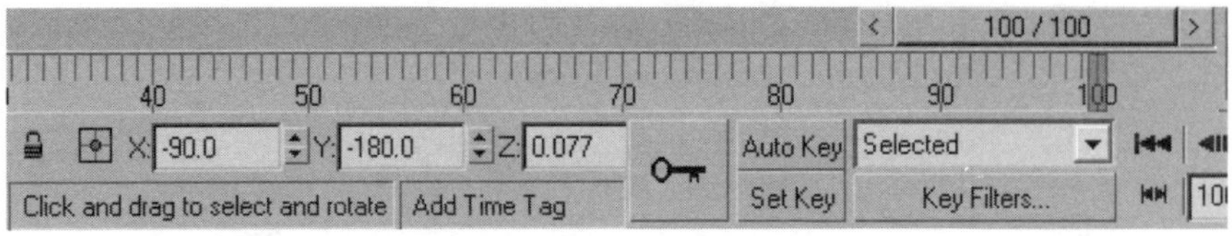

Figure 1.38: Auto Key Button Deactivated

9. Activate the Perspective viewport. Click the **Play Animation** button and see the Torus ring and Sphere rotate in opposite direction.
10. Save the file as **ch01_lab_ex3_sol.max**.

The animation strip in Figure 1.39 shows the complete animation.

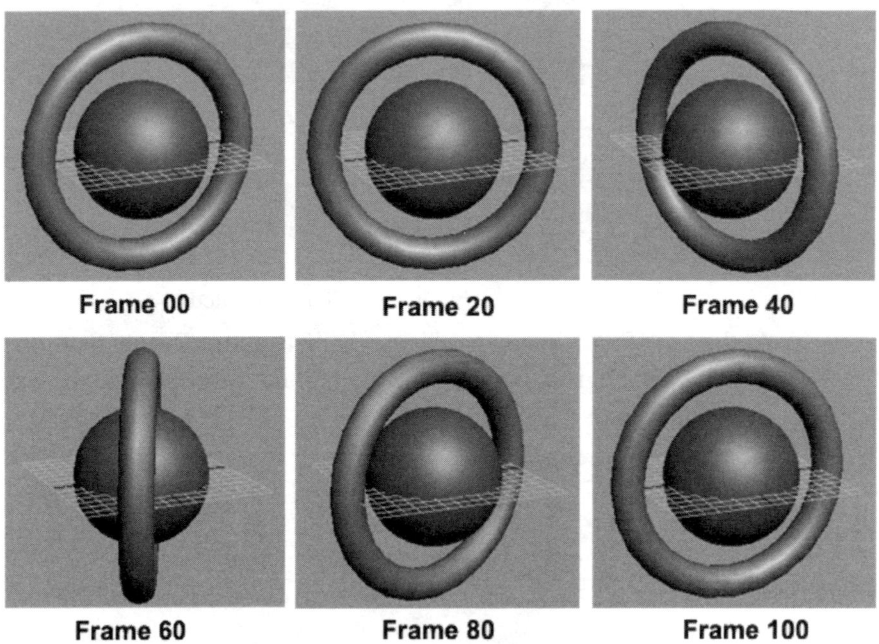

Figure 1.39: Final Rendered Frames of the Animation

Lab Activity Checklist

S. No.	Tasks	Completed	
		Yes	No
1.	Created an object		
2.	Rotated the object		

Project

Scenario

You need to create a logo of a company that bounces down the stairs and zooms into the camera. The logo is then converted into a product that represents the campaign.

Activities

- Create a storyboard of the animation that they need to create. (In the storyboard, draw the objects that need to be included in the animation. In addition, also write the type of animation that needs to be created. Draw the same roughly on paper.)
- Build the necessary model required for the animation.
- Animate the logo by using move transform, rotate transform, and squash transform.

Using Track View

2

You learned that animation is the changes in the scene happening at defined instances of time over a specified time frame. You also learned that keyframes are created when changes are defined to objects in the time line. Between these keyframes, 3ds max creates interim motion frames by using interpolation methods. Previously, you used the viewports and the Autokey mode to define changes to objects at instances of time. Another way to create and control animations in 3ds max is using Track View.

At the end of this chapter, you will be able to:

- Describe the need for using Track View.
- Use Track View to create and control animations.
- Describe the interface of the Curve Editor.
- Explain the working of the Curve Editor.
- Describe the interface of the Dope Sheet.
- Explain the working of the Dope Sheet.

2.1 Introducing Track View

2.2 Controlling Animation Using Track View

2.1 Introducing Track View

While creating complex animation, you would need more than simple movements to get the desired animation. For example, consider a bird flying and banking while it takes a turn. It is time-consuming and difficult to create animations with complex movements using viewports. Another example would be when you release a ball onto a ground from a height, the ball falls down and hits the ground. Based on the elastic properties of the material of the ball, the bounce sequence will be affected. A less elastic ball will bounce less and a more elastic ball will bounce more.

In such cases of complex requirement where creating and editing animations through viewports become extremely cumbersome and time consuming, you can use Track View to control almost every aspect of the animation complexity.

Track View is used to create and edit complex animations in 3ds max. The Track View window provides features to control motion characteristics and allows you to control keyframes in terms of location in the timeline. The duration in which the animation takes place is called timeline.

Track View provides the necessary control to edit other aspects of animation other than simple movements like position rotation and scale. It features other useful functionality, such as curves to change and effect keyframes globally without having to edit any key manually.

Before proceeding ahead, you will learn to create a simple animation and with that as an example the nuances of Track View can be learned. You will learn to animate an object over a period of time. In 3D animation, an object can be primarily animated by transforming (moving), rotating, or scaling (resizing) it.

In the simplest of all animations, you will be moving an object that is a box over a period of time. To do this, perform the following steps:

1. Open a new .max file. Create a simple box in the top viewport.

2. Select the object you want to animate. In this case, select the box as this is the only object in the scene, as shown in Figure 2.1.

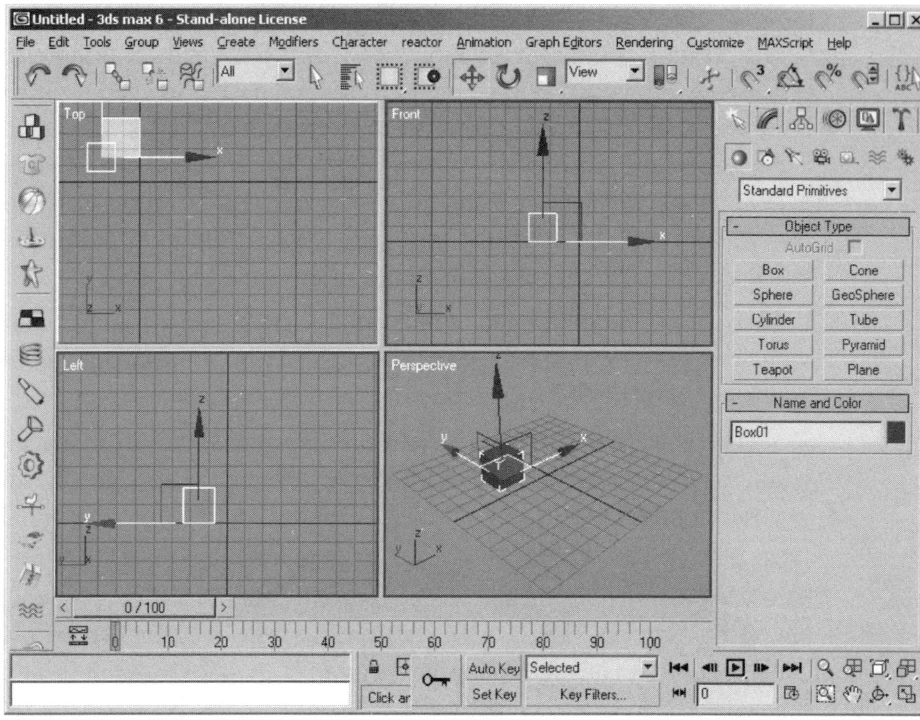

Figure 2.1: Select Object

3. Click **Auto Key**, as shown in Figure 2.2. The Auto Key button enables the animation mode wherein you can change the scene contents over a duration of time. At any specified instance of time, for example, at 50th frame, change the object's location or parameters. The information stored is called a keyframe. 3ds max then generates the frame l in between the keyframes to ensure a smooth transition between the keyframes.

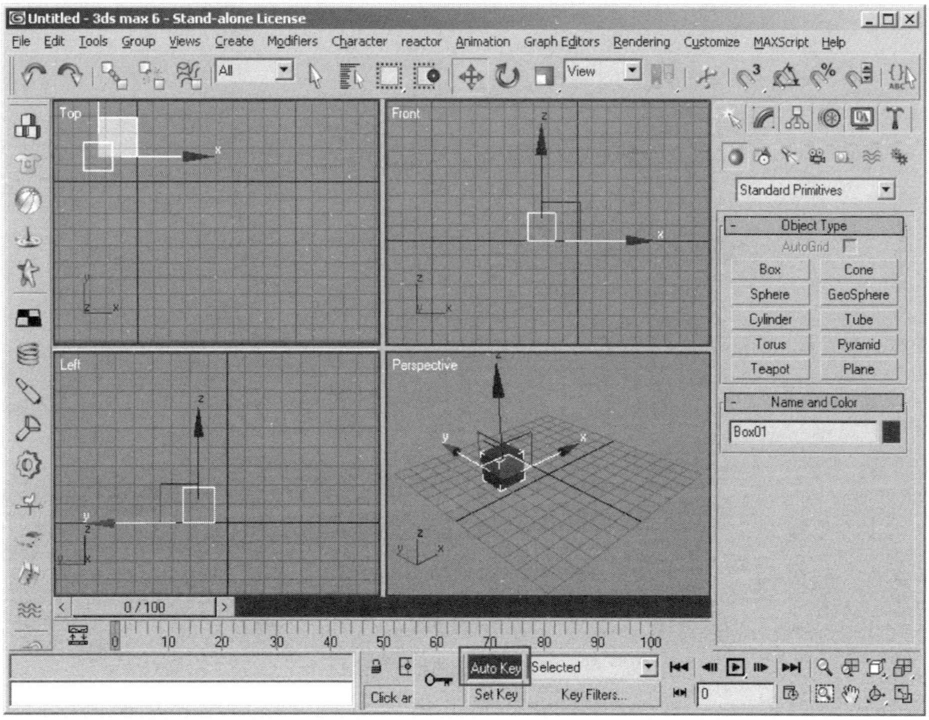

Figure 2.2: Auto Key Button

4. To start the animation process, move the time slider to a different location other than 0 on the time rule. In Figure 2.3, the time slider is kept at Frame 50 as an animation with 100 frames in total.

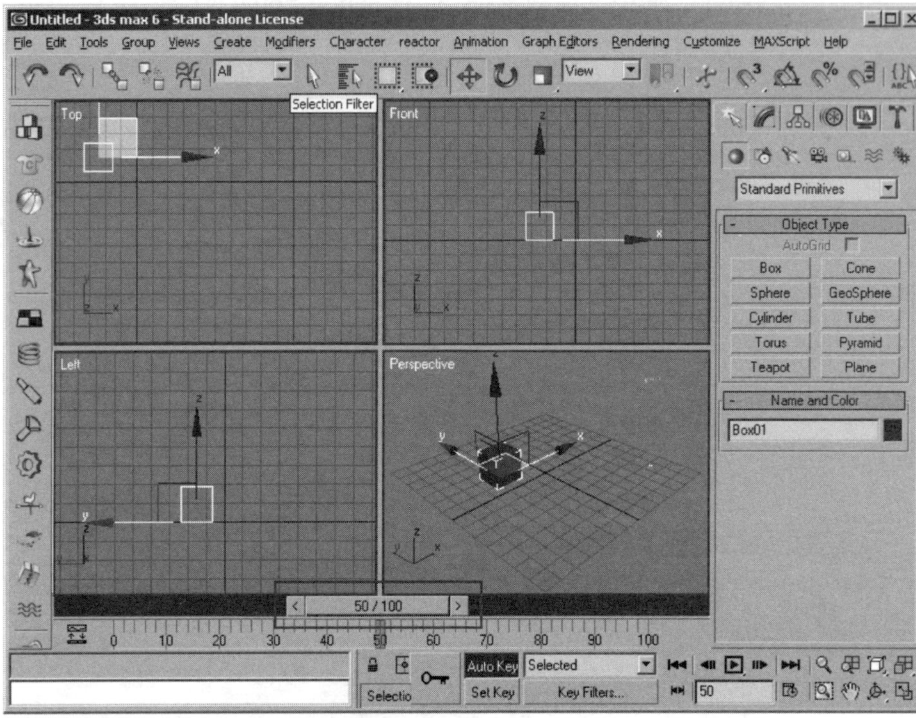

Figure 2.3: Time Slider on the Time Ruler

5. Click and use the **Move** tool to move the object to a different location on the viewport, as shown in Figure 2.4.

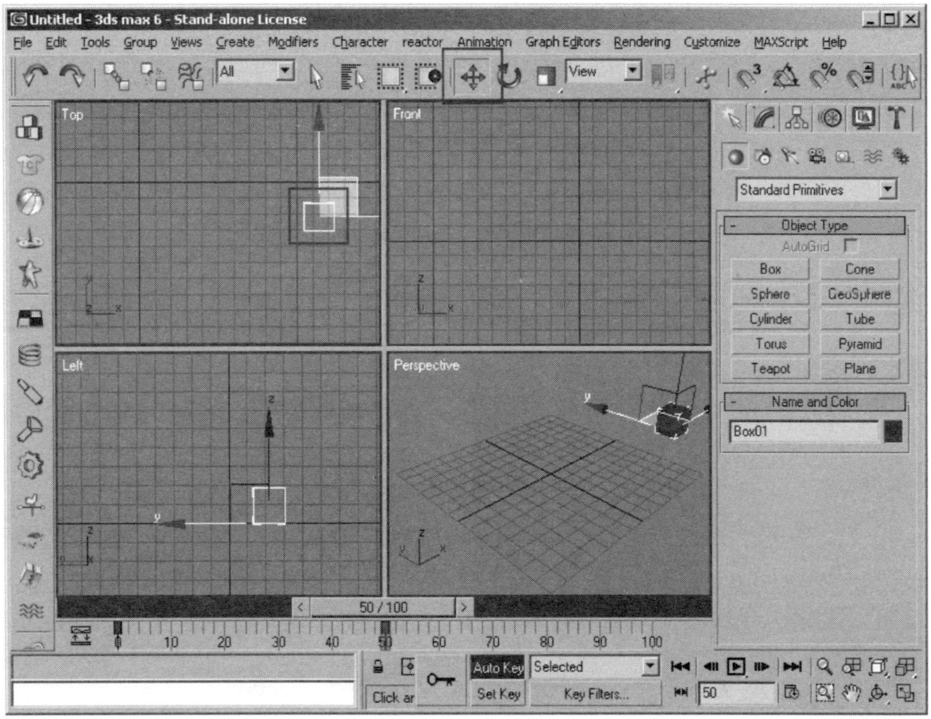

Figure 2.4: Move Tool

6. Repeat steps 4 and 5. While repeating step 4, place the time slider at Frame 100, as shown in Figure 2.5.

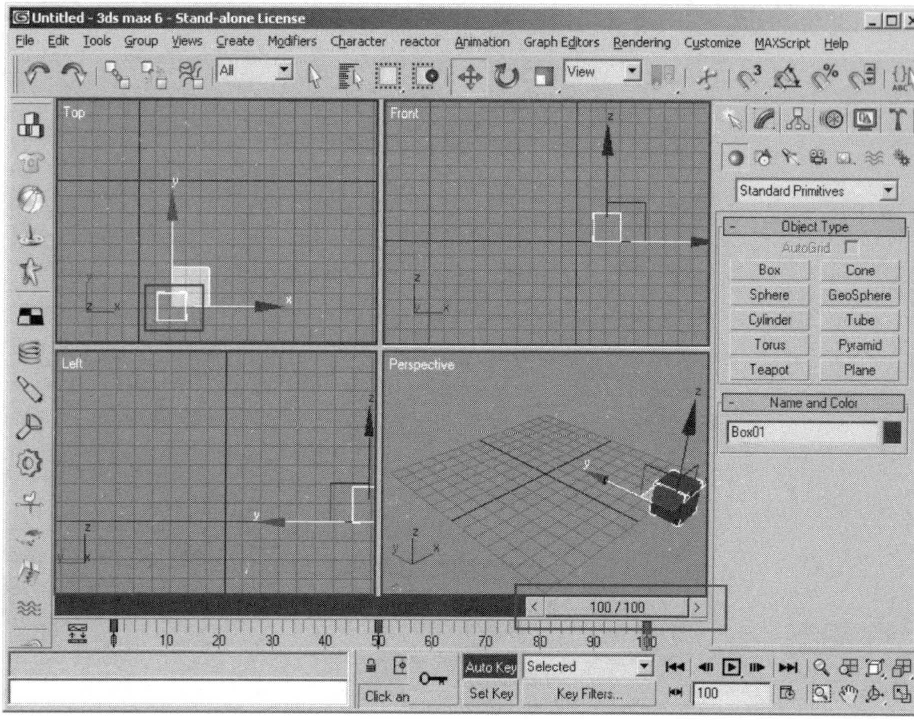

Figure 2.5: Time Slider

7. Click **Auto Key** to switch it off.

   Next, you can play the animation by using the **Play** button. You will see that the box automatically moves to the new location step-by-step, frame-by-frame, which gives the feeling of motion.

8. Save the file using the filename **ch02_my_simple_animation.max**. As shown in Figure 2.6, the small box-like figures which are marked beneath the frame numbers in timeline are called keyframes. 3ds max created the entire animation by using these keyframes.

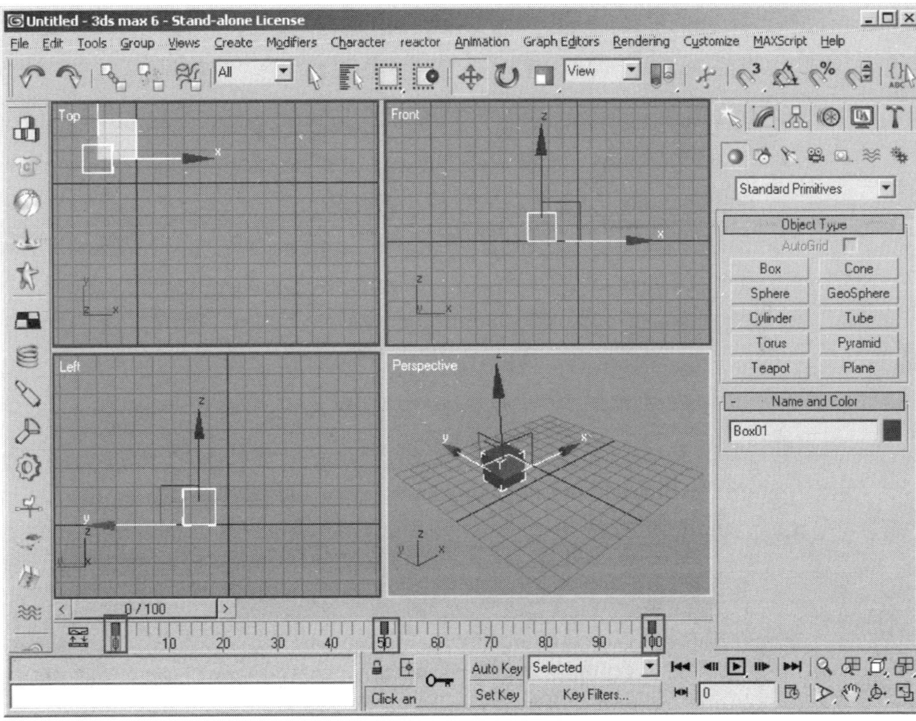

Figure 2.6: Keyframes

You will notice that at frame 0, frame 50, and frame 100 different locations for the box were assigned. 3ds max automatically created the necessary intermediate locations and the animation. The key information about the position of the object is defined at the three frames 0, 50, and 100. Therefore, the frames are called keyframes. Similarly, the size of the box can be altered with the same keyframe concept to change in time and another animation can be created.

That was quite simple.

However, imagine you realize that there was a mistake while creating the previous animation. You actually had to create 5 points during the entire 100 frames of animation such that the box moved from one location to another 5 times in the entire duration of 100 frames. Typically, you would once again use the viewports to switch on the autokey mode using the Auto Key button and create keyframes for the 5 points.

However, while you do so, you will realize that as the animation requirements increase in complexity, it becomes difficult to manipulate and control the animation.

Imagine you had a requirement where you would want the following things to happen during the animation:

- The Box moves slowly from the first location to the second one.
- The Box moves fast from the second to the third location.
- The Box starts fast from the third location but settles slowly at the fourth location.
- The Box starts slowly from the fourth location, at midway it moves fast, and finally settles at the fifth location slowly.

The first two requirements are easy to implement. They can be achieved using a lesser number of frames for the fast motion and a higher number of frames for the slow motion, using the viewports and the autokey mode. The last two requirements are not possible to handle visually using the viewports.

You can use Track View to achieve these four requirements.

In this chapter, you will be familiarized with the interface elements in Track View.

It is interesting to note here that in most of the studios where professional animations are created, professionals always use Track View to control animations.

Going beyond Track View, 3ds max provides powerful scripting facility where extremely complex animations can be achieved using programmatic methods. A simple example of this would be an event-based animation where an event of one object affects the animation sequences of another object. Such concepts are used by the broadcast and film industry for creating animations, which otherwise would be impossible to achieve using either the viewports or Track View. However, such functionality will require an in-depth knowledge of the 3ds max programming environment. You can find more information on scripting environment within 3ds max in the standard 3ds max help documentation.

Practice Questions

1. List two reasons to use Track View.
2. List the two modes of Track View.
3. Why would you use Curve Editor over simple viewports?
4. Explain the purpose of Edit Window and Time Ruler in Curve Editor.

2.2 Controlling Animation Using Track View

There are two types of Track View:

- Curve Editor
- Dope Sheet

These two types provide different ways to control your animations. In this section, these types of Track View will be discussed in detail.

2.2.1 Track View Curve Editor

Describe the interface and working of the Curve Editor.

The Curve Editor is a powerful tool to control animations. It gives functionality to animate objects which is beyond the scope of using the simple viewport animation methods. Using the Curve Editor, you can control the timing and the magnitude of an animation. The curves that are created based on the keys in keyframes control how 3ds max controls motion between keyframes.

To open the Curve Editor mode, perform the following steps:

1. Open the **ch02_my_simple_animation.max** scene that you created in the last section, as shown in Figure 2.7.

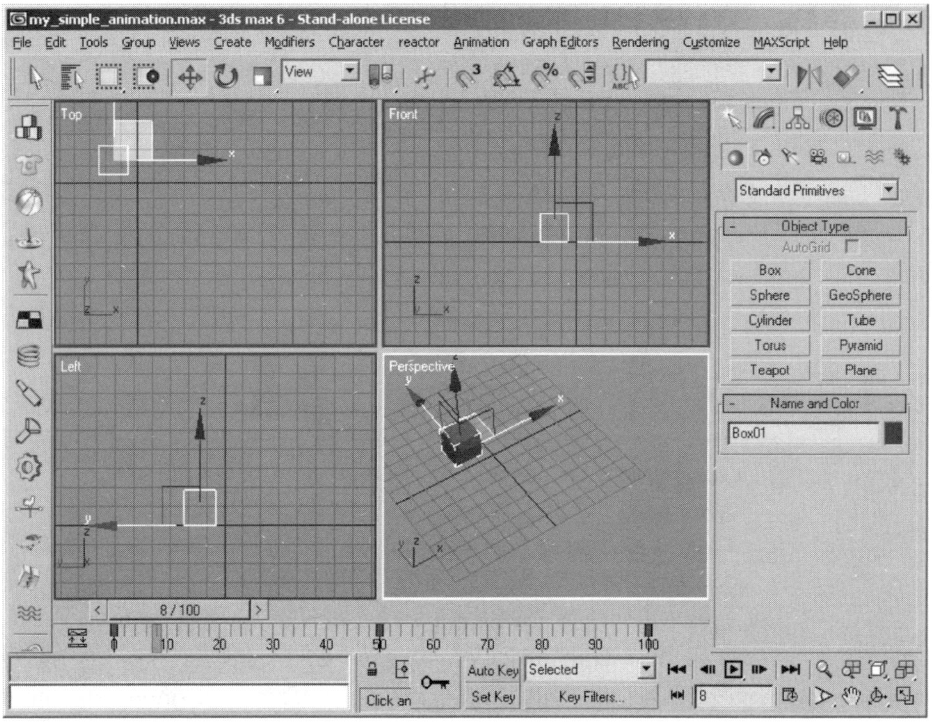

Figure 2.7: My_simple_animation.max

2. Open the Track View - Curve Editor window. Select **Graph Editors → Track View - Curve Editor**, as shown in Figure 2.8.

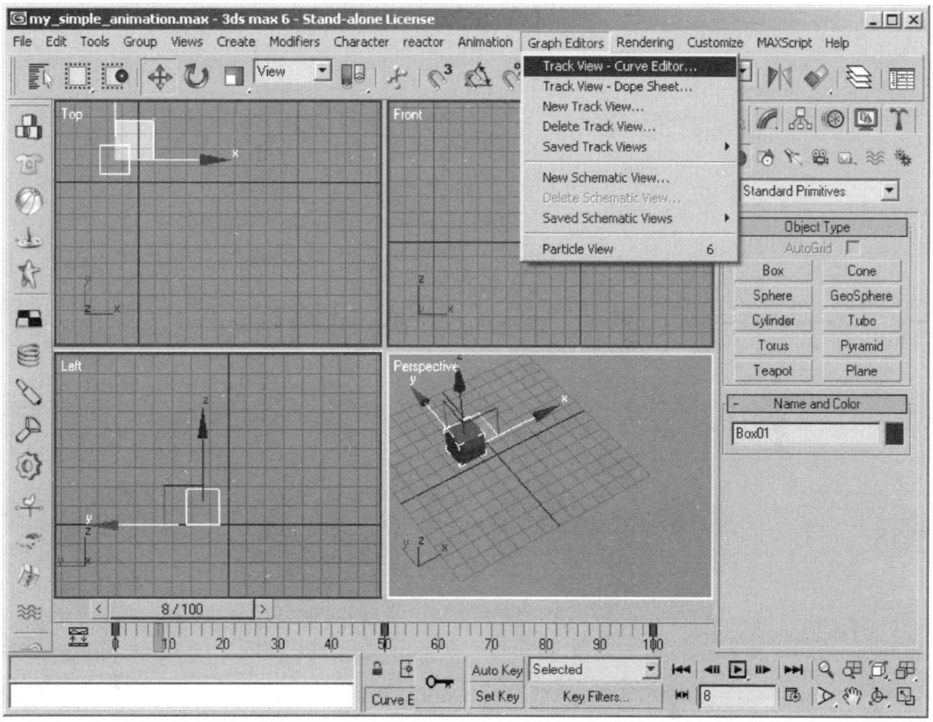

Figure 2.8: Opening Track View - Curve Editor

The Curve Editor creates and shows curves that are formed by connecting to keys for a specific changing parameter of an object that has been animated. For example, if you have moved the object from one location to another, the keys for the motion are created, using which animation curves are created. These curves define how the interpolation in-between the keyframes will take place. When you move or change keys, the underlying curves also change to accommodate the new changes. Using the Curve Editor, you can change the magnitude of keys and move the instance of time where an animation keyframe exists.

You first need to understand the interface of the Curve Editor.

Elements of the Curve Editor Interface

The various elements of the Curve Editor interface are shown in Figure 2.9.

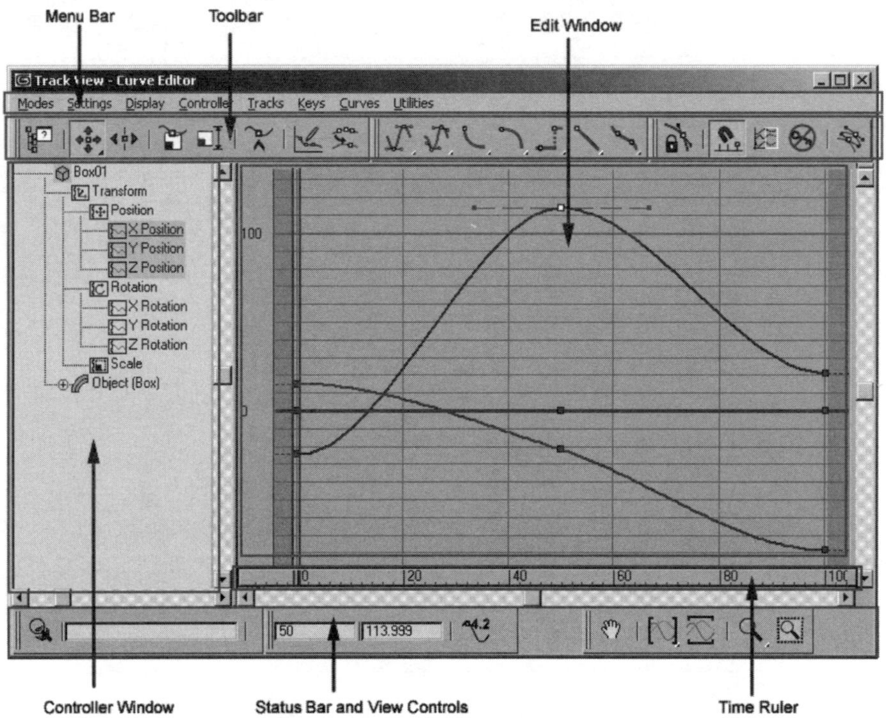

Figure 2.9: Elements of the Curve Editor Interface

The description of the various elements:

- Menu bar: The menu bar consists of items that are useful while working in Track View.
- Toolbar: The toolbar consists of tools that are used while editing individual keys.
- Controller window: The Controller window consists of the list of objects and other scene elements from which keys can be created or have been created in a tree kind of format.
- Edit window: The Edit window holds the main keys that are based on the keyframes of the animation. The Edit window shows the curves related with the keys in the Curve Editor mode.
- Time Ruler: Time Ruler displays the time or frame at which keys are located. It shows the entire time line before and after the active time segment. Active time segment is the duration for which the animation duration has been defined.

- Status bar and View controls: The Status toolbar displays the status of various keys like the frame number at which the key is present and the current value of the key at the keyframe. The View controls are used to control the view in the Edit window and provide functions such as zooming.

Menu Bar

Some common items on the menu bar are as follows:

- Modes: This helps you to select either Curve Editor or Dope Sheet to work.
- Settings: This provides facilities to control the handling of items in the Track View window.
- Display: This enables you to make choices for the animation to be shown as curve, icon, and tangent. It appears only in Curve Editor.
- Controller: This helps you to assign, copy, and paste controllers and to add loops. Controllers are powerful alternatives to the keyframing methods because they are used to assign rules to an animation.
- Tracks: This facilitates you to add Note and Visibility tracks. Visibility tracks are used to show and hide objects during a time frame.
- Keys: This helps you to include soft selection, align to cursor, snap frame, and add or remove the slide and scale keys.
- Curves: This enables you to apply and remove the Ease and Multiplier curves.
- Utilities: This helps create or randomize out-of-range keys.

Toolbar

Some common tools found on the toolbar are shown in Table 2.1.

Icon	Tool	Description
	Filter	Used to display and filter the content displayed in the Controller window. Useful when you have a large number of objects in the scene and selectively want to display keys only for certain objects based on some filtering criteria.
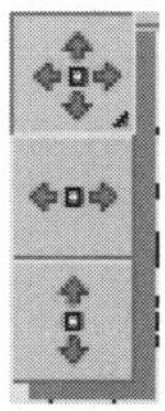	Move Keys	Used to move keys in the Edit window. Allows you to move keys vertically and horizontally, which can be selected from the move keys flyout.
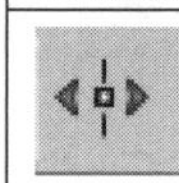	Slide Keys	Used to move keys along with the keys that are lying to one end of the animation. The selection of keys until one end of the animation is based on the direction in which the slide keys are used.
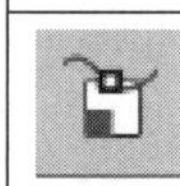	Scale Keys	Used to move proportionally all selected keys along one direction. If you have multiple keys selected at multiple instances of time, the scale tool will increase time between the keys proportionally based on the existing difference.
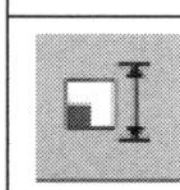	Scale Values	Scales values of the keys proportionally without effecting time. When you scale values, the effects of the animation increase rather than any change in the final time duration.
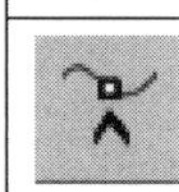	Add keys	Used to add keys to animation curves. Adding a key will increase keyframes in the animation.
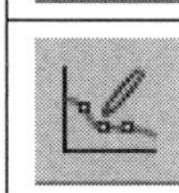	Draw Curves	Draw curves or edit existing keys by using the freehand curve drawing methods. Usually not preferred as it will create a large number of keys and will not create smooth animations.
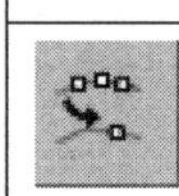	Reduce Keys	Based on a threshold value, will reduce the number of keys that you have created on a curve. Useful to reduce keys when you have a large number of undesirable keys in a curve and when you use the freehand curve.

Table 2.1: Common Tools

Controller Window

The Controller window determines which curve and track is available for display and editing.

You can expand and rearrange hierarchy items by right-clicking any of the objects in the Controller window, as shown in Figure 2.10.

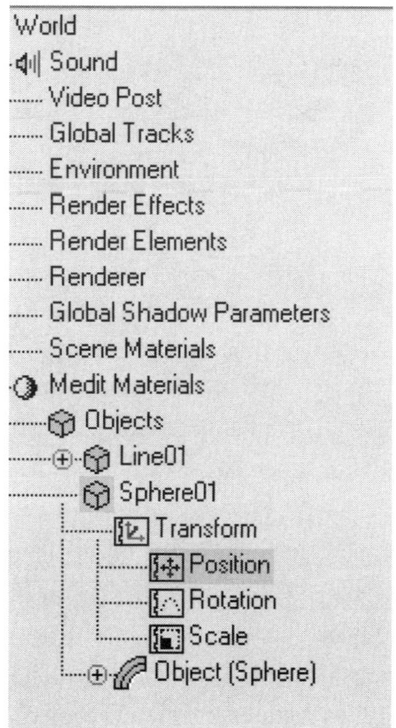

Figure 2.10: Controller Window

Edit Window

The Track View Edit window displays function curves and keys. You can either select or change the animation values and timing in this window. The Edit window also indicates the active time segment.

Figure 2.11 shows the active time segment highlighted in a different color.

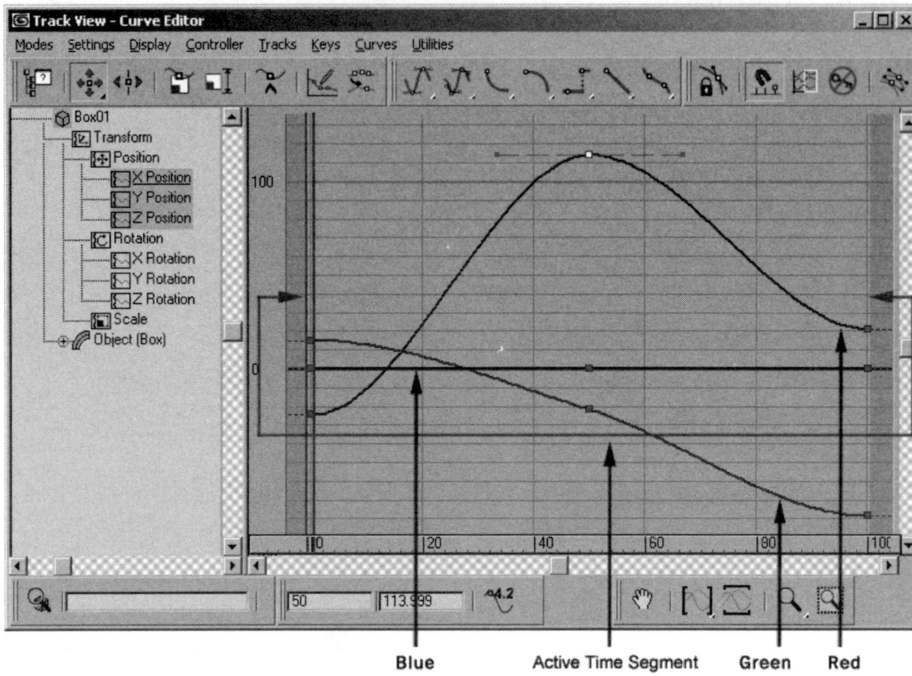

Figure 2.11: Active Time Segment

Time Ruler

Time ruler is used to measure time. Time ruler can be dragged vertically to align it with any track. Time ruler can be increased to measure keys against time.

Along with the ruler, you can use the time slider to scroll the view of the Edit window to various times in the animation, as shown in Figure 2.12.

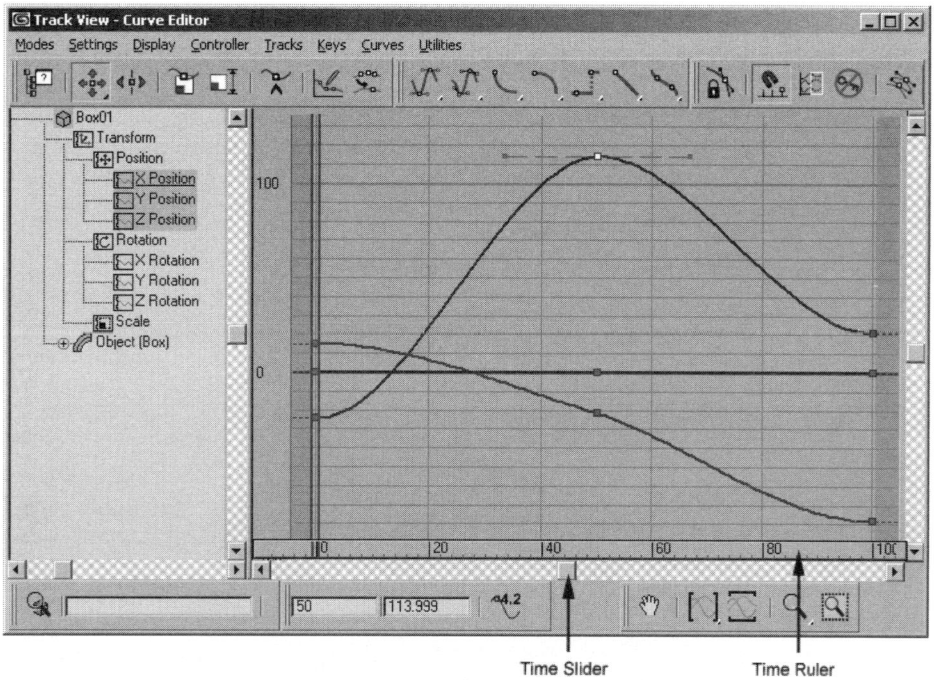

Figure 2.12: Time Slider and Time Ruler

Status Bar and View Controls

The Status Bar controls provide information in keys and their values.

The View controls are used to manage and view the Edit window. It has functions such as pan, zoom, zoom extents horizontally, and zoom extents vertically.

Working of the Curve Editor

After learning the interface of the Curve Editor, you need to understand how you can work with it. To give a simple example, suppose you were to walk from point A to point B; you can walk and reach B in several ways as mentioned below:

- You could walk in a straight line from A to B with the same speed throughout the animation.
- You could walk in a zigzag motion with the same speed.
- You could start running from A and while you are near B you could slow down and start walking.

- You could have a hopping motion from A to B.

You can use the Curve Editor to edit the keys and the curves in the Edit window to achieve such complex animations of an object.

The following steps demonstrate the use of Track View Curve Editor:

1. Open the sample file **ch02_my_anim_start.max**.

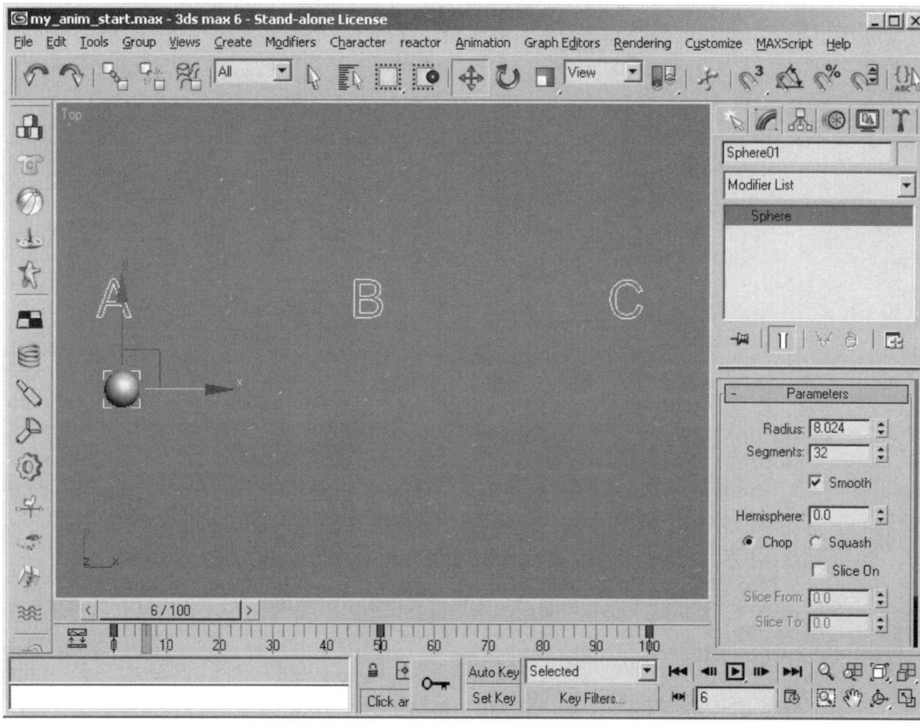

Figure 2.13: Opening my_anim_start.max

2. Use the **Play** button to play the animation. The sphere moves gradually from A to B and then from B to C, as shown in Figure 2.14.

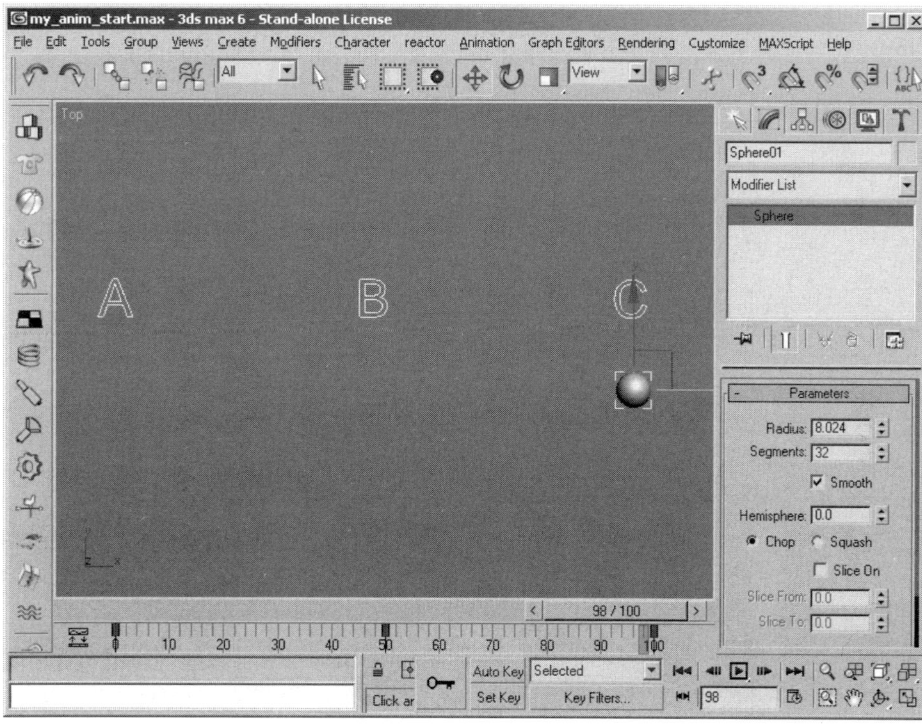

Figure 2.14: Play Button

3. Use the Graph **Editors → Track View - Curve Editor** menu option to open the Track View window, as shown in Figure 2.15.

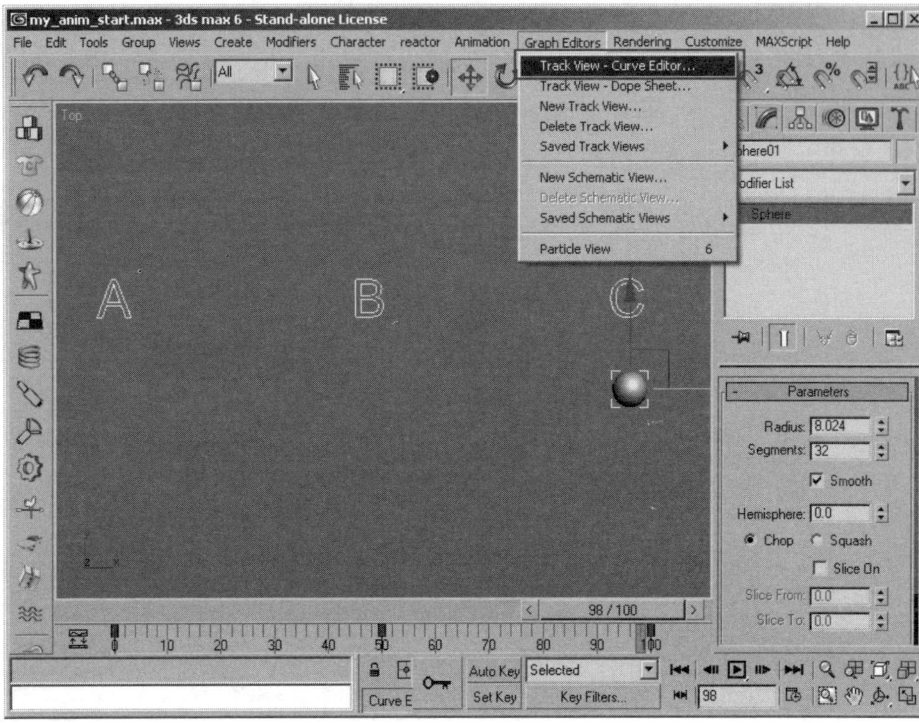

Figure 2.15: Curve Editor

4. You can see some curves in the Edit window. The red curve represents motion in the X-axis. The green curve represents motion in the Y-axis and the blue curve in the Z-axis.

If you look at the top viewport, the animation flows along the X-axis only, as shown in Figure 2.16. Therefore, the rest of the curves are straight lines. You will work on these straight lines later to edit them.

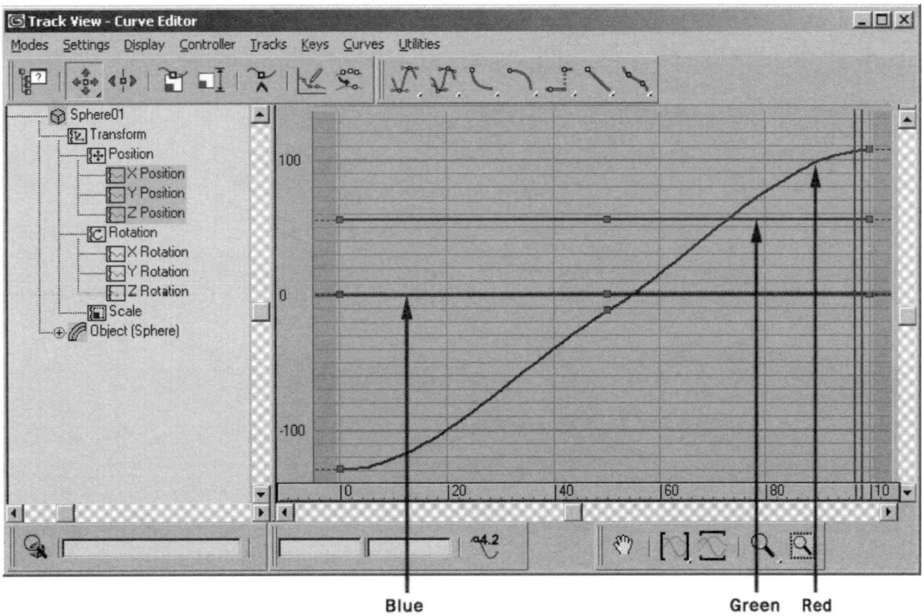

Figure 2.16: Curves in Edit Window

5. Click the **X Position** item in the Controller window. The window shows the red curve because you have selected to work on the X-axis curve, as shown in Figure 2.17.

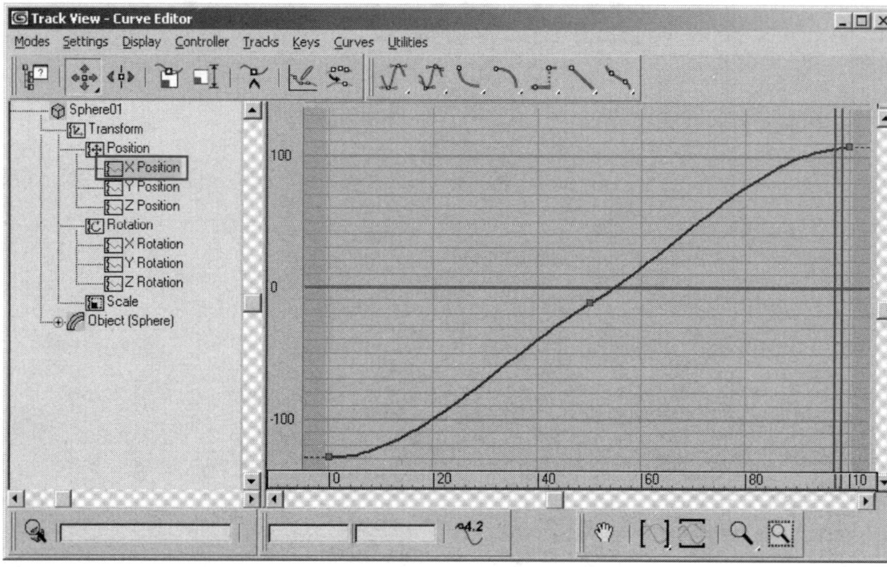

Figure 2.17: X Position

6. The keys seen in the red curve are based on the keyframes in the animation. Click the middle key to select it, as shown in Figure 2.18.

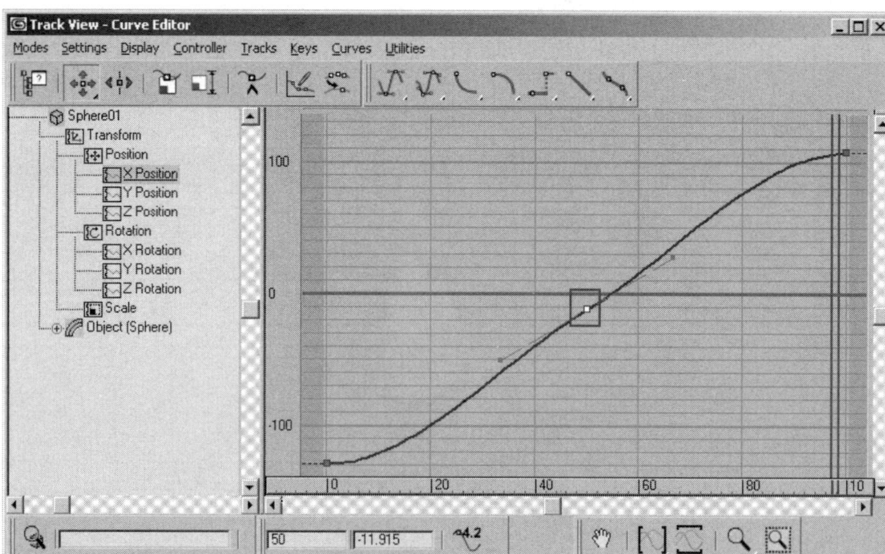

Figure 2.18: Middle Key

7. Using the **Move Keys** tool to move the selected key to the left of the current position, place the key at frame 20, as shown in Figure 2.19.

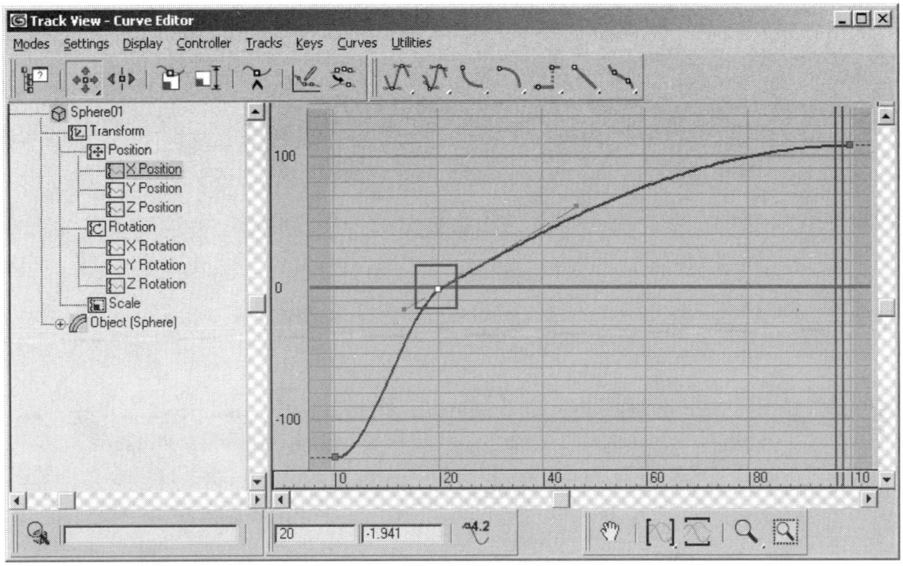

Figure 2.19: Move Keys

8. Play the animation by using the **Play** button. You will notice that the sphere moves very fast from A to B and then moves very slow between B and C.
9. Click the **Add Keys** icon in the toolbar, as shown in Figure 2.20.

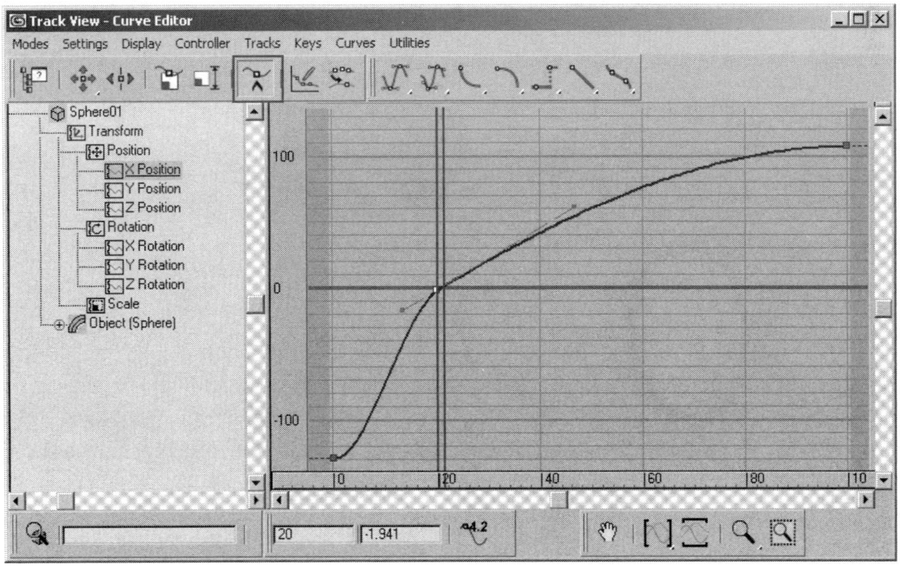

Figure 2.20: Add Keys

10. Click the red curve at frame 60 to add a key at frame 60, as shown in Figure 2.21.

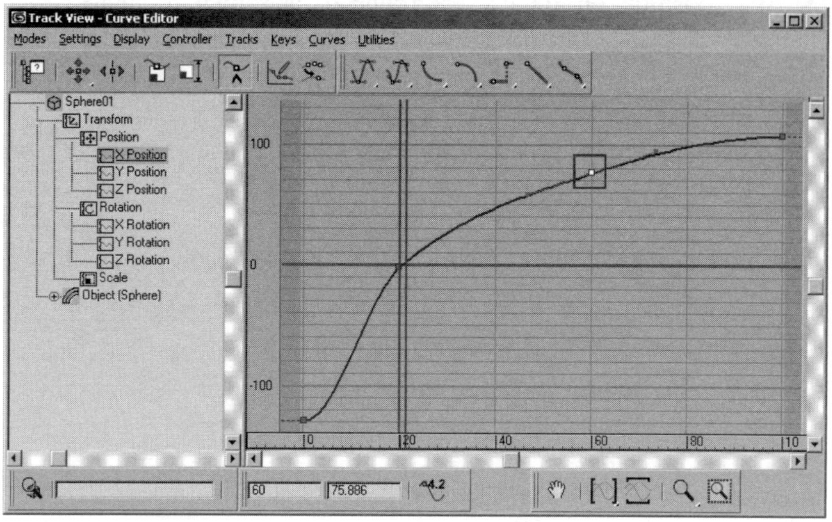

Figure 2.21: Frame 60

11. Use the **Move Keys** to move the key below the straight dark line to a position, as shown in Figure 2.22.

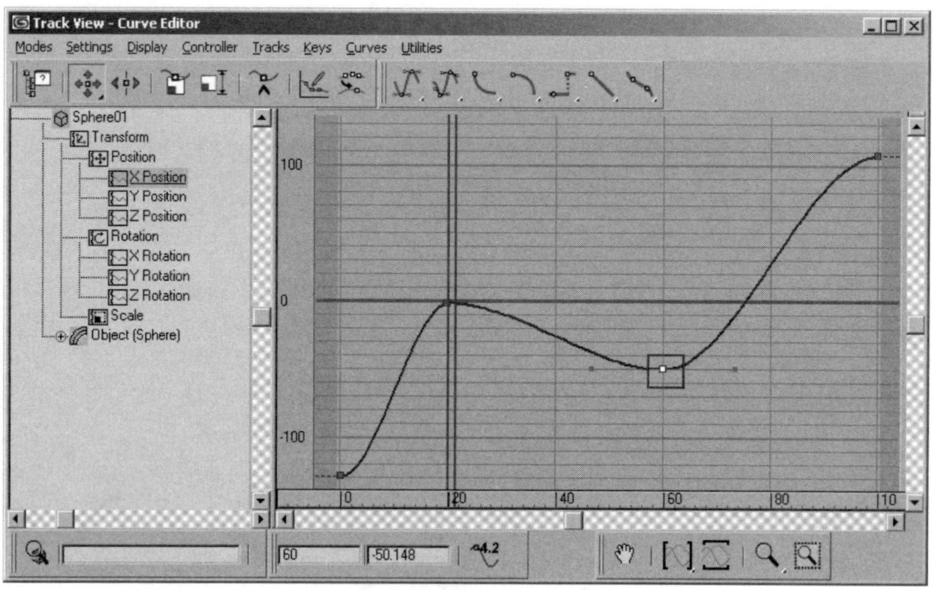

Figure 2.22: Move Key

12. Click **Play** to play the animation. Notice that the motion of the sphere moves from A to B and comes back midway between A and B and then finally moves to C. In the Main window timeline, you can see that keyframes are automatically created at 20 and 60, as shown in Figure 2.23.

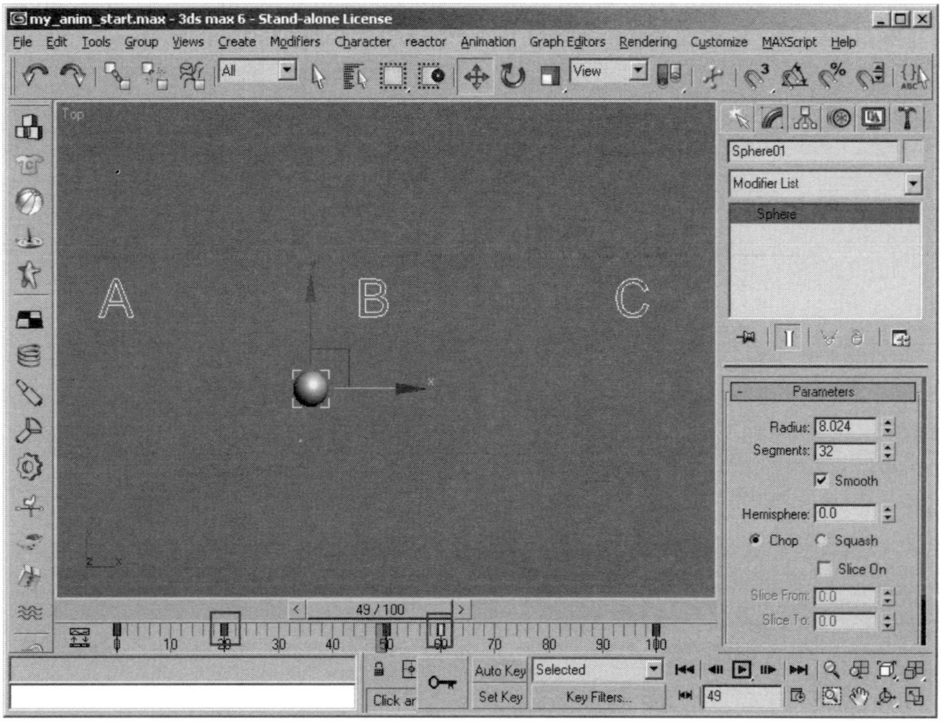

Figure 2.23: Created Keyframes

13. Next, control the motion from frame 60 to 100 in such a way that it starts very fast from 60 and then decelerates when it reaches to frame 100 which is location C. Watch carefully at the selected key. You will see a blue line with two handles at each end with each selected key, as shown in Figure 2.24. These handles are called the Bezier handles, which you can edit to further control the animation curve. The Bezier handles control the interpolation mechanism in 3ds max that is used to calculate intermediate frames between keyframes.

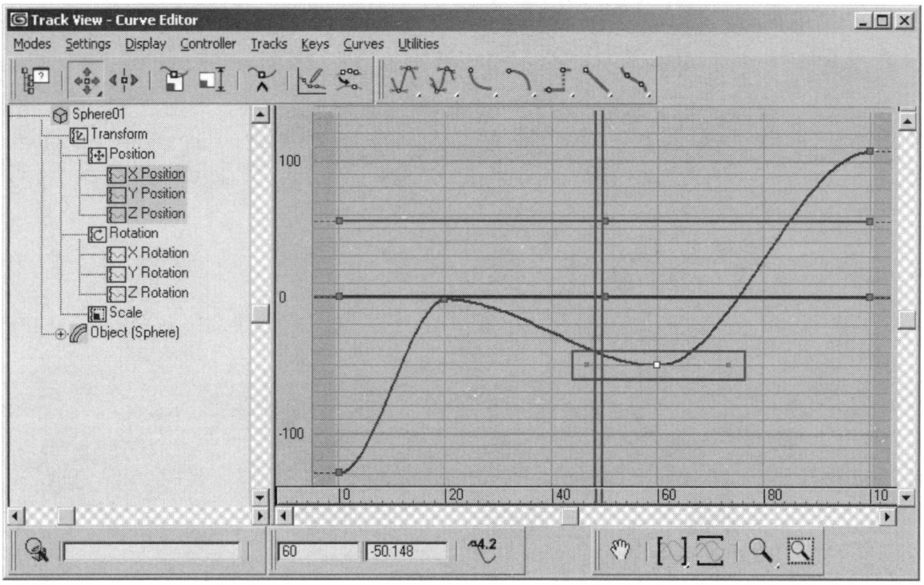

Figure 2.24: Bezier Handles

14. Select the last key along the X-axis by clicking it, as shown in Figure 2.25.

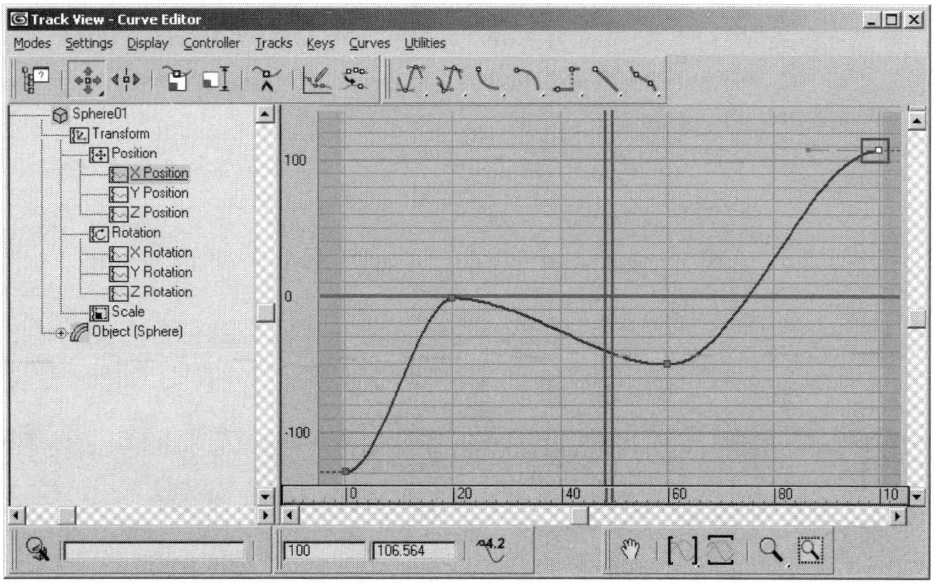

Figure 2.25: Last Key Along X-axis

15. Place the cursor over the blue handle that you see associated with the last key. The cursor changes to a select mode. Click and drag the handle and place it as shown in Figure 2.26.

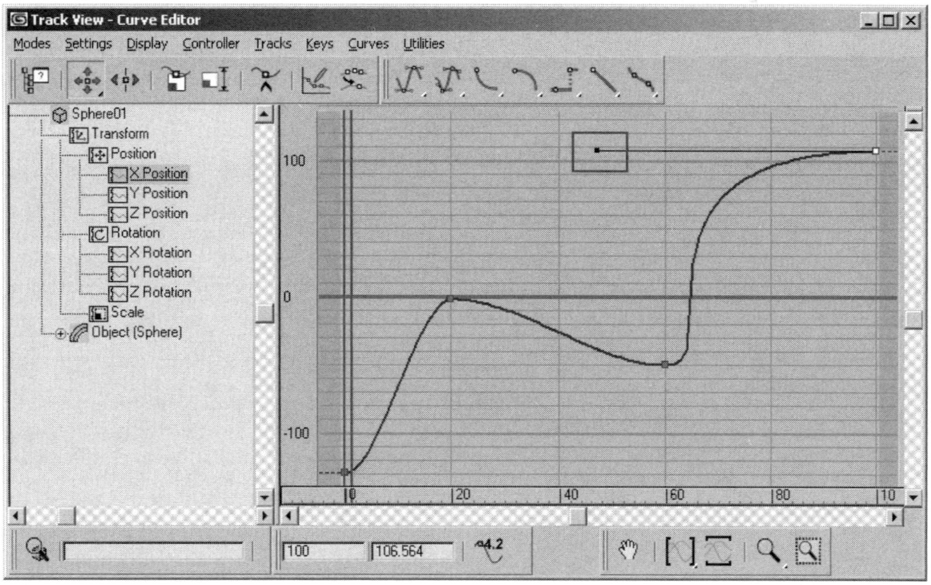

Figure 2.26: Drag Handle

16. Click **Play**. You will see that the sphere starts very fast from frame 60 and then slows down in a deceleration mode and reaches point C very slowly. You can edit the rest of the keys similarly to control motions at each key.

To create the zigzag motion along Y-axis from frame 60 through frame 100 perform the following steps:

1. Click the **Y Position** item in the Controller window, as shown in Figure 2.27.

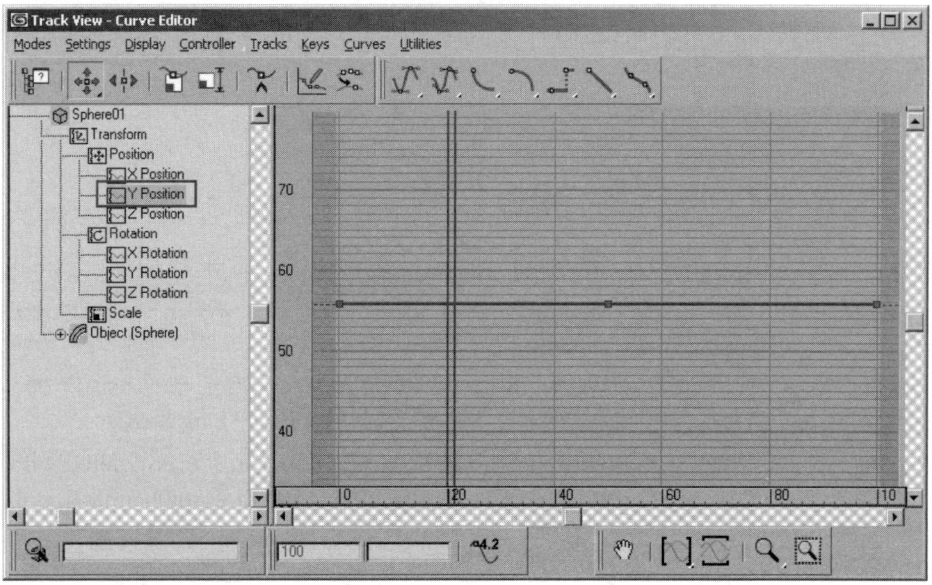

Figure 2.27: Controller Window

2. Use **Add Keys** to add four keys between frame 60 and 100, as shown in Figure 2.28.

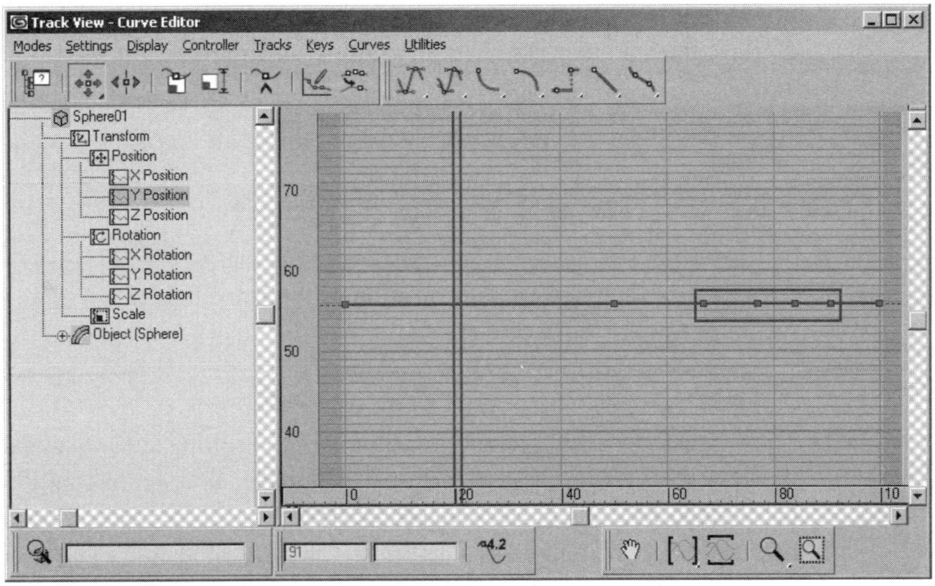

Figure 2.28: Add Keys

3. Select each key and place them using the **Move Keys** tool, as shown in Figure 2.29.

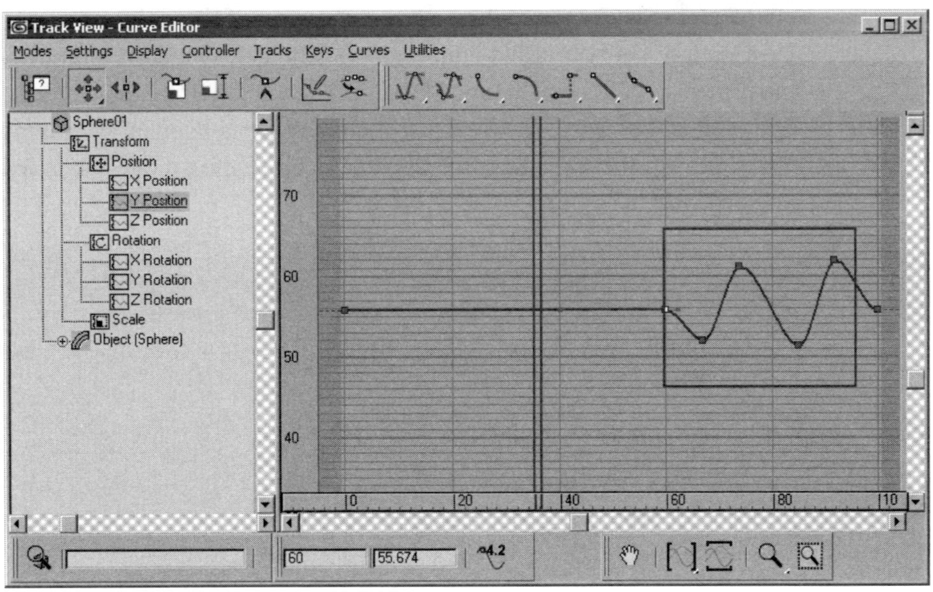

Figure 2.29: Move Keys

4. Click **Play** to play the animation. You will see that while traversing between frame 60 and frame 100, the sphere takes a zigzag motion along the Y-axis.
5. Save the animation as **ch02_my_anim_end.max**.

You have learned to control animations using Track View Curve Editor.

2.2.2 Track View Dope Sheet

Describe the interface and working of the Dope Sheet.

The Dope Sheet is an alternative method of controlling keys. It actually represents all the keys in a spreadsheetlike format which makes it easier to control animation if only the timing of keys is to be changed. In the Curve Editor mode, you saw that the keys had the horizontal and vertical entities. The horizontal entity was used for time and the vertical entity was used as a value based on the controller assigned. However, in the Dope Sheet, the display is based on the horizontal entity. Therefore, it allows easy methods of positioning keys in the timeline. For example, you have a crowd of characters in your scene where all the characters follow the same animation style. However, to get believable animation in this scenario, there should be variations in their movements, which can be done by editing each key for each character. You can use the Dope Sheet to control the time at which the events happen by moving the keys in time. You can shift the same key for each character in the time frame to avoid the undesirable unison effect.

To open the Dope Sheet, perform the following steps:

1. Open the **ch02_my_simple_animation.max** scene that you created in the last section, as shown in Figure 2.30.

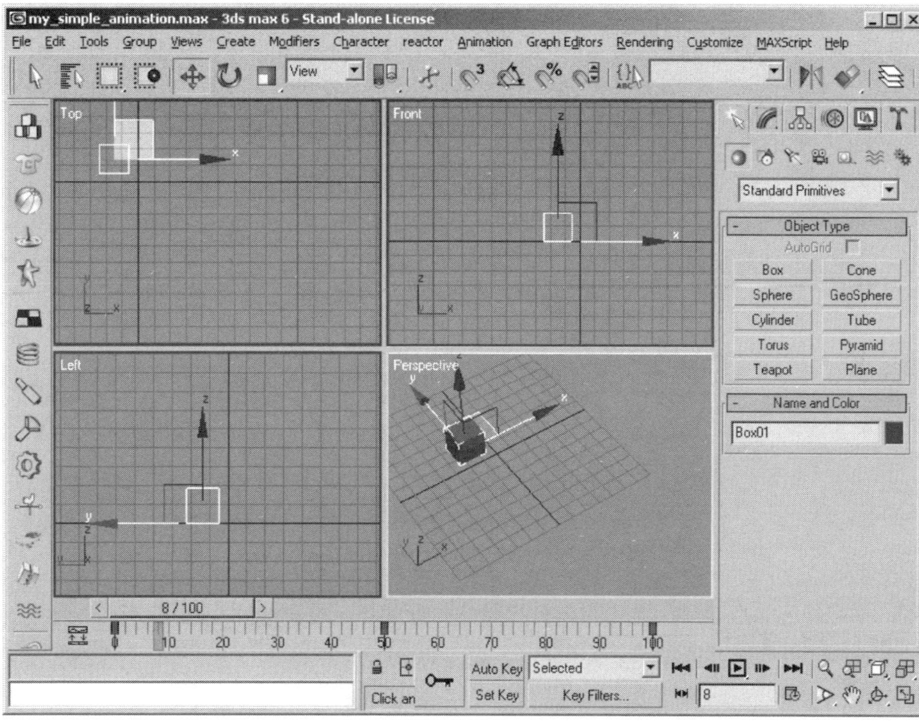

Figure 2.30: Opening my_simple_animation.max

2. Open the Track View - Dope Sheet editor using the **Graph Editors menu → Track View - Dope Sheet** menu option, as shown in Figure 2.31.

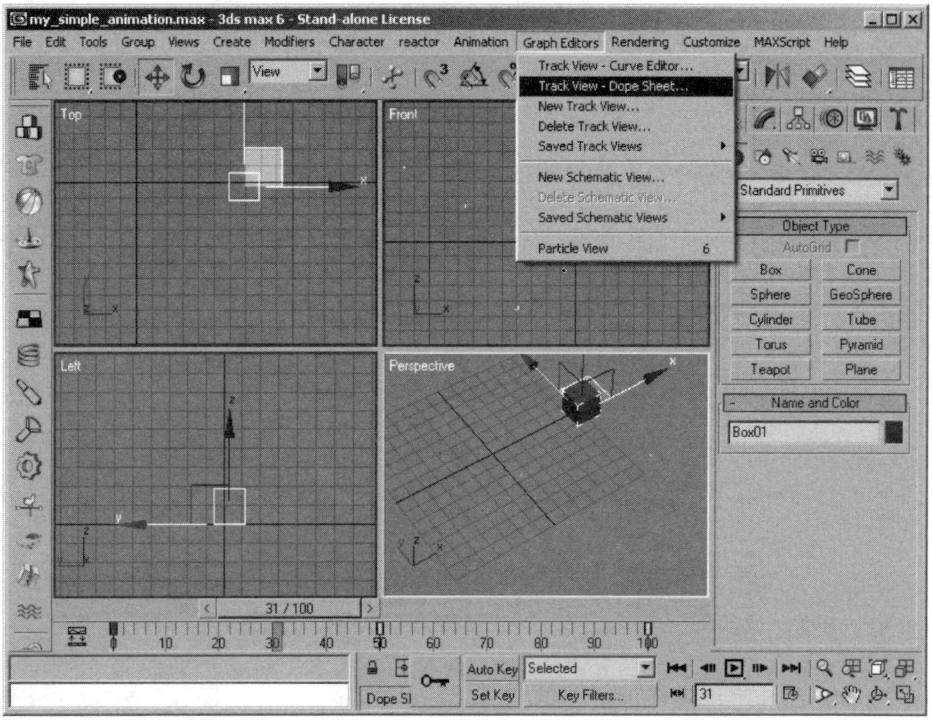

Figure 2.31: Dope Sheet

Elements of the Dope Sheet Interface

The visual elements of the Dope Sheet window are similar to the Curve Editor window but some changes exist in the toolbars and the Edit window.

Changes in the Toolbar

Some of the changes in the keys part of the toolbar are as follows:

-  : **Edit Keys -** Allows you to change single key.
- 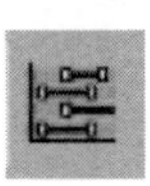 : **Edit Ranges -** Allows you to change a range of keys. This is useful when you want to quickly change timings of a complete animation track.

Changes in the Edit Window

The Edit window in the Dope Sheet is a completely different representation of the scene animation tracks. While in the Curve Editor you could edit curves connected to keys, in the Dope Sheet you can only control the key's timing. In other terms, using the Dope Sheet, you can speed up or delay a complete animation or an animation at specific keyframes. You cannot visually change the magnitude of the key's values using the Dope Sheet. However, you can have some control over the magnitude of the keys using the Key Status tools. Figure 2.32 shows the Dope Sheet window.

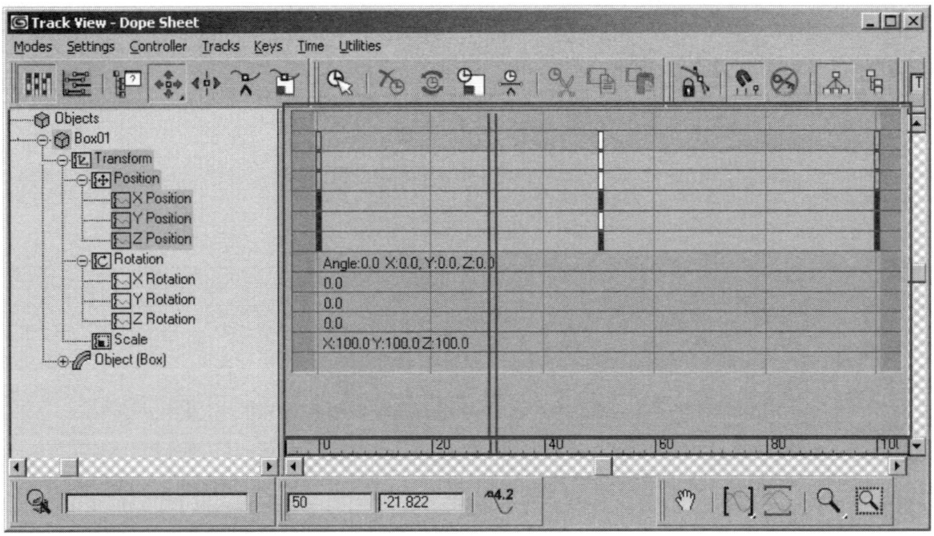

Figure 2.32: Track View - Dope Sheet

Time Ruler, the Controller window, the Status bar, and the navigation tools are all similar to the Curve Editor window.

Working of the Dope Sheet

The Dope Sheet allows another way of controlling animations. The Dope Sheet is a conventional approach to editing in terms that a similar style was used by the film industry to keep track of all events in a scene. It is similar to an exposure sheet used in classical animation by Disney for recording the dialogue and camera actions.

While the Curve Editor provides a lot of flexibility in editing curves, the Dope Sheet displays keys in the format similar to a spreadsheet from which individual keys can be accessed and edited.

Figure 2.33 shows the Dope Sheet window of the example scene modified above using the Curve Editor.

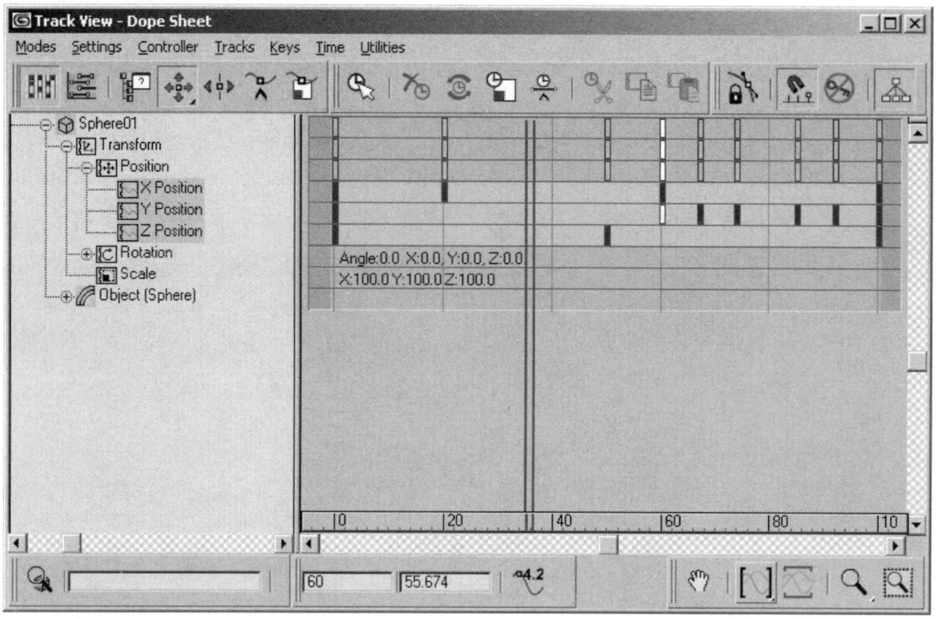

Figure 2.33: Track View - Dope Sheet

You can see that the keys created along the Y-axis by using the Curve Editor are visible in a spreadsheet form, as shown in Figure 2.34.

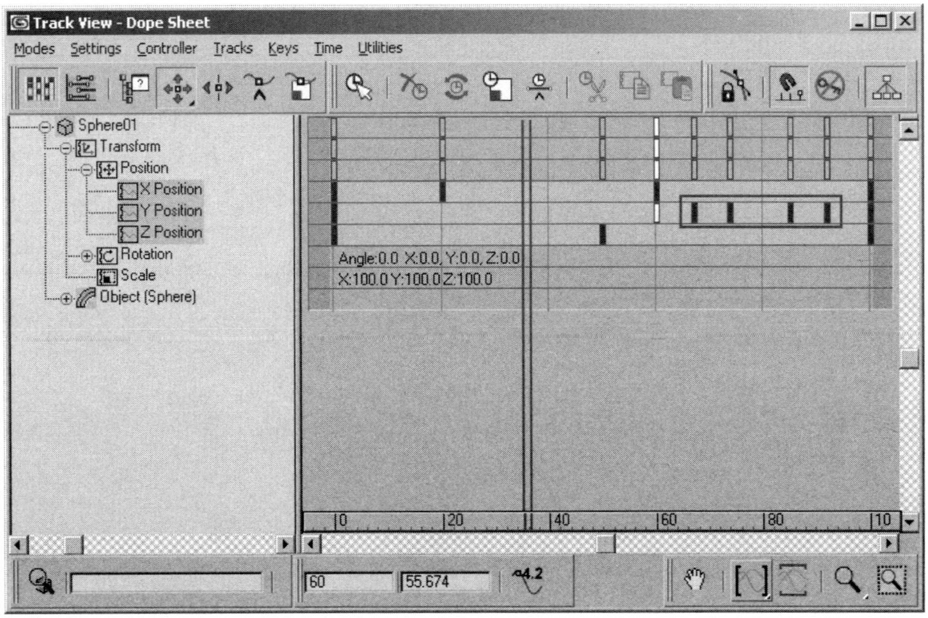

Figure 2.34: Keys in Spreadsheet Form

You can access each of these keys and move them to different time locations in the scene to further control the animation.

For example, the image in Figure 2.35 shows the same keys moved to different locations in the time frame. Therefore, the zigzag motion is witnessed in the full time frame. You can use the Move Keys tool to move the keys to a different location in the timeline.

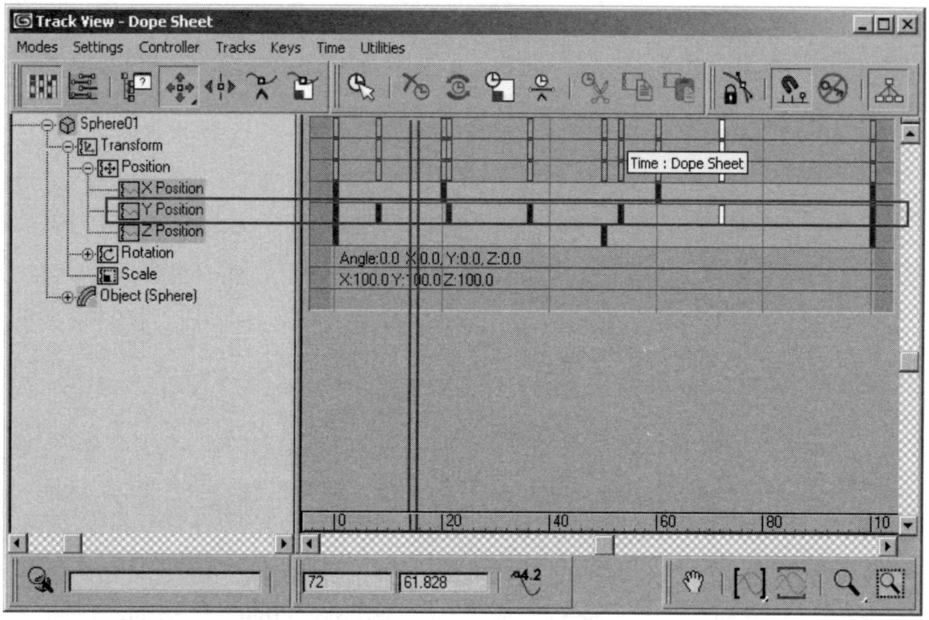

Figure 2.35: Movement of Keys

If you open the Track View - Curve Editor window, you will see the underlying curve has also been affected due to the motion of keys.

Figure 2.36 shows the changed curve after the keys are moved in the Dope Sheet.

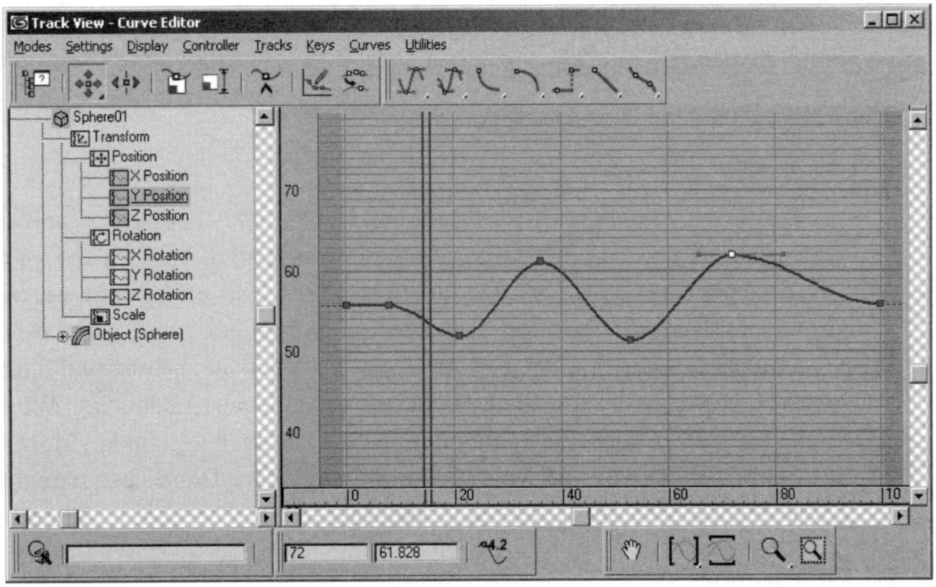

Figure 2.36: Changed Curve Editor

Why would one use the Dope Sheet when the same can be achieved using the Curve Editor?

You would typically use the Dope Sheet when you want to control only the timing of the keyframes. The Dope Sheet window does not show curves, and motion is affected only horizontally, therefore you do not risk the change of keys' magnitude values. You can only change the time at which the key resides.

Imagine you need 20 boxes moving. To make a believable crowd of such boxes moving, you would normally create copies of the same animated box 20 times and place them side by side. However, when you play the animation, all of them will move in unison making the motion unrealistic. Therefore, to get realistic motion, you would need to get subtle differences in their motions. Using the Dope Sheet, you can achieve realistic motion of 20 boxes. You can select each object and move the timing of the same key of each object to a slightly different location from the rest of the objects. This helps achieve a motion which will result in a believable animation.

The Curve Editor is precise, but it is difficult to manage control over the keys in the animation. The Dope Sheet gives fast and easy access to changing an animation.

2.2.3 Optimizing Performance of Track View

Describe the enhanced tools in Track View.

Track View provides the ease and multiplier curves to optimize animations. These curves are special function curves that are applied to initiate time for animation and displacement values for other function curves. This enables the use of global effects to the entire animation range. The ease and multiplier curves can be used to adjust the animation speed or change of locations of objects in an animated scene after the curves are created for the specified animation. Imagine a ball bouncing. When you create such an animation, curves are generated for the motion based on keyframes. These curves can be further adjusted without working on the keyframes again to change how the animation gets affected in the time duration at and around the keyframes.

Using Ease Curves

This function alters the time of the selected function curve. An ease curve fluctuates the time of a superior function curve. Standard function curves chart an animated limit value and changes to the time of a function curve over time. Imagine you were animating a ball moving on the ground and slowing down to rest. In the sequence of the animation if you create two keyframes—one at the beginning and one at the end, the ball would start and stop abruptly. The ease curve allows you to create the required animation of the ball starting fast and gradually slowing down before coming to a standstill. The Ease curve allows scaling time efficiently so that the animations such as mentioned above can be accomplished with ease and less effort.

Using Multiplier Curves

This function is used to scale the value of the selected function curve. The value of a multiplier curve is considered as a scale factor applicable to the value of its superior function curve. You can also use the ease and multiplier curves in the Curve Editor mode that enables you to edit its keys, ranges, and properties as done for any other animation track.

Applying a Curve to an Animation

You can assign the ease or multiplier curves to existing motion curves by performing the following steps:

1. In the Curve Editor Controller window, choose the track you want to ease. As shown in Figure 2.37, select all three XYZ position curves.

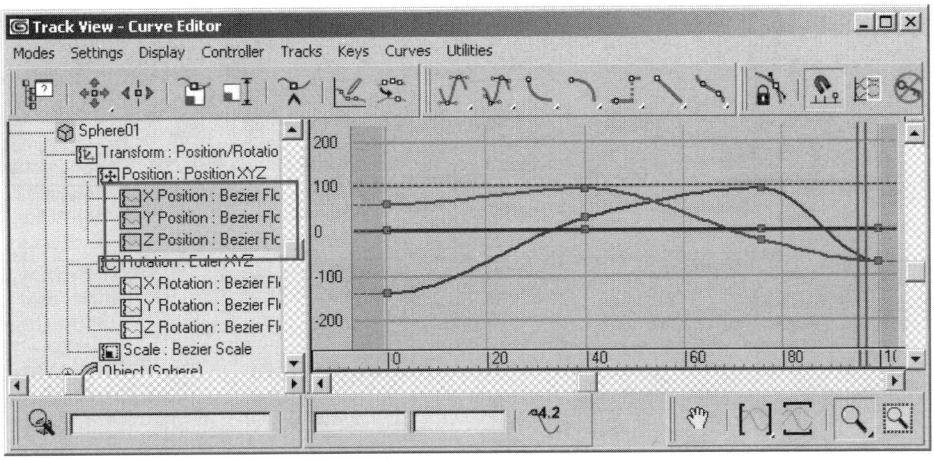

Figure 2.37: Curve Editor Controller

2. On the Curves menu, select **Apply - Ease Curve** or **Apply - Multiplier Curve**, as shown in Figure 2.38.

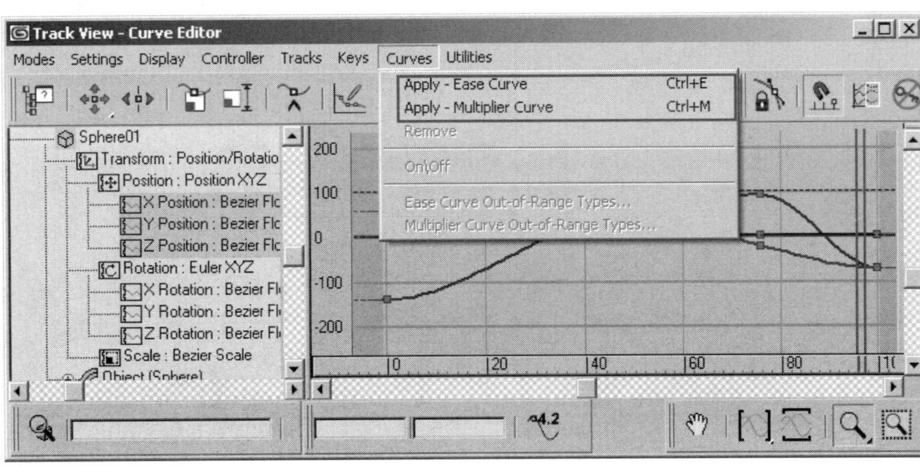

Figure 2.38: Apply - Ease Curve and Apply - Multiplier Curve

3. In the Controller window, extend the selected tracks to view the ease curve, as shown in Figure 2.39.

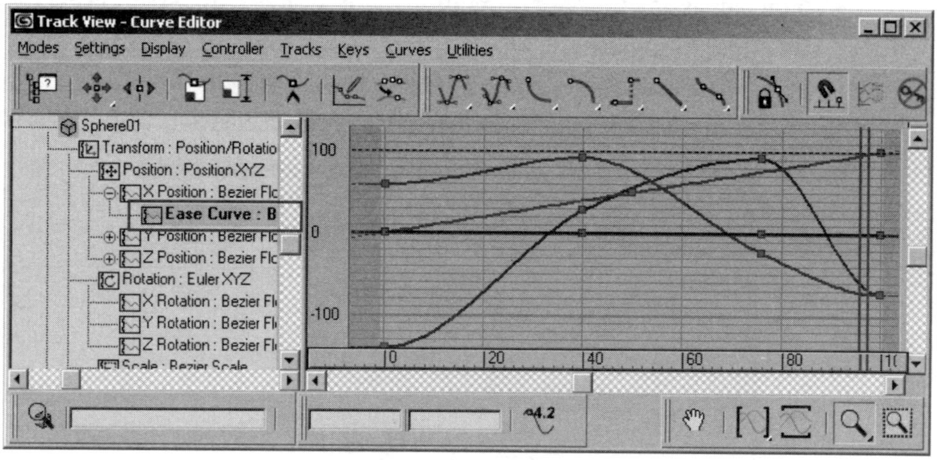

Figure 2.39: Ease Curve

4. Hold down the CTRL key and click the ease curve and the controller track.
5. Arrange the keys or points on the ease curve to get the required result in the controller curve, as shown in Figure 2.40.

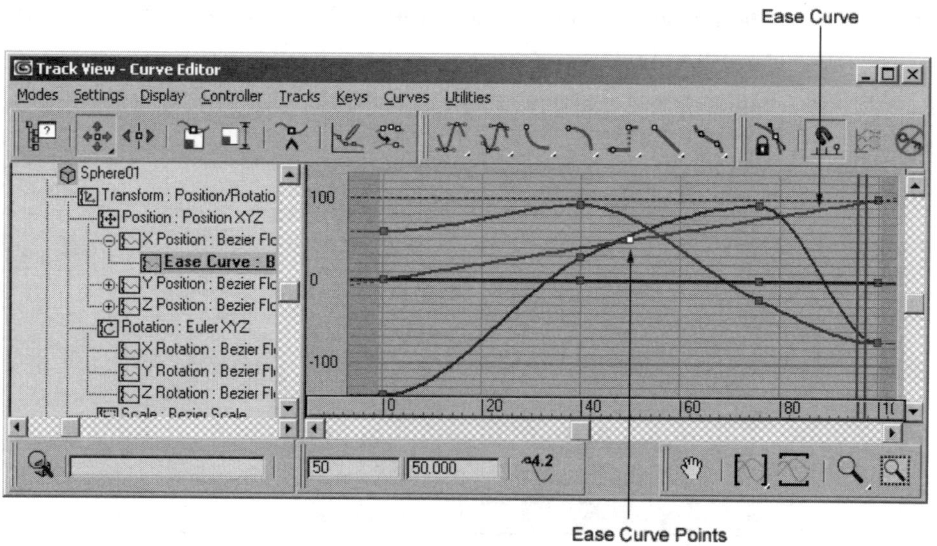

Figure 2.40: Controller Curve

To make changes in the effect, you have to add or move keys in the Edit window.

Deleting a Curve

You can delete an ease or multiplier curve at any time using the Remove menu option. In addition to removing, you can also choose to activate or deactivate the effect of the ease or multiplier.

Follow the given steps to carry out the function of removing an ease curve or multiplier:

1. Select one or more ease or multiplier curve tracks in the Controller window Hierarchy list you want to remove, as shown in Figure 2.41.

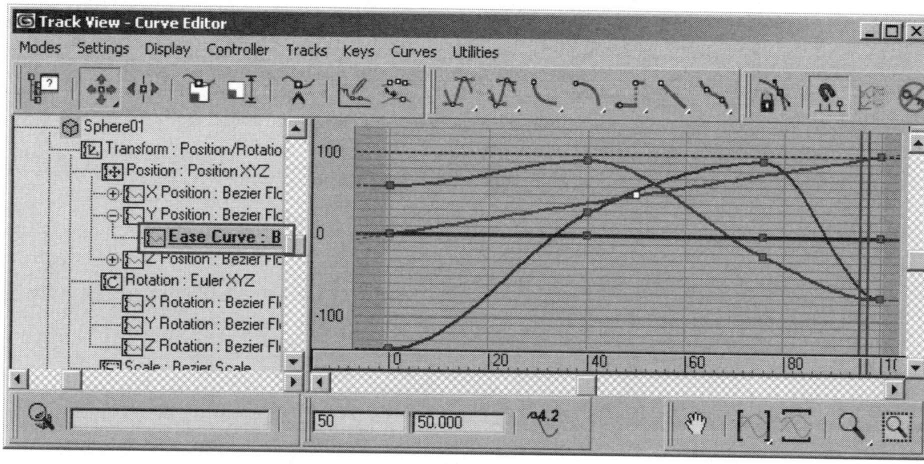

Figure 2.41: Multiplier Curve Tracks

2. Choose **Curves → Remove**, as shown in Figure 2.42.

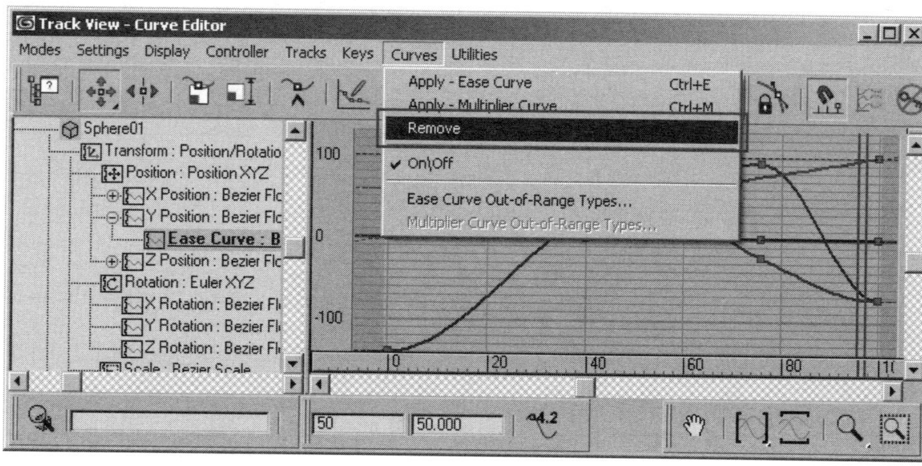

Figure 2.42: Remove Curve

The selected Ease or Multiplier curve is removed, as shown in Figure 2.43.

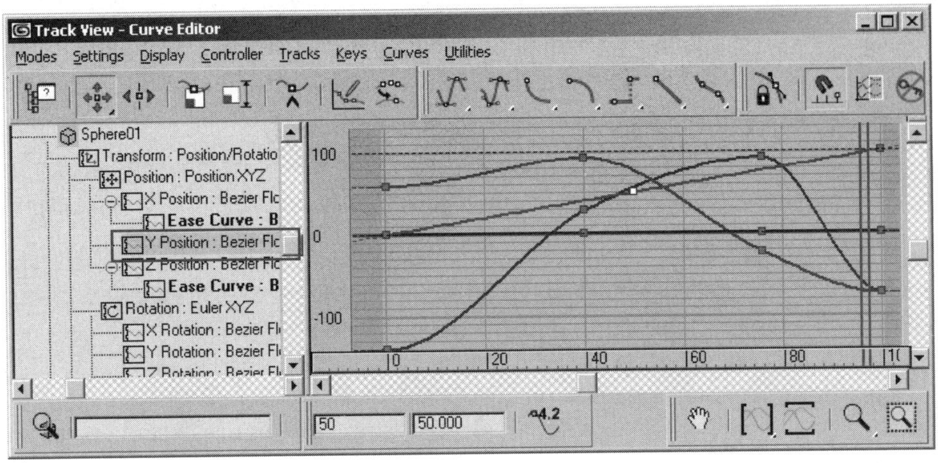

Figure 2.43: Removed Curve

3. You can activate or inactivate the effect of the ease or multiplier curves using **On\Off** (curves) without removing the curve, as shown in Figure 2.44.

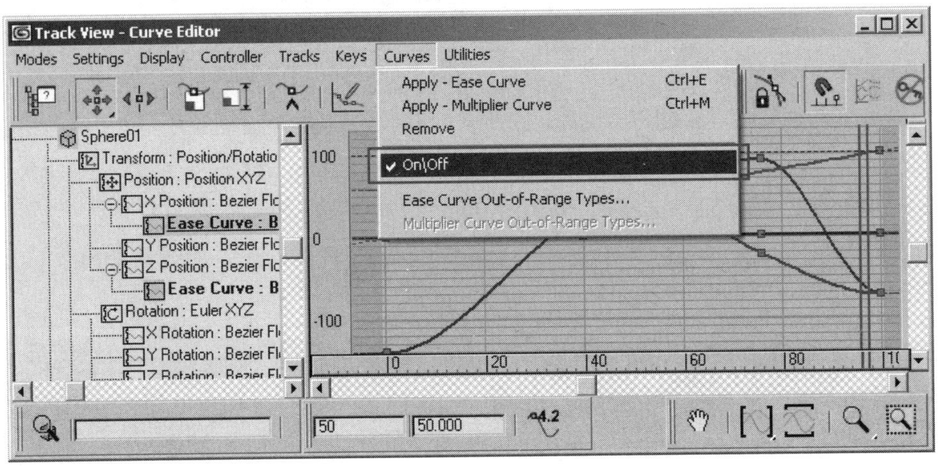

Figure 2.44: Selecting On\Off

You learned to remove and activate or deactivate an ease or multiplier curve.

Practice Questions

1. List one situation when you would use Dope Sheet instead of Curve Editor.
2. List the toolbar buttons that allow you to make changes in the keys part and how.
3. You can optimize animations using ______ and ______ curves.
4. You cannot activate or deactivate an ease or multiplier curve. (True/False)

Summary

- Track View is useful in complex animations where creating and editing animations through viewports is cumbersome and time-consuming. You can use Track View to control almost every aspect of the animation complexity.
- There are two types of Track View:
  - Track View - Curve Editor
  - Track View - Dope Sheet
- The Curve Editor provides functionality to animate objects. Using the Curve Editor, you can control the timing and magnitude of an animation. The curves, which are created based on the keys in keyframes, determine how 3ds max controls motion between keyframes.
- The Dope Sheet is an alternative method of controlling keys. It represents all the keys in a spreadsheet-like format which makes it easier to control animation if only timing of keys is to be changed.
- Track View provides the ease and multiplier curves to optimize animations. These curves are special function curves that are applied to initiate time for animation and displacement values for other function curves.
- The ease curve function alters time of the selected function curve. An ease curve fluctuates the time of a superior function curve.
- The multiplier curve function is used to scale the value of the selected function curve. The value of a multiplier curve is considered as a scale factor applicable to the value of its superior function curve.
- You can remove or activate or deactivate an ease or multiplier curve any time.

References

- Murdock, Kelly L., 3ds Max 5, Bible. Wiley Publishing Inc., USA. 2003.
- Animator's Survival Kit, Richard Williams, Faber & Faber, 2002.
- http://www.miralab.unige.ch/5teaching/assdb/htmls/StudentFiles/Cours_3DSMax/A03_Trackview.pdf (February 10, 2004)
- http://www.maxhelp.com/content/tutorials/express/express.htm (February 10, 2004)
- http://www.arch.kth.se/vmav/anime2/anime2.html (February 10, 2004)
- http://www.lowend.se/3d_festival_notes/3df_03_12principles.html (February 10, 2004)
- http://www.izware.com/faqs/cache/14.html (February 10, 2004)

Assignments

1. List the two functions that you can perform in ease and multiplier curves.
2. List the various steps for removing an ease and a multiplier curve.
3. Define the following components of the toolbar:
   a) Filter
   b) Draw Curves
   c) Scale Keys
4. Identify the steps to apply an ease curve or a multiplier curve.
5. Identify the various ways of applying ease and multiplier curves.
6. List the Amplify values that affect scaling.
7. Define the Curve Editor interface with a diagram.
8. Define the following components of the menu bar:
   a) Modes
   b) Setting
   c) Controller
   d) Curves

Lab Exercise

Exercise 1

Objective

Animate a ball.

Problem Statement

Animate a ball such that it bounces three times before it halts to rest and with every bounce it reaches a lower height.

Lab Setup

3ds max 6

Procedure

1. Open the file **ch02_lab_ex1_model.max** provided in the CD, as shown in Figure 2.45.

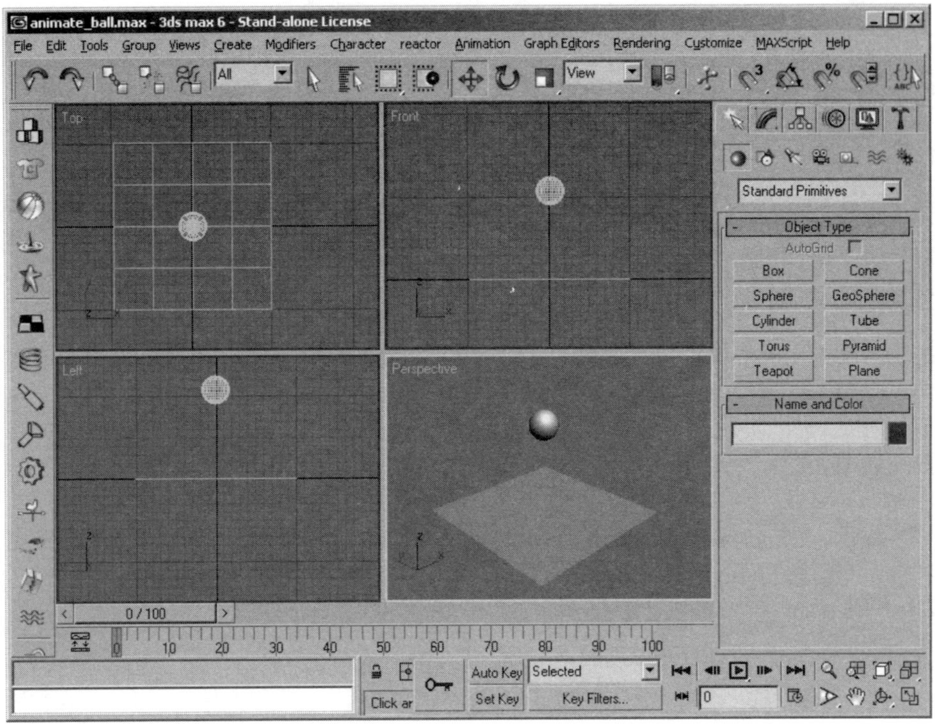

Figure 2.45: animateball.max

2. Click the ball to select it, as shown in Figure 2.46.

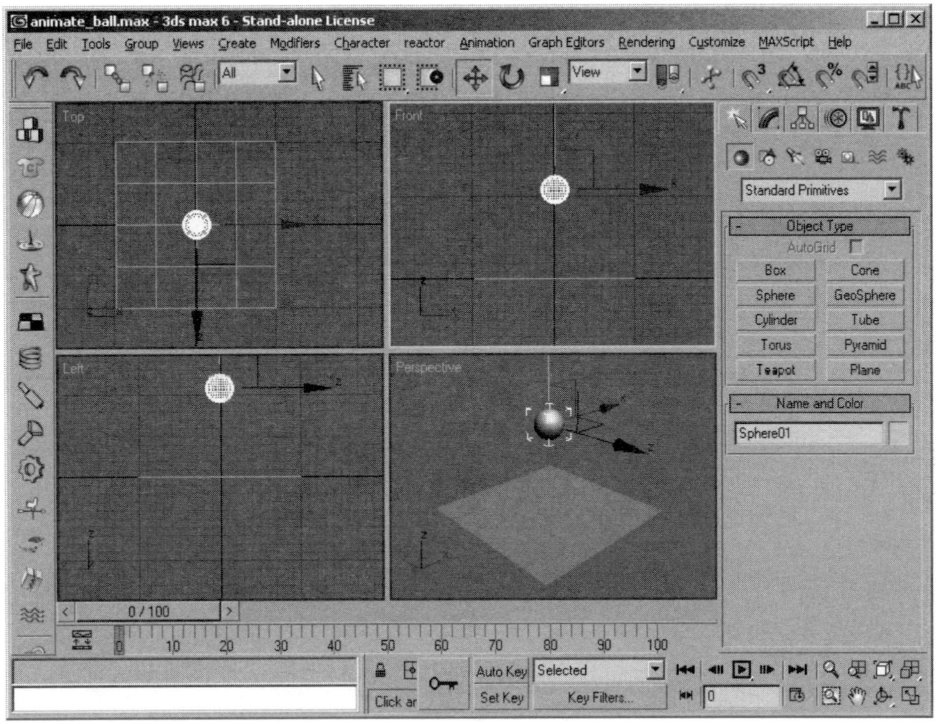

Figure 2.46: Ball

3. Click the **Auto Key** button, as shown in Figure 2.47.

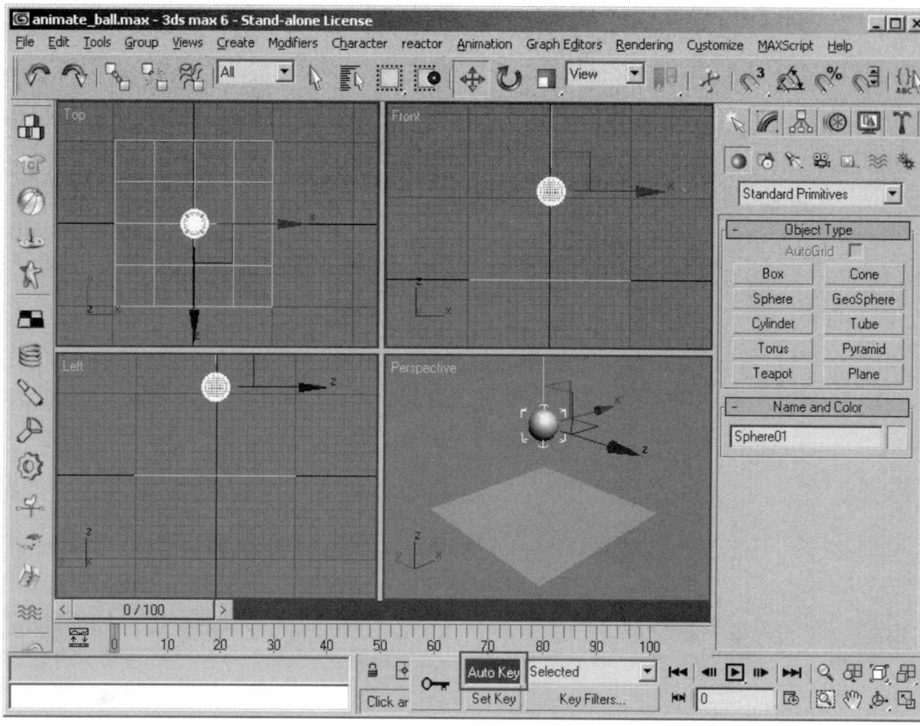

Figure 2.47: Auto Key

4. Scroll down the animation slider to the frame 100, as shown in Figure 2.48.

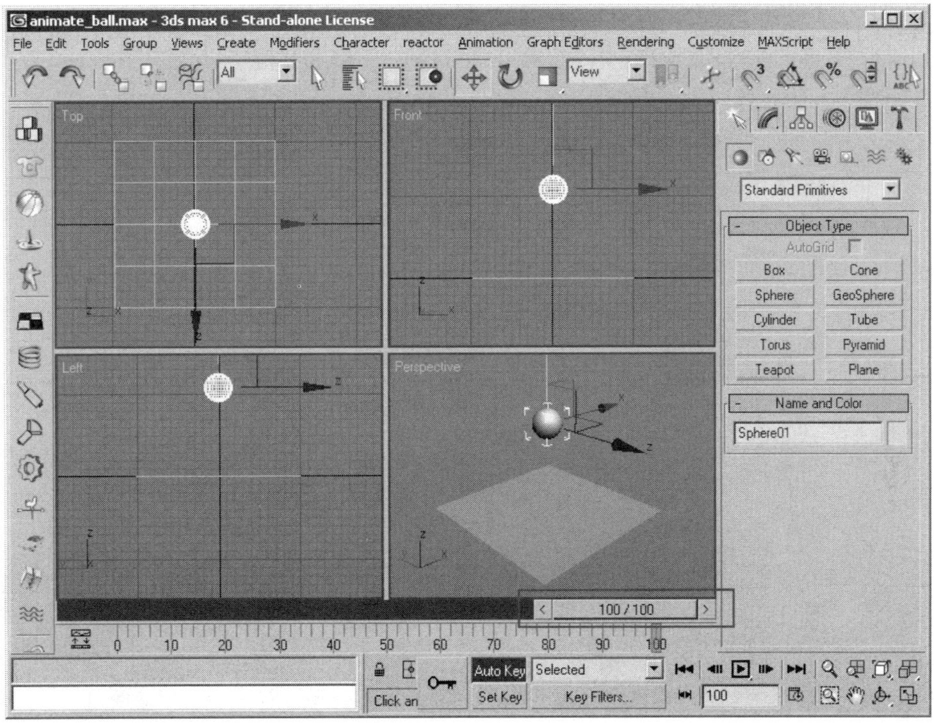

Figure 2.48: Frame 100

5. Use the move tools to exactly position the ball on the surface of the plane, as shown in Figure 2.49.

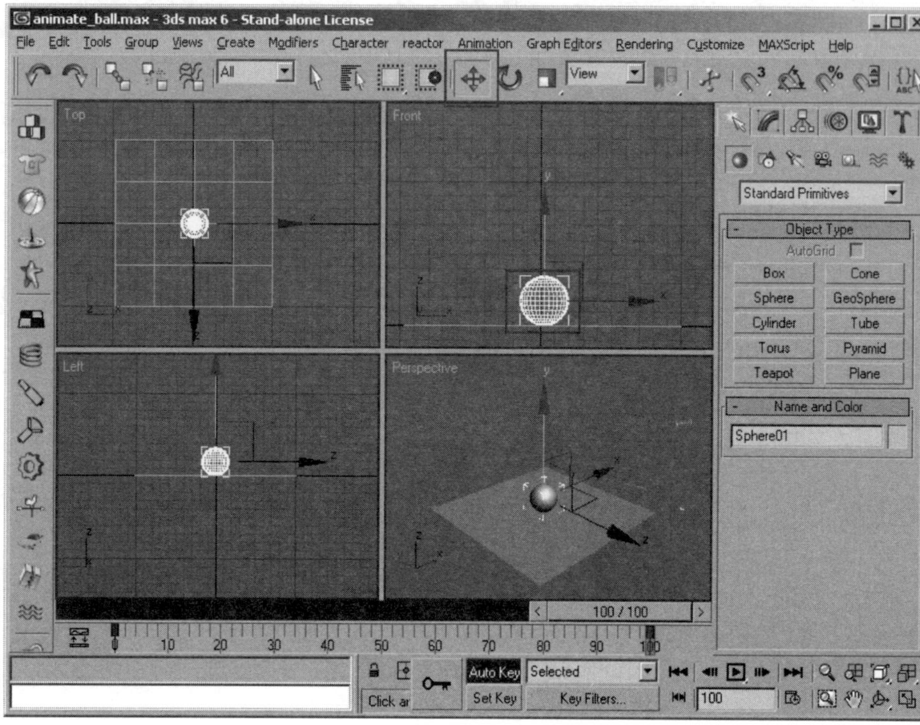

Figure 2.49: Move Tools

6. Click the **Auto Key** button to move out of the animation mode, as shown in Figure 2.50.

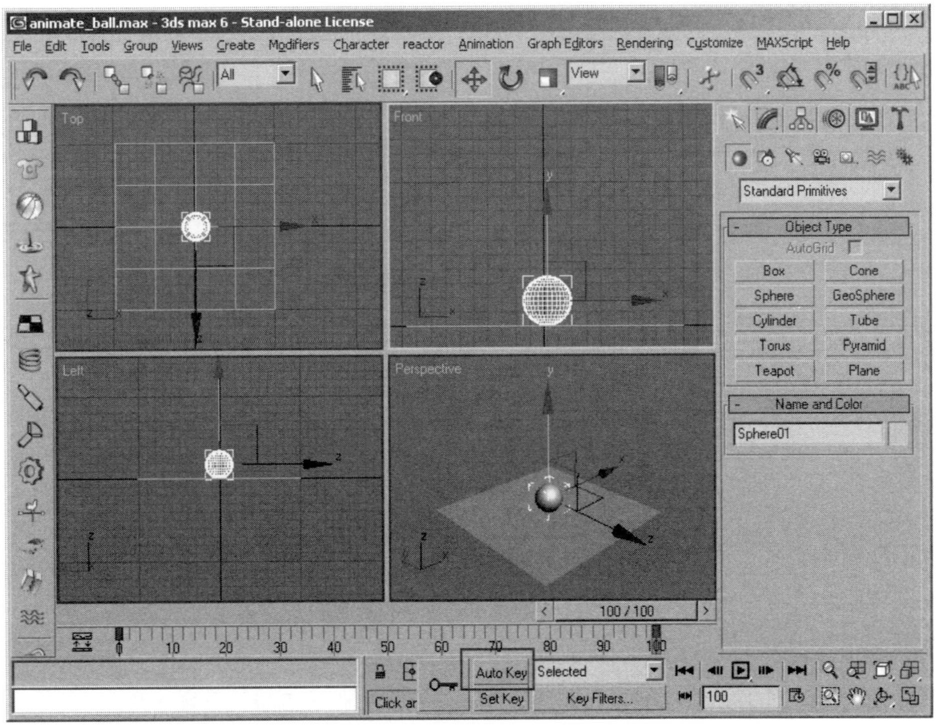

Figure 2.50: Auto Key

7. Click **Graph Editors → Track View - Curve Editor** to open the Curve Editor, as shown in Figure 2.51.

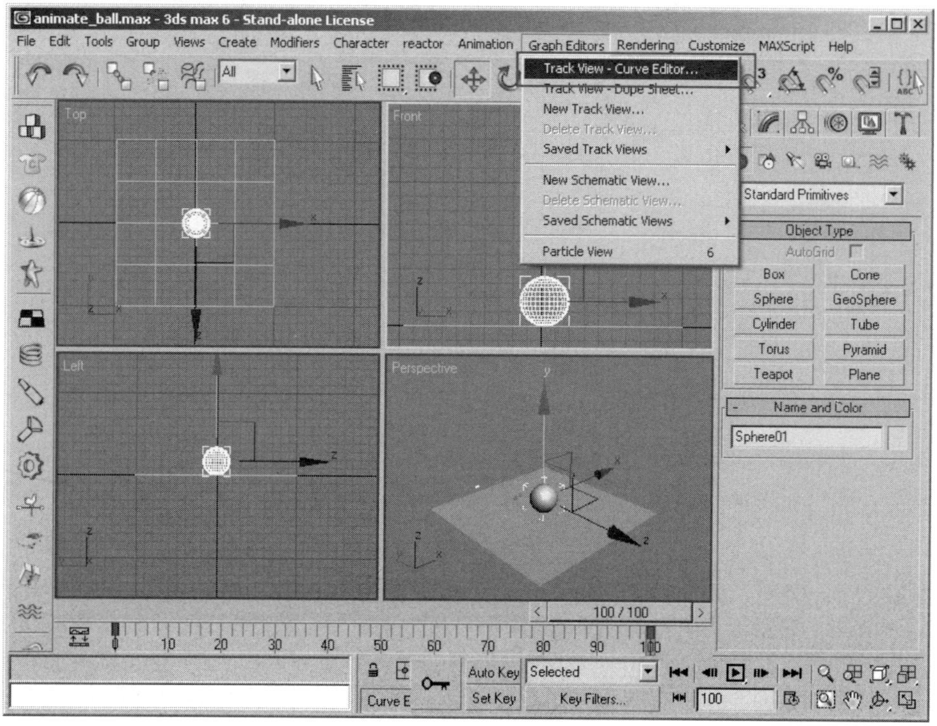

Figure 2.51: Curve Editor

8. In the Controller window, click the **Z Position** item under the Ball object to show only the Z-axis, as shown in Figure 2.52.

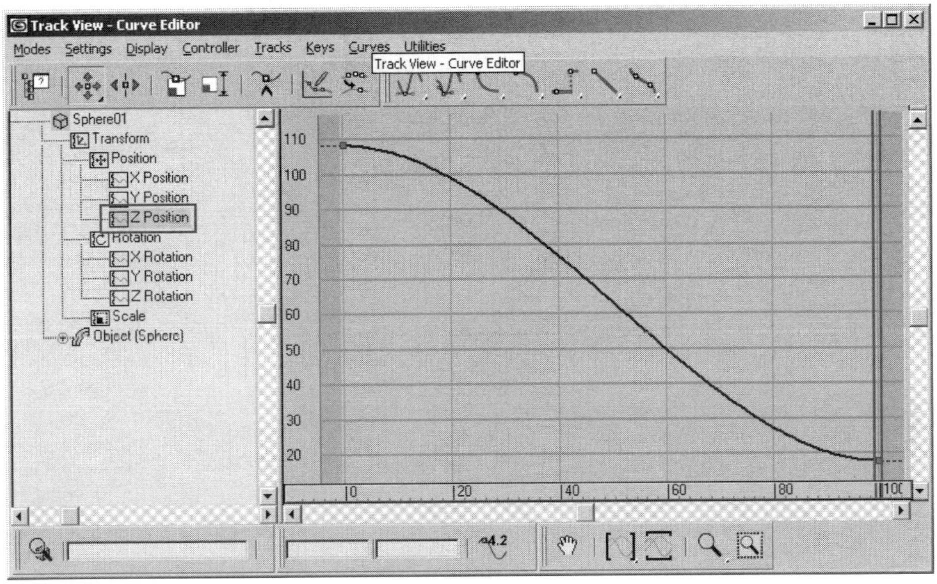

Figure 2.52: Z-axis

9. Click the **Add Keys** button. Add keys onto the curve, as shown in Figure 2.53.

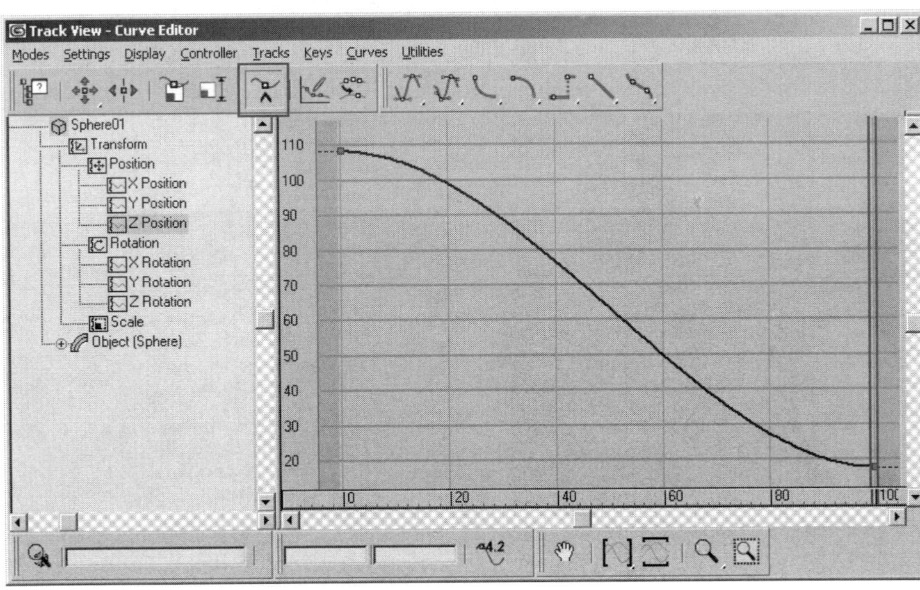

Figure 2.53: Add Keys

10. Move your cursor over the curve and add 4 keys, as shown in Figure 2.54.

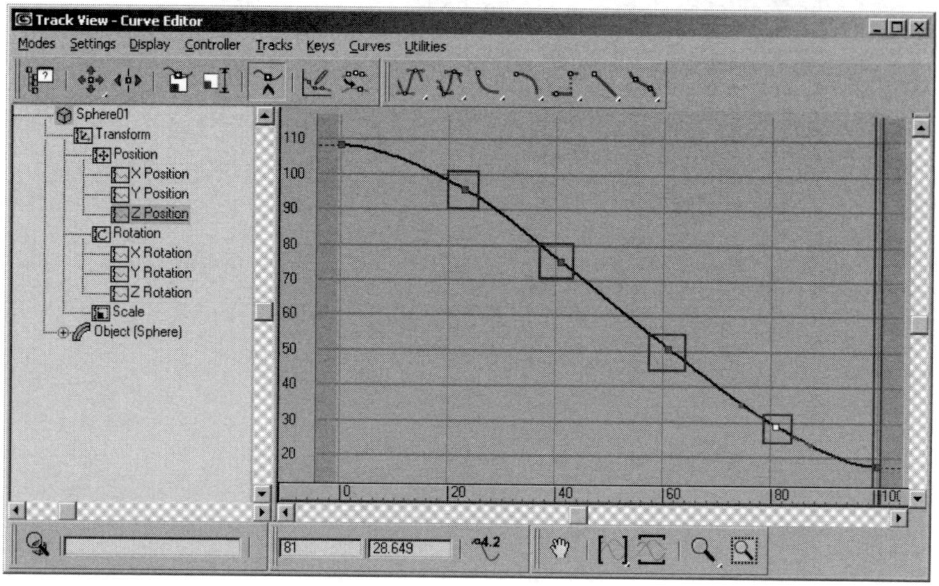

Figure 2.54: Blue Curve

11. Click the **Move Keys** button, as shown in Figure 2.55.

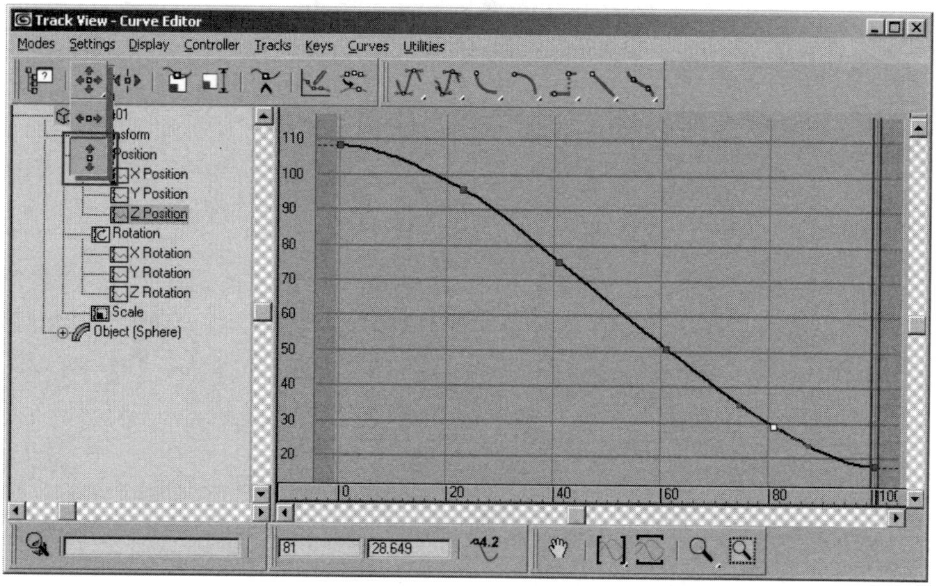

Figure 2.55: Move Keys

12. Select each key and move to its location, as shown in Figure 2.56.

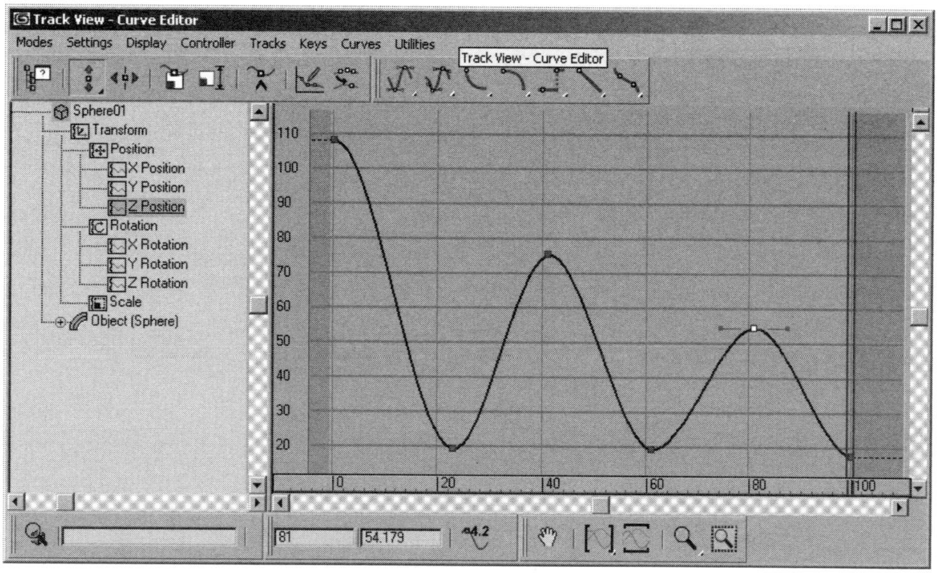

Figure 2.56: Keys Selection

13. Adjust the tangents of each key so that they are as shown in Figure 2.57 and Figure 2.58.

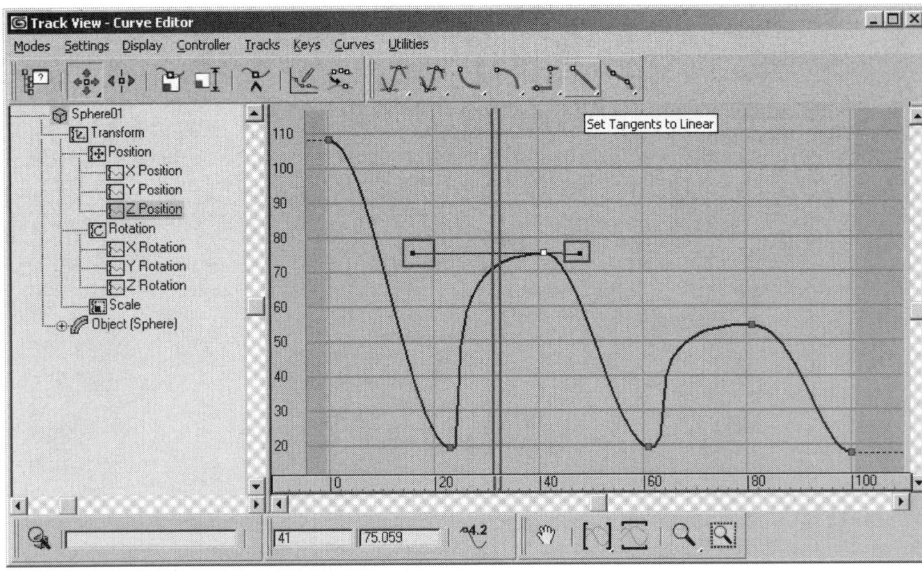

Figure 2.57: Adjust Tangents

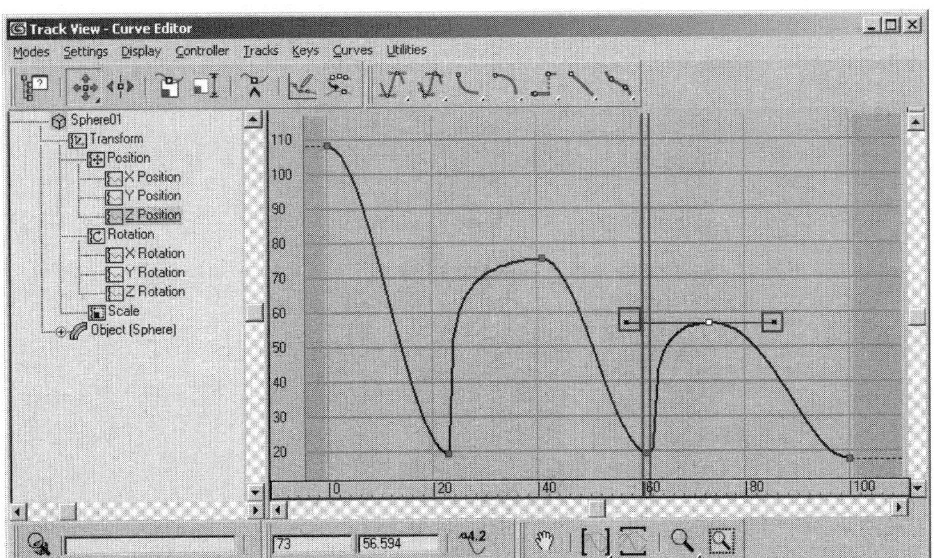

Figure 2.58: Adjust Tangents

14. Use the **Play** button to see your animation, as shown in Figure 2.59.

Figure 2.59: Play

15. Stop the animation and adjust the keys and their tangents to get the desired motion of a ball bouncing in real life.
16. Save the animation as **ch02_lab_ex1_sol.max**.

Lab Activity Checklist

S. No.	Tasks	Completed	
		Yes	No
1.	Animated the Initial Frames at 0 and 100		
2.	Opened Track View and selected the Right Curve		
3.	Added the required number of keys		
4.	Adjusted the keys according to the requirement		
5.	Adjusted the tangents of the keys according to the requirement		
6.	Re-tweaked the animation keys and curves to get the desired bouncing effect		

Project

Activities

- Analyze the animation and fix the squash effect by using the Curve Editor.

Controllers and Constraints

3

An animation requires a path and a direction to navigate. In animation, the path and direction are limited by constraints and controllers. Constraints limit an object to the dimensions of another object depending on the constraint that is being used. Controllers help in deciding the properties of the object to be animated, such as its scale, rotation, and transformation.

At the end of this chapter, you will be able to:

- Define different types of controllers.
- Animate using Path constraints.
- Differentiate between different types of animation controllers.
- Apply controllers using the motion panel and the track view.

3.1 Animation Controllers

3.2 Animation Constraints

3.1 Animation Controllers

Controllers let you fine-tune or modify animations, such as changing the direction or size of an object. For example, a ball that bounces vertically can be adjusted to bounce horizontally. To do this, you need to create a controller for the ball object in the animation. In this chapter, you will learn to use different types of controllers to provide a variety of effects to the animated objects.

3ds max automatically assigns every object a default animation controller. You can modify the default controller to change the object's position, shape, or rotation.

3ds max places keys on the track bar to indicate a change in the scene. As a scene becomes more complex, the number of keys increases making it difficult to place individual keys for every object. You can facilitate this task by applying controllers to objects.

Controllers let you add multiple animation effects to an object by loading more plug-ins. Controllers also provide parameters that create different animation effects.

3.1.1 Types of Animation Controllers

Define the various types of animation controllers.

Animation controllers use numerical values to create an animation effect on a parameter or a track. You can use a single value or multiple values. The following list describes 3ds max controllers:

- Float controllers manage the parameters or tracks in which one floating value needs to be controlled. Floating values provide the effect of alternate actions, such as on and off. For example, you can set a value, 10, for the on state and a value, 20, for the off state. When the value is 10, the animation turns on a specific effect, such as jump. When the value is 20, the animation stops jumping but moves linearly.
- Point3 controllers manage any of the three values of the parameters or tracks, for example, R, G, and B color. Point3 controllers alternate between red, green, and blue color.
- Position controllers place the parameter or track on the x, y, or z axes.

- Rotation controllers manage the rotation angle of the object or parameter.
- Scale controllers manage the size of the object or parameter.
- Transform controllers manage multiple values, such as position, rotation, or scale, in one step.

In addition to the kinds of values that they manage, controllers can be classified by the number of tracks that they affect:

- Single-track controllers control one track and manage one value. They include Position, Rotation, and Scale (PRS) controllers.
- Multiple-track controllers manage multiple tracks and multiple values. Transform controllers that control the x, y, and z axes are one of the multiple-track controllers.

Special controllers do not fall into either of the other categories. These controllers perform various functions, such as providing audio effects, jumps, fading, or linear effects.

3.1.2 Applying Controllers

Apply controllers using the motion panel and the Track View dialog box.

You can assign, manage, and edit the animation controllers using either of the following tools:

- Motion panel
- Track View dialog box

Applying Controllers Using the Motion Panel

You can access the Motion panel by clicking the wheel icon on the Command panel. The Motion panel provides two sets of options associated with the Parameters and Trajectories buttons. The Parameters options are used to apply controllers, while the Trajectories options allow you to adjust an animation path. The Motion panel applies to all types of controllers. In this section, you will learn to use the Motion panel and apply controllers using this panel.

Parameters Options

In the Parameters mode, the Motion panel displays the Assign Controller rollout along with the active controller rollouts. To activate options in the Parameters mode, you need to create and select an object in a viewport. However, the Assign Controller rollout is visible without any active controllers. Figure 3.1 displays the Motion panel with the Parameters button.

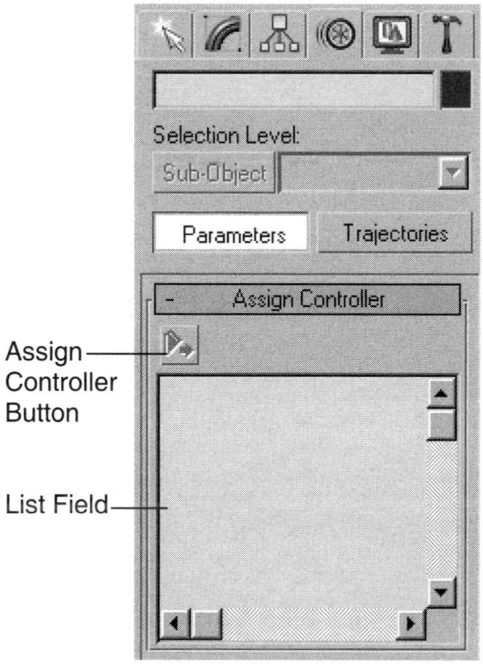

Figure 3.1: Motion Panel

When an object is created in any of the viewports, the Motion panel displays the parameters of the PRS controller so you can modify an object's position, size, or rotation. The PRS parameters are displayed by default.

Figure 3.2 displays the Motion panel after an object has been created. Notice that the Assign Controller rollout is active.

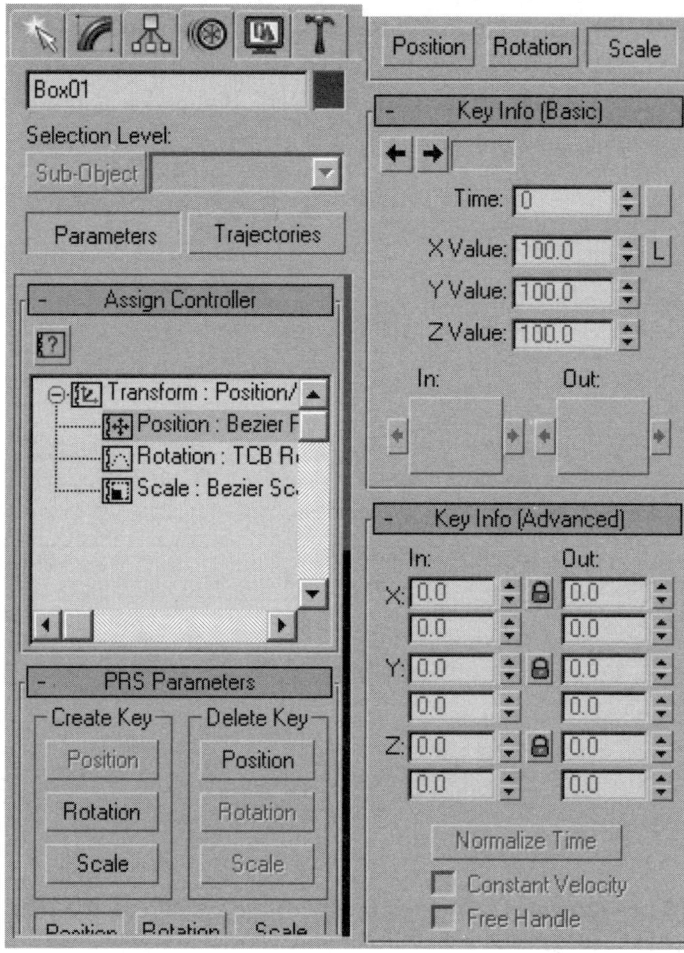

Figure 3.2: Motion Panel in the Parameters Mode with Objects in Viewports

The Motion panel rollouts in the Parameters mode are:

- Assign Controller
- PRS Parameters
- Key Info (Basic)
- Key Info (Advanced)

Assign Controller Rollout

The Assign Controller rollout enables you to select a controller from the Assign Controller dialog box. This dialog box is displayed when you select a track, such as Position, Rotation, or Scale, from the Transform list, and click the Assign Controller button. The Assign <*track name*> Controller dialog box displays only the controllers applicable to the selected track. The track name is visible in the title of the dialog box. For example, if you select the Position track, 3ds max displays the Assign Position Controller dialog box. Figure 3.3 shows the Assign Position Controller dialog box.

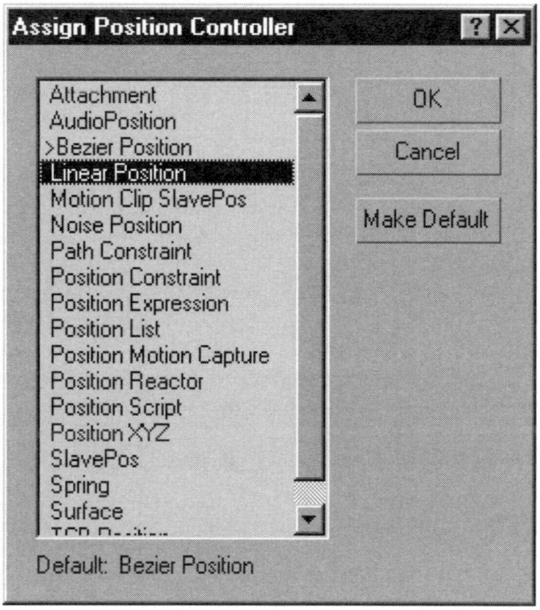

Figure 3.3: Assign Position Controller Dialog Box

The default controllers can be changed using the Assign Controllers dialog box. You can do this by selecting a controller, and then clicking the **Make Default** button.

You can edit the controller settings by clicking the Animation tab in the Preferences dialog box. Access the Preferences dialog box from the Customize menu.

PRS Parameters Rollout

The PRS Parameters rollout enables you to add or delete the position, rotation, and scale keys on the track bar. The PRS Parameters rollout is highlighted in Figure 3.4.

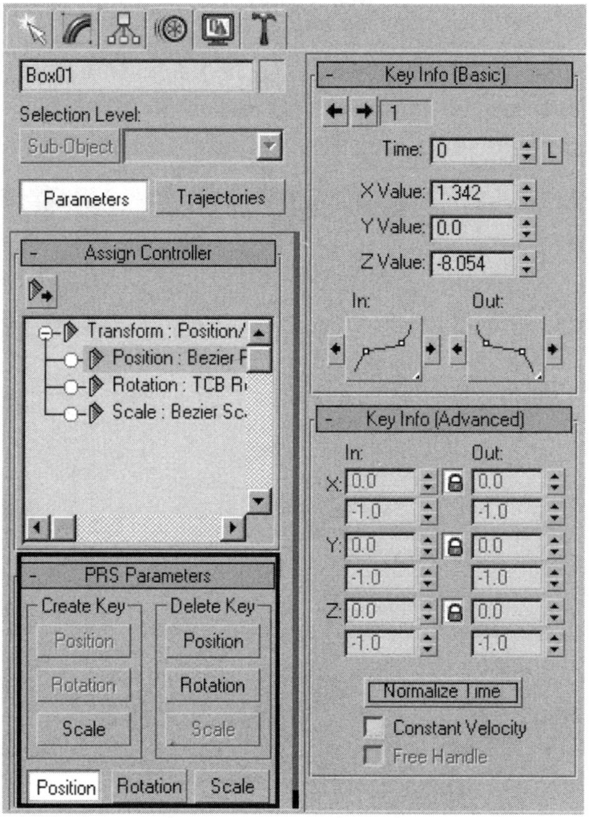

Figure 3.4: PRS Parameters Rollout

The Create Key and Delete Key buttons allow you to add or delete the keys for position, rotation, or scale for a selected frame. The key type is active in either Create or Delete. You can apply the keys to a frame only once; as soon as a key is applied, its button becomes inactive in the Create key set and is activated in the Delete key set.

The Position, Rotation, and Scale buttons decide the type of Key Info (Basic) and Key Info (Advanced) rollouts displayed below the PRS Parameters rollout.

Key Info (Basic) Rollout

The following Key Info (Basic) rollout options allow you to define and edit key values, placement, and behavior of objects:

- The arrows allow you to navigate between the keys.
- The Time list box specifies the time placement of the key on the track bar.
- The x, y, and z values specify the key value by defining the x-, y-, and z-axes.

The Key Info (Basic) rollout is highlighted in Figure 3.5.

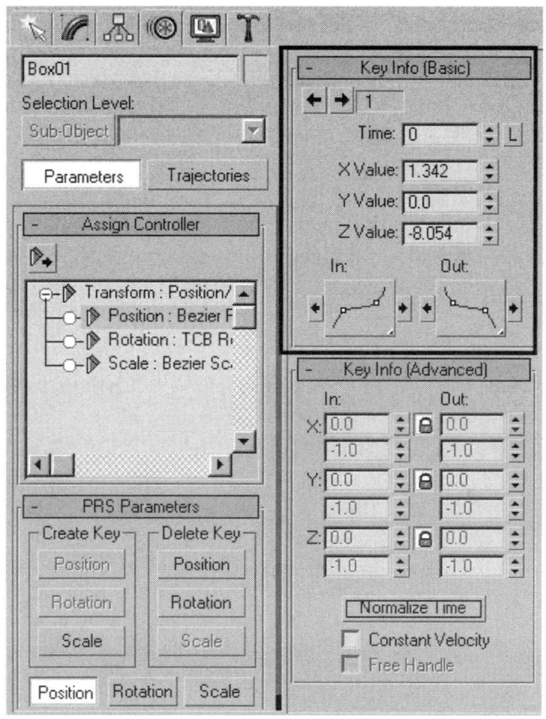

Figure 3.5: Key Info (Basic) Rollout

- The In and Out options specify how an animation will behave as it goes into and comes out of the key position. These behavior patterns are called key tangents. You can choose from six different key tangents. The custom tangent is editable. The arrow buttons on either side of the key tangents allow you to paste the selected key tangent to the previous and the next keys on the track bar.

Figure 3.6 displays the seven key tangents.

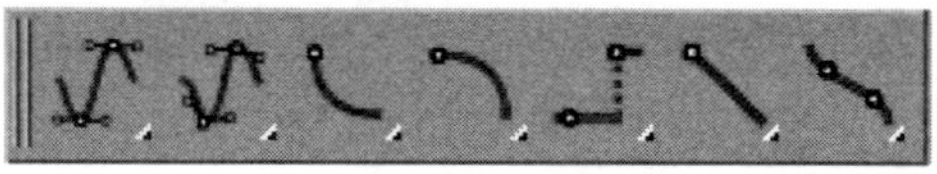

Figure 3.6: Seven Key Tangents

Table 3.1 lists the seven key tangents along with their functions.

Name of the Key Tangent	Function
Set Tangents to Auto	Enables the editing of the tangents.
Set Tangents to Custom	Sets the key to custom tangents.
Set Tangents to Fast	Enables you to set key tangency to fast in, fast out, or both in and out.
Set Tangents to Slow	Enables you to set key tangency to slow in, slow out, or both in and out.
Set Tangents to Step	Enables you to set key tangency to step in, step out, or both in and out.
Set Tangents to Linear	Enables you to set key tangency to linear in, linear out, or both in and out.
Set Tangents to Smooth	Enables you to set key tangency to smooth. This is used to even up the discontinuous motion.

Table 3.1: Key Tangents and Their Functions

Key Info (Advanced) Rollout

The Key Info (Advanced) rollout provides the following options to adjust the key values:

- The In/Out option allows you to specify the exact setting of the key tangent when a custom tangent is used. The Key Info (Advanced) rollout is highlighted in Figure 3.7.

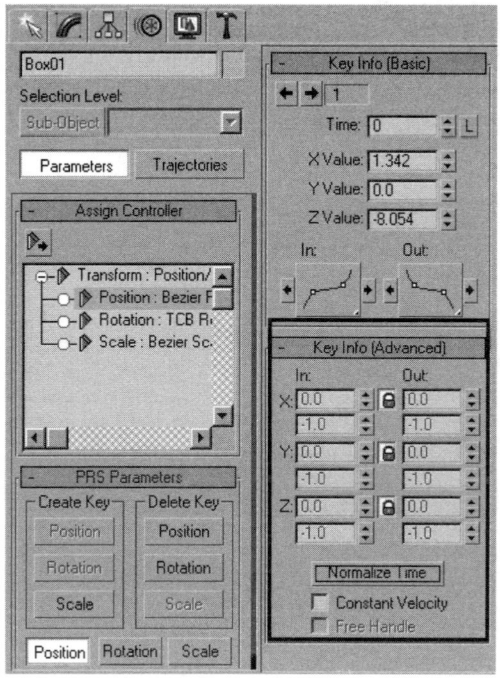

Figure 3.7: Key Info (Advanced) Rollout

- The Lock button with In and Out makes the two values exactly the same, but with one positive and the other negative.
- The Normalize Time option makes the animation smooth by placing the keys on the track bar according to the desired time as precisely as possible.
- The Constant Velocity option gives the object constant velocity between two keys.
- The Free Handle option is used to adjust the key tangents automatically, according to the time.

The Key Info (Basic and Advanced) settings are also available on the track bar, through the pop-up menu accessible by right-clicking the selected key.

Trajectories Options

The Motion panel Trajectories rollout enables you to adjust the path of an animation sequence. When you click the Trajectories button, the animation path is visible as a spline, with the keys represented as nodes. You can observe these changes in the animation path in Figure 3.8.

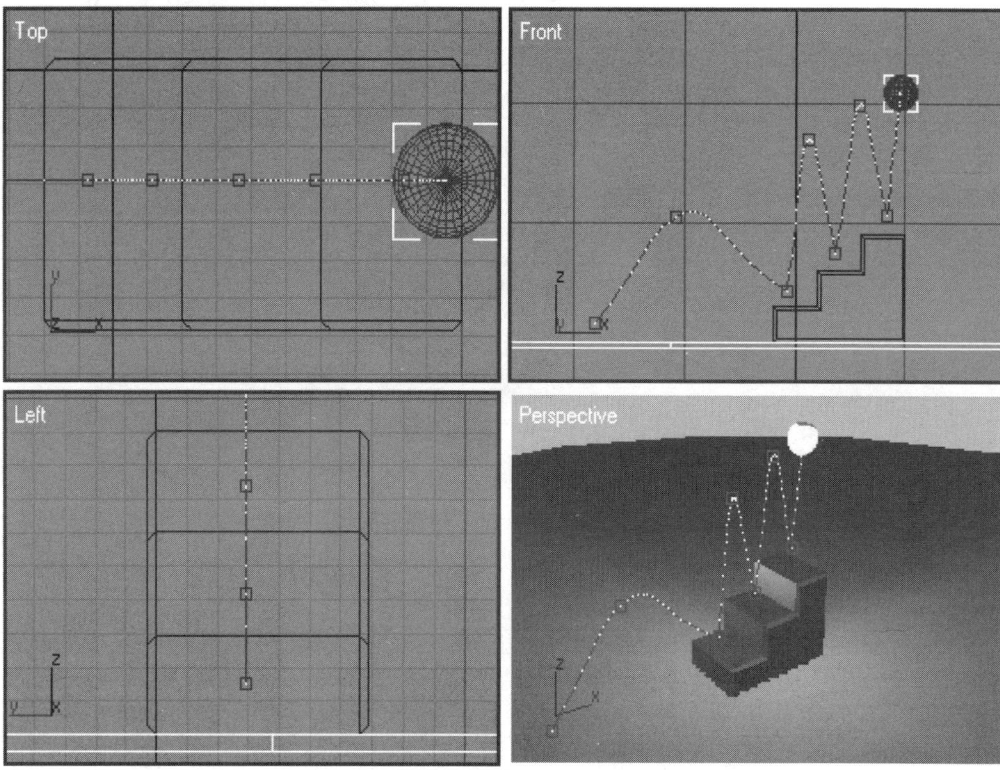

Figure 3.8: Viewports Displaying the Animation Path as a Spline with Trajectories

The animation path is visible as a red and white dotted line and there are boxes to indicate the keys.

Figure 3.9 displays the Trajectories rollout in the Motion panel.

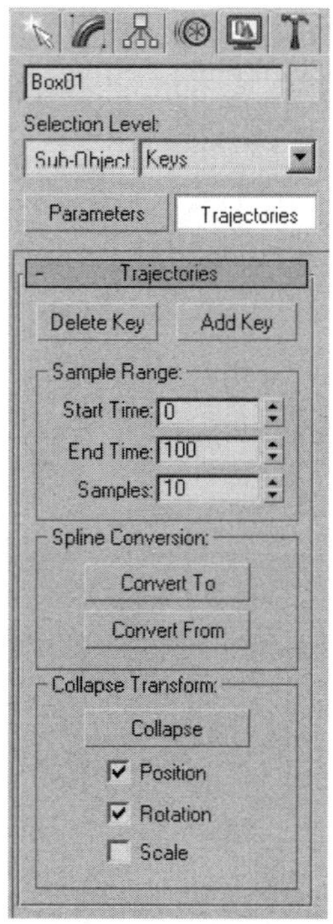

Figure 3.9: Trajectories Rollout in the Motion Panel

The various options in the Trajectories rollout are:

- The Sub-Object list box lets you select which sub-object to edit. The only option available for the current selection is Keys.
- The Delete Key button allows you to delete the selected key.
- The Add Key button adds keys to the animation path.

- The Sample Range box defines the settings used for the Spline Conversion and Collapse Transform options. This box has the following options:
  - The Start Time and End Time list boxes specify the range of frames to be covered in the conversion and transform functions.
  - The Samples list box defines the closeness with which the frames are sampled for spline conversion.
- The Spline Conversion box converts the animation path into a spline or from another spline. It has the following options:
  - The Convert To button converts the animation path into a spline.
  - The Convert From button converts a spline into an animation path.
- The Collapse Transform box is used to edit the keys of an animation created with the transform controller. The Collapse button collapses an animation into an editable trajectory path with keys.
- The Position, Rotation, and Scale check boxes allow you to specify which tracks to use for creating a trajectory using the Collapse button.

TIP: You can also view an object's trajectory by right-clicking the object to see the Object Properties dialog box.

Creating a Simple Animation

To assign Position controllers to an animation using the Motion panel, perform the following steps:

1. Open the file, ch03_position_start.max.

   You can see the ball in the viewports, as shown in Figure 3.10.

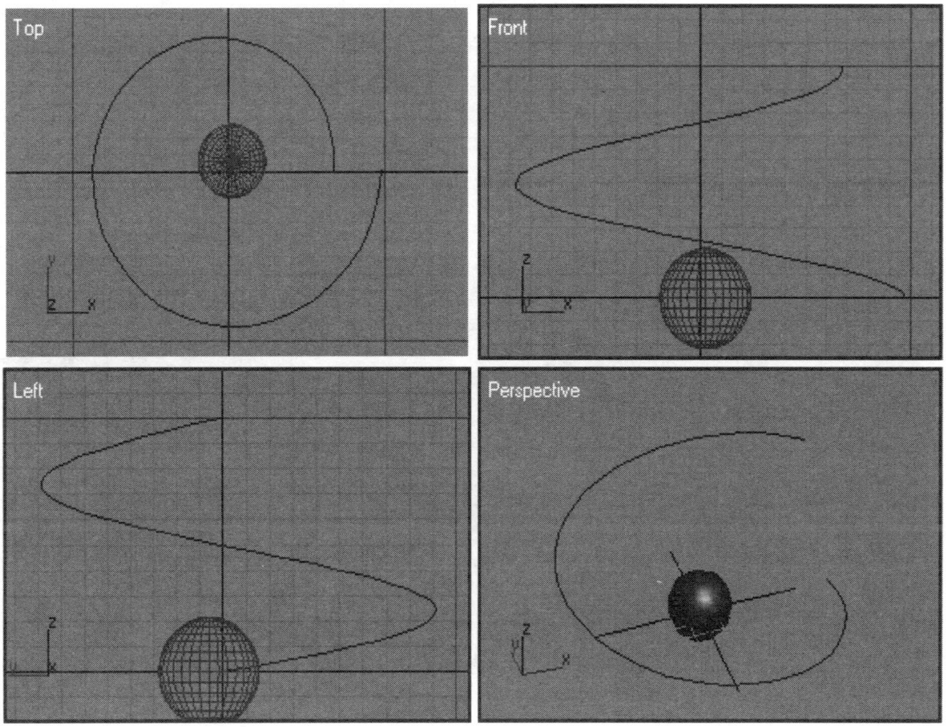

Figure 3.10: Ball in the Viewports

2. Click **Auto key** button.
3. Move the Time Slider to frame **50**.
4. Click the **Select and Move** button  and move the ball on the y-axis.

5. At frame 100, bring the ball back to its original position, as shown in Figure 3.11.

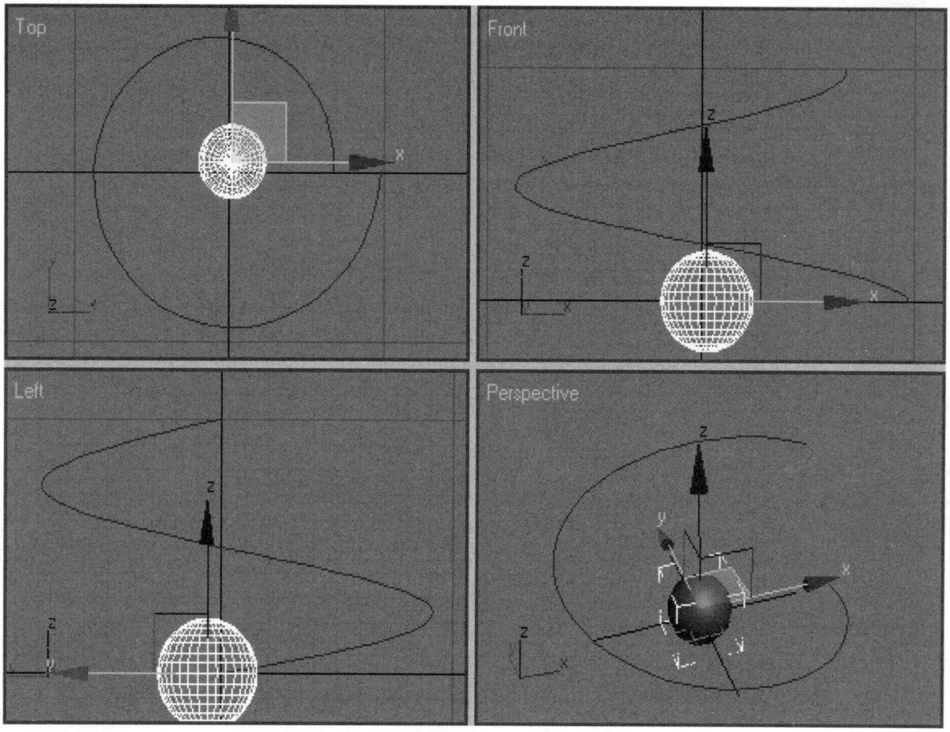

Figure 3.11: Ball in the Viewports

6. Click **Auto key** button.
7. To view the animation, click **Play Animation** in the playback controls.

Assigning Controllers

After a simple animation has been created, the next task is to add controllers to it using the Assign Controllers dialog box. To assign controllers to the animation using the Motion panel, perform the following steps:

1. Click the **ball** to select it and then right-click the **Sphere01** and select properties from the drop-down menu to view the Object Properties dialog box, as shown in Figure 3.12.

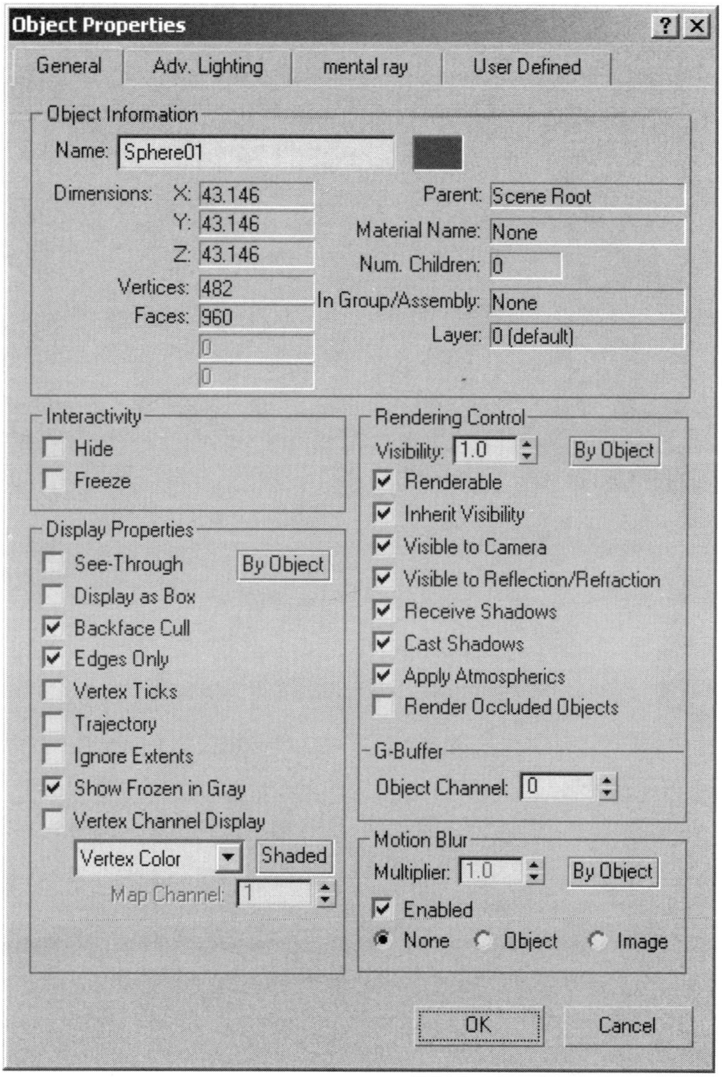

Figure 3.12: Object Properties Dialog Box

2. On the Display Properties group box, select the **Trajectory** check box. This check box is located in the Display Properties box of the Object Properties dialog box.
3. Click **OK**.
4. Navigate to the Motion panel, and from the Assign Controller rollout, select the **Position** track.
5. Click **Assign Controller.**
6. In the Assign Position Controller dialog box, change the controller from Bezier to **Linear Position** controller, as shown in Figure 3.13.

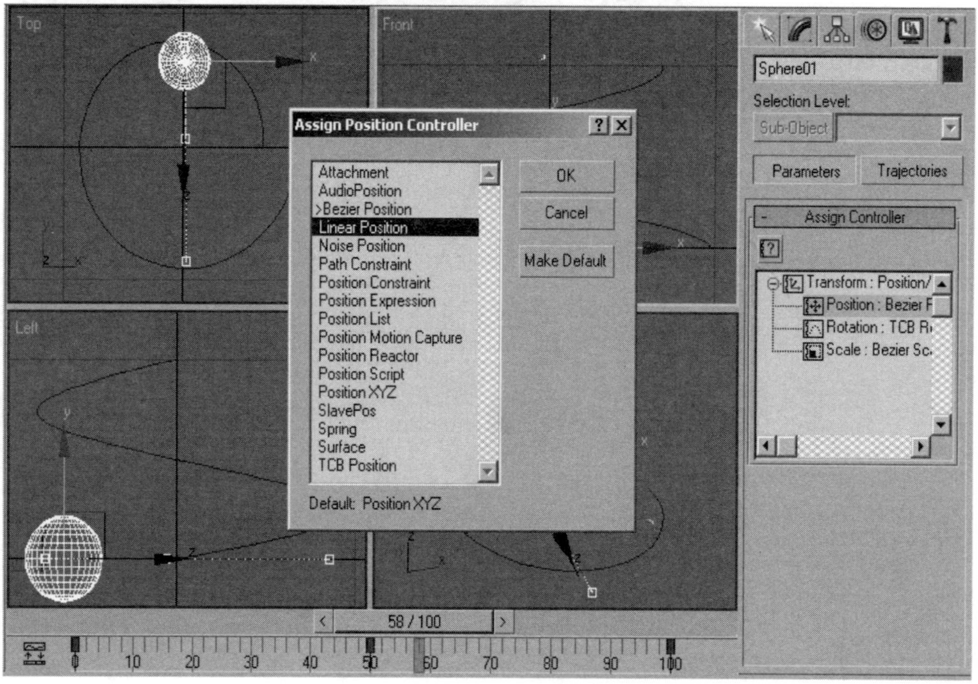

Figure 3.13: Assign Position Controller Dialog Box

7. Click **OK**.

Figure 3.14 displays the effect of the Linear Position controller on the object trajectory.

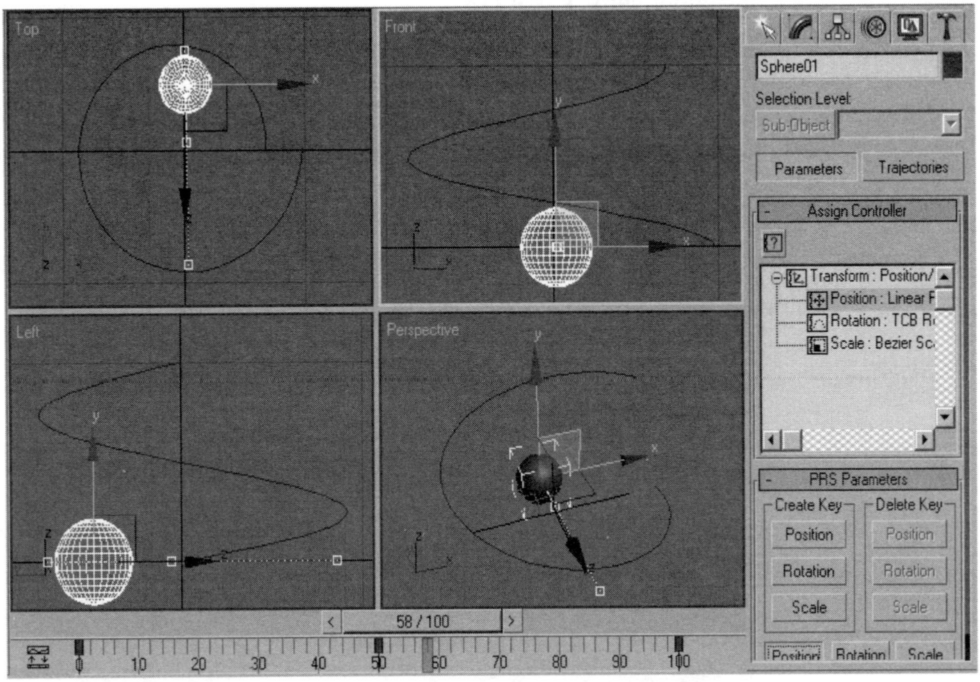

Figure 3.14: Object Trajectory

8. Click **Assign Controller**, and in the Assign Position Controller dialog box that displays, change the controller from Linear Position to **Position XYZ**.

9. The Position XYZ controller allows you to edit the position on any or all the three axes individually. Click **OK**.
10. Click the **plus** sign on the Position track in the Motion panel. The Position track expands to display tracks for all the three axes: x Position, y Position, and z Position. You can edit the position of the ball on any or all of the three axes. Figure 3.15 displays the effect of the Position XYZ controller on the object trajectory.

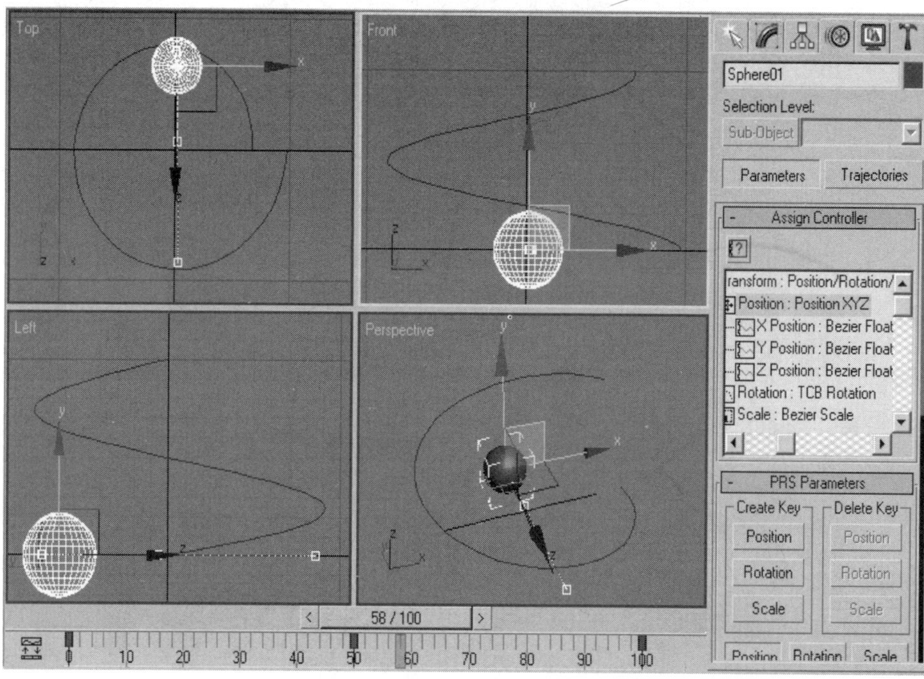

Figure 3.15: Effect of the Position XYZ Controller

11. Click the **Play Animation** button to view the animation.
12. Save the file as **ch03_position_end.max**.

Applying Controllers Using the Track View

In addition to the Motion panel, you can use the Track View option to manage objects and parameters. This option presents all the components of the animation in a hierarchical sequence. Figure 3.16 shows the options available in the Track View dialog box.

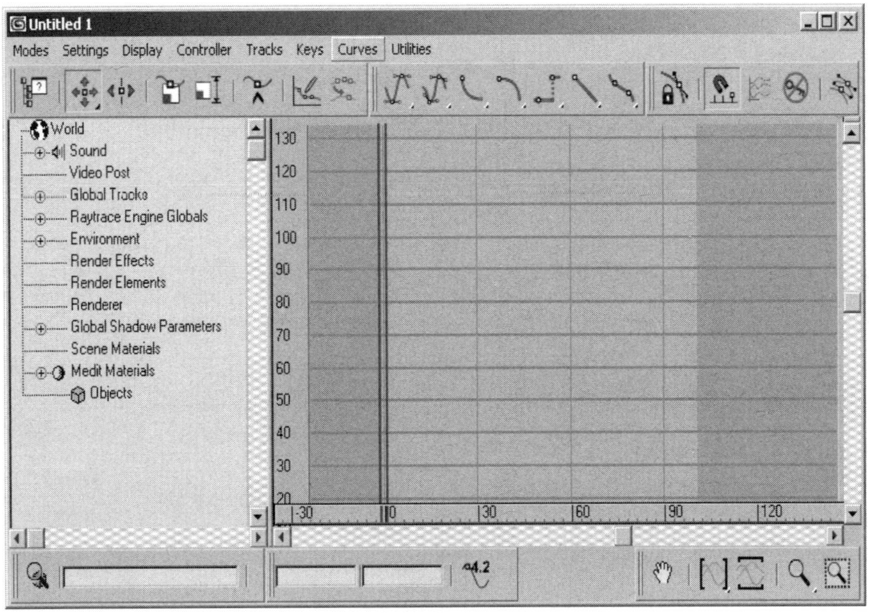

Figure 3.16: Track View Dialog Box

The main options available in the Track View dialog box are:

- Toolbar
- Sequence
- Tracks
- Time bar
- Status bar

Toolbar

Toolbar buttons let you manage tracks. Some of the buttons are global and remain standard irrespective of the mode, while others change depending on the edit mode. By default, the Track View dialog box is in the edit keys mode.

Table 3.2 lists the global buttons available in the Track View dialog box.

Button	Name	Functionality
	Filters	Displays the Filters dialog box, which allows you to select the tracks to be displayed in the Track View dialog box.
	Copy Controller	Copies the selected track.
	Paste Controller	Pastes the copied track.
	Assign Controller	Assigns controllers using the Assign Controller dialog box, similar to the Motion panel.
	Delete Controller	Deletes the selected track.
	Make Controller Unique	Makes the pasted instance track independent of the track from which it was copied.
	Parameter Curve Out-of-Range Types	Decides the behavior of an object when it is out of range.
	Add Note Track	Adds a note track below the selected track to take notes.
	Delete Note Track	Deletes the selected note track.
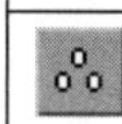	Edit Keys	Activates the edit keys mode for the editing of the keys of the animation.
	Edit Time	Activates the edit time mode for editing the time span of the animation.
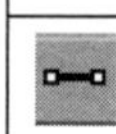	Edit Ranges	Activates the edit ranges mode for editing the range or span of the animation.
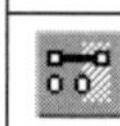	Position Ranges	Activates the position ranges mode for editing the range of the animation without touching the key placement.
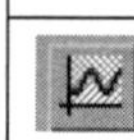	Function Curves	Activates the function curves mode which displays the values of the tracks as editable curves.
	Snap Frames	Makes the changes occur only at specific frames and not in between them.
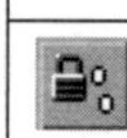	Lock Selection	Locks the selected tracks selection from further change.
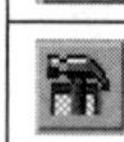	Track View Utilities	Provides access to the Track View Utilities dialog box to select the utilities.

Table 3.2: Global Buttons in the Track View Dialog Box

Edit Modes

The Track View dialog box provides five edit modes for editing an animation. These modes are accessible from the buttons on the toolbar in the Track View dialog box. When you select a particular mode, its corresponding buttons are visible on the toolbar.

The edit modes are:

- Edit Keys: Enables you to edit the key placement.
- Edit Time: Enables you to edit the timing of an animation.
- Edit Ranges: Enables you to edit the range of the selected object or parameter, which signifies its life span in the animation.
- Position Rangcs: Enablcs you to edit the range of the selected object or parameter without touching the keys.
- Function Curves: Enables you to view the tracks as graphs depending on the type of controller. These graphs and curves can be managed and adjusted as needed within the animation.

Table 3.3 displays the buttons in different modes of the Track View dialog box.

Button	Name	Function	Mode
	Add Visibility Track	Adds a visibility track for the selected object.	Edit Keys
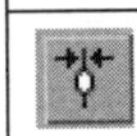	Align Keys	Aligns all the keys at one position.	Edit Keys, Function Curves
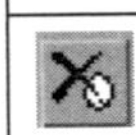	Delete Keys	Deletes the selected key.	Edit Keys, Function Curves
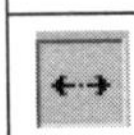	Move keys	Allows the horizontal movement of a key to change its placement.	Edit Keys
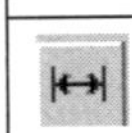	Slide Keys	Slides the selected keys to one side of the time bar.	Edit Keys
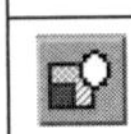	Scale Keys	Scales the selected keys in relation to their placement.	Edit Keys
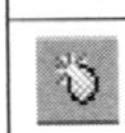	Add Keys	Enables the Add key mode, which adds a key at the click position.	Edit Keys, Function Curves
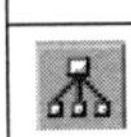	Modify Subtree	Allows the editing of a parent to affect the child.	Edit Keys, Edit Time, Edit Ranges

Button	Name	Function	Mode
	Properties	Displays the Properties dialog box for the selected track.	Edit Keys, Function Curves
	Delete Time	Deletes the selected block of time.	Edit Time
	Cut Time	Cuts the selected block of time.	Edit Time
	Copy Time	Copies the selected block of time.	Edit Time
	Paste Time	Pastes the selected block of time.	Edit Time
	Reverse Time	Reverses the flow of the selected block of time.	Edit Time
	Select Time	Allows the selecting of a block of time by dragging.	Edit Time
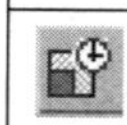	Scale Time	Scales the selected block of time.	Edit Time
	Insert Time	Enables the Insert Time mode which adds time at the selected point.	Edit Time
	Exclude Left/ Right End Point	Excludes the left-most or the right-most key of the selected group of keys.	Edit Time
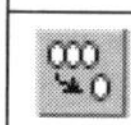	Reduce Keys	Reduces the number of keys in an animation.	Edit Time
	Recouple Ranges	Rearranges the range bar to flow with the first and last key placements.	Position Ranges
	Freeze Nonselected Curves	Freezes the nonselected curves from mistaken editing.	Function Curves
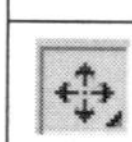	Move Keys	Moves the keys on the curves in either direction.	Function Curves
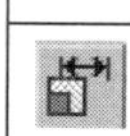	Scale Keys	Scales the key position horizontally.	Function Curves
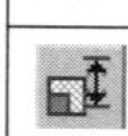	Scale Values	Scales the value vertically.	Function Curves

Button	Name	Function	Mode
	Show Tangents	Displays the handles for the curves.	Function Curves
	Lock Tangents	Locks the curve from further editing.	Function Curves
	Apply Ease/ Multiplier Curve	Applies an ease or multiplier curve.	Function Curves
	Delete Ease/ Multiplier Curve	Deletes an ease or multiplier curve.	Function Curves
	Enable/Disable Curve Toggle	Enables the activation and deactivation of the ease and multiplier curves.	Function Curves
 	Ease/Multiplier Curve Out-of-Range	Allows the selection of the out-of-range type using a dialog box.	Function Curves

Table 3.3: Edit Mode Buttons on the Track View Toolbar

Sequence

Sequence provides a hierarchical representation of all the objects and parameters in the scene. Table 3.4 lists the tracks and explains their functions.

Track Name	Functionality
World	Holds all sub-tracks.
Sound	Uses a sound file for the animation.
Global Tracks	Holds the tracks for all the different types of controllers, such as float and position, allowing them to be used globally.
Video Post	Manages the Video Post parameters.
Environment	Holds tracks for the various components of the environment, such as ambient light.
Render Effects	Contains the tracks for the rendering of the effects used in an animation.
Render Elements	Displays the tracks for all the components that are to be rendered separately using the render elements.
Renderer	Allows the animation of the render parameters by the use of tracks.
Global Shadow Parameters	Globally sets the shadow for different lights in the animation.
Scene Materials	Displays the tracks for all the materials used in the scene.
Medit Materials	Holds tracks for the materials in the Material Editor that may or may not be used in the animation.
Objects	Displays all the object tracks hierarchically.

Table 3.4: Tracks and Their Functionality

The hierarchical tracks in the sequence also have icons attached to them. You can judge the type of track by its icon. Table 3.5 lists the various track icons.

Icon	Name
	World track
	Sound track
	Container that holds multiple tracks
	Controller can be applied to this track
	Material track
	Object track
	Note track
	Modifier track
	Map track

Table 3.5: Track Icons and Their Names

Tracks

You can view the values of the selected object in the tracks. The display depends on the kind of mode active in the Track View dialog box. In the Function Curves mode, the values are represented by curves, which can be edited using their handles.

Time Bar

The time bar in the Track View dialog box displays the time span available for the animation according to the time settings in the Time Configuration dialog box. The time for the animation is also set in the Time Configuration dialog box.

Status Bar

The status bar in the Track View dialog box provides the various options for viewing and selecting the different tracks and their values. The different tasks that can be performed using the status bar in the Track View dialog box are:

- Viewing selected tracks, values, and keys after zooming using the Zoom tools
- Selecting tracks, time, and frame number
- Giving instructions by the prompt line about the next step
- Panning tracks

- Viewing the status of the selected key

Editing Animations in the Track View Dialog Box

The Track View dialog box buttons enable editing of animations. The Track View dialog box provides you more options to edit the controllers and track values.

To edit an animation, perform the following steps:

1. Open the file, **ch03_ball&steps.max**.
2. Select the ball in the viewport, and right-click it to view the Object Properties dialog box.
3. If the Trajectory check box is not selected, then select the **Trajectory** check box, and click **OK**. The animation path becomes visible as a red and white dotted line in the viewports, as shown in Figure 3.17.

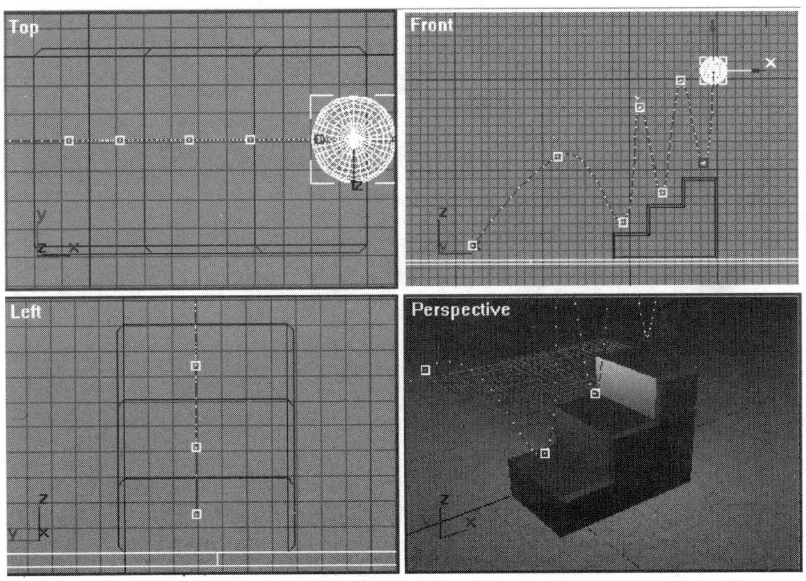

Figure 3.17: Animation Path

4. Open the Track View dialog box using the **New Track View** command on the Graph Editors menu. The track view is shown in Figure 3.18.

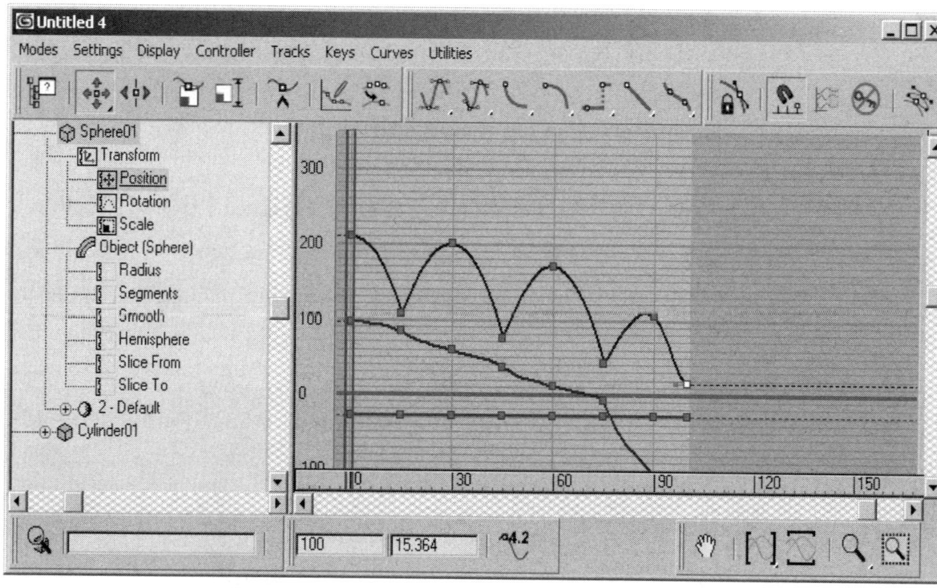

Figure 3.18: Sphere01 Track in the Track View Dialog Box

5. Select the second key from any one of the three curves.
6. Click **Set Tangents to Fast** button. The result is shown in Figure 3.19.

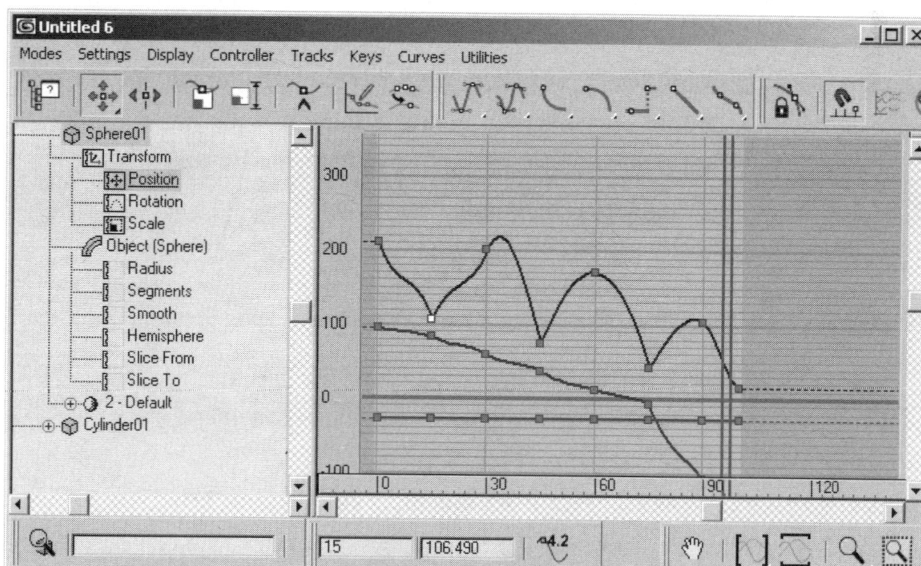

Figure 3.19: Effect of Set Tangents to Fast Button

7. Similarly, apply the Set Tangents to Fast key to all the even keys, 2, 4, 6, and 8, in the animation.
8. Close the Track View dialog box.
9. In the playback controls, click **Play Animation** to view the animation effect. Notice that after you apply the Position controller, the animation is smoother and proceeds with a realistic flow.

Editing Animations Using Motion Panel and Track View

Controllers can be manipulated using either or both of the Motion Panel and Track View dialog boxes. To edit an animation using the Motion panel and the Track View dialog boxes in conjunction, perform the following tasks:

- Create an animation to edit.
- Edit the animation by modifying the controllers using the Motion panel and the Track View dialog boxes.

Creating an Animation

To create the animation, perform the following steps:

1. Load the file, **ch03_scale.max**. You can see the bird in the viewports.
2. Click **Auto key** button.
3. Click **Select and Move** button.
4. Click the **bird**.
5. Move the Time Slider to frame 50, and with the **Select and Uniform Scale** button, scale the bird to increase its size.
6. At frame 100, scale the bird to decrease its size.
7. Click **Auto key** button.
8. Click the **Play Animation** button to view the animation.

Editing an Animation

To edit the animation, perform the following steps:

1. Select the Scale track in the Motion panel, and click the **Assign Controller** button to view the dialog box.
2. Select the **Scale XYZ** controller, and click **OK**.
3. After selecting the Scale XYZ controller, you can observe that three sub-tracks, X Scale, Y Scale, and Z Scale are added to the Scale track, one for

each axis, using which the scale of the object can be modified. Select **New Track View…** from the Graph Editors menu, as shown in Figure 3.20.

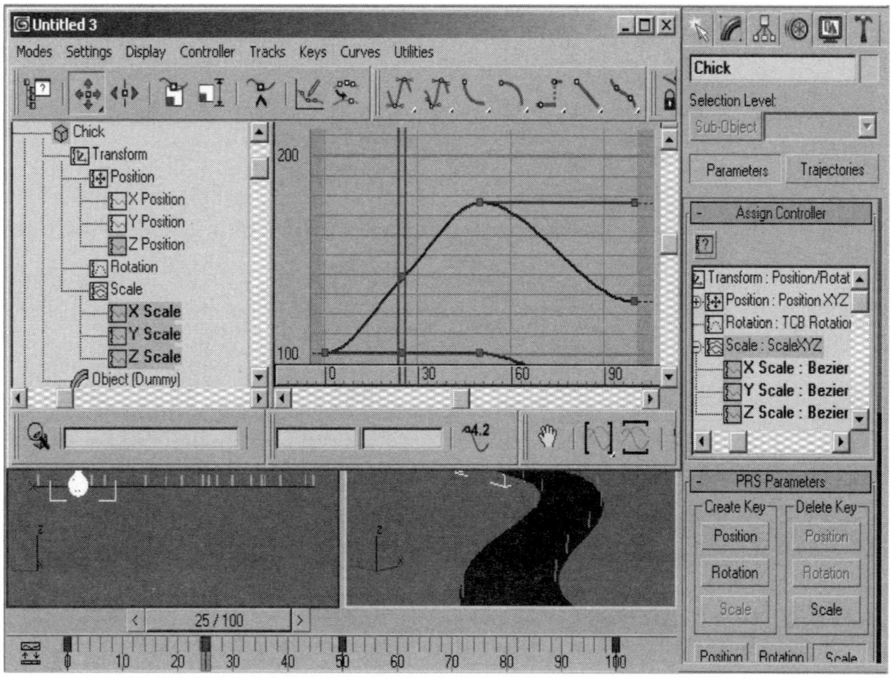

Figure 3.20: Effect of Scale XYZ Controller

4. Click the **Y Scale** track to display the curve for the Y Scale track selected in the Track View dialog box, as shown in Figure 3.21.

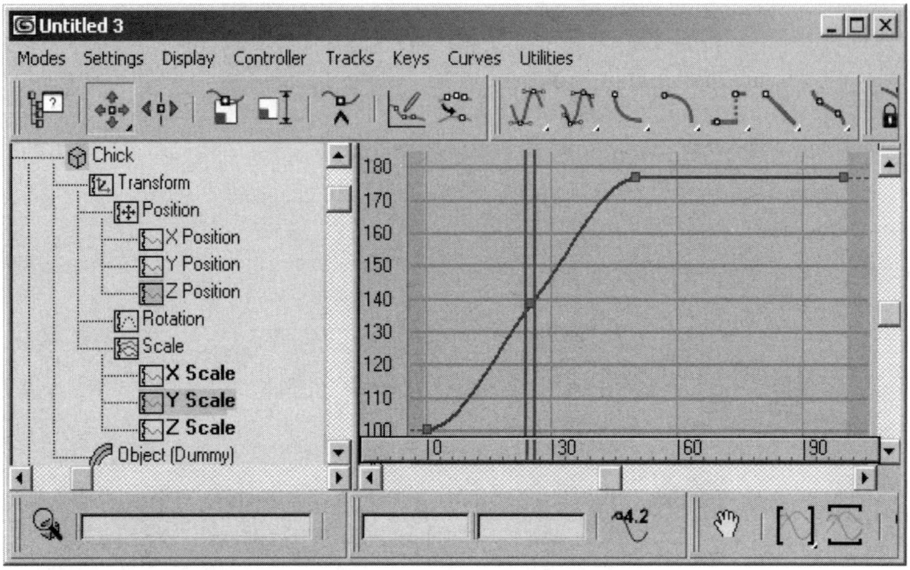

Figure 3.21: Y Scale Track in the Function Curves Mode

5. In the Track View dialog box, reduce the Y Scale value to make the curve less pronounced, as shown in Figure 3.22.

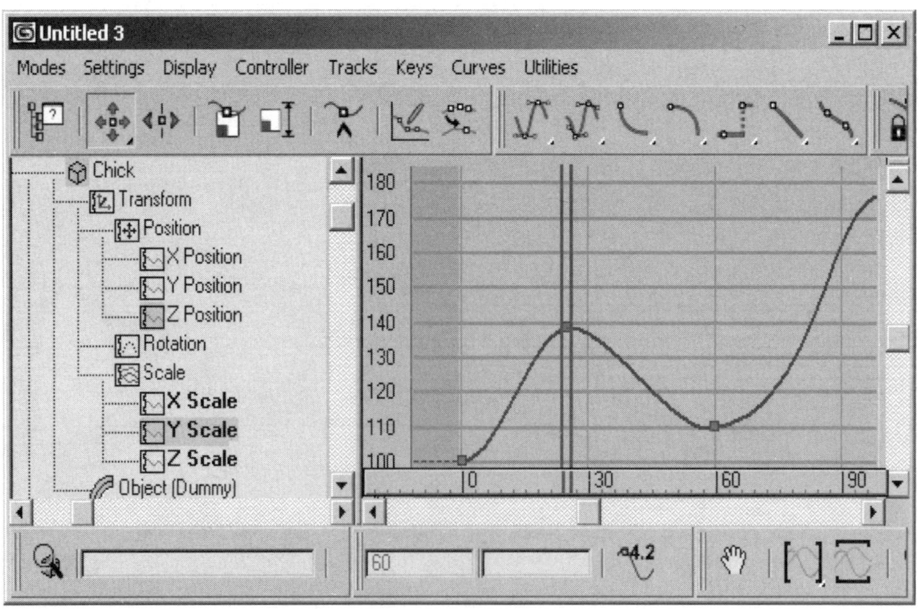

Figure 3.22: Scaled Y Scale Track

6. Close the Untitled 3 window.
7. Click **Play Animation** to view the animation.

Practice Questions

1. List the different types of controllers.
2. List the different ways of applying the controllers.
3. List the various options of trajectories rollout.
4. What are the tasks that can be performed using status bar?
5. Give out the functionality of the various tracks:
    a. scene material
    b. sound
    c. render effects
    d. video posts

3.2 Animation Constraints

Constraints control movement of an object by linking it with a target object. You can control an animation sequence to perform movement according to the constraint assigned to it. This is especially useful in situations where you might also need to restrict the animation to limited areas. For example, an animation of a ping-pong match needs to show a ball bouncing on the table and reaching a player. To show the ball landing on the table and bouncing up, you need to override system defaults that would show unrealistic motion. The movement of the ball needs to be assigned restrictions or a limited area. In 3ds max, you can apply restrictions to animation with the help of constraints.

3.2.1 Types of Constraints

Define the types of constraints.

There are seven types of constraints in 3ds max. These constraints are:

- Attachment
- Surface
- Path
- Position
- Link
- LookAt
- Orientation

Attachment Constraint

The attachment constraint controls the position of the constrained object by attaching it to the face of the target object, so that the constrained object cannot move away from the target object. The face of an object refers to the renderable surface of the object. For example, in an animation of a dog chasing a car, the attachment constraint ensures that the dog moves according to the movement of the car and never beyond a certain distance from the car.

A constrained object is the one on which you set the constraint.

The Motion panel displays the various options of the attachment constraint. Figure 3.23 displays the Attachment Constraint rollout.

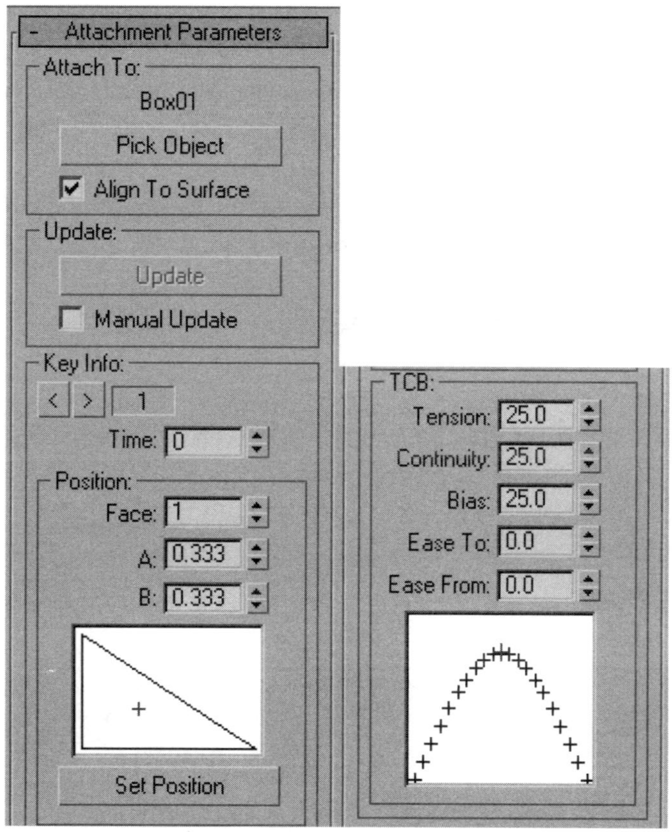

Figure 3.23: Attachment Constraint Rollout

Table 3.6 lists the options of the Attachment Constraint rollout and their functions.

Option	Function
Attach To	Aligns a constrained object according to the orientation of the target object.
Update	Updates the scene in the viewports.
Key Info	Enables you to navigate between keys.
Position	Specifies the position of the constrained object on the face of the target object.
TCB	Enables you to set the same settings as the TCB controller with Tension, Continuity, Bias, and Ease to and from.

Table 3.6: Options in the Attachment Constraint Rollout

Surface Constraint

The surface constraint enables you to link an object to the surface of the target object. When you apply the surface constraint, the constrained object is placed according to the parameter or overall boundary of the target object.

Figure 3.24 displays the Surface Constraint rollout.

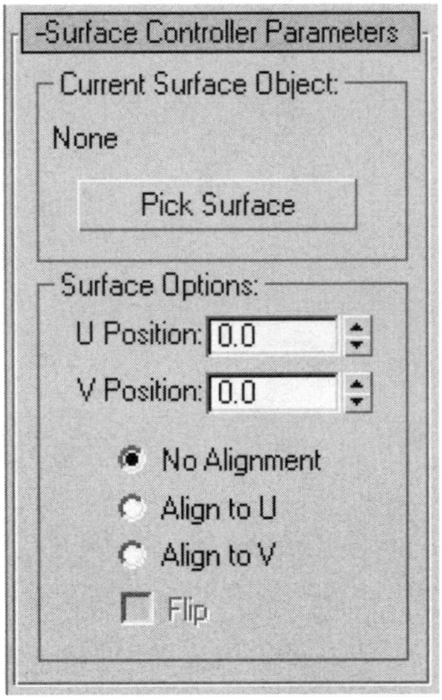

Figure 3.24: Surface Constraint Rollout

Table 3.7 lists the options of the Surface Constraint rollout and their functions.

Option	Function
Current Surface Object	Displays the current target object and allows you to select another target object.
Surface Options	Enables you to define the dimension and alignment options according to which the object should be constrained.
Text	Displays the name of the selected object.
Pick Surface	Selects the object you want used as a surface.
U Position	Adjusts the position of the controlled object along the U coordinates of the surface object.
V Position	Adjusts the position of the controlled object along the V coordinates of the surface object.
No Alignment	When on, the controlled object is not reoriented, regardless of its position on the surface object.
Align to U	Aligns the local Z axis of the controlled object with the surface normal of the surface object, and the X axis with the U axis of the surface object.
Align to V	Aligns the local Z axis of the controlled object with the surface normal of the surface object, and the X axis is aligned with the V axis of the surface object.
Flip	Flips the alignment of the local Z axis of the controlled object. This check box is not available if No Alignment is turned on.

Table 3.7: Options in the Surface Constraint Rollout

Path Constraint

The Path constraint enables you to constrain the object to a spline so that it follows the spline and remains attached to it, even when the spline is changed. An object may be constrained to multiple paths. For example, if you create an animation of the solar system, the Path constraint prevents the planets from moving out of their respective orbits.

Figure 3.25 displays the Path Constraint rollout.

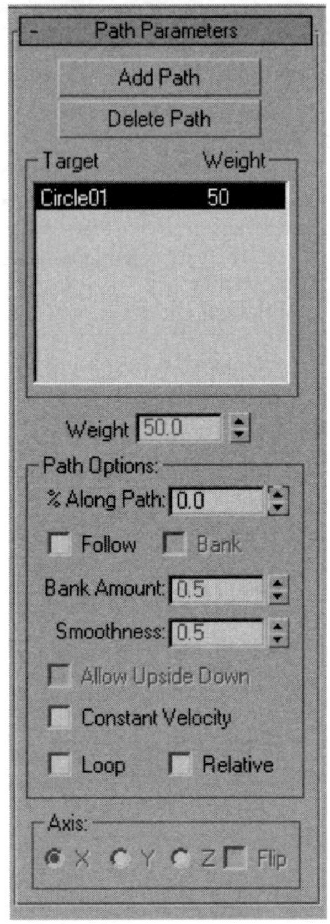

Figure 3.25: Path Constraint Rollout

Table 3.8 lists the options of the Path Constraint rollout and their functions.

Option	Function
Add/Delete Path	Adds or deletes the target paths from the list.
Weight	Determines the influence level of each path.
Path Options	Specifies the movement of the object on the path through various settings such as Follow, which aligns the object to the path, Bank, which makes the object rotate on the path, and Loop, which makes the object turn around as it reaches the end of the path.
Axis	Aligns the object with a path or the reverse of the path.

Table 3.8: Options of the Path Constraint Rollout

Position Constraint

The Position constraint allows you to constrain an object to the position of one of more target objects. For multiple targets, the influence of each individual target is determined by the weight value of each target. For example, if you are animating a car moving along a road, you will need to animate the wheels first and make the body of the car move along with the wheels. However, if you link the car to the wheels, the body of the car will also rotate along with the wheels. To avoid this, you can use the Position constraint so that the body of the car moves along with the wheels but does not rotate. Figure 3.26 displays the Position Constraint rollout.

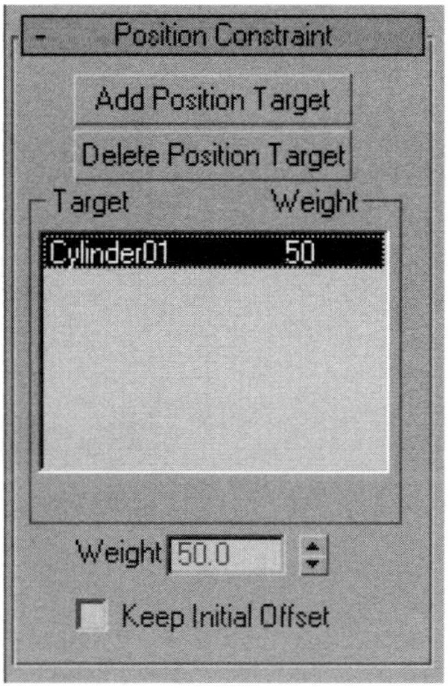

Figure 3.26: Position Constraint Rollout

Table 3.9 lists the options of the Position Constraint rollout and their functions.

Option	Function
Add Position Target	Adds targets to constrain the object.
Delete Position Target	Deletes targets used to constrain the objects.
Weight	Determines the relative influence of different targets by weight.
Keep Initial Offset	Retains the original placement of the constrained object with regard to the target.

Table 3.9: Options of the Position Constraint Rollout

Link Constraint

The Link constraint allows you make the constrained object inherit the position, rotation, and scale of the target. During the course of the animation, you can link different targets and transfer hierarchical links. For example, you need to animate the motion of a pair of hands catching a basketball and throwing it. Consider that the ball and model of the hands are already created and the ball's motion is animated. The animation should depict the ball coming into the pair of hands, the hands moving with the ball, and throwing the ball. With the Link constraint, you can animate the hands so that when the ball reaches the hands, it starts moving according to the movement of the hands.

Figure 3.27 displays the Link Constraint parameters rollout.

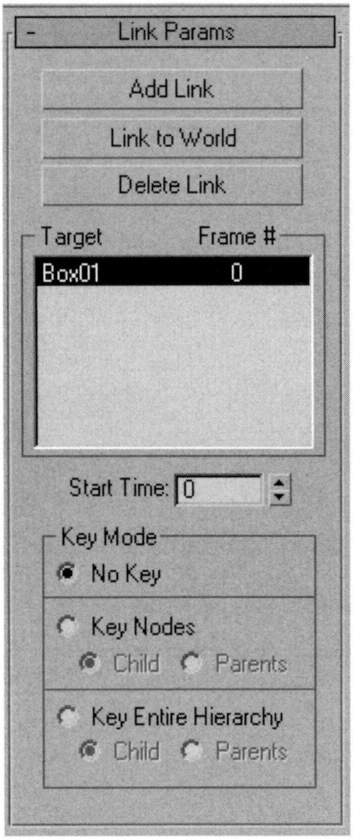

Figure 3.27: Link Constraint Parameters Rollout

Table 3.10 lists the options of the Link Constraint rollout and their functions.

Option	Function
Add Link	Adds new targets for the link constraint.
Delete Link	Deletes targets that you have used for link constraint.
Start Time	Defines the frame number from which the linking begins for the selected target in the list above.
Key Mode	Enables to define key frames for the components in the link.

Table 3.10: Options of the Link Constraint Rollout

LookAt Constraint

The LookAt constraint allows you to constrain an object to the target object, so that the constrained object is always facing the target. For example, if you want to add spectators to a ping-pong match, their heads should move from left to right according to the movement of the ball across the table. You can do so using the LookAt constraint. With this constraint, you can link the heads of spectators to the ball so the animation depicts the heads moving in accordance with the movement of the ball across the table.

Figure 3.28 displays the LookAt Constraint rollout.

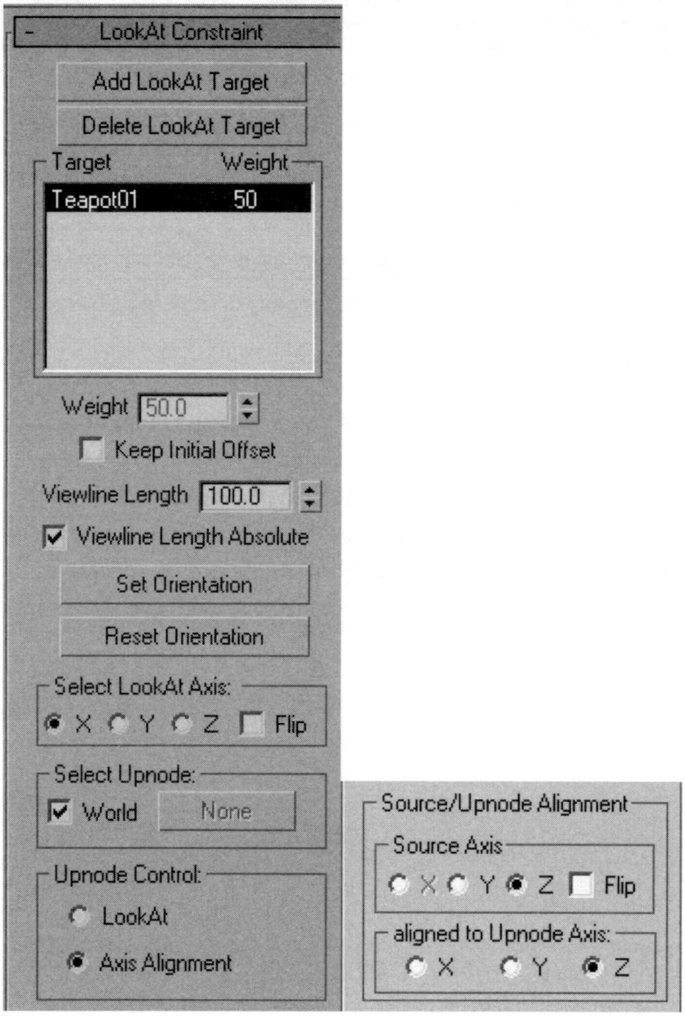

Figure 3.28: LookAt Constraint Rollout

Table 3.11 lists the options of the LookAt Constraint rollout and their functions.

Option	Function
Add LookAt Target	Enables to select a target object for applying the LookAt constraint.
Delete LookAt Target	Deletes the target object being used in the LookAt constraint.
Weight	Defines weight values for each of the targets.
Keep Initial Offset	Maintains the original placement of the constrained object with regard to the target.
Viewline Length	Defines the length of the line attaching the constrained object with the target.
Viewline Length Absolute	Defines a fixed length for the line attaching the constrained object with the target irrespective of the length value.
Set Orientation	Sets the orientation of the constrained object with regard to the target.
Reset Orientation	Resets the orientation of the constrained object with regard to the target.
Select LookAt Axis	Selects the axis which is pointing towards the target.
Select Upnode	Selects the up direction object as the world, the default upnode, or manually selects another.
Upnode Control	Controls the upnode.
Source/Upnode Alignment	Defines the axis and alignment of the upnode.

Table 3.11: Options of the LookAt Constraint Rollout

Orientation Constraint

The Orientation constraint allows you to constrain an object so that the constrained object always rotates or is orientated with the target object. Consider the wheels of a battle tank. It has different sized wheels rotating simultaneously. However, the smaller wheels rotate faster than the larger wheels. This can be animated using the Orientation constraint. Using this constraint, you can animate the wheels so that the smaller wheels rotate in accordance with the bigger wheels. However, since the circumferences of the smaller wheels are much less than that of the larger wheels, the speed of rotation of the smaller wheels is much faster.

Figure 3.29 displays the Orientation Constraint rollout.

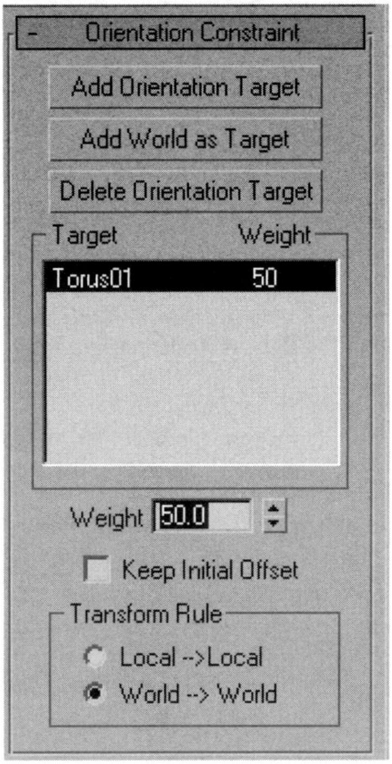

Figure 3.29: Orientation Constraint Rollout

Table 3.12 lists the options of the Orientation Constraint rollout and their functions.

Option	Function
Add Orientation Target	Adds new targets for orientation constraint to use.
Add World as Target	Adds the world as the target for orientation constraint.
Delete Orientation Target	Deletes targets used in orientation constraint.
Weight	Defines weight values for individual targets.
Keep Initial Offset	Maintains the original placement of the constrained object with respect to the target.
Transform Rule	Determines whether the constrained object rotates according to the world coordinates or the local coordinates.

Table 3.12: Options of the Orientation Constraint Rollout

The way you apply each constraint is a little different depending on their functionality and use. However, the basic requirement for applying constraints remains the same. All constraints require the presence of a target object with which they can be bound and which in turn can control the movement of the constrained object.

The moment a constraint is selected either from the Animation menu or through the Assign Controller dialog box, a constraint relative rollout appears in the Motion Panel. This rollout allows you to define and edit the properties of the constraint used.

Uses of Constraints

Constraints allow you to perform more than one type of movement modification to an object. After the object is animated, all the functions of the linked object are carried out according to the target object. In the example of the ping-pong ball, the table on which the ball bounces is the target object.

3ds max provides different types of constraints. You can select a constraint from the Constraints submenu on the Animation menu, the Motion panel, and the Track view. When you select a constraint, a rollout appears on the Motion panel. This rollout allows you to define and adjust the properties of the constraint used.

Each constraint has its own functionality, but the basic application for applying constraints is the same. All constraints require the presence of a target object with which they can be bound and which in turn can control the movement of the constrained object.

3.2.2 Animating with the Path Constraints

Animate an object using Path constraint.

To assign the Path constraint to objects by using the Motion panel, perform the following steps:

1. Open the file, **ch03_path_start.max**. The file depicts a helix and a sphere in the viewports.
2. In the viewport, select the sphere and click the **Motion panel** tab.

3. In the Assign Controller rollout, select the **Position** track, as shown in Figure 3.30.

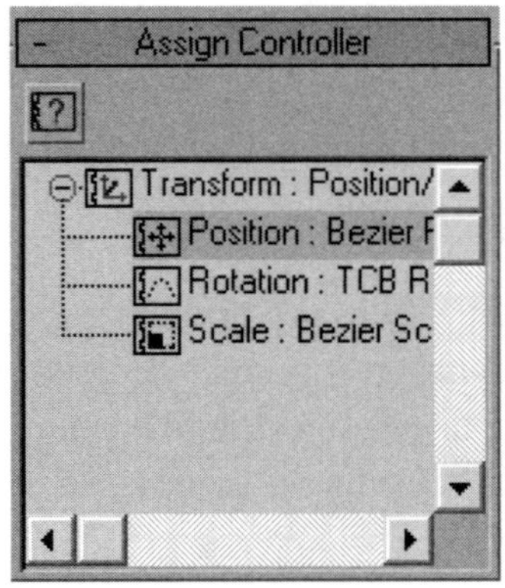

Figure 3.30: Assign Controller Rollout

4. Click the **Assign Controller** button. The Assign Controller dialog box is displayed, as shown in Figure 3.31.

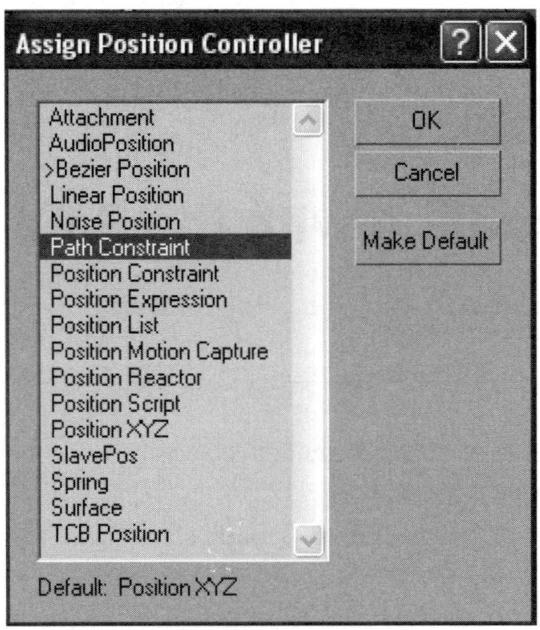

Figure 3.31: Assign Position Controller Dialog Box

5. In the Assign Controller dialog box, select **Path Constraint** and click **OK**.

Path Constraint appears in the Position Track and its rollout is added in the Motion panel.

6. In the Path Parameters rollout, click the **Add Path** button and select the helix.

   By default, the Bezier Position is assigned to the position track. The helix is added to the rollout in the target list, as shown in Figure 3.32.

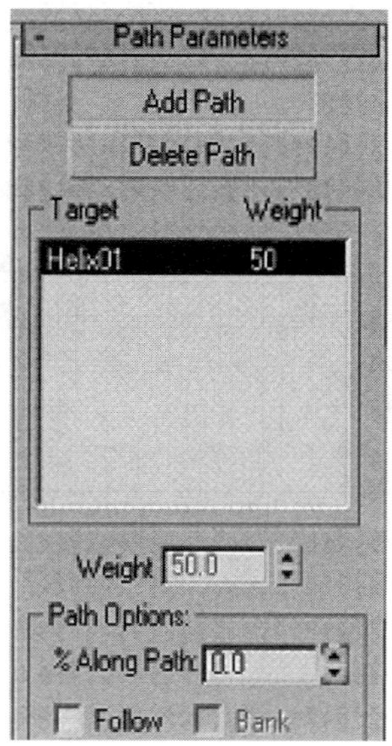

Figure 3.32: Helix Added as a Path in the Path Parameters Rollout

7. Click the **Play Animation** button to view the animation.
8. Click the **Quick Render (Production)**  button to render the animation.
9. Save the file as **ch03_path_end.max**.

Figure 3.33 displays the rendered view of the animation created by applying Path constraint to the objects.

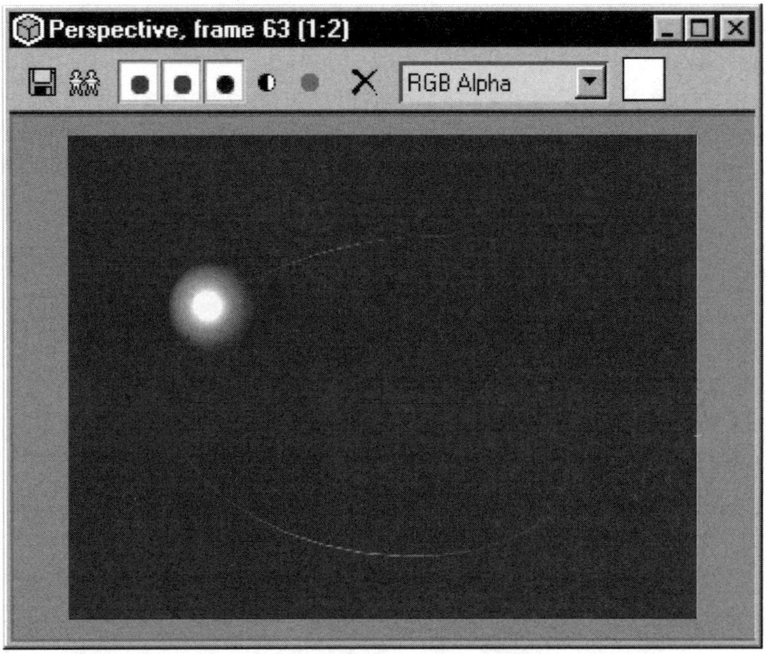

Figure 3.33: Rendered View of the Helix and the Sphere Animation Using the Path Constraint

3.2.3 Animating with the Surface Constraint

Animate an object using a surface constraint.

To roll a sphere around a cylinder, using surface constraints, perform the following steps:

1. Open the file **ch03_surface_start.max**, as shown in Figure 3.34.

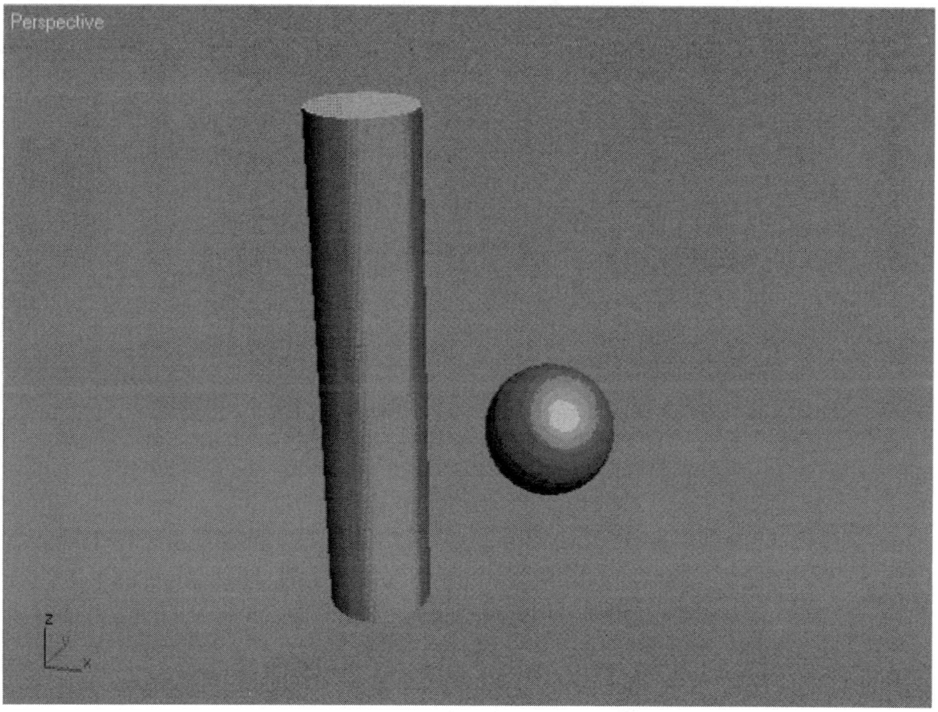

Figure 3.34: surface_start.max File

2. Select the sphere object.

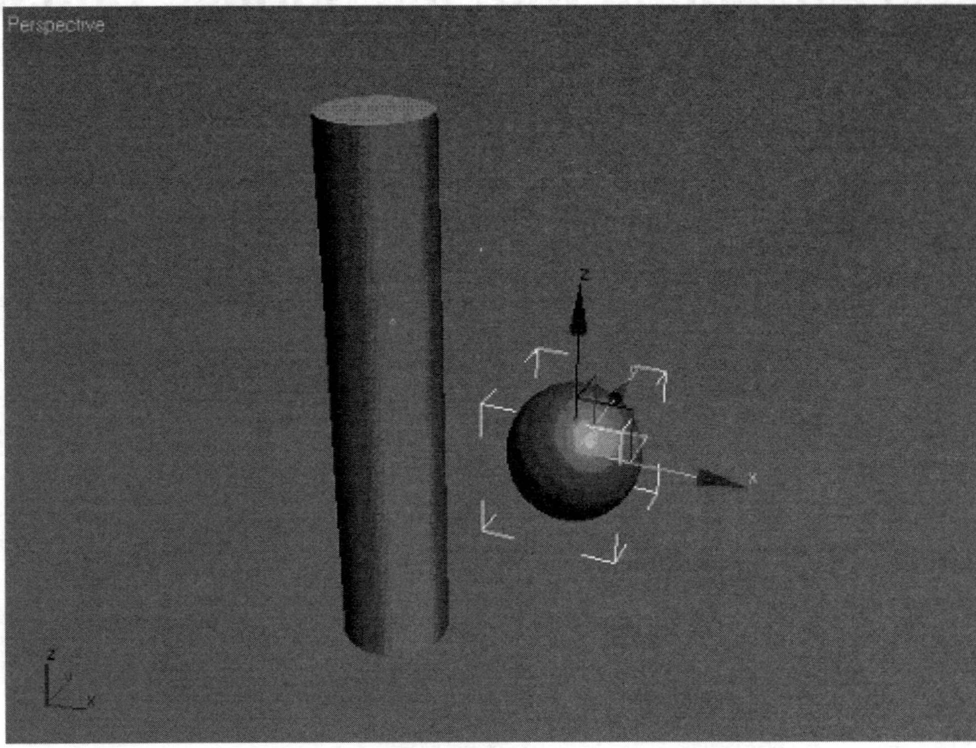

Figure 3.35: Selecting the Sphere Object

3. Select **Surface Constraint** from the drop-down menu Animation → Constraints, as shown in Figure 3.36.

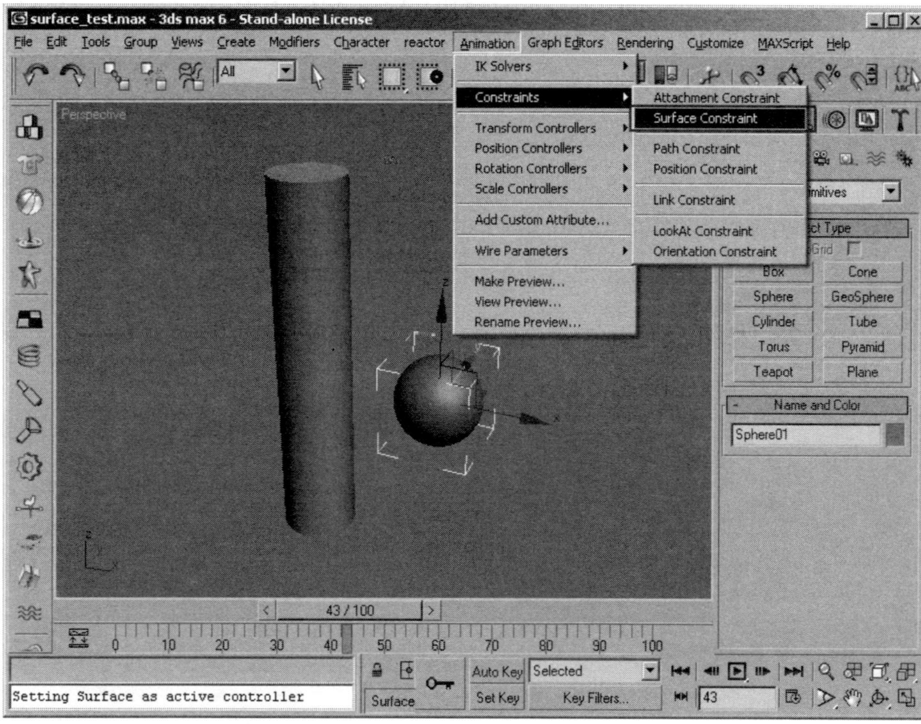

Figure 3.36: Selecting Surface Constraint

4. Click the cylinder object.
5. The sphere will be at the bottom of the cylinder. Type **40** in the V position in the Surface Options section in the Motion Parameters panel. This shifts the sphere around the middle of the cylinder.
6. Click **Auto Key**.
7. Move the time slider to 100.
8. Enter **200** in the U position.
9. Click **Auto Key** to go out of animation mode.
10. Click **Play Animation** to play the animation using the button. The sphere now rotates around the cylinder over a given period of time.
11. Save the file as **ch03_surface_end.max**.

Practice Questions

1. How can you activate the Assign Position Controller dialog box?
2. List two uses of constraints.
3. What is the function of Add World as Target option of the Orientation Controller tab?
4. List the various types of constraints that can be used in an animation.
5. What is the functionality of the LookAt constraint?

Summary

- Controllers have built-in animations, which are applied to the object or parameter to which they are assigned.
- All animations have controllers assigned to them by default as soon as they are animated, depending on the kind of function that they perform.
- Controllers are classified into six types depending on the type of data that they use:
  - Float controllers
  - Point3 controllers
  - Position controllers
  - Rotation controllers
  - Scale controllers
  - Transform controllers
- Controllers can also be classified by the number of tracks they can manage:
  - Single-track controllers
  - Multiple-track controllers
  - Special controllers
- Controllers can be assigned using the:
  - Motion panel
  - Track View dialog box
- Both the Motion panel and the Track View dialog box use the Assign Controller dialog box to assign controllers to objects.
- The Assign Controller dialog box changes according to the selected track, displaying only the applicable controllers.
- The Make Default button in the Assign Controller dialog box makes the selected controller the default controller for the current type of tracks.
- The Motion panel is mainly used to apply Transform controllers.
- The Track View dialog box allows the editing and application of all controllers.
- The Motion panel has two sets of options:
  - Parameters options
  - Trajectories options

- The Track View dialog box has five edit modes that enable you to edit animations in different ways:
    - Edit keys
    - Edit time
    - Edit Ranges
    - Position Ranges
    - Function Curves
- The Function Curves mode displays the track values as curves that can be adjusted using their handles.

References

- http://www.hash.com/htmlHelp/v10.0/GeneratedHtml/PathConstraintA.htm (February 10, 2004)
- http://www.hash.com/htmlHelp/v9.5/GeneratedHtml/PathConstraintP.htm (February 10, 2004)
- http://www.hash.com/htmlHelp/v10.0/GeneratedHtml/SurfaceConstraintA.htm (February 10, 2004)
- http://www.hash.com/htmlHelp/HTMLHelp/mas00232.htm (February 10, 2004)
- http://www.trl.ibm.com/projects/modeling/cute/index_e.htm (February 10, 2004)
- http://www.worldof3d.com/resources/docs/Designer/anim_controller.htm (February 10, 2004)
- http://tutorial.stavit.cz/page.asp?category=0900 (February 10, 2004)

Assignments

1. Identify the steps used to apply Path constraints.
2. List the various types of constraints available in 3ds max.
3. What are the functions of the Add Position Target and Delete Position Target buttons in the Position Constraint rollout?
4. How can you apply controllers using the Motion Panel?
5. What are Tangents and how can you see the tangents of associated to keys on the curves?
6. What is the purpose of adding keys?
7. What is the purpose of the Trajectory option in the Motion Panel?
8. List the various steps used to assign controllers.
9. What is the purpose of the Follow option in the Path Constraint?
10. List an example where you would use a surface constraint.

Lab Exercises

Exercise 1

Objective

- Identify the uses of the Euler XYZ Rotation controller in 3ds max.
- Apply the Euler Parameters rollout to animations using the Motion panel.

Problem Statement

Using Euler XYZ Rotation rotate a box 500 degrees around the X-axis and 90 degrees around the Z-axis.

Lab Setup

3ds max 6.0

Procedure

To rotate a box, perform the following steps:

1. Create a box, and then select the rotation track in the **Motion panel → Parameters → Assign Controller** rollout.
2. Click **Assign Controller**, and then select **Euler XYZ** in the Assign Controller dialog box. Click **OK**.
3. Turn on **Auto Key**.
4. Select **Rotation** at the bottom of the PRS Parameters rollout.
5. In the Euler Parameters rollout, select the **X axis**.
6. In the Create Key group of the PRS Parameters rollout, click **Rotation**.
7. A rotational key is created. Move the time slider to frame 50.
8. Again, in the Create Key group of the PRS Parameters rollout, click **Rotation**.
9. In the Key Info (Basic) rollout, enter **500** in the value field.
10. Select the **Z-axis** in the Euler Parameters rollout, and then enter **90** in the value field of the Key Info (Basic) rollout.

11. Play the animation. The box rotates 500 degrees around the X-axis and 90 degrees around the Z-axis. In this case the X-axis is rotated first, and then the Z-axis is rotated.

Lab Activity Checklist

S. No.	Tasks	Completed	
		Yes	No
1.	Applied the Euler Parameters Controller option		
2.	Applied the PRS Parameters rollout		

Exercise 2

Objective

- Apply Assign controllers in 3ds max.

Problem Statement

- Animate a sphere over the surface of a cylinder.

Lab Setup

3ds max 6.0

Procedure

To animate a sphere over the surface of a cylinder, perform the following steps:

1. In the Top viewport, create a cylinder and a sphere.
2. Open the **Motion panel**. Select the **sphere**, expand the Assign Controller rollout and the Transform heading in the list.
3. Click **Position** in the list window, and then click **Assign Controller**.
4. Select **Surface** and then click **OK**.
5. The Surface Controller Parameters rollout replaces the Key Info rollout. Click **Pick Surface**, and then select the cylinder.
6. Turn on **Auto Key**, and place the time slider at frame 0.

7. Use the V Position spinner to move the sphere to a starting position at the bottom of the cylinder.
8. Place the time slider at frame 100.
9. Use the V Position spinner to place the sphere at the top of the cylinder.
10. Set U Position to **300**.
11. Turn off **Auto Key** and play the animation. The sphere moves over the surface of the cylinder in a helical path.

Lab Activity Checklist

S. No.	Tasks	Completed	
		Yes	No
1.	Applied the Assign Controller rollout option		
2.	Applied the Surface Controller Parameters rollout		
3.	Specified appropriate parameters in Surface Controller rollout		

Exercise 3

Objective

- Apply controllers to animations using the Motion panel.
- Use the Parameters and the Trajectories options of the Motion panel.
- Apply controllers to animations using the Track View dialog box.

Problem Statement

Create an animation of a pendulum in a clock. Move the pendulum from the extreme left to the extreme right.

- The model of the clock is present in the file, ch03_lab_ex3_model.max, in the student CD provided to you.

Lab Setup

3ds max 6.0

Procedure

1. Open the file **ch03_lab_ex3_model.max**.
2. Click the **Auto Key** button.
3. Take the time slider to frame 12.
4. Right-click the pendulum and select the **rotate** option from the drop-down menu.
5. Rotate the pendulum to 30 degrees. Figure 3.37 displays the pendulum selected on frame 12.

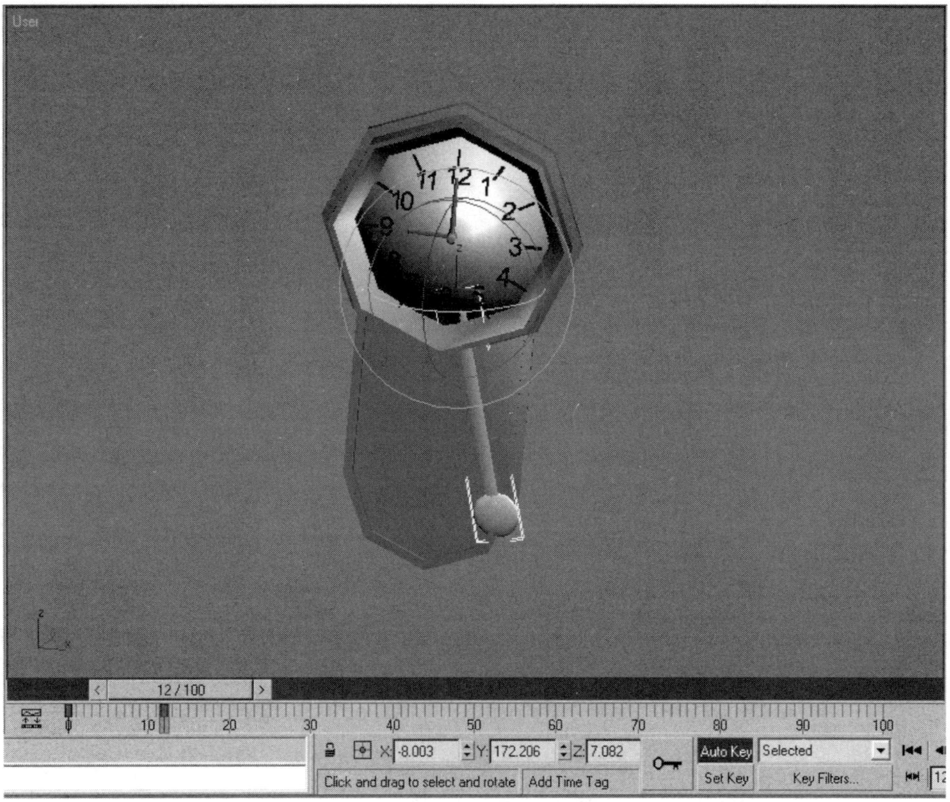

Figure 3.37: Pendulum at Frame 12

6. On frame 24, rotate the pendulum and rotate it to 60 degrees in the reverse direction, as shown in Figure 3.38.

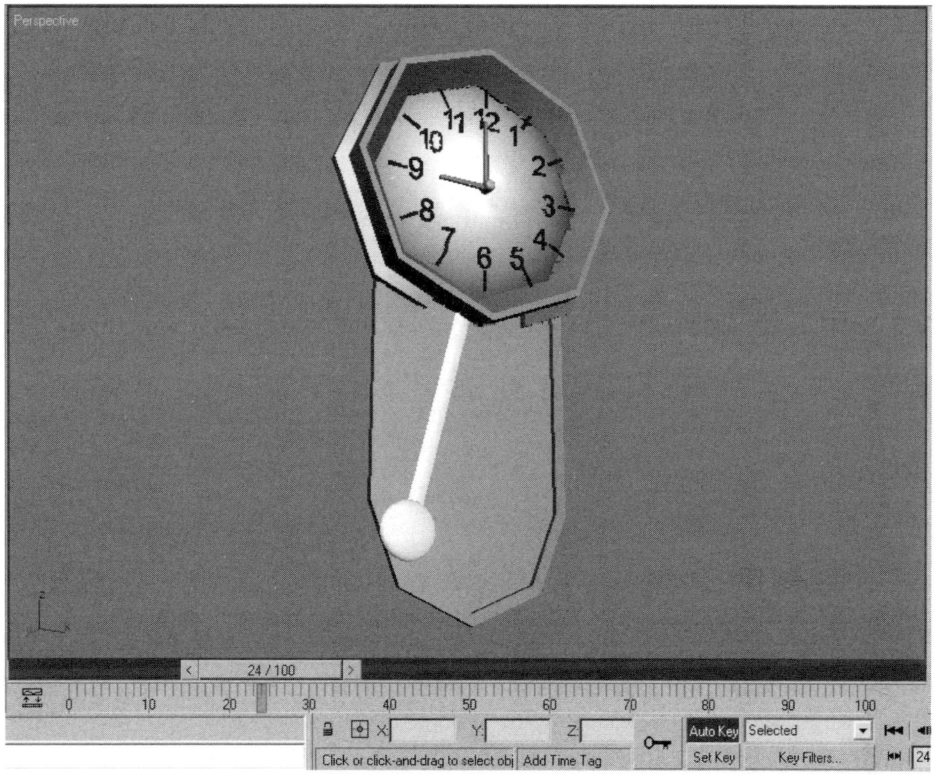

Figure 3.38: Rotating the Pendulum at Frame 24

7. Navigate the Motion panel and select **Rotation** from the Assign Controllers rollout.

8. Click the **Assign Controller** button and select the **Euler XYZ** option of the Rotational Controllers key, as shown in Figure 3.39. The Euler XYZ option is used to provide angular rotation and also helps edit rotational curves.

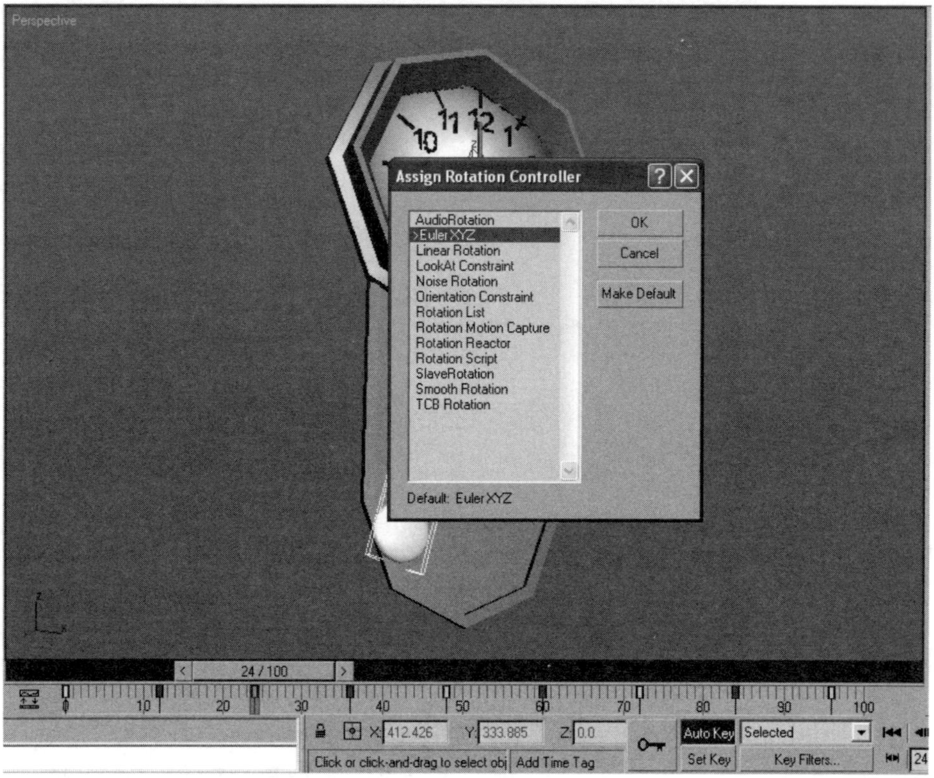

Figure 3.39: Selecting the Euler XYZ Option

9. Click **Auto Key** button.
10. Click **Play Animation** to view the animation.
11. Save the file as **ch03_lab_ex3_sol.max**.

Lab Activity Checklist

S. No.	Tasks	Completed	
		Yes	No
1.	Create an animation of a pendulum in a clock		
2.	Move the pendulum from the extreme left to the extreme right		

Exercise 4

Objective

- Apply constraints to an animation.

Problem Statement

Create an animation of the text, NEWS rotating around a globe. Animate the text by using the Path constraint in 3ds max. The model of the globe is available in the file, ch03_lab_ex4_model.max, in the Student CD provided to you.

Lab Setup

3ds max 6.0

Procedure

1. Open the file, **ch03_lab_ex4_model.max**, as shown in Figure 3.40.

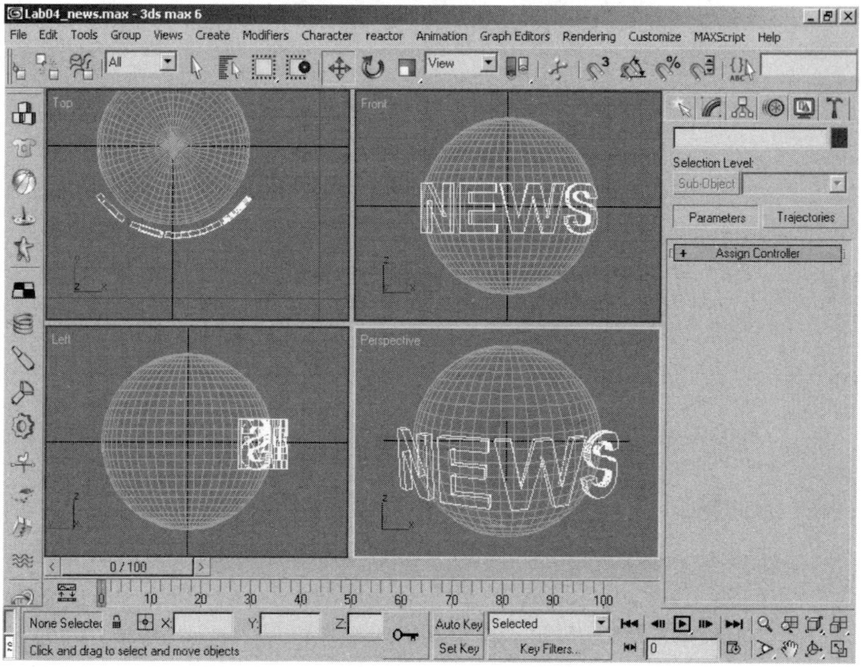

Figure 3.40: Scaled Y Scale Track

2. Click the **Create** button to show the Object Type rollout, as shown in Figure 3.41.

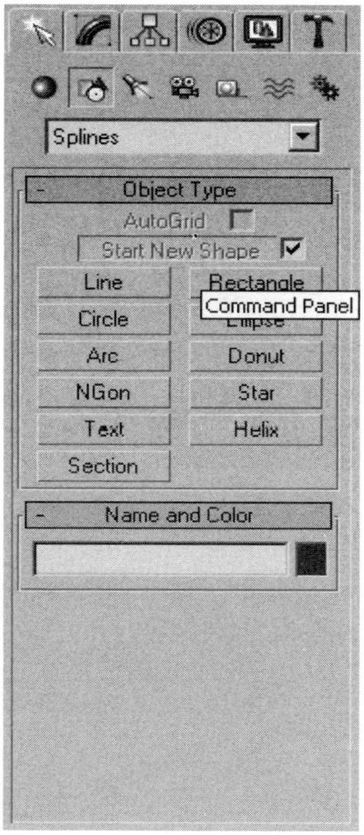

Figure 3.41: Object Type Rollout

3. Click **Circle**.
4. Click at the **Origin** of the axis in the perspective view and create a circle.

5. Change the radius of the circle in the Parameters rollout to **69**, as shown in Figure 3.42.

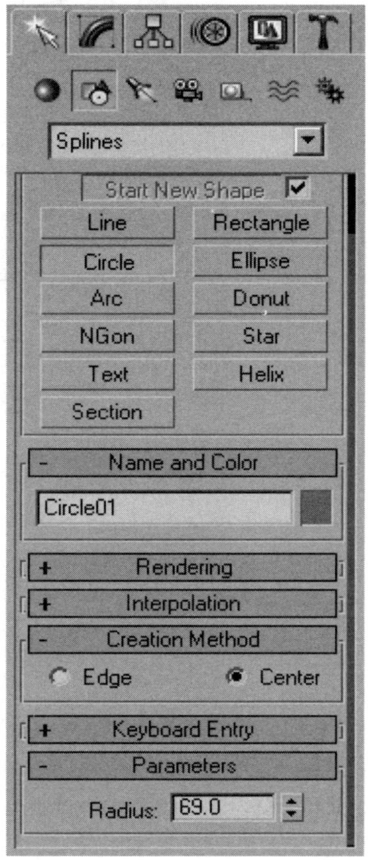

Figure 3.42: Parameters Rollout

6. Press **Enter**.
7. If Position is not highlighted in the Assign Controller rollout, then click **Position** in the Assign Controller rollout.
8. Click **Assign Controller** to display the Assign Position Controller dialog box.
9. In the Assign Position Controller dialog box, select **Path Constraint** and click **OK**.
10. Click **Add Path**.

11. Select the **Follow** check box in the Path Parameters rollout. Figure 3.43 displays the Path Parameters rollout.

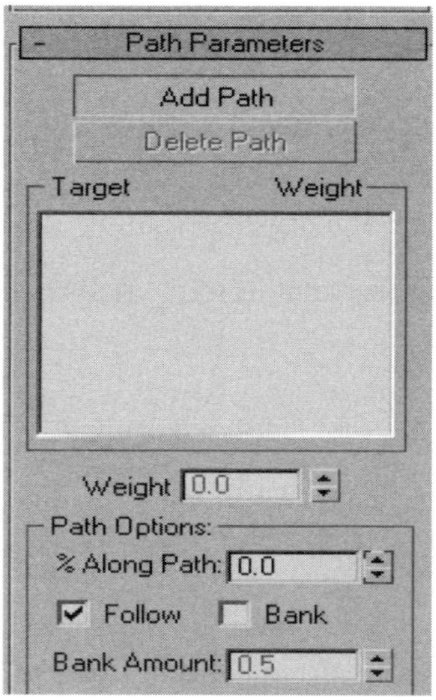

Figure 3.43: Path Parameters Rollout

12. Select the **spline** created by you.
13. Click **Play Animation** to view the animation.
14. Save the file as **ch03_lab_ex4_sol.max**.

Lab Activity Checklist

S. No.	Tasks	Completed	
		Yes	No
1.	Applied the Assign Position Controller option		
2.	Applied the Path constraint		
3.	Specified appropriate parameters in the Path Parameters rollout		

Exercise 5

Objective

- Use surface constraints.

Problem Statement

Use the surface constraint to move one sphere around another sphere along the surface of the sphere.

Lab Setup

3ds max 6.0

Procedure

To move one sphere around another sphere, perform the following steps:

1. Open a new max file.

2. Create two spheres in the top viewport, as shown in Figure 3.44.

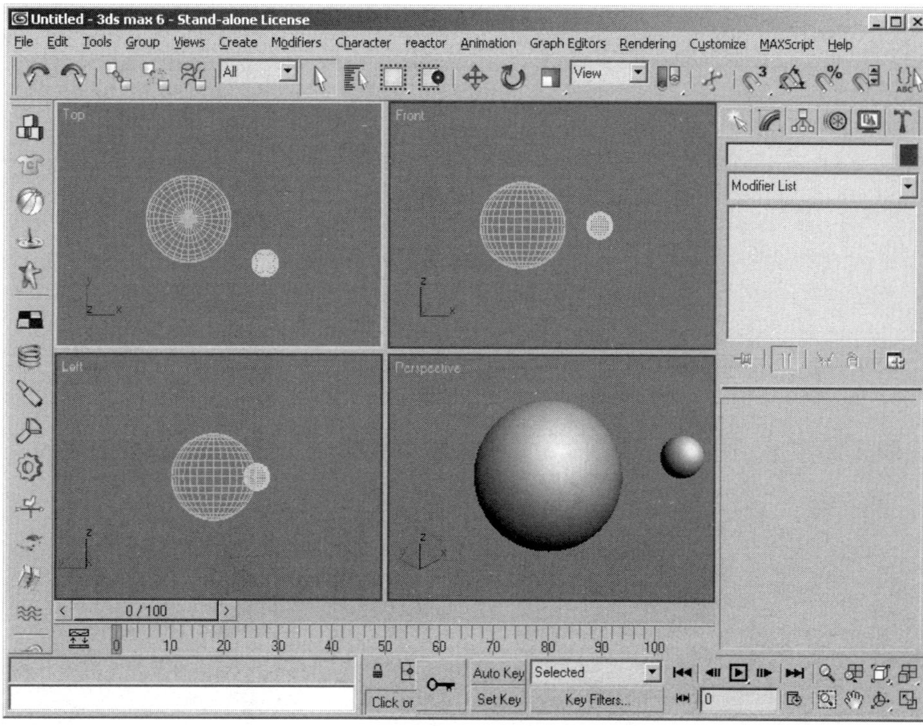

Figure 3.44: Creating Spheres

3. Select the small sphere by clicking it.
4. Click the **Motion** tab.

5. Expand the Transform option in the Assign Controller roll out, as shown in Figure 3.45.

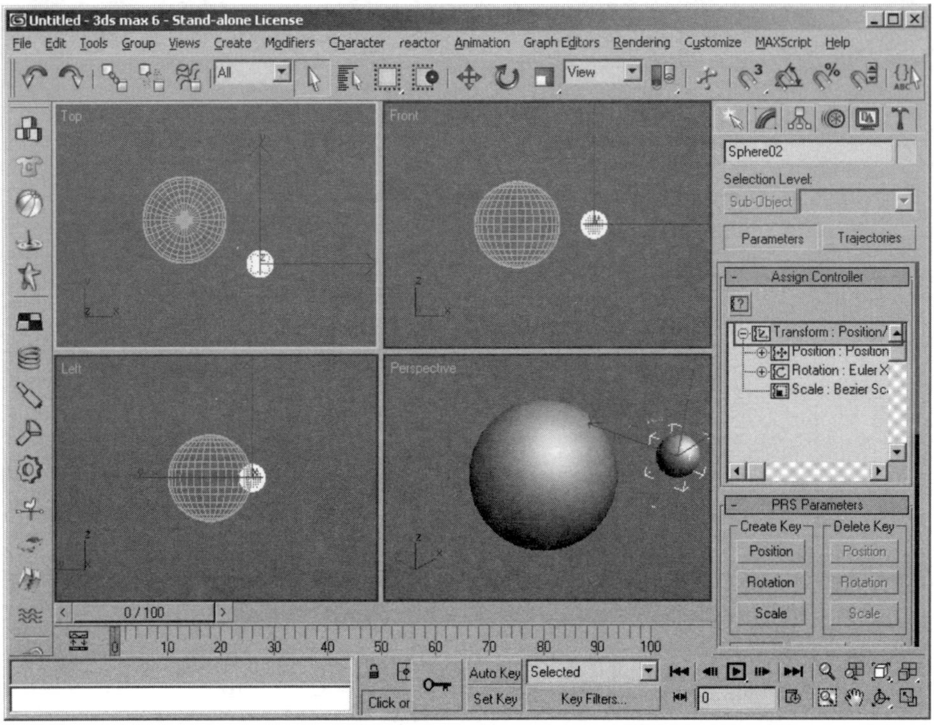

Figure 3.45: Expanding the Transform Assign Controller

6. Click **Position**.
7. Click **Assign Controller**.

8. Select **Surface** and click **OK**, as shown in Figure 3.46.

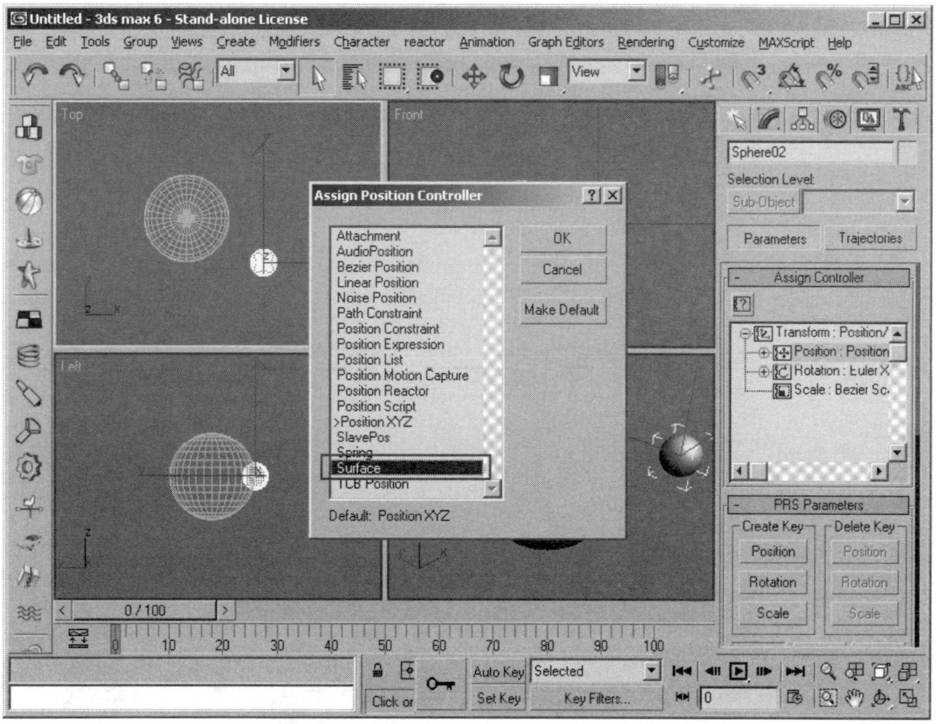

Figure 3.46: Assign Position Controller Dialog Box

9. Scroll down in the Motion Parameters rollout until you see the section Current Surface Object.
10. Click **Pick Surface**.

11. Click the big sphere. The small sphere re-orients itself to the bottom of the big sphere, as shown in Figure 3.47.

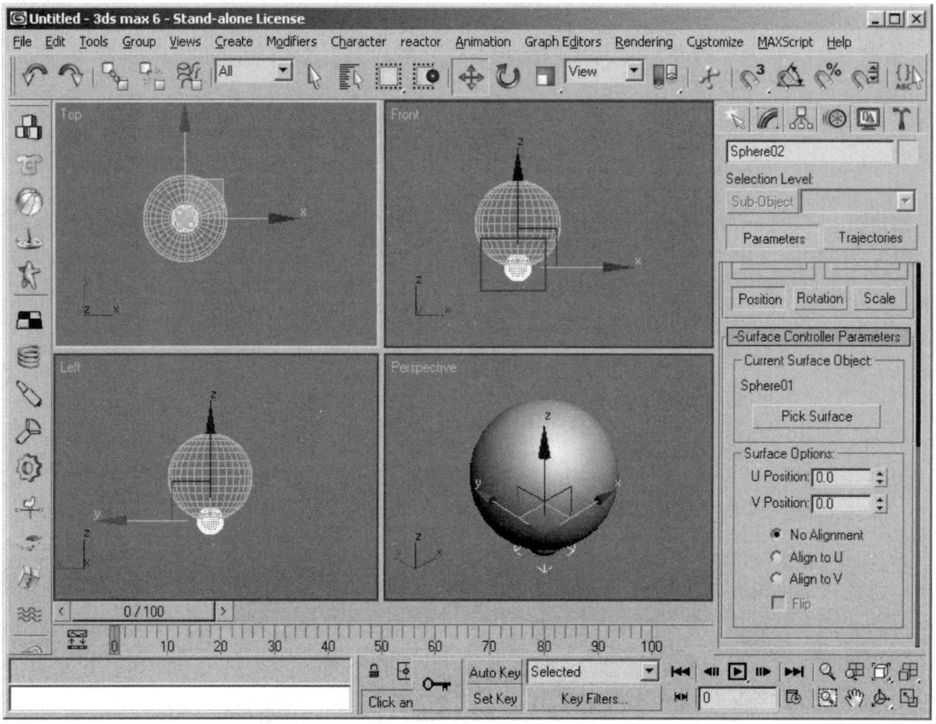

Figure 3.47: Clicking the Big Sphere

12. In the Surface Options section, specify a value of **50** in the V position text box. The small sphere is now vertically aligned properly with the big sphere, as shown in Figure 3.48.

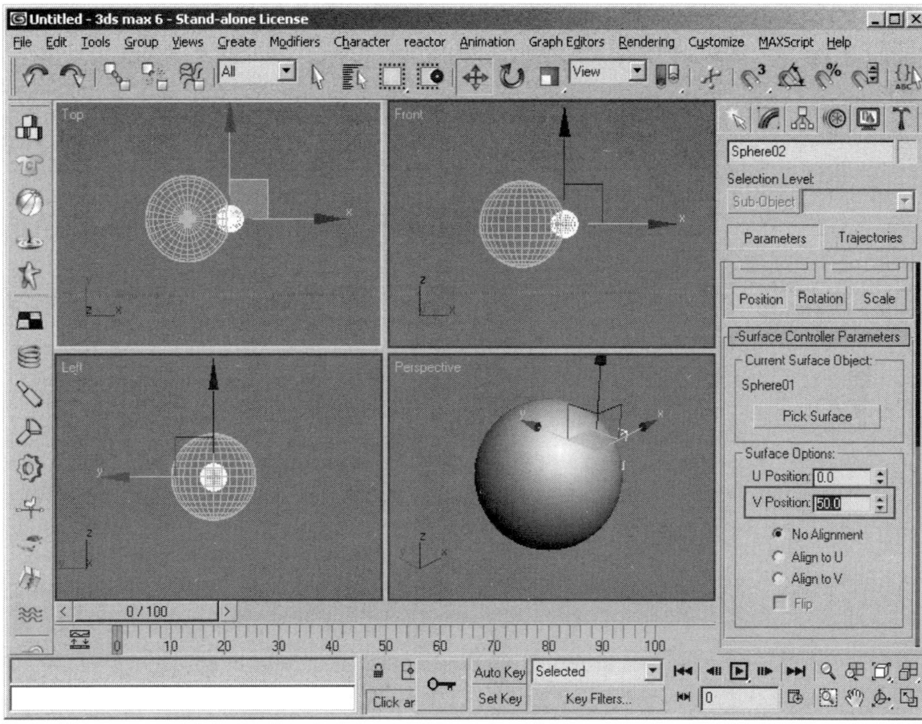

Figure 3.48: Sphere Aligned Properly

13. At frame 0, click **Auto Key** to start animation.
14. Place the time slider at frame 100.
15. In the Surface Options section, specify a value of **100** in the V position text box. The sphere is now aligned at the top of the big sphere.
16. Set U Position to **300**.
17. Turn off **Auto Key** and play the animation. The sphere moves over the surface of the cylinder in a helical path.
18. Save the file as **ch03_lab_ex5_sol.max**.

Lab Activity Checklist

S. No.	Tasks	Completed	
		Yes	No
1.	Created 2 spheres		
2.	Applied the surface constraint		
3.	Specified appropriate parameters in the Surface Parameters rollout		

Exercise 6

Objective

- Use Path constraints to animate an object.

Problem Statement

- Open the sample 3ds max scene with a spline curve, a basic model of an airplane, and a basic model of a hut. Use Path constraints to animate the plane so that it flies over the hut along the spline curve.

Lab Setup

3ds max 6.0

Procedure

To animate a plane, perform the following steps:

1. Open the file **ch03_lab_ex6_model.max**.
2. Switch to the top perspective and Zoom out so that you can see all the elements in the scene completely.
3. Click the plane object to select it.
4. Click the **Animation → Constraints → Path Constraint** menu command.
5. Now the cursor is ready to take a spline curve as the path. Click the **Path** curve. The plane orients itself to the spline curve.

6. Play the animation by clicking the **Play** button. You will see that although the plane is flying along the path specified, it still does not follow and bank according to the path properly, as shown in Figure 3.49.

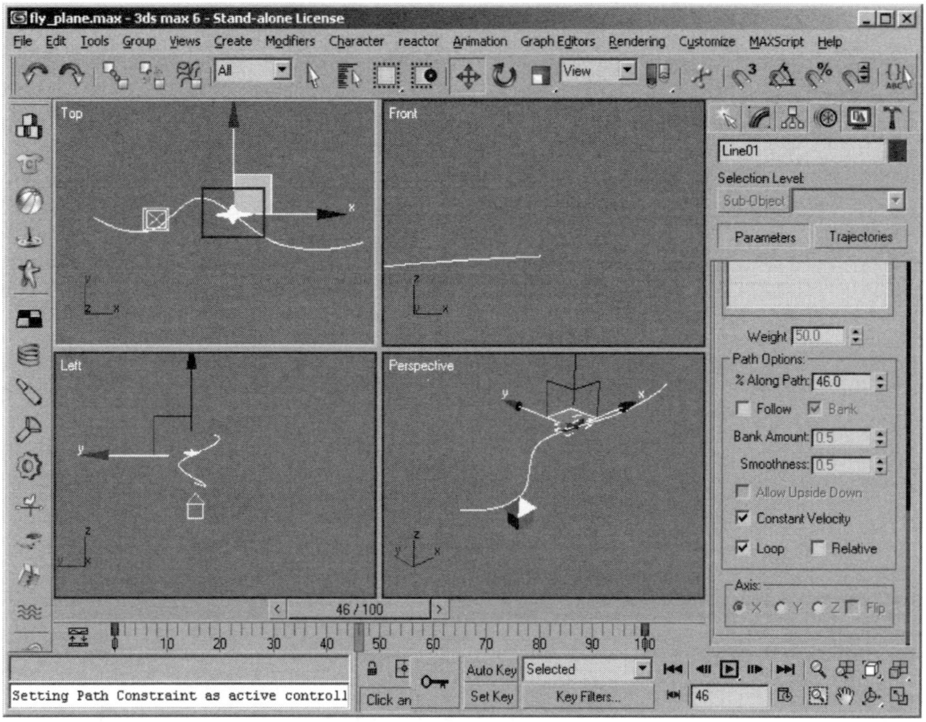

Figure 3.49: Plane Flying Along the Path

7. With the Plane still selected, click in the **Motion panel**.
8. In the Parameters section, scroll down till you see the Path options section.

9. In the Path Options section, click **Follow** and then click **Bank**, as shown in Figure 3.50.

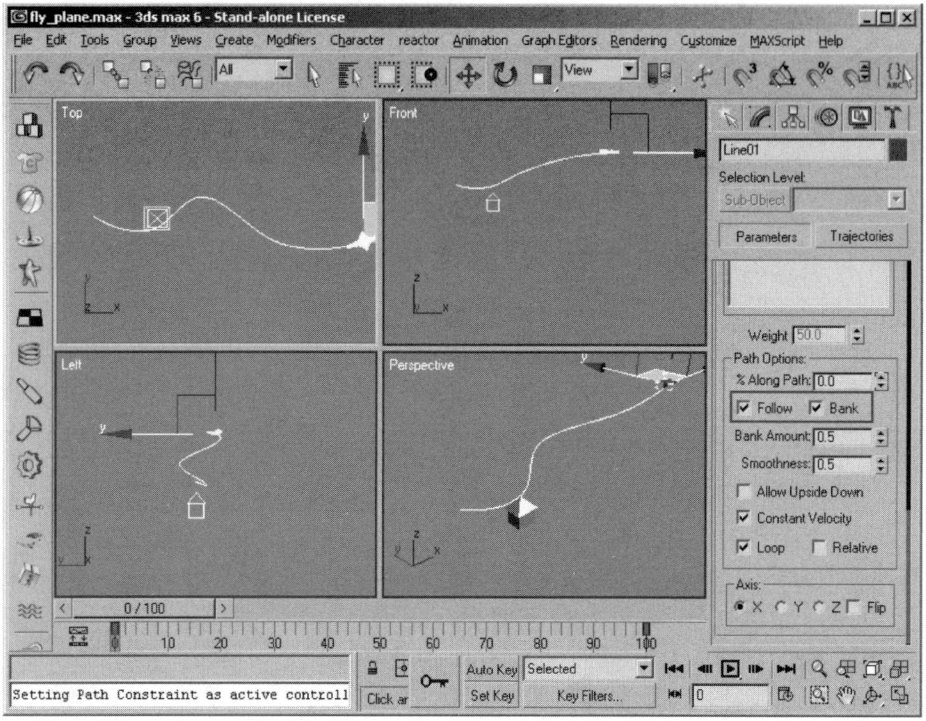

Figure 3.50: Clicking Follow and Bank

10. The plane is now properly following and banking according to the path. However, it is flying with its tail in front. Click **Flip** and this corrects the direction of the plane.
11. Click **Play** to play the animation.
12. Save the file as **ch03_lab_ex6_sol.max**.

Lab Activity Checklist

S. No.	Tasks	Completed	
		Yes	No
1.	Applied the Path constraint		
2.	Selected the path properly		
3.	Set the Follow, Banking and Flip options properly		

Exercise 7

Objective

- Apply the LookAt constraint to the animation.
- Apply controllers to animations using the Motion panel.

Problem Statement

- Open the sample 3ds max scene with a cannon and a flying saucer. The flying saucer is animated to move around the scene in 100 frames. Extend the animation so that the cannon always looks at the flying saucer and is ready to fire.

Lab Setup

3ds max 6.0

Procedure

To create the animation, perform the following steps:

1. Open the Max file named **ch03_lab_ex7_model.max**.
2. Click in the **Perspective** viewport to activate it and maximize it.
3. Click **Play Animation** to view the animation of the flying saucer. Click **Stop/Pause** to stop the animation.

4. Select the **Cannon object** by clicking on it in the Perspective Viewport. If you are unable to select the object visually, use the menu command Edit → Select By → Name and select the cannon from the visible list of objects, as shown in Figure 3.51.

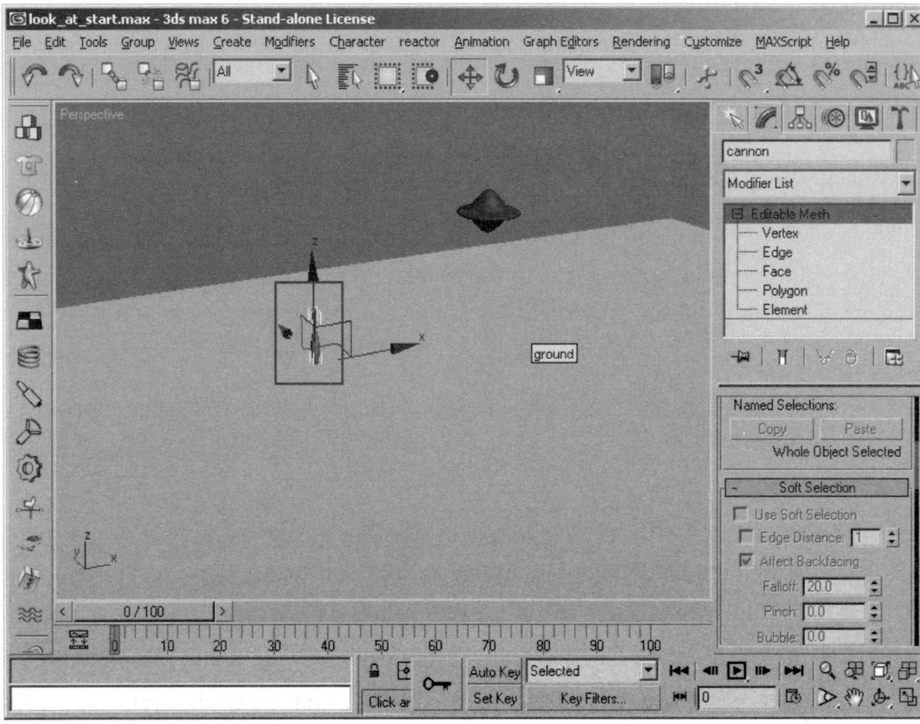

Figure 3.51: Selecting the Cannon Object

5. Click the **Motion** tab, as shown in Figure 3.52.

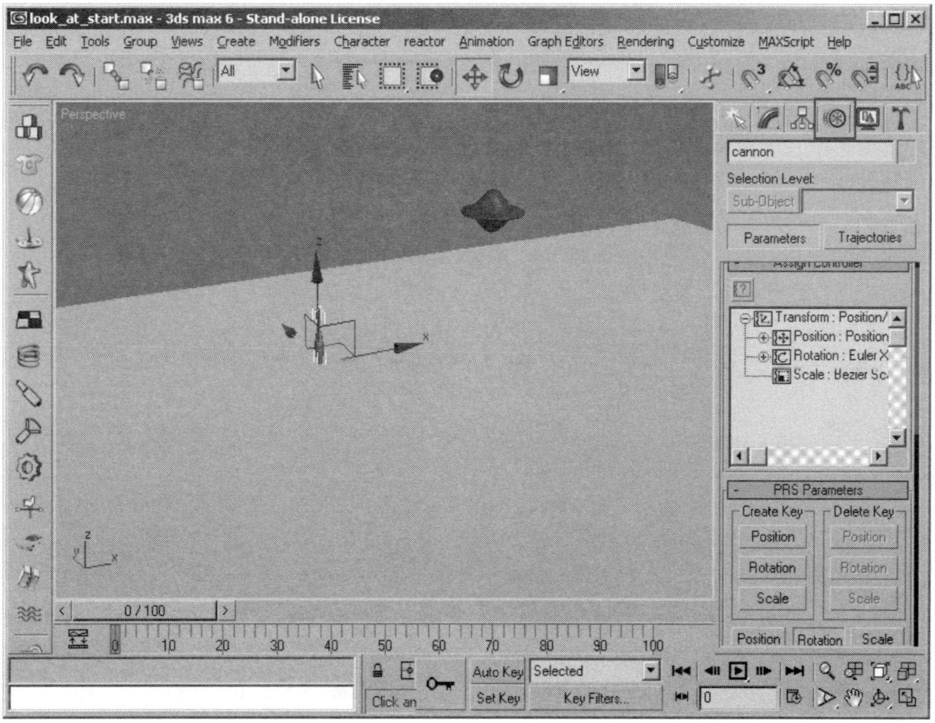

Figure 3.52: Selecting the Motion Tab

6. In the Assign Controller section, click **Rotation**, as shown in Figure 3.53.

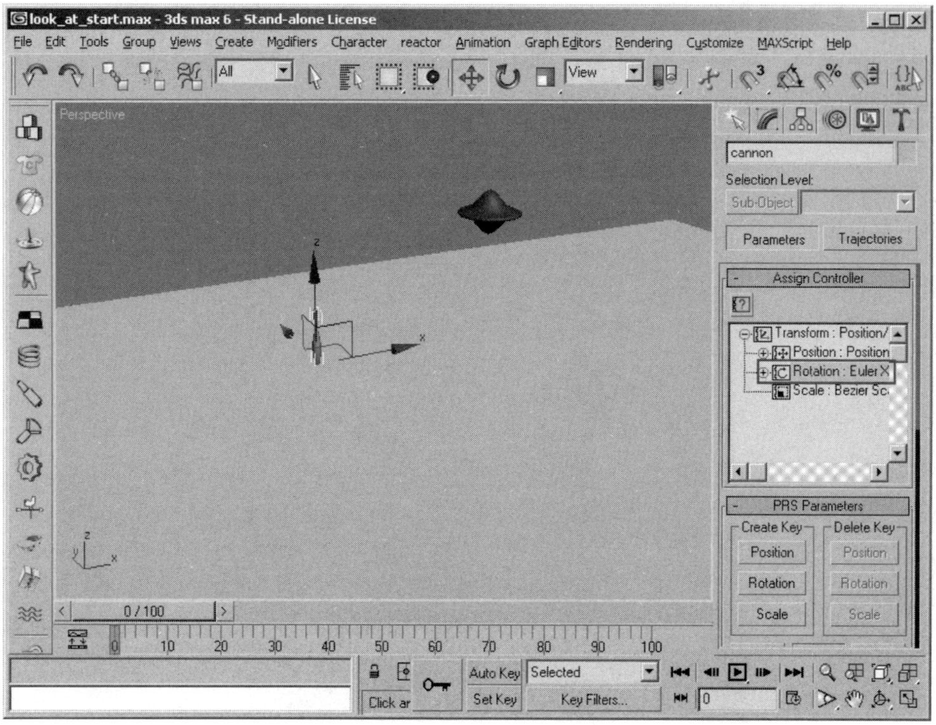

Figure 3.53: Selecting Rotation

7. Click **Assign Controller**.

8. The Assign Rotation Controller dialog box is displayed. From the list of available controllers select **LookAt Constraint** and click **OK**, as shown in Figure 3.54.

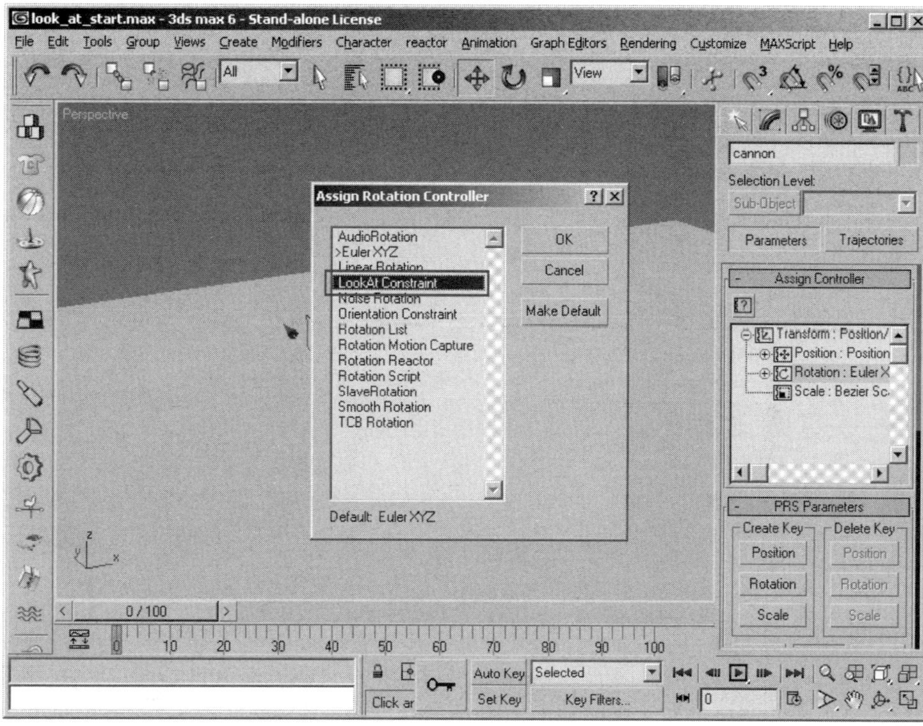

Figure 3.54: Selecting LookAt Constraint

9. In the parameters of the LookAt Constraint section click **Add LookAt Target**.

10. In the viewport, click the saucer object. You will immediately see that the orientation of the cannon is not correct, as shown in Figure 3.55.

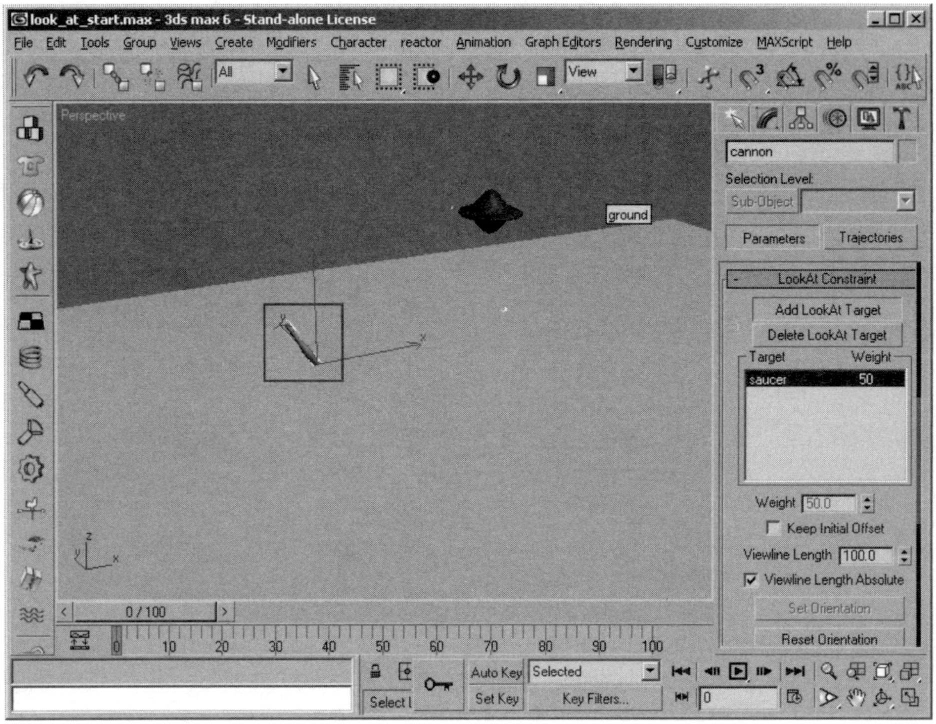

Figure 3.55: Orientation of the Cannon Incorrect

11. Scroll down to the Select LookAt Axis section in the parameters section and click the **Z** ratio button to enable the Z-axis. The cannon is not properly oriented, as shown in Figure 3.56.

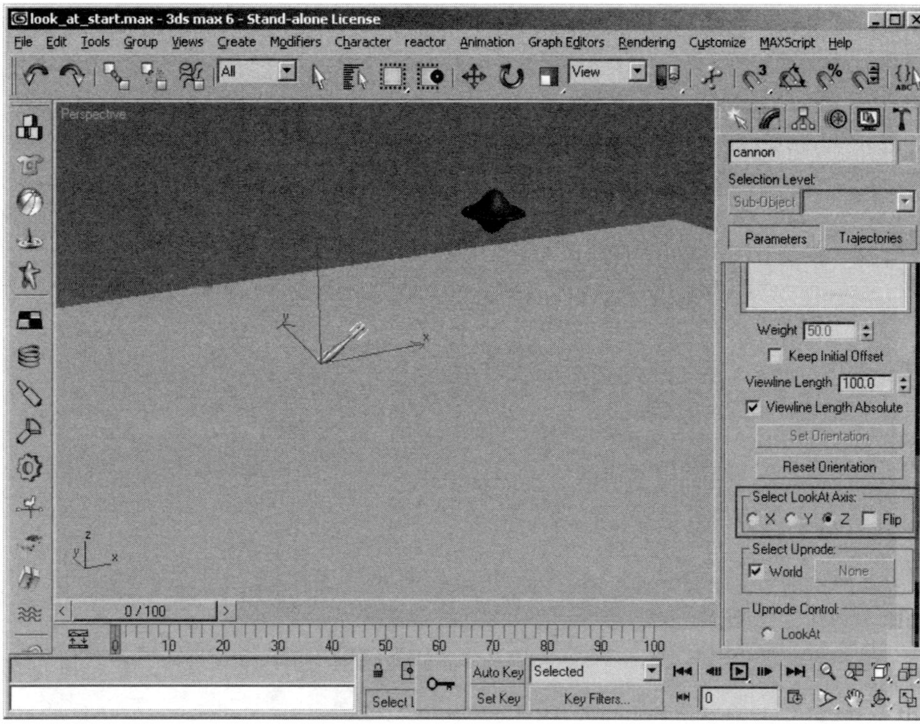

Figure 3.56: Cannon Not Properly Oriented

12. Click the **Modify tab** to come out of the Motion tab.

13. Play the animation using the **Play** button. You will see that now the tip of the cannon is always pointing at the saucer object and is ready to fire. Figure 3.57 shows the animation at frame 43.

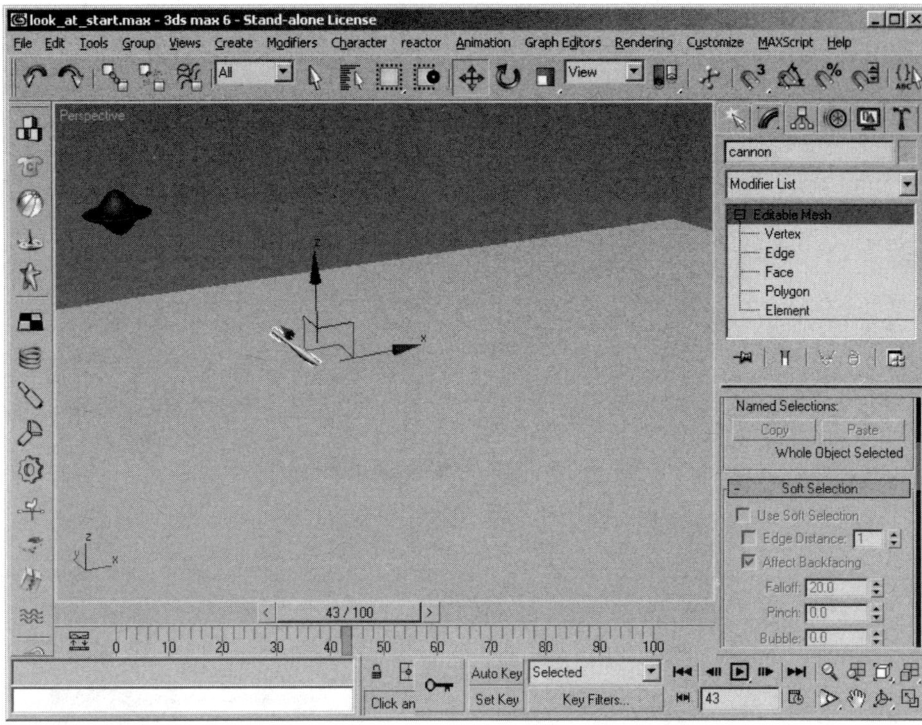

Figure 3.57: Animation at Frame 43

14. Save the file as **ch03_lab_ex7_sol.max**.

Lab Activity Checklist

S. No.	Tasks	Completed	
		Yes	No
1.	Applied the Assign Rotation Controller option		
2.	Applied the LookAt constraint		
3.	Selected the LookAt Target correctly		
4.	Assigned the right Axis options for the right alignment		

Exercise 8

Objective

- Assign Path constraints through the Motion panel on an animation.

Problem Statement

Create a Solar System and make the planets revolve around the sun with the help of Path constraints.

Lab Setup

3ds max 6.0

Procedure

To create a solar system, perform the following steps:

1. Select File → Reset.
2. Towards the Front of the viewport, make 10 Spheres of radius mentioned below:
   a. Sphere 1 of radius 35
   b. Sphere 2 of radius 5
   c. Sphere 3 of radius 8
   d. Sphere 4 of radius 12
   e. Sphere 5 of radius 8
   f. Sphere 6 of radius 20
   g. Sphere 7 of radius 15
   h. Sphere 8 of radius 12
   i. Sphere 9 of radius 10
   j. Sphere 10 of radius 5
3. Align sphere 1 at the center of the world space.

Figure 3.58 shows the 10 spheres you have created.

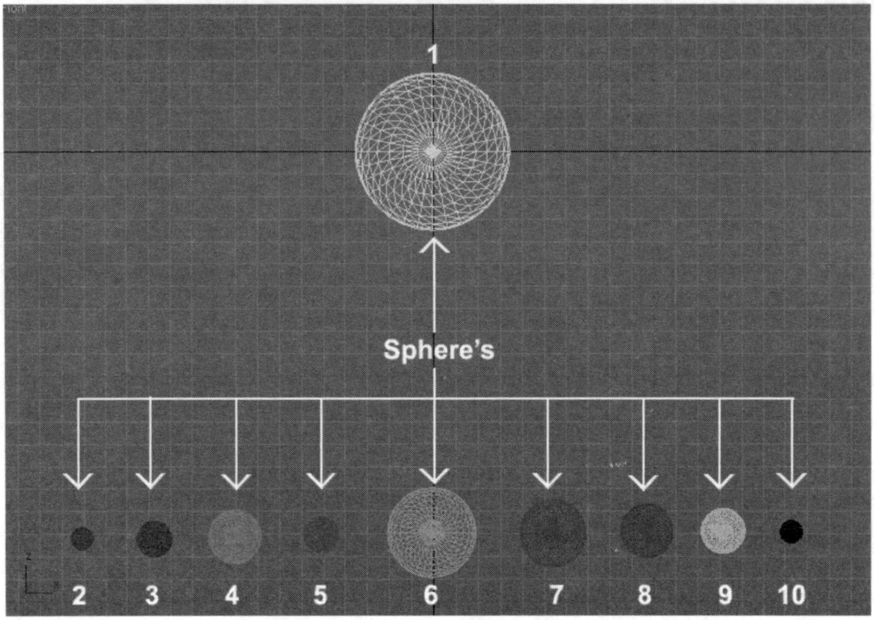

Figure 3.58: 10 Spheres

4. Towards the Top of the viewport, make 9 Circular Paths of radius mentioned below:

   k. Path 1 of radius 70

   l. Path 2 of radius 110

   m. Path 3 of radius 150

   n. Path 4 of radius 180

   o. Path 5 of radius 230

   p. Path 6 of radius 270

   q. Path 7 of radius 300

   r. Path 8 of radius 340

   s. Path 9 of radius 370

Figure 3.59 shows the 10 Paths you have created.

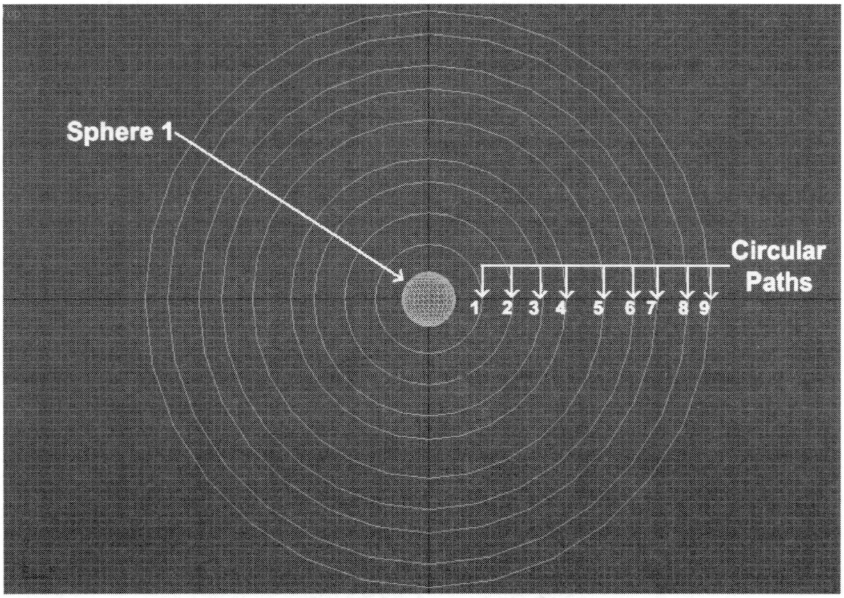

Figure 3.59: 10 Paths Created

5. Towards the top of the viewport, select **Sphere 2** and choose **Animation menu → Constraints → Path Constraints**.

You are now in Select Target mode.

6. Towards the top of the viewport, select **Circle Path 1**. Sphere 2 automatically aligns itself to the selected path, as shown in Figure 3.60.

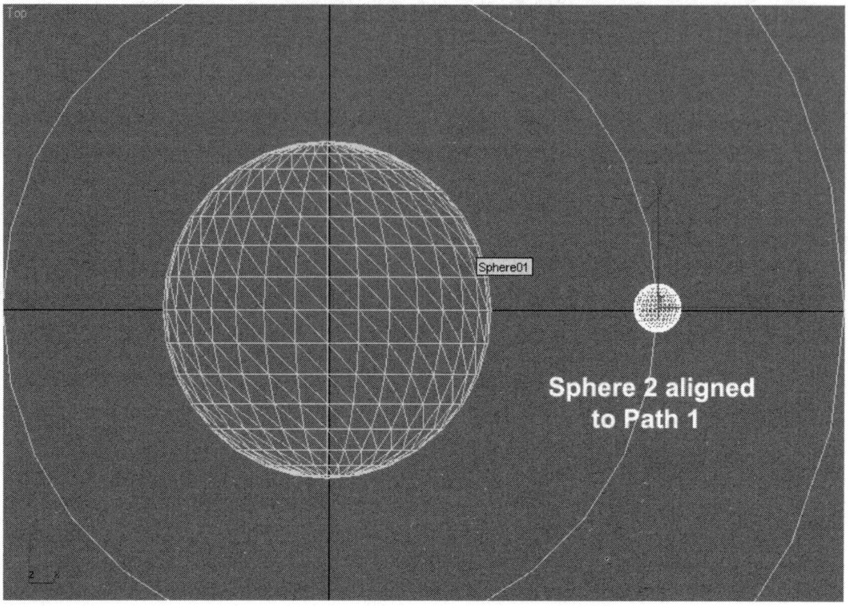

Figure 3.60: Sphere 2 Aligned to Path 1

7. In the Path options group, specify the % Along Path to **30**.
8. Move the time slider and you will see sphere 2 revolve around sphere 1.
9. Towards the top of the viewport, select Sphere 3, choose **Animation → Constraints → Path Constraints**. Select Circle path **2**.
10. In the Path options group, specify the % Along Path to **70**.
11. Towards the top of the viewport, select **Sphere 4**, choose **Animation → Constraints → Path Constraints**. Select Circle path **3**.
12. In the Path options group, specify the % Along Path to **110**.
13. Towards the top of the viewport, select Sphere 5, choose **Animation → Constraints → Path Constraints**. Select Circle path **4**.
14. In the Path options group, specify the % Along Path to **50**.
15. Towards the top of the viewport, select Sphere 6, choose **Animation → Constraints → Path Constraints**. Then select Circle path **5**.
16. In the Path options group, specify the % Along Path to **90**.
17. Towards the top of the viewport, select Sphere 7, choose **Animation → Constraints → Path Constraints**. Select Circle path **6**.
18. In the Path options group, specify the % Along Path to **25**.

19. Towards the top of the viewport, select Sphere 8, choose **Animation → Constraints→ Path Constraints**. Select Circle path **7**.
20. In the Path options group, specify the % Along Path to **60**.
21. Towards the top of the viewport, select Sphere 9, choose **Animation → Constraints → Path Constraints**. Select Circle path **8**.
22. In the Path options group, make the % Along Path to **40**.
23. Towards the top of the viewport, select Sphere 10, choose **Animation → Constraints → Path Constraints**. Select Circle path **9**.
24. In the Path options group, specify the % Along Path to **80**.
25. After assigning Path constraints to all the spheres, activate your Perspective viewport by clicking the **Play** button and see the solar system animation play, as shown in Figure 3.61.

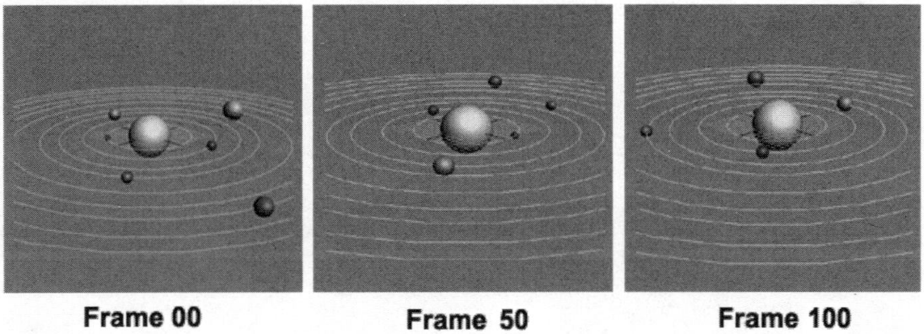

Figure 3.61: Three Different Frames of Solar Animation

Lab Activity Checklist

S. No.	Task	Completed	
		Yes	No
1.	Created objects		
2.	Applied Path constraints		

Project

Activities

- Modify the animation by using the trajectories and path controller/constraints.

Structuring for Animation

4

Hierarchies play an important role in creating and managing various parts of an animation. They also help in rearranging various objects according to their importance in an animation.

Helper objects play a supporting role in an animation. They are useful in positioning objects and measuring dimensions. At the end of this chapter, you will be able to:

- Establish links in an animation using the linking strategy and link inheritance mechanisms.
- Identify the features of the Dummy helper object.
- List the types of hidden helper objects that aid animation.
- Identify the features of the slider, cone angles, and atmosphere helper objects.
- Create an animation using dummies and point helpers.

4.1 Hierarchies

4.2 Standard Helper Objects

4.3 Advanced Helper Objects

4.1 Hierarchies

Hierarchies are logical sets of linked objects. You use hierarchies to animate a set of linked objects so that the motion realistically flows throughout the grouping. For example, consider what happens when you take a step and move your leg. Is your leg the only object that moves? Obviously, your toes, foot, ankle, and knee also move along with the leg. When your leg changes position, corresponding changes occur in the position of your toes, foot, ankle, and knee. Similarly, while creating animations, you need to link related objects so that the motion automatically flows through the linked objects.

You can create a hierarchy of objects or bones. For example, you need a hierarchy of bones to create a dinosaur, whereas you need a hierarchy of objects to create a hand pump. The Bones system is helpful in character animation.

This chapter introduces you to hierarchies and the techniques to create hierarchies in 3D.

4.1.1 Components of a Hierarchy

Identify the components of a hierarchy.

Hierarchies are based on the concept of parent and child relationships. Changes to the parent object are automatically and naturally transmitted to child objects. In a 3D environment, a parent object can have multiple child objects, while a child object can have only one parent object. Moreover, an object can be both a parent and child at the same time. A parent object that controls all subordinate child objects is present at the root of each hierarchy.

Figure 4.1 illustrates the components of a hierarchy.

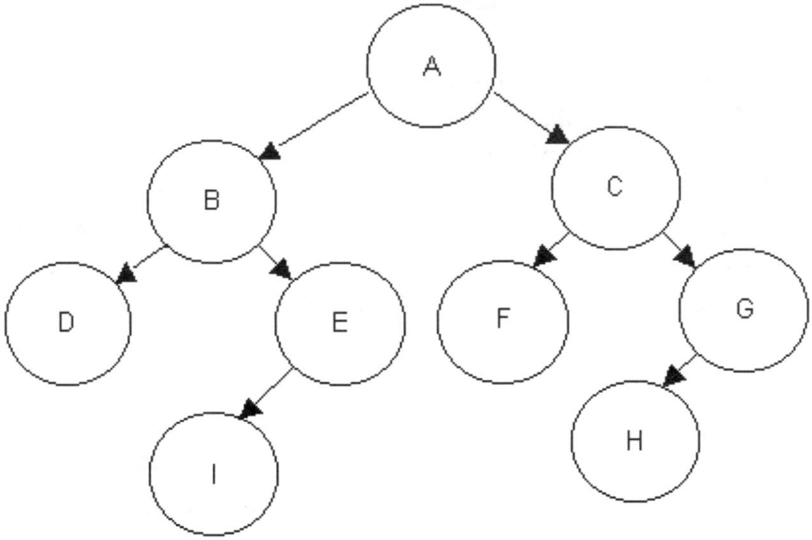

Figure 4.1: Components of a Hierarchy

The components of a hierarchy are:

- Root object: The root object is located at the top of the hierarchy. It has only child objects and no parent object. In Figure 4.1, A is the root object.
- Parent object: Parent objects in a hierarchy control one or more child objects, and sometimes other parent objects. In Figure 4.1, A, B, C, E, and G represent parent objects.
- Child object: A child object is managed by a parent object, and it can be a parent to other child objects. In Figure 4.1, B, C, D, E, F, G, H, and I represent child objects.
- Links: Links define the relationship between the parent and the child object. Links help in passing on the various transformations from the parent to the child object.
- Pivots: Pivots form the center point of an object. They also act as the connecting points between the child and parent objects.
- Ancestors: Ancestors refer to all the parent objects above a selected child object. This includes the parents of parents, until the top of the hierarchy is reached. For example, in Figure 4.1, E, B, and A are ancestors of I.
- Descendants: All the child objects below a selected parent object become its descendants. This includes the children of children, right down to the bottom of the hierarchical chain. For example, in Figure 4.1, F, G, and H are descendants of C.

- Subtree: A subtree refers to all the objects below the selected parent object in a hierarchy. The path between the parent and the child objects in a hierarchy is called a branch.
- Leaf: A leaf in a hierarchy refers to a child object that has no child objects beneath it. It is the last object in the branch. In Figure 4.1, D, F, H, and I depict leaves.

4.1.2 Kinematics

Identify the types of hierarchies.

After you link objects to form a hierarchy, you need to manipulate the hierarchy to depict movement or animation. You can manipulate a hierarchy with the help of *kinematics*. In 3ds max, kinematics governs the animation of a hierarchy with the help of internal mathematical formulae.

You can use kinematics to animate a hierarchical chain in two ways, from the top or from the bottom:

- Forward kinematics: When kinematics is applied from the top, the process is referred to as *forward kinematics*. In this, the movement of the selected parent object determines the movement of all the child objects beneath it.
- Inverse kinematics: When kinematics is applied from the reverse direction, that is, from bottom to top, it is referred to as *inverse kinematics*. In this case, the selected child object determines the movement of all the parent objects above it in the hierarchical chain.

Forward Kinematics

Forward kinematics governs the default animation of a hierarchy. In this, the inheritance feature passes on the transformations from the parent object to its child objects, depending on their relationship in the hierarchy. For forward kinematics to function, it is important that all the pivot points of the bone objects are properly positioned at the joints between the two objects.

Forward kinematics is used only for transformations. Transformations include a change in the position, rotation, and scale of the parent object. When a parent object is modified in any of these ways, all the child objects in the subtree follow suit. No other change in the modifiers or creation parameters of the parent object is reflected in the child objects.

Similar transformations in the child object do not bind the parent object. Any transformations applied to a child object remain constrained to the particular child object and its subsequent child objects. These transformations are not passed on to the parent object. The child is not bound to the parent, and has an independent identity. The child object may even move ahead, leaving its parent behind.

Inverse Kinematics

Inverse kinematics (IK) controls the hierarchy from the child to the parent. It is an animation method based on hierarchical linkages, which requires all the pivot points to be properly positioned for smooth functioning. In inverse kinematics, the child object defines the position, movement, and orientation of the parent object. It is easier to manipulate a hierarchical chain using inverse kinematics because it allows you easily to create complicated animations. This is because you can make changes in the desired object or bone instead of creating numerous keyframes. The changes will then be reflected in the entire chain.

Inverse kinematics uses the following tools:

- IK solvers
- IK methods

IK Solvers

IK solvers allow you to apply inverse kinematics or IK solutions to the components of a hierarchy across frames. These solutions, applied with controllers, help perform transformations, such as position and rotation, on the various links and other components in the hierarchical chain. You can access the IK solvers from the Animation menu in 3ds max.

3ds max has three types of IK solvers:

- History-dependent (HD): This is a smooth but slow process that is best suited for short animations because it takes more time and memory.
- History-independent (HI): This is a fast process that independently looks at each frame. It is best suited for long animations.
- IK limb solver: This process works on two bones or objects. It is best used to animate limbs.

IK solvers are plug-ins. You can expand them by including third-party IK solvers or those that you create.

IK Methods

You can use IK methods to animate and manipulate hierarchies without applying IK solvers. You can access the IK methods from the Hierarchy panel.

Two types of IK methods are available in 3ds max:

- Interactive IK: This process animates by computing solutions only for keyframes.
- Applied IK: This process animates by computing solutions for all the hierarchical objects in every frame.

4.1.3 Animating Hierarchies

Create and link hierarchies.

You need to create and link a hierarchy to animate it. You will learn to create and animate hierarchies by using the Bones system.

Creating Hierarchies

3ds max allows you to create complex hierarchies that contain a large number of objects. You can create hierarchies by:

- Linking and unlinking objects
- Creating hierarchies with bones

The topic on bones is explained in detail in Chapter 7, Skinning a Model.

Linking and Unlinking Objects

The simplest way to create a hierarchy in 3ds max is to create normal objects and link them using the Select and Link buttons on the main toolbar. These buttons allow you to link child objects with parent objects.

You can disconnect an object from its parent links by using the Unlink Selection button. Unlinking only affects an object's parent links, the child objects are not affected.

Table 4.1 summarizes the functionality provided by the Link and Unlink buttons.

Icon	Name	Functionality
	Select and Link	Allows you to link a child object with a parent object
	Unlink Selection	Allows you to unlink an object from its parent

Table 4.1: Linking and Unlinking Buttons on the Main Toolbar

To link objects, perform the following steps:

1. Click **Select and Link** on the Main toolbar. You are now in the linking mode.
2. Select the object for which you want to establish links.
3. Drag the mouse pointer from the first object to the object that you want to make the parent object. As you drag, observe that a line is attached to the cursor and the cursor changes to the link icon when it is over any object.
4. Select the second object. As you release the mouse button, the second object, which has now become the parent for the first object, flashes. This indicates that the linking is successful.

To unlink objects, perform the following steps:

1. Click the **Unlink** button on the Main toolbar. You are now in the unlinking mode.
2. Select the object that is to be detached from its parent object. As you select the object, its link with its parent object is broken, but not with its child objects.

Creating a Hierarchy with Bones

You can also create a hierarchy using the Bones system. You can access the Bones system from the Systems category of the Create panel, as shown in Figure 4.2.

You can also access the Bones system by using the Create Bones command in the Animation menu.

Figure 4.2: Create Bones Command

To create a hierarchy with the Bones system, click the Bones button, and then click the desired spot in the viewport. After defining the starting point, click again to define the end-point of the particular bone. Continue the same process to create more bones. New bones are child objects of earlier bones, and are created from the end-point of the latest bone. You can complete the hierarchical chain of bones by right-clicking the end-point of the latest bone. In such a hierarchy, if you move one bone, all the bones linked to it accordingly move.

The placement of the pivot point is very important in an animation. The pivot point is located at the base of a bone object. Bones rotate around this pivot point. You can consider the bones to be linked joints, which are similar to splines and are not renderable unless specified.

Bone Parameters Rollout

As you click the Bones button in the Systems category of the Create panel, the bone settings become available in the Bone Parameters rollout.

The Bone Parameters rollout, as shown in Figure 4.3, allows you to modify the bones even after you have created them.

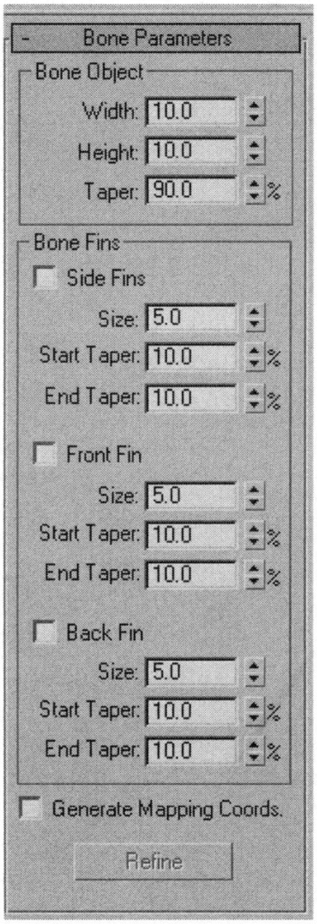

Figure 4.3: Bone Parameters Rollout

The options available in the Bone Parameters rollout are:

- Bone Object: These options allow you to define the width, height, and taper of the selected bone object.
- Bone Fins: These options allow you to add side, front, and back fins to the selected bone object. You can also decide the size and taper of the fins added.
- Generate Mapping Coords: These options allow you to generate mapping coordinates for the bone materials.
- Refine: This button allows you to divide the bone at the point where you click on it.

After creating a hierarchy with the Bones system, you can apply different modifiers and materials, such as the skin modifier, before rendering the animation.

Creating Bones from Objects

3ds max allows you to create bones from other objects by using the options in the Object Properties dialog box. Right-click an object and choose Properties from the menu to open the Object Properties dialog box. Figure 4.4 shows the Object Properties dialog box.

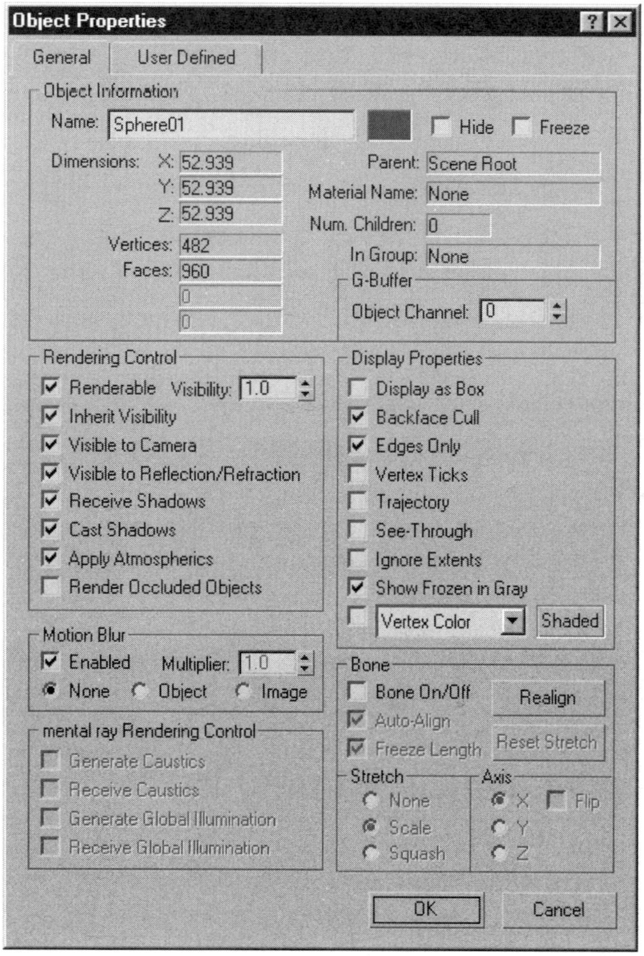

Figure 4.4: Object Properties Dialog Box

Select the Bone On/Off check box to activate the Bone section. The options available in this section are:

- Bone: The following options enable you to manipulate objects to behave as bones.
  - Bone On/Off: Makes an object behave as a bone
  - Auto-Align: Aligns the pivot points of the adjacent bones
  - Freeze Length: Prevents the length of the bone from being changed
  - Realign: Allows you to realign the bone to the default
  - Reset Stretch: Allows you to reset the stretch of the bone to the default
- Stretch: This option allows you to choose the stretching techniques that are available when the Freeze Length option is cleared.
  - None: Applies no stretching
  - Scale: Allows you to scale the bone while stretching
  - Squash: Allows the bone mass to be adjusted in size as the bone is stretched, making the bone broader as the size is reduced and longer as it is increased
- Axis: This option allows you to select the axis along which the different stretching techniques will be implemented.
  - X/Y/Z: Selects any one of the three axes to apply the techniques
  - Flip: Flips the stretch on the selected axis

You can also use the Bone Options command on the Animation menu to convert an object into bones.

Applying Animations in Hierarchies

In this topic, you will learn to use various techniques to create animations. You can apply animations in hierarchies by using any of the following methods:

- Animating with a linked hierarchy
- Animating the bone hierarchy with a dummy
- Animating with IK solvers

Animating with a Linked Hierarchy

To animate a hierarchy by linking and unlinking objects, perform the following steps:

1. Link objects to create a hierarchy.
2. Adjust the pivots of the objects in the hierarchy.
3. Link the objects to animate the hierarchy.

To link objects to create a hierarchy, perform the following steps:

1. Open the file, **ch04_hierarchy_start.max**. This file depicts a chick.
2. Select the chick. Click **Group** → **Ungroup** to ungroup the object. The resultant object is shown in Figure 4.5.

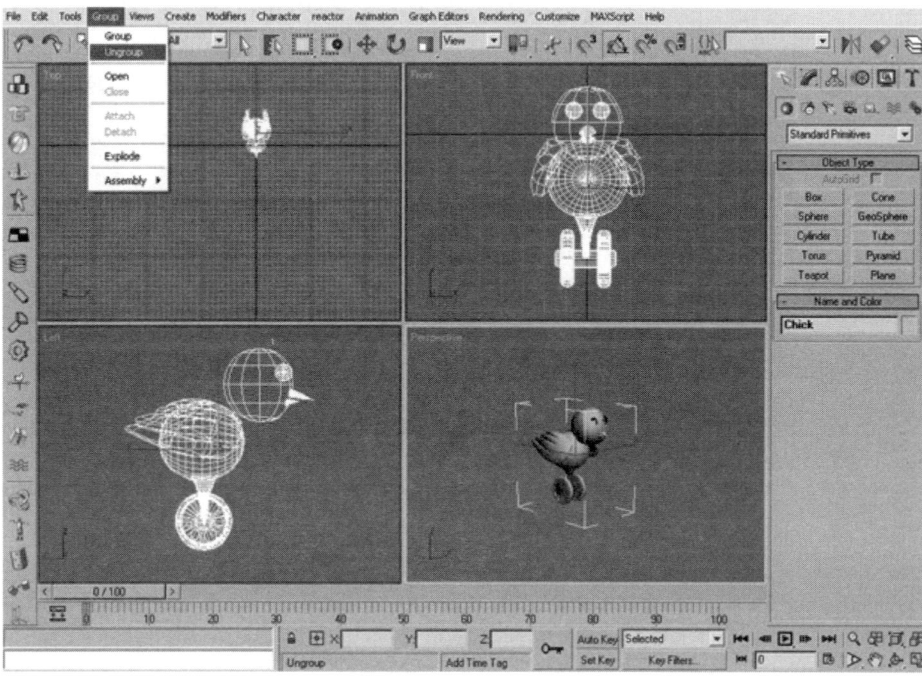

Figure 4.5: Ungrouping the Object

3. To link the beak and the head of the chicken, select both the upper and lower beaks, and then select the **Link** tool on the Main toolbar.
4. With the Link tool activated, select the beak and drag it to the head of the chick.

Notice that the icon changes to the Link icon and a dotted line is attached to the cursor as you select the first object, as shown in Figure 4.6.

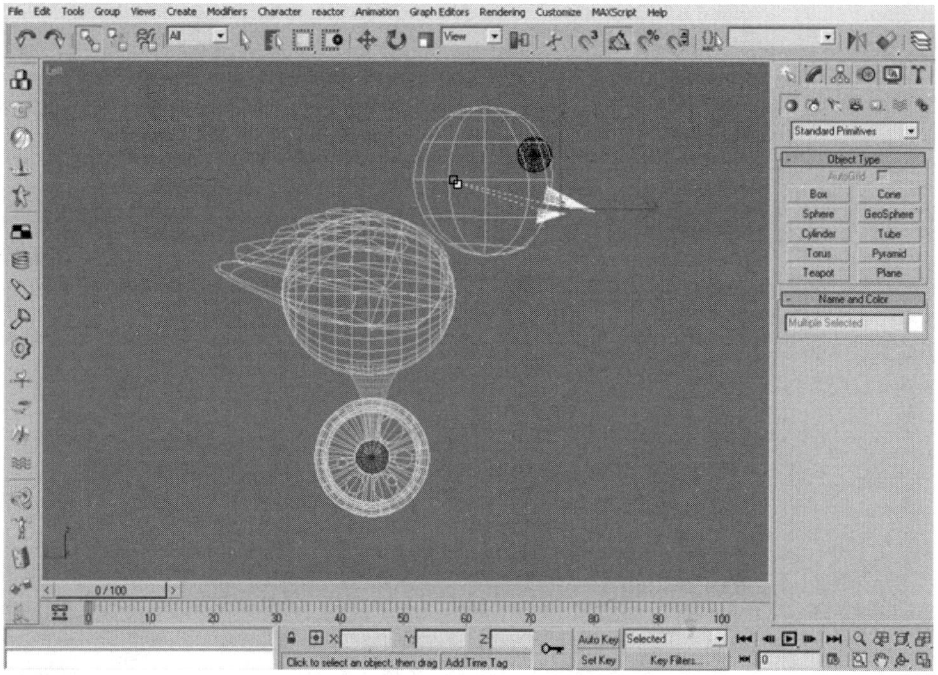

Figure 4.6: Linking Beak and Head

5. Similarly, link the eyes to the head, the head to the body of the bird, and the wings to the body of the bird.

Figure 4.7 shows the chick with the wings linked to the body.

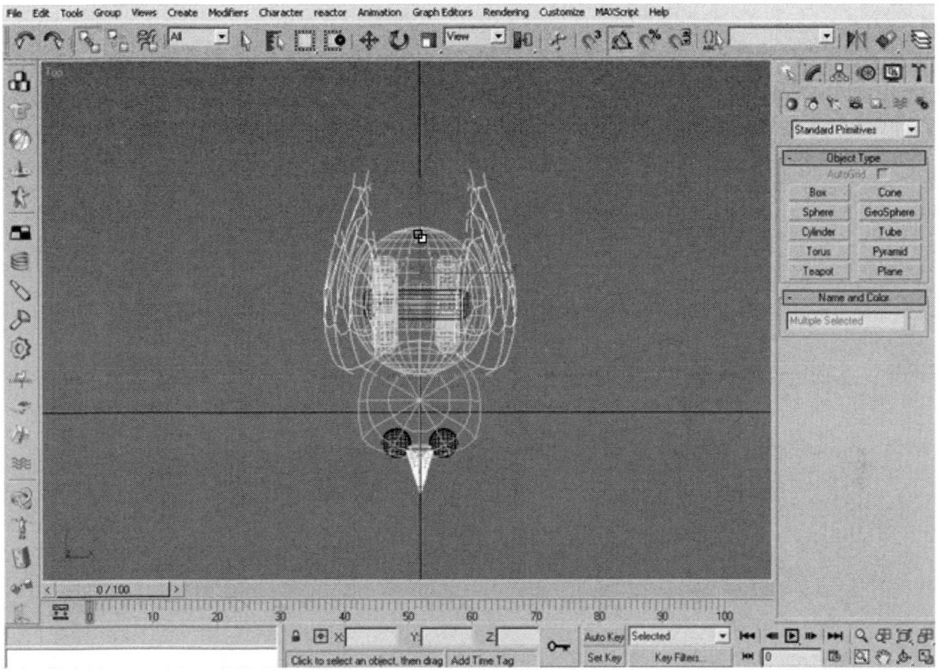

Figure 4.7: Linking the Wings to the Body

After linking the objects, align the pivot of the wheels to the center of the objects so that the wheels turn uniformly. To adjust the pivots of the wheel, perform the following steps:

1. Click the **Hierarchy Panel** tab to activate it.
2. Click **Pivot** on the Hierarchy panel to adjust the pivot of the wheel in the hierarchy.
3. In the Adjust Pivot rollout that opens, perform the following steps to align the pivot of the wheel to the center of the object:

   a. In the Move/Rotate/Scale options, click **Affect Pivot Only**.

b. In the Alignment options, click **Center to Object**. Figure 4.8 shows the adjusted pivot.

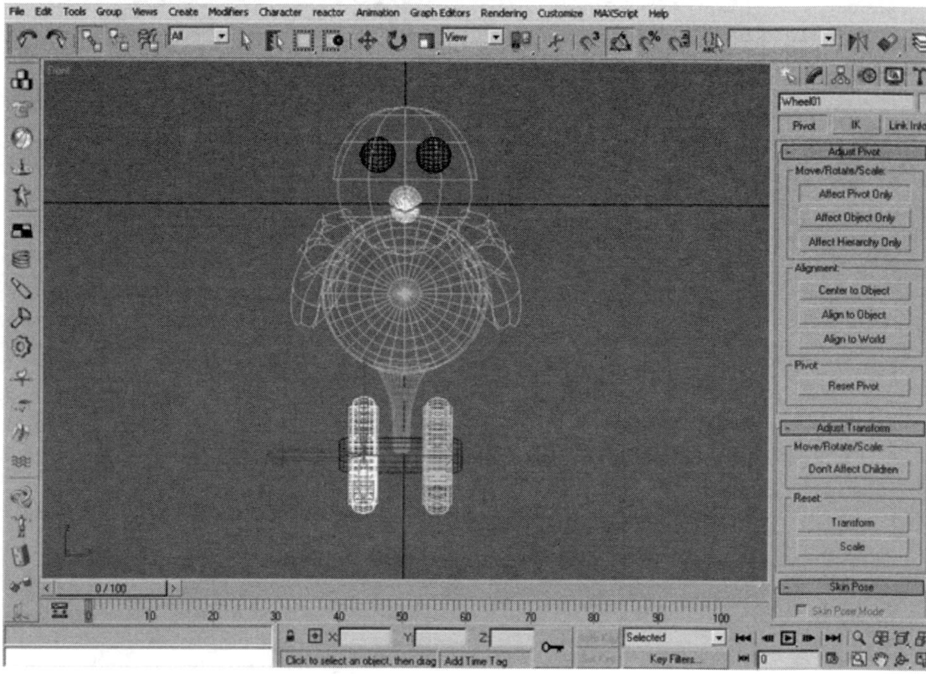

Figure 4.8: Adjusting the Pivot

4. Similarly, adjust the pivot of the other wheel.

Linking the Objects to Animate the Hierarchy

To link objects to animate the hierarchy, perform the following steps:

1. Using the **Link** tool, link both the wheels to the roller.
2. Link the roller to the stand.
3. Link the stand to the body. Observe that as you move the body of the chick, all other parts of the chick move correspondingly.

Figure 4.9 shows the stand being linked to the body of the chick.

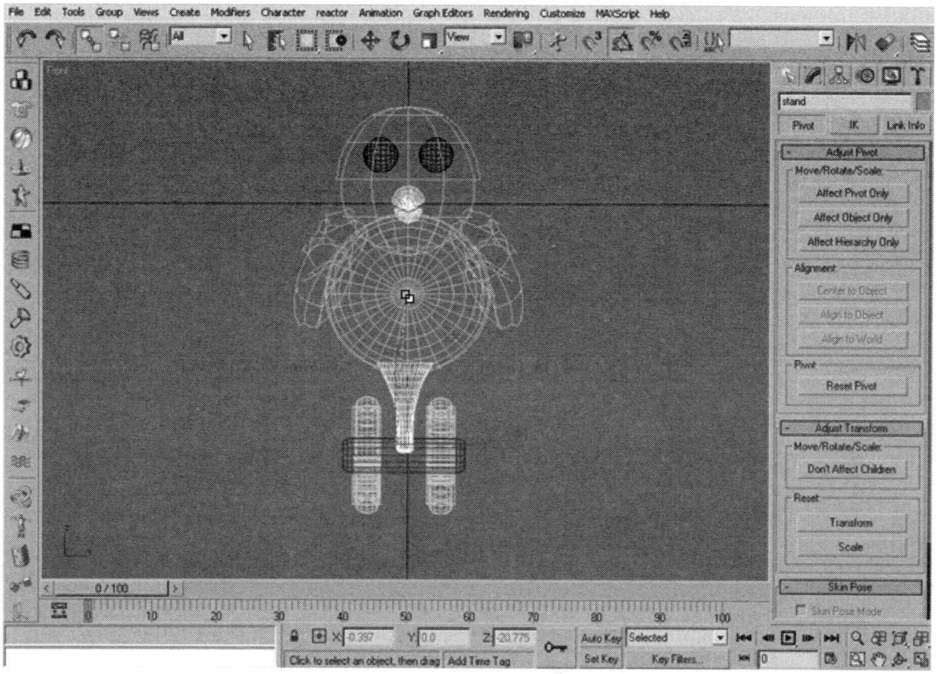

Figure 4.9: Stand Linked to the Body

4. Select the left wing, and then click **Unlink Selection** on the Main toolbar to unlink the left wing from the rest of the body. Notice that the left wing no longer moves with the rest of the body.

You can view the subtree in the Select Objects dialog box, as shown in Figure 4.10.

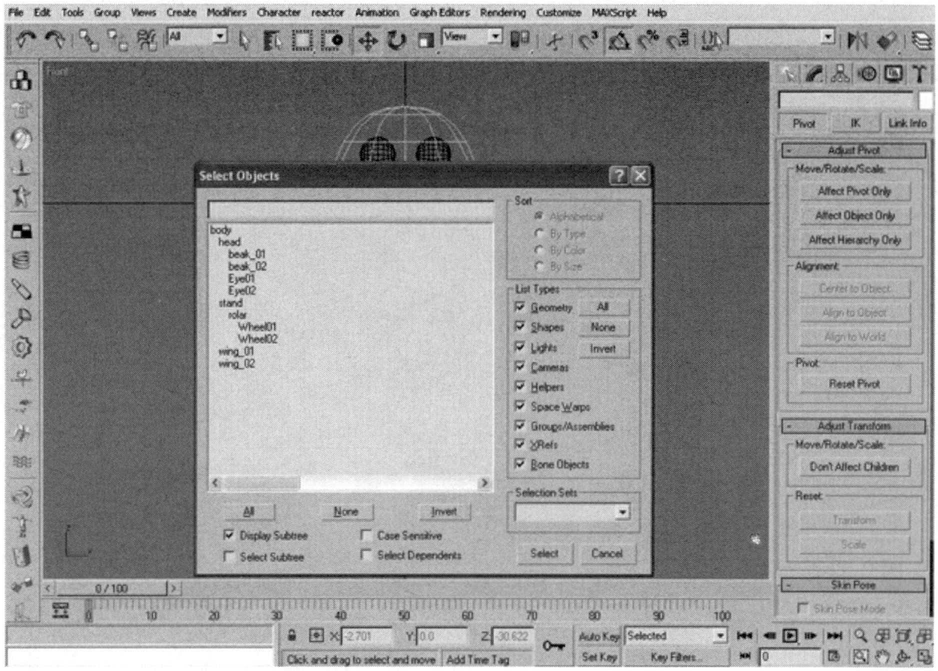

Figure 4.10: Select Objects Dialog Box

5. Click **Link Info** on the Hierarchy panel to adjust the movement of the wings in the hierarchy.
6. In the Link Info mode of the Inherit rollout, clear the X check box on the Move panel. This makes the wing movable when the chick is moving on the Y and Z axes, but not on the X-axis. One object at a time.
7. Save the file as **ch04_hierarchy_final.max**.

See figure 4.9 on pg. 4.19

Figure 4.11 shows the detached wing of the chick.

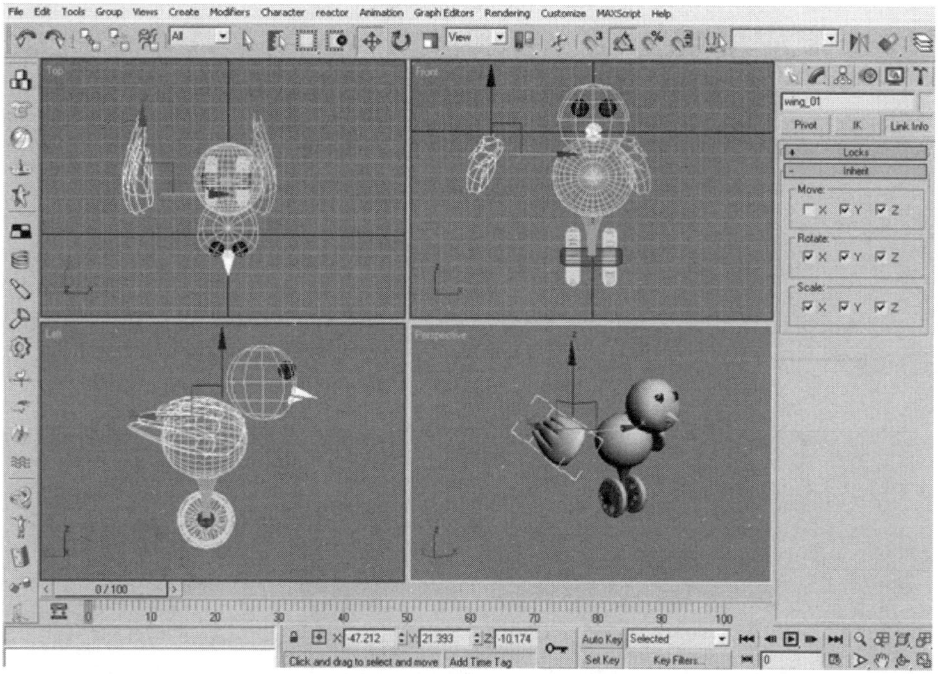

Figure 4.11: Detached Wing

Animating a Bone Hierarchy with a Dummy

Another method to animate the bone hierarchy is by using a dummy. To animate a bone hierarchy by using a dummy, perform the following steps:

1. Create a dummy and bones.
2. Link the bones and the dummy.
3. Apply the Skin modifier, and then animate.

Creating Dummy and Bones

To create a dummy and bones, perform the following steps:

1. Open the file, **ch04_hand_start.max**.
2. In the Create Panel, from the Helpers category, click **Dummy** to create a dummy of the hand.

The Dummy button is shown in Figure 4.12.

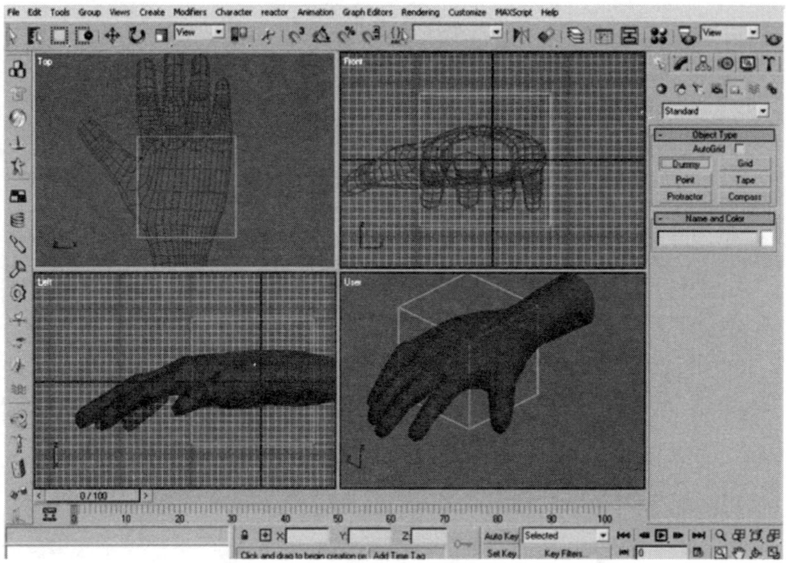

Figure 4.12: Dummy Button

3. In the Create panel, from the Systems category, click **Bones** to create bones.
4. In the Top viewport, create bones for the thumb and the fingers, as shown in Figure 4.13.

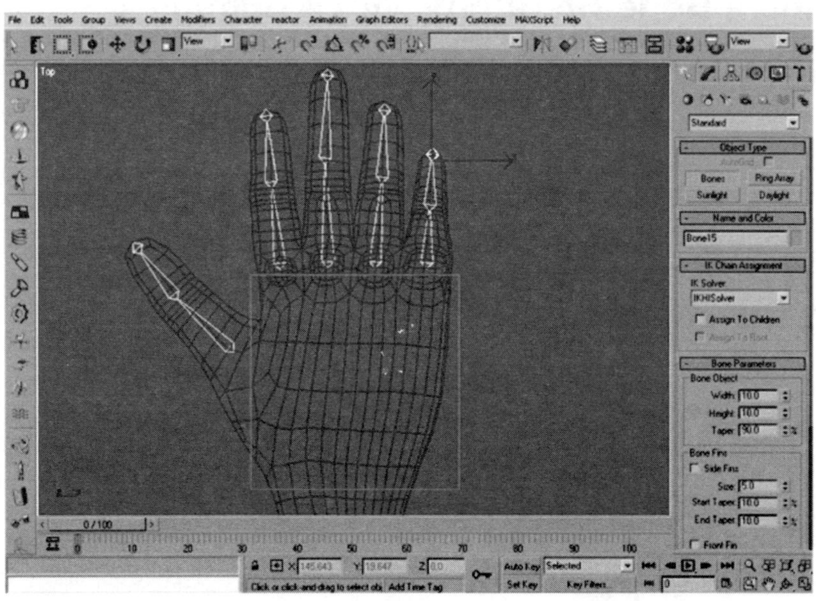

Figure 4.13: Creating Bones for Thumb and Fingers

Linking the Bones and the Dummy

To link the dummy and the bones after you create them, perform the following steps:

1. Select the root bones, and link them to the dummy, as shown in Figure 4.14.

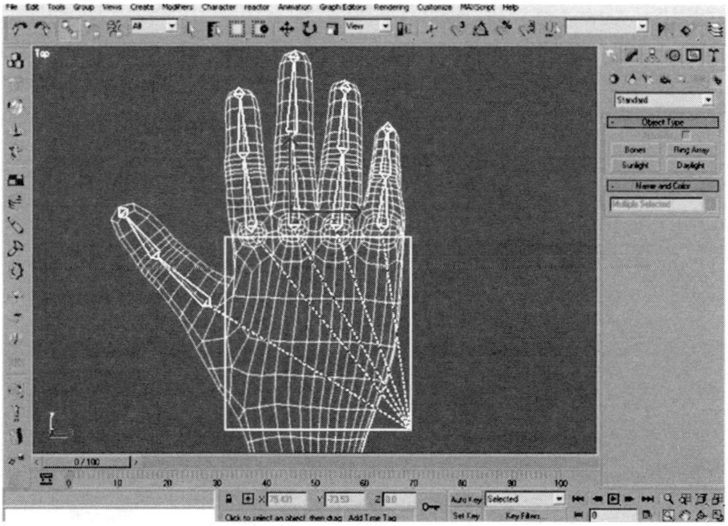

Figure 4.14: Linking Root Bones to the Dummy

2. Adjust and position the bones in the center of the fingers, as shown in Figure 4.15.

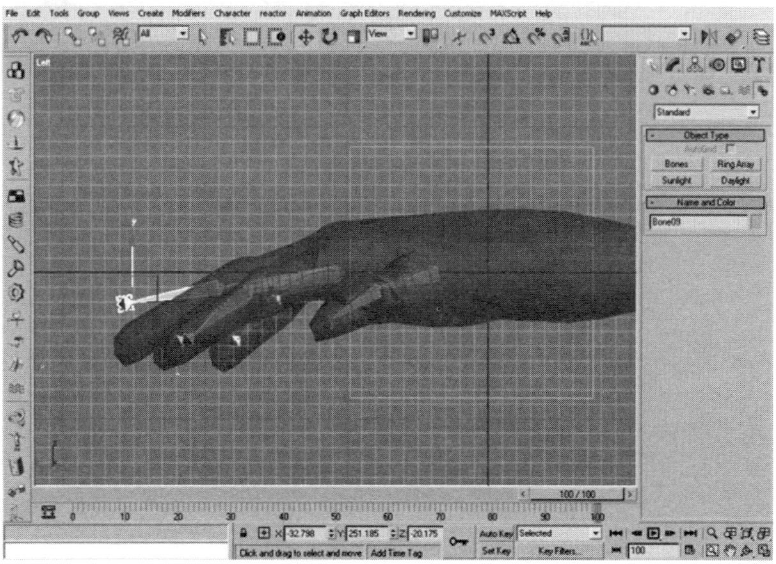

Figure 4.15: Positioning the Bones

Applying the Skin Modifier and Animating

Next, to apply the Skin modifier and animate the bones, perform the following steps:

1. Select the hand. Apply the Skin modifier to it by using the Modifier menu.

Figure 4.16 shows the selected hand to which the Skin modifier has been applied.

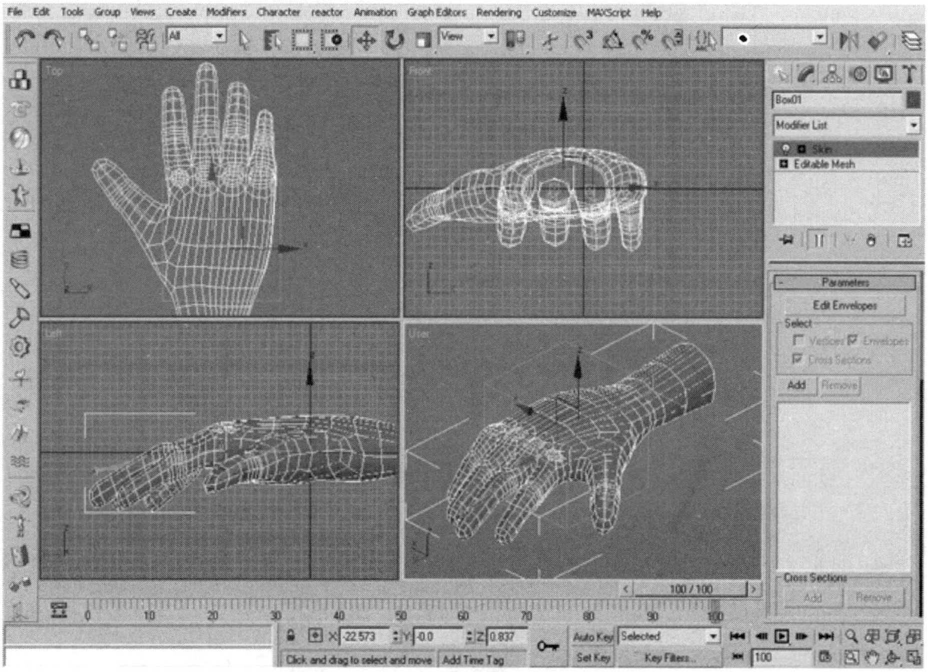

Figure 4.16: Applying the Skin Modifier

Select Mesh Smooth

Or Physique - Standard Biped

Skin - IK Bones

2. Click **Add**. This button is located in the Modify panel in the Skin modifier parameters rollout. The Select Bones dialog box is displayed, as shown in Figure 4.17.

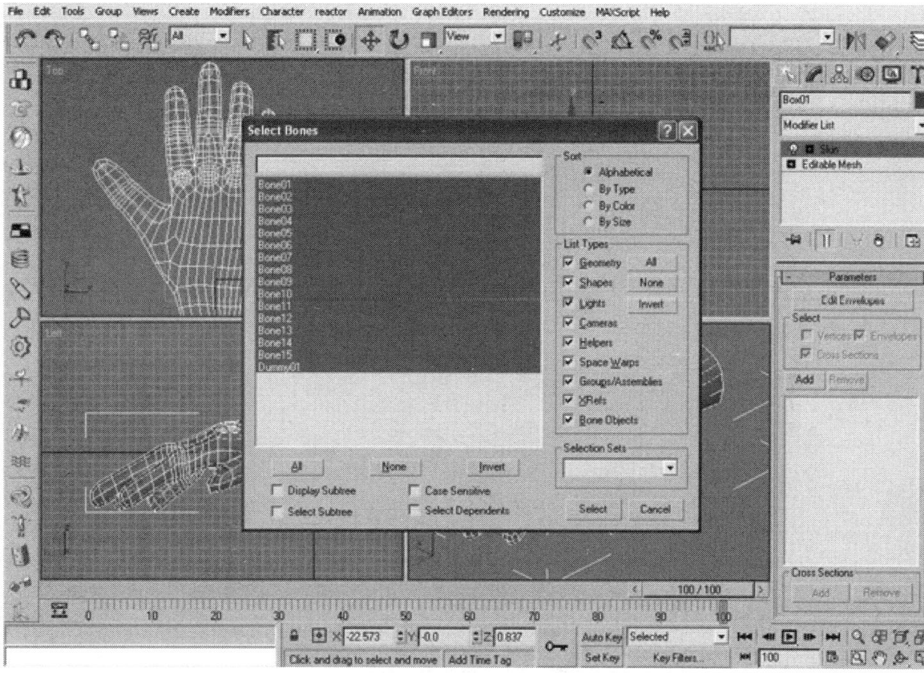

Figure 4.17: Select Bones Dialog Box

3. Select all the bones and the dummy.
4. Click **Edit Envelopes**, and then edit the specific envelopes for the bones and the dummy, such that all the envelopes cover the mesh.

Figure 4.18 shows the envelopes covering the mesh.

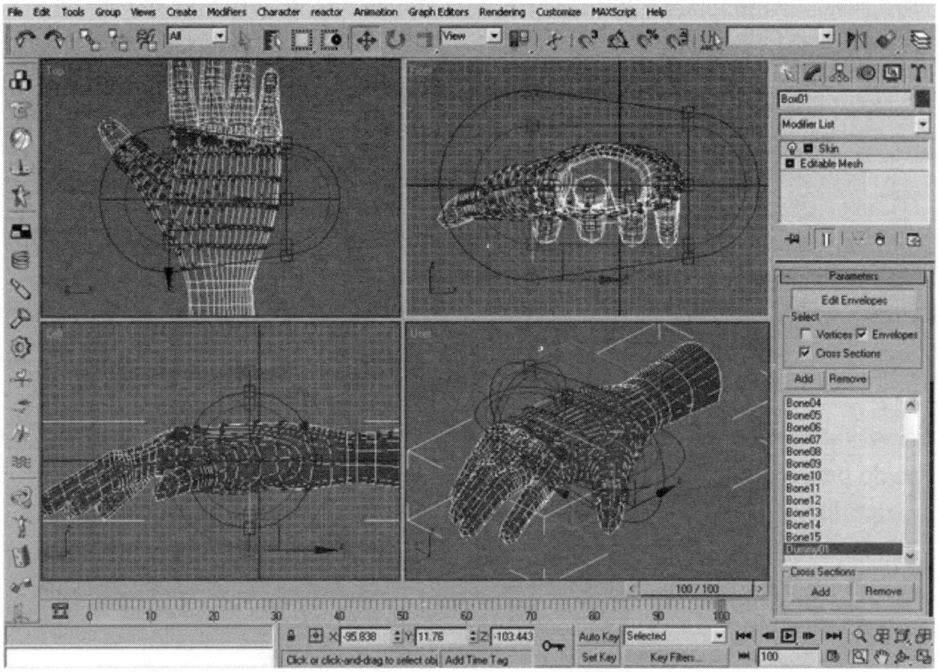

Figure 4.18: Envelopes Covering the Mesh

5. Animate the finger bones according to your requirements.
6. Save the file as **ch04_hand_final.max**.

You can view the linkage pattern of the dummy as the main bone in the Schematic View dialog box, as shown in Figure 4.19.

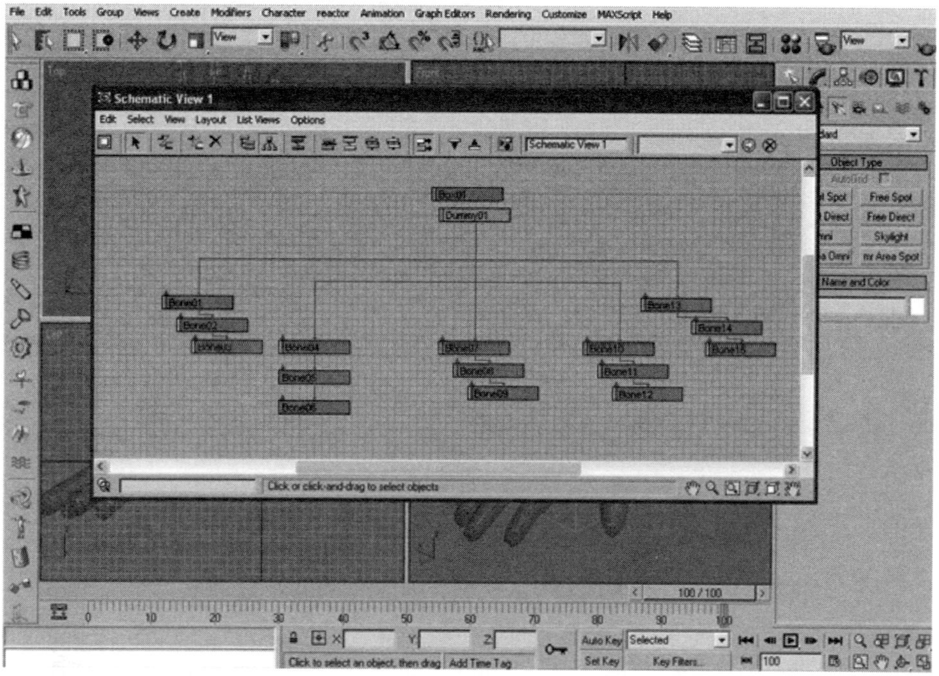

Figure 4.19: Schematic View Dialog Box

Animating with IK Solvers

Another method that you can use to create animations is to animate objects with IK solvers. To observe the difference in the animation of the three IK solvers, perform the following steps:

1. Load the file, **ch04_solverIK_start.max**.
2. Observe that there are three simple chains in the file. All the components of the chains are properly linked to their respective parts.
3. In the viewports, select the topmost ring in the HI chain.
4. Click **Animation → IK Solvers → HI Solver**.

The IK Solvers submenu is shown in Figure 4.20.

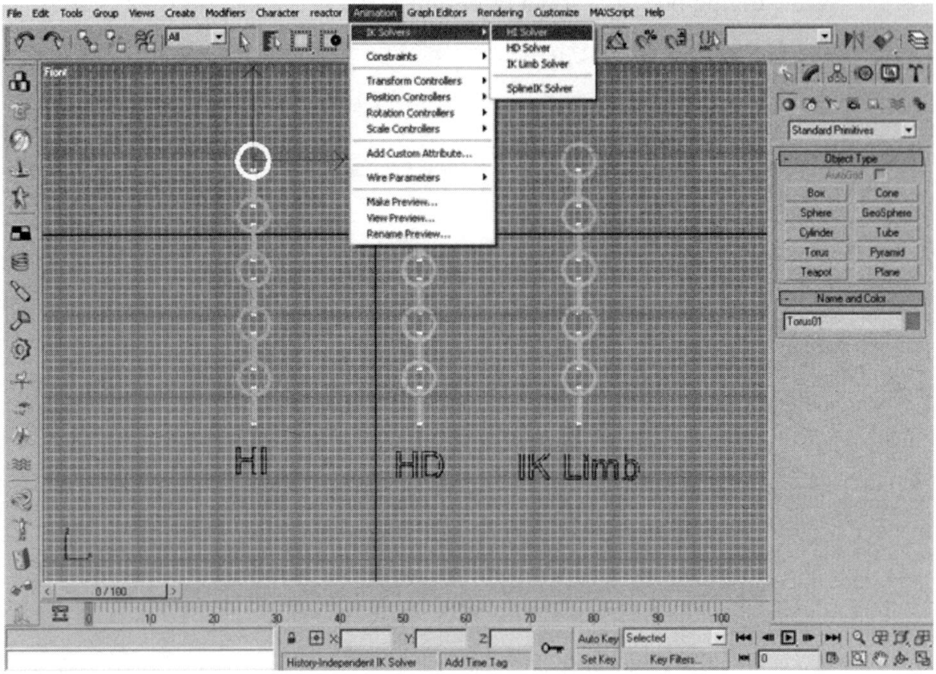

Figure 4.20: IK Solvers Submenu

5. Then, click the last ring in the HI chain.
6. Similarly, select the first ring of the rest of the two chains and assign corresponding IK solvers to them.
7. Select the last ring of the selected chain to close the assigning process.
8. Save the file as **ch04_solverIK_end.max**.

Observe that there are three handles, one for each of the respective chains. You can move these handles to view the difference in their motion.

Practice Questions

1. What are hierarchies?
2. List the components of a hierarchy.
3. What is kinematics? How many types of kinematics are there in 3ds max?
4. Write the steps for linking and unlinking objects.
5. What are IK solvers and IK methods?

4.2 Standard Helper Objects

Helpers are simple objects that help you build complex models and animate complex scenes. Helpers are objects with a supporting role. They act as an assistant or an extra helping hand, making it easy for an animator to work in the 3ds max environment. Helper objects cannot be modified or rendered.

The standard helper objects contain the following objects:

- Dummy objects
- Grid objects
- Point objects
- Tape objects
- Compass objects
- Protractor objects

4.2.1 Dummy Helper Object

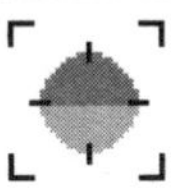

- Explain the use of Dummy helper objects.
- List the steps to create a dummy object in space.

A dummy object is designed as a wire frame cube with a pivot point at its center. It has a name but no parameters. It helps to transform objects, for example, a wire frame acts as an indication for transform effects. Dummy helper objects cannot be modified or rendered. For example, you can create a dummy object that the camera could follow through an animation sequence.

Dummy objects are always formed as cubes. The proportions of a dummy object can be altered by using non-uniform scaling.

To create a dummy object in space, perform the following steps:

1. To create a dummy, go to the Create Panel and click Helpers, as shown in Figure 4.21.

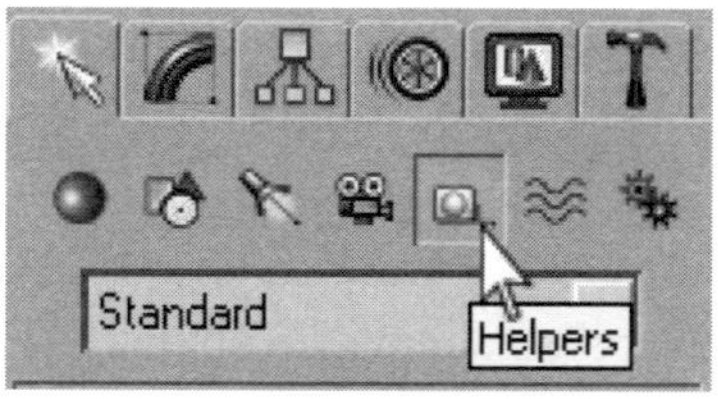

Figure 4.21: Helpers Icon

2. In the Helpers palate, click Dummy, as shown in Figure 4.22.

Figure 4.22: Dummy Button

3. Drag and release the left mouse button at the location at which you want the dummy object. Figure 4.23 shows a Dummy helper object.

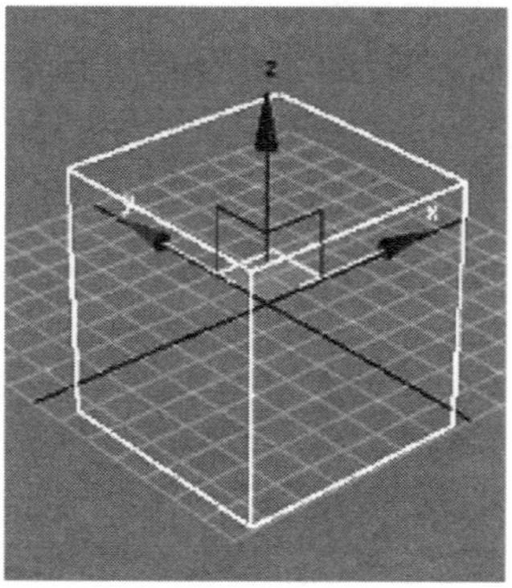

Figure 4.23: Dummy Helper Object

4.2.2 Grid Helper Object

- Explain the use of Grid Helper objects.
- Perform the steps to create a grid in space.

Also known as User Grid or Custom Grid, the Grid is a 2D parametric object with adjustments for overall size and grid spacing. You can move and orient user grids anywhere in world space. You can create any number of grid objects in your scene. You can name, save, and delete grid objects. The Grid helper object is used to create and align different objects to the active grid.

Do not use scaling to resize a grid object. Scaling enlarges or reduces the apparent size of the grid object, but has no effect on grid spacing.

For example, you can create a box and rotate it at a certain angle, and then simultaneously create a cylinder on top of the box, at the same angle, with the help of a grid helper object. To activate it in the top viewport, in the create panel helper rollout select the AutoGrid check box and now make a cylinder on top of the box. The cylinder created is automatically aligned to the box.

To create a grid in space, perform the following steps:

1. In the Helpers palate, click **Grid**, as shown in Figure 4.24.

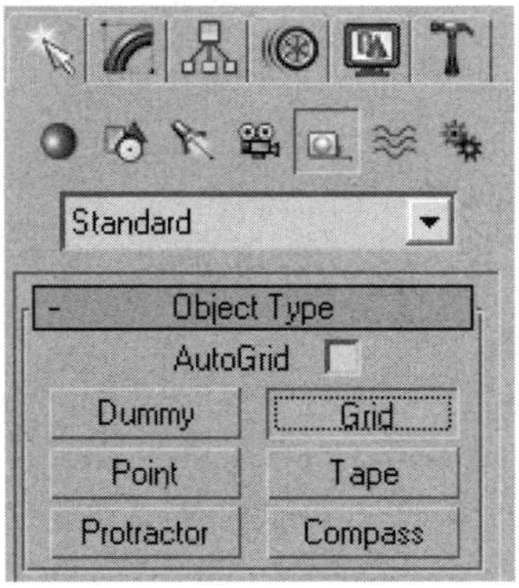

Figure 4.24: Grid Button

2. In a viewport, click and drag the left mouse button to create a rectangle. This creates and selects a grid object, which appears divided into four quadrants, with coordinate axes at the center, as shown in Figure 4.25.

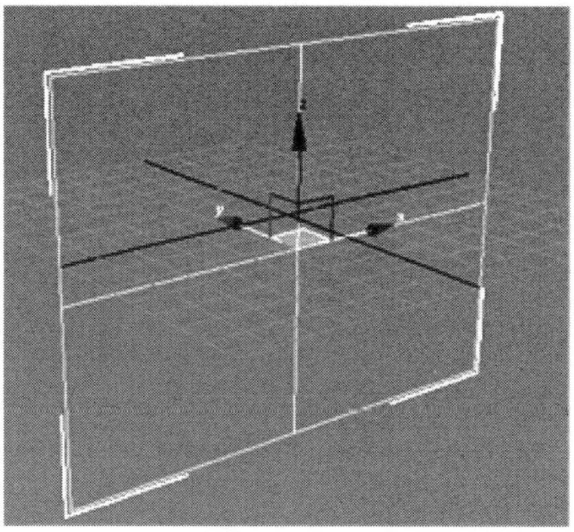

Figure 4.25: Creating a Grid Object

Figure 4.26 displays the Grid Parameters rollout.

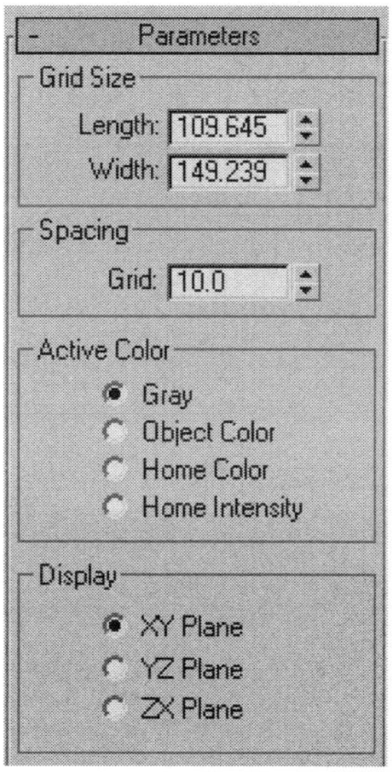

Figure 4.26: Grid Parameters Rollout

The following types of display are present in the Grid parameters rollout:

- Grid Size group:
  - Length/Width: Specifies the length and width of the grid.
- Grid Spacing group:
  - Grid: Specifies the size of the smallest square in the visible grid.

- Active Color group:
  - Gray: The active grid object is displayed in two shades of gray.
  - Object Color: The main grid lines use the assigned color, while the secondary lines use a lighter intensity color.
  - Home Color: The grid object uses the custom color assigned to the home grid in the Customize User Interface dialog box.
  - Home Intensity: The grid object uses the grid intensity settings assigned to the home grid in the Customize User Interface dialog box.
- Display group:
  - XY Plane, YZ Plane, and ZX Plane: Determines which of the three planes of the grid object are displayed in the viewport.

4.2.3 Point Helper Object

- Explain the use of Point objects.
- Perform the steps to create a point in space.

The Point object is similar to the Dummy object. It has only two modifiable parameters, and does not render. The axis tripod identifies the point object, and the tripod and its length are the only parameters that can be altered in the Parameters rollout. The main purpose of the point object is to mark positions and define the point in space.

Point objects are easy to lose. Be sure to name the object so that it is easy to locate using the Select by Name dialog box.

To create a point in space, perform the following steps:

1. In the Helpers panel, click **Point**, as shown in Figure 4.27.

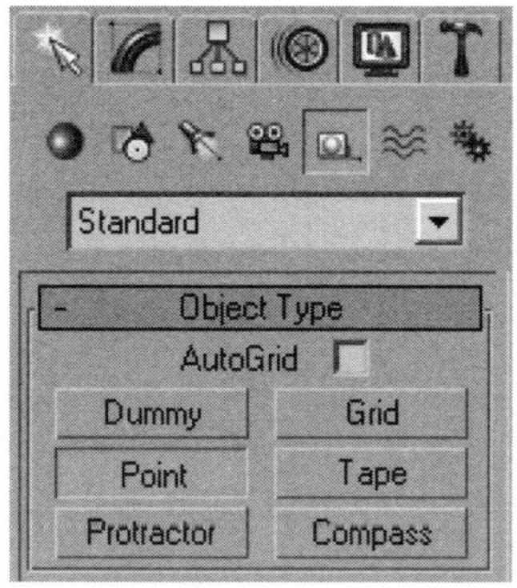

Figure 4.27: Point Button

2. In the Parameters rollout, select the type of display, such as Box, as shown in Figure 4.28.

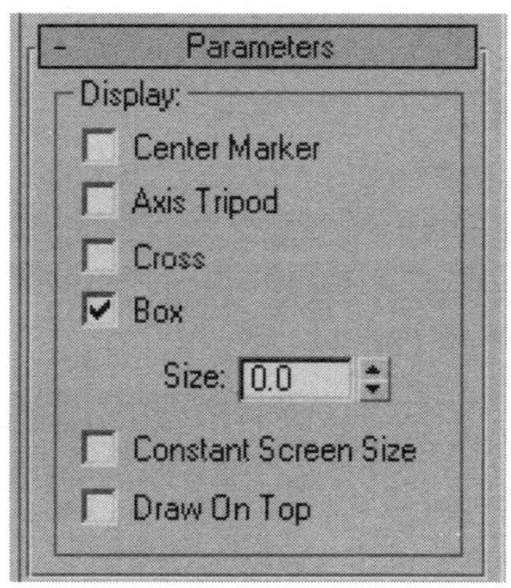

Figure 4.28: Type of Display

3. Use the size spinner to adjust the size of the point object, as shown in Figure 4.29.

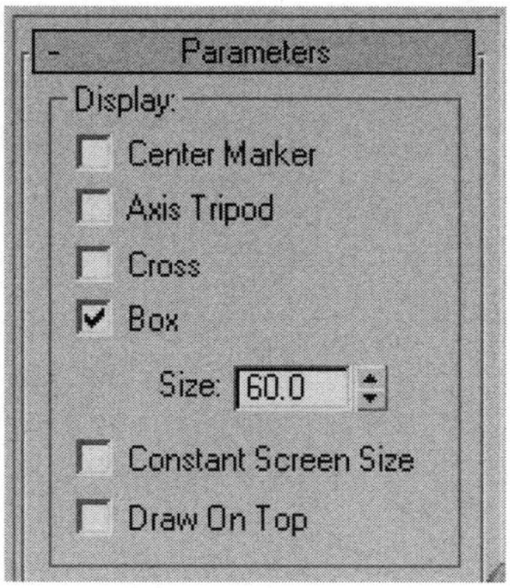

Figure 4.29: Using the Size Spinner

The default size of the point object is 20.

---

4. Drag and release the left mouse button to the location at which you want the point object, as shown in Figure 4.30.

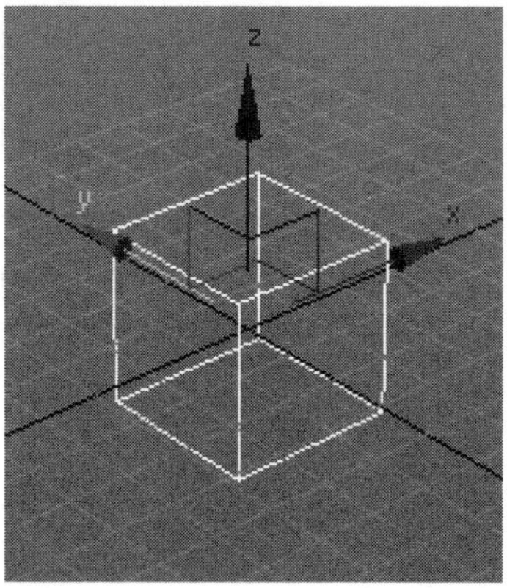

Figure 4.30: Creating the Point Object

There are four types of display in the Display group box:

- Center Marker: This marker displays a small X marker at the center of the object.
- Axis Tripod: This displays the tripod axis, and indicates the orientation and location of the point object.
- Cross: This displays the axis-associated cross.
- Box: This is at the center of the point object, and displays the axis-associated box.

4.2.4 Tape Helper Object

- Explain the use of Tape objects.
- List the steps to measure the distance between two objects.

The Tape object is used to measure distances. For example, you can use the Tape object to measure the distance between two objects or the length of an object, as shown in Figure 4.31.

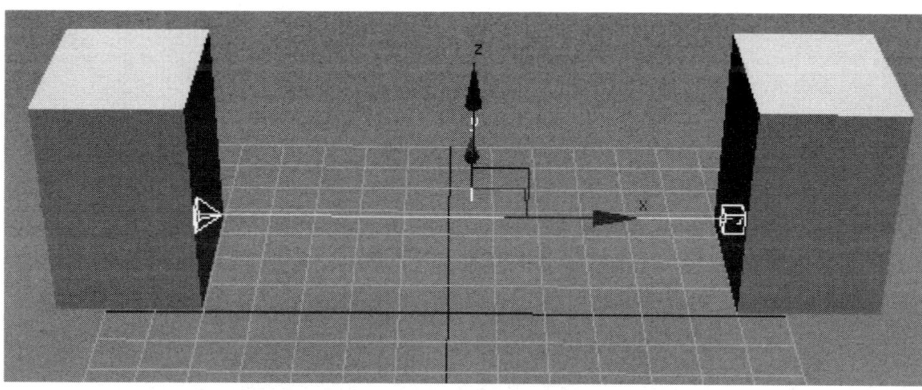

Figure 4.31: Distance Between Two Objects

The tape is composed of two named objects, named as Tape # # and Tape # #.Target, by default. The target and the tape are connected by a line that indicates the distance between the objects. Both ends of the connecting line are selected when you click it. This enables both the ends to move as one unit. You can have as many tape objects in a scene as you want. The tape objects do not render. Select the tape, and open the Modify panel to the tape statistics.

To create and use the Tape helper object, perform the following steps:

1. In the Helpers panel, click **Tape**, as shown in Figure 4.32.

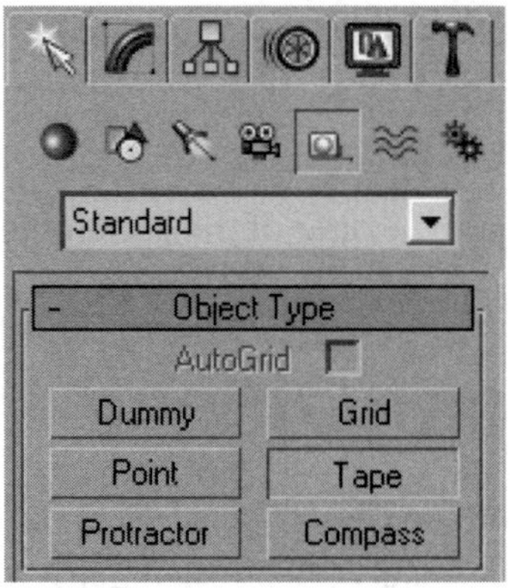

Figure 4.32: Tape Button

2. Drag the mouse between two points to create the tape, and then release the mouse button to create the target.
3. Set the length of the Tape object using the Specify Length option, as shown in Figure 4.33.

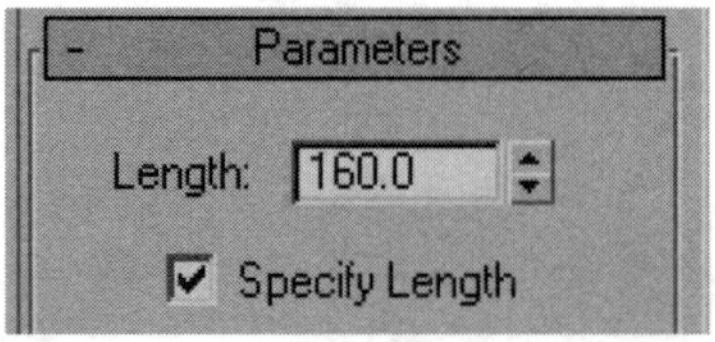

Figure 4.33: Specify Length Option

4. Move any of the ends to a new location where the line stretches to a new location, which is shown in the Length field, as shown in Figure 4.34.

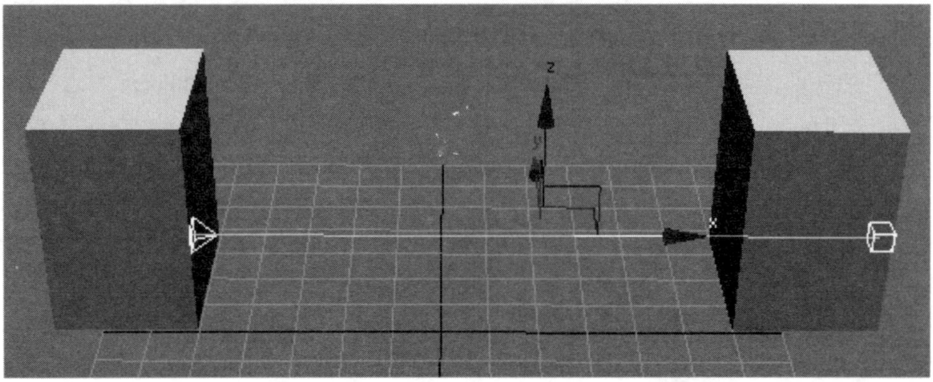

Figure 4.34: Moving the Ends

4.2.5 Compass Helper Object

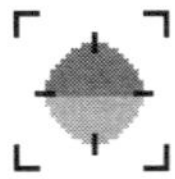

- Explain the use of the Compass Helper object.
- List the steps to create a compass.

The Compass object identifies the direction, that is, North, South, East, or West, on a planar, star-shaped object. The Compass object is mainly used in conjunction with the Sunlight System. The point of reference of the compass indicates the point of reference of the scene in the Sunlight System.

To create a compass helper object, perform the following steps:

1. In the Helpers palate, click **Compass**, as shown in Figure 4.35.

Figure 4.35: Compass Button

2. Drag the mouse to define the radius of the compass in the Parameters rollout, as shown in Figure 4.36.

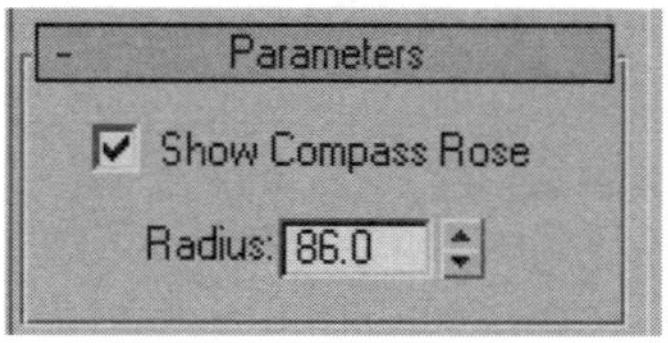

Figure 4.36: Radius of the Compass

3. Rotate the compass object to orient it, as shown in Figure 4.37.

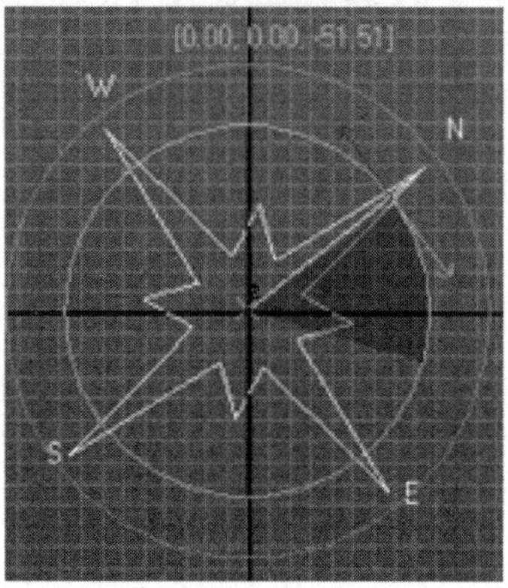

Figure 4.37: Rotating the Compass

4.2.6 Protractor Helper Object

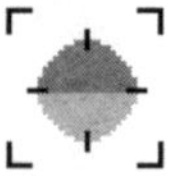

- Explain the use of the Protractor helper object.
- List the steps to use the Protractor helper object.

The protractor is used to measure the angle readouts between points. It is also used to find an angle of line in space. The Protractor helper object has a translucent view that emulates real protractors. The program can draw clockwise and counterclockwise gradations. You can study mathematical facts by making use of this graphic.

The names of the two objects are displayed on the buttons. The angle formed by the two objects is displayed in the Angle field.

To use the Protractor helper object, perform the following steps:

1. In the Helpers panel, click **Protractor**, as shown in Figure 4.38.

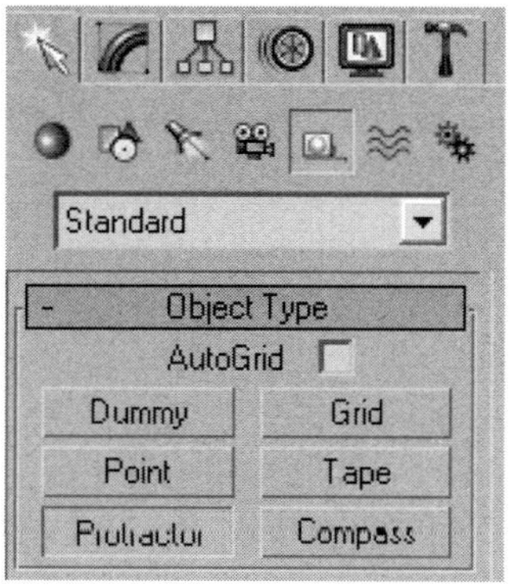

Figure 4.38: Protractor Button

2. Click in the viewport to create the protractor icon, as shown in Figure 4.39.

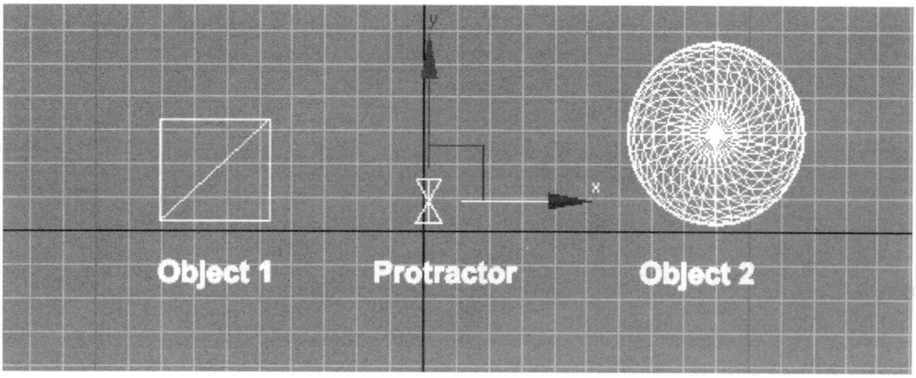

Figure 4.39: Creating the Protractor Icon

3. In the Parameters rollout, click **Pick Object 1**, and then select the first object whose angle is to be measured, as shown in Figure 4.40.

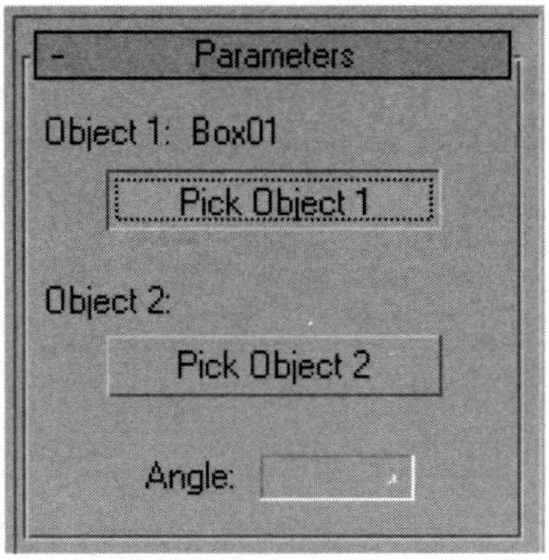

Figure 4.40: Selecting the First Object

4. In the Parameters rollout, click Pick Object 2, and then select the second object whose angle is to be measured. The angle between the two objects is automatically displayed in the parameters rollout. In this example, the angle is measured as 158.623. Figure 4.41 shows the protractor making an angle between the two objects.

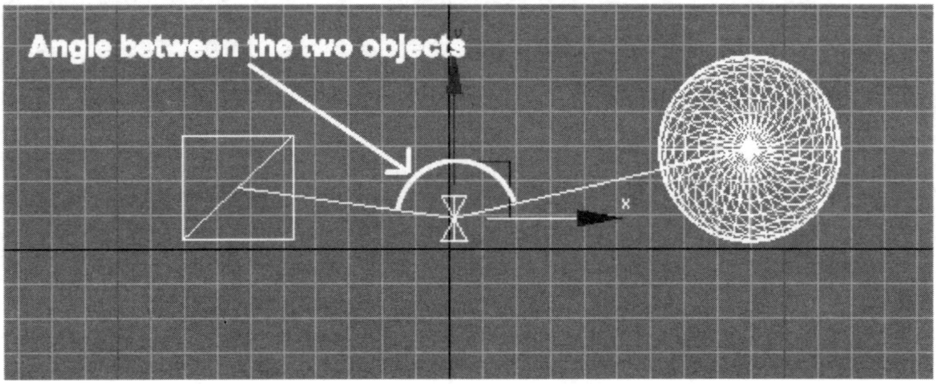

Figure 4.41: Protractor Making an Angle Between Two Objects

The angle between the two objects is displayed in Figure 4.42.

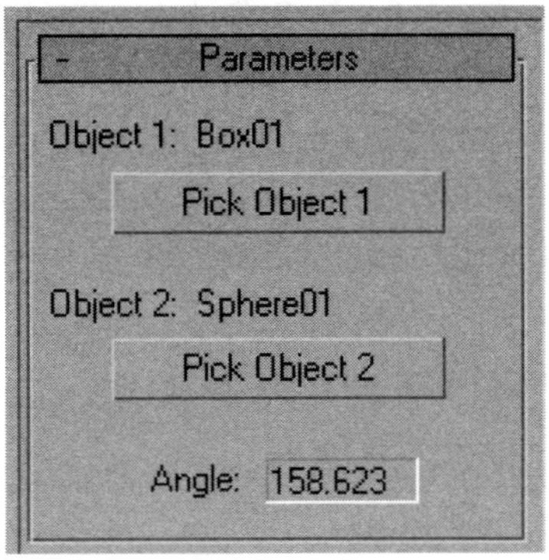

Figure 4.42: Angle Between Two Objects

Practice Questions

1. What is the Dummy object?
2. How many types of standard helper objects are available in 3ds max?
3. What is a Tape object? How can you use it to measure the distance between objects?
4. What is a Protractor object? How would you find the angle between two objects using a Protractor object?
5. Discuss the Grid Parameters rollout in detail.

4.3 Advanced Helper Objects

There are some advanced helpers in 3ds max that help in adding advanced features, such as fire effects and volume fog, to your 3d scenes. For example, the atmospheric effects help you restrict the effects, such as fog and fire, to a particular region in your scene.

The various advanced helpers available are:

- Manipulator Helper Objects
- Atmospheric Apparatus
- Camera Match Helper
- Assembly Heads
- Particle Flow

In this section, you will learn about the Slider Manipulator and Cone Angles Manipulator of the Manipulator Helper objects, and the BoxGizmo, SphereGizmo, and CylGizmo of the Atmospheric Apparatus helper objects.

4.3.1 Manipulator Helper Objects

- Identify the types of Manipulator helper objects.
- Create the various types of Manipulator helper objects.

Manipulator helper objects can be created to manipulate other objects in the 3ds max environment. You get visual feedback in viewports when you add customized controls to your scene with the help of manipulators.

There are three Manipulator helper objects available:

- Slider Manipulator
- Cone Angle Manipulator
- Plane Angle Manipulator

Slider and Cone Angle helpers are known as Manipulator helpers. They are available as a subcategory under the Helpers category of the Create panel.

Figure 4.43 shows the Manipulator Helper panel.

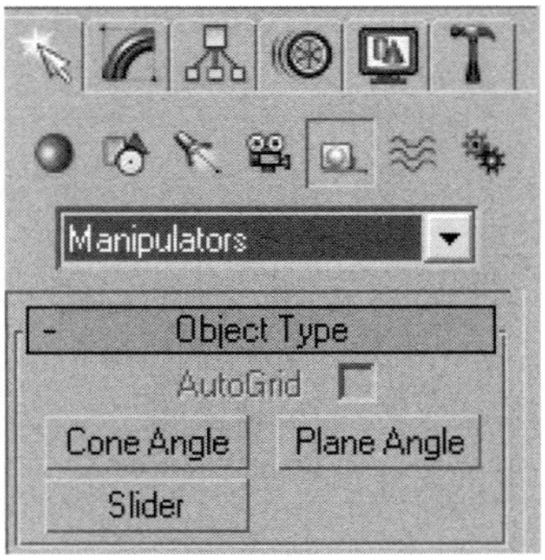

Figure 4.43: Manipulator Helper Panel

Slider Manipulator

Slider manipulator appears in the active viewport. You can give a name to this manipulator. The specified name will appear in the viewports above the slider objects. A default value can also be set along with the maximum and minimum values. You can also create a custom control by wiring its value to the parameter of another object.

Figure 4.44 shows the Slider Manipulator Parameters rollout.

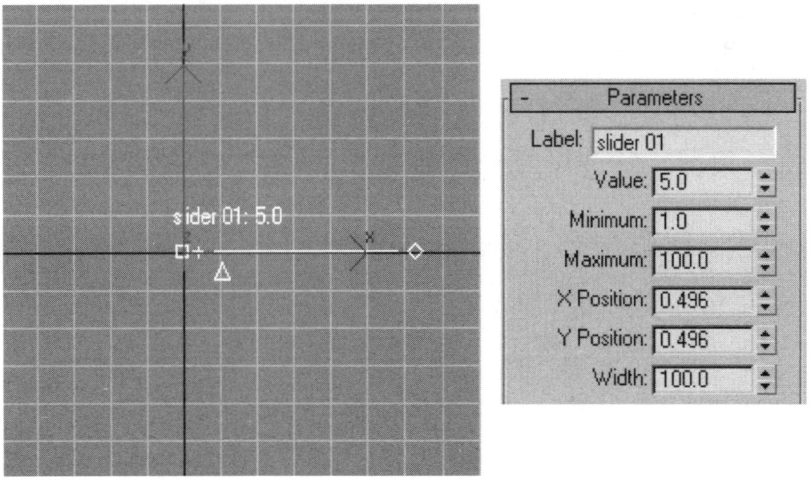

Figure 4.44: Slider Manipulator Parameters Rollout

The Slider consists of the above-mentioned components. The label and the value are stated in the Slider. The Slider's value can be adjusted by dragging the triangle below the slider bar. Each Slider should be labeled to indicate which dummy it will control.

To create a Slider manipulator, perform the following steps:

1. Choose **Manipulator** from the Helpers group box.
2. In the Object Type rollout, click **Slider**, as shown in Figure 4.45.

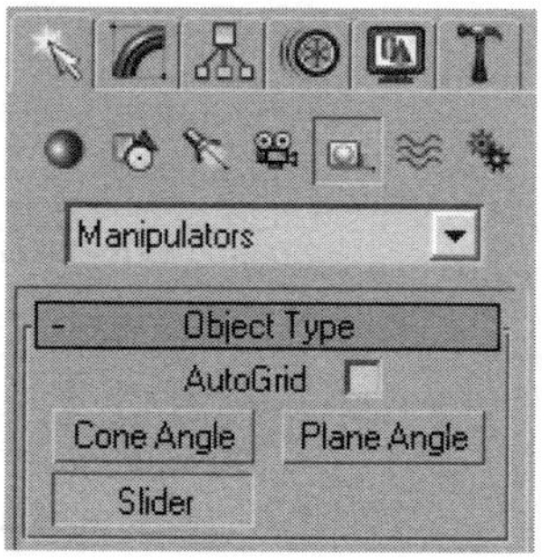

Figure 4.45: Slider Button

3. Click the viewport in which you want to create the slider, as shown in Figure 4.46.

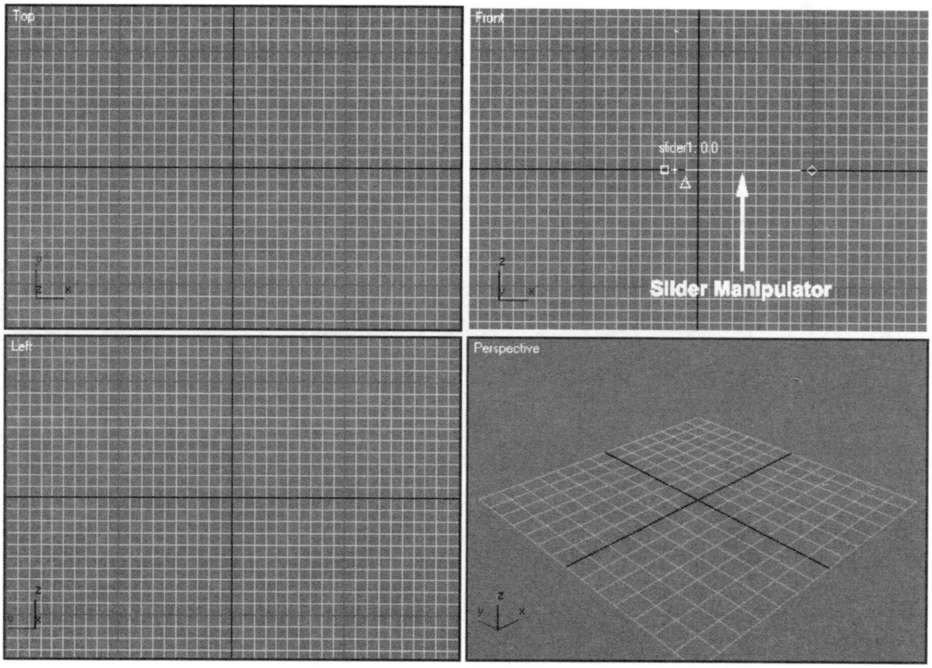

Figure 4.46: Creating the Slider

4. Click any other viewport. The slider appears in the currently active viewport.

The default width of the slider manipulator is 100 units.

Cone Angle Manipulator

Cone angle measures the angle between two edges of a spotlight beam. You can change the angle of the beam by moving the Cone Angle manipulator.

The angle, distance, and the aspect can be set for the Cone Angle helper. The default cone is a circle, but it can also be made into a square.

Figure 4.47 shows the Cone Angle Manipulator Parameters rollout.

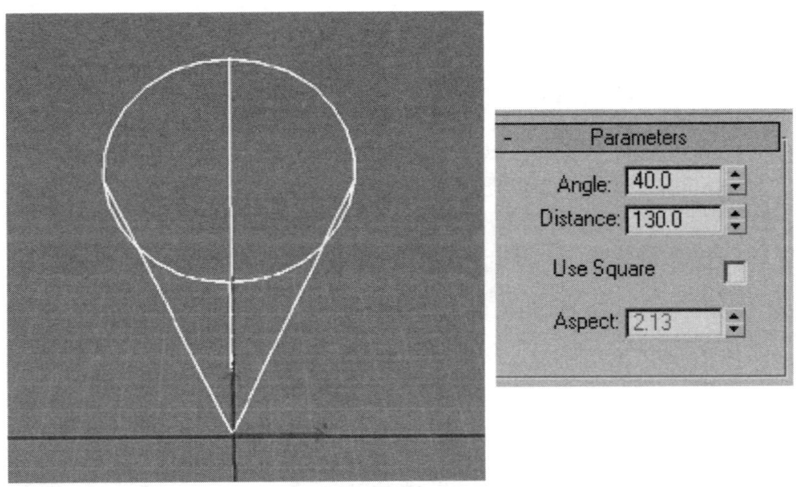

Figure 4.47: Cone Angle Manipulator Parameters Rollout

To create the Cone Angle manipulator, perform the following steps:

1. Choose **Manipulator** from the Helpers group box.

2. In the Object Type rollout, click **Cone Angle**, as shown in Figure 4.48.

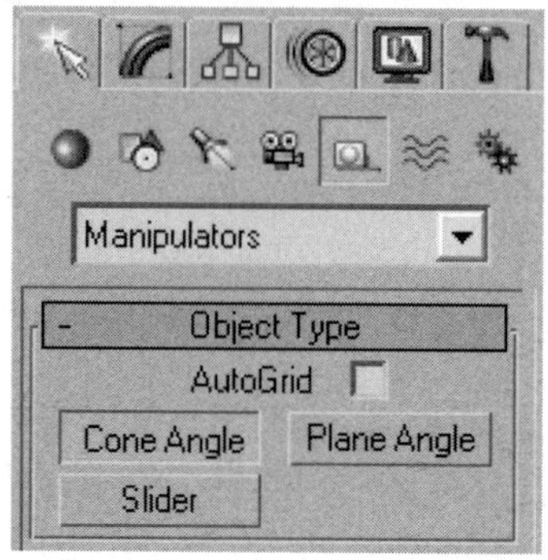

Figure 4.48: Cone Angle Button

3. Select the viewport in which you want to create the Cone Angle and drag and release the mouse. The cone is created in that viewport, as shown in Figure 4.49.

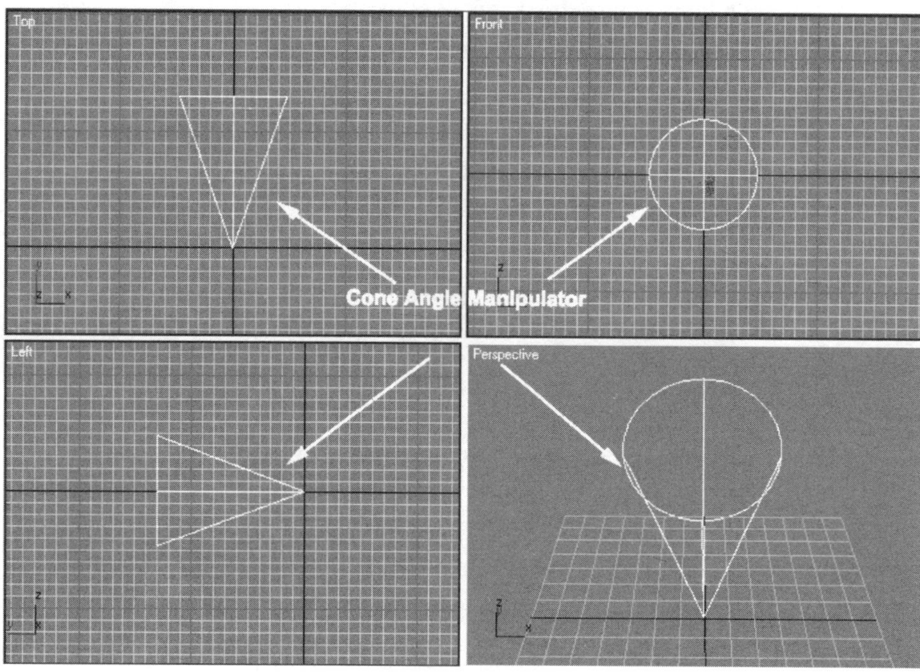

Figure 4.49: Creating the Cone

The Cone Angle manipulator is created along the negative Z-axis of the viewport.

4.3.2 Atmospheric Effects

Apply atmospheric effects in animations.

Atmospheric effects are placed in the Atmospheric Apparatus gizmo in the Helpers panel. This specifies the location of the applied effect. For example, if you apply fog or combustion in your scene, these gizmos set the boundaries for the applied effect and limit the spread of fog or combustion in your scene.

The three Atmospheric Apparatus gizmos available are:

- BoxGizmo
- SphereGizmo
- CylGizmo

Figure 4.50 shows the Atmospheric Apparatus Helper panel.

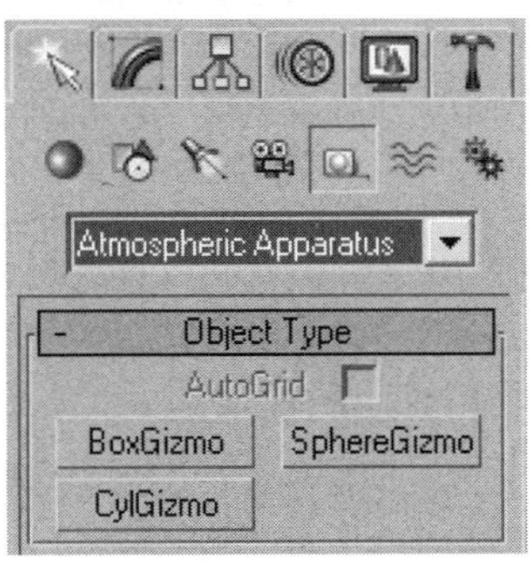

Figure 4.50: Atmospheric Apparatus Helper Panel

BoxGizmo

BoxGizmo creates a box-shaped gizmo in the scene. To create the BoxGizmo, drag the mouse horizontally in the viewport, and then release it. Then, drag it in the vertical position to set the height, and then click.

Figure 4.51 shows a BoxGizmo.

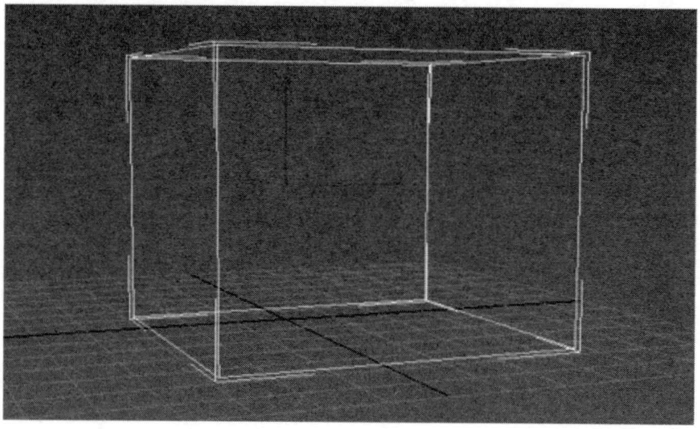

Figure 4.51: BoxGizmo

Selecting the gizmo and opening the Modify panel reveals two different rollouts: one to label atmospheric effects and the other for defining the basic parameters such as gizmo dimensions as shown in Figure 4.52.

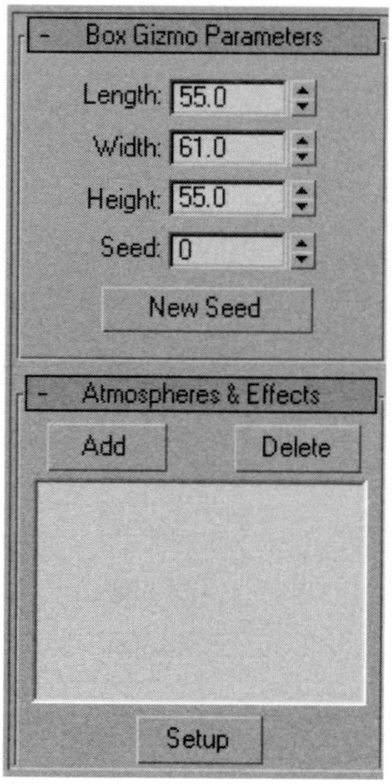

Figure 4.52: Box Gizmo Parameters Rollout

To add a new atmosphere, perform the following steps:

1. Select the **BoxGizmo**, as shown in Figure 4.53.

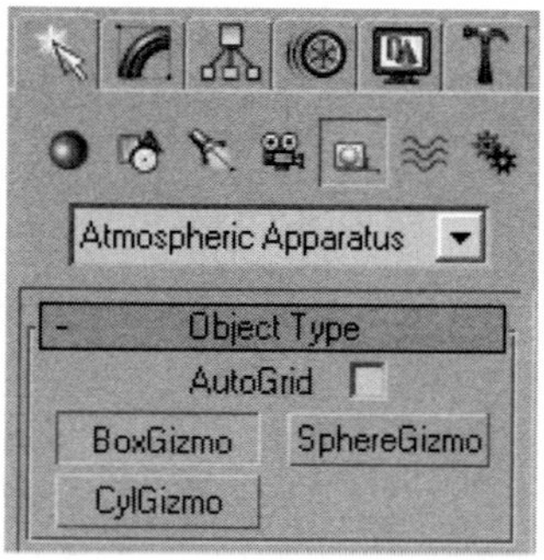

Figure 4.53: BoxGizmo Button

2. Drag the mouse in any viewport to create the box gizmo as shown in Figure 4.54.

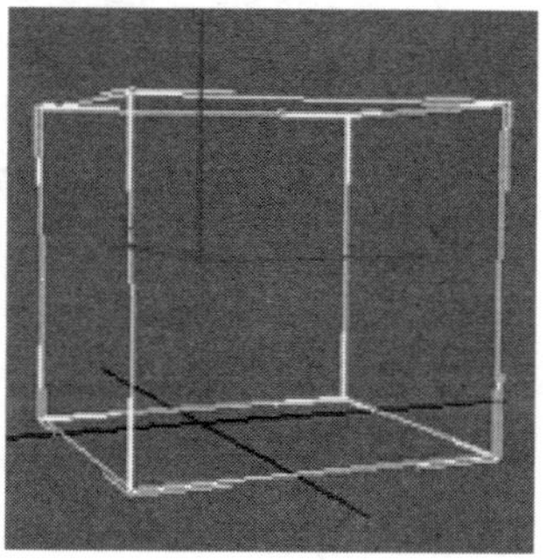

Figure 4.54: Creating the Box Gizmo

3. Click **Add** in the Modify panel under the Atmospheres & Effects rollout, as shown in Figure 4.55.

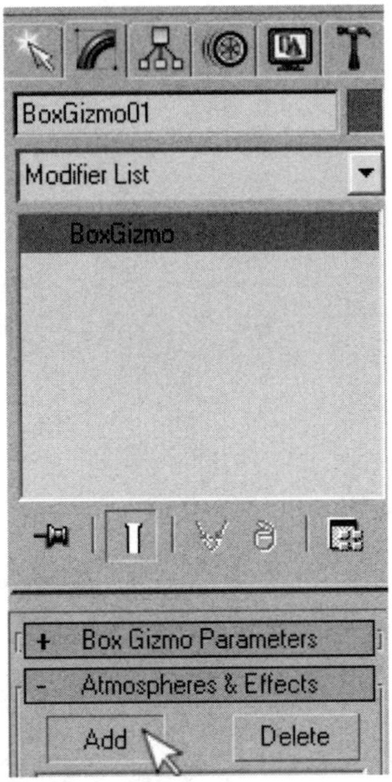

Figure 4.55: Modify Panel

4. Choose the required atmospheric effect from the displayed list, and then click **OK**. Figure 4.56 shows the Fire Effect in the Box gizmo.

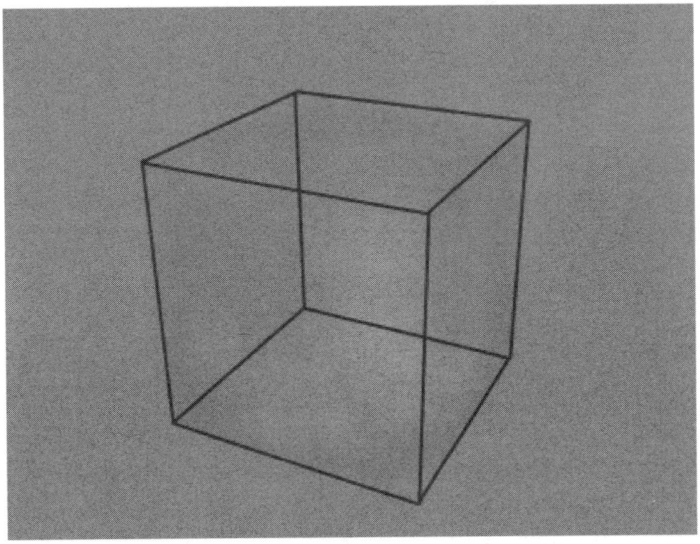

Figure 4.56: Fire Effect in the Box Gizmo

Each Gizmo Parameters rollout has a Seed value and the New Seed button. The Seed value sets a random number that is used to compute the atmospheric effects. The New Seed button automatically generates a random seed. If two gizmos have the same value, they have nearly identical results.

SphereGizmo

SphereGizmo creates a sphere-shaped gizmo in the scene. To create the SphereGizmo, drag the mouse horizontally in the viewport, and then release it. Then, move the spinner to adjust the radius. Figure 4.57 shows a SphereGizmo.

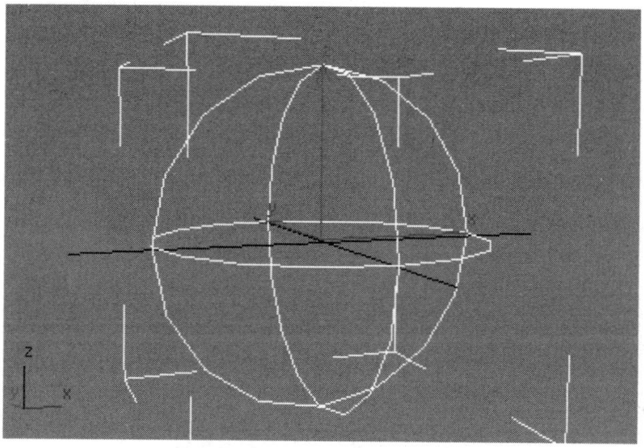

Figure 4.57: SphereGizmo

Selecting the gizmo and opening the Modify panel reveals two different rollouts: one to label atmospheric effects and the other for defining the basic parameters such as gizmo dimensions as shown in Figure 4.58.

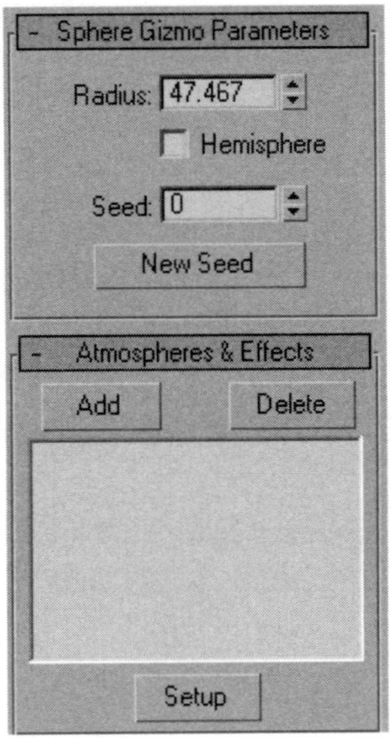

Figure 4.58: Sphere Gizmo Parameters Rollout

To add an existing atmosphere, perform the following steps:

1. Select **SphereGizmo**, as shown in Figure 4.59.

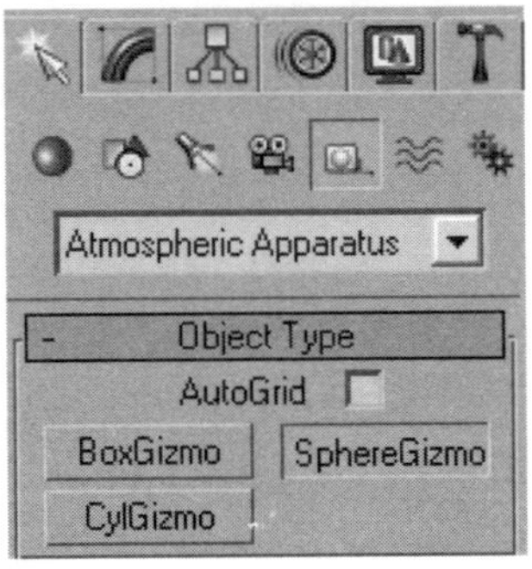

Figure 4.59: Selecting the SphereGizmo

2. Drag the mouse in any viewport to create the SphereGizmo, as shown in Figure 4.60.

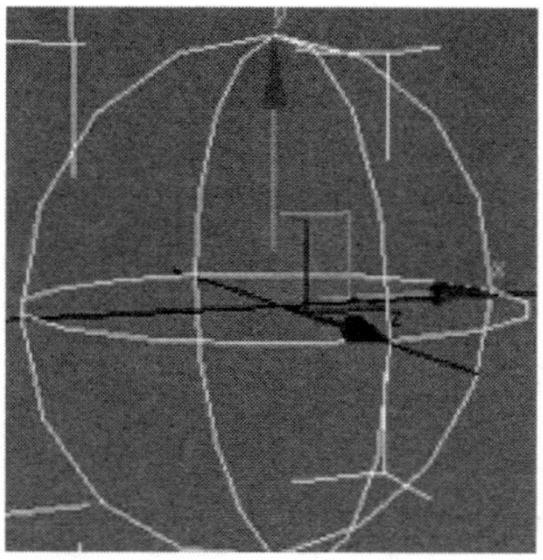

Figure 4.60: Creating the SphereGizmo

3. Click **Add** in the Modify panel under the Atmospheres & Effects rollout, as shown in Figure 4.61.

Figure 4.61: Modify Panel

4. Choose the required atmospheric effect from the displayed list, and then click **OK**.

Figure 4.62 shows the Fire Effect in the Sphere gizmo.

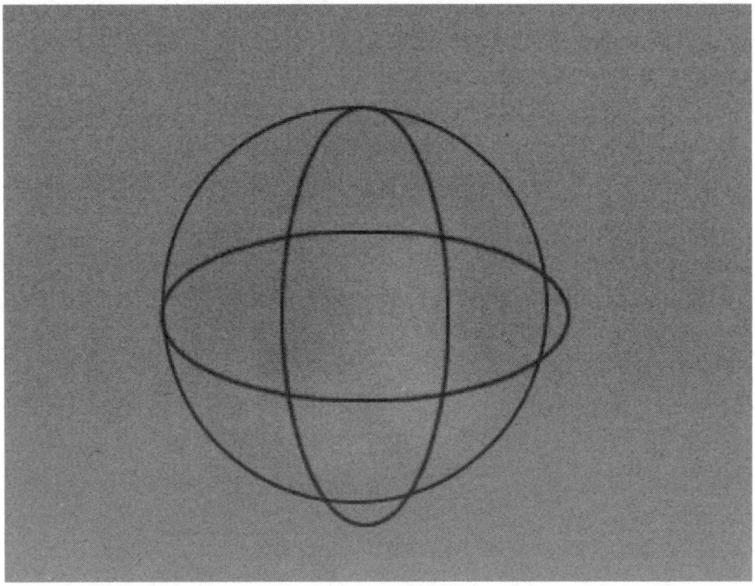

Figure 4.62: Fire Effect in the Sphere Gizmo

CylGizmo

CylGizmo creates a cylinder-shaped gizmo in the scene. To create the CylGizmo, drag the mouse horizontally in the viewport and then release it. Drag it again in the vertical position to set the height, and then click to end the creation.

Figure 4.63 shows a CylGizmo.

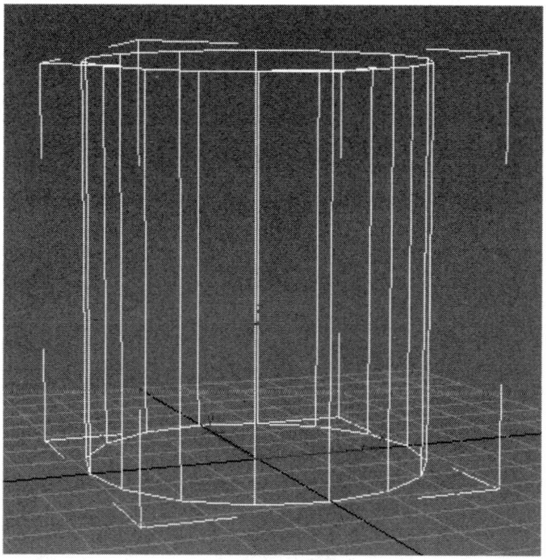

Figure 4.63: CylGizmo

Selecting the gizmo and opening the Modify panel reveals two different rollouts, one to label atmospheric effects and the other for defining the basic parameters such as gizmo dimensions as shown in Figure 4.64.

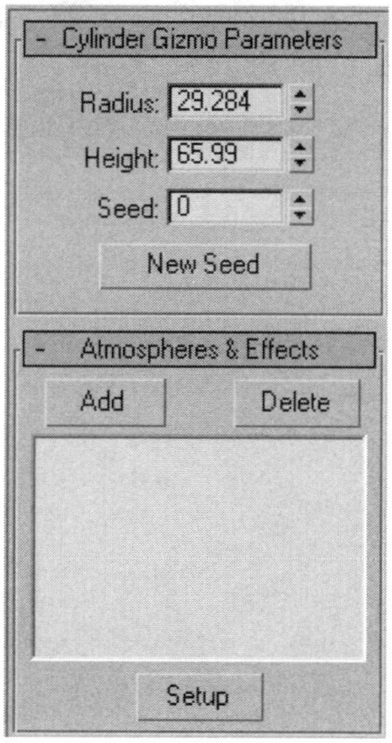

Figure 4.64: Cylinder Gizmo Parameters

To add an existing atmosphere, perform the following steps:

1. Select **CylGizmo**, as shown in Figure 4.65.

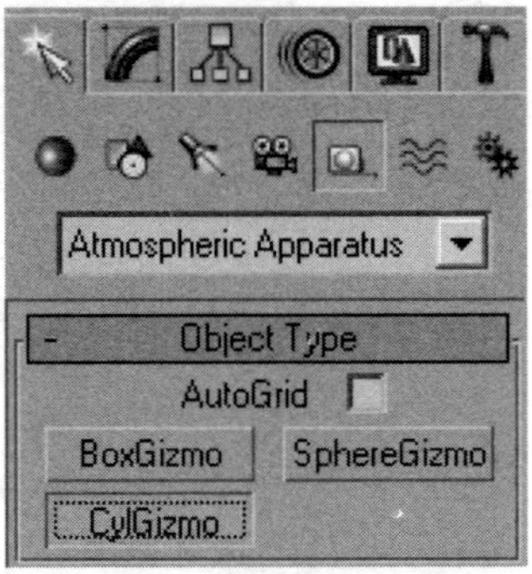

Figure 4.65: Selecting CylGizmo

2. Drag the mouse in any viewport, as shown in Figure 4.66.

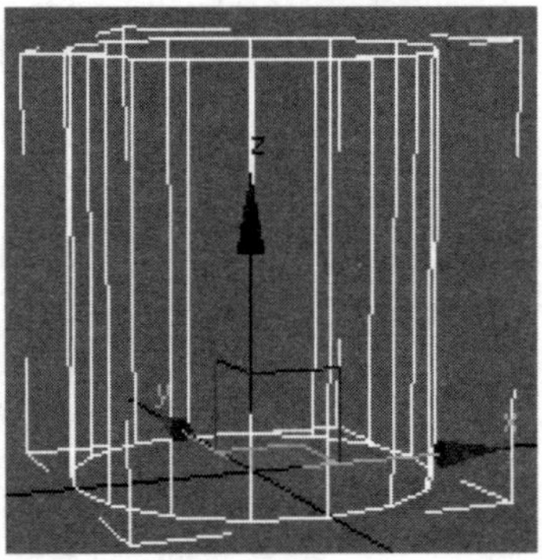

Figure 4.66: Creating the CylGizmo

3. Click **Add** in the Modify panel under the Atmospheres rollout.

4. Choose the required atmospheric effect from the displayed list, and then click **OK**. Figure 4.67 shows the Fire Effect in the CylGizmo.

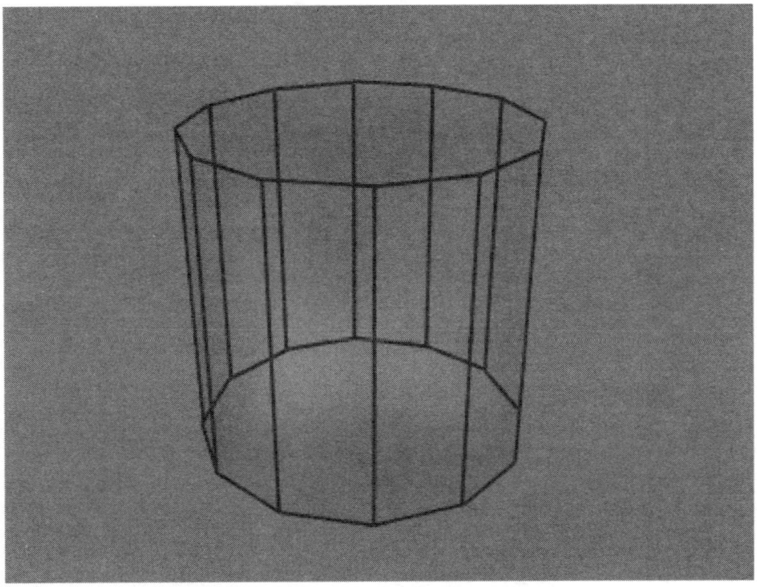

Figure 4.67: Fire Effect in the CylGizmo

The Add Atmospheric dialog box contains the following atmospheric effects by default:

- Volume Fog
- Fire Effect

Volume Fog

Fog is used to produce the hazy layer in a scene, similar to real life fogs. Volume Fog gives more control over the exact position of the fog. It provides an effect in which the density of the fog is not constant.

Select Volume Fog, and then click Setup to open the Volume Fog parameters rollout, as shown in Figure 4.68.

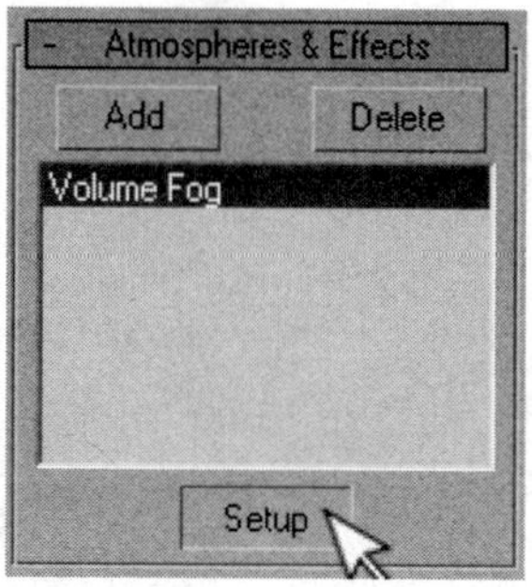

Figure 4.68: Atmospheres and Effects Rollout

The Volume Fog Parameters rollout is shown in Figure 4.69.

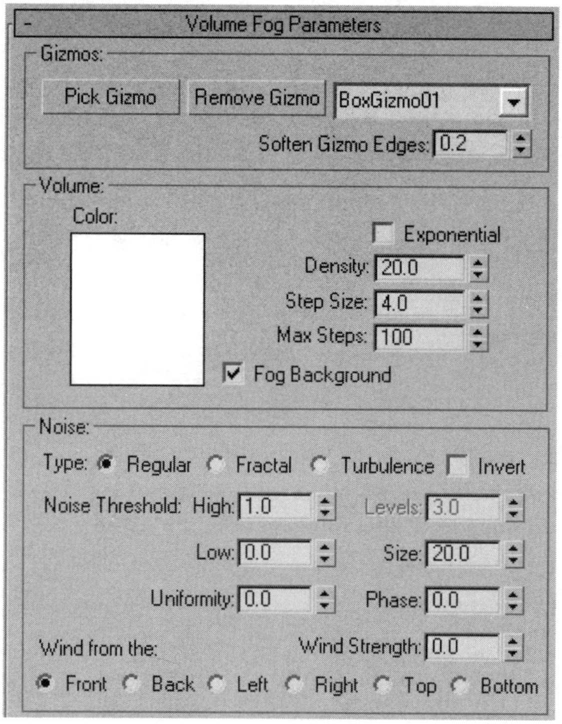

Figure 4.69: Volume Fog Parameters Rollout

The Volume Fog Parameters rollout displays the groups, as discussed in the subsequent topics.

Gizmos Group

Following are the options in the Gizmos group:

- Pick Gizmo: Click this button to enter Pick mode and click an atmospheric apparatus created in the scene. This apparatus will contain the Volume fog when you render. The name of the apparatus gets added to the apparatus list.
- Remove Gizmo: This removes the selected apparatus from the Volume Fog effect. Select the apparatus in the list, and then click Remove Gizmo.
- Soften Gizmo Edges: This feathers the edges of the Volume Fog effect. The higher the value, the softer the edges will be.

Volume Group

Following are the options in the Volume group:

- Color: This is used to set the color of the fog. Click the color swatch, and then select the color you want to set for the fog.
- Exponential: You can activate this check box only when you want to render transparent objects in the Volume Fog effect. This exponentially increases the density with distance. When it is turned off, the density increases linearly with distance.
- Density: This controls the fog density. The range of values is 0 to 20.
- Step Size: This determines the granularity of the fog. A large step size creates coarse fog.
- Max Steps: This limits the amount of sampling so that it does not take a long time to compute the fog. This is especially useful when the fog is of low density.
- Fog Background: This applies the fog function to the background of the scene.

Noise Group

Following are the options in the Noise group:

- Type: Click one of the three noise types, that is, Regular, Fractal, or Turbulence, to apply it.
- Noise Threshold: This limits the noise effect. The range of values is from 0 to 1.0.
- High: This sets the high threshold.

- Low: This sets the low threshold.
- Uniformity: The value ranges from -1 to 1. The smaller the value, the more transparent is the smoke volume.
- Levels: This is enabled only for Fractal or Turbulence noise. This sets the number of times the noise is iteratively applied.
- Size: This determines the size of the whirls of the smoke or fog. The smaller the value, the smaller is the whirl.
- Phase: This controls the speed of the wind, which directly affects the fog. If there is no wind, the fog will churn at one place.
- Wind Strength: This controls how fast the smoke moves away from the wind direction.
- Wind from the: This defines the direction from where the wind is blowing.

Fire Effect

Fire is used to produce the animated effects of smoke and fire. It is used to show the effect of sun, fireballs, clouds, and explosions. Select Fire Effect, and then click Setup to open the Fire Effect Parameters rollout, as shown in Figure 4.70.

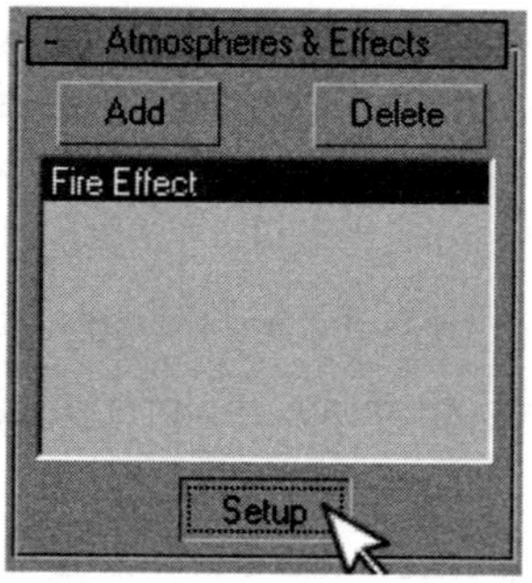

Figure 4.70: Atmospheres and Effects Rollout

The Fire Effect Parameters rollout is shown in Figure 4.71.

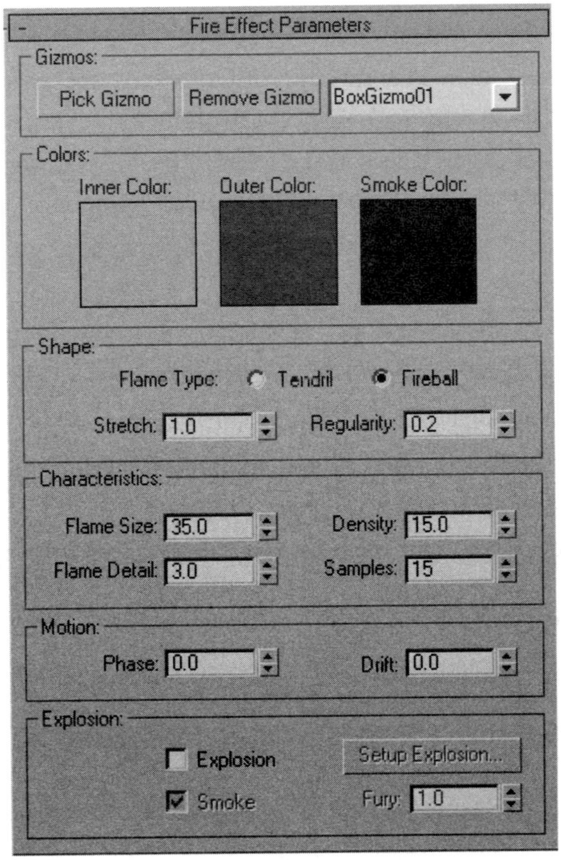

Figure 4.71: Fire Effect Parameters Rollout

The Fire Effect Parameters rollout displays the groups, as discussed in the subsequent topics.

Gizmos Group

Following are the options in the Gizmos group:

- Pick Gizmo: Click this to enter the Pick mode. Then, click an atmospheric apparatus created in the scene. This apparatus will contain the Fire Effect when you render the object. The name of the apparatus is added to the apparatus list.
- Remove Gizmo: This removes the selected apparatus from the Fire Effect. Select the apparatus in the list, and then click Remove Gizmo.

Colors Group

Following are the options in the Colors group:

- Inner Color: This sets the color of the densest part of the effect. This color represents the hottest part of the flame.
- Outer Color: This sets the color of the sparsest part of the effect. This color represents the dissipating edge of the flame.
- Smoke Color: This sets the color of smoke for use with the Explosion option.

Shape Group

Following are the options in the Shape group:

- Flame Type: This sets the type of flame, that is, Tendril or Fireball.
- Stretch: This scales flames along the Z-axis of the apparatus. You can use this option to give an oval shape to Fireballs.
- Regularity: This modifies how the flames fill the apparatus. The range is 1.0 to 0.0.

Characteristics Group

Following are the options in the Characteristics group:

- Flame Size: This sets the size of individual flames inside the apparatus. The larger the apparatus, the larger the flame size required.
- Flame Detail: This controls the amount of color change and edge sharpness seen within each flame.
- Density: This sets the opacity and brightness of Fire Effect. The size of the apparatus affects the density.
- Samples: This sets the rate at which the effect is sampled. Higher values produce more accurate results, but take longer to render.

Motion Group

Following are the options in the Motion group:

- Phase: This controls the rate of change for Fire Effect. You can choose two different values at two different keyframes to animate this parameter.
- Drift: This sets how flames are rendered along the Z-axis of the fire apparatus. Low values give a slow-burning, cool fire. High values give a fast-burning, hot fire.

Explosion Group

Following are the options in the Explosion group:

- Explosion: This automatically animates the size, density, and color, based on the animation of the Phase value.
- Smoke: This controls whether the explosion creates smoke.
- Set Up Explosion: Opens a dialog box, in which you can enter the start time and end time for the explosion to take place.
- Fury: This varies the churning effect of the Phase parameter. Values less than 1.0 cause slower churning, and values greater than 1.0 cause faster churning.

4.3.3 Creating an Animation with the Dummy Helper

Create an animation with the Dummy helper.

In this topic, you will test the Pythagorean Theorem by using the Dummy helper.

To test the Pythagorean Theorem, perform the following steps:

1. Create a file with a simple box of dimensions, 30*20*10, as shown in Figure 4.72.

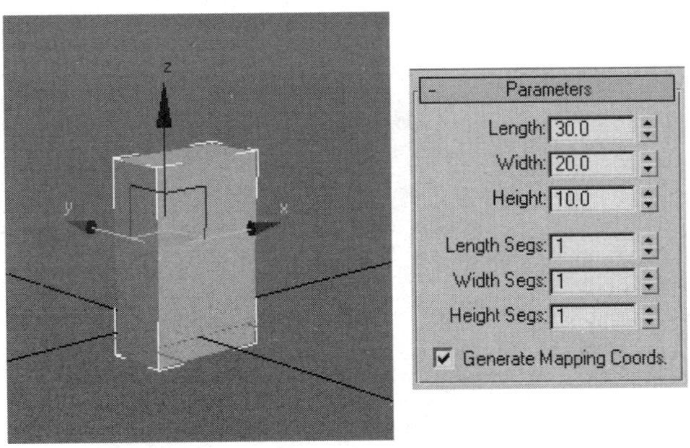

Figure 4.72: Creating a Simple Box

2. To open the Grid and Snap Settings dialog box, right-click any of the snap buttons on the Main toolbar, as shown in Figure 4.73.

Figure 4.73: Snap Button

3. Set the snap feature to snap the vertices by selecting the Vertex option, as shown in Figure 4.74.

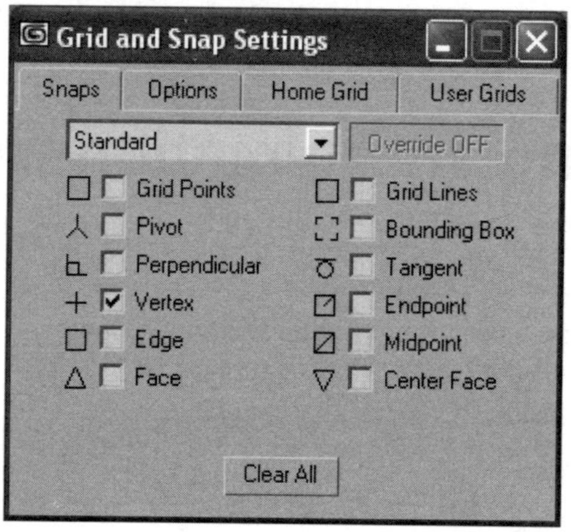

Figure 4.74: Grid and Snap Settings Dialog Box

4. Close the Grid and Snap Settings dialog box and enable the 3D Snap feature.
5. Select the **Tape** object from the Helpers group box, as shown in Figure 4.75.

Figure 4.75: Selecting the Tape Object

6. Move the cursor over the upper-left corner of the object in the viewport. Then, click on the blue-vertex that emerges, as shown in Figure 4.76.

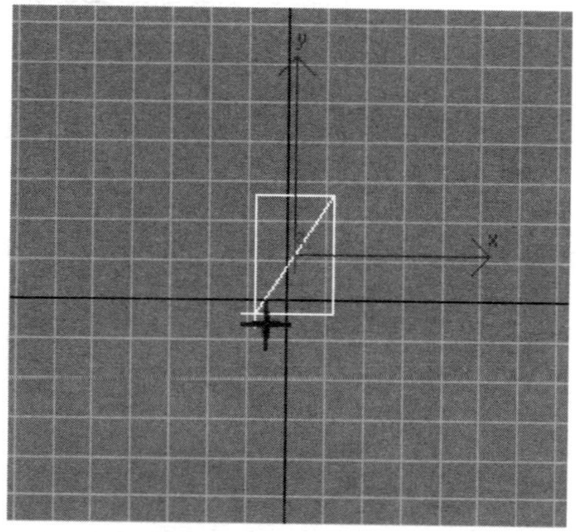

Figure 4.76: Blue-Vertex

7. Drag the mouse to the lower-left corner, and then click on the blue-vertex that emerges, as shown in Figure 4.77.

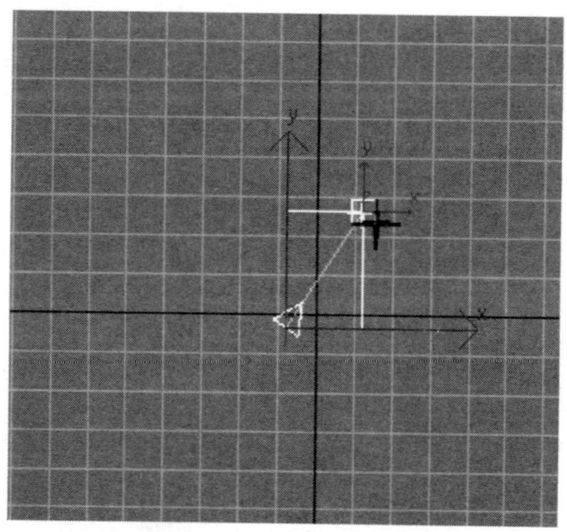

Figure 4.77: Lower-Left Corner

8. Observe the dimension in the Parameters rollout, as shown in Figure 4.78.

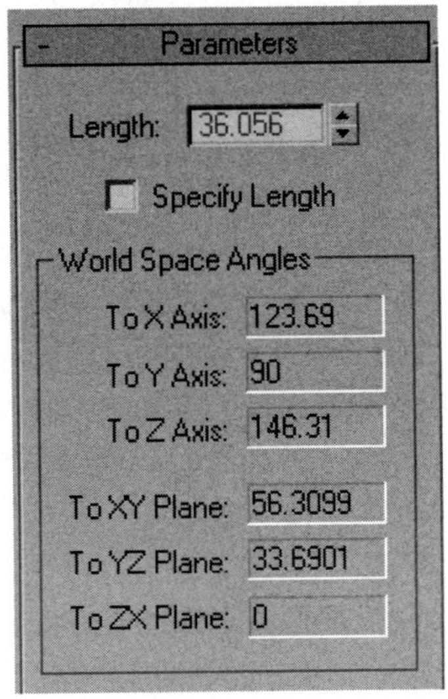

Figure 4.78: Parameters Rollout

The Pythagorean theorem states that the sum of the squares of the sides of a right triangle equals the sum of the hypotenuse squared.

Practice Questions

1. What is Volume Fog? Mention the steps to create a Volume Fog.
2. What is a Cone Angle manipulator? What are the steps to create a Cone Angle manipulator?
3. What is the Atmospheric Apparatus gizmo? How many types of Atmospheric Apparatus gizmos are there in 3ds max?
4. What is Fire Effect? Mention the steps to create a Fire Effect.

Summary

- Hierarchies are logical sets of linked objects. You use hierarchies to animate a set of linked objects so that the motion realistically flows throughout the grouping.
- Hierarchies are based on the concept of parent and child relationships. Changes to the parent object are automatically and naturally transmitted to child objects.
- You can manipulate a hierarchy with the help of *kinematics*. In 3ds max, kinematics governs the animation of a hierarchy with the help of internal mathematical formulae.
- You can use kinematics to animate a hierarchical chain in two ways:
  - Inverse Kinematics
  - Forward Kinematics
- Inverse kinematics uses the following tools:
  - IK solvers
  - IK methods
- There are two IK methods available in 3ds max:
  - Interactive IK
  - Applied IK
- You can create hierarchies by:
  - Linking and unlinking objects
  - Creating hierarchies with bones
- 3ds max allows you to create bones from other objects by using the options in the Object Properties dialog box.
- You can apply animations in hierarchies by using any of the following methods:
  - Animating with a linked hierarchy
  - Animating the bone hierarchy with a dummy
  - Animating with IK solvers
- To animate a bone hierarchy by using a dummy, perform the following steps:
  1. Create a dummy and bones.
  2. Link the bones and the dummy.
  3. Apply the Skin modifier, and then animate.

- The standard helper objects contain the following objects:
  - Dummy objects
  - Grid objects
  - Point objects
  - Tape objects
  - Compass objects
  - Protractor objects
- The various Advanced Helpers available are:
  - Manipulator Helper Objects
  - Atmospheric Apparatus
  - Camera Match Helper
  - Assembly Heads
  - Particle Flow
- There are three Manipulator Helper Objects available:
  - Slider Manipulator
  - Cone Angle Manipulator
  - Plane Angle Manipulator
- Atmospheric effects are placed in the Atmospheric Apparatus gizmo in the Helpers panel. The three Atmospheric Apparatus gizmos available are:
  - BoxGizmo
  - SphereGizmo
  - CylGizmo

References

- http://ligwww.epfl.ch/~thalmann/papers.dir/04.hierarchy.pdf (February 10, 2004)
- http://archweb.arch.virginia.edu/~ejm9k/arch545/handouts/actors.html (February 10, 2004)
- http://unreal.epicgames.com/skeletal/setup.html (February 10, 2004)
- http://udn.epicgames.com/pub/Content/AnimBrowserReference/ (February 10, 2004)
- http://www.jhaywood.com/croiProjectEyes03.htm (February 10, 2004)
- http://www.digimation.com/software/asp/product.asp?product_id=234&category_id=1 (February 10, 2004)

Assignments

1. What does a Compass helper object do? What are the steps to create a compass?
2. What is a Cone Angle manipulator? What are the steps to create a Cone Angle manipulator?
3. What is BoxGizmo under Atmospheric effects? What are the steps to create a new atmosphere?
4. What is Fire under Atmospheric effects? What are the steps to create Fire Effects?
5. What is the Grid helper object? Explain with the help of an example.
6. Discuss the Bone Parameters rollout in detail.
7. Discuss the Bone section in the Object Properties dialog box.
8. What are the various methods of applying animations in hierarchies?
9. List the steps to apply the Skin modifier.

Lab Exercises

Exercise 1

Objective

- Animate the sunlight system to show an entire day.

Problem Statement

You are required to animate the Sunlight system to show an entire day in a short number of frames. You can focus on a tree in Florida and Los Angeles on the eve of the New Year. The tree will not move, but the shadows can be observed.

Lab Setup

3ds max 6.0

Procedure

To animate the sunlight system, perform the following steps:

1. Create a cone object, as shown in Figure 4.79.

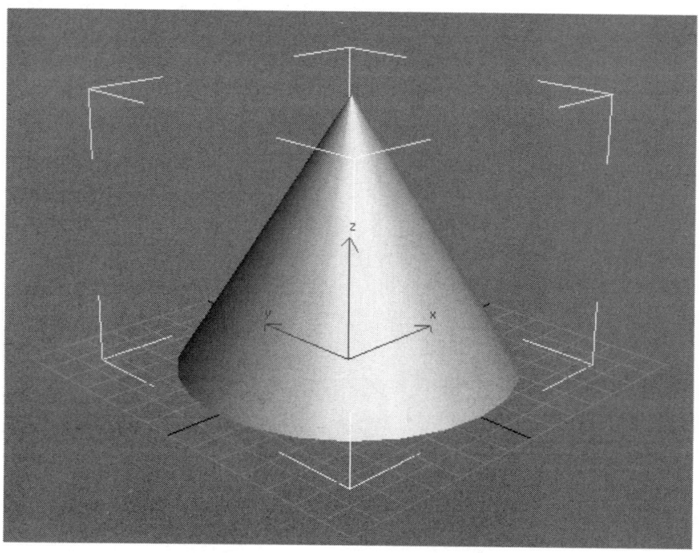

Figure 4.79: Creating a Cone Object

2. In the Create Panel, select the Systems category, and then add a Sunlight system to the scene.

   The Sunlight System is applied to the scene, as shown in Figure 4.80.

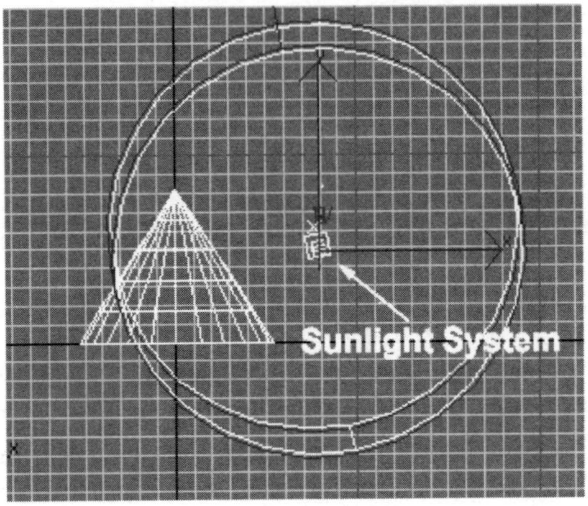

Figure 4.80: Applying the Sunlight System

3. Create a Compass helper by dragging in the Top view. Then, create another Sunlight system, as shown in Figure 4.81 to Figure 4.82.

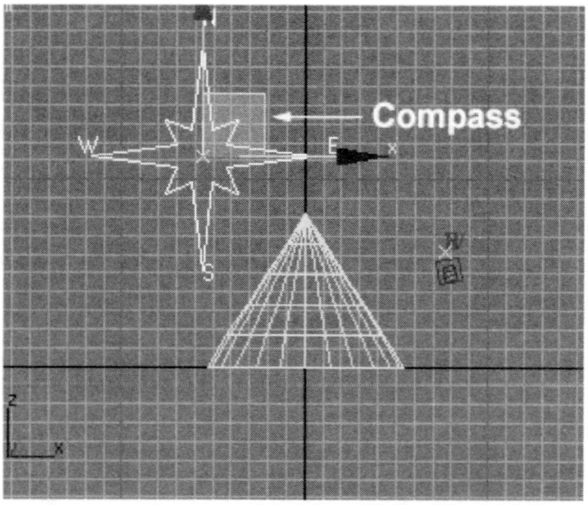

Figure 4.81: Creating Another Sunlight System

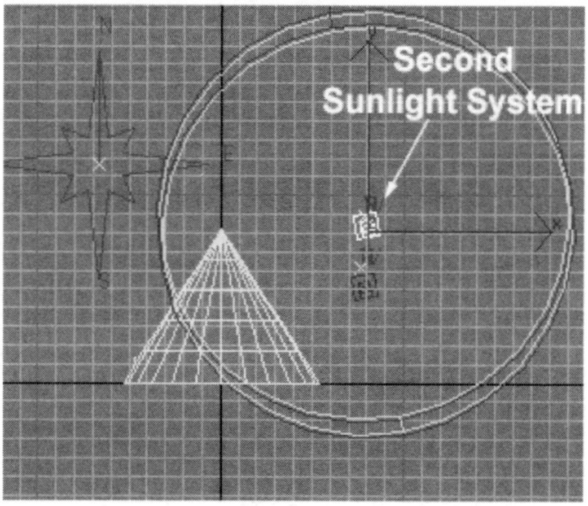

Figure 4.82: Second Sunlight System

4. Enter 12/31/2003 for the date and 05/00/00 as early morning time in the Control Parameter rollout, as shown in Figure 4.83.

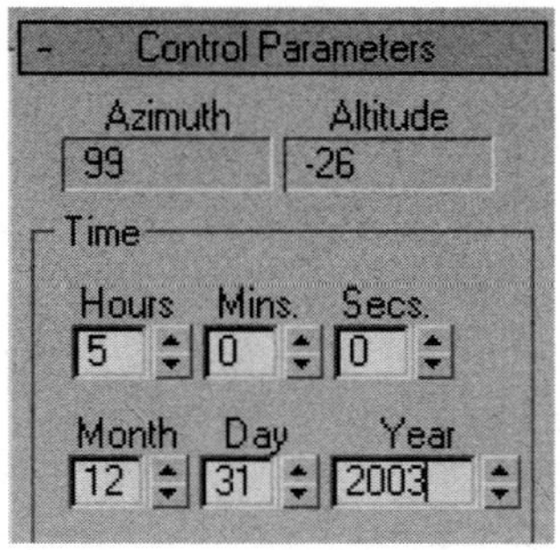

Figure 4.83: Control Parameters Rollout

5. Click Get Location, locate Florida in the Cities list, and then click **OK**, as shown in Figure 4.84.

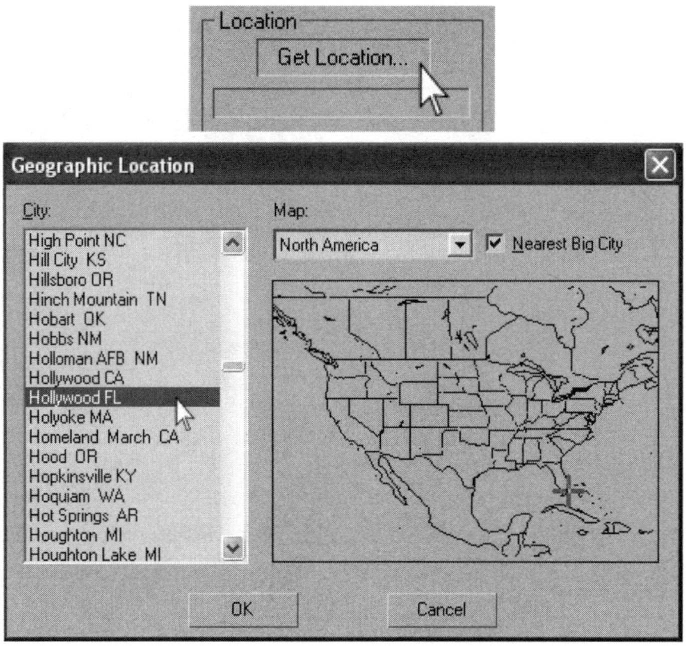

Figure 4.84: Specifying Location

6. Click Auto Key, and then move the Time Slider to frame 100, as shown in Figure 4.85.

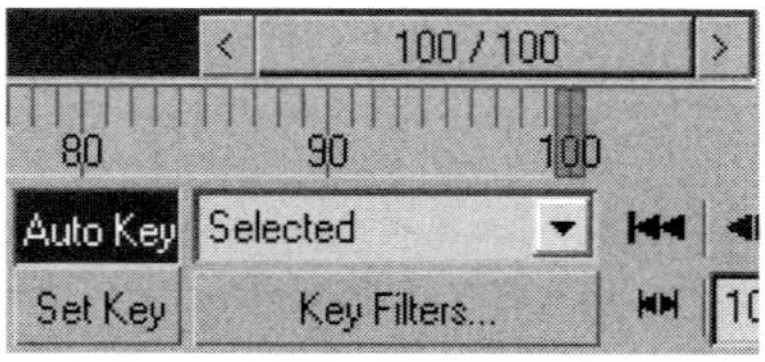

Figure 4.85: Frame 100

7. Change the time value to an evening hour in the Control Parameters rollout, as shown in Figure 4.86.

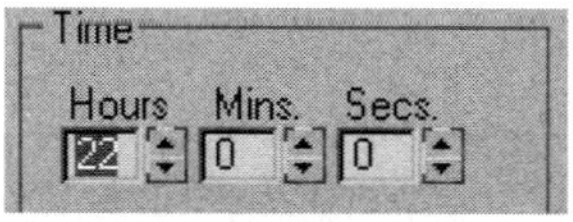

Figure 4.86: Specifying Time

8. Click Auto Key again to disable the animation mode.
9. To view the animation, click Play in the animation controller menu.

   Figure 4.87 shows a few rendered frames of the above animation.

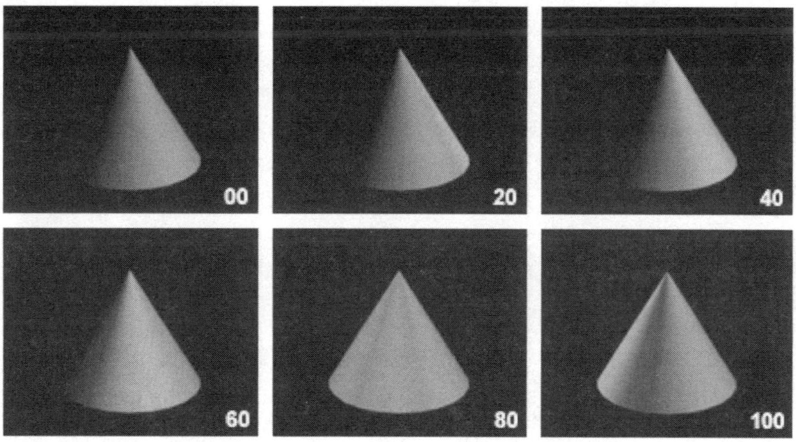

Figure 4.87: Rendered Frames of the Animation

10. Save the file as **ch04_lab_ex1_sol.max**.

By looking at the Altitude value for each hour, you can evaluate when the Sun goes up and comes down. A negative value indicates that the Sun is below the horizon.

Conclusion/Observation

You can use the Compass helper to provide an orientation for positioning the Sun in a Sunlight System.

Lab Activity Checklist

S. No.	Tasks	Completed	
		Yes	No
1.	Created objects		
2.	Applied Compass Helper		

Exercise 2

Objective

- Apply IK Solver.

Problem Statement

Create the motion of a piston moving along its shaft. A sample piston is available in the file, ch04_lab_ex2_model.max in the Student CD provided to you. Use the LookAt constraint and the HI Solver option of the IK Solver to create the desired effect.

Lab Setup

3ds Max 6.0

Procedure

To Apply IK solver, perform the following steps:

1. Open the file **ch04_lab_ex2_model.max**.
2. Link dummy01 of the piston to its plate in the image. View the plate, dummy01, dummy02, the shaft, and the piston. These parts are labeled in Figure 4.88.

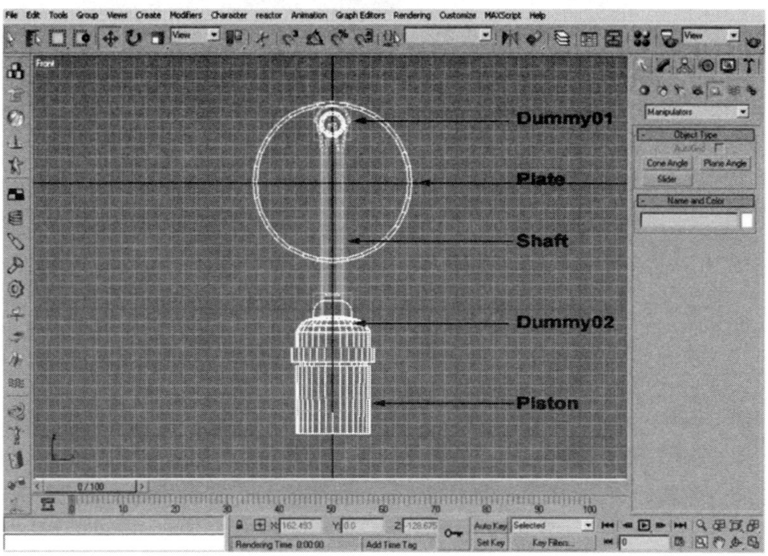

Figure 4.88: Linking dummy01 to the Plate

3. Link the piston to dummy02, as shown in Figure 4.89.

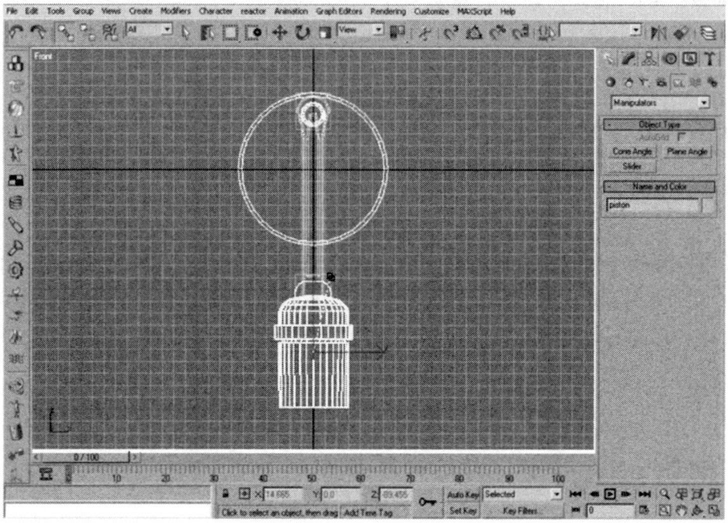

Figure 4.89: Linking dummy02 to the Piston

4. Link dummy02 to dummy01, because these should move up and down in coordination. Figure 4.90 displays dummy03 linked to dummy01.

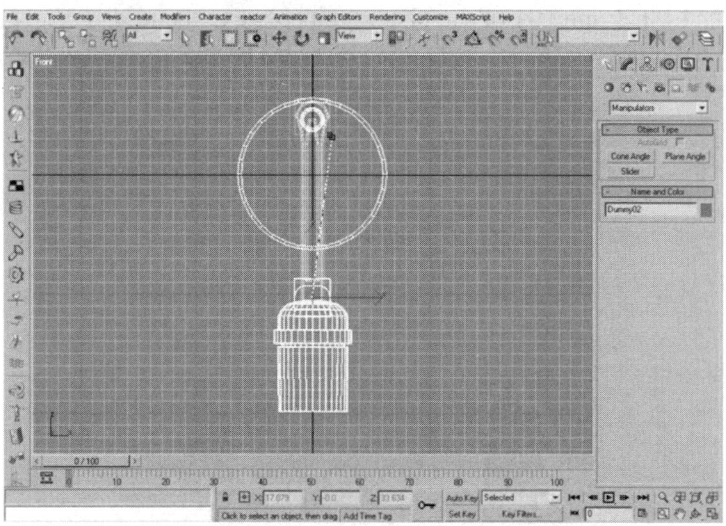

Figure 4.90: Linking dummy02 to dummy01

5. Link the shaft to dummy02. Figure 4.91 displays the shaft linked to dummy02.

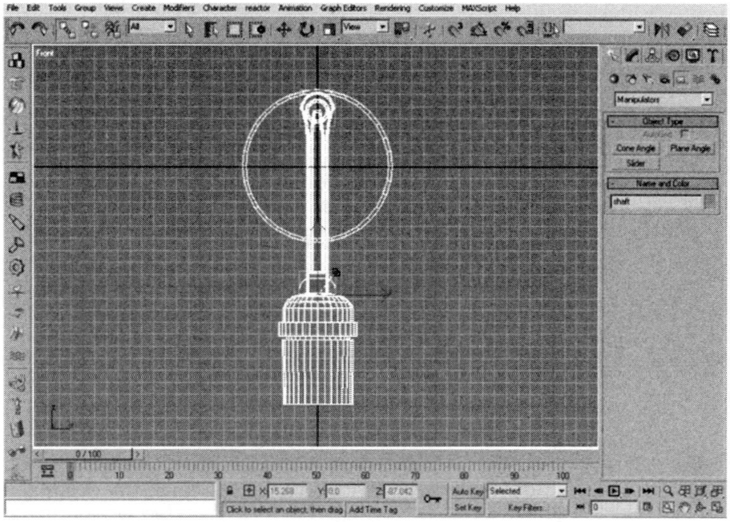

Figure 4.91: Linking the Shaft to dummy02

6. Clear the **Rotational Inherit** check box in the Hierarchy panel (Link info) option of dummy01, as shown in Figure 4.92.

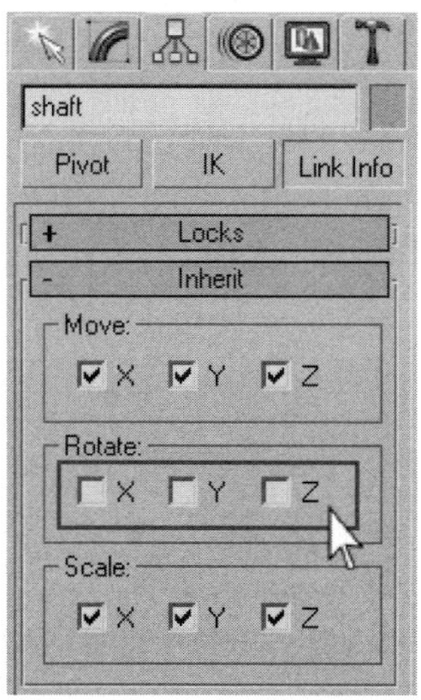

Figure 4.92: Hierarchy Panel of dummy01

7. Clear x Move Inherit of dummy02, as shown in Figure 4.93.

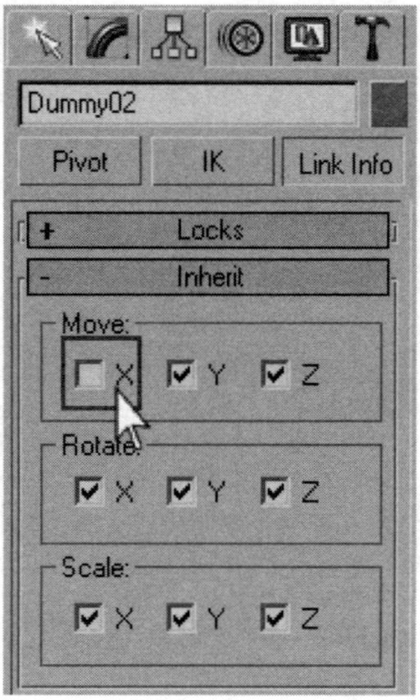

Figure 4.93: Hierarchy Panel of dummy02

8. Select Shaft as the target in its initial position. Apply the **LookAt** constraint to the shaft, as shown in Figure 4.94.

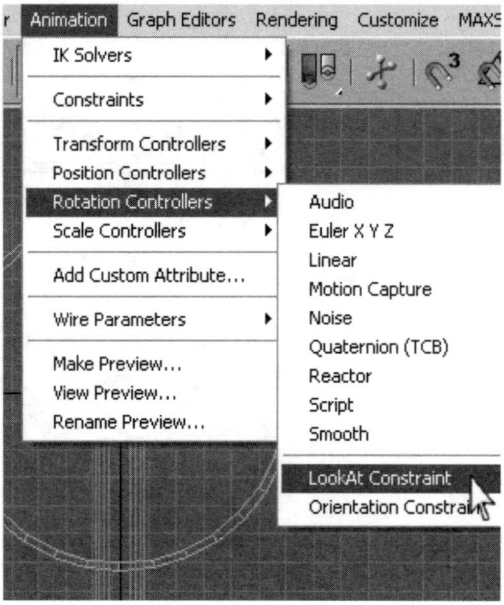

Figure 4.94: Applying the LookAt Constraint

9. Click the Y-axis in the Select LookAt Axis group of the LookAt Constraint rollout, if the shaft does not move as desired.
10. Move the Time slider to 100 and activate the **Auto Key**.
11. Select the plate and rotate it at an angle of –359° in the Z-Axis. Deactivate the **Auto Key** button.
12. Click **Play Animation** to view the animation.
13. Save the file as **ch04_lab_ex2_sol.max**.

Lab Activity Checklist

S. No.	Tasks	Completed	
		Yes	No
1.	Linked the various objects		
2.	Applied the LookAt constraint		

Project

Activities

- Apply materials to the scene.
- Add an atmosphere to the scene.
- Render the animation.

Character Animation

5

Correct modeling helps create high-quality characters. Modeling involves the creation of bones, which are an essential component of a character model. The bone system in 3ds max functions as a skeletal framework that supports the entire structure of character animation.

At the end of this chapter, you will be able to:

- Define various types of modeling techniques.
- Create a character model.
- Use modifiers in the modeling process.
- Differentiate between segmented and seamless character modeling.
- Understand the functions of the bone system.
- Use objects as bones.

5.1 Character Model

5.2 Introducing Bones

5.1 Character Model

A character can be modeled using various methods, such as polygonal, spline patch, Non-Uniform Rational B-Spline (NURBS), and sub-division modeling. The method selected depends on the output medium and the preference of the modeler.

By creating a model, you translate the physical attributes and shape defined in a character sketch to a 3D form.

5.1.1 Modeling Techniques

Define the various modeling techniques.

High-Resolution and Low-Resolution Models

High-resolution (high-res) and low-resolution (low-res) are two categories of models. Though a high-res model produces better output, it consumes valuable system resources and slows down the speed and performance of the system.

In 3D terminology, a model is a data file that contains information required to view and render an object. A model may have thousands of vertices. Calculating such a large amount of data requires a lot of memory and slows down viewport interaction. Thus, it is a good idea to increase the polygon (poly) count only at the time of rendering.

Generally, a low-res model refers to an object that consists of 800–1500 triangles. Low-res models are ideal for 3D real-time games. These games are generally played on standard computers with the minimum system resources. Modelers use low poly objects in a game to make it appear more interactive and appealing. With the advent of powerful 3D accelerator cards and faster CPUs, a game can now easily support a model consisting of 2000—3000 triangles.

The polygonal and mid-resolution spline patch techniques are used to build low-res models. The NURBS and sub-division techniques are used to build high-res models.

The following modeling techniques are available:

- Polygonal modeling
- Spline patch modeling

- NURBS modeling
- Sub-division modeling

Polygonal Modeling

Polygonal modeling is a simple yet quick method to create models for character animation, regardless of their geometry. However, this method is ineffective in creating complex organic shapes such as the human face.

Polygonal modeling is used to create both high-res and low-res models. It is the most interactive and easy-to-use tool to model an object. Polygonal modeling has a few disadvantages. An object is made up of small flat surfaces, and these are visible when the camera approaches the object surface. To avoid this, you need to increase the polygon resolution, which requires additional system resources. You can increase the poly resolution of an object by applying the MeshSmooth or HSDS modifier.

Spline Patch Modeling

Spline patch modeling helps create smooth and organic shapes, which is difficult to achieve using polygonal modeling. You can create complex surfaces by adding details such as wrinkles to the model. A patch surface is resolution-independent. Thus, when the camera approaches the object, the faceting on the surface of the object is not visible. The surface topology of even a mid-resolution model appears smooth.

A patch surface can be deformed in a way that a poly object cannot. Polygons need to be co-planar, where the edges always appear as straight lines. But, a patch surface provides better control. An object can be bent even at the edges and need not be co-planar.

NURBS Modeling

NURBS modeling is the ideal method to create models with complex organic shapes. It is not effective in creating simple models. NURBS is now an industry standard to model complicated mechanical equipment, biological organic models, intricate architectural structures, and film-quality character modeling.

Sub-Division Modeling

Sub-division modeling is a modeling concept based on the polygonal modeling technique. Polygonal modeling converts a low-res primitive object to either polymesh or mesh. As the level of detail added to the object increases, the resolution also increases. The sub-division modeling method creates characters similarly. Sub-division modeling is a global term that defines the process of dividing larger polygons into smaller polygons to provide more control to the modeler. Sub-division modeling offers the best techniques of NURBS and polygonal modeling.

In the next topic, you will learn how to create a model for animation.

5.1.2 Creating a Suitable Model for Animation

Describe how to create a suitable model for animation.

When you model a character, you need to pay close attention to two views, the front view and the side view. In character models, the side view is also called the profile view. The front view displays the entire character. The profile view displays the various curves and bends in the character.

Figure 5.1 shows the front view and the profile view of a model to be created. Before you start creating the model, note the proportions of the character sketch. For example, observe that the length of the torso is three times that of the face. Create the model corresponding to the sketch, which will help reduce the number of final adjustments required later.

Figure 5.1: Character Sketch

In the character sketch, observe that the character's arms are outstretched and legs spread apart. This is called the binding pose. This pose avoids issues of overlapping envelopes between the torso and the arm when skinning the model.

Another advantage of the binding pose is that the model requires less deformation during animation, which prevents possible tearing of the model. For example, you need to animate a model with its arms above the head. When you create the model in the binding pose, you need to rotate the shoulder by only 90 degrees. However, when you create the model with the arms alongside the torso, you need to rotate the shoulder by 180 degrees. Increasing the angle of rotation increases the amount of deformation. Thus, it is a good idea to create a model in the binding pose.

Creating a model involves creating the following:

- The torso
- The arms
- The legs
- The neck
- The body
- The face

The order in which the various parts are created may differ.

While creating a model, the torso is created first because it forms the base from which the arms, the legs, and the neck are created.

Creating the Torso

To create the torso, perform the following steps:

1. Open 3ds max 6.
2. In the Create panel, select Standard Primitive, and then click the **Box** button to create a box object in the Top viewport.
3. Set the parameter of the object by entering the following values in the Parameter rollout.
    - Length = 50
    - Width = 50
    - Height = 55
    - Length segments = 1

- Width segments = 2
- Height segments = 4

The new object is similar to the one shown in Figure 5.2. You need to modify this object to create the shape of a belly by converting it into an editable poly.

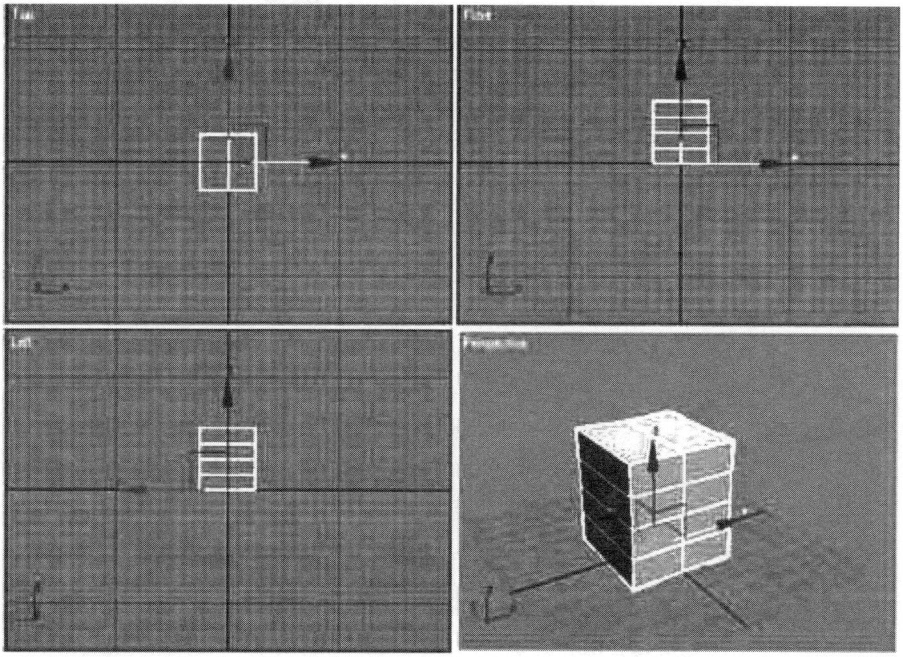

Figure 5.2: Creating the Box Primitive

4. Select the box primitive and right-click to open the **Quad** menu. From the Convert To menu option, select Convert To Editable Poly. The box primitive is now converted to a non-parametric editable object.

Create Background Image for character to trace it.

Use Symmetry while creating character.

Views
View Port Backgrounds/Files/Open /Match Bitmap

5. Select the left-side vertices of the object and delete, as shown in Figure 5.3.

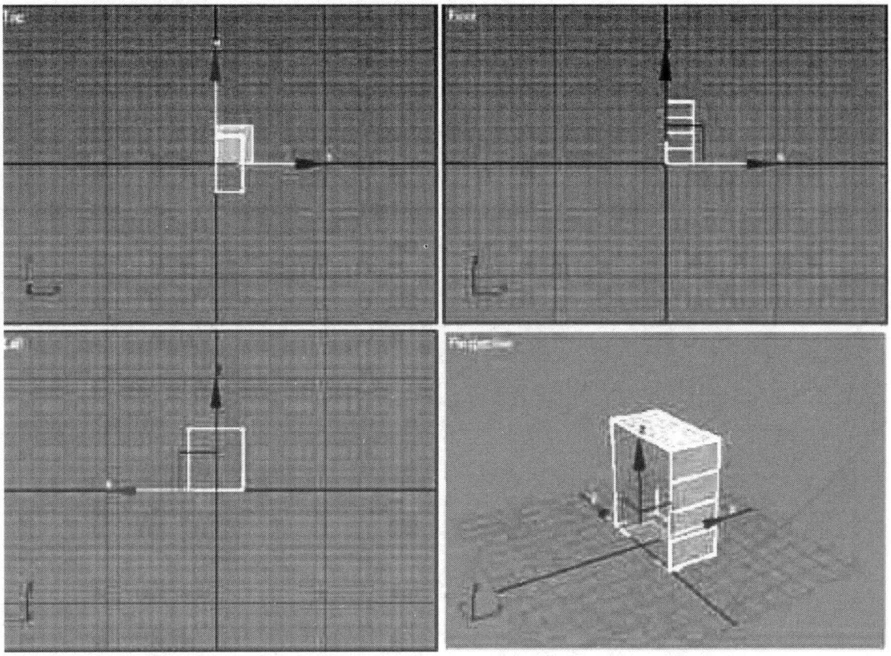

Figure 5.3: Deleting Selected Vertices

6. You need to use an instanced mirror clone to create the other side of the character. Then, create a mirror copy using the Mirror tool on the toolbar.
7. Maximize the Front viewport and select the right side of the box. From the vertex sub object, select the third and fourth vertices from the right side and move along the x-axis.

Now, select the first vertex and move inward to create a shape, as shown in Figure 5.4.

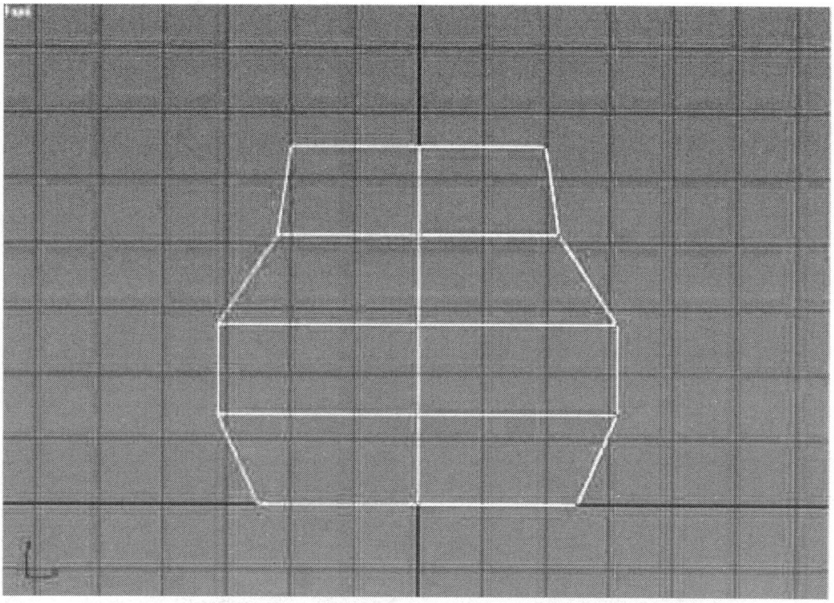

Figure 5.4: Adjusting the Vertices in the Front Viewport

8. Maximize the right viewport and adjust the second and third segments to create the belly area for the character. To do this, you need to select the third and fourth vertices and move along the x-axis.

Then, select all the right-side vertices of the object and pull inward to make the object thinner from the right side, as shown in Figure 5.5.

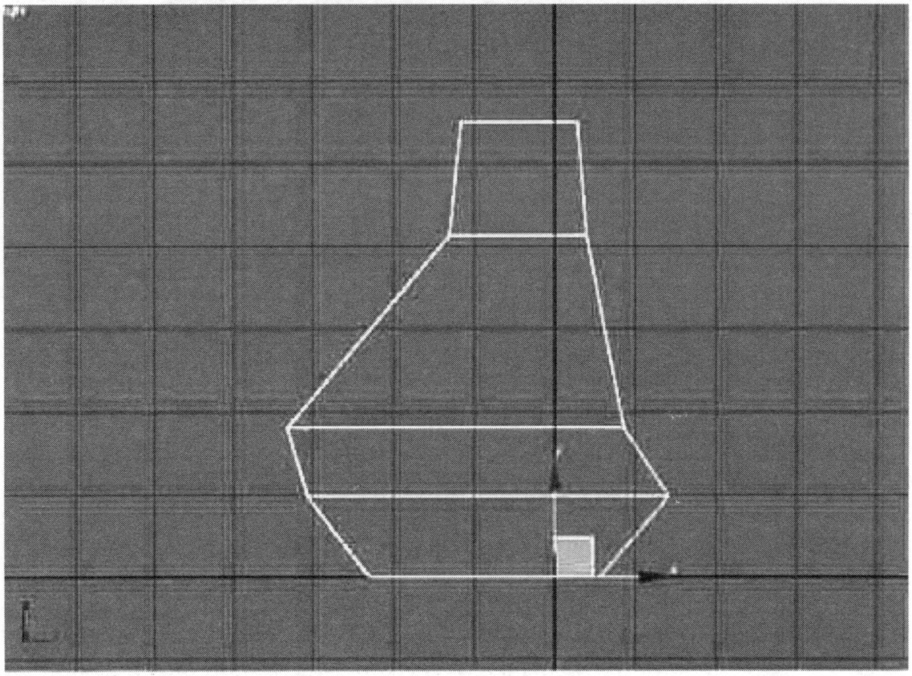

Figure 5.5: Adjusting the Vertices in the Right Viewport

9. The torso is now complete. Assign the MeshSmooth modifier with the Iteration value as 2 to smooth the object, as shown in Figure 5.6.

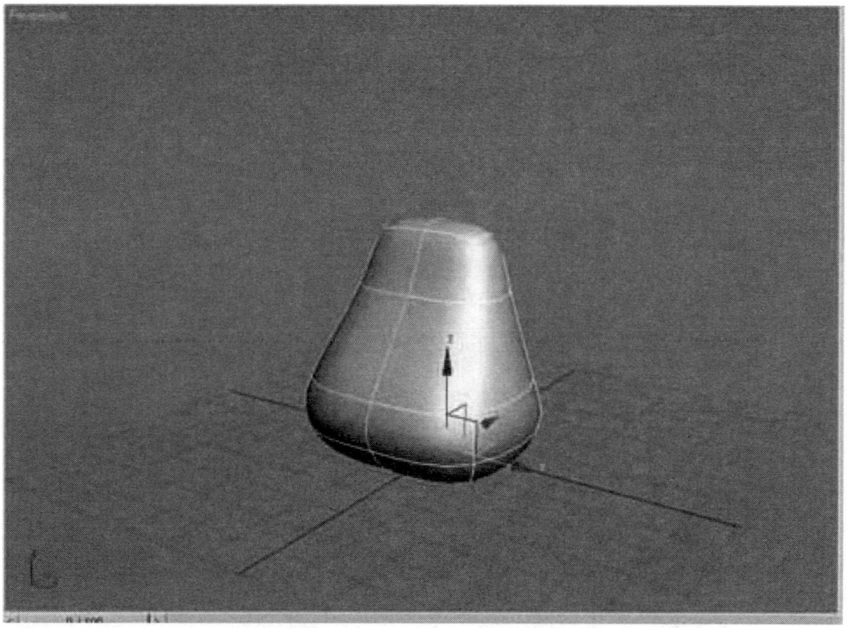

Figure 5.6: Assigning the MeshSmooth Modifier

Save the file containing the torso. Always save your work after making changes to the model. If you make any unintentional or erroneous modifications, you can retrieve the model by opening the most recently saved file.

Creating the Arms

Now you need to extrude the arm from the torso. The arm consists of the shoulder, the elbow, and the wrist joints. The model should deform at these joints. To create the arms, perform the following steps:

1. Select the Polygon mode from the Editable Poly modifier menu option, and then select the poly from the shoulder region. Press F2 to highlight the selected polygon in red, as shown in Figure 5.7.

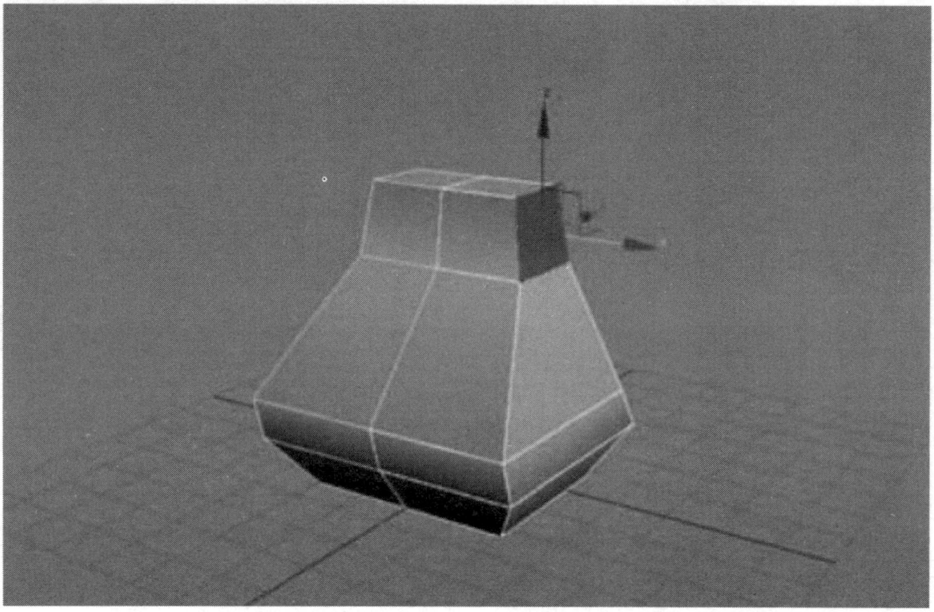

Figure 5.7: Selecting a Polygon for the Upper Arm

2. Click the **small box** icon beside the Extrude button. The Extrude Polygon dialog box appears. Set Extrusion Height to 4, and click the **Apply** button. Again, specify Extrusion Height as 4, and click the **Apply** button. In the Front viewport, push the newly created vertices downward to straighten the arm, as shown in Figure 5.8.

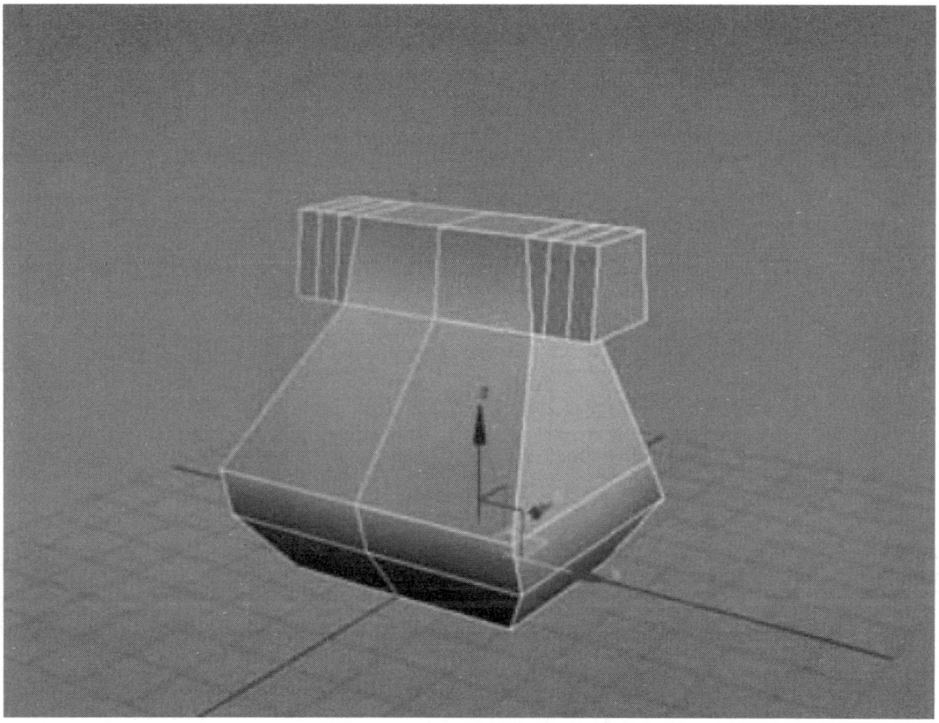

Figure 5.8: Extruding the Upper Arm

Extruding the upper arm twice by four units instead of extruding it once by eight units increases the number of polygons, which increases the smoothness. This is because the MeshSmooth modifier transforms the polygons to smooth curves.

3. Ensure that the polygon is still selected. In the Bevel dialog box, specify the Height spinner as 15 and –2.0 as Outline. Then, click the **Apply** button. This creates the elbow region. To create a smooth deformation in the elbow area, extrude again by 4 and click the **OK** button, as shown in Figure 5.9.

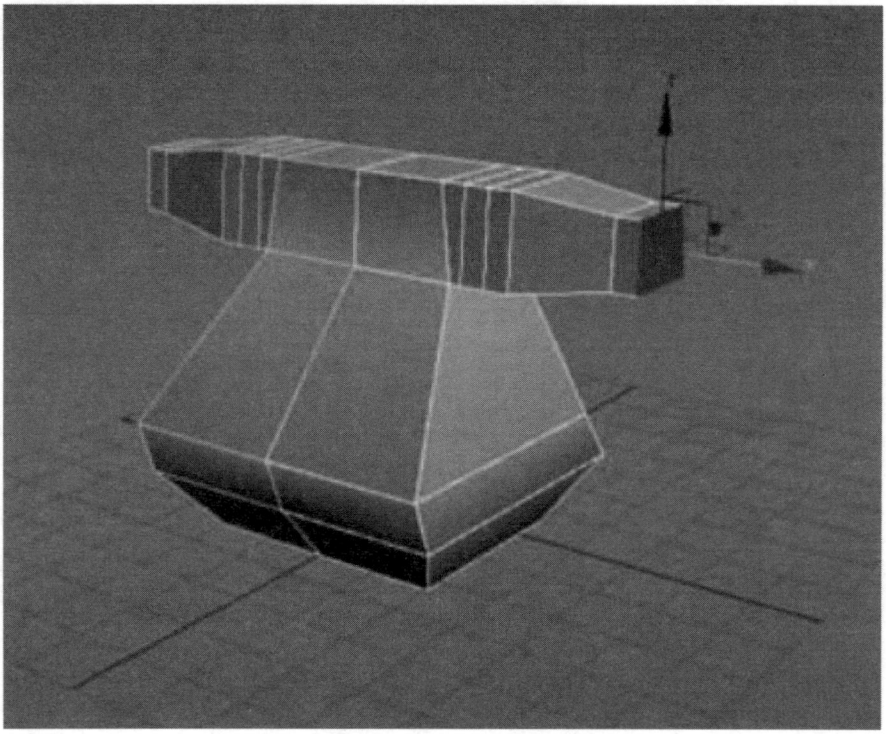

Figure 5.9: Beveling the Selected Polygon

4. Note that the polygon is already selected. Now, create the forearm. Click on the small box beside the Bevel tool under the Edit Polygons rollout to open the Bevel dialog box. Specify the Height value as 20 and the Outline spinner as –2.0. Click the **OK** button to close the Bevel dialog box, as shown in Figure 5.10.

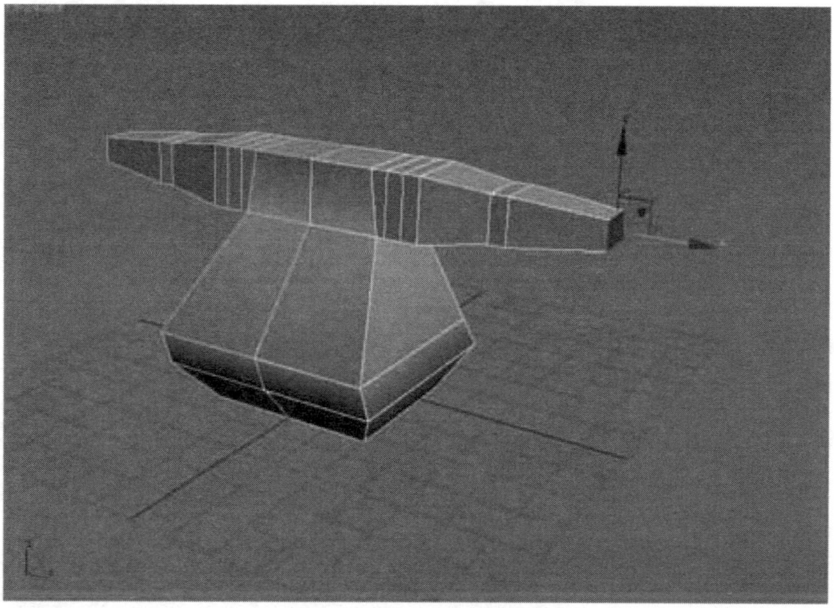

Figure 5.10: Extruding the Forearm

5. Zoom in to the lower arm region and click on the **small box** beside the Extrude tool under the Edit Polygons rollout to open the Extrude dialog box to create the wrist. Extrude the poly by 2.0, click on **Apply**, again set 10.0 units for the extrusion height, and click on **OK**. Tweak the vertices to create a shape, as shown in Figure 5.11.

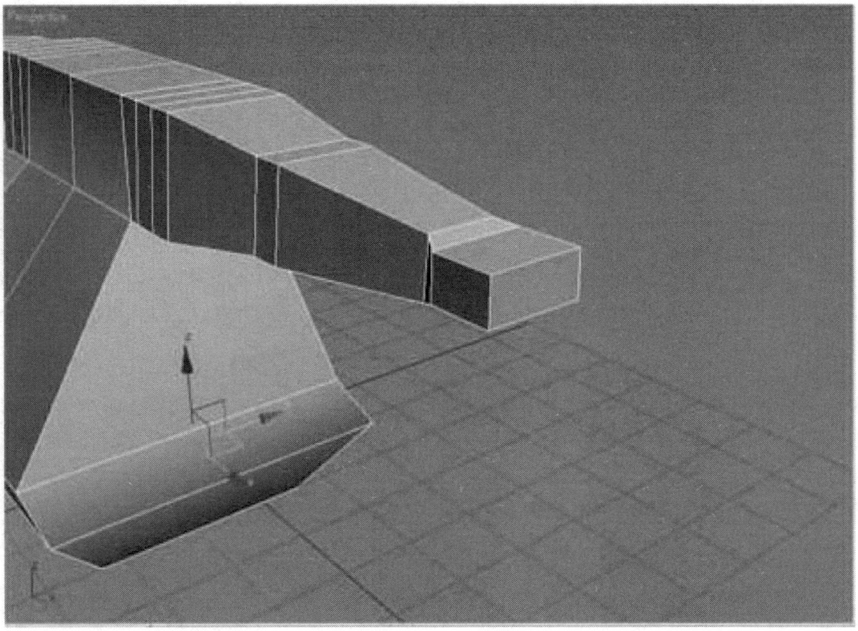

Figure 5.11: Creating the Wrist

6. You need to extrude the thumb and fingers from the polygon that forms the palm. To create the thumb and fingers, select the top and bottom edges of the polygon in the Edge mode and open the Connect Edges dialog box by clicking on the **small box** beside the Connect tool under the Edit Edges rollout. Specify the Connect Edge Segment value as 2, and click the **OK** button. This creates smaller polys that are required to extrude the fingers, as shown in Figure 5.12.

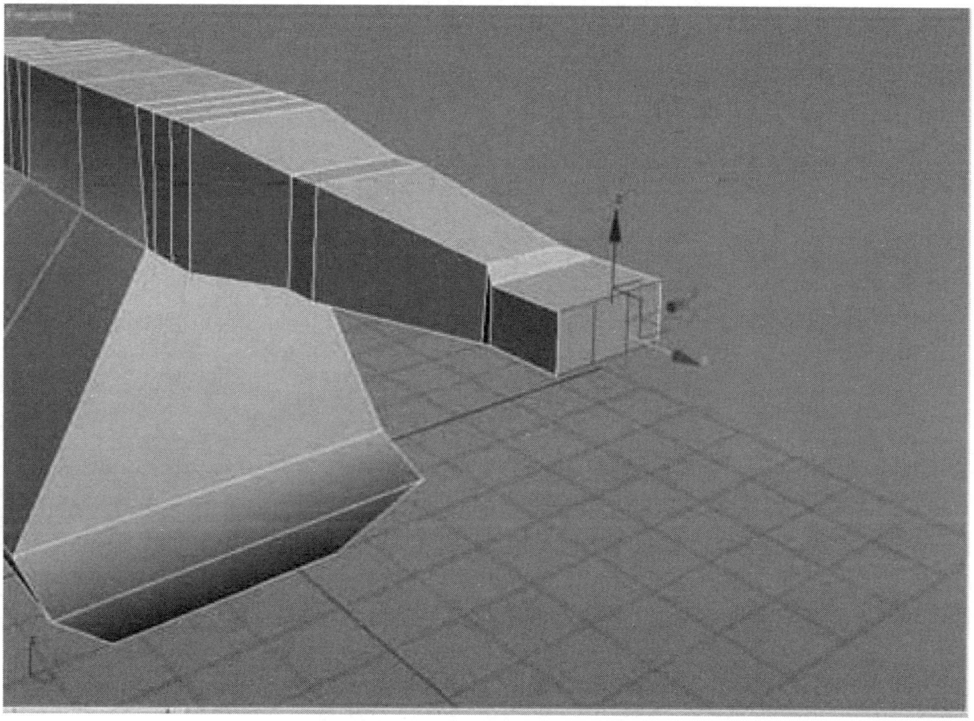

Figure 5.12: Using the Connect Tool to Cut Polygons

7. Select two polys to create two fingers. Click the **Bevel tool** dialog box as you did before and bevel the polys by specifying 1.0, 4.0, and 1.0 for the Height spinner respectively and 0.0 for the Outline spinner in all three cases. Finally, specify the height as 4.0 and 1.0 and the outline as 0.0 and –1.0 respectively, in the Bevel dialog box. Click the **OK** button to complete the procedure. Tweak the vertices at the fingertips in the Top viewport to create an object, as shown in Figure 5.13.

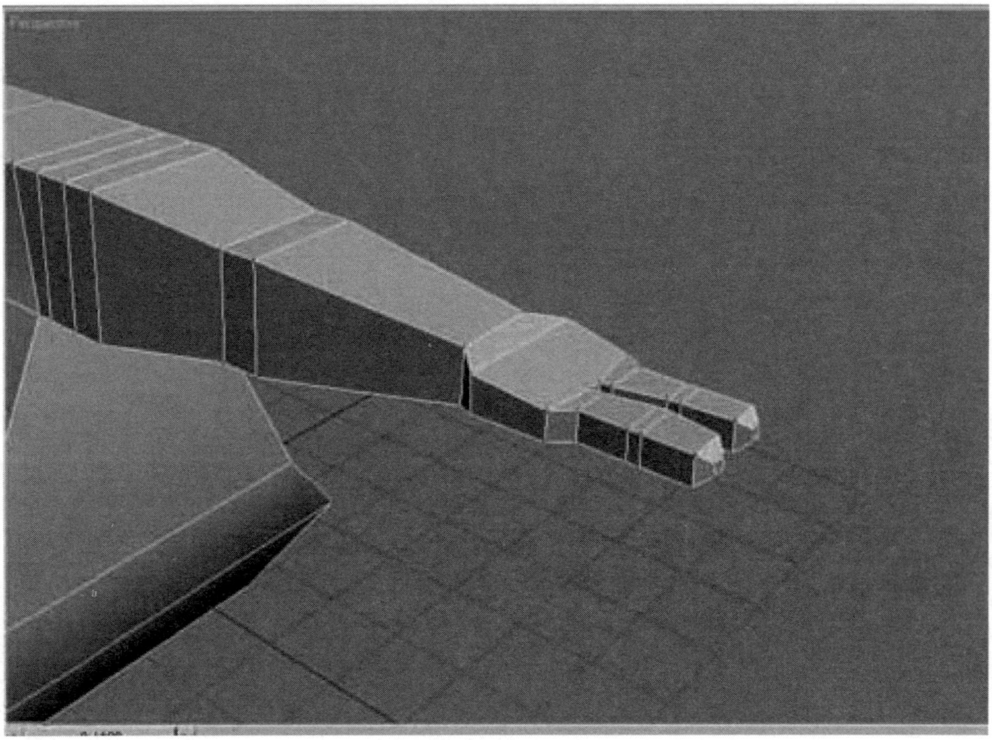

Figure 5.13: Modeling the Fingers

8. Select the polygon to extrude the thumb, as shown in Figure 5.14.

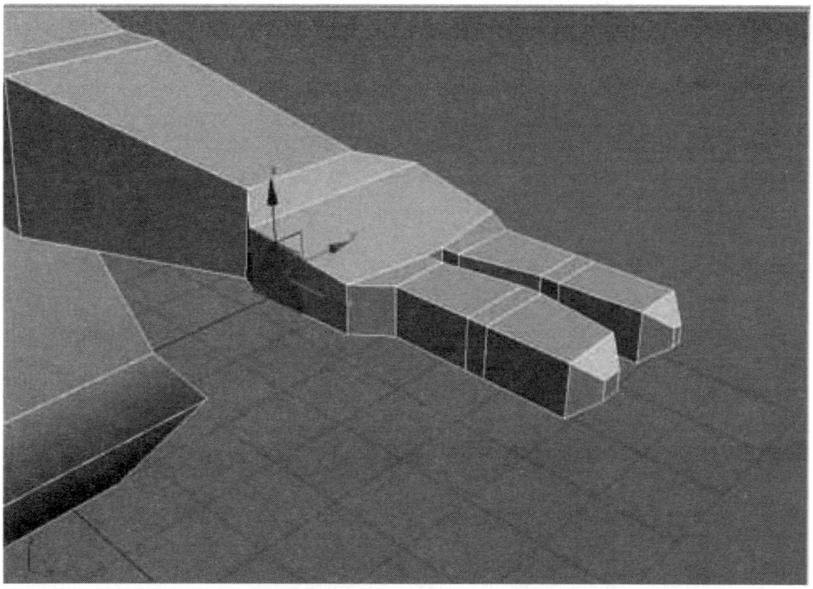

Figure 5.14: Extruding the Thumb

9. Select the polygon, as shown in Figure 5.15, and cut the selected polygon in two using the Quick Slice tool located under the Edit Geometry rollout of the Editable Poly panel.

Figure 5.15: Using Quick Slice to Divide a Poly

10. Select the newly created polygon on the left and extrude it by 1 unit and 4 units, respectively from the Extrude tool dialog box. Finally, bevel the poly by specifying 1 for the height and –1.0 for the outline. This creates the thumb, as shown in Figure 5.16.

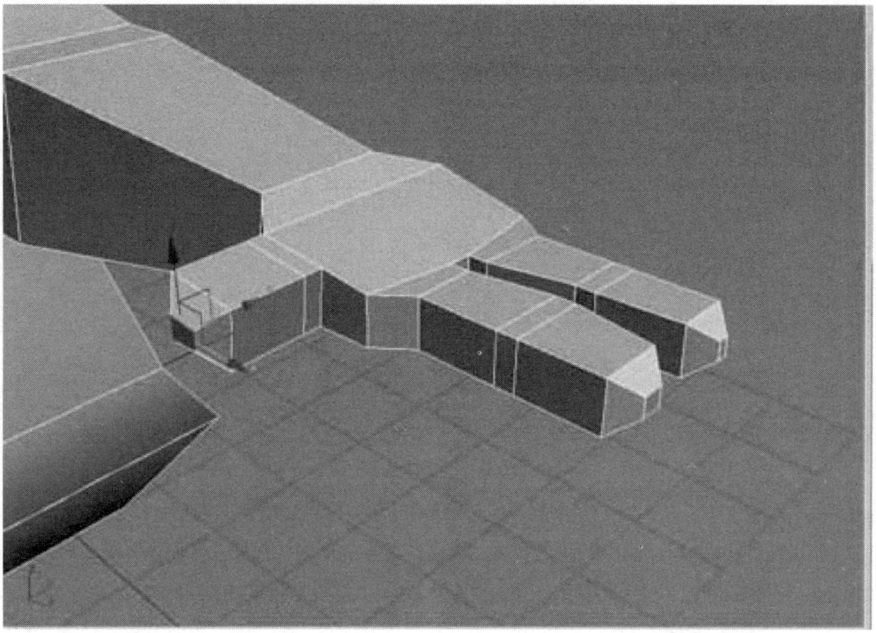

Figure 5.16: Beveling the Thumb

Creating the Legs

To create the legs, you need to perform the following steps:

1. Select the poly from the bottom of the object. Use the Quick Slice tool to cut the polygon, as shown in Figure 5.17.

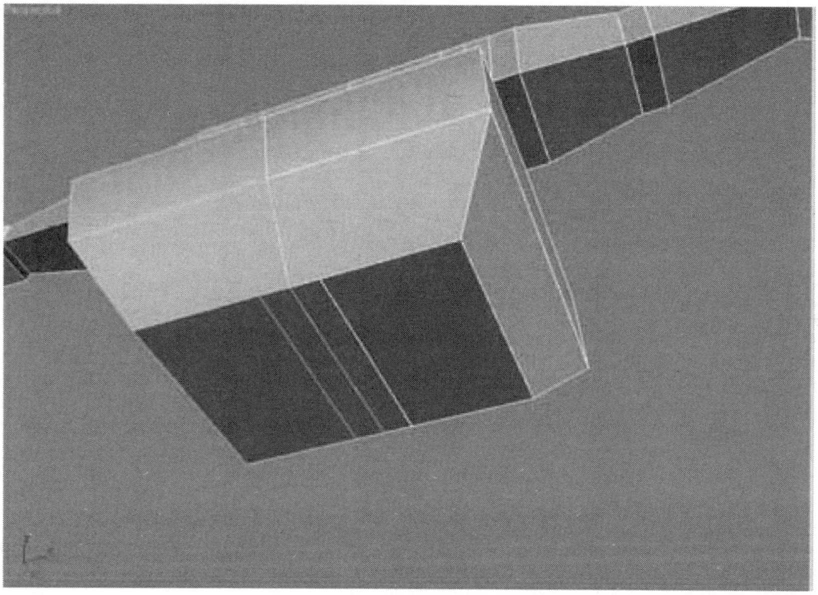

Figure 5.17: Using the Quick Slice Tool to Cut the Bottom of the Torso

2. Select the poly, and open the Extrude tool dialog box. Specify 4.0, 3.0, and 4.0 units in the Extrusion Height parameter, respectively by clicking on the **Apply** button each time. Finally, set Extrusion Height to 20.0 and click on the **OK** button to close the dialog box. Now, adjust the newly created vertices in the Front viewport to create a shape, as shown in Figure 5.18.

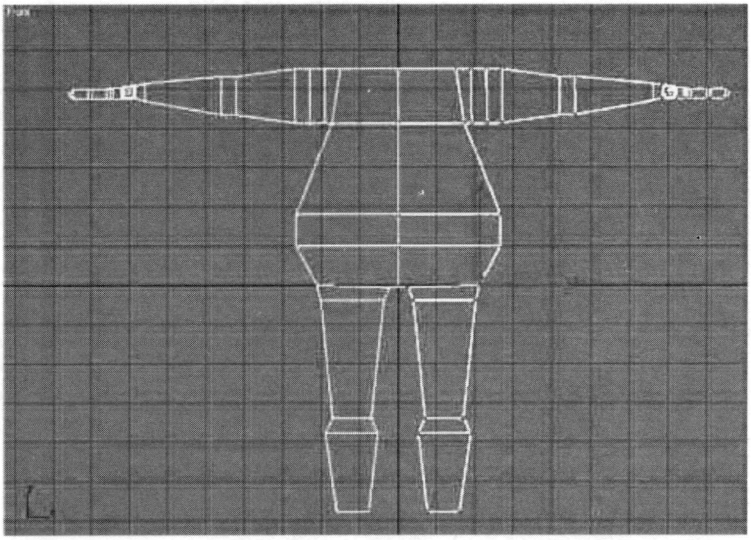

Figure 5.18: Tweaking the Vertices of the Legs in the Front Viewport

3. Maximize the Right viewport and adjust the vertices, as shown in Figure 5.19.

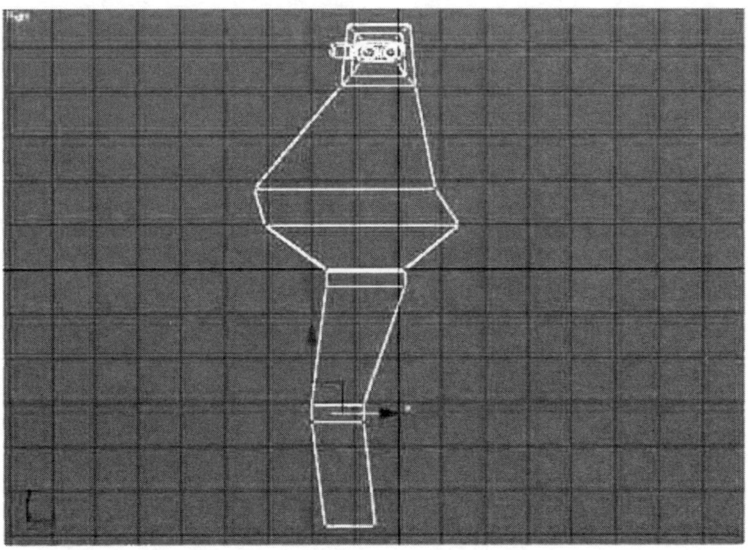

Figure 5.19: Adjusting the Vertices of the Legs in the Right Viewport

4. Zoom in to the foot region in the Perspective viewport and extrude the selected poly by another 2.0 and 4.0 unit in the Extrusion Height spinners respectively, as shown in Figure 5.20.

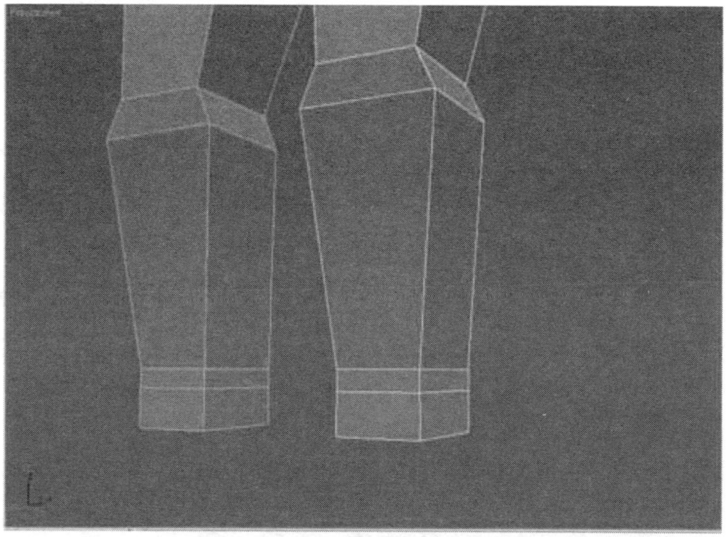

Figure 5.20: Extruding the Foot

5. Select the facing poly and extrude it by another 4.0 and 10.0 unit in the Extrusion parameter from the Extrude tool dialog box, as shown in Figure 5.21.

Figure 5.21: Creating the Foot Portion and the Ankle

6. Next, extrude the bottom of the foot polygon by 2.0 units and use the MeshSmooth modifier to create a sharp edge. Adjust the top vertices of the foot region to create a shape, as shown in Figure 5.22.

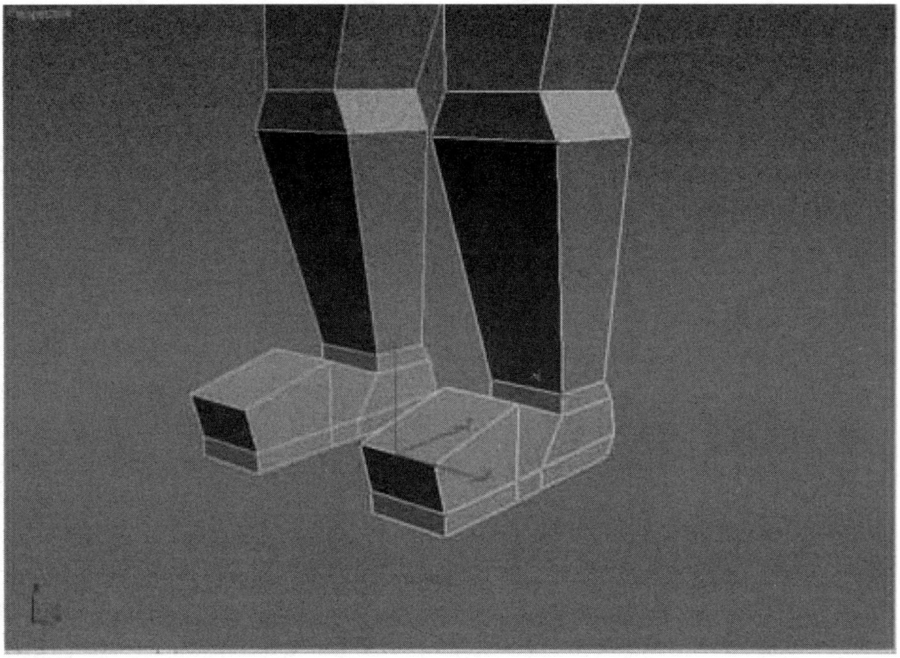

Figure 5.22: Adjusting the Vertices for the Foot

Creating the Neck

To create the neck region, you need to perform the following steps:

1. Select the polygon from the top of the body object. Extrude the poly by 2.0, and click **Apply**. Extrude the poly again by 5.0 units in the Extrusion Height spinner, as shown in Figure 5.23.

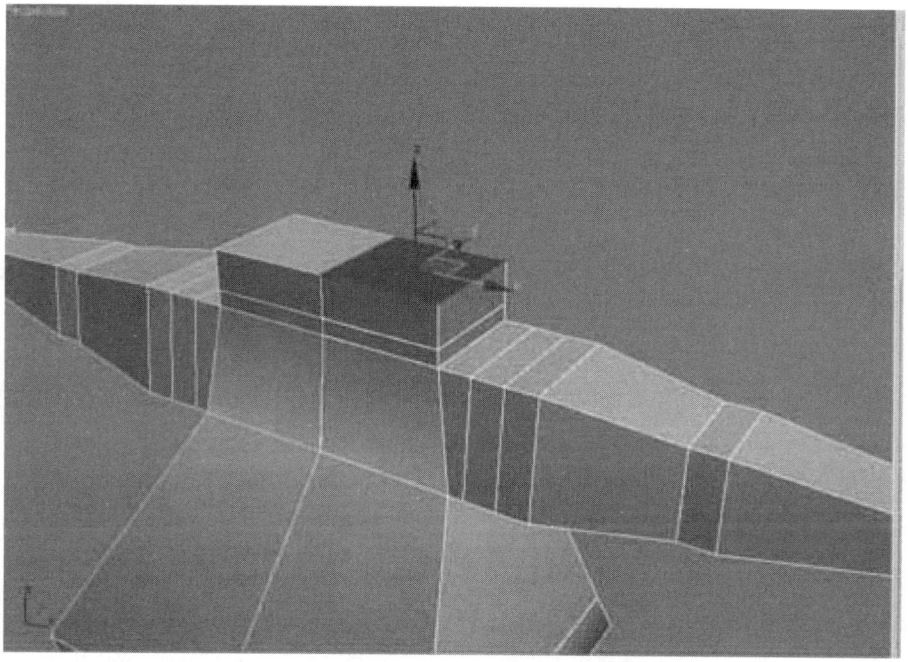

Figure 5.23: Extruding the Neck Region Twice

2. In the Perspective viewport, delete the selected polys, as shown in Figure 5.24.

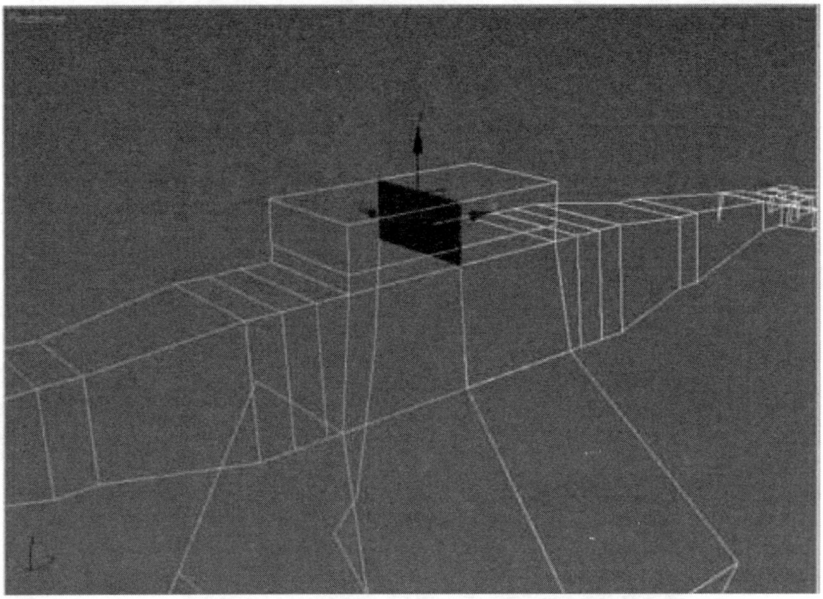

Figure 5.24: Deleting the Selected Polygons

3. Adjust the vertices from the neck region in the Front and Right viewports, as shown in Figure 5.25.

Figure 5.25: Adjusting the Vertices to Create a Round Shape

Creating the Body

You need to round out the belly region, which currently appears flat. To do this, you need to perform the following steps:

1. Select the vertices that define the middle region of the body and drag along the y-axis by 8 units.
2. To create the navel, select the vertex in the middle of the belly region and specify 2.0 as the Chamfer amount, as shown in Figure 5.26.

Figure 5.26: Chamfering a Vertex for the Navel

3. Select the new poly and click the **Bevel** dialog box. Set the height as –0.9 and the outline as –0.2, as shown in Figure 5.27. Click the **OK** button to close the dialog box.

Figure 5.27: Beveling the Polygon for the Navel

4. Select the poly and delete the selected poly, as shown in Figure 5.28.

Figure 5.28: Deleting the Selected Polygon

5. Adjust the vertices in the Front viewport and apply the MeshSmooth modifier to create a shape, as shown in Figure 5.29.

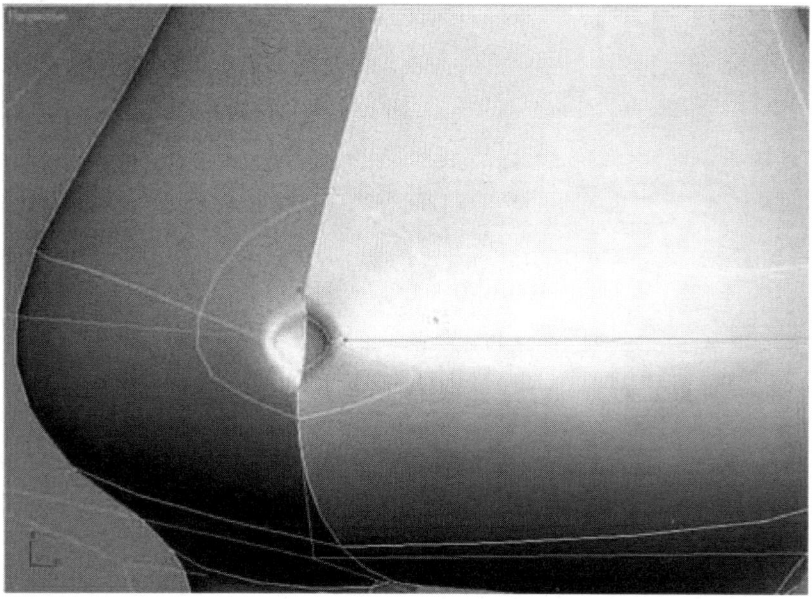

Figure 5.29: Applying the MeshSmooth Modifier

6. Similarly, round out the vertices in the rear portion of the body. Select the middle vertices and drag along the y-axis by 4.0 units, as shown in Figure 5.30.

Figure 5.30: Creating the Rear

Creating the Face

The face is a separate object. It is easier to create a face using a sphere than by extruding from the neck region. To create the face, you need to perform the following steps:

1. Create a sphere with a radius of 15 and a segment of 14. Convert it to a poly and delete the vertices from one side as you did while creating the body, as shown in Figure 5.31.

Figure 5.31: Deleting Half the Vertices of the Face to Maintain Symmetry

2. Create an instanced clone, and place it on top of the neck. Go to the Edge mode of the Editable Polygon object. Select the By Vertex option below the Mode icons. Then, click a vertex to create the eye socket. This will select all the four edges, as shown in Figure 5.32.

Figure 5.32: Selecting Edges Using the By Vertex Method

3. Click the small box beside the Connect tool. This opens the Connect Edges dialog box. Specify 2 for the Connect Edge Segment parameter. This connects the four edges, as shown in Figure 5.33.

Figure 5.33: Using the Connect Tool to Create a Connection Between the Edges

4. Select and push the middle vertex backward to create the eye socket. Adjust the other vertices to create a round shape. Assign the MeshSmooth modifier to create a shape, as shown in Figure 5.34.

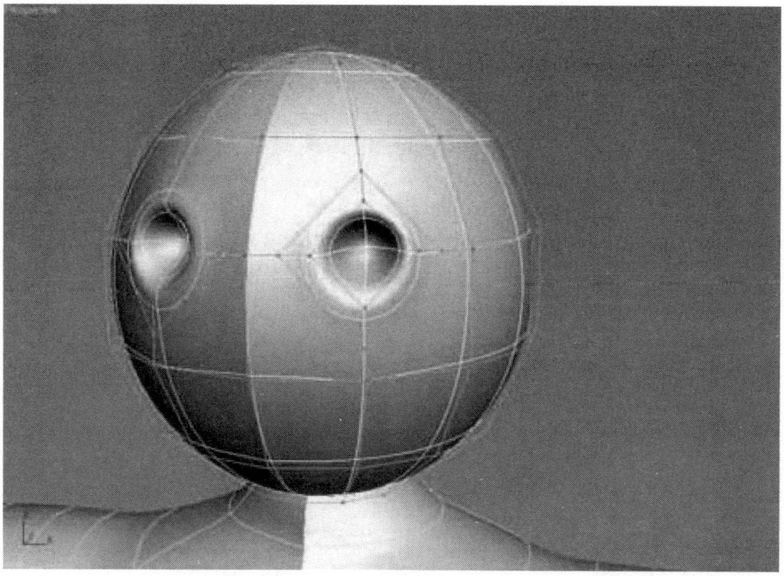

Figure 5.34: Pushing the Middle Vertex of the Eye Socket Backwards

5. Now, adjust the vertices of the face in the Front viewport, as shown in Figure 5.35.

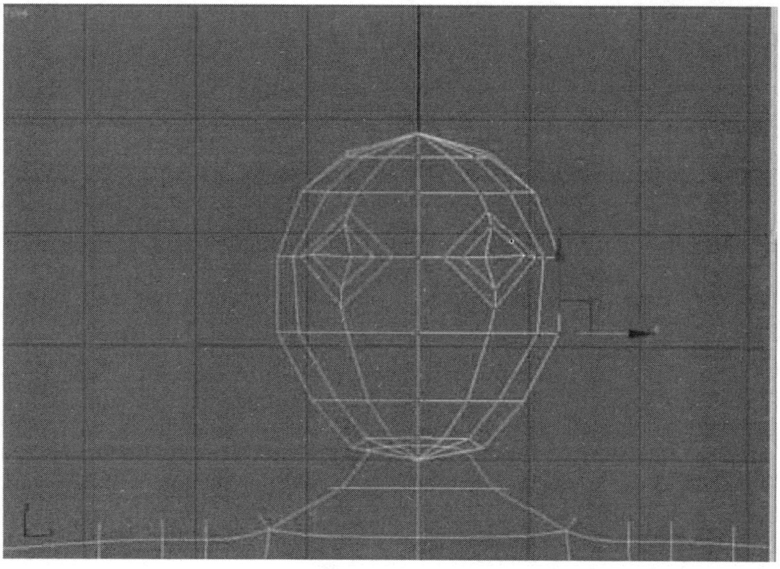

Figure 5.35: Adjusting the Vertices of the Face in the Front Viewport

6. Next, adjust the vertices in the Left viewport, as shown in Figure 5.36.

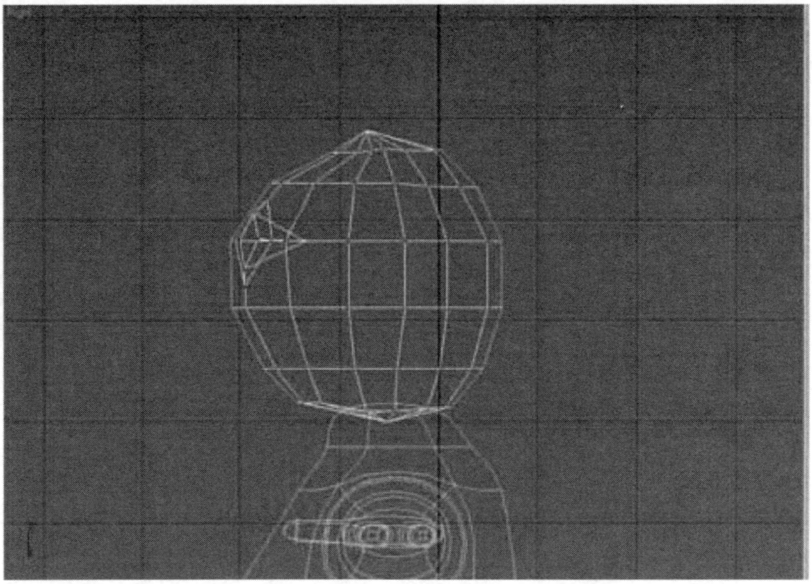

Figure 5.36: Adjusting the Vertices of the Face in the Left Viewport

7. Make two cuts in the mouth area using the Quick Slice tool. This tool is located in the Edit Geometry rollout of the Editable Poly panel. Adjust the vertices, as shown in Figure 5.37.

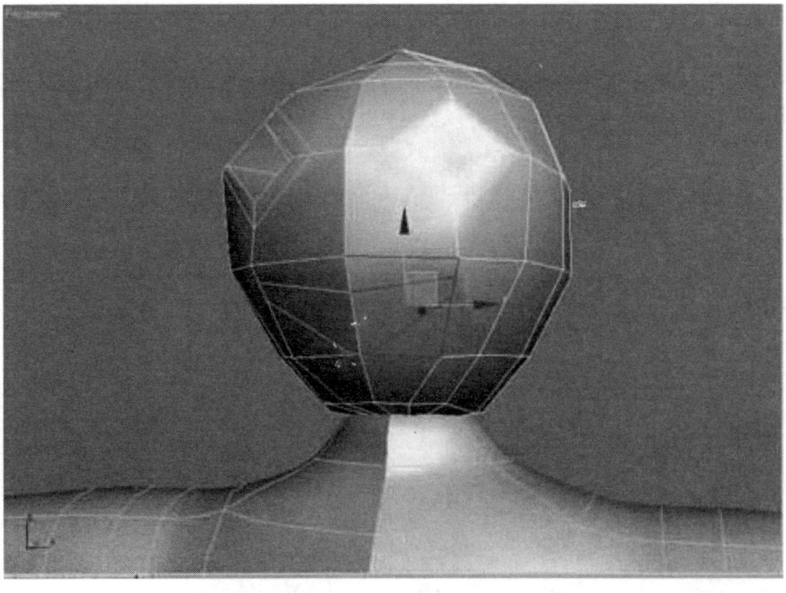

Figure 5.37: Using the Quick Slice Tool to Cut the Polygon for the Mouth Region

8. Select the new poly created in the previous step using the Quick Slice tool and open the Bevel dialog box under the Edit Polygon rollout. Specify –2.0 in the Height spinner and 0.0 in Outline. Click the **Apply** button. Then, specify –0.5 for the height and –0.05 for the outline. Click the **OK** button to close the dialog box.
9. Now, delete the inner poly, as shown in Figure 5.38.

Figure 5.38: Deleting the Selected Polygons

10. Next, create the nose region. Select the vertex above the mouth region. Apply Chamfer located in the Edit Vertices rollout. Specify the Chamfer amount as 2.0 to create a shape, as shown in Figure 5.39.

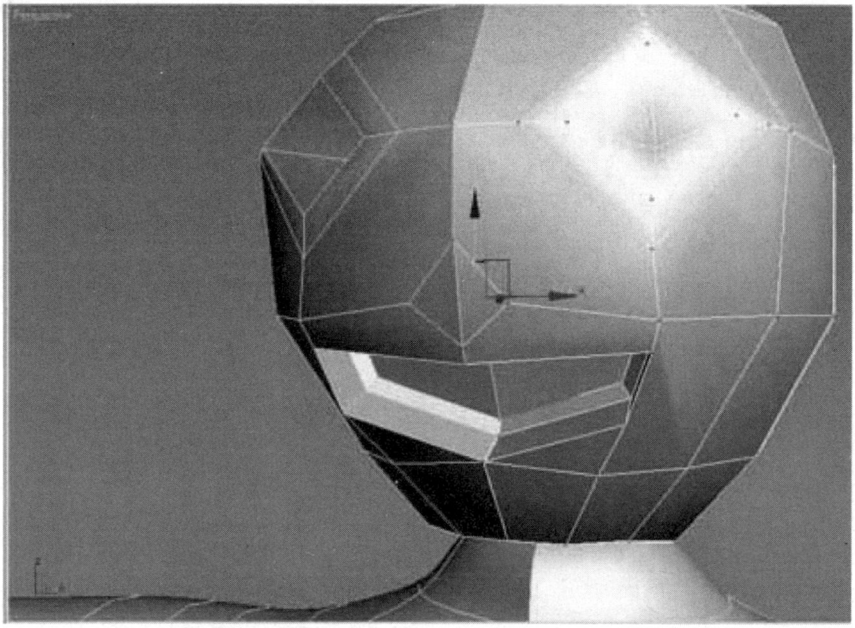

Figure 5.39: Chamfering the Vertex at the Nose Region

11. Select the Bevel option. Specify 4.0 for the height and –0.5 for the outline, as shown in Figure 5.40. Click the **OK** button to close the dialog box.

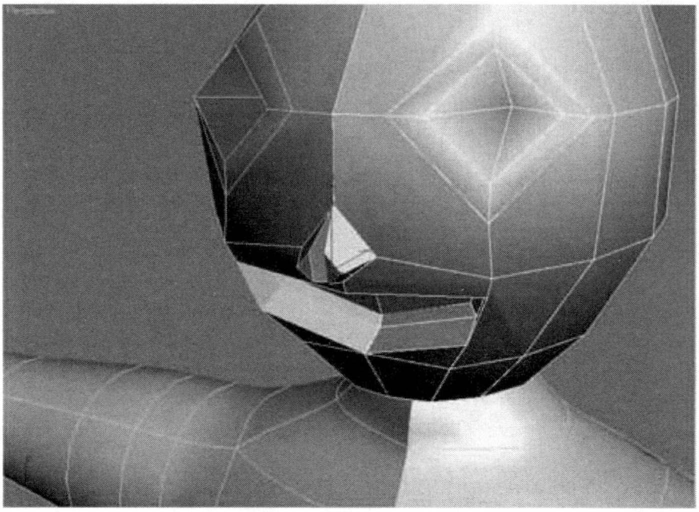

Figure 5.40: Extruding the Newly Created Poly for the Nose

12. Then, select and delete the inner polys, as shown in Figure 5.41.

Figure 5.41: Deleting the Inner Polys

13. Adjust the vertices to close the gap in the nose region and refine the shape, as shown in Figure 5.42.

Figure 5.42: Tweaking the Vertices at the Nose Tip to Refine the Shape

14. Now, you need to model the ears. Select the polygon and cut through the middle using the Quick Slice tool, as shown in Figure 5.43.

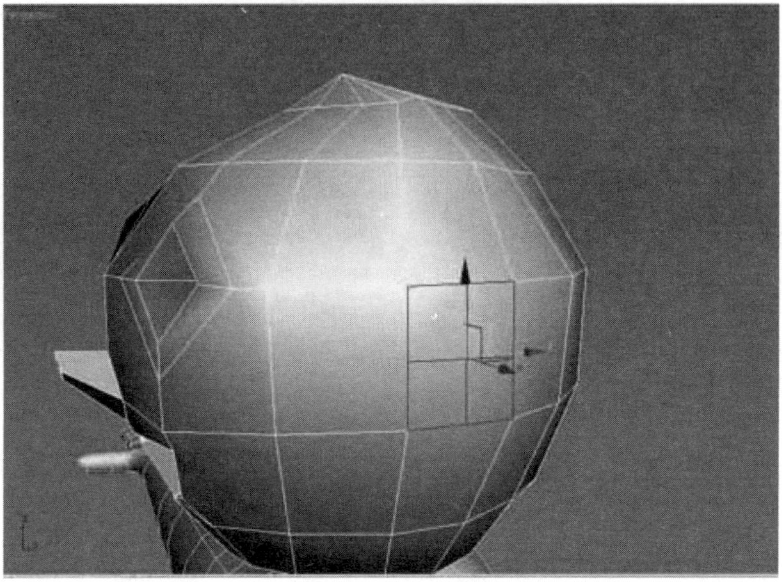

Figure 5.43: Dividing the Poly Using the Quick Slice Tool

15. Select the newly created poly. In the Bevel dialog box, set the height to 1.0 and the outline to 0.0. Click the **Apply** button. Again, set the height to 1.5 and the outline to – 0.5, as shown in Figure 5.44. Click **OK** to close the dialog box.

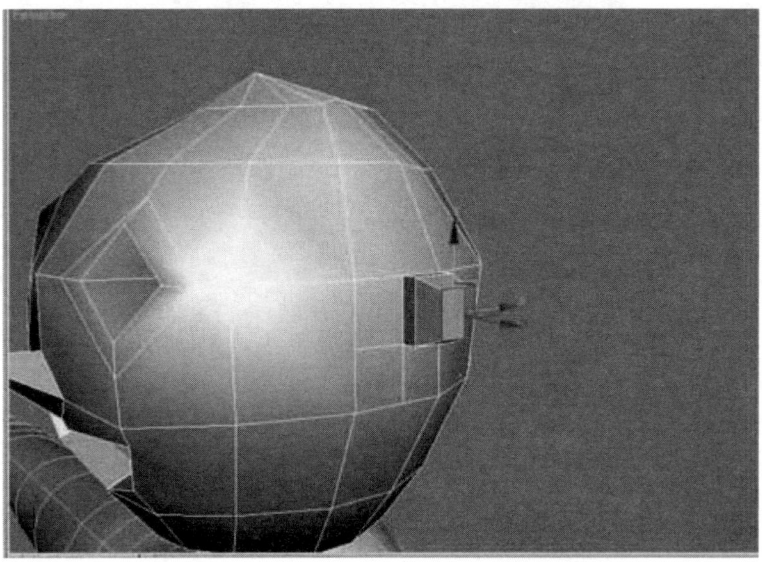

Figure 5.44: Extruding the Polygon for the Ear

16. In the Front viewport, adjust the ear, as shown in Figure 5.45.

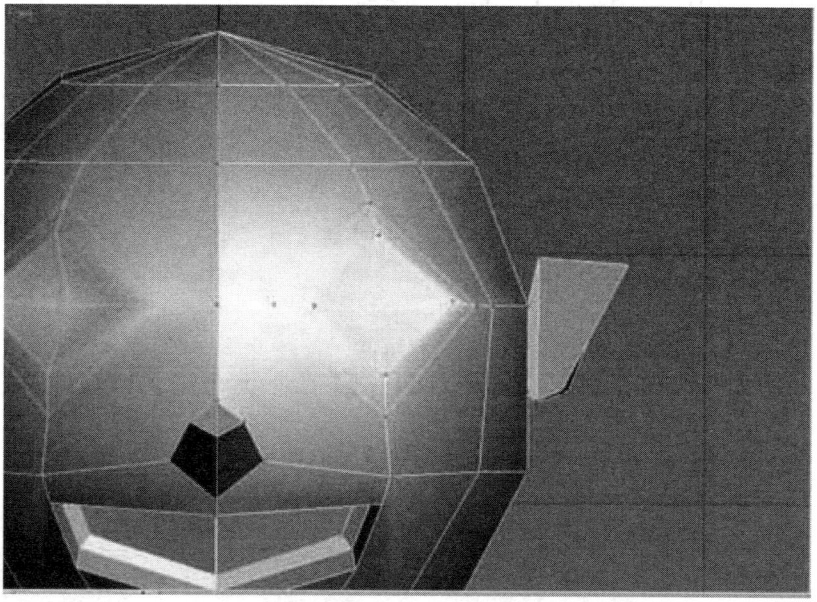

Figure 5.45: Adjusting the Vertices of the Ear Region

17. Select the poly, as shown in Figure 5.46, and use the **Inset** tool to set the inset amount as 0.5.

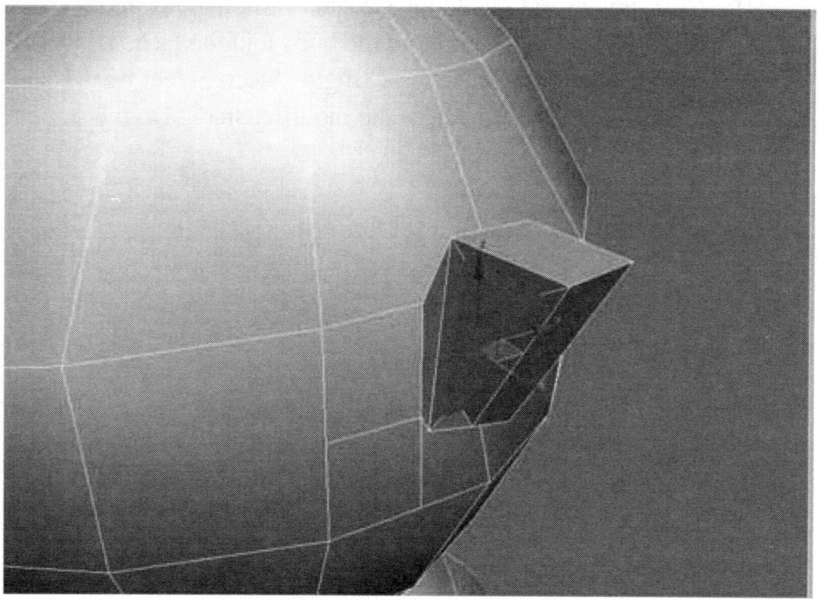

Figure 5.46: Using the Inset Tool on the Facing Polygon

18. Select the new poly created in the previous step using the Inset tool and apply Bevel. Set the height to **–0.75** and the outline to **–0.1**, as shown in Figure 5.47.

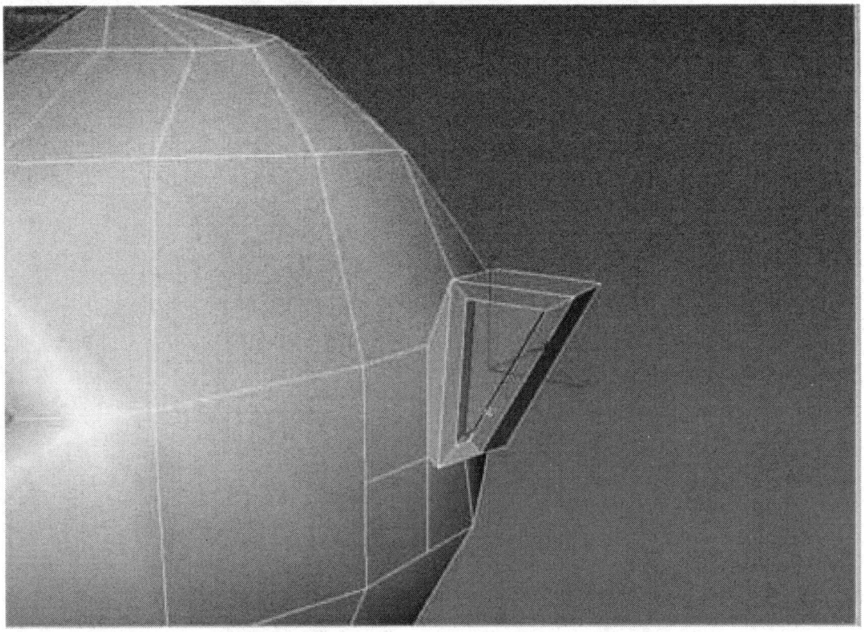

Figure 5.47: Beveling the New Polygon

19. Next, you need to weld the two sides of the body and the face. Delete the MeshSmooth modifier from the body and the face. To weld the two halves, you need to attach the object as a single object. Select **box01** and click the **Make Unique** tool located below the modifier stack. Do the same for the face object.

20. Now, select **box01** and click the **Attach** tool in the Edit Geometry rollout. Click **box02**. This attaches the two halves, but the vertices are still not welded. Select all the middle vertices and click the **Weld** tool, as shown in Figure 5.48.

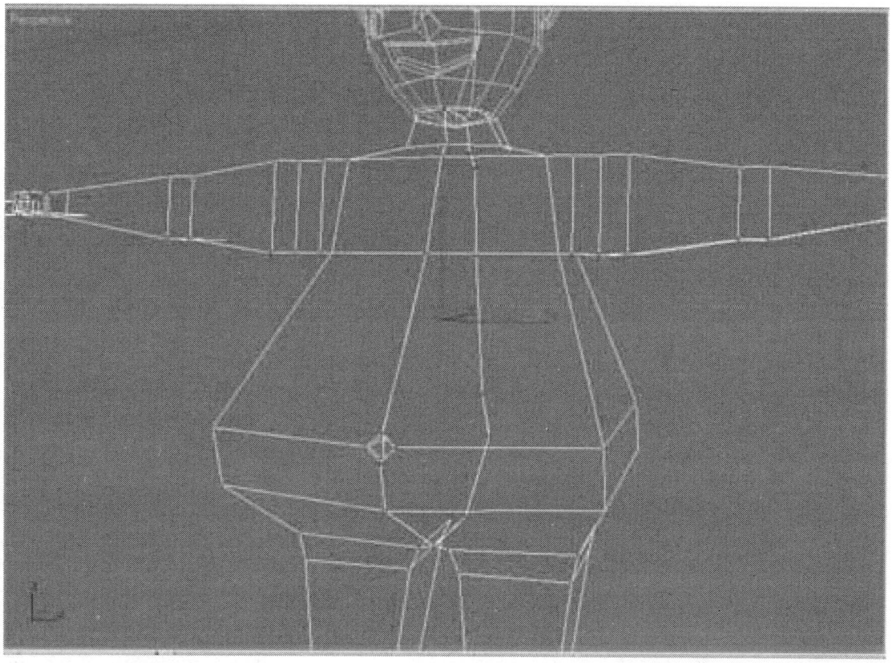

Figure 5.48: Selecting and Welding the Vertices at the Middle

21. Perform the same procedure for the face, and connect the two halves.

22. Now, create a sphere in the Front viewport with a radius of 2.70 and a segment of 32. Create another sphere with a bigger radius of 2.80 for the eyelid. Specify 0.5 for the Hemisphere parameter, as shown in Figure 5.49.

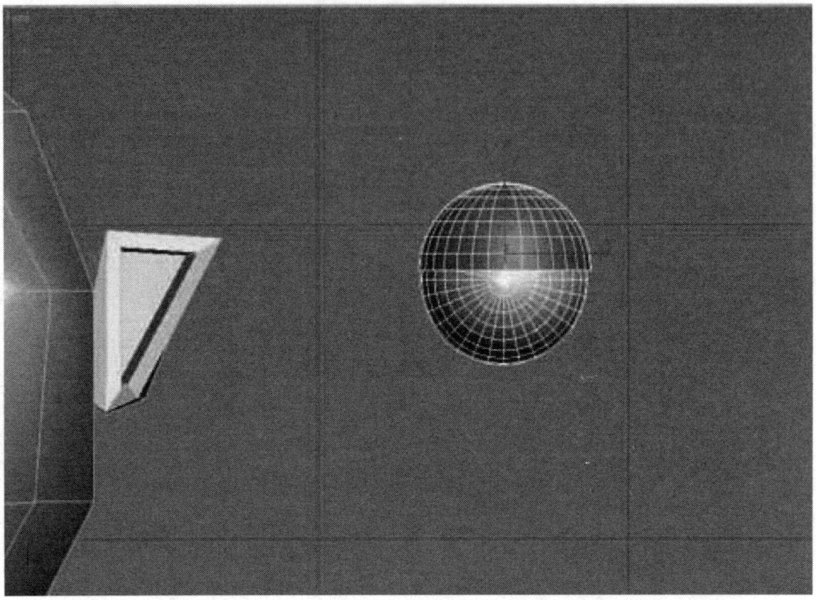

Figure 5.49: Creating Two Spheres for the Eye and the Eyelid

23. Select both of the spheres and position them properly in one eye socket using the Front and Right viewports. Scale both of the spheres by 73 percent and rotate them slightly. Make an instanced clone of both of the spheres for the second eye socket. Change the color of both of the spheres, as shown in Figure 5.50.

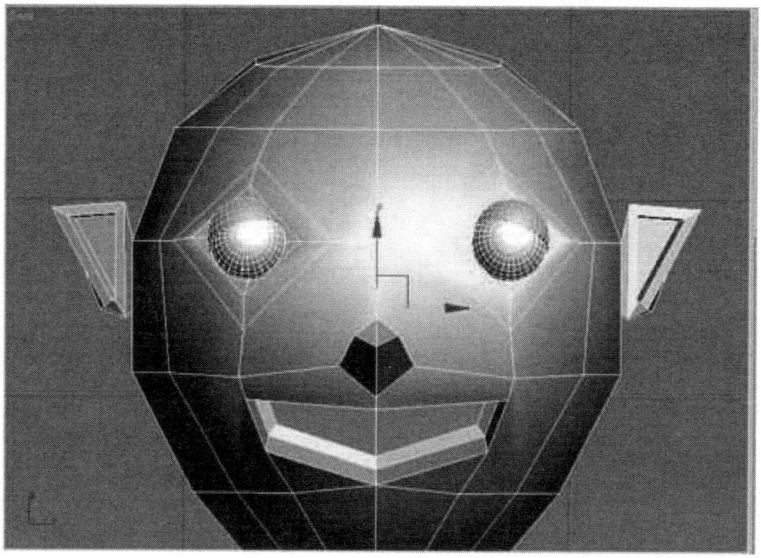

Figure 5.50: Positioning and Rotating the Eyes in the Sockets

24. Next, you need to create the hair. Select the top vertex of the head object, as shown in Figure 5.51.

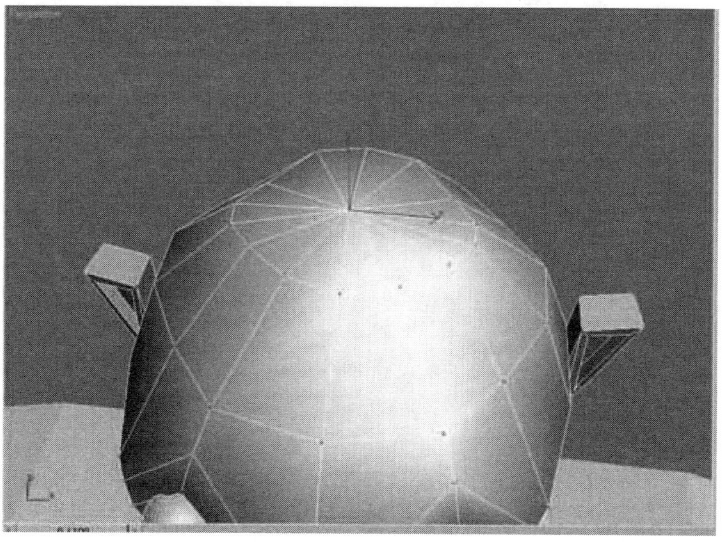

Figure 5.51: Selecting the Vertex at the Top

25. Pull the selected vertex upward. Adjust the surrounding vertices in the Front and Right viewports, as shown in Figure 5.52.

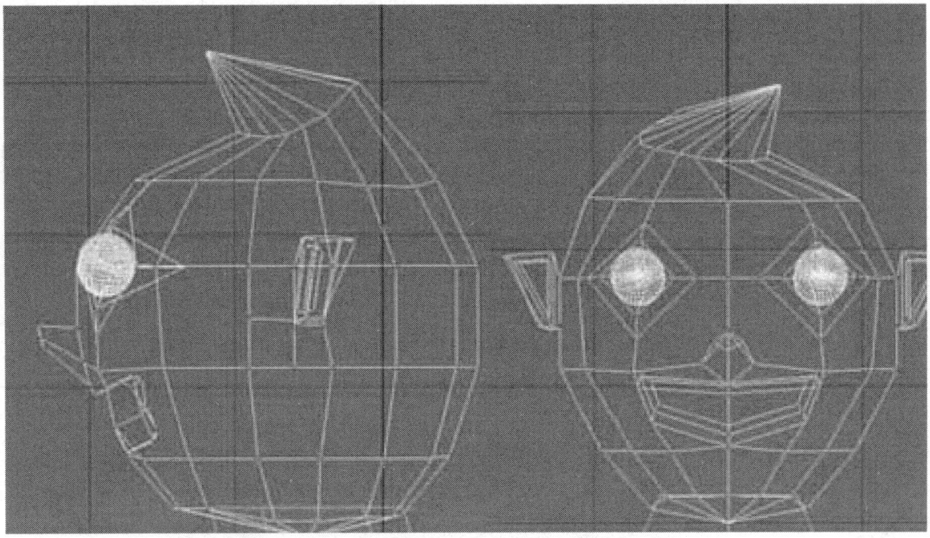

Figure 5.52: Adjusting the Vertices in the Front and Right Viewports

26. Figure 5.53 shows the hair as created at this stage.

Figure 5.53: Creating the Hair

27. Now you need to add the MeshSmooth modifier to the face and body parts. Set the Iteration parameter to 2.0.

Figure 5.54 shows the finished model.

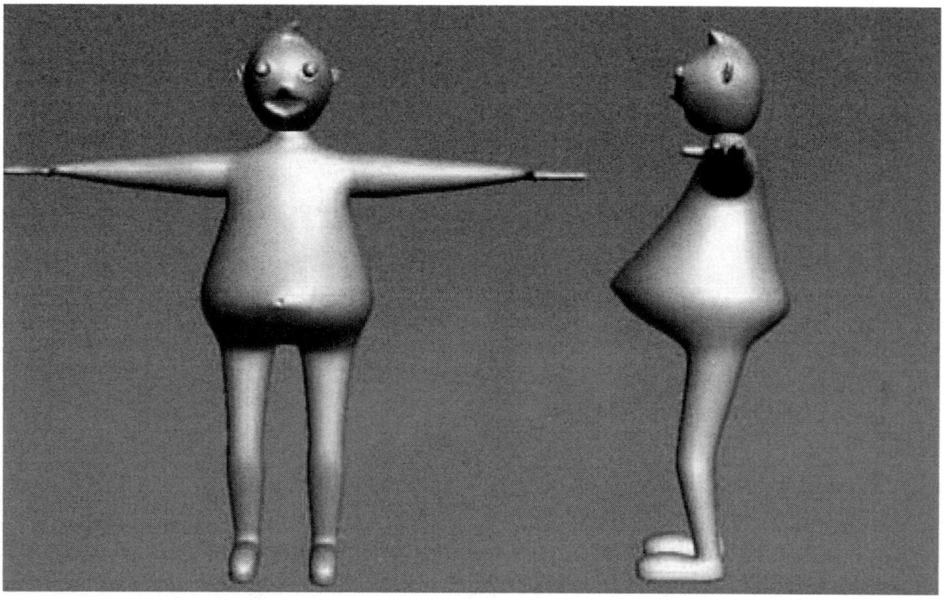

Figure 5.54: The Finished Model

You can open the completed model file, ch05_characterMakingFinished.max, on the student CD.

5.1.3 Modifiers Used in Character Modeling

Define the various modifiers of 3ds max 6 that are indispensable in character modeling.

Modifiers are tools that are used to deform and reshape objects as required. In the object-oriented approach of 3ds max 6, modifiers are separate objects and do not possess a distinct coordinate system. They adopt the local coordinate system of the object to which they are applied.

There are several modifiers, such as:

- MeshSmooth
- Symmetry
- MultiRes

MeshSmooth Modifier

The MeshSmooth modifier is used in the polygonal modeling method. Generally, polys are flat-faceted co-planar surfaces and do not render as smooth and seamless objects, as shown in Figure in 5.55.

Figure 5.55: Rough Edge of a Polygon Object

The MeshSmooth modifier smoothens an object by adding faces along the corners and edges. This modifier can be applied to the whole object or to selected parts of the object. It chamfers both edges and vertices and smoothens sharp corners.

In 3ds max 6, the MeshSmooth modifier can also be used to produce non-uniform rational mesh smooth (NURMS) objects.

NURMS is a method of the Sub-division method of the MeshSmooth modifier. The MeshSmooth modifier provides model control vertices that can have varying weights on vertices, similar to a NURBS object.

The MeshSmooth modifier acts much like a NURBS object when the NURMS algorithm is selected from the Subdivision method spinner. NURMS can apply the vertex weight method. This is a powerful tool that enables you to change the weight of a vertex to modify the surface. The NURMS method is selected, as shown in Figure 5.56.

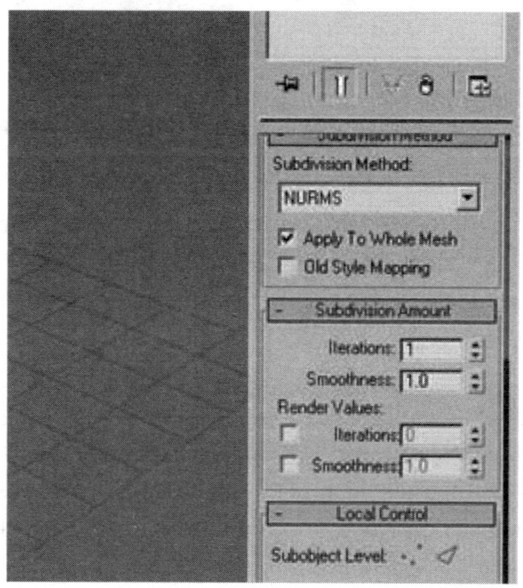

Figure 5.56: Selecting the NURMS Sub-Division Method

A vertex is modified by changing the Weight value located under the Local Control rollout inside the Vertex sub object mode of the MeshSmooth modifier, as shown in Figure 5.57.

Figure 5.57: Increasing the Vertex Weight of an Object

To clearly understand how to use the MeshSmooth modifier, create a sphere and a cube and apply MeshSmooth to both. The cube's sharp corners become rounded. The sphere's geometry becomes more complex without its shape being changed significantly.

Placing an animated deformer before a mesh-smoothed object on which control-level editing has been performed can result in distorting the mesh-smoothed object. If you use deformers for animation, it is advisable to place the deforming modifiers after the MeshSmooth modifier in the stack.

Iteration parameters specify the number of times a modifier is to be applied to an object, without actually having to add the modifier in the modifier stack. For example, if you want to apply the MeshSmooth modifier twice on an object, just set the Iteration spinner to 2.You need to exercise caution when setting the Iteration value, because each time the iteration is run, the object is sub-divided four times. This results in longer calculation time.

In real-time playback, the application software drops a frame to keep pace with the frame rate setting. If a file is heavy, real-time playback results in many frames being omitted, which results in jerky movements.

The Iteration value ranges from 0 to 10. A value of 10 can crash the system in the case of a complex model. To observe the effectiveness of the MeshSmooth modifier, apply the modifier to an object with many sharp edges.

To apply the MeshSmooth modifier to an object, perform the following steps:

1. Create a box with five segments each in length, width, and height under the Parameters rollout.
2. Select the MeshSmooth modifier from the modifier, and apply it to the object.
3. Specify the Sub-division method as NURMS and Iterations as 1. Observe how the edges of the object are smoothed, as shown in Figure 5.58.

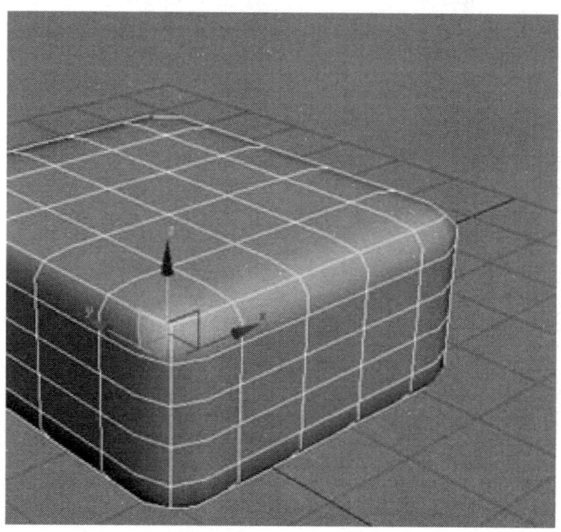

Figure 5.58: Effect of the NURMS Method When Iteration Is Set to 1

4. Increase the Iteration value to 2. This makes the object denser and rounds the corners more. With Isoline Display turned off, observe the newly sub-divided segments, as shown in Figure 5.59.

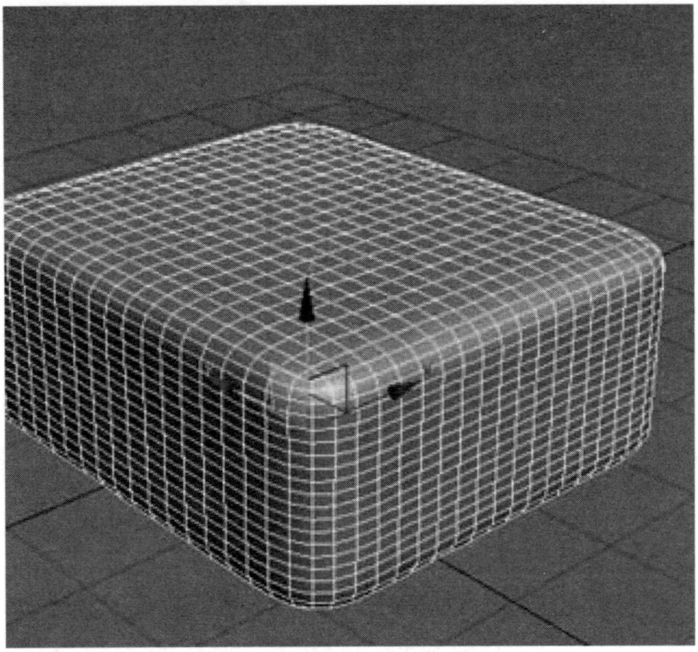

Figure 5.59: Effect of the NURMS Method When Iteration is Set to 2

To apply the MeshSmooth modifier to a selected part of the object, you need to perform the following steps:

1. Create a box with the segments as in the earlier procedure. Convert it to an editable mesh by right-clicking the box and selecting the Convert to Editable Mesh option from the Quad menu.

2. Go to the poly sub object and select a few faces at the corner, as shown in Figure 5.60.

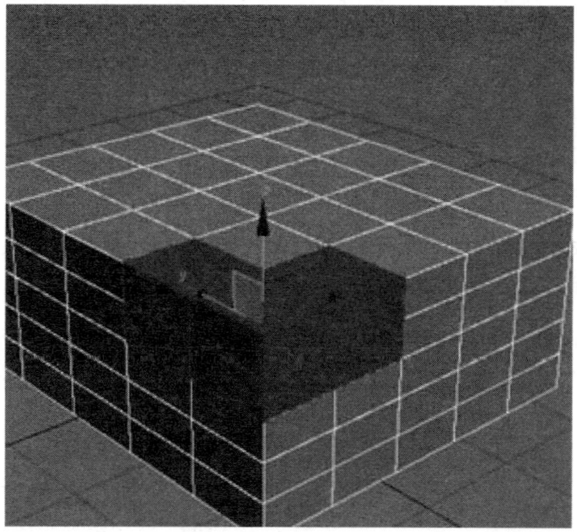

Figure 5.60: Few Faces of the Box Object Selected

3. Exit the sub object mode without deselecting the polys, and assign the MeshSmooth modifier.
4. Specify NURMS as the Sub-division method, and specify the Iteration parameter as 1. Deselect the Apply To Whole Mesh parameter. The modifier will now be applied to only the selected polys of the box, as shown in Figure 5.61.

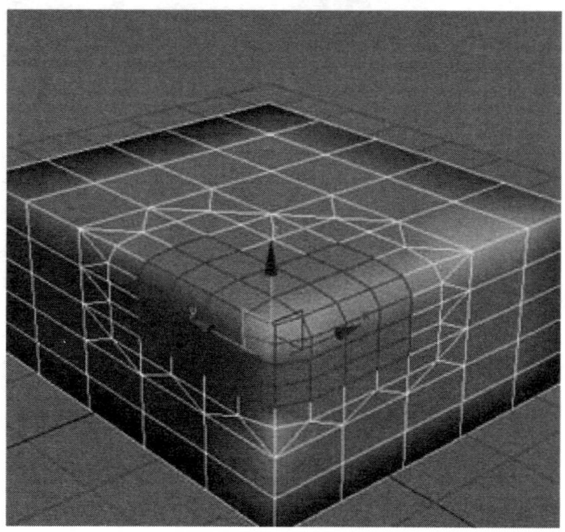

Figure 5.61: Applying MeshSmooth to Selected Polys

The Symmetry Modifier

The Symmetry modifier is used to create symmetrical organic objects and mechanical models. This modifier generates a mirrored instance of the object and removes overlapping regions. It works similar to the Instance method of the Mirror tool. The changes made to one side of the object are automatically mirrored on the other side.

The Symmetry modifier is more flexible and powerful than the Mirror tool located on the toolbar and offers the following features:

- It mirrors an object based on the x-, y-, or z-axis.
- It can slice a mesh and remove either side, if required.
- It automatically welds common vertices where the two instanced halves meet, thus eliminating the need to manually weld the two halves.
- You can animate the modifier's gizmo to apply animated slice effects to the object.

To use the Symmetry modifier, perform the following steps:

1. Create a teapot in the Top viewport. Retain the default values of all the parameters, and apply the Symmetry modifier.
2. The teapot will now have two spouts, one on each side. The Mirror axis specifies the axis plane based on which the mirroring occurs, as shown in Figure 5.62.

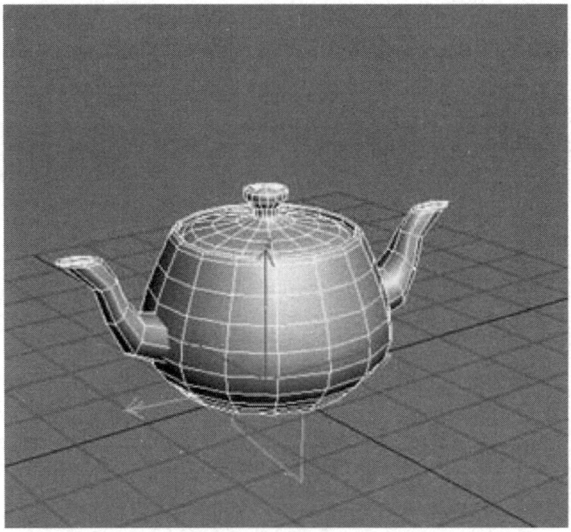

Figure 5.62: Applying the Symmetry Modifier to the Teapot

3. Select and expand the "+" sign in the modifier stack. You will get the Mirror sub object. Moving the Mirror gizmo will transform the two instanced objects along the selected axis, as shown in Figure 5.63.

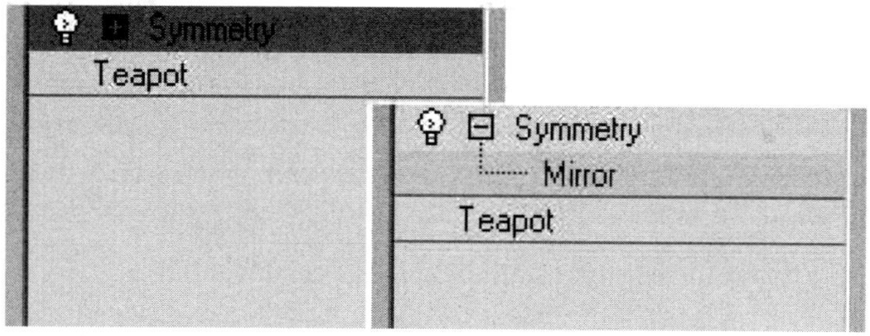

Figure 5.63: Collapse Overlapped Vertices

4. The Weld Seam option works when the Slice along mirror option is checked. This removes the overlapped sections and welds the common vertices, as shown in Figure 5.64.

Figure 5.64: Symmetry Modifier's Weld Method Collapsing Overlapped Vertices

The MultiRes Modifier

The MultiRes modifier is used to reduce the polygon count of an object. It is a parametric method of down resing a model. It does not disturb UVW coordinate mapping in the process. This modifier can be used on the whole object or on parts of the object.

To apply the MultiRes modifier, you need to:

1. Create a sphere in the Top viewport and retain the default values of all the parameters.
2. Apply the MultiRes modifier to the sphere. Go to the Generation Parameters rollout and click the **Generate** button. This initializes the modifier and calculates the number of polygons. The calculation time depends on the complexity and the number of polys in the object.

   Now, Vert Percent, Vert Count, and other information are displayed in the MultiRes Parameters rollout, as shown in Figure 5.65.

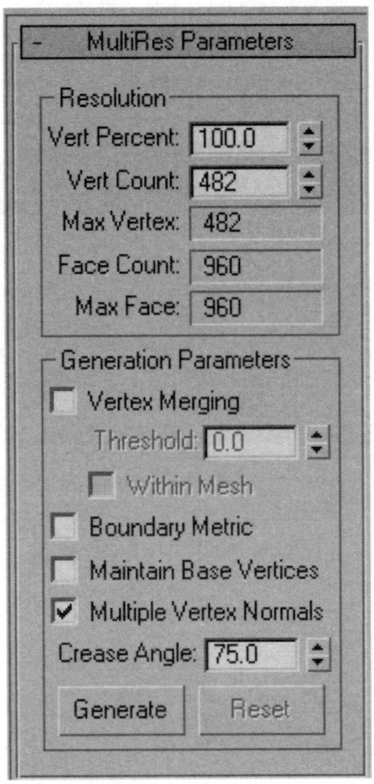

Figure 5.65: MultiRes Modifier Dialog Box

3. Next, go to the MultiRes Resolution rollout and change the vertex percent to 55 or change the vertex count to 262 in the Vert Count spinner.

4. The changes to the spinner values are updated to the object in all the viewports.

To apply the MultiRes modifier to selected parts of an object, you need to perform the following steps:

1. Create a sphere in the Top viewport, and apply the MultiRes modifier.
2. Then, click the "+" sign in the modifier stack area beside the MultiRes text. The vertex sub object appears.
3. Go to the Vertex sub object of the MultiRes modifier, and select a few vertices from the top of the sphere. Check the Maintain Base Vertices option under the Generation Parameter rollout, and click the **Generate** button in the Generation Parameters rollout. The vertices are selected, as shown in Figure 5.66.

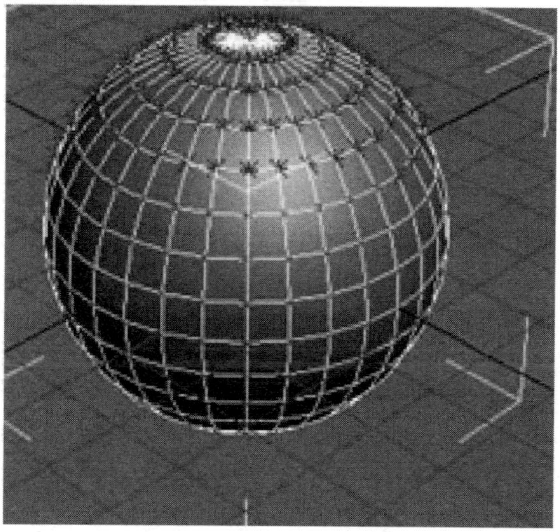

Figure 5.66: Applying MultiRes to the Selected Vertices of an Object

In Figure 5.67, you can see that the Maintain Base Vertices option is checked.

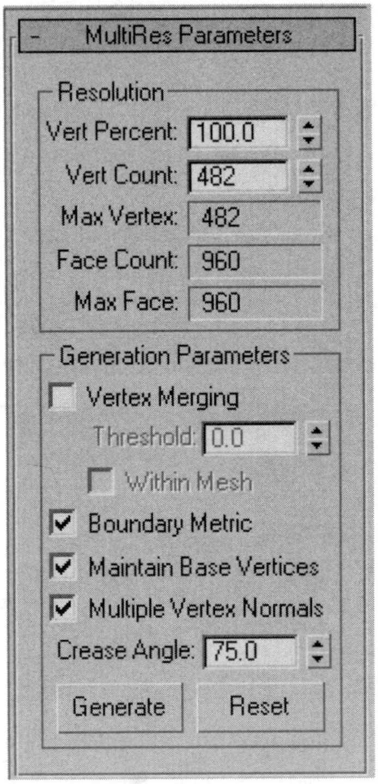

Figure 5.67: Maintain Base Vertices Option Checked

4. The selected vertices are marked in red. Reducing the vertex count or percent value does not at first affect the selected vertices, as shown in Figure 5.68.

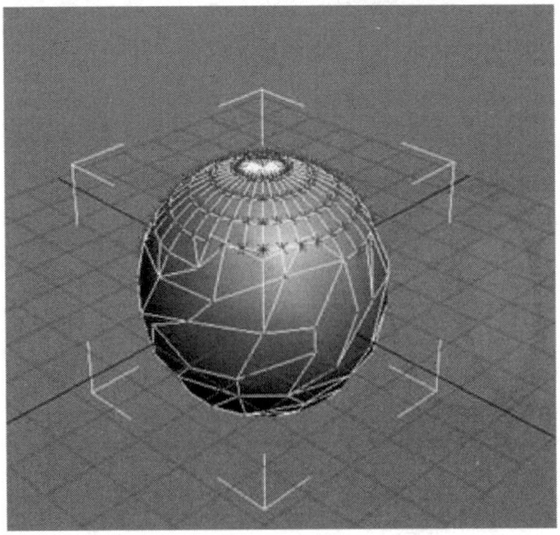

Figure 5.68: Resolution of the Region Covered by Base Vertices Unchanged

In this way, you can maintain specific parts of a mesh in the base resolution while changing the resolution of other parts.

The following method is used to reduce the number of polys and merge vertices when gaps appear in the object:

1. Create two spheres in the Top viewport. Convert one sphere to a mesh, and attach the other sphere as an element. Then, go to the Element mode, select an element, and bring it closer to the other elements by dragging them along the x-axis so that there is an overlapped region, as shown in Figure 5.69.

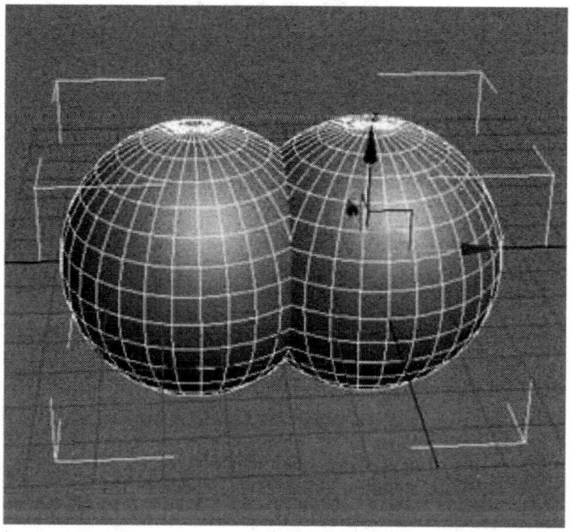

Figure 5.69: Placing Two Elements to Overlap a Region

2. Next, apply the MultiRes modifier, and check the Vertex Merging and Within Mesh options. Click the **Generate** button. Specify 0.5 for the Threshold spinner.

As you reduce the Count spinner, the sphere elements converge to become a single mesh, as shown in Figure 5.70.

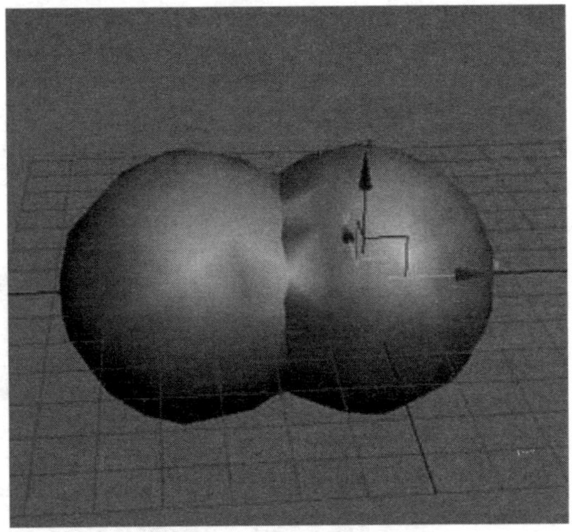

Figure 5.70: Merging the Vertices in the Mesh

These are the methods of using the MultiRes modifier.

The MultiRes modifier is ideally used for a single skinned object.

5.1.4 Types of Characters

Define the various types of characters.

There are two types of characters used in 3D modeling.

- Segmented
- Seamless

A segmented character type is built in small parts that are later linked with the skeleton using external deformers or constraints. Seamless characters are modeled as single mesh objects. The parts may be modeled separately, but they are attached and welded as a single object to maintain surface continuity.

Segmented Character Type

In the segmented character type method, the different parts of the body are created as separate objects. This provides the modeler greater control over specific parts of the model. The separate objects can be created in a single file or imported or merged from other files.

This method is popular in the game industry where characters are sub-divided into multiple parts, the standard requirement generally being three parts. This is because game programming allows for movement of a character's head and torso independent of the lower body. The texturing of a segmented character is also easier. The low-poly method is generally used for this character type, and the MultiRes modifier is ideal for modeling such characters.

All the characters of *Quake III: Arena* were created using the segmented method. Another benefit of using the segmented method is that you can build four sets of arms, legs, heads, and torsos, and combine the various parts in different ways to produce numerous characters.

Seamless Character Type

Seamless characters are created as a single mesh, with all the parts of the character attached. Generally, high-resolution models used for film and commercials are created this way.

The character, Gollum, in the film, *The Lord of The Rings*, is a seamless high-resolution character.

The advantage of seamless modeling is that it deforms the skin of a character more naturally and conforms to the skeleton more accurately. The NURBS and Sub-division methods are ideal modeling methods for this type of character.

Practice Questions

1. List the various modeling techniques.
2. State the difference between low-res and high-res modeling and their use in the animation industry.
3. What are the advantages of using patch modeling over poly modeling?
4. What is the importance of the MeshSmooth and MultiRes modifiers?
5. Differentiate between segmented and seamless characters types.

5.2 Introducing Bones

After creating a character, you need to animate the model. The process of character rigging links the two processes of creating and animating a character. Rigging is the complex process of binding a character mesh with a skeleton framework, which provides the required support and motion to the mesh model. This is similar to the network of human bone and flesh.

Muscles receive electrical signals from the brain, which instructs the bones and moves the various body parts.

In 3ds max 6, the bone is a tool that enables you to deform an object. Several modifiers can be used to deform an object, but they cannot deform a surface as required. A character needs a set of linked objects so that they can be attached and move freely on their pivot points. As shown in Figure 5.71, a human arm consists of three joints: the shoulder, the elbow, and the wrist.

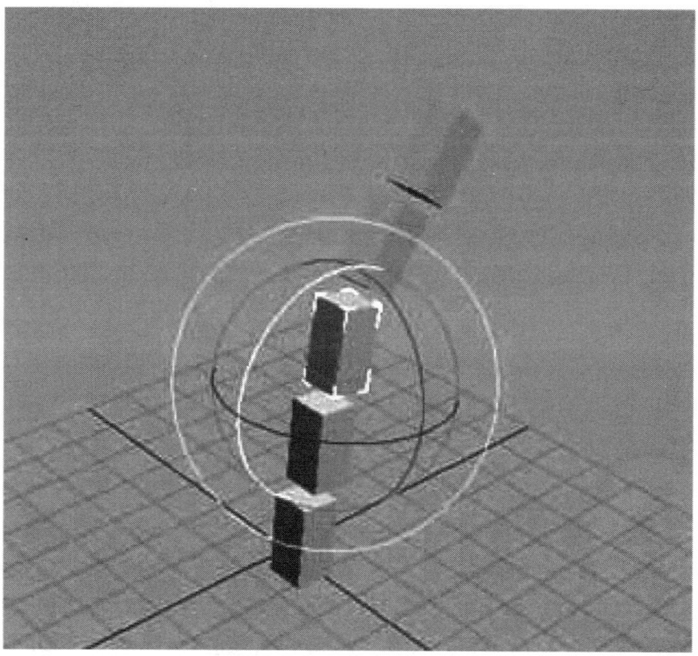

Figure 5.71: Linking Box Objects to Form a Hierarchy

If a single object is used, the hand cannot bend realistically. There are various methods of building this set of objects. You can create several box objects and place them on top of each other. This structure will enable the pivot points to work like a lever. The box objects are linked in a hierarchy so that moving the lower box moves the neighboring box. The bone system is pre-jointed and is a hierarchical linkage of bone objects that are already attached to each other based on the parent-child relationship. This tool is ideal for building a skeleton network. It supports the character model and provides motion.

A bone system combines several objects, helpers, controllers, and constraints to produce an object with a specific behavior.

5.2.1 Creating a Bone System

Define the process to create a bone system.

To create a bone system, you need to perform the following steps:

1. Launch 3ds max 6, go to the system panel, and click the **Bones** button. This activates the bone system, as shown in Figure 5.72.

Figure 5.72: Bone Creation Tool in the System Command Panel

2. Maximize the Front viewport, and click in the top-half of the viewport. This creates the root bone and any subsequent click at a different location creates an additional new bone as a child of the previous bone object.

By multiple clicks, a single bone chain is created, as shown in Figure 5.73.

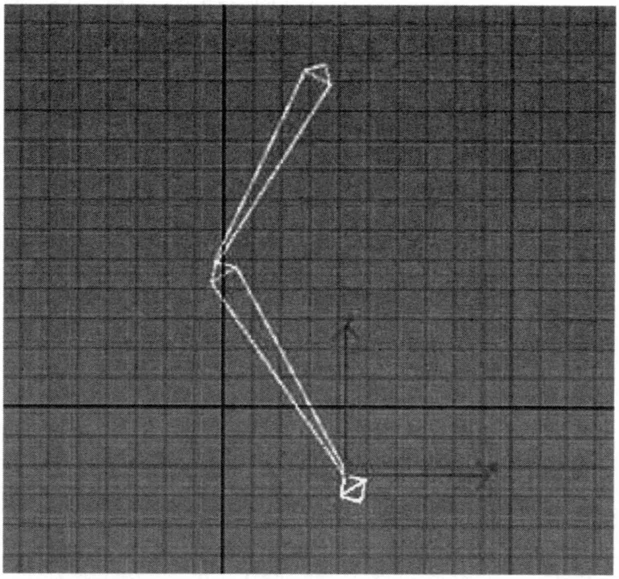

Figure 5.73: After the Bone Creation Process

3. Right-click to end the creation process. This will create a small bone object at the end of the hierarchy. This is required by the IK solver. However, if the IK solver is not required in a particular chain, this small bone can be deleted.

A solver applies the IK solution to the bone to translate a bone and its parents.

To modify the bone object, select a bone link from the hierarchy and go to the Modifier panel. Figure 5.74 shows the options of the bone system in the Modifier panel.

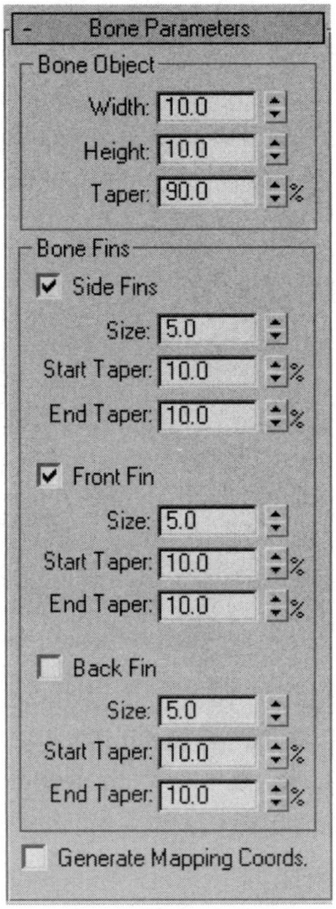

Figure 5.74: Modifier Panel of the Bone System

The various parameters of the bone have various functions, such as:

- Width: Sets the width of the bone object in the local z-axis. This provides volume to the bone skeleton. For a huge skeleton, this value can be increased to match the character mesh. The default value is 10.0.
- Height: Sets the height of the bone object along the local y-axis. By default, the height is 10.0. This value can be changed based on the mesh.
- Taper: Makes one end of the bone thinner than the other. It also helps determine the parent-child flow of the hierarchy. Setting this value to a positive number will reduce the scaling at one end. A negative value will enlarge the end. A taper value of 0 will shape the bone as a box.
- Fins: Add visual aids to a bone object. It is difficult to judge a bone's orientation without using fins. Fins can be added to the front, back, and sides of the bone

object. For example, when animating the tail of a dragon, fins show the actual rotational axis.

  - Side Fins: Adds a set of fins to both sides of the bone object
  - Back Fins: Adds a set of fins to the back of the bone object
  - Front Fins: Adds a set of fins at the front of the bone object
  - Size: Controls the size of individual fins
  - Start Taper: Sets the starting taper of the fins
  - End Taper: Sets the ending taper of the fins

- Generate Mapping Coords: Bones are renderable and also support texturing. This parameter creates mapping coordinates on the bone object to be used by textures.

The Character → Bone Tools menu contains more controls for bone objects.

5.2.2 Object as a Bone

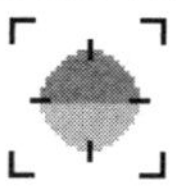

Define the use of an object as a bone.

In 3ds max 6, any object can be used like a bone and given all the properties of a standard bone object. This is possible because the IK solver is now not the sole property of the bone object and some of its functionality can be used on other objects.

The controls to use a standard object as are found in the Object Properties rollout of the Bone Tools panel under the Character menu, are shown in Figure 5.75.

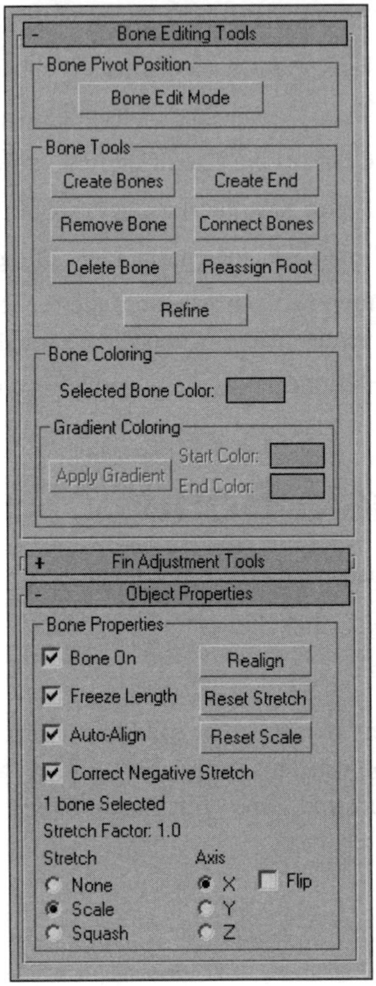

Figure 5.75: Object Property Dialog Box of the Bone Tools Panel

The functionality of different parameters is explained below:

- Bone On: Turning on this check box converts an object to a bone. It enables the user to display objects as bone links. To do this, go to the Link Display rollout of the Display panel and check the Display links option. Checking this option for all the objects will display the bone connections between them. If the Link Replaces Object option is checked, then the objects are totally replaced by non-renderable bone links. Turning it off will remove the bone properties from the object. For a standard bone object, this option is checked by default.

- Freeze Length: When this option is turned on, the bone object maintains its original length. When it is turned off, the length of the bone object varies due to the translation of the child bone that is next in hierarchy.
- Auto-Align: It automatically rotates the joint of the selected link to align with the next child links in the hierarchy. If this option is turned off for a particular link, translating the child links may distort the unchecked link.
- Stretch: This parameter determines the type of stretching that takes place on an object. None means no stretch is possible. The Scale option allows the object to scale on one axis. And the Squash option is an algorithm that makes an object fatter when the height is shortened and thinner as it gets longer. Checking this option will enable this operation on the bone behavior.
- Flip: Selecting this option flips the stretch along the selected axis.
- Axis: This option lets you select the axis base on which the stretching takes place.
- Correct Negative Stretch: This corrects the geometry when the object is stretched in the negative direction as a result of the translation of the next child link.
- Realign: This option realigns the multiple selected objects on a particular axis selected from the radio button below.
- Reset Stretch and Reset Scale: This option removes any stretch and scale changes from the link and brings it back to the initial value and position.

Practice Questions

1. State the importance of a hierarchy in character animation.
2. Give the functionality of the bone system in 3ds max.
3. Narrate the importance of Fins as a visual aid in the bone system.
4. Define the way an object is used as a bone.

Summary

- There are several modeling techniques, such as:
    - Polygonal models
    - Spline and Patch models
    - NURBS models
    - Sub-division modeling
- High-res and low-res models are two categories on which characters are built.
- Polygon models are used both for high-res and low-res models. They provide the most interactive and easy-to-use tool to model objects.
- Patch modeling is used to create smooth and organic shapes, which is difficult to achieve using Polygon modeling.
- Non-Uniform Rational B-Spline (NURBS) modeling is used to create models with complex organic shapes.
- Sub-division modeling is a global term that defines the process of dividing large polygons into smaller polys to provide more control to the modeler.
- Creating a model involves creating the torso, arms, legs, neck, body, and face.
- There are several modifiers used in character modeling, such as:
    - MeshSmooth
    - Symmetry
    - MultiRes
- The different character types are segmented and seamless.

References

- 3D Graphics and Animation: From Starting Up to Standing Out, Mark Giambruno, New Riders Publishing, 1997.
- http://www.3dcafe.com/asp/tutorials/maya/charactermodeling/charactermodeling.asp (February 10, 2004)
- http://www.3dtotal.com/team/Tutorials/benmathis/benmathis_1.asp (February 10, 2004)
- http://www.cgnetworks.com/story_custom.php?story_id=1429&page=1 (February 10, 2004)
- http://ligwww.epfl.ch/~thalmann/papers.dir/Computing.Surveys.pdf (February 10, 2004)
- http://www.evl.uic.edu/aej/527/lecture02.html (February 10, 2004)
- http://students.cec.wustl.edu/~cs453/lectures/18Animation.pdf (February 10, 2004)
- http://asifa.net/israel/pixelsandlead-part2.html (February 10, 2004)
- http://download.blender.org/documentation/html/x1485.html (February 10, 2004)
- http://www.learning-maya.com/rigging.php (February 10, 2004)
- http://www.steven-tubbrit.pwp.blueyonder.co.uk/Tutorials/Tutorial_04.htm (February 10, 2004)
- http://support.realityfactory.ca/tutorials/schade/bones_animation/ (February 10, 2004)
- http://www.cane-toad.com/tuteRig_Facial.htm (February 10, 2004)

Assignments

1. State whether the following sentences are True or False:
   a. The output medium is an important consideration while selecting a character modeling technique.
   b. High-resolution models are generally not used in commercials.
   c. The Lara Croft model in the Tomb Raider game is a sub-division model.
2. List the various character-modeling methods of 3ds max.
3. Why is NURBS a better method to create characters for films?
4. What are the functions of modifiers in 3ds max?
5. Fill in the blanks:
   a. The MeshSmooth modifier is used to ________ a low-res character to a _________.
   b. The two types of characters are ________ and seamless.
   c. The process of binding the bone hierarchy with the character mesh is called _______.

Lab Exercises

Exercise 1

Objective

- Modify a character model using the Symmetry modifier.
- Differentiate between the use of the Symmetry modifier and the Mirror tool.

Problem Statement

Modify a character model using the Symmetry modifier of 3ds max 6. The ch05_lab_ex1_model.max file, which is required to complete the exercise, is available in the student CD.

Lab Setup

3ds max 6

Procedure

To modify a character model using the Symmetry modifier, perform the following steps:

1. Open the **ch05_lab_ex1_model.max** file on the CD, as shown in Figure 5.76.

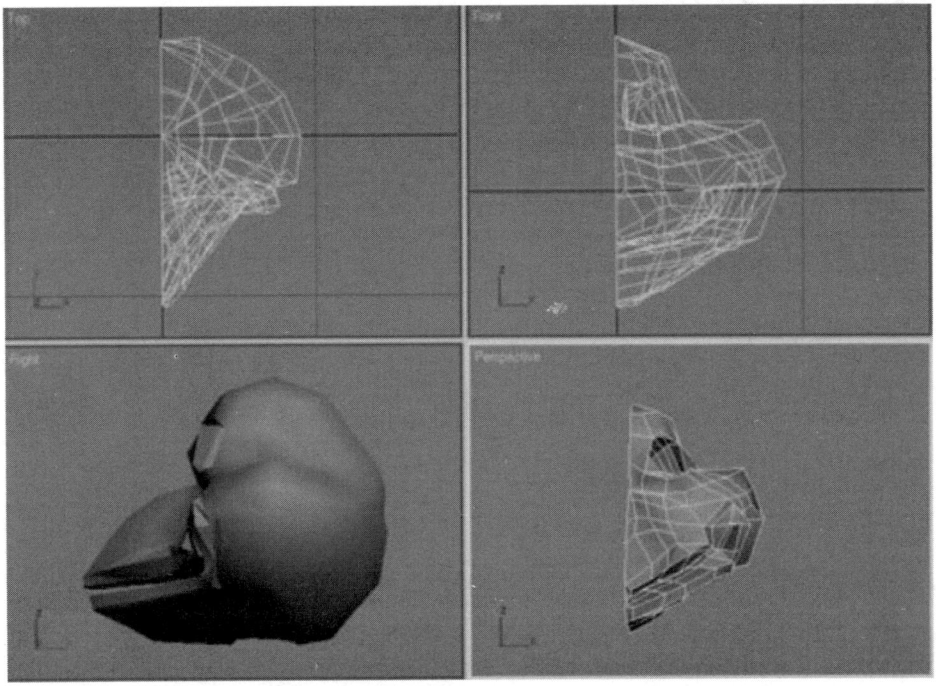

Figure 5.76: Ch05_lab_ex1_model.max File

Observe the model. It is the half head of a cartoon character created using the polygonal modeling method. Only the half portion is built because both sides of the head are the same and the other side can be replicated using a modeling technique like the Symmetry modifier.

2. Select the object named toonHeadLeftSide, go to the modifier list, and click the **Symmetry** option, as shown in Figure 5.77.

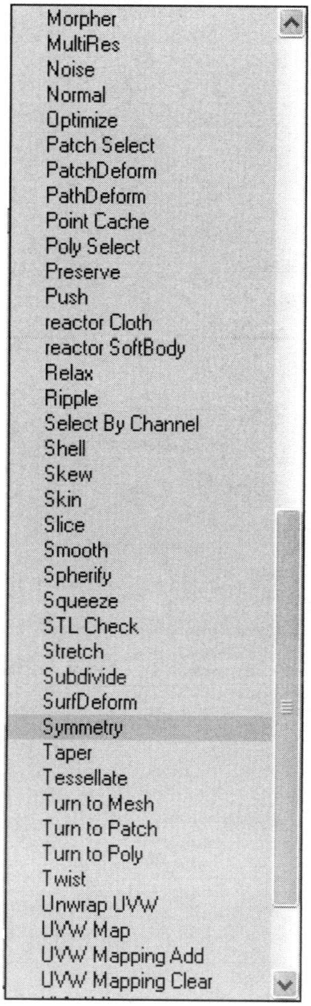

Figure 5.77: Selecting Symmetry from the Modifiers List

Now, you should get something like Figure 5.78 in your viewports.

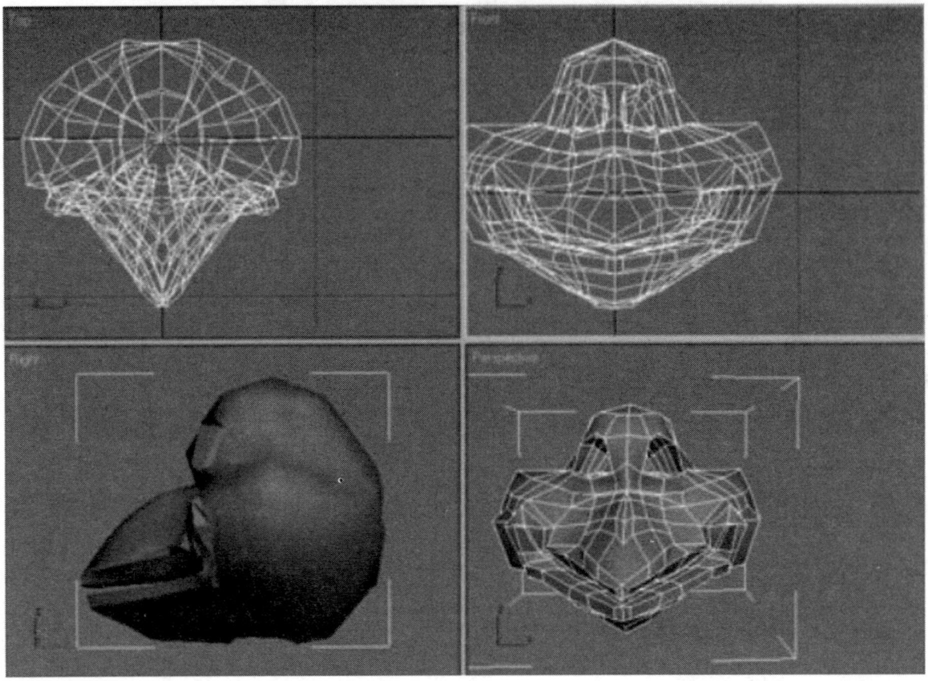

Figure 5.78: After Applying the Symmetry Modifier

The modifier creates an instance mirror copy of the model along the specified mirror axis, as shown in Figure 5.79.

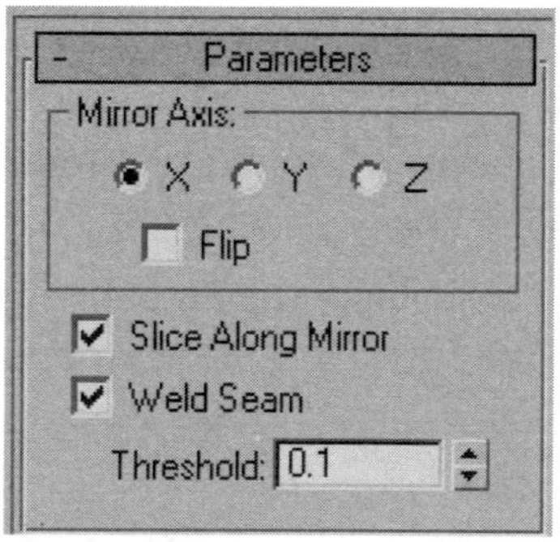

Figure 5.79: Symmetry Modifier Option Panel

3. Now, go to the Vertex sub object mode of Editable Mesh and keep the Show end result on/off button on. Refer to Figure 5.80.

Figure 5.80: Show End Result Toggle

Keeping this option on will display the changes made in the current mode after any modifier higher in the stack is applied.

4. Maximize the Perspective viewport, click a set of vertices, and move it on the x-y axis.

The vertices will be modified in the mirrored portion of the model also. This is what the Symmetry modifier does.

5. Finally, exit the subobject mode and go to the Mirror subobject of the modifier, as shown in Figure 5.81. Drag the Mirror gizmo along the x-axis, and see the result.

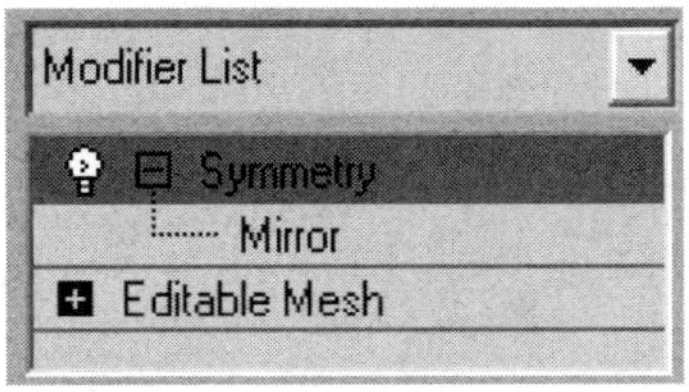

Figure 5.81: Mirror Subobject of the Symmetry Modifier

This will increase the distance between the two slices, as shown in Figure 5.82.

6. Undo the last step, and exit the sub object mode. Now, save the max file using a different file name.

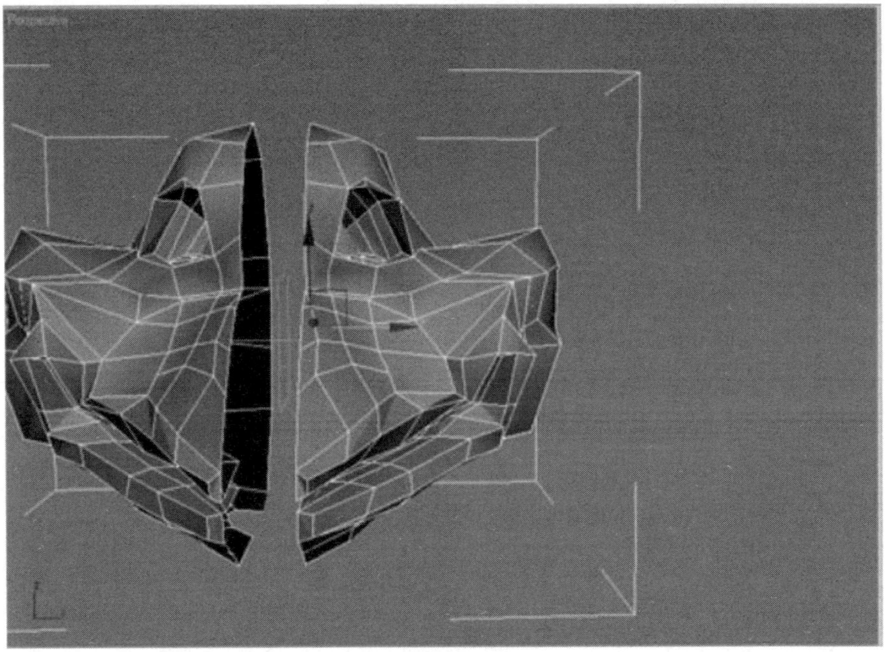

Figure 5.82: After the Mirror Gizmo Is Moved Along the X-Axis

7. Save the file as **ch05_lab_ex1_sol.max**.
8. Exit 3ds max 6.

Lab Activity Checklist

S. No.	Tasks	Completed	
		Yes	No
1.	Modified the character model using the Symmetry modifier		
2.	Identified the difference between the use of the Symmetry modifier and the Mirror tool		

Exercise 2

Objective

- Implement the MeshSmooth modifier in character modeling.

Problem Statement

Modify a character model using the MeshSmooth modifier of 3ds max 6. The ch05_lab_ex2_model.max file that is required to complete the exercise is available in the student CD.

Lab Setup

3ds max 6

Procedure

The steps for modifying a character using the MeshSmooth modifier are:

1. Open the **ch05_lab_ex2_model.max** from the CD, as shown in Figure 5.83.

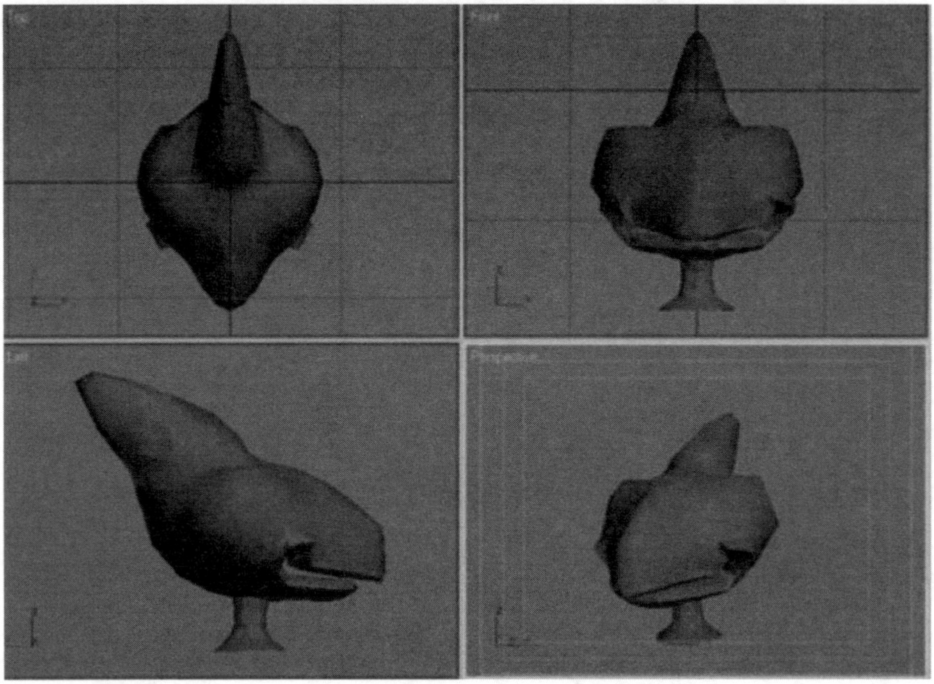

Figure 5.83: ch05_lab_ex2_model.max File Opened in the Viewport

This is the head of a character model. It is built using the polygon method, and you can see the faceted flat surface.

2. Press **F9** for a quick render, and you will see the rough edges of the mesh. Refer to Figure 5.84.

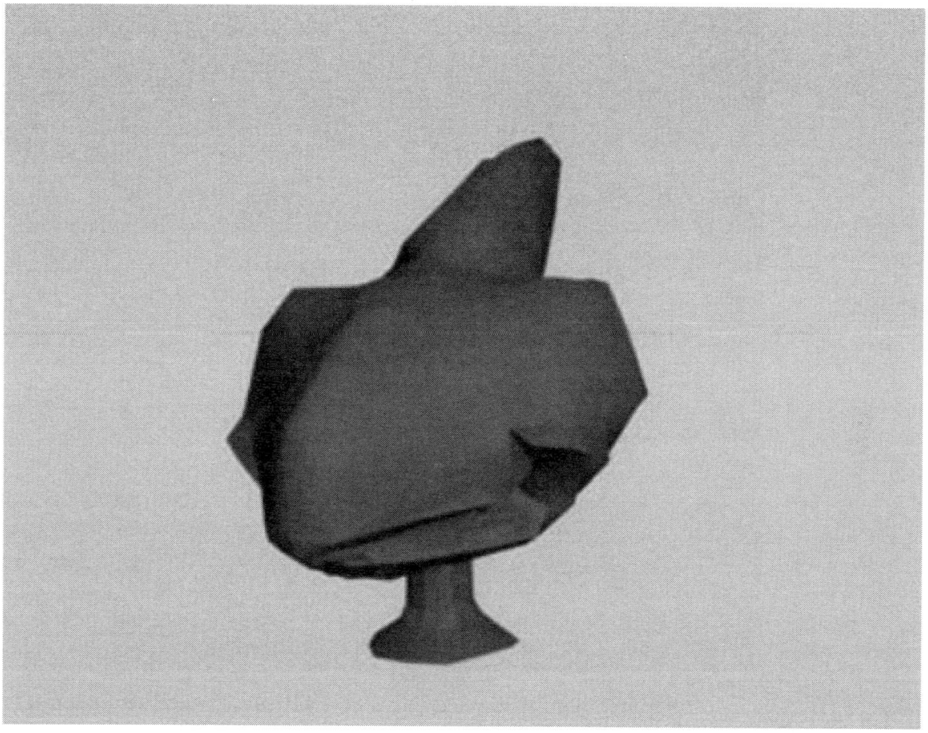

Figure 5.84: Rendered Without MeshSmooth

Now, the MeshSmooth modifier is applied to convert this low-res character to high-res.

3. Select the model, go to the modifier list, and click **MeshSmooth.** Press **F4** to display the edges in the viewport, as shown in Figure 5.85.

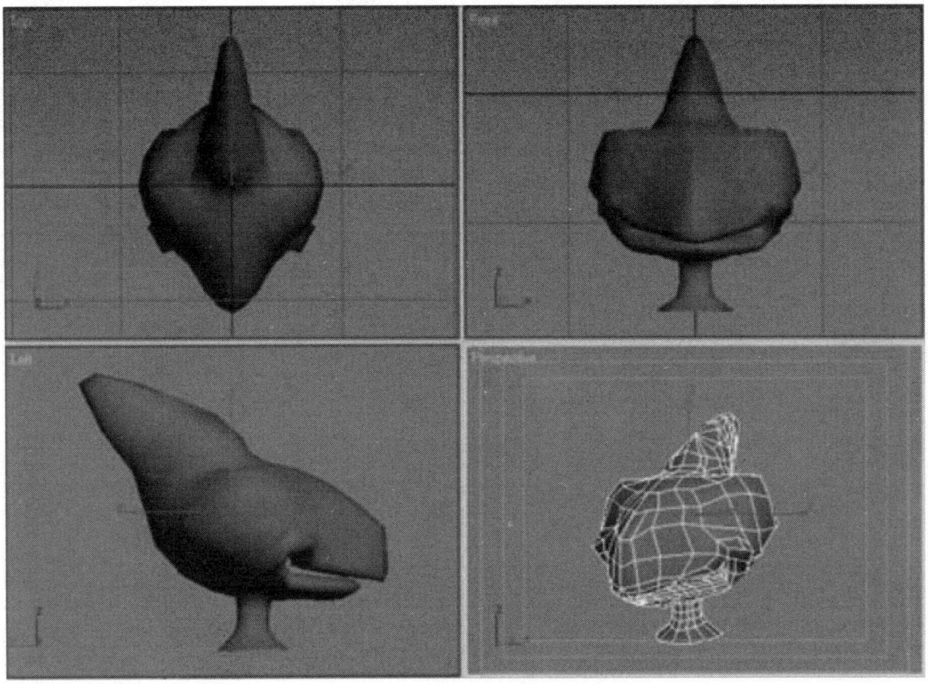

Figure 5.85: F4 Pressed to Display Edges After MeshSmooth Is Applied

4. Maximize the Perspective viewport and select NURMS from the Subdivision Method list, as shown in Figure 5.86.

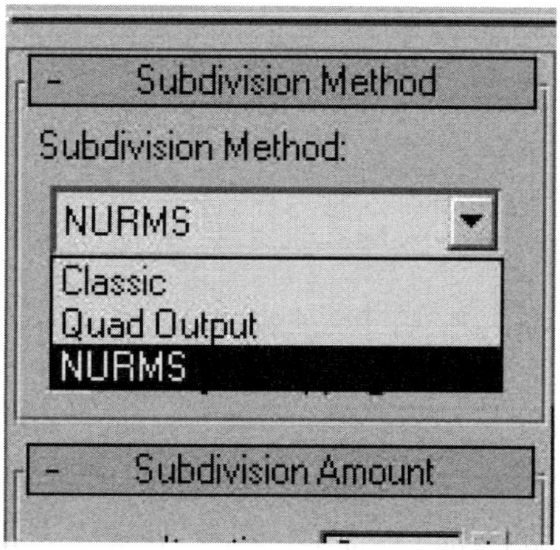

Figure 5.86: Subdivision Methods List

This will apply the NURMS algorithm of the subdivision method.

5. Now, under Subdivision Amount rollout, increase the Iterations spinner to 1, as shown in Figure 5.87.

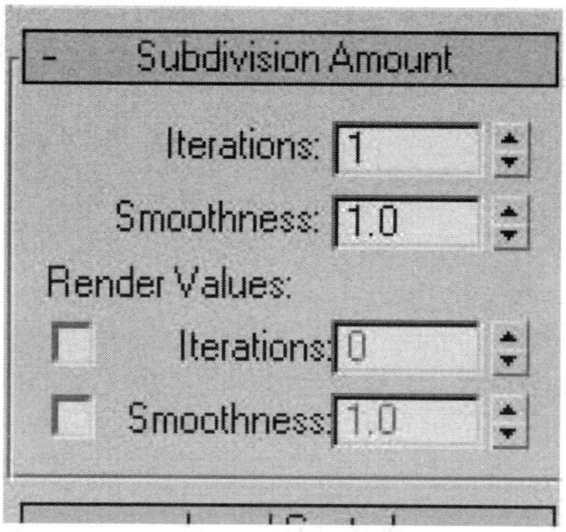

Figure 5.87: Iterations Spinner Under the Subdivision Amount Rollout

By default, the Iterations value remains at 0. Increasing the Iterations value will smoothen out the geometry by adding faces and edges in the sharp portions of the model.

Refer to Figure 5.88 to see the model before iterations is increased.

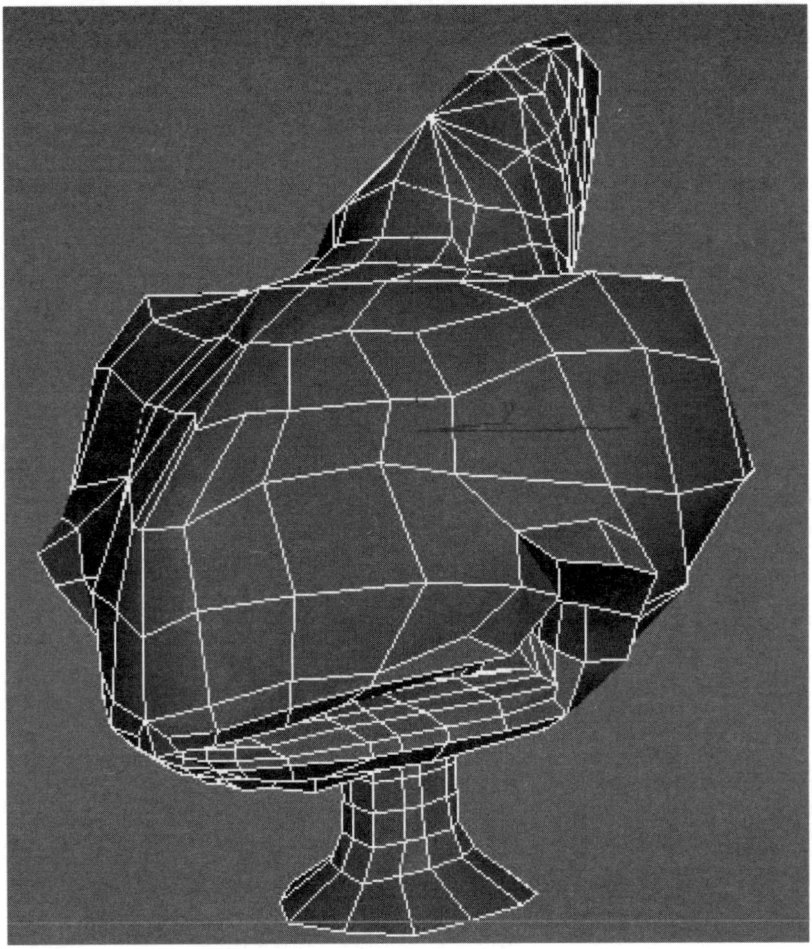

Figure 5.88: Before Iterations Is Applied

7. Refer to Figure 5.89 to see the smoothness in the surface of the model after iterations is applied.

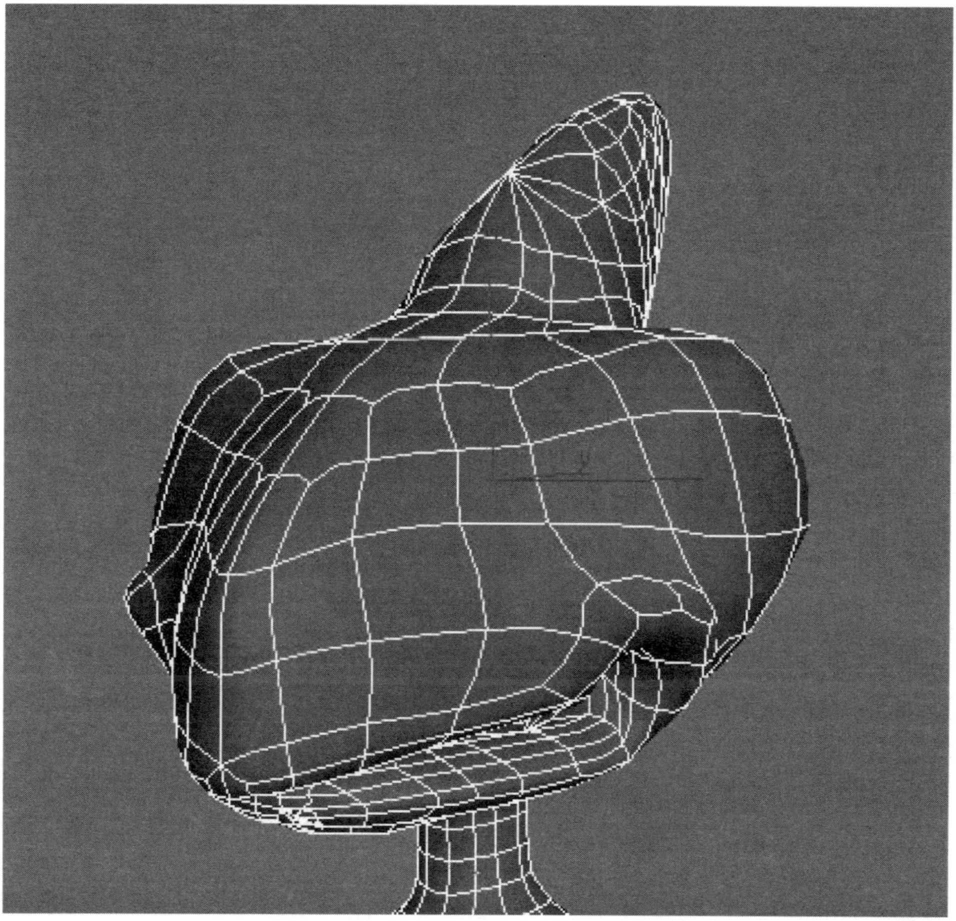

Figure 5.89: After Iterations Is Applied

8. In the Local Control rollout, click the Isoline Display option, as shown in Figure 5.90.

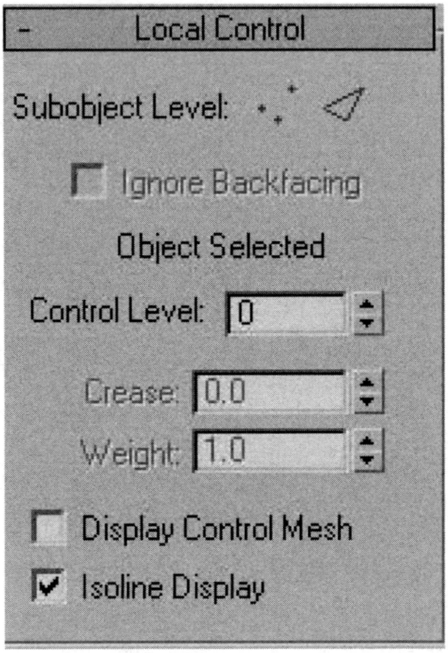

Figure 5.90: Local Control Rollout

This will show the newly created faces and edges, as shown in Figure 5.91.

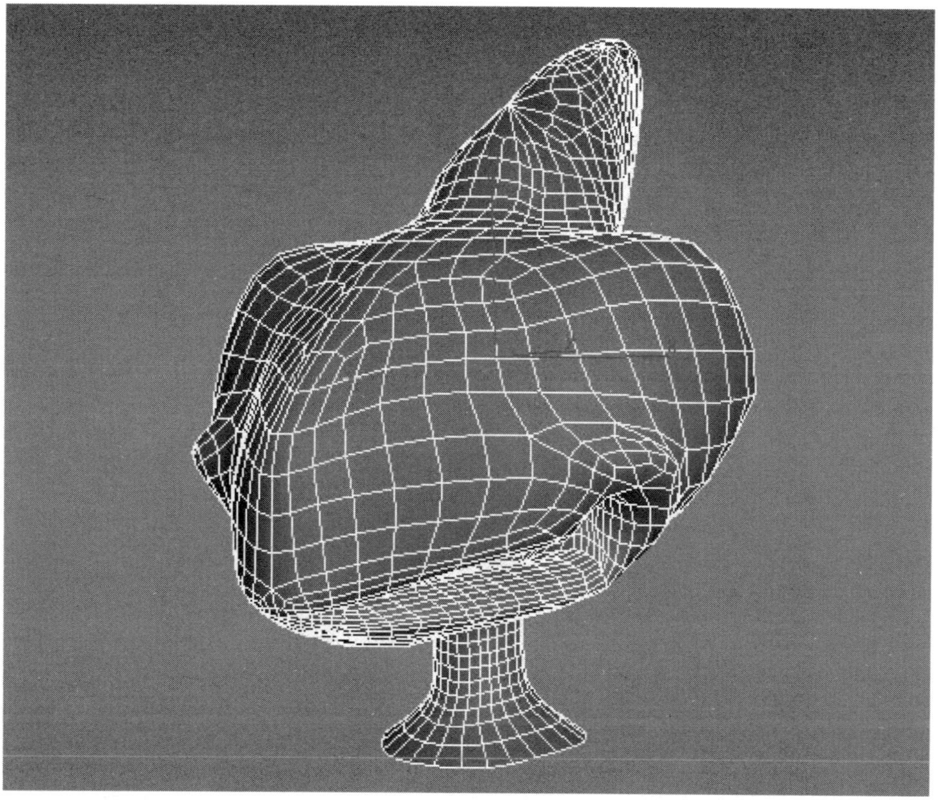

Figure 5.91: Newly Created Faces After Isoline Display Is Unchecked

9. Increase Iterations to 2. Render to see the effect in Figure 5.92.

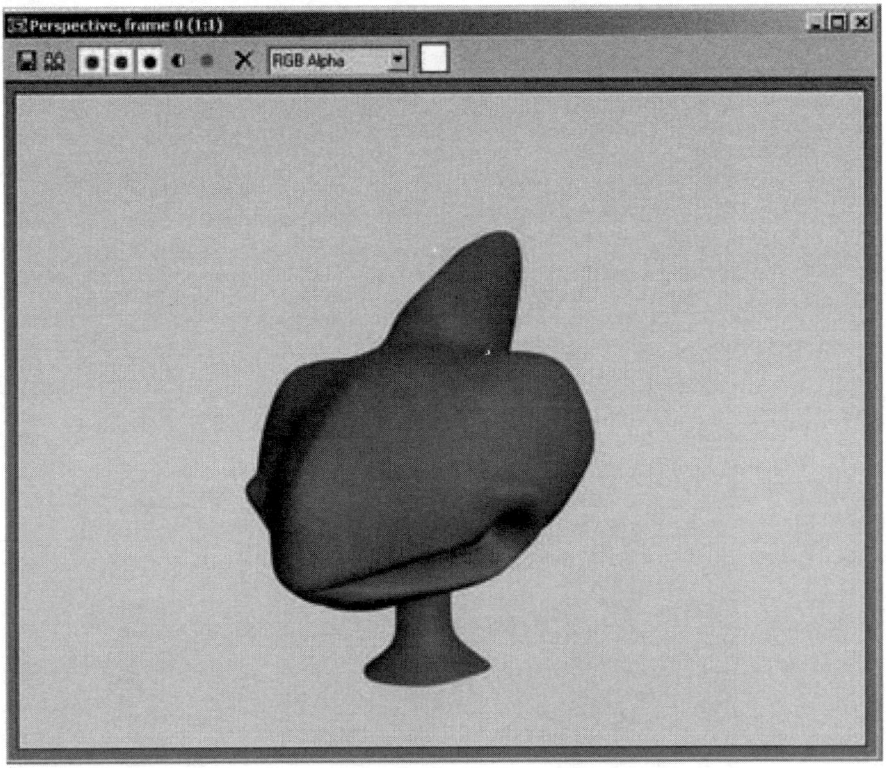

Figure 5.92: Rendered Image at Iterations 2

10. Go to the Vertex subobject level of MeshSmooth, as shown in Figure 5.93.

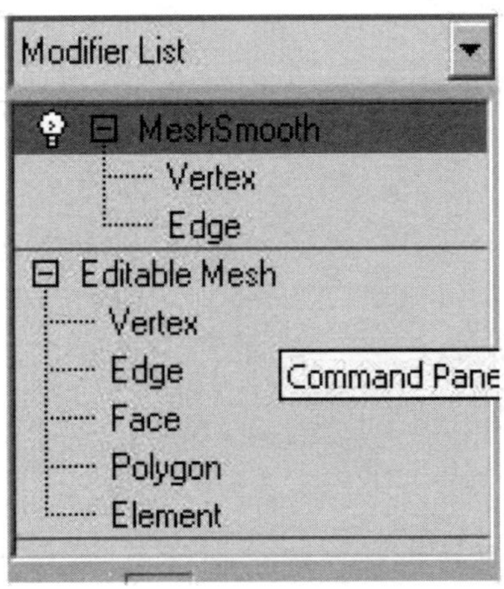

Figure 5.93: MeshSmooth Subobject Mode

11. Select a group of vertices and move them. Observe how smoothly the geometry surface changes, as shown in Figure 5.94.

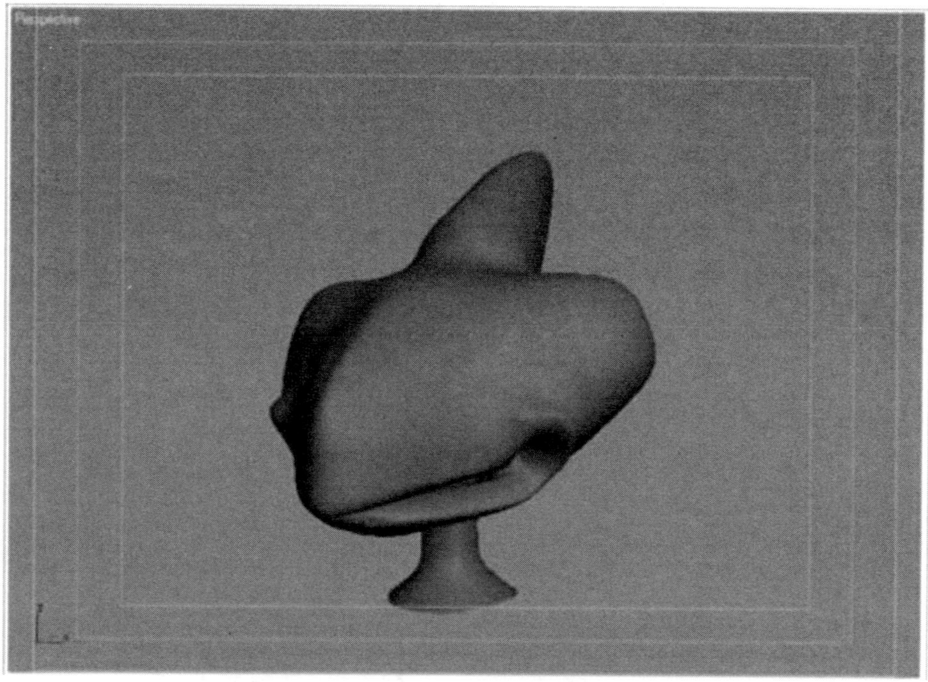

Figure 5.94: After the Vertices Are Tweaked

12. Exit the subobject mode, deselect the object, and press F4 to hide the edges in the viewport.
13. Save the file as **ch05_lab_ex2_sol.max**, and quit 3ds max 6.

Lab Activity Checklist

S. No.	Tasks	Completed	
		Yes	No
1.	Applied the Symmetry modifier to the character model to show how it helps model the symmetrical structure		
2.	Applied the MeshSmooth modifier to the character model to show how a low-res polygon model is converted to a high-res model		

Exercise 3

Objective

- Identify the importance of using modifiers in the character modeling process.
- Implement the MultiRes modifier in character modeling.
- Use the Polygon Counter utility to display object resolution.

Problem Statement

Modify a character model using the MultiRes modifier of 3ds max 6. The ch05_lab_ex3_model.max file that is required to complete the exercise is available in the student CD.

Lab Setup

3ds max 6

Procedure

To modify a character using MultiRes modifier, perform the following steps:

1. Open the **ch05_lab_ex3_model.max** file on the student CD. A medium-resolution head of a cartoon character is displayed in the viewport, as shown in Figure 5.95.

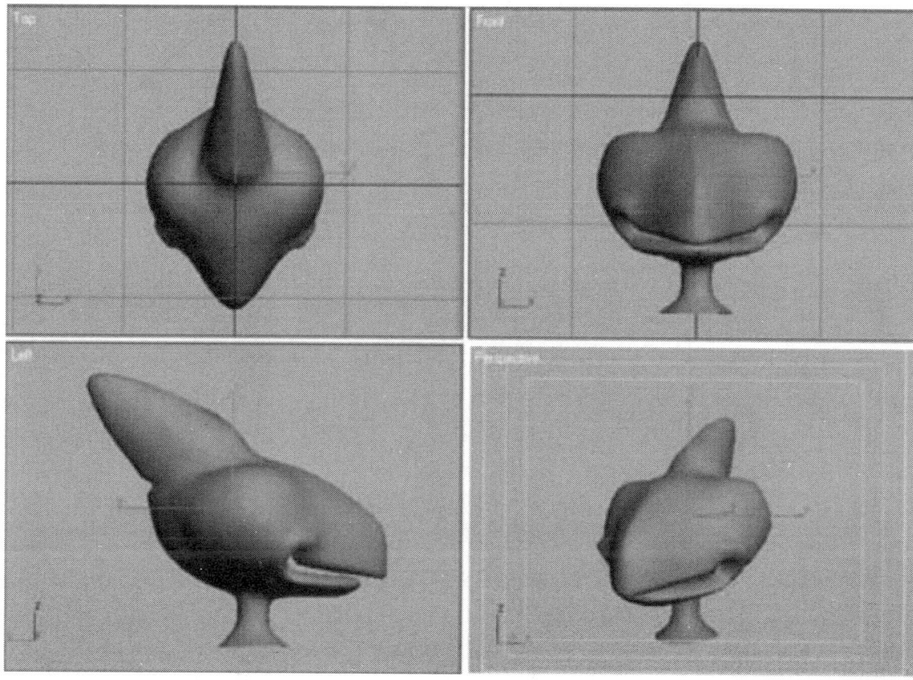

Figure 5.95: ch05_lab_ex3_model.max Opened in Viewport

Observe the model. It is a medium-resolution polygon model.

2. Maximize the Perspective viewport and press **F4** to see the edges of the model, as shown in Figure 5.96.

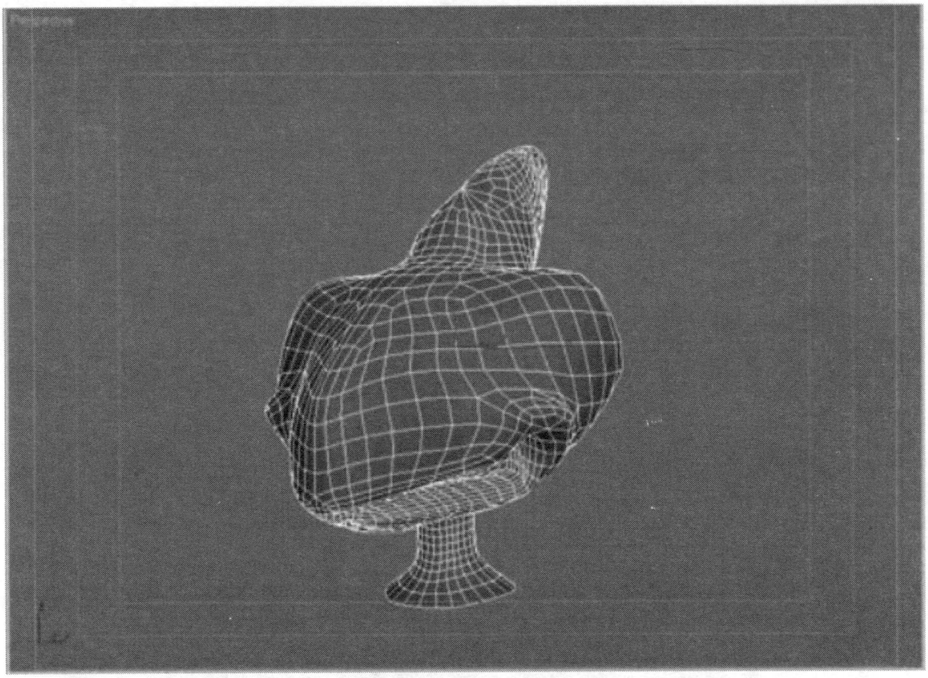

Figure 5.96: Displaying the Edges of the Model

3ds max 6 provides a utility that is used to display the polygon numbers of an object.

3. Go to the Utility panel located in the Command panel.

4. Click the **Configure Button Sets** button. This opens the Configure Button Sets dialog box, as shown in Figure 5.97.

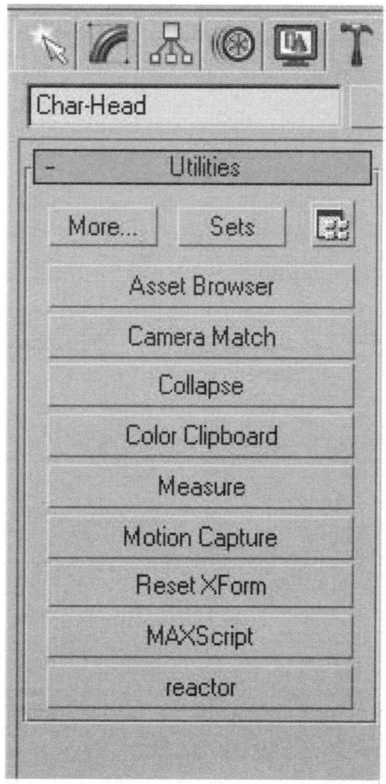

Figure 5.97: Utilities in the Utility Panel

5. Refer to Figure 5.98. In the left column, select and double-click the Polygon Counter. This replaces Asset Browser from the first slot on the right side.

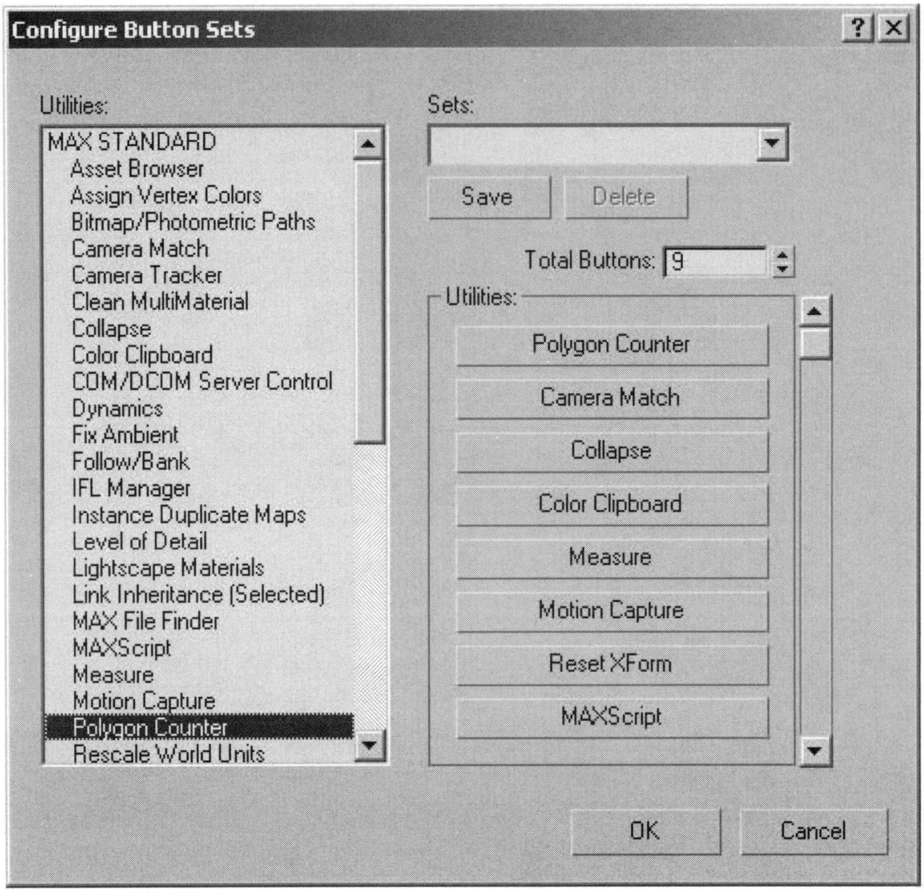

Figure 5.98: Configure Button Sets Dialog Box

6. Now, click **Polygon Counter** in the Utility panel. This opens the Polygon Count dialog box, as shown in Figure 5.99.

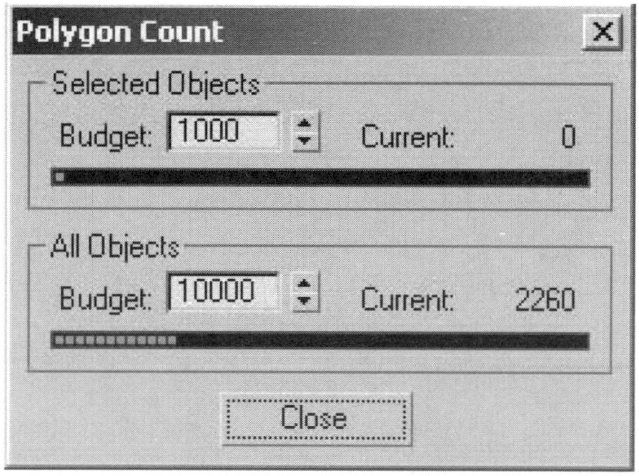

Figure 5.99: Polygon Count Dialog Box

7. Now, select the Char-Head object in the viewport. The Polygon Count dialog box is updated to display the number of polys in the object. Polygon Counter is a very important tool that is used to determine the object density. It shows the poly count of the selected object or a group of objects, as shown in Figure 5.100.

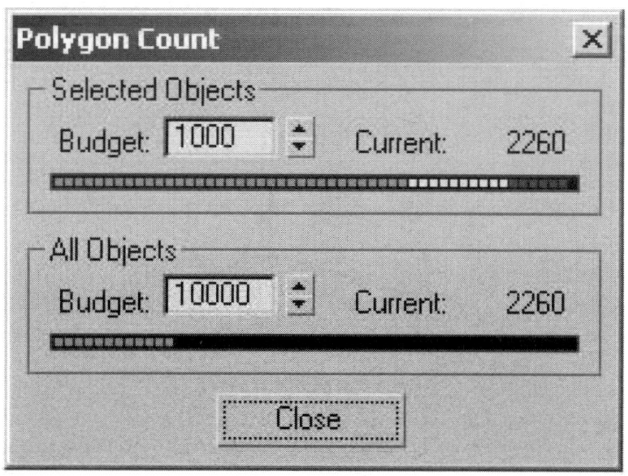

Figure 5.100: Displaying the Polygon Count for the Selected Object

8. Close the Polygon Count dialog box. Go to the Modifier panel and select the MultiRes modifier from the Modifier list, as shown in Figure 5.101.

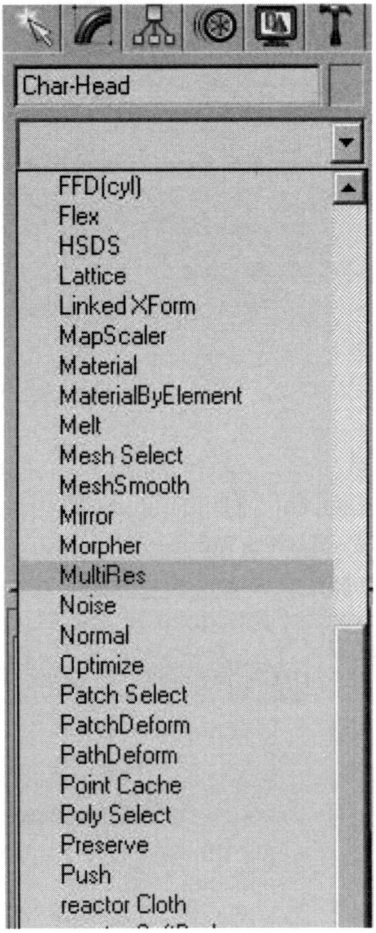

Figure 5.101: Selecting the MultiRes Modifier from the Modifier List

9. Next, click the **Generate** button under Generation Parameters, as shown in Figure 5.102.

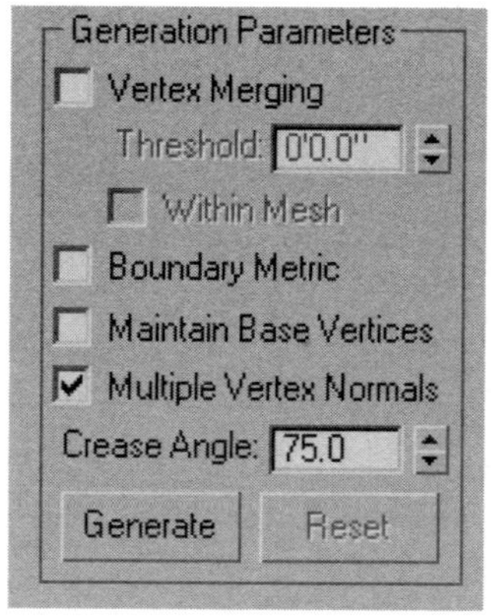

Figure 5.102: Generate Button in the MultiRes Panel

10. The object statistics are computed and displayed in the Resolution rollout, as shown in Figure 5.103.

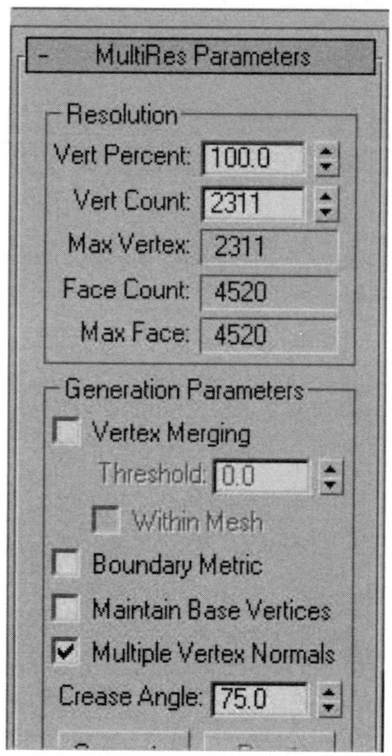

Figure 5.103: Displaying Vertices and Polygon Statistics

11. Using the Vert Percent parameters, you can reduce the number of vertices on the object. For example, if you specify 75 as the Vert Percent, 25 percent of the vertices are removed from the model, as shown in Figure 5.104.

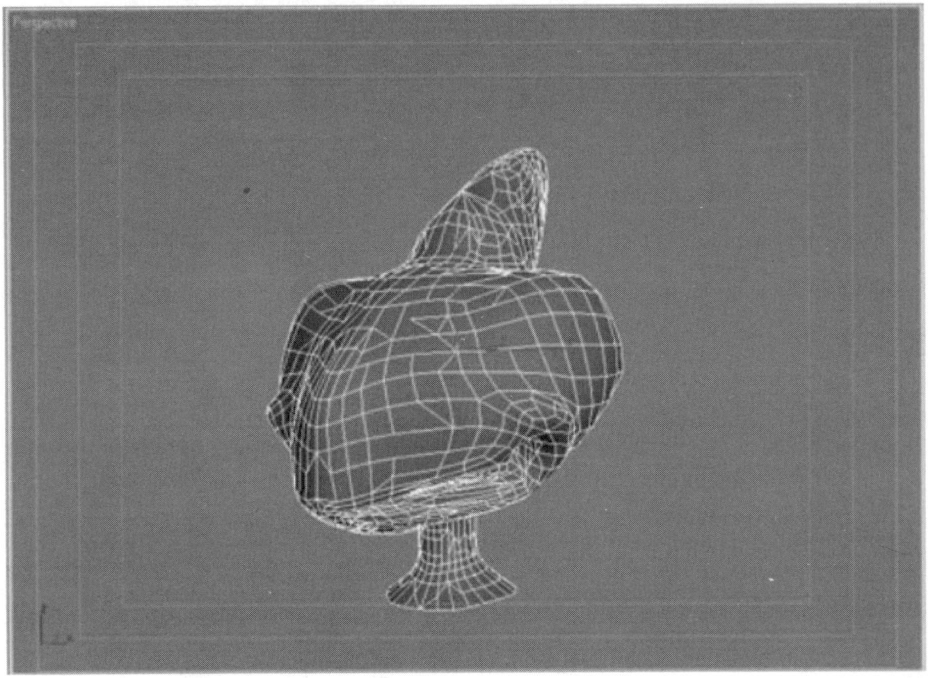

Figure 5.104: Specifying Vert Percent as 75

Now, the modifier automatically merges several edges of the model along its surface.

12. Change Vert Percent back to 100. The Vert Count spinner displays the number of vertices. Specify 1000 in the Vert Count spinner and notice the changes in the Vert. Percent spinner as a percentage of the total vertices is calculated. See Figure 5.105.

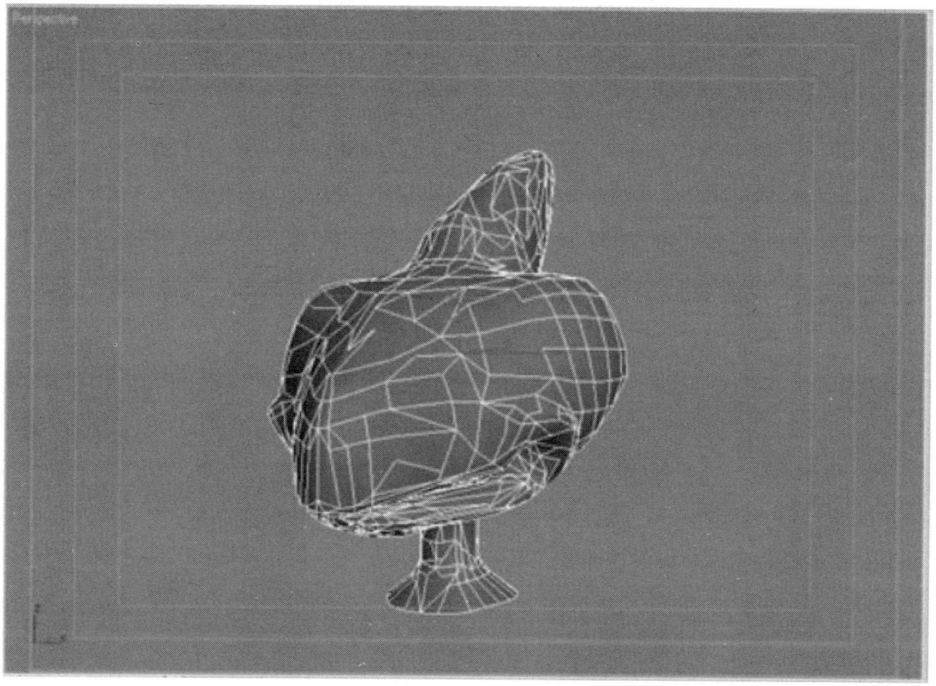

Figure 5.105: Reducing Vert Count to 1000

13. Reset the Vert Percent value to 100. Go to the Vertex subobject of MultiRes in the modifier stack, as shown in Figure 5.106.

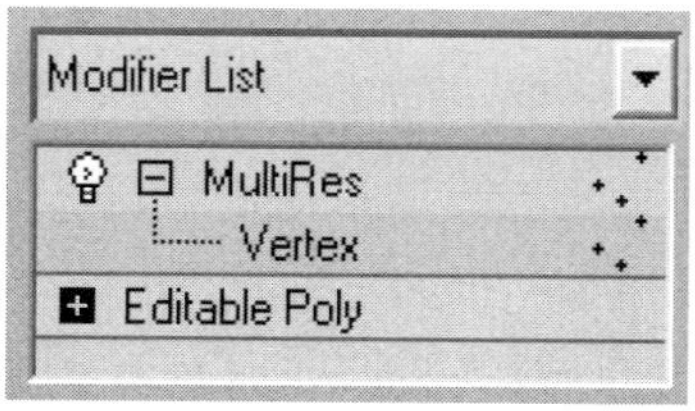

Figure 5.106: Vertex Subobject of the MultiRes Modifier

14. Select a few vertices from the top of the model, as shown in Figure 5.107.

Figure 5.107: Selecting a Few Vertices from the Top of the Head

15. Check the Maintain Base Vertices and Multiple Vertex Normals parameters and click the **Generate** button.

16. Now, reduce Vert Percent to 50. This does not affect the selected vertices initially.

The resolution affects only the non-selected areas of the object, as shown in Figure 5.108.

Figure 5.108: Unchanged Region of the Selected Vertices

17. Save the file as **ch05_lab_ex3_sol.max**.

Lab Activity Checklist

S. No.	Tasks	Completed	
		Yes	No
1.	Specified the Polygon count for the model		
2.	Applied the MultiRes modifier		
3.	Specified the various parameters		

Exercise 4

Objective

- Create a character face using the spline patch modeling method.

Problem Statement

Create a character model using the spline patch modeling method of 3ds max. The ch05_lab_ex4_model.max file required to complete the exercise is available in the student CD provided to you.

Lab Setup

3ds max 6

Procedure

To create the face of the character, perform the following steps:

1. Open the **ch05_lab_ex4_model.max** file from the student CD. You will get a spline outline of a character face, as displayed in Figure 5.109.

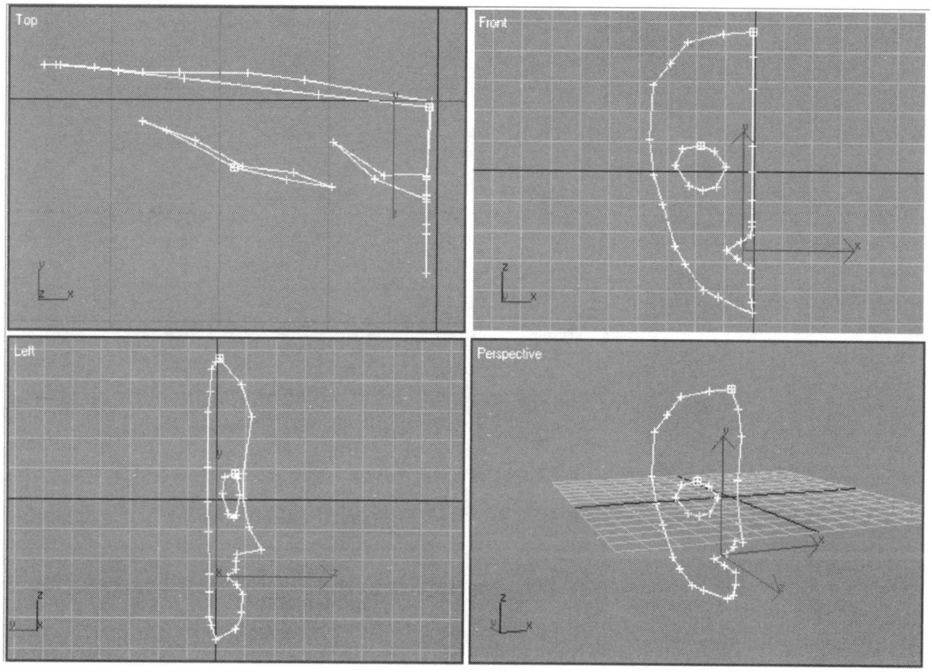

Figure 5.109: File Opened from the CD

2. You have to create the complete network of the face and apply a surface to the face. Observe the model from different views, and plan a proper and economic way of interconnecting the vertices without making the model too heavy.
3. Maximize the Perspective viewport. Find the snap toggle tool from the toolbar of 3ds max and click it to activate it.

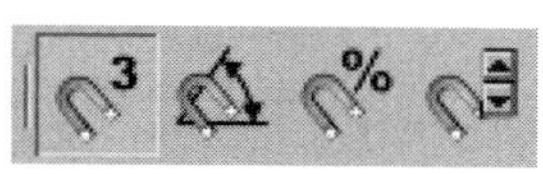

Figure 5.110: Snap Toggle Tool on the 3ds max Toolbar

4. Now, right-click on it to open the Grid and Snap Settings options, as shown in Figure 5.111.

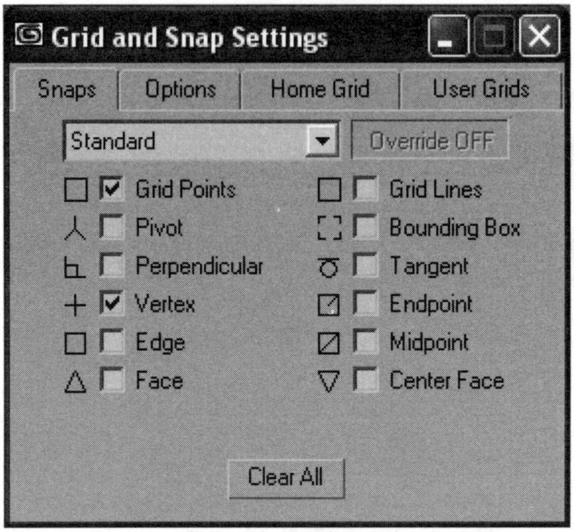

Figure 5.111: Grid and Snap Setting Options

5. Check the Vertex box, and set the Snap Strength value to 20 under the General rollout in the Option tab, as displayed in Figure 5.112.

Figure 5.112: Snap Strength Set to 20 Pixels

6. Select Create Line from the Geometry rollout of the line option from the Modifier panel, and move the cursor to the vertex at the corner of the eye. You will see a blue cross forming at the vertex, and it will snap the cursor to the vertex. Click to start creating a line, which will start from that corner vertex, as displayed in Figure 5.113.

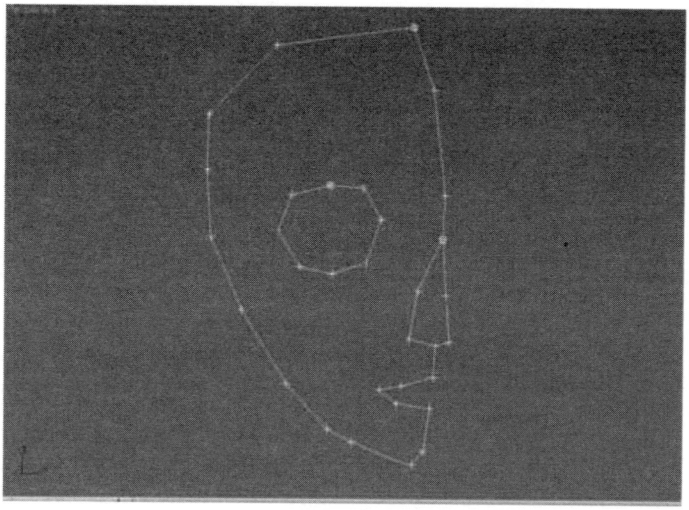

Figure 5.113: Vertex Selected and Cursor Snapped to Show the Vertex in Blue

7. Now, click on the vertex at the outer edge, as shown in Figure 5.114. A line is drawn between the two edges, thus connecting them. Right-click to end the process.

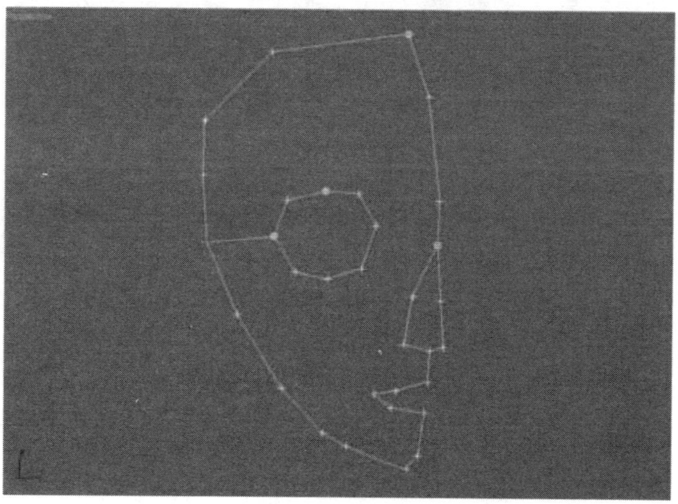

Figure 5.114: First Connection Made

8. In the same way, connect the following vertices, as shown in Figure 5.115.

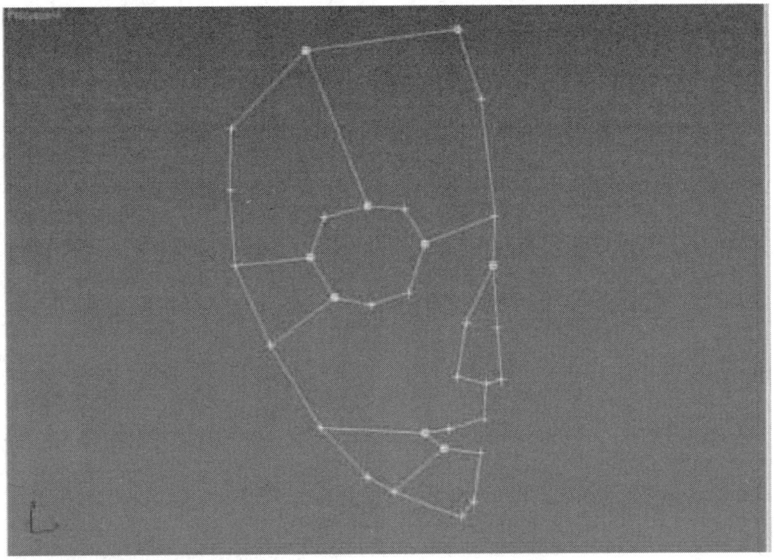

Figure 5.115: More Vertices Connected the Same Way

9. Create some vertices at the points shown in Figure 5.116.

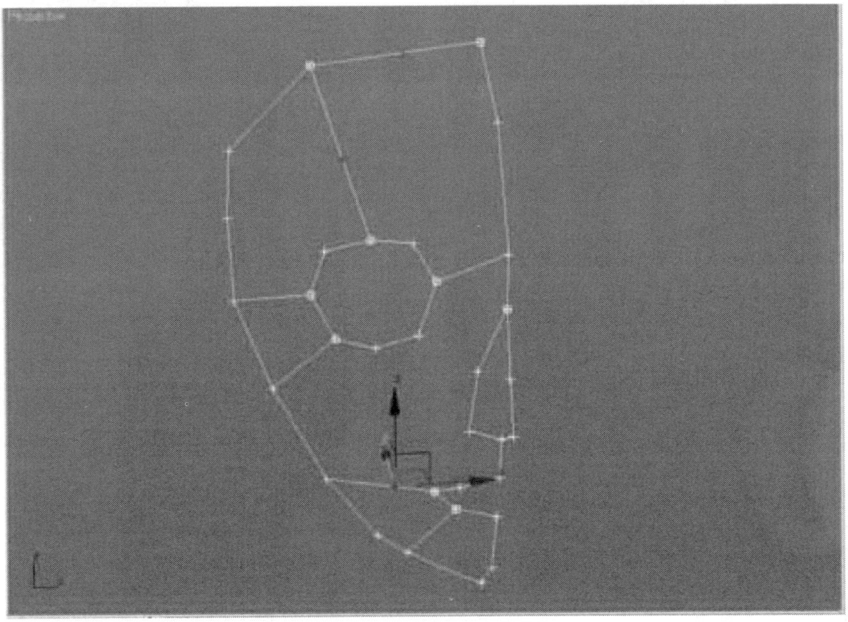

Figure 5.116: Newly Added Vertices Shown in Red

10. Connect them, as shown in Figure 5.117.

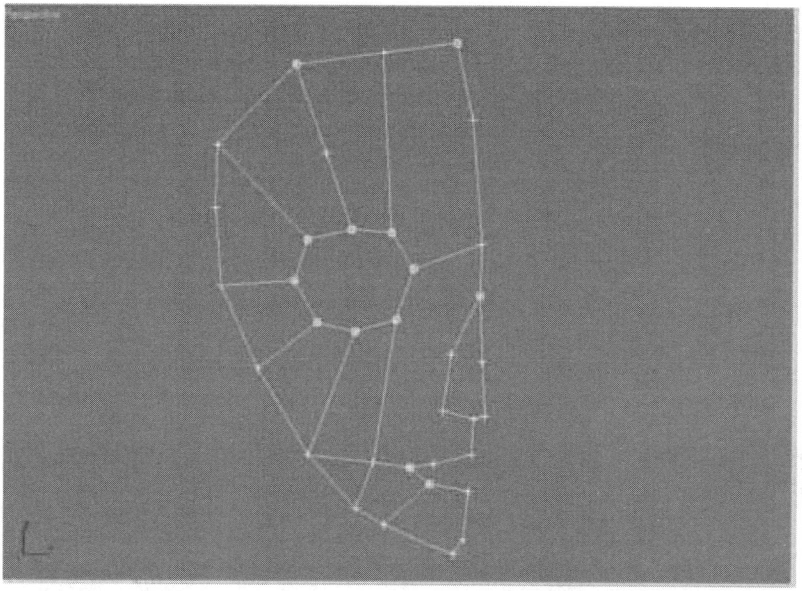

Figure 5.117: More Vertices Connected to Get the Basic Network

11. Zoom in to the eye region and select the segments from the Segment sub object, as shown in Figure 5.118.

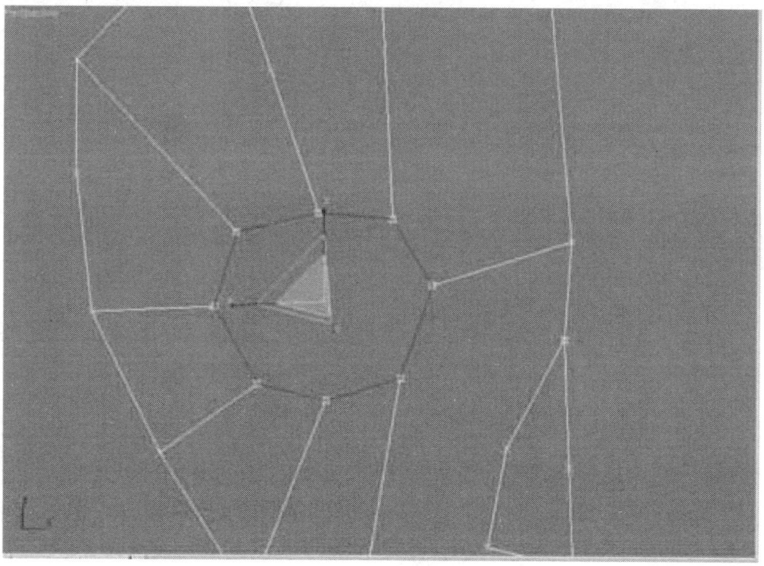

Figure 5.118: Segments Around the Eye Selected

12. Keeping the Shift key pressed, scale the segments to create a copy of the segments. This creates another segment ring around the eye, as shown in Figure 5.119.

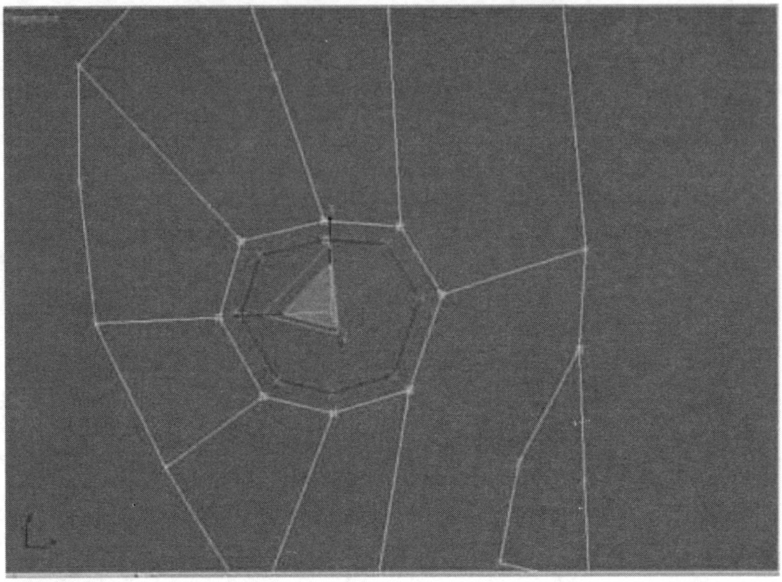

Figure 5.119: Segments Copied Using the Shift + Scale Method

13. Connect the vertices, as shown in Figure 5.120.

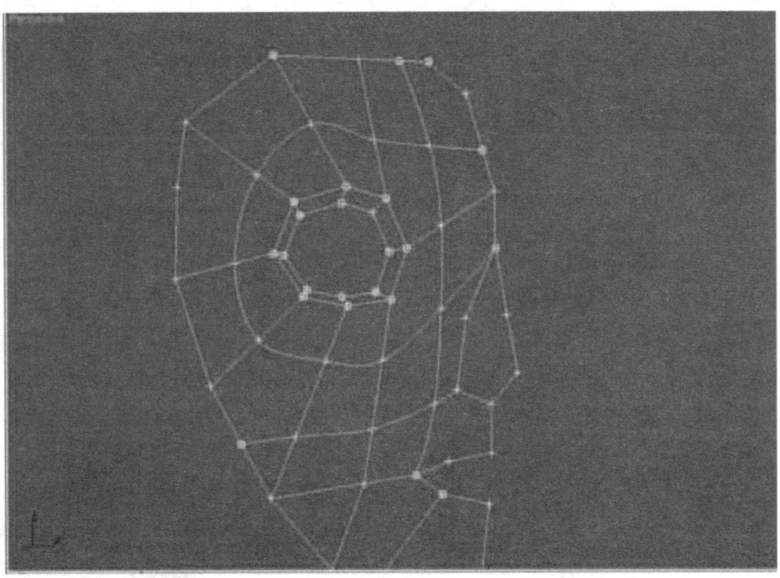

Figure 5.120: Vertices Connected to Make the Eye Socket More Prominent

14. Add more segments to increase the resolution of the model.
15. Refine the nose area and get the basic shapes, as shown in Figure 5.121.

Figure 5.121: Nose Area Refined

16. Assign the Surface modifier from the modifier list. This creates a surface based on the spline networks. But there are some gaps in the surface due to improper edges, as shown in Figure 5.122.

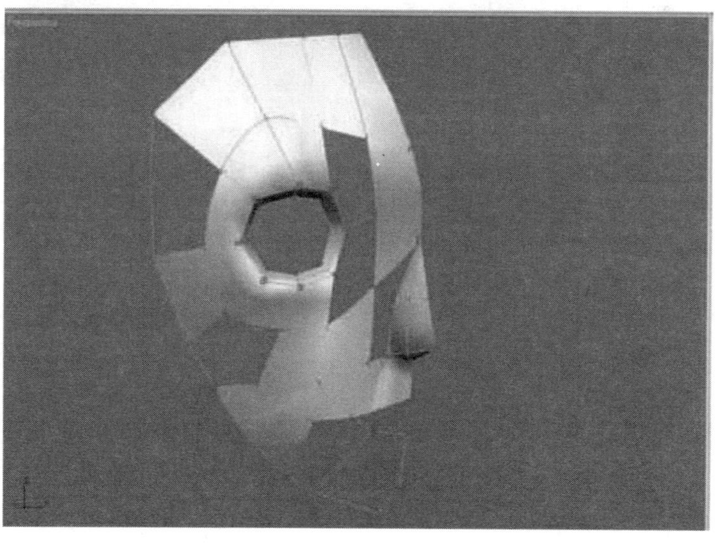

Figure 5.122: New Connections Made to Close the Gaps

17. Add more detail to the lips area, as shown in Figure 5.123.

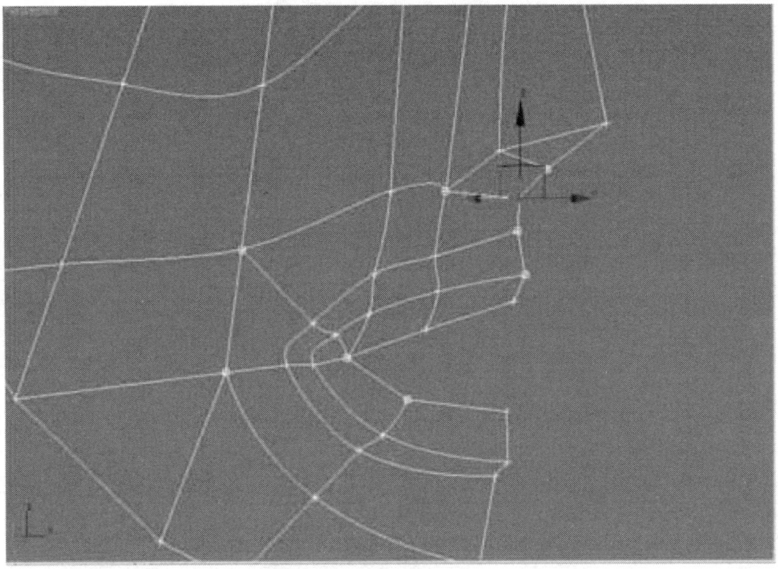

Figure 5.123: Resolution of the Lips Area Increased

18. Finally, adjust the vertices near the cheek and forehead to get a rounder look, as shown in Figure 5.124.

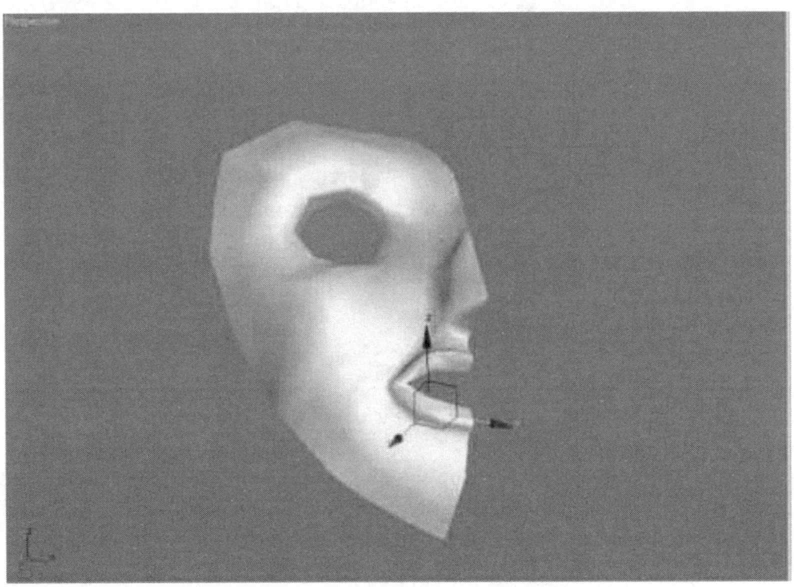

Figure 5.124: Cheek and Forehead Area Made Rounder

19. Finally, in the last step, make a copy of the face using the Mirror tool. Figure 5.125 shows the final model.

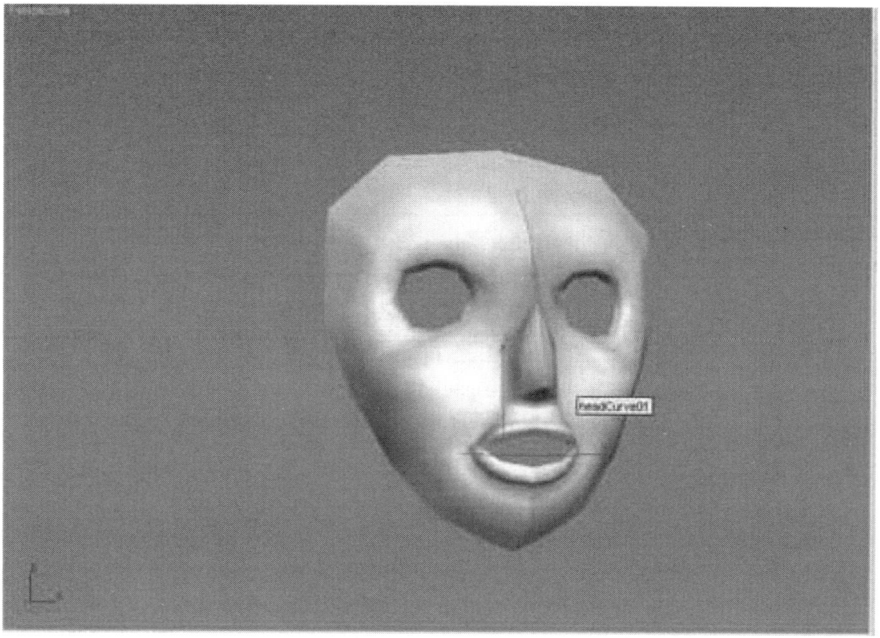

Figure 5.125: Final Face

20. Save the file as **ch05_lab_ex4_sol.max**.

Lab Activity Checklist

S. No.	Tasks	Completed	
		Yes	No
1.	Applied the Symmetry modifier to the character model to show how it helps to model a symmetrical structure		
2.	Applied the MeshSmooth modifier to the character model to show how a low-resolution polygon model is converted into a high-resolution model		
3.	Applied the MultiRes modifier to a character to show how it is used to reduce the resolution of an object		
4.	Modeled a character face using the spline patch modeling method		

Project

- Create a character model using the polygon modeling method of 3ds max 6.0.

Activities

- Create a basic head structure.
- Add details such as eyes, ears, and the mouth.
- Create the torso using a separate box.
- Extrude the arms and legs partly.
- Add fingers and toes.
- Save the file using characterProject.max.

Forward and Inverse Kinematics

6

After you link objects to form a hierarchy, you need to manipulate the hierarchy to depict movement or animation. You can manipulate a hierarchy with the help of kinematics. In 3ds max, kinematics governs the animation of a hierarchy. For example, in character animation all the parts of a hand move in coordination with the main arm. This coordinated movement is controlled by kinematics. At the end of this chapter, you will be able to:

Define the goals of Inverse and Forward Kinematics.

Apply end effectors.

Apply manipulator helpers.

Apply different types of IK solvers.

Animate a walk cycle.

6.1 Introducing Forward Kinematics

6.2 Introducing Inverse Kinematics

6.3 Types of IK Solvers

6.4 Walk Cycle

6.1 Introducing Forward Kinematics

When you create a tree of linked objects or bones, you create a hierarchy. For example, an arm has an upper arm, a forearm, a hand, and fingers attached as child objects. If you move the arm, all the child objects move accordingly. All the child objects share the properties of the parent. This movement is a result of kinematics. The following are the two types of kinematics:

- Forward Kinematics: When kinematics is applied from the top, the process is referred to as Forward Kinematics (FK). In FK, the movement of the selected parent object determines the movement of all the child objects under it.
- Inverse Kinematics: When kinematics is applied from the reverse direction, which is from the bottom to the top, it is referred to as Inverse Kinematics (IK). In this case, the selected child object determines the movement of all the parent objects above it in the hierarchical chain.

In this section, you will learn about the control and coordination of animation using FK. The hierarchy of an arm is the best example of FK.

6.1.1 Defining Forward Kinematics

Define Forward Kinematics.

In FK, when a parent object moves, its children must follow. If the child wants to move on its own, the parent remains static. For example, in a hierarchical linkage of a human figure, when the torso (the parent) bends over, the head (the child) moves along with it, but you can turn the head without affecting the torso.

Before applying FK to a set of objects, you must know the concept of hierarchical linkage.

Applying FK

To apply FK, you first link the two objects to create a parent-child relationship using the hierarchical panel. After the objects have been linked, you have to set the pivot points in the object. The pivot points help in providing a realistic motion to the various child and parent objects.

To apply pivot points, select the Pivot button in the hierarchy panel, as shown in Figure 6.1.

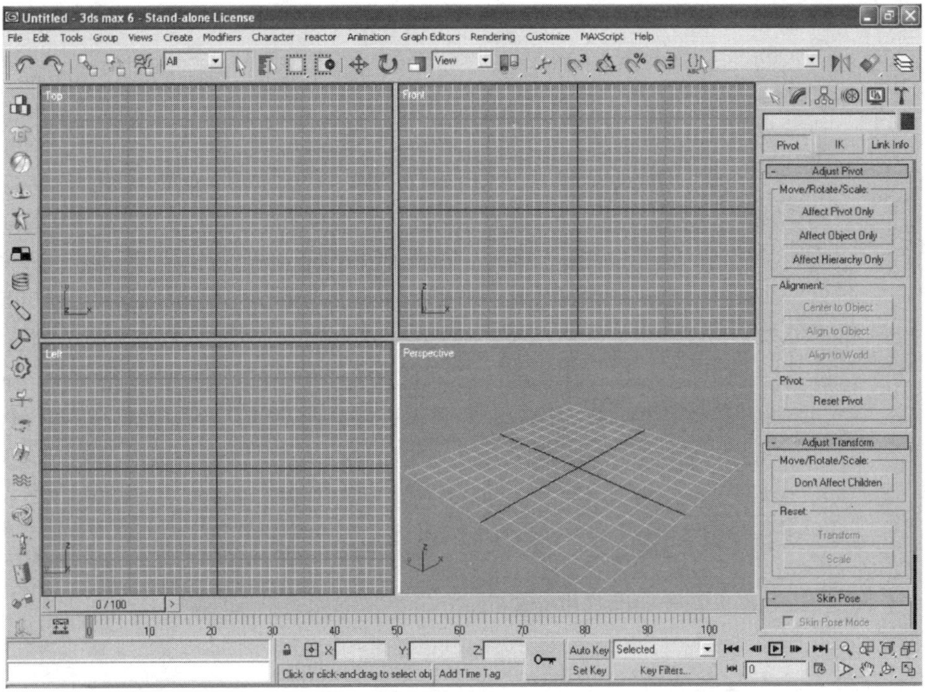

Figure 6.1: Hierarchy Panel

You use the pivot to:

- Set the rotation and the scaling point
- Set the location of a modifier center
- Define an object's relationship with its linked children
- Define the joint location for IK

The Adjust Pivot rollout buttons in the hierarchy panel can orient an object's pivot point. This has no effect on any child linked to that object.

Adjusting an object's pivot on any frame changes it for the entire animation. Use caution when adjusting the pivot of an animated object. Adjusting the pivot on one frame might produce unexpected results in another part of the animation. If possible, you should adjust the pivot point to the location you want before you start to animate.

The Pivot panel has three rollouts:

- Adjust Pivot rollout
- Adjust Transform rollout
- Skin Pose rollout

You cannot animate the functions under the Adjust Pivot rollout because adjusting an object's pivot on any frame changes the pivot for the entire animation. Figure 6.2 shows a pivot point positioned at the top of a sphere.

Figure 6.2: Pivot Point on a Sphere

You can reposition the pivot point to increase the flexibility of an object. To reposition an object's pivot point:

1. Select an object, and then turn on **Adjust Pivot rollout → Affect Pivot Only**.
2. Move or rotate the pivot.

You can also use Align, Normal align, and Align to view on the toolbar to align a pivot.

The Adjust Pivot interface has the following options, as shown in Figure 6.3.

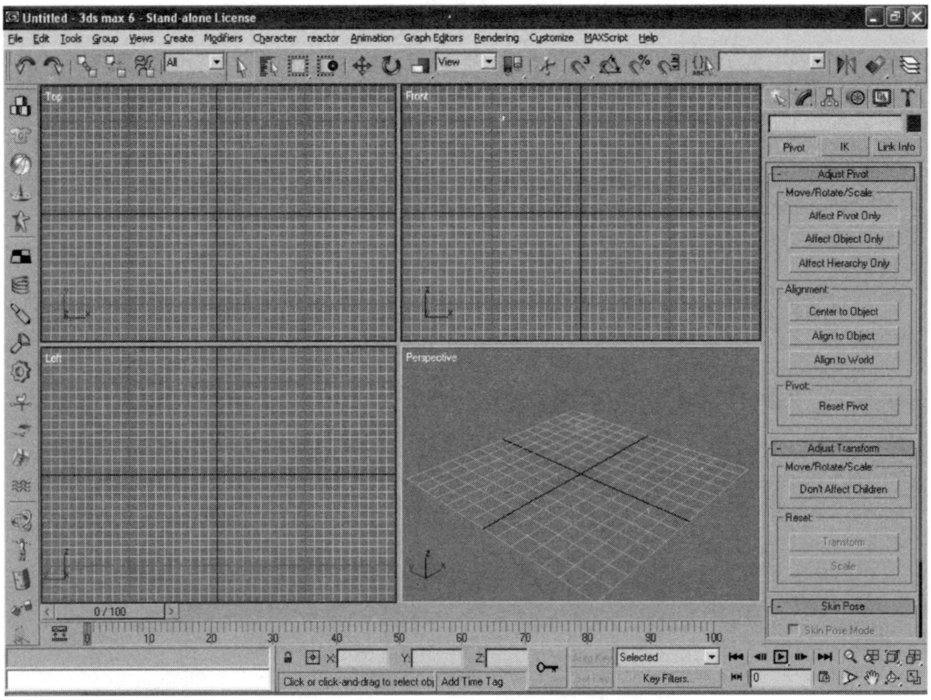

Figure 6.3: Options on the Adjust Pivot Interface

- Move/Rotate/Scale group: Each of the buttons in the Move/Rotate/Scale group box is highlighted when active. This determines the part of the object affected by the three buttons in the Alignment area, as well as the Transform and Align commands on the Main toolbar.
- This group has the following sub options:
  - Affect Pivot Only: Affects only the pivot points of the selected objects.
  - Affect Object Only: Affects only the selected objects and not the pivot points.
  - Affect Hierarchy Only: Affects only the Rotation and Scale tools. It applies the rotation or scale to the hierarchy by rotating or scaling the position of the pivot point without rotating or scaling the pivot point itself.

- Alignment group: The effect of these buttons depends on whether you chose Affect Pivot Only or Affect Object Only. They do not apply to Affect Hierarchy Only.
    - Center to Object: Moves the pivot to the center of its object.
    - Align to Object: Rotates the pivot to align with the object's transformation matrix axes.
    - Align to World: Rotates the pivot to align with the world coordinate axes.
- If you chose Affect Object Only, the buttons work as follows:
    - Center to Pivot: Moves the center of the object to its pivot location.
    - Align to Pivot: Rotates the object to align its transformation matrix axes with the pivot.
    - Align to World: Rotates the object to align its transformation matrix axes with the world coordinate axes.

The Affect Hierarchy Only button is rarely used.

- Pivot group: Consists of the Reset Pivot button which resets the pivot point to the position and orientation it held when the object was first created. This is not affected by the state of the Affect Pivot Only and Affect Object Only buttons.

Practice Questions

1. What is meant by Forward Kinematics?
2. Explain the use of pivot.
3. What is the impact of adjusting an object's pivot?
4. List the rollouts available in the pivot panel.

6.2 Introducing Inverse Kinematics

FK involves transforming linked hierarchies. Whenever you move, rotate, or scale a linked hierarchy, the children move with the parent, but the child object can be transformed independent of its parent. In FK, the inheritance feature passes on the transformations from the parent object to its child objects, depending on their relationship in the hierarchy. FK governs the animation of a hierarchy in a default manner. However, IK enables a child object to control its parent object. So, in IK, you can drag the hand to the exact position and the other parts will follow.

For example, consider a tree with branches and leaves. In FK, if the bark of the tree is moved, the branches and the leaves move along with it. But, in the case of IK, if you move the leaves, the branches and the bark move with the leaves.

The built-in bones of 3ds max are a system of Helper objects that are linked hierarchically. Kinematics animation is the term used when you animate objects that are linked in a hierarchy by using rotation to pose them. If you use real-time IK, you need to use bones because real-time IK is implemented as a controller assigned to the bones at certain times.

IK provides a quick and easy way to create animations. You need to define the goal of an action by positioning the end effectors of an articulated chain and then 3ds max calculates how to position the rest of the chain to reach the goal.

In this section, you will study the goals of IK and how to display IK controls. You will study the use of end effectors, manipulator helpers, joint constraints, and IK solutions.

6.2.1 Applying Inverse Kinematics

Define the goals of Inverse Kinematics goals.

IK uses a goal-directed method in which the animator positions a child object and 3ds max calculates the position and orientation of the parent objects. The final position of the hierarchy after all the calculations have been solved is referred to as the IK solution.

The IK Display Options rollouts can enable, disable, and set the size of the gizmos used when working with IK solvers. Using this rollout, you can enable the end effector, the goal, the swivel angle manipulator, and the IK solver.

The IK system is a very powerful animation tool. You use this tool to animate the position of an IK goal, which, in turn, controls the rotation of an entire hierarchy of objects. You can also make the goal follow the last object in a hierarchy when the object's rotations are animated.

The IK goal is the procedure that controls all the bones linked in a hierarchy. It is a history-independent (HI) system. Instead of rotating the joints of an object to make a pose, the joints are posed by positioning a lower bone in the chain, causing the upper bones to rotate.

For example, to pose the arm of a puppet, you would grab and move its wrist instead of rotating first the chest, then the shoulder and the upper arm. You also use IK to fix the chain's end to an object moving relative to it.

IK is used for goal-driven animation.

IK Solver Plane Group

The IK Solver rollout has the following properties:

- Swivel Angle: Controls the solver plane that determines the direction of the knee or the elbow in a human limb. You can manipulate the swivel angle in the viewport by turning on Swivel Angle Display in the Display Options rollout and then turning on the Manipulate mode. When the swivel angle manipulator is displayed in the viewport, you can interactively animate the handle to animate the solver plane.
- Pick Target: Enables you to select another object to use to animate the swivel angle.
- Use: Turns the use of the target on and off.
- Parent Space: Defines the space the swivel angle is relative to. You need to use this on chains with multiple solvers, so that the swivel angle manipulations on one chain do not affect another.
- IK Goal: Defines the swivel angle parent space relative to the IK goal.
- Start Joint: Defines the swivel angle parent space relative to the start joint.

Figure 6.4 shows the IK Solver rollout properties.

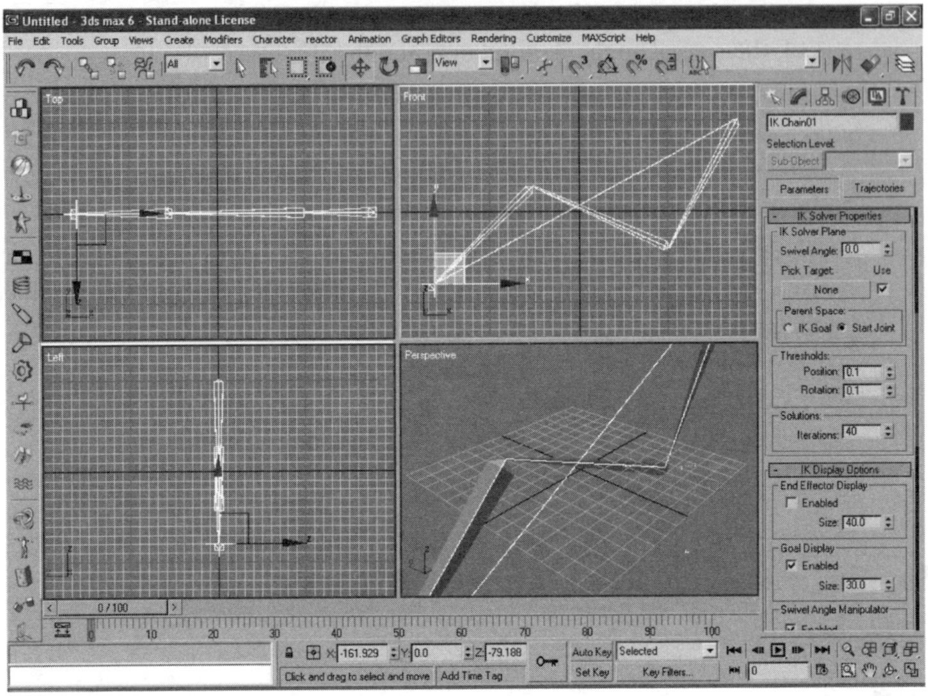

Figure 6.4: Solver Rollout Properties

You need to pin the IK structure to animate follow objects in applied IK. When an object is pinned, you need to select any object in your kinematics chain and click the Apply IK button. 3ds max then calculates the IK solution for each frame of the animation and places transform keys for every object in the IK chain.

6.2.2 Displaying IK Controls

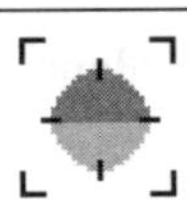

Display IK controls.

After the creation of a bones hierarchy, you can enable, disable, or set the size of the gizmos used when working with IK solvers. You need to use the IK Display Options rollout to enable or disable the End Effector, Goal, Swivel Angle Manipulator, and IK Solver components. All these components help in the application of IK. The end effectors control the movement of the entire chain in IK. Manipulator helpers help in the creation of the characters in the character animation. Figure 6.5 shows the IK Display Options rollout.

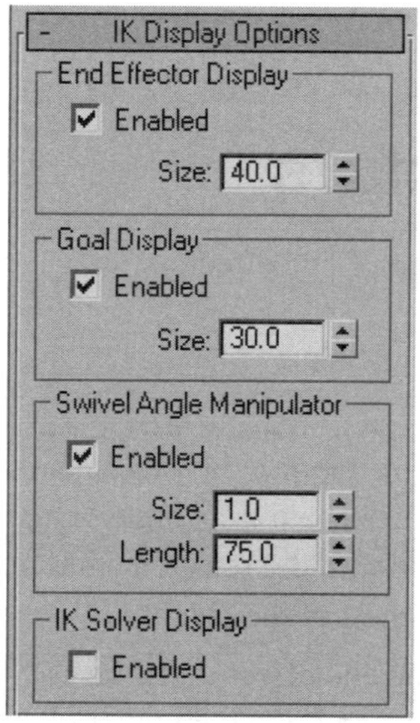

Figure 6.5: IK Display Options Rollout

The IK Display Options rollout has the following properties:

- End Effector Display group: Controls the appearance of the end effectors in the IK chain. It is turned off by default. This group has the following options:
  - Enabled: Turns the display of the end effectors on or off
  - Size: Controls the size of the end effector gizmo in the viewport
- Goal Display group: Controls the appearance of the goals in the IK chain. It is on by default. This group has the following options:
  - Enabled: Turns the display of goals on or off
  - Size: Controls the size of the goal gizmo in the viewport
- Swivel Angle Manipulator group: Controls the display of the swivel angle manipulator in the IK chain. It is switched on by default. You need to check Turn on and then check the Manipulate mode to see the swivel angle manipulator. This group has the following options:
  - Enabled: Marks the swivel angle manipulators on or off.
  - Size: Controls the size of the manipulator's handle in viewports.
  - Length: Controls the length of the manipulator in viewports.

- IK Solver Display group: Controls the appearance of the IK Solver display and the line drawn between the start and end joints. Select the Enabled option when there are multiple chains that you need to see at the same time.

6.2.3 End Effectors

Describe the use of end effectors.

An end effector is the pivot point of a selected child object at the end of a kinematics chain. The kinematics chain is a single branch of a hierarchy used for animation with IK. The chain starts with the selected child object and travels up through the ancestors until it reaches the start of the chain.

When you move the end effector, the History-Dependent IK solver then uses IK calculations to move and rotate all other objects in the kinematics chain to react to the object you moved. The end effector has the following two transforms:

- One that connects it to its parent
- One that connects it to the end effector parent

By default, the end effector parent is none (equivalent to World); you can assign this in the Motion panel. You use the end effector to create an effector at the end of the chain, which can be animated. To use the end effector, perform the following steps:

1. Select Systems on the object rollout under the Create panel, and select Bones.
2. Mark the Assign to root and Assign to children check boxes.
3. Click once in the Left viewport to create the base of the chain. After the base has been set, move the mouse off the base of the chain. A triangular-shaped bone appears and follows the pointer.
4. Anchor the second bone by clicking below the first bone.

5. Click below and to the right of the second bone to anchor the third bone, as shown in Figure 6.6.

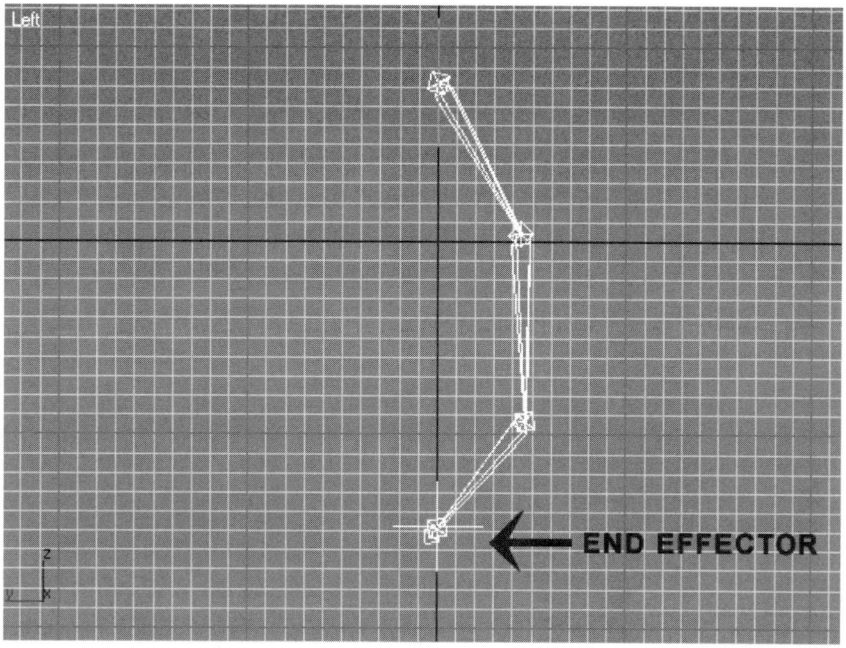

Figure 6.6: Anchoring the Third Bone

6.2.4 Manipulator Helpers

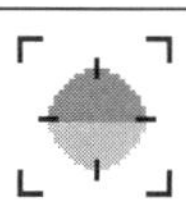

Link Point helpers to viewport sliders.

Manipulators are one of the types of helpers in 3ds max. You use manipulators to create character animation. They store the minimum or maximum value of an attribute of a bone. You can also add some interactive controls, such as custom attribute sliders and viewport sliders. Viewport sliders provide animators with an easy way to see and adjust values. The slider rollout has the following options:

- Label: The slider label that appears in viewports. The default value is none.
- Value: The value of the slider, based on the position of the slidable triangle. The default value is 0.0.
- Minimum: The minimum possible value of the slider. The default value is 0.0.

- Max: Maximum possible value of the slider. The default value is 100.0. When the minimum is 0.0 and the maximum is 100.0, the slider value can represent a percentage.
- X Position: The slider's X location in the active viewport.
- Y Position: The slider's Y location in the active viewport.
- Width: The slider's width, in 3ds max units. The default value is 100.0.
- Snap: When on, the slider "snaps" to the incremental values delegated by the Snap Value setting. The default value is on.
- Snap Value: The increment used by the slider when Snap is on. The default value is 0.01.
- Hide: When on, hides all of the slider except for the label and the Move and Show/Hide components. The default value is off.

If you link the X-axis rotation value of each Point helper to a viewport slider, it gives you an easy way of posing the foot bones. To link Point helpers to viewport sliders, perform the following steps:

1. Create the bone hierarchy of a leg.
2. Attach the IK solver to it.
3. Maximize the Left viewport.

4. Click **Helpers** on the **Create** panel, and then choose **Manipulators** from the drop-down list, as shown in Figure 6.7.

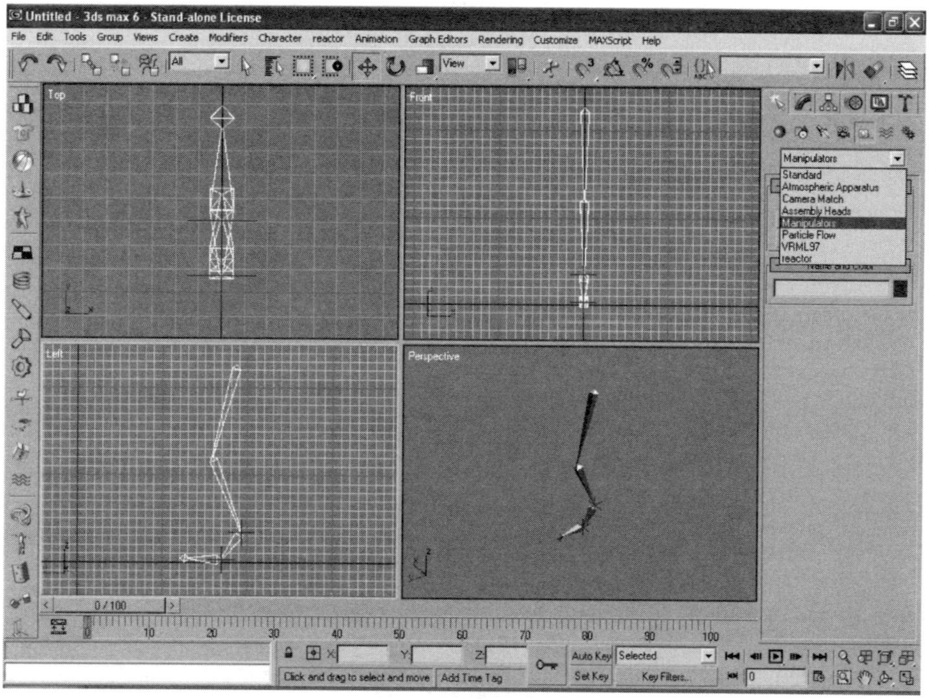

Figure 6.7: Manipulators

5. In the object rollout, click **Slider**, as shown in Figure 6.8.

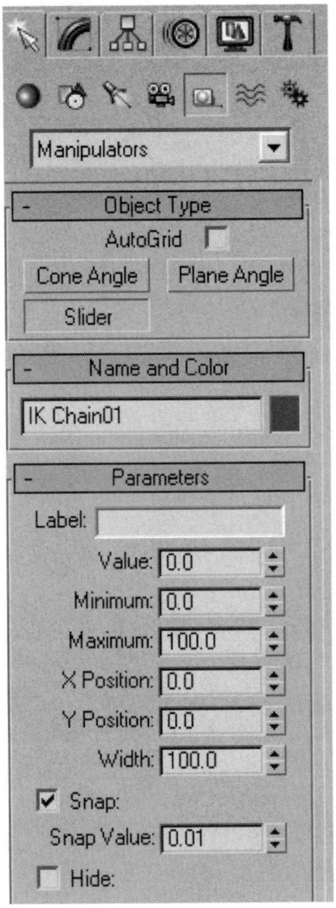

Figure 6.8: Slider Option

6. Create the slider over the top right of the viewport and open the **Modify** panel.

7. Type **Ankle** in the Name field of the Parameters rollout, as shown in Figure 6.9.

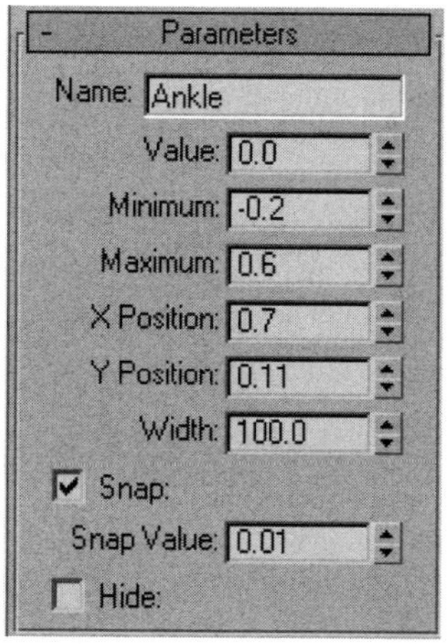

Figure 6.9: Name Field of the Parameters Rollout

8. Change the slider's object name to **ankle slider** in the Object Name field.
9. Create one more slider for the heel.
10. Select the second slider.
11. Type **Heel** in the Name field of the Parameters rollout.
12. In the Object Name field, change the slider's object name to **heel slider**.

After you specify the required information for the link point, helpers are attached to viewport sliders. You need to use Parameter Wiring to make the viewport sliders work. To use Parameter Wiring:

1. Select Animation → Wire Parameters → Parameter Wire.
2. Expand the **Objects** branch of the hierarchy.
3. Right-click **null_heel_right**, and select the **Expand Tracks** option.
4. Select the **X Rotation** track.

Figure 6.10 shows the World parameters panel with the highlighted X Rotation track.

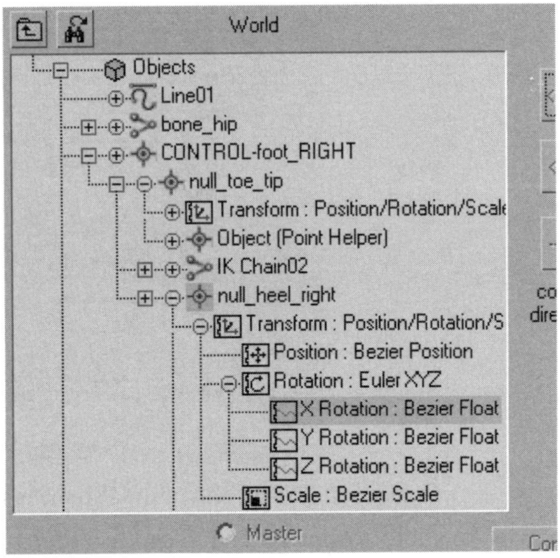

Figure 6.10: Selection of the X Rotation Track

5. Expand the **heel slider** option.
6. Highlight the value track for the heel slider. Figure 6.11 shows the World parameters panel with the highlighted Value track.

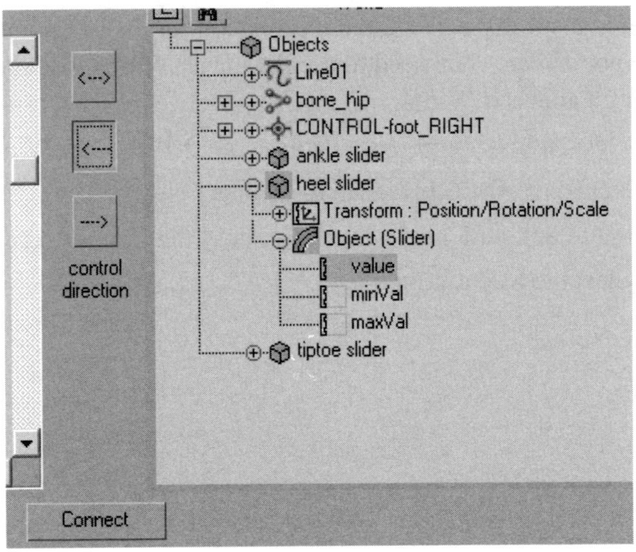

Figure 6.11: Selection of the Value Track

7. Click on the left arrow at the center of the Parameter Wiring dialog box. This is highlighted in yellow.
8. Click the **Connect** button.
9. You need to repeat the steps to use Parameter Wiring for the remaining sliders.

6.2.5 Joint Constraints

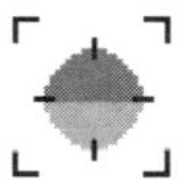

Define joint constraints.

You need to define joint constraints in sliding joints and rotational joints. By default, each joint has six degrees of freedom. The two objects that make up a joint can each move or rotate along the X-, Y-, or Z-axis. When an axis is enabled, the two objects can be transformed freely in all three axes in position and rotation. Enabling and disabling local transform axes is also referred to as setting the degree of freedom (DoF) for an object. When an axis is locked, the object can't be transformed to that particular axis. The axis setting for all other sliding and rotational joints are the same.

Figure 6.12 shows the Rotational Joints rollout.

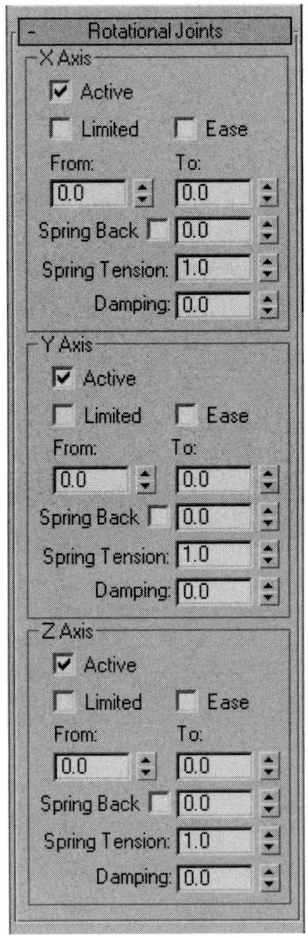

Figure 6.12: Rotational Joints Rollout

The Rotational Joints rollout has the following options:

- x-axis, y-axis and z-axis groups: The Sliding Joints rollout and the Rotational Joints rollout contain identical group boxes to control the X-, Y-, and Z-axis. It has the following options:
  - Active: Activates an axis (X/Y/Z) and allows the selected object to slide on or rotate about the activated axis.
  - Limited: Limits the range of motion or rotation allowed on an active axis. You need to use this in conjunction with the From and To spinners. Most joints are limited in their range of motion along an active axis. For example, a piston slides only within the length of its cylinder.

- Ease: Causes a joint to resist motion as it approaches its From and To limits. This simulates an organic joint, or a worn mechanical joint, moving or rotating freely in the middle of its range of motion but moving less freely at the extremes of its range.
- From and To spinners: Determine the position and rotation limits. You need to use this option in conjunction with the Limited function.
- Spring Back: Activates a spring back. Each joint has a rest position. As the joint moves further from the rest position, an increasingly larger force pulls the joint back to its rest position, like a spring.
- Spring Back (spinner): Sets the rest position for the joint. For rotational joints, this is the orientation of the joint in degrees; for sliding joints, it is the position in units.

If you are using the HD Solver, you must turn on Show Initial State to see the effect on the geometry during the adjustment (Motion panel → IK Controller Parameters rollout).

- Spring Tension: Sets the strength of the "spring". Higher values cause the spring to pull harder as the joint moves further from its rest position. A setting of 0 turns off the spring; very high settings can turn the joint into a limit because you can reach the point where the spring is too strong to allow the joint to move past a certain point.
- Damping: Applies resistance over a joint's full range of motion or rotation. Simulates the natural effect of joint friction or inertia. As a joint corrodes, dries out, or is put under a heavy load, it resists motion along its active axes.

From the IK Solver rollout, you define a joint constraint. To prevent unnatural motions, you need to define a joint constraint to enable you to constrain this motion. For example, suppose you need to constrain an elbow bending backwards. To constrain an axis, select the object that includes the pivot point for the joint. In the appropriate rollout, locate the section for the axis that you want to restrict and clear the Active option. If an axis' Active option is clear, the axis is constrained. By selecting the Limited option, you can also limit the motion of joints.

When the Limited option is selected, the object can move only within the bounds set by the From and To values. The ease option causes the motion of the object to become slow as it approaches either limit. To define a joint constraint, perform the following steps:

1. Create a hierarchy of bones.
2. Select any bone of the hierarchy.
3. Select IK from the Hierarchy Panel. The IK rollout appears, as shown in Figure 6.13.

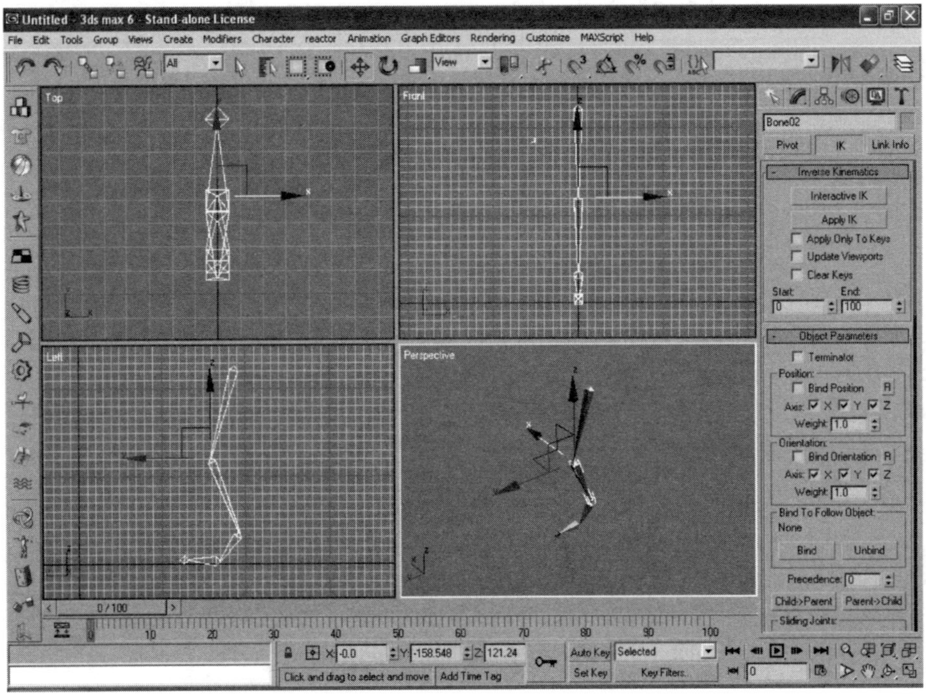

Figure 6.13: IK Rollout

Weights

It sets the influence of the follow object (or end effector) on its assigned object, and on the rest of the chain. A setting of 0 turns off the binding. Using this value you can set the relative influence of multiple follow objects or end effectors and their priority in solving the IK solution. The higher the relative Weight value, the higher the priority.

The Weight settings are relative; there is no point in using them if there is only one follow object or end effector in the IK hierarchy. If you have a single History Dependent IK chain with both Position and Rotation end effectors on a single joint, you can give them different weights to give priority to either the position or the rotation solution.

You can adjust the Weight value for multiple joints. Select two or more objects in the hierarchy, and the Weight value represents the commonality of the selection set.

Differences in the Weight values only have an effect when there is no solution that satisfies two or more opposing end effectors in the chain. In this case, the end effector with the greatest weight "wins."

Practice Questions

1. Define Inverse Kinematics.
2. Describe the goals of IK.
3. List the transforms of End effector.
4. Describe the role of manipulator helpers in creation of character animation.

6.3 Types of IK Solvers

IK solvers allow you to apply IK solutions to the components of a hierarchy across frames. These solutions, applied with controllers, help perform transformations such as position and rotation on the various links and other components in the hierarchical chain. You can access the IK solvers from the Animation menu in 3ds max.

3ds max has the following four types of IK solvers:

- History-dependent (HD): A smooth but slow process that is best for short animations because it takes more time and memory.
- History-independent (HI): A fast process that looks at each frame independently and is best for long animations.
- IK Limb solver: A process that works on two bones or objects. It is best when animating limbs.
- Spline IK solver: A process that uses splines to control the movements of the bone hierarchies.

IK solvers are basically plug-ins. You can expand them by including third-party IK solvers or even those that you create yourself.

6.3.1 History-Dependent IK Solver

Apply a History-Dependent IK solver.

You use the HD IK solver for short animation sequences because it is history-dependent. If you use the solver at a later stage in an animation, it takes longer to calculate the solution.

The HD IK solver shows up as a controller in the Motion panel. The settings are contained in the rollout named IK Controller Parameters, which will be visible in the Motion panel if you select one of the end effector gizmos.

The end effector gizmo is the object that you move to control the IK chain. It is displayed as a set of crossing axes.

You can access the IK Controller Parameters rollout in the Motion panel. Any parameter changes will affect all bones in the current structure. The Show Initial State option displays the initial stage of the linkage and enables you to move it. The Lock Initial State option prevents any linkage other than the end effectors from moving.

Figure 6.14 shows the IK Controller Parameters rollout.

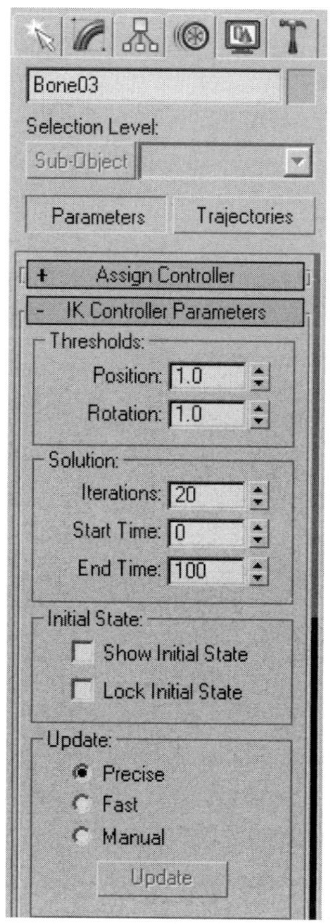

Figure 6.14: IK Controller Parameter Rollout

When you first create a bones system, an end effector is set to the last joint automatically. To make a bone an end effector, select the bone and click the Create button. If the bone is already an end effector, the Delete button will be active.

6.3.2 History-Independent IK Solver

Describe History-Independent IK solver.

The History-Independent (HI) IK solver looks at each key frame independently when making its solution. You can animate linked chains with this IK solver, applied by positioning the Goal object. The solver will then key frame the position of the pivot point of the last object in the chain to match the Goal object.

You can apply IK solvers to any hierarchy of objects. IK solvers are applied automatically to a bones system when you create the system. When you choose IK Solver, a dotted line appears from the selected object. You can drag this line within a viewport and click another object within the hierarchy to be the end point. Because this solver is history-independent, it is swift, irrespective of the number of frames. It is stable and jitter-free in viewports.

6.3.3 IK Limb Solver

Describe the IK Limb solver.

You use the IK Limb solver to work with limbs such as arms and legs. It is used on chains of three bones such as the hip, the upper leg, and the lower leg. Only two of the bones in the chain actually move. The goal for these three joints is located at the pivot point for the third bone.

The IK Limb solver considers the first joint as a spherical joint, which can rotate along three different axes. The second joint can only bend in one direction.

6.3.4 Spline IK Solver

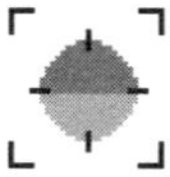

Apply the spline IK solver.

You can use the HI solver for the arms and legs, but not for the tails, where the animation will not be so smooth. Tails are unique because they start out large and gradually reduce in size. For tails, the Spline IK solver works well. In the Spline IK solver, the dummy objects are replaced with vertices called nodes, which control the curvature of the chain. The more the number of nodes, the easier it is to make an animation. The nodes in the Spline IK can be moved anywhere in the viewport by enabling more flexibility in animation. Rotating or scaling nodes has no effect on the spline or structure.

You can control a bone structure by a spline using the Spline IK solver. You can assign this solver before the creation of bones or after the creation of bones. To apply the Spline IK solver before the creation of a bone structure, perform the following steps:

1. Click the **Systems** button under the **Create** panel or select the **Bone** tools option under the **Character** button on the menu bar.

2. From the IK Chain Assignment rollout, choose **SplineIKSolver** as the IK Solver, as shown in Figure 6.15.

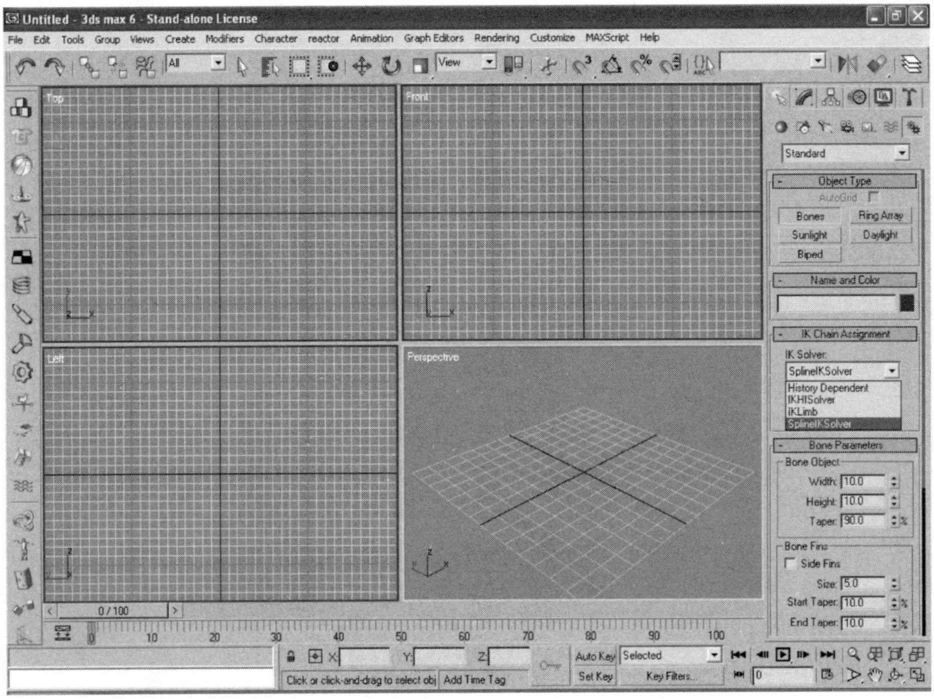

Figure 6.15: Applying SplineIKSolver

3. Select the **Assign to Children** check box.
4. Create a series of bones in the suitable viewport consisting of the desired number of bones.
5. Right-click the structure.

The Spline IK Solver dialog box will display, as shown in Figure 6.16.

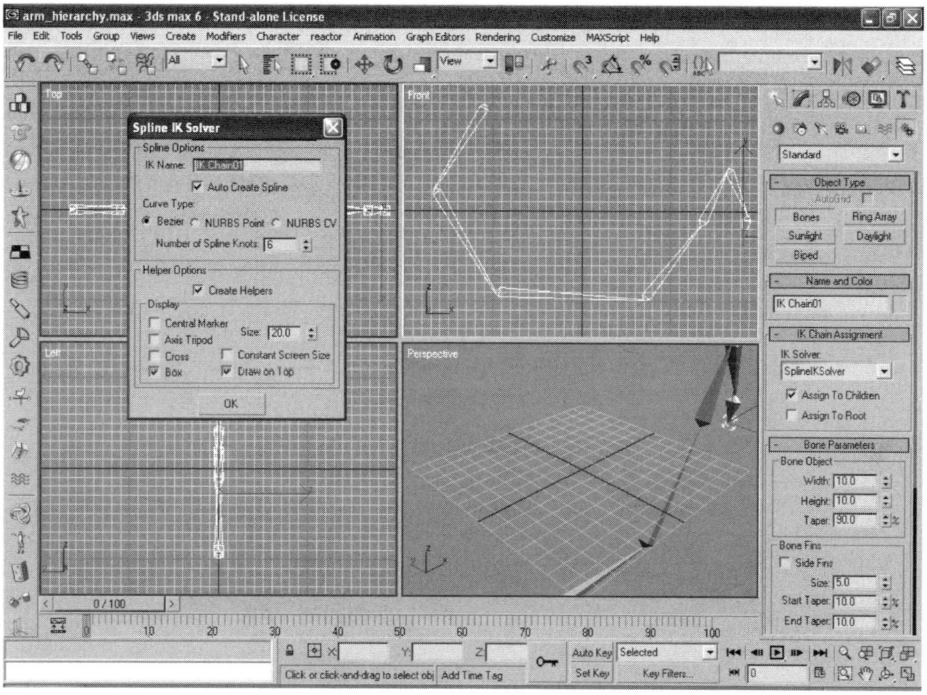

Figure 6.16: Spline IK Solver Dialog Box

6. Select the **Auto Create Spline** option so that a spline and the helpers to control the spline will be created.
7. Choose the **Curve** type, which can be Bezier, NURBS Point, or NURBS CV, and will appear in the viewport.
8. Set a value for the **Number of Spline Knots** as required, to control the movement of the curve.
9. Mark the **Create Helpers** option. This creates the helpers that are used to move the bone series.
10. Choose the display type and size, and click the **OK** button.

After you complete the procedure, a spline is created in the shape of the bone series. On the spline are box-shaped Point helpers, as shown in Figure 6.17. You need to select a box helper on the spline and move it using the Move tool. The shape of the spline changes, which in turn changes the shape of the bone series.

The bone series will also be animated according to the helper's movement.

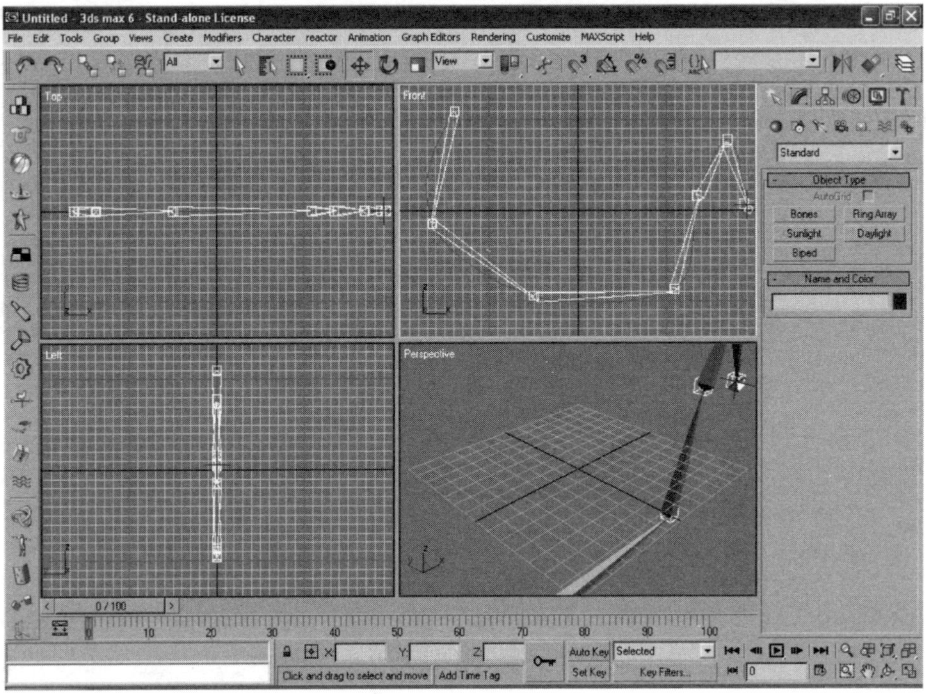

Figure 6.17: Box-Shaped Point Helpers

Another way to use this IK solver is with an existing bone structure. From the spline curve, select the first bone where you want the solver to be applied. Then, select **Animation → IK solver → Spline IK**. In the viewport, a dotted dragging line appears. Move the dotted line to the last bone that you want to include and then drag the dotted line to the spline that you want to use.

The bone structure then assumes the shape of the spline curve. A helper object will be positioned at the location of each curve vertex. These helper objects let you refine the shape of the curve.

Practice Questions

1. List the types of IK Solvers.
2. Where is IK Controller Parameters rollout available?
3. You use the end effector gizmo to control the IK chain. (True/False)

6.4 Walk Cycle

The walk cycle is one of the most common actions for a character. You need to use the Set Key tool to animate a basic walk cycle. This lets you set both the position and the rotation of objects simultaneously during the animation process.

As the structure of the bones has already been set up, animating a walk cycle is straightforward. You need to animate only the feet and the hips. A character's walk conveys a great deal about its personality.

6.4.1 Walking Mechanism

Define a walk cycle.

A walk can be described as controlled falling because while walking, a character leans forward when taking the first step. The weight of the upper parts of the body gets transferred to the foot where the knee absorbs the shock. This phenomenon is repeated with the other foot as well. A walk is a complex phenomenon. When the feet have to move across the ground, the hips, the spine, the arms, the shoulders, and the head all move in synchronization to maintain balance in the system. Although complex, if you break down each of these movements, the mechanics of walking become clear.

6.4.2 Animating a Simple Walk Cycle

Animate a walk cycle.

There are various means to achieve a walk cycle. They are:

- Motion capture
- Inverse Kinematics
- Transformation animation

Transformation animation is generally the best choice when animating something mechanical because it yields very precise control over the motion of the animated objects. We are going to use the IK method.

Timing a Walk

You use the pose-to-pose method to animate a walk cycle. To animate a walk using contact poses, perform the following steps:

1. Pose the individual character part on frame 1.

Ensure that the forward leg is in contact with the ground; else it will appear that the character is leaning.

---

2. Advance the time 12 frames and do the next heel strike pose. Key everything on your character.
3. Pose the heel strike in the 12th frame.
4. Pose the individual character in a passing posture in the 7th frame.

Ensure that the shoulders and the hips are in opposite directions. Drop the shoulder and the hips laterally.

In frame 10, add the striding pose between the passing and contact postures. At this stage, the hips start moving towards the centerline. The body in turn gets prepared to catch itself with the other foot.

Setting Up the IK Chain

To set up the IK chain, perform the following steps:

1. Open the file, **leg.max**.

The max file displays the area below the hip area. The structure of the leg is shown in Figure 6.18.

Figure 6.18: Hierarchy of the Leg

2. Click the **Key Filters** button, which is next to the Set Key button, in which you can select the check box for the position, rotation, custom attributes and modifiers, as shown in Figure 6.19.

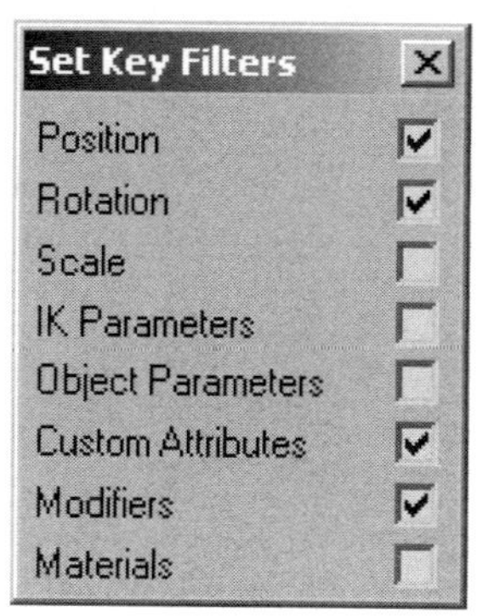

Figure 6.19: Set Key Filters Option

3. When the Set Key mode is used, the key will be created only for the above selected options.
4. Turn on the Set Key mode by pressing the Set Key button, below the viewport.

The Set Key Mode toggle, the Time slider background, and the active viewport outline turn red to indicate that the Set Key mode is on.

Animating the Extreme Poses

We are going to animate the character at frame 40, where the character's right leg is in the passing position. You need to use eight poses to animate the walk, which will require four extreme poses.

When the term, forward, is used in these steps, it means forward from the character's point of view.

To animate the extreme poses, you need to perform the following steps:

1. Move the time slider to frame 50.
2. Activate the Left viewport.
3. Select the hip control and move it forward and slightly down.
4. Move the right leg to step completely on the ground (the temporary surface).

The back leg should be completely straight, with the heel slightly lifted, as shown in Figure 6.20.

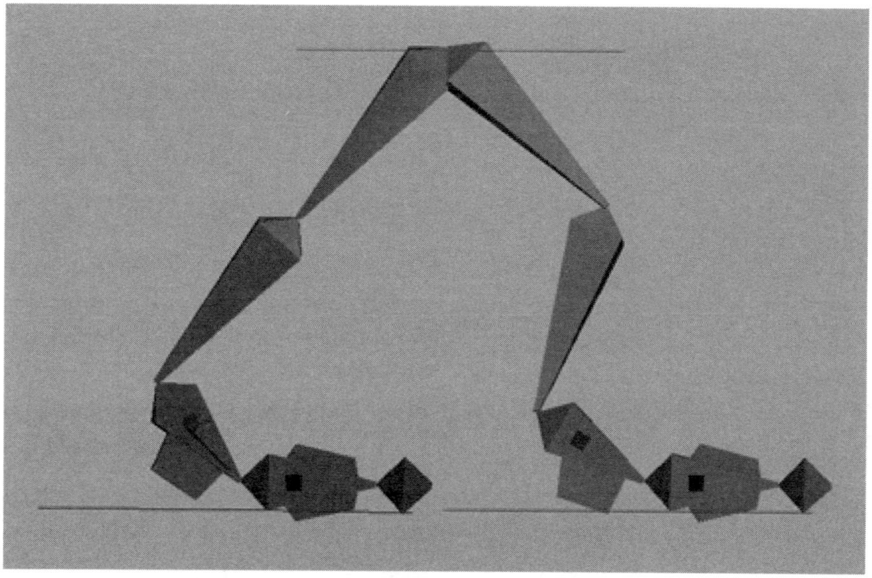

Figure 6.20: Leg Structure

5. Select both the foot controls and the hip control, and click the **Set Key** button in the lower part of the viewport, as shown in Figure 6.21.

Figure 6.21: Set Key Button

6. When the **Set Key** button is pressed, the button turns red for a few seconds, as shown in Figure 6.22.

Figure 6.22: Active Set Key Button

7. Move the time slider to the 60th frame.
8. Select the hip control, and move it up and slightly forward, and move the left leg to the passing position.
9. Select the hip and foot controls, and click the **Set Key** button.

The structure of the leg will be as shown in Figure 6.23.

Figure 6.23: Leg Structure at the 60th Frame

10. Move the time slider to the 70th frame.
11. Select the hip control, and move it down and forward.
12. Move the left leg to step on the ground, keeping the back leg straight. The back heel might come up a little.
13. Select the hip and foot controls, and click the **Set Key** button.

The structure would be as shown in Figure 6.24.

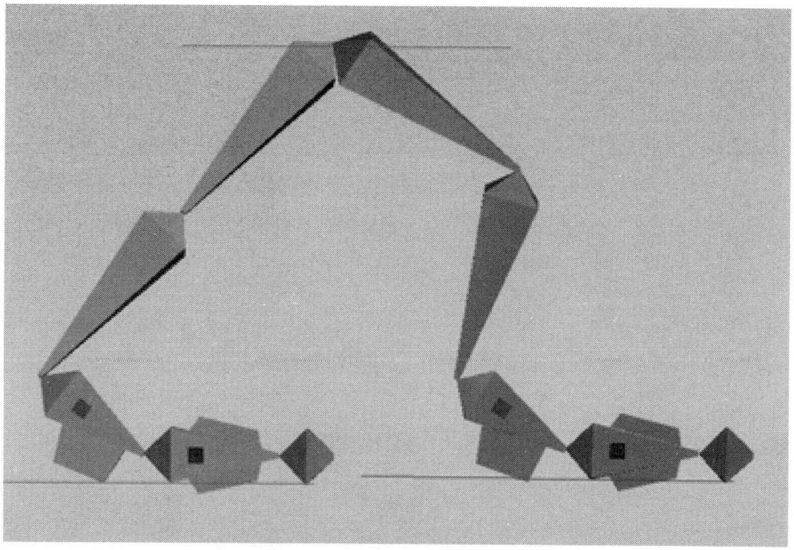

Figure 6.24: Leg Structure at the 70th Frame

14. Move the time slider to the 80th frame.
15. Select and move the hip control up and forward, and move the right leg to the passing position.
16. Select the hip and foot controls, and click the **Set Key** button.

The structure would be as shown in Figure 6.25.

Figure 6.25: Leg Structure at the 80th Frame

17. Drag the time slider to see the alien's legs move through the extreme poses.

You have created a rough walk cycle, but the walk cycle is still a little stiff. You need to add more fluid motion with in-between poses.

Animating the Poses in Between

As we saw, there is stiff movement between the poses; we do need some changes between the poses.

1. Select the right foot control.
2. Move the time slider to the 50th frame, select all the keys at frame 50 on the trackbar, hold down Shift, and move the key to the 45th frame on the trackbar.

It is not necessary to click the Set Key after copying a key.

3. Move the time slider to the 45th frame.
4. On the Modify panel, change the Roll attribute to –100.0.
5. Click the **Set Key** button. The leg structure is shown in Figure 6.26.

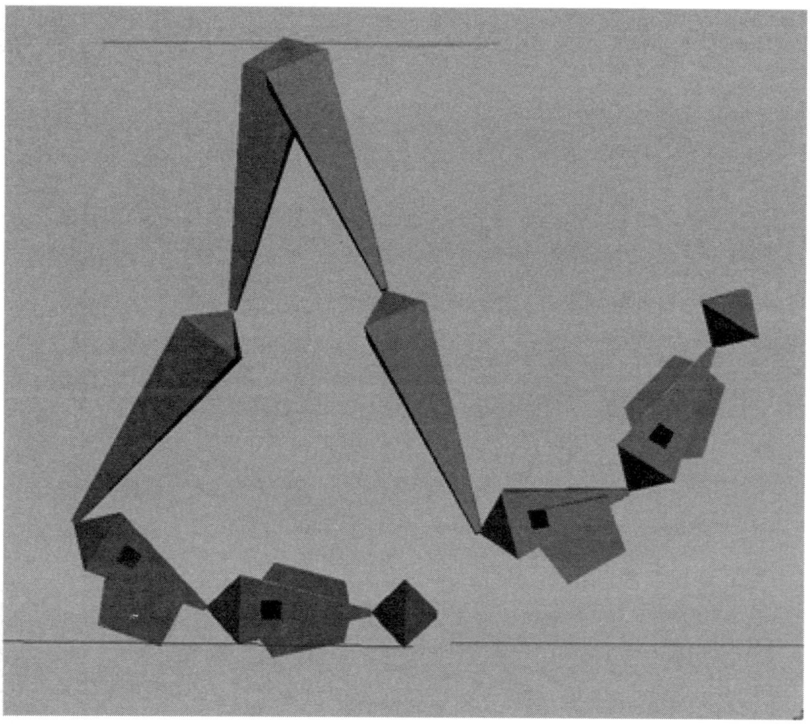

Figure 6.26: Leg Structure

6. Select the left foot control, and copy the key on frame 50 and shift drag to frame 55.
7. Move the time slider to the 55th frame.
8. On the Modify panel, increase the Roll attribute to make the heel come up off the ground.

The example in the illustration uses a value of 75.0, but the best value for your rig might vary, depending on how far apart the foot controls have been placed. Watch the Front viewport while changing the value, and roll the foot enough to come off the ground but not so much as to make the character's knee bend inward.

9. Click **Set Key** after you have set the Roll attribute. The structure of the leg is shown in Figure 6.27.

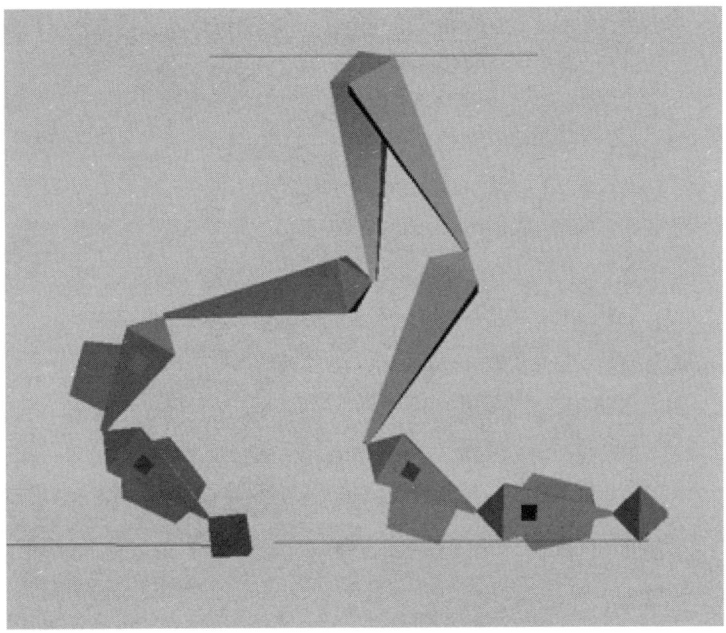

Figure 6.27: Leg Structure

10. Copy the key at frame 70, and move to frame 65.
11. Go to frame 65 and change the Roll attribute to **–100.0**.

12. Click the **Set Key** button, the leg structure will be as shown in Figure 6.28.

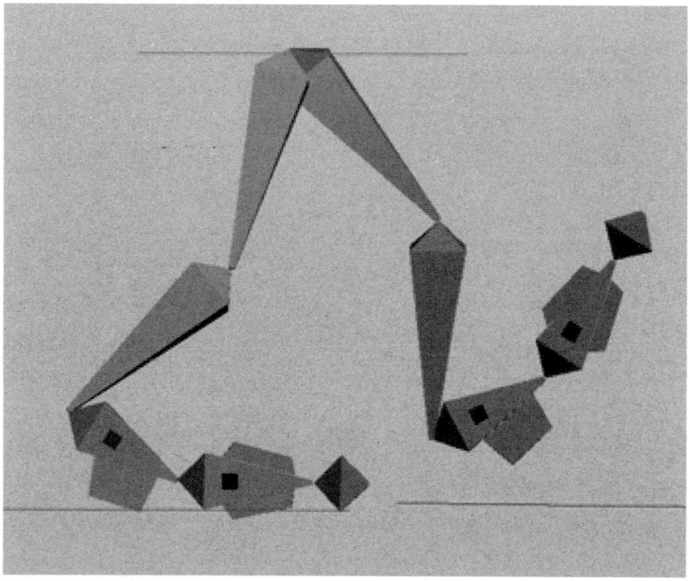

Figure 6.28: Leg Structure

13. Select the right foot control, and copy the key at frame 70 to frame 75.
14. Move the time slider to the 75th frame.

15. Increase the Roll attribute and click the **Set Key** button, the leg structure is shown in the Figure 6.29.

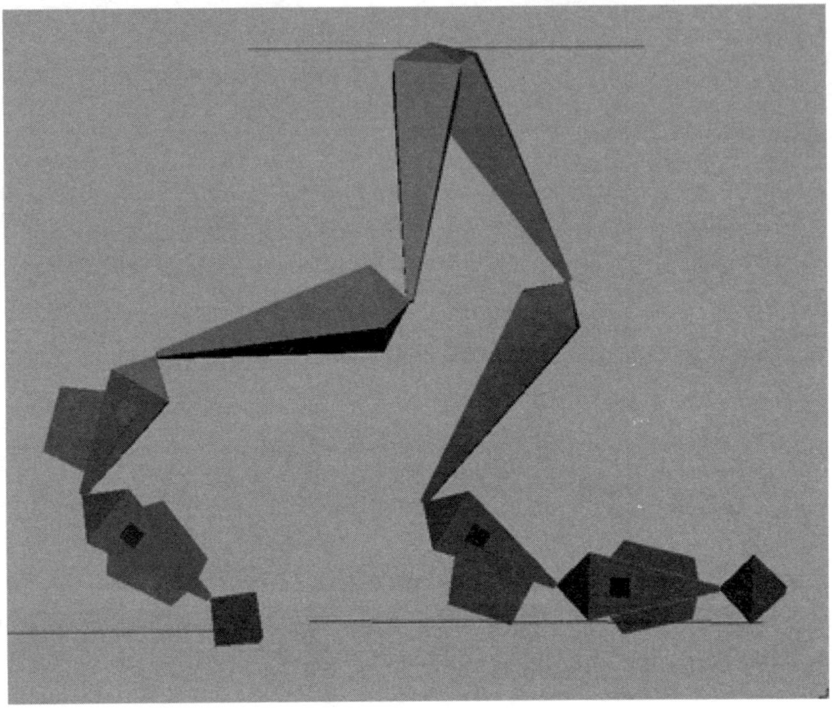

Figure 6.29: Leg Structure

A smooth walk cycle is created with the smooth in between animations. Next, we shall give more realism.

Shifting the Weight

After the bulk of the animation is done, you can use the Set Key method without the Set Key mode being turned on. This will set a key for the current transform only. To shift the weight, perform the following steps:

1. Click the **Set Key** button to turn it off.
2. Move the time slider to the 40th frame.
3. In the Front viewport, move the hips to the right to compensate for the weight being on one leg only.

4. Click **Set Key**. Figure 6.30 shows the weight compensation.

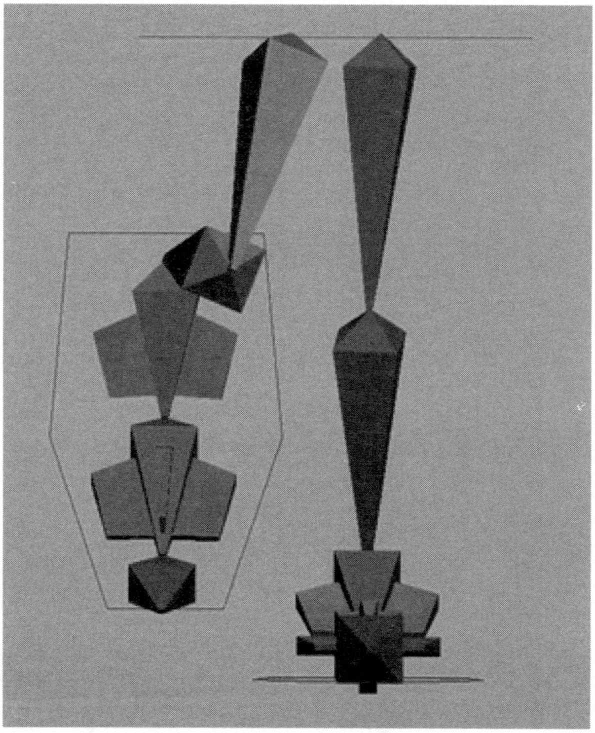

Figure 6.30: Weight Compensation

5. Move the time slider to the 60th frame, move the hips over the standing leg, and click on the Set Key button to record your animation.
6. Move the time slider to the 80th frame, move the hips over the standing leg, and click **Set Key** to record your animation.

To add the finishing touches, perform the following steps:

1. Move the time slider to the 40th frame.
2. In the Front viewport, rotate the right foot to make it flick outward.

Click **Set Key**. The leg structure is shown in Figure 6.31.

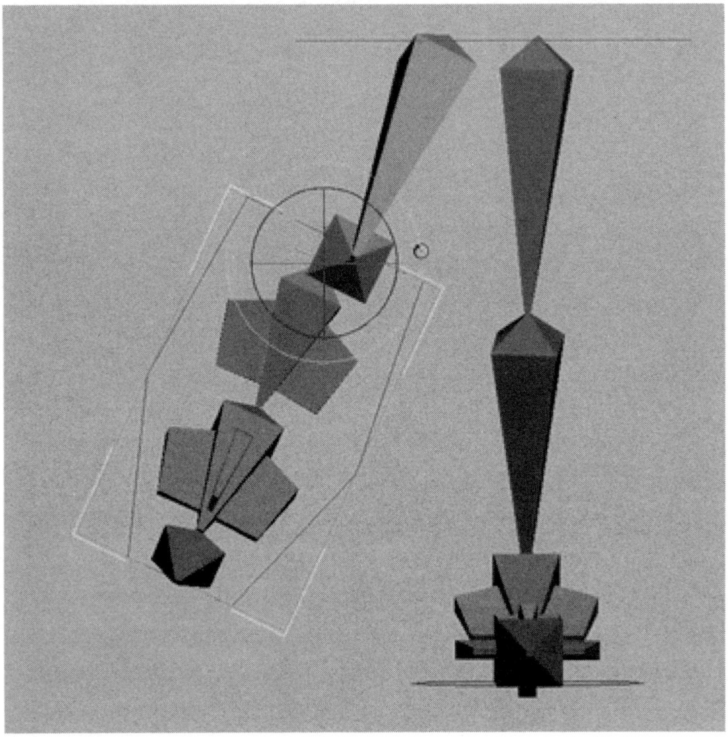

Figure 6.31: Flicking the Right Foot

3. On frame 60, rotate the left foot outward in the same fashion, and click on the **Set Key** button.
4. Perform the same for the right foot on frame 80. The basic walk cycle is complete.
5. Play the animation, and see how it plays.
6. Save the max file.

Practice Questions

1. Define a walk cycle.
2. List the means to achieve a walk cycle.
3. While animating a walk cycle, you should ensure that the shoulders and the hips are in opposite directions. (True/False)
4. The Set Key Mode toggle, the Time slider background, and the active viewport outline turn red to indicate that the Set Key mode is off. (True/False)

Summary

- Forward Kinematics (FK) causes objects at the bottom of a linked structure to move along with their parent.
- The hierarchy of an arm is a good example of FK.
- Any hierarchy of objects can be turned into Bones by selecting the hierarchy and clicking the Bone On button in the Object Properties rollout found in the Bone Tools dialog. The Hierarchy contains commands to control the behavior of links.
- You use the hierarchical panel to link two objects creating a parent-child relationship. When you apply a transformation to the parent it is transmitted to the child.
- The uses of linking are:
  - Simulating jointed structures
  - Creating complex motions
  - Setting rotational and sliding parameters for bones
- Pivots are used to:
  - Set the rotation and scaling points
  - Set the location of modifier centers
  - Define relationships
- A hierarchy is the complete set of linked objects that include all parent-child relationships.
- Objects that are not linked to any other objects are, by default, children of the world object, which is an imaginary object that holds all objects.
- IK enables a child object to control its parent object. So, in IK you can drag the hand to the exact position, and the other parts will follow.
- The goal is the procedure, which controls all the bones linked in a hierarchy. It is a HI system.
- The end effector is the pivot point of the selected child object at the end of a kinematics chain.
- A Manipulator is one of the types of Helpers in 3ds max. You use the manipulator helpers to create character animation.

- You need to define the Joint Constraints in the Sliding Joints and Rotational Joints. By default, each joint has six degrees of freedom. The two objects that make up the joint can each move or rotate along their X-, Y-, or Z-axes.
- Weights set the influence of the follow object (or end effector) on its assigned object, and on the rest of the chain.
- IK Solvers are of the following types:
    - History Dependent IK solver
    - History Independent IK solver
    - IK Limb solver
    - Spline IK solver
- A walk cycle is one of the most common actions for a character. You need to use the Set Key tool to animate a basic walk cycle.
- The various methods to achieve a walk cycle are:
    - Motion capture
    - Inverse kinematics
    - Transformation animation

References

- http://www.siggraph.org/education/materials/HyperGraph/animation/rick_parent/forwardAnimation.html (February 10, 2004)
- http://virtual.cvut.cz/odl/partners/fuh/course_main/node17.html (February 10, 2004)
- http://www.olympus.net/personal/mortenson/preview/definitionsf/forwardkine.html (February 10, 2004)
- http://caad.arch.ethz.ch/info/maya/manual/UserGuide/CharSetup/SkeletonPose.fm1.html (February 10, 2004)
- http://freespace.virgin.net/hugo.elias/models/m_ik.htm (February 10, 2004)
- http://ourworld.compuserve.com/homepages/crestline/ik.htm (February 10, 2004)
- http://www.webreference.com/3d/lesson58/ (February 10, 2004)
- http://www.maxhelp.com/content/tutorials/iksolvers/iksolvers.htm (February 10, 2004)
- http://caad.arch.ethz.ch/info/maya/manual/UserGuide/CharSetup/SkeletonPose.fm4.html (February 10, 2004)
- http://www.3dtotal.com/team/Tutorials/bipedrigging/bipedrigging_1.asp (February 10, 2004)
- http://www.3dtotal.com/team/Tutorials/rigging101/Rigging105.asp (February 10, 2004)
- http://www.kicrea.com/articles/rigging/bases/rigging_bases_us.php3 (February 10, 2004)
- http://www.anticz.com/Walks.htm (February 10, 2004)
- http://www.tvcd.com/TextTut/CatRun/RunTutorial.htm (February 10, 2004)
- http://www.anzovin.com/reviews/column9.html (February 10, 2004)
- http://www.awn.com/tooninstitute/lessonplan/walk.htm (February 10, 2004)
- http://www.cyberloonies.com/3dsmax.html (February 10, 2004)

Assignments

1. What is Forward Kinematics?
2. What do the suboptions do?
3. What is a root object?
4. How many degrees of freedom does a joint have by default?
5. What is Interactive IK?
6. Define end effectors.
7. What are the various types of IK solvers?
8. What is the Limb solver?
9. Why is it important to develop a character's gait?
10. What are the various means to achieve a walk cycle?

Lab Exercises

Exercise 1

Objective

- Animate a hierarchy using FK.

Problem Statement

Animate a robotic arm using FK. For this, you need to perform the following tasks:

- Create individual objects.
- Create the animation hierarchy.

Creating Individual Objects

To create the individual objects, you need to perform the following steps:

1. Reset the 3ds max scene.
2. Create a box in the center of the Top viewport using the 3D Snap tool, as shown in Figure 6.32 and from the Grid and Snap Settings dialog box, select **Grid Points**, as shown in Figure 6.33.

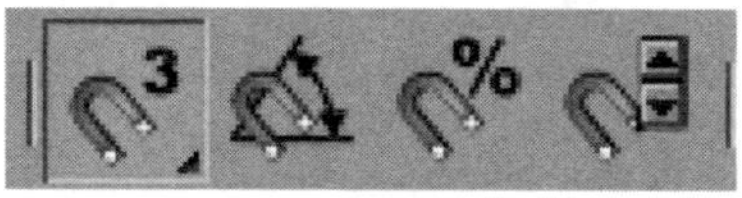

Figure 6.32: 3D Snap Tool

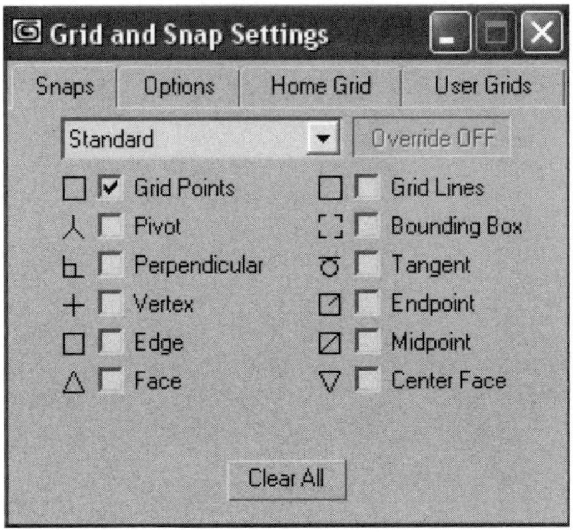

Figure 6.33: Grid and Snap Settings Window

This box will be treated as the platform of the arm, so name it **Platform**.

3. Create another box in the center of the platform. This box should be taller than the previous box. Name it **Base**, which you can rotate on top of the platform. Align Base at the top of the platform using the 3D Snap or the Align tool. You have to keep in mind that all the objects should be centered on the World origin based on the XY plane. Figure 6.34 shows the viewports.

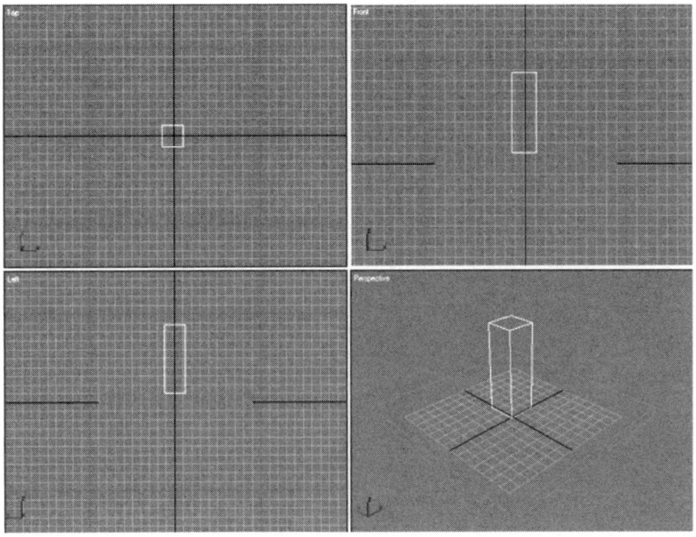

Figure 6.34: Four Viewports

4. Create a big cylinder at the top of the Base object so that it covers the top faces of Base. You have to place the cylinder such that there are no gaps visible in the model when the animation is rendered.
5. Name the cylinder **Shoulder**. Its position should be at the center of the XY plane. Figure 6.35 shows the viewports with the cylinder placed.

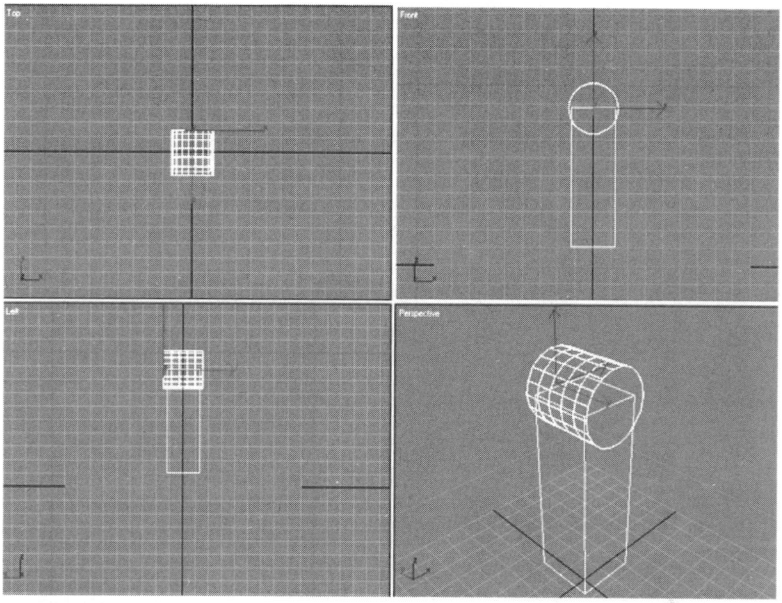

Figure 6.35: Four Viewports

6. Create another rectangular box. Place the box on top of Shoulder so that they overlap a bit. There should not be a gap between the two objects.

7. Rename the box **Arm**. Figure 6.36 shows the viewports with the rectangular placed.

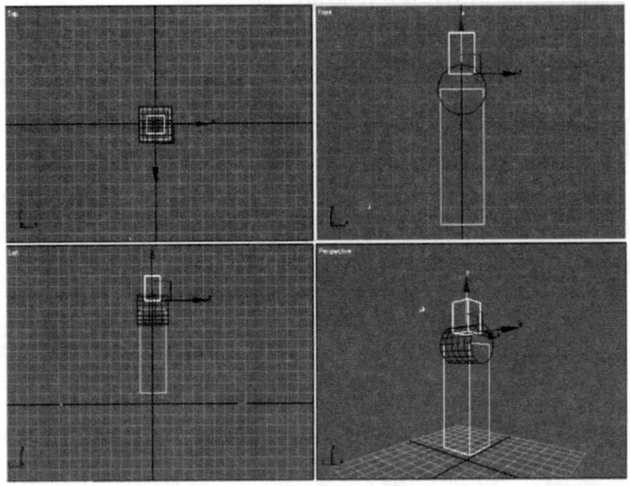

Figure 6.36: The Four Viewports

8. Use the same procedure for creating the shoulder, to create another cylinder on top of the Arm object in the Front viewport.
9. Rename the new cylinder **Elbow**. Center it as shown in Figure 6.37.

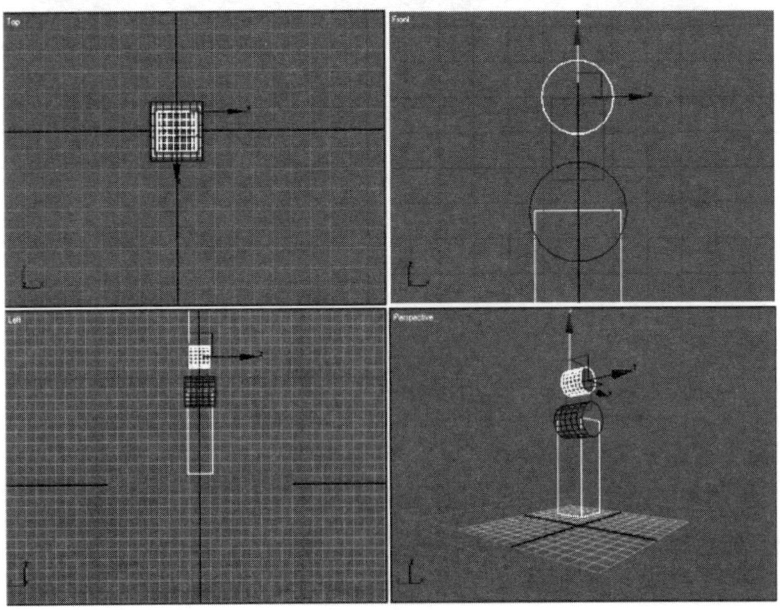

Figure 6.37: Four Viewports

10. Create one more box in the Top viewport. The box should be thin and tall as the Base object.
11. Rename the new box **Forearm** and move it up into position so that it slightly overlaps the Elbow joint.

    Figure 6.38 shows the viewports with the new box, Forearm.

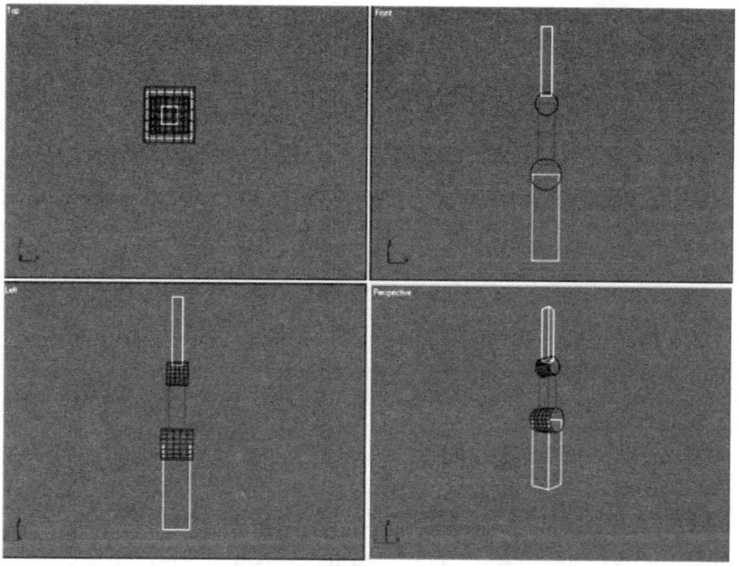

Figure 6.38: Four Viewports

12. Create another cylinder in the Top viewport, and move it to the top of the Forearm. It should look like a disc.

13. Rename it **Wrist**. Figure 6.39 shows the four viewports with the Wrist object.

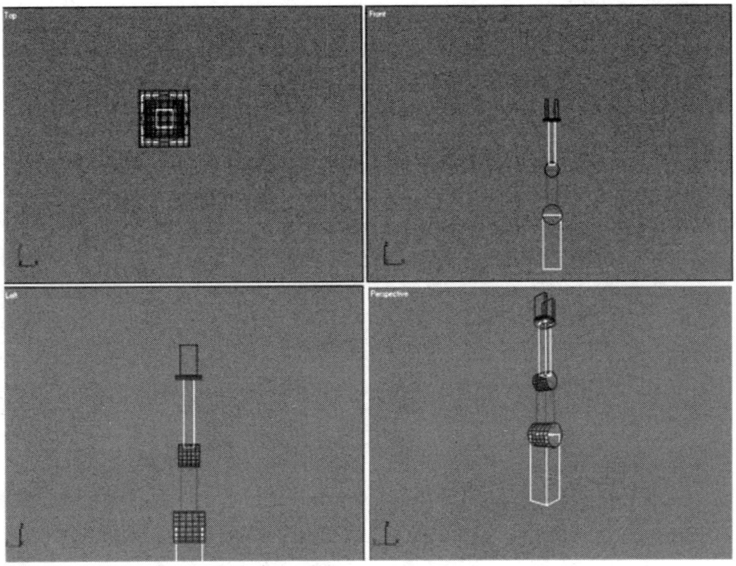

Figure 6.39: Wrist Object

Creating the Animation Hierarchy

After you have created the above objects, you need to create the animation hierarchy by performing the following steps:

1. On the Main toolbar, click the **Select and Link** button, as shown in Figure 6.40. The status line reads, "Click to select an object, then drag to assign it a parent."

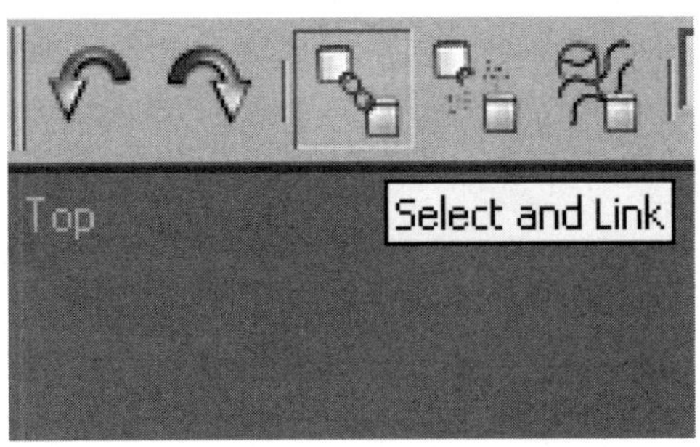

Figure 6.40: Select and Link Button

2. With the help of the **Zoom** tool, zoom the Front viewport to see the palm clearly. Link Palm and Thumb to Wrist, using the **Select and Link** button. Here, Wrist is the parent of Palm and Thumb.

Using the above procedure link the objects as follows:

- Forearm is the parent of Wrist.
- Elbow is the parent of Forearm.
- Arm is the parent of Elbow.
- Shoulder is the parent of Arm.
- Base is the parent of Shoulder.
- Platform is the parent of Base.

When you link the above objects, click the **Select by Name** button. The Select Objects dialog box opens.

3. Select the **Display Subtree** option to view the hierarchy, as shown in Figure 6.41.

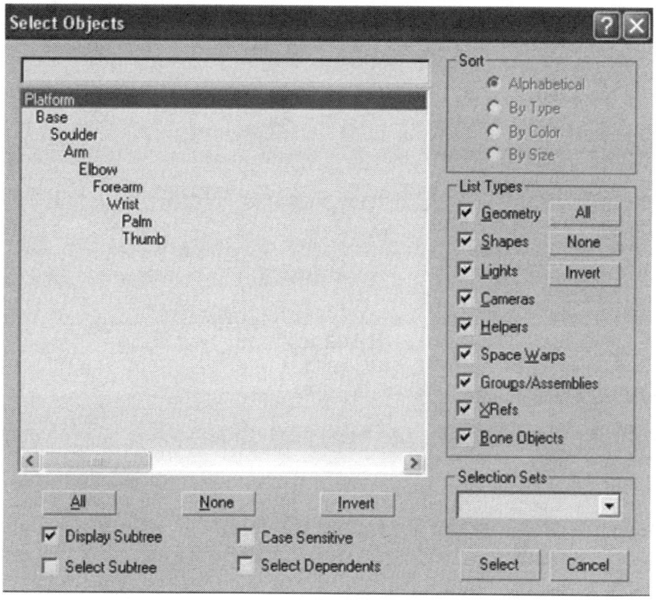

Figure 6.41: Select Objects Dialog Box

4. Save the file as **ch06_lab_ex1_sol.max**.

When you select and move the Platform object, because all the other objects in the arm are descendants of the Platform object, the entire hierarchy moves as a single object.

5. Select and move an object in the middle of the hierarchy, such as Elbow. All the objects that are descendants of Elbow move with it, but the ancestors of Elbow remain in place.

Lab Activity Checklist

S. No.	Tasks	Completed	
		Yes	No
1.	Created individual object		
2.	Created the animation hierarchy		

Exercise 2

Objective

- Set up a leg and foot.

Problem Statement

Set up a leg and foot for a character. For this, perform the following steps:

- Create a leg and foot skeleton.
- Align the IK goals.
- Create animation controls for the leg and the foot.
- Link each IK goal to a Point helper.
- Link the Point helpers to the viewport sliders.
- Wire the viewport sliders.
- Change the range of the viewport sliders.

Creating a Leg and Foot Skeleton

To create a leg and foot skeleton, perform the following steps:

1. Create a reference of the leg in the Left viewport by using **Spline → Line** tool. Figure 6.42 shows the Left viewport.

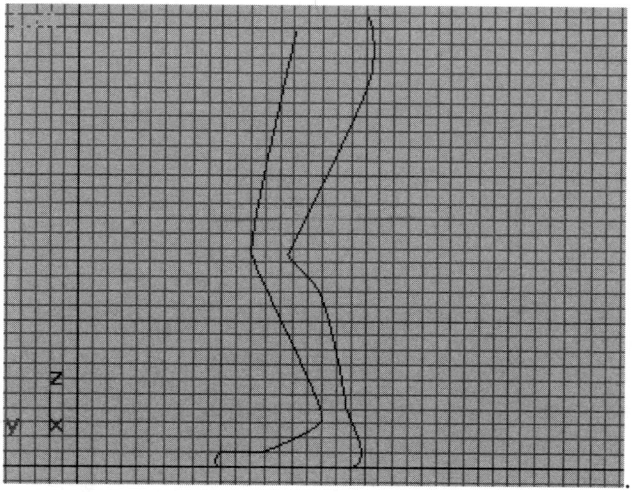

Figure 6.42: Left Viewport

2. Select **Bone Tools** from the Character menu. The Bone Tools dialog box opens, as shown in Figure 6.43.

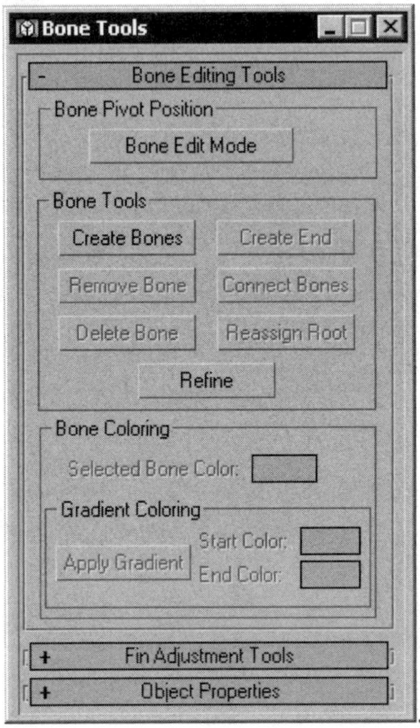

Figure 6.43: Bone Tools Dialog Box

3. In the Bone Tools group of the Bone Editing Tools rollout, select **Create Bones**.
4. Use the leg template as a reference. Click once at the hip; then click, in sequence, the knee, the ankle joint, the ball of the foot, and the tip of the toes.
5. Right-click to complete your bone chain. This creates a fifth, small bone at the end of the toes.
6. Right-click again to turn off bone creation.
7. Go to the **Modify** panel. Starting from the hip, rename the bones to bone_hip, bone_knee, bone_ankle, bone_toes, and bone_toe_tip.
8. Save the file as ch06_lab_ex2_sola.max.

Align the IK Goals

You must apply an IK solver to selected parts of the skeleton for the leg and foot to behave interactively. When an IK solver is assigned to a hierarchy of bones, it is called an IK chain. You need to create three IK chains for the leg and the foot to function properly.

An IK goal is created at the base of bone_ankle. When you select this IK bone, a line appears between bone_hip and bone_ankle.

Figure 6.44 shows the IK goal.

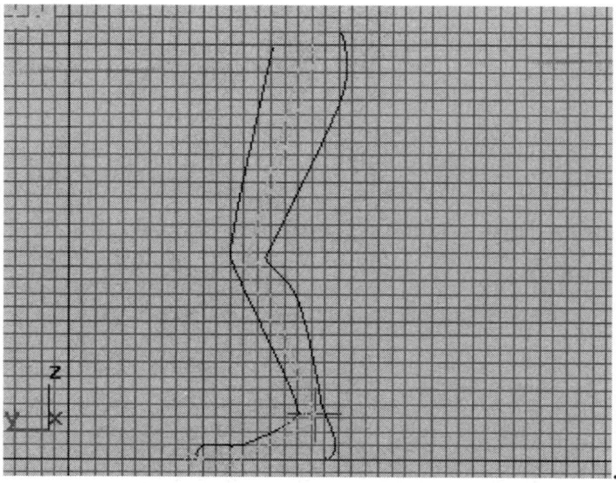

Figure 6.44: IK Goal

Next, you need to align the IK goals to the world. For this setup, this alignment is an important step because it will affect how custom attributes and parameter wiring work with the rotation values. Align the IK goals by performing the following steps:

1. Open the previous file, **ch06_lab_ex2_sol.max**. Select all three IK goals.
2. Open the **Hierarchy** panel.
3. Make sure **Pivot** is selected.
4. In the Adjust Pivot rollout, click **Affect Pivot Only**.
5. In the Alignment group, click **Align To World**.
6. Turn off Affect Pivot Only.

Creating Animation Controls for the Leg and the Foot

If you are unfamiliar with IK, you might move the IK goals around to see how IK works. You might also move bone_hip around to see how IK rotates each bone to maintain the foot's position in space. Note that you cannot move any bone other than bone_hip, because it's the root of the hierarchy. The IK solvers are controlling the other bones.

For animation, it is important to have controls that are easy to use and quick to manipulate. Often, with complex characters, you can have hundreds of controls for an entire character. These might be facial-animation shapes, bone rotation and scale XYZ values, IK goal position XYZ values, and constraints. It is a good practice to simplify controls whenever possible. This simplifies the task of posing your character.

To create animation controls for the leg and the foot:

1. On the Create panel, choose **Helpers** and then click **Point**. Make sure **Cross** is the only option selected for the Point helper.
2. In the Left viewport, using the leg template as reference, create a Point helper at the base of the heel. Figure 6.45 shows the Point helper.

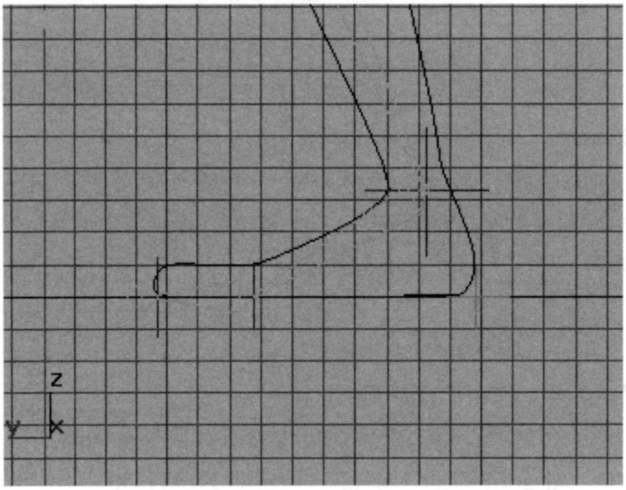

Figure 6.45: Point Helper

3. Rename the Point helper as **CONTROL_foot_RIGHT**. This will help you recognize the control when it is listed in the Track view or the Schematic view.
4. Create another Point helper exactly over the IK goal named IK Chain02. It is important that they be exactly over each other so that their pivot points are positioned in the same spot. This Point helper will control the up-and-down motion of the heel.

5. Rename the Point helper to **null_heel_right**.
6. Create another Point helper exactly over the IK goal named **IK Chain03**. Rename the Point helper to **null_toe_tip**.

Linking each IK Goal to a Point Helper

The Point helpers will be used to drive the position of the IK goals through hierarchical rotations. This is why it is very important that each Point helper's pivot point matches exactly with each IK goal.

To link each IK goal to a Point helper, perform the following steps:

1. On the Main toolbar, click **Select And Link**. Select **IK Chain01** and link it to **null_heel_right**.
2. Select and link **IK Chain03** to **IK Chain02**.
3. Select and link null_heel_right to null_toe_tip.
4. Select and link **IK Chain02** to **null_toe_tip**.
5. Select and link null_toe_tip to CONTROL_foot_RIGHT.

The entire leg and foot setup is complete. It is time to add some interactive controls. In 3ds max, you can add custom attribute sliders, or viewport sliders. Viewport sliders provide animators with an easy way to see and adjust values. Figure 6.46 shows the viewport sliders.

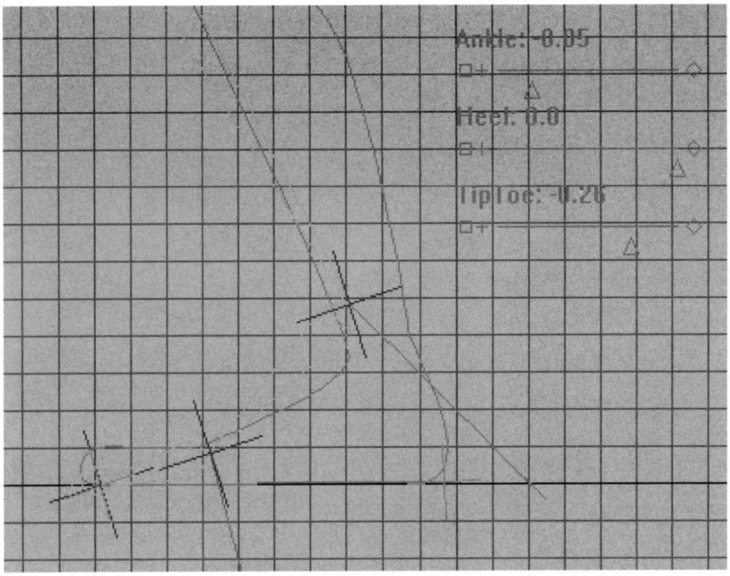

Figure 6.46: Viewport Sliders

Linking the Point Helpers to the Viewport Sliders

Linking the X-axis rotation value of each Point helper to a viewport slider gives you an easy way of posing the foot bones. To link the Point helpers to the viewport sliders:

1. Continue from the previous procedure.
2. Maximize the Left viewport. You'll be working in this viewport only.

3. On the Create panel, click **Helpers**, and then choose **Manipulators** from the drop-down list, as shown in Figure 6.47.

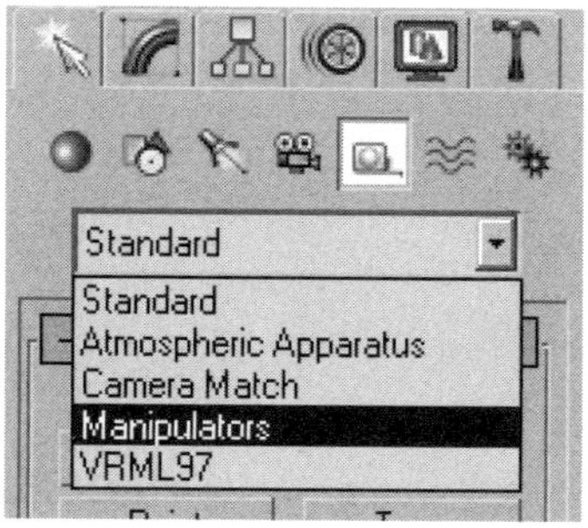

Figure 6.47: Manipulators

4. In the Object Type rollout, click **Slider**.
5. At the top-right side of the viewport, create three viewport sliders in a column with the first at the top, as shown in Figure 6.48. Right-click in the viewport to stop adding sliders.

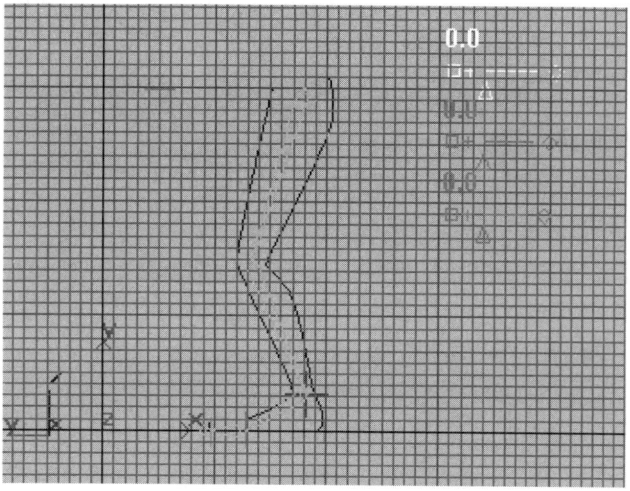

Figure 6.48: Viewport Sliders

6. Select the top slider and open the **Modify** panel.
7. In the Name field of the Parameters rollout, enter **Ankle**.
8. In the Object Name field (at the top of the Modify panel, under the icon tabs), change the slider's object name to **ankle slider**.

The Object Name field refers to the slider object's name, not its Name parameter. The Name parameter is displayed only in the viewport. The slider is still an object and needs a name to distinguish it in areas such as the Track view, parameter wiring, and the Schematic view.

9. Select the middle slider.
10. In the Parameters rollout → Name field, enter **Heel**.
11. In the Object Name field (at the top of the Modify panel, under the icon tabs), change the slider's object name to **Heel slider**.
12. Give the bottom slider the Name parameter of TipToe and the Object Name parameter of tiptoe slider.

Wire the Viewport Sliders

To make the viewport sliders work, you need to use Parameter Wiring to connect each slider to the rotation axis of its corresponding Point helper. To wire the viewport sliders:

1. Select null_heel_right.
2. From the Animation menu, choose **Wire Parameters → Parameter Wire** dialog.
3. On the left side of the dialog box, expand the **Objects** branch of the hierarchy. Right-click null_heel_right and choose **Expand Tracks**.

The null_heel_right object is inside the null_toe_tip hierarchy because it is a child of that object.

4. Click the **X Rotation** track, as shown in Figure 6.49.

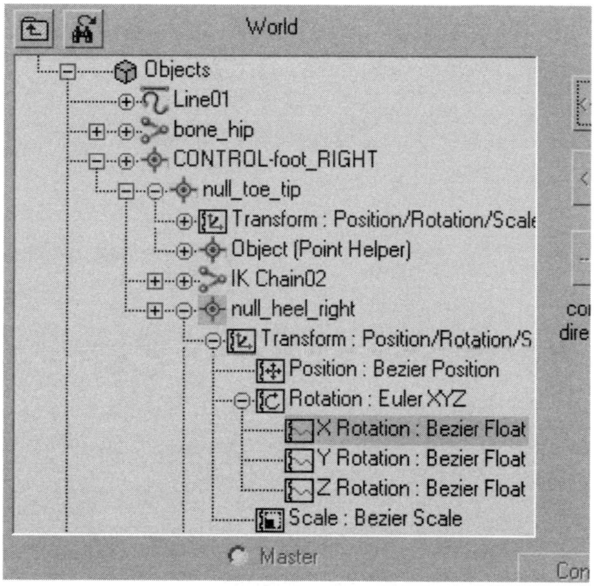

Figure 6.49: Parameter Wiring Dialog

5. On the right side of the Parameter Wiring dialog box, expand the **Objects** branch. Right-click heel slider and choose **Expand Tracks**.

6. On the right side of the dialog, highlight the **Value** track for the heel slider, as shown in Figure 6.50.

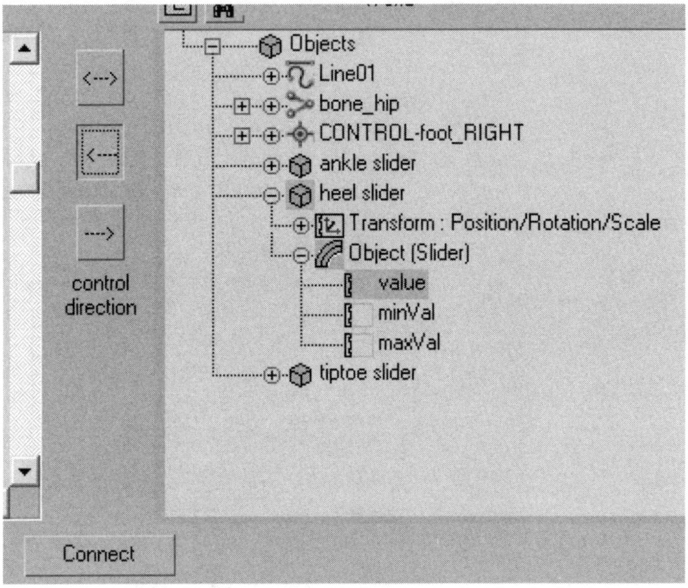

Figure 6.50: Object Field

7. In the center of the Parameter Wiring dialog box, click the arrow that points left.
8. Click **Connect**.

Repeat the preceding steps for the two remaining sliders. Link the X Rotation of null_toe_tip to the tiptoe slider value. Then link the X Rotation of CONTROL_foot_RIGHT to the ankle slider value.

Changing the Range of the Viewport Sliders

Each viewport slider has the minimum and maximum value settings that define the range of the slider. By default, the range is 0 to 100. This is too high and should be altered so that the sliders accurately rotate each foot bone. To change the range of the viewport sliders:

1. Select the ankle slider manipulator.
2. On the Modify panel, set Minimum to **–0.2** and Maximum to **0.6**.
3. Select the heel slider, and set Minimum to **–0.5** and Maximum to **0.2**.
4. Select tiptoe slider, and set Minimum to **–1.0** and Maximum to **0**.

5. On the Main toolbar, turn on **Select and Manipulate**, and then drag the triangular slider components to animate the foot using IK. When you're done, turn off Select and Manipulate.
6. Save the file as **ch06_lab_ex2_solb.max**.

You are ready to animate the leg by manipulating the sliders using key framing animation.

Lab Activity Checklist

S. No.	Tasks	Completed	
		Yes	No
1.	Created a leg and foot skeleton		
2.	Aligned the IK goals		
3.	Created animation controls for the leg and the foot		
4.	Linked each IK goal to a Point helper		
5.	Linked the Point helpers to the viewport sliders		
6.	Wired the viewport sliders		
7.	Changed the range of the viewport sliders		

Project

Activities

- Create a bone hierarchy of the character you modeled in Chapter 5. To do this, you need to perform the following tasks:
  - Create bone structures for the legs.
  - Assign IK solvers for the leg bones.
  - Create a bone structure for the torso.
  - Create a bone hierarchy for the arms.
  - Add more detail by adding finger bones.
  - Create the skeleton by linking all the hierarchies.

Skinning a Model

7

Skinning refers to the movement of the covering object in synchronization with the underlying bone structure. You need to use different skin modifiers to skin different models. After you have created a model using a hierarchy of bones, you need to cover the bones with objects that have skin modifiers applied to the objects. The skin modifier is a skeletal deformation tool. It is used to create a skin to encapsulate a skeletal system. While skinning models, deformable objects are bound to the skeleton so that it can be animated to affect the mesh.

At the end of this chapter, you will be able to:

- Identify various aspects of the application of skin modifiers.
- Identify the features of the skin modifier using various weight painter and weight table options.
- Identify the features and uses of the joint, bulge, and morph angle.

7.1 Introduction to the Skin Modifier

7.2 Deformations

7.1 Introduction to the Skin Modifier

The skin modifier is useful for creating skin to encapsulate a skeletal system. When a skin modifier is applied to an object, a capsule-shaped envelope gets attached to the object. An envelope is a single sub-object available for the skin modifier. An envelope is an area that surrounds the bone and defines which vertices of the skin object should be moved with the bone. In the envelope sub-object mode, you can edit the size and the influence of the envelope.

When envelopes overlap, their surfaces blend together. These envelopes can be attached to NURBS, meshes, patches, bones, or splines. When you move a bone with a skin attached to it, the skin follows the bone movement accordingly.

In this section, you will learn to apply and adjust the weight, which is the influence over vertices, of the skin modifiers.

7.1.1 Applying the Skin Modifier

Apply the skin modifier.

When you work with skeletons, a collection of bones has a skin attached to it. Any mesh, patch, or NURBS object can be made a skin using the skin modifier. After you attach a skin to a collection of bones, you can move the bones and the skin will follow the bones movement. When you work with the skin modifier, you need to consider the skinning of sub-objects, editing envelopes, and weights.

You can apply the skin modifier using the Modifier drop-down list, as shown in Figure 7.1.

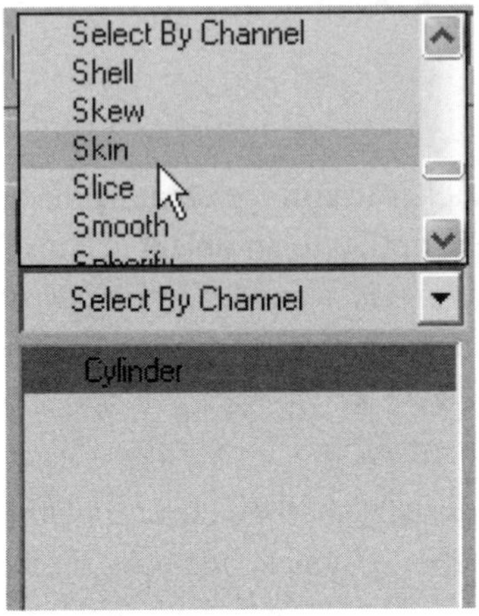

Figure 7.1: Modifier List

The skin modifier rollout has five components, as shown in Figure 7.2.

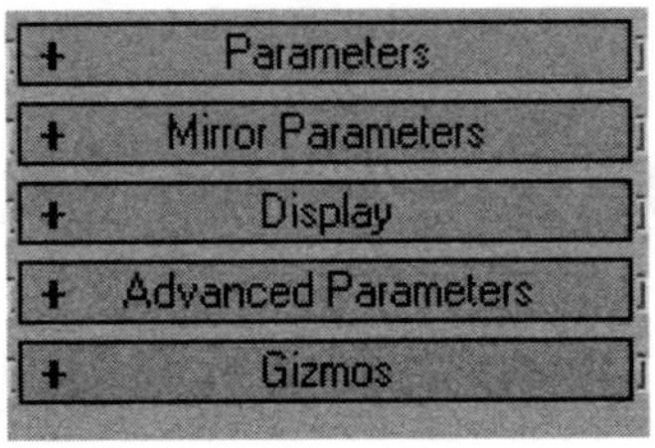

Figure 7.2: Components of the Skin Modifier Rollout

The Parameters rollout has been discussed in Chapter 3.

The different components of the skin modifier rollout are:

- Display: Enables you to define components that are visible in the view ports. The Display rollout is shown in Figure 7.3.

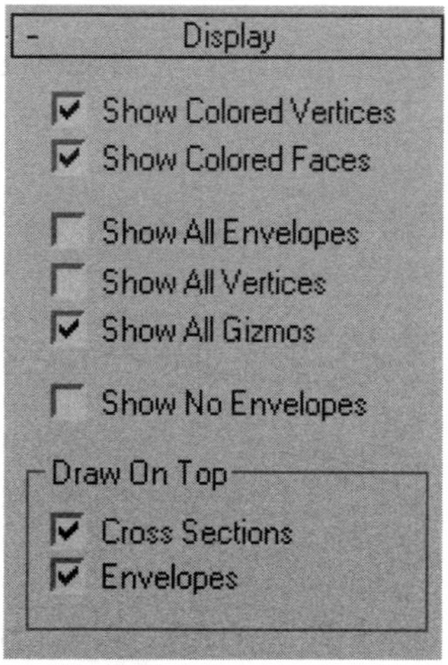

Figure 7.3: Display Rollout

The different options of the Display rollout are:

- Show Colored Vertices: Displays the colored vertices of the model with respect to their respective bones in view ports according to their weights.
- Show Colored Faces: Displays a colored face of the model with respect to their respective bones in view ports according to their weights.
- Show All Envelopes: Displays all envelopes simultaneously.
- Show All Vertices: Draws a small tick mark at every vertex. On a patch surface, it draws all the handles.
- Show No Envelopes: Hides envelopes even when an envelope is selected.
- Show All Gizmos: Displays all the gizmos in addition to the currently selected gizmo.
- Draw on Top Group: Determines which elements will be drawn on top of all other objects in view ports.
- Cross-Sections: Forces cross-sections to be drawn on top.
- Envelopes: Forces envelopes to be drawn on top.

- Mirror Parameters: Is used to apply mirror images to an object. The Mirror Parameters rollout is shown in Figure 7.4.

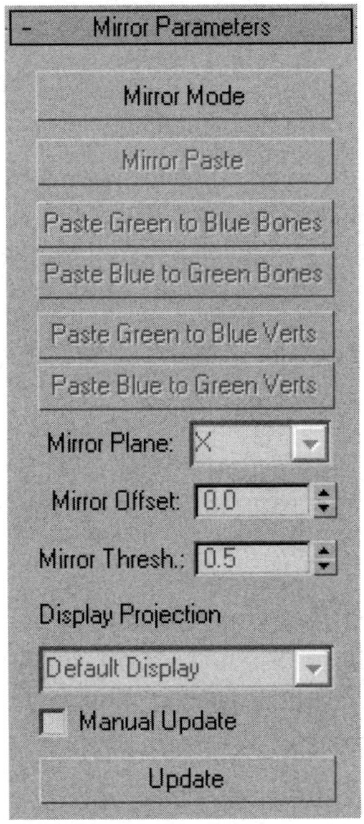

Figure 7.4: Mirror Parameters Rollout

The mirror mode is very useful in giving a symmetrical look to the skinning process. This option is used to achieve a symmetrical influencing style for some models. For example, in human beings, to divide the body vertically into two equal halves.

The various options of the Mirror Parameters rollout are:

- Mirror Mode: Mirrors the envelopes and vertex assignments from one side of the mesh to another.
- Mirror Paste: Allows you to paste selected envelope and vertex assignments to the opposite side of the body.
- Paste Green to Blue Bones: Pastes the envelope settings from blue bones to green.
- Paste Blue to Green Bones: Pastes the envelope settings from green bones to blue.
- Paste Green to Blue Verts: Pastes the individual vertex assignments from all green vertices to the corresponding blue vertices.

- Paste Blue to Green Verts: Pastes the individual vertex assignments from all blue vertices to the corresponding green vertices.
- Mirror Plane: Determines the plane that will be used to determine the left and right sides.
- Mirror Offset: Shifts the mirror plane along the mirror plane axis.
- Mirror Thresh: Sets the relative distance that the mirroring tools will look when setting vertices as left or right. If some vertices in the mesh, other than those at the mirror plane, are not colored blue or green when you turn on the mirror mode, you can increase the mirror thresh value to include a larger area of the character.
- Display Projection: When Display Projection is set to Default Display, selecting vertices on one side of the mirror plane automatically projects the selection to the opposite side.
- Manual Update: Turn on this option to update the display manually.
- Update: When Manual Update is turned on, you can use this button to update the display with new settings.
- Advanced Parameters: Enables you to manage bones, vertices, and envelopes, by performing resetting, saving, and loading functions.

The Advanced Parameters rollout is shown in Figure 7.5.

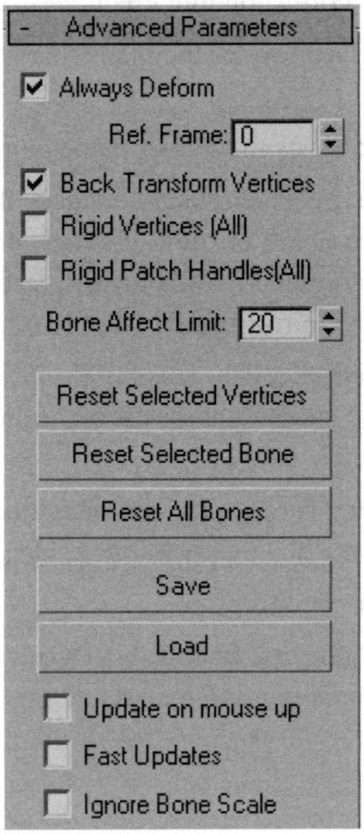

Figure 7.5: Advanced Parameters Rollout

The different options of the Advanced Parameters rollout are:

- Always Deform: Used to edit the transformation relationship between bones and controlled points. This relationship is initially set when the skin is applied. To change the relationship, the end user can deactivate Always Deform, move the object or the bones, and reactivate. The new transformation relationship is applied.
- Back Transform Vertices: Enables you to link the mesh to the bone structure. When you link the mesh to the bone structure, any movement of the bones causes the mesh to move twice as far as it should, as the mesh moves once with the bones and once with the link. Selecting this option prevents the mesh from moving twice.
- Rigid Vertices (All): Causes vertices to have assignments to only one bone, where the envelope has the most influence. The weight of the vertices is not distributed over more than one bone, and the deformation of the skinned object

is rigid, if this option is selected. This is mainly used for games that do not support weighted point transformation.

- Rigid Patch Handles (All): Forces patch handle weights to equal the knots weights on a patch model.
- Bone Affect Limit: Limits the number of bones that can affect a vertex.
- Reset Selected Vertices: Resets the weight of selected vertices to the envelope defaults. You can use this to reset weights after manually changing vertex weights.
- Reset Selected Bone: Resets associated vertex weights back to the original weights calculated for the selected bone's envelope.
- Reset All Bones: Resets all vertex weights back to the original weights calculated for all the envelopes associated with a bone.
- Save/Load: Enables you to save the envelope position and shape. If you load an envelope onto a different system of bones, a Load Envelope prompts you to match the incoming bones to the current bones.
- Update on Mouse Up: Helps keep workflow moving quickly by avoiding unnecessary updates. When the mouse button is pressed down, no updates will take place. When the mouse button is released, updates will occur.
- Fast Updates: Turns off the view port display of weighted deformations and gizmos and uses rigid deformation when not rendering.

■ Gizmos: Enables you to apply three kinds of deformers to the vertices of the object.

The Gizmos rollout is shown in Figure 7.6.

Figure 7.6: Gizmos Rollout

The options of the Gizmos rollout are:

- Joint Angle Deformer: Is applied to joint vertices.
- Bulge Angle Deformer: Creates a bulge in the bone by lifting the vertices.

To apply the skin modifier, perform the following steps:

1. Create a cylinder (NURBS, mesh, or patch object) in your view port, as shown in Figure 7.7.

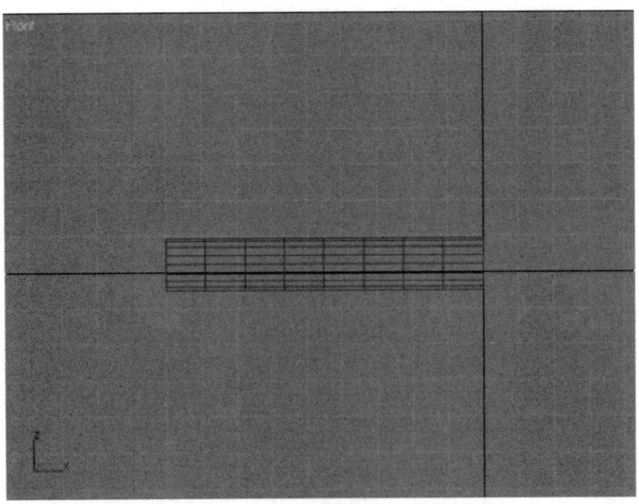

Figure 7.7: Mesh Object (Cylinder)

2. Create bones as a skeletal system.
3. Place the skeleton inside the object so that the skeleton can influence the object.

   Figure 7.8 shows the skeleton and the mesh object.

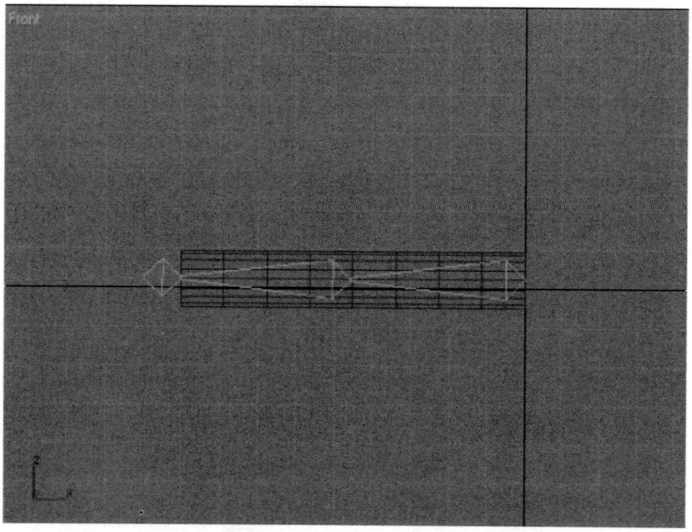

Figure 7.8: Skeleton and Mesh Object

4. Select the mesh object.
5. Select the skin modifier from the Modify panel, as shown in Figure 7.9.

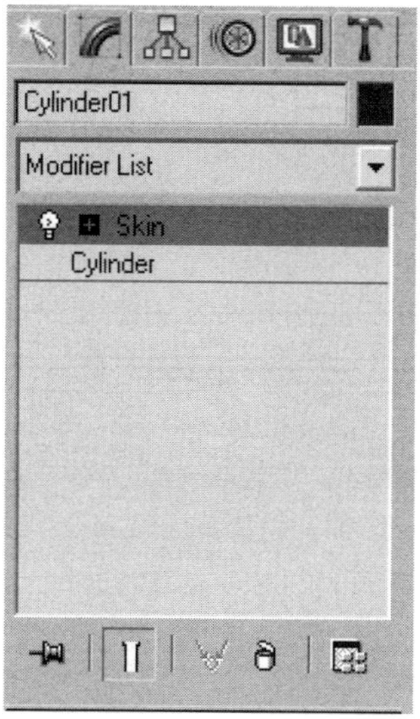

Figure 7.9: Skin Modifier

6. Click the Add button and choose the skeleton object in the Parameters rollout, as shown in Figure 7.10.

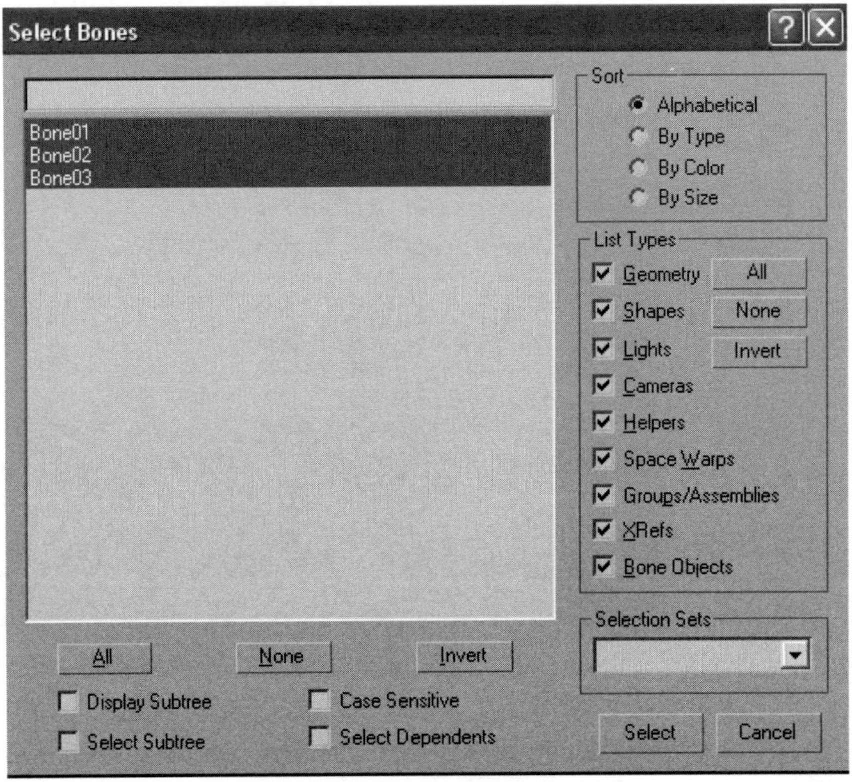

Figure 7.10: Select Bones Dialog Box

7. Click **Edit Envelopes** and select an envelope to modify the volume where each bone can influence the surrounding geometry, as shown in Figure 7.11.

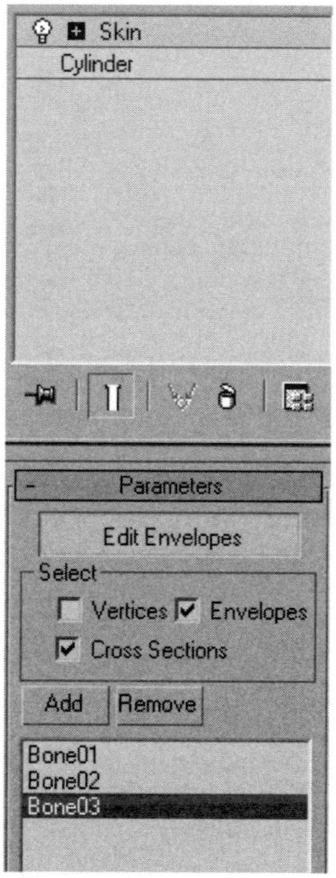

Figure 7.11: Parameters Rollout

Editing Envelopes

Editing an envelope influences the skeleton by adding and removing bones to and from the skin. The parameters rollout includes a list of bones that are assigned to the skin modifier. You can add and remove bones from this list using the Add Bone and Remove Bone buttons. You can edit an envelope using the Edit Envelope button.

Figure 7.12 shows a cylinder surrounding three bone objects with a skin modifier applied.

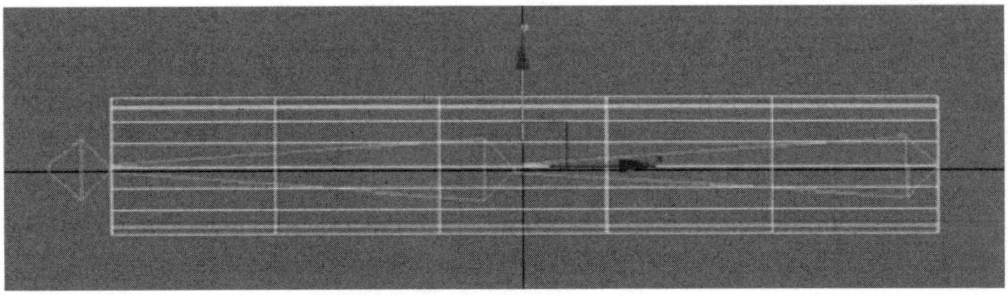

Figure 7.12: Cylinder Surrounding Three Bone Objects with a Skin Modifier Applied

You need to click the Add Bone button to include the three bones within the skin modifier list. The first bone is selected within the list.

When you click the Edit Envelope button, the envelope for the first bone is revealed.

For each envelope, you can add a cross section using the Add Cross Section button. This button lets you select a cross section shape within the view ports. The Remove Cross Section button removes an added cross section from the envelope. Figure 7.13 shows the Cross Sections rollout with the Add and Remove button.

Figure 7.13: Cross Sections Rollout

When the envelope is visible within the view port, you will see that it consists of two capsule-shaped areas within each other. At each end of these areas there are four small square handles that can bc dragged to change the cross section radius. The radius of the selected cross section is displayed in the Radius field within the Envelope Properties section of the parameters rollout.

The view port shades vertices included with the envelope as red and vertices not included within the envelope blue. These colors are the visual clues that help you see exactly which sections of skin will move with the bones.

The Envelope Properties section of the parameters rollout includes five icon buttons, as shown in Figure 7.14. The first button toggles between Absolute and Relative. All vertices that fall within the outer envelope are fully weighted when the Absolute toggle is selected, but only those within both envelopes are fully weighted when the Relative toggle is selected.

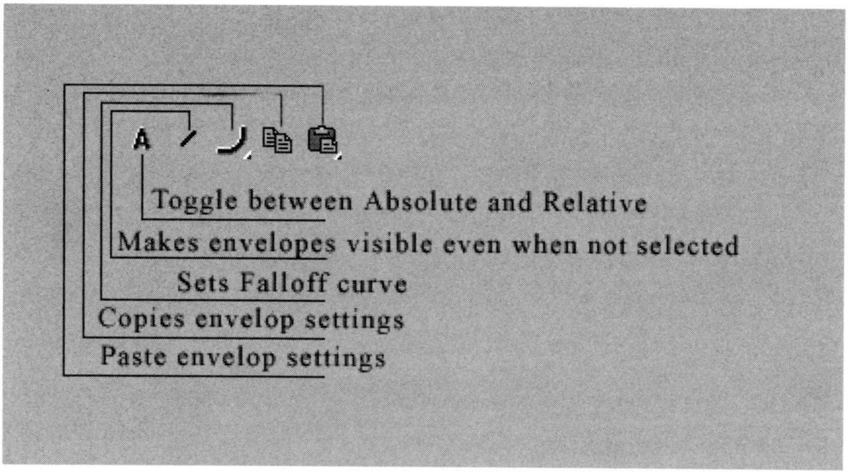

Figure 7.14: Envelope Properties Section

The second icon button enables envelopes to be visible even when not selected. This helps you see the adjacent bones overlap. The third icon button sets the Falloff curve for the envelopes. The options within this envelope are:

- Fast out: Steep fall off curve of the envelope.
- Slow out: Gradual fall off curve for the envelope.
- Linear: Linear fall off curve for the envelope.
- Sinual: Sinusoidal fall off curve for the envelope.

You can use the last two icon buttons to copy and paste envelopes settings to other bones. The fly-out options for the Paste button include:

- Paste (to a single bone)
- Paste to all bones
- Paste to multiple bones (opens a selection dialog box)

When you select the squash option in the Object Properties dialog box, you can set a squash value, which determines the amount of squash applied to the object.

7.1.2 Weighing the Skin Modifier

Describe how to weigh the skin modifier.

Envelopes assign weights to each vertex of the skin to define how strongly the envelope influences the vertex. A vertex weight can range from 0 to 1. The weight of 0 means the bone doesn't affect the vertex at all. At 0.5, the vertex is affected partially by the bone, and partially by one or more other bones. At a weight of 1, only that bone influences the vertex. Each vertex can have weights from several different bones, but all the weights must add up to 1. In an envelope, red vertices have a weight of 1 or approximately 1, while blue vertices have a weight close to 0 or 0. The color of the vertices can visually help you show the influence of an envelope over the vertices. For example, red implies that the envelope controls the vertices, whereas blue implies that vertices are not at all controlled.

Figure 7.15 shows the weight properties of selected vertices.

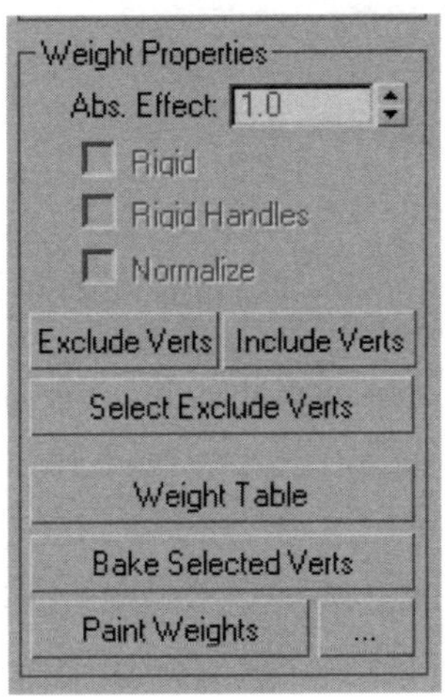

Figure 7.15: Weight Properties of Selected Vertices

The options of the Weight Parameters rollout are:

- Abs. Effect: Enables you to enter an absolute weight for the selected bone to selected vertices.
- Rigid: Enables the selected vertices to be influenced by only one bone. This bone should be the one which has the maximum influence.

- Rigid Handles: Enables the handles of selected patch vertices to be influenced by only one bone. This bone should be the one with the maximum influence.
- Normalize: Forces the total weights of each selected vertex to add up to 1.
- Exclude Verts: Takes the currently selected vertices and adds them to the exclusion list for the currently selected bone. Any vertices in this exclusion list will not be affected by this bone.
- Include Verts: Takes the selected vertices out of the exclusion list for the selected bone. The bone can then affect these vertices.
- Select Exclude Verts: Takes the currently excluded vertices and selects them.
- Weight Table: Displays a table for viewing and changing weight for all bones in the skeletal structure.
- Bake Selected Verts: Click to bake the current vertex weight. Baked weights are not affected by envelope changes, only by changes to Abs. Effect or weights in the Weight Table.
- Paint Verts: You can click and drag the cursor over vertices in the view ports to brush on weight for the selected bone.

Using the Weight Table

You use the weight table for the skin modifier to change vertex weights for several vertices and bones at a time. The weight table button opens the weight table interface. This table displays all the vertices for the skinned object.

To set a weight, you need to locate the vertex for the bone and click in the cell and type the new value. If you click a cell and drag it to the left or right, the weight value changes. Weight values can be changed between cells. Right-clicking a cell sets its value to 0 and right-clicking with the Ctrl key sets its value to 1.

Figure 7.16 shows the table that appears when you click the Weight Table button.

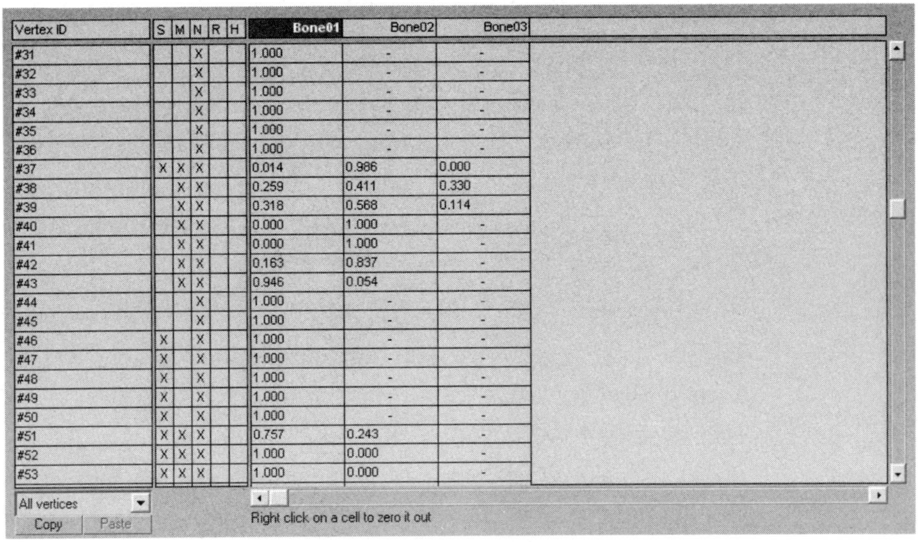

Vertex ID	S	M	N	R	H	Bone01	Bone02	Bone03
#31			X			1.000	-	-
#32			X			1.000	-	-
#33			X			1.000	-	-
#34			X			1.000	-	-
#35			X			1.000	-	-
#36			X			1.000	-	-
#37	X	X	X			0.014	0.986	0.000
#38		X	X			0.259	0.411	0.330
#39		X	X			0.318	0.568	0.114
#40		X	X			0.000	1.000	-
#41		X	X			0.000	1.000	-
#42		X	X			0.163	0.837	-
#43		X	X			0.946	0.054	-
#44			X			1.000	-	-
#45			X			1.000	-	-
#46	X		X			1.000	-	-
#47	X		X			1.000	-	-
#48	X		X			1.000	-	-
#49	X		X			1.000	-	-
#50	X		X			1.000	-	-
#51	X	X	X			0.757	0.243	-
#52	X	X	X			1.000	0.000	-
#53	X	X	X			1.000	0.000	-

Figure 7.16: Weight Table

Painting Weights

Painting weights is a process where you can assign weight to individual vertices of a skinned object. It is used to get the exact deformation of skin when you transform your skeleton. You can also assign weights to the vertices to move the vertices in the skin with the bone. Using the Paint Weights button, you can paint with a brush over the surface of the skin object. The paint strength value sets the value for each brush stroke. This value can be positive (up to 1.0) for vertices that will move with the bone, or negative (up to –1.0) for vertices that will not move with the bone. The radius and feather settings define the size and softness of the brush.

To the right of the Paint Weights button is the painter options button, as shown in Figure 7.17.

Figure 7.17: Paint Weights Button

Click the painter options button to open the Painter Options dialog box, as shown in Figure 7.18.

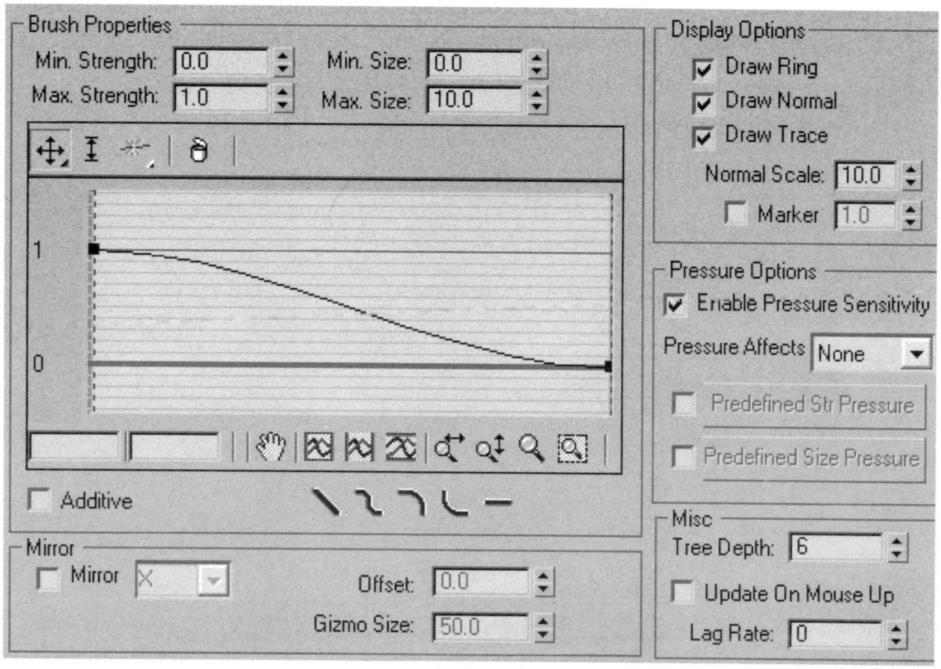

Figure 7.18: Painter Options Dialog Box

The Min/Max Strength and Min/Max Size value determine the minimum and maximum weight values and paint gizmo sizes. You can define the brush falloff using the curve. This keeps the weights from making abrupt changes. Under the curve are several buttons for defining the shape of the falloff curve. These buttons are:

- Linear
- Smooth
- Slow
- Fast
- Flat

The Display Options section includes options that determine the look of the painting gizmo. You can enable pressure sensitivity for the brush gizmo. The options are:

- None
- Strength
- Size
- Both

Using the graph, you can predefine strength and size pressure curves, and then select to use them. You can also set an offset and the gizmo size. This is handy for muscles that you want to deform symmetrically. The Tree Depth, Update on Mouse Up, and Lag Rate options control how often the scene and painted strokes are updated.

Practice Questions

1. List the different components of the skin modifier rollout and provide a brief description for each of them.
2. What are Gizmos and what are their rollout options?
3. State the effect of editing envelopes. List the buttons that can be used to edit envelopes.
4. Explain the purpose of a weight table.

7.2 Deformations

Deformation denotes any change in shape of an object. When you create the model of a character, it has a particular shape, but when you animate the character the shape changes. Suppose there is a model of a hand which is straight, but when it bends the shape is deformed. In 3D Studio Max, you use a skin modifier to deform objects. When the skin modifier is applied to a mesh and bone, the mesh becomes capable of deformation as the bone moves.

An envelope is an area that surrounds the bone. It defines which vertices of the skin object are to be moved along with the bone. The initial shape and position of the envelope depends on the type of bone object. Bones create a linear envelope that extends along the longest axis of the bone geometry. Spline objects create envelopes that follow the curve of the spline. Primitive objects create an envelope that follows the longest axis of the object. You can also deform the mesh based on the angle of the bones.

There are three deformers that allow you to shape the mesh based on bone angles. The Joint and Bulge Angle deformers use a lattice. When you add a gizmo, you will find some cross points on it, which are called lattices. You can select them and move them as needed, and thereby deform the mesh.

Figure 7.19 shows the lattice of a deformer.

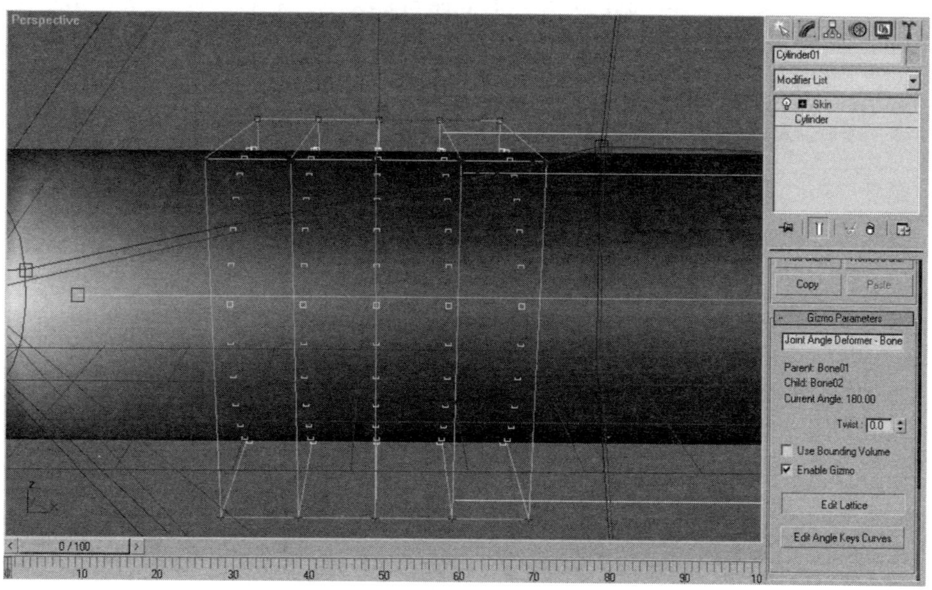

Figure 7.19: Lattice of a Deformer

A lattice that supports the freeform deformation of a mesh object is called a freeform deformation lattice (FFD).

The Morph Angle Deformers morph the mesh at specified angles. Using modifiers, you can create a copy of the mesh and deform the mesh using standard tools that create morph targets. Figure 7.20 shows the lattice of a deformer.

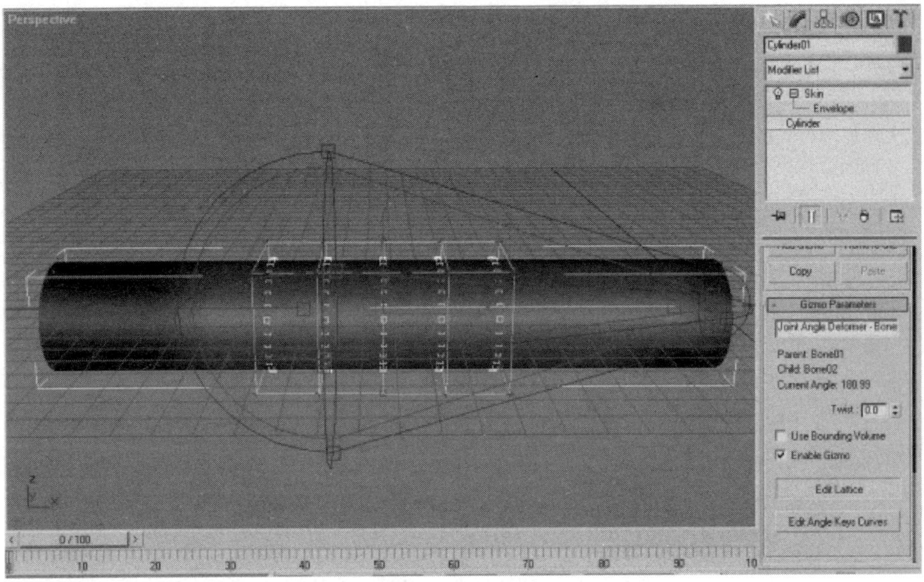

Figure 7.20: Lattice of a Deformer After Using Modifiers

7.2.1 Modifying the Skin Object

Modify the skin object without affecting the envelopes.

To apply the skin modifier and adjust the skin and/or bones without affecting the envelopes, you need to perform the following steps:

1. Select the object to which the skin modifier is applied.
2. In the Advanced Parameters rollout, turn off the Always Deform option.
3. Apply any necessary transforms to the mesh/patch object or bones objects.
4. Turn the Always Deform option on.

To apply the skin modifier to a cylinder with a bones skeleton, perform the following steps:

1. On the Create Panel, under Standard Primitives, click **Cylinder**.
2. Click and drag 20 units to create the base of the cylinder in the middle of the Top view port.
3. Release the mouse button and drag up 130 units to establish the height of the cylinder.
4. Set Height Segments to **20** on the Parameters rollout, as shown in Figure 7.21. This provides the mesh detail for a smooth surface deformation.

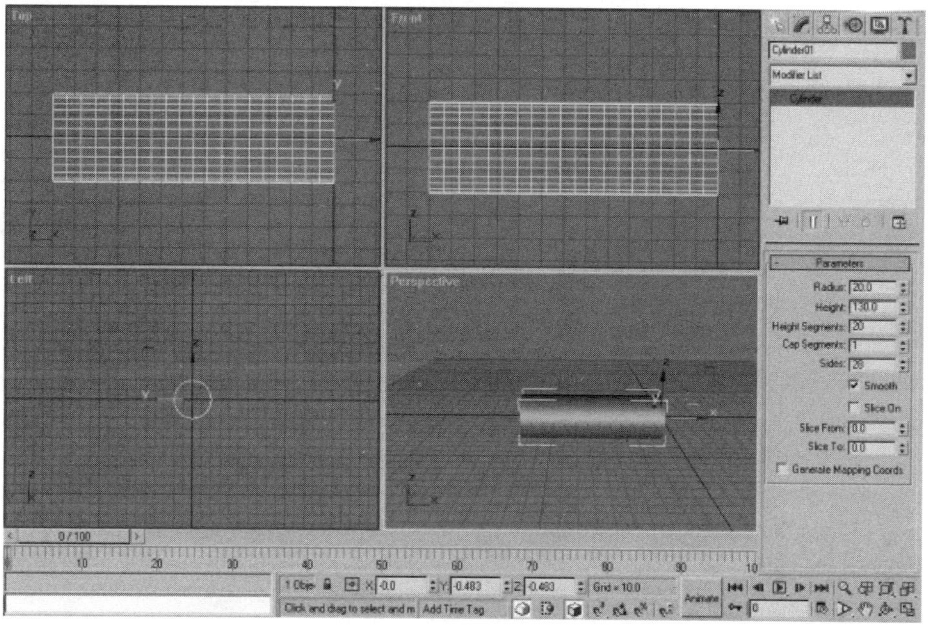

Figure 7.21: Smooth Surface Deformation

5. On the Create panel, under Systems, click **Bones**. Ensure that an IK Solver is chosen in the IK Solver list. Click Bones.
6. In the Front view port, click successively three times: below the cylinder, in the middle of the cylinder, and above the top of the cylinder.

7. Right-click the front viewport to end bones creation. Three bones are displayed, as shown in Figure 7.22. Two of them are within the middle of the cylinder.

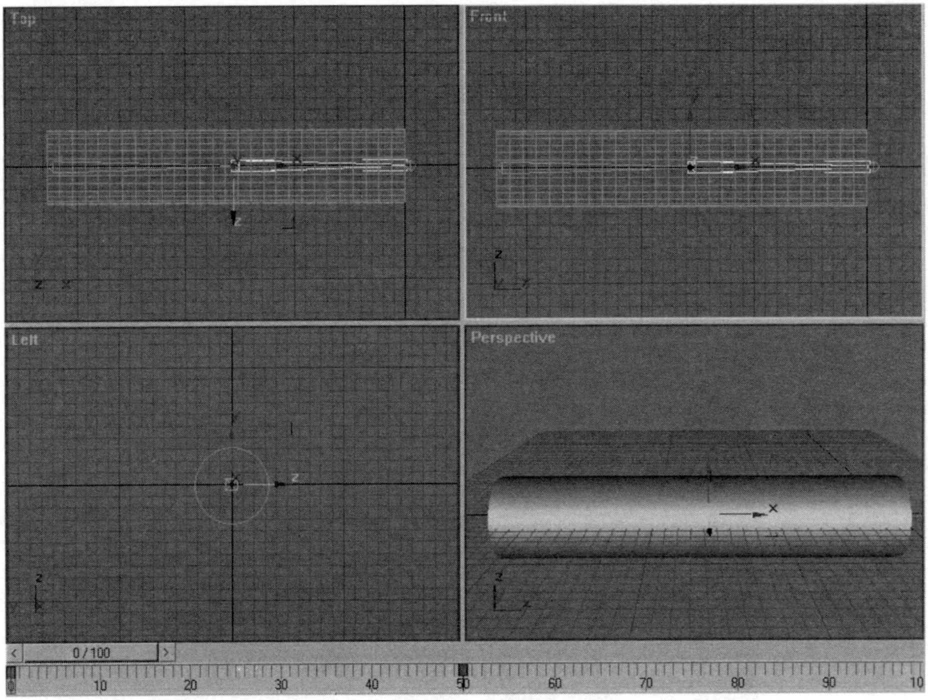

Figure 7.22: Three Bones Created

8. Select the cylinder.

9. Choose **Skin** from the modifier list on the Modify panel, as shown in Figure 7.23.

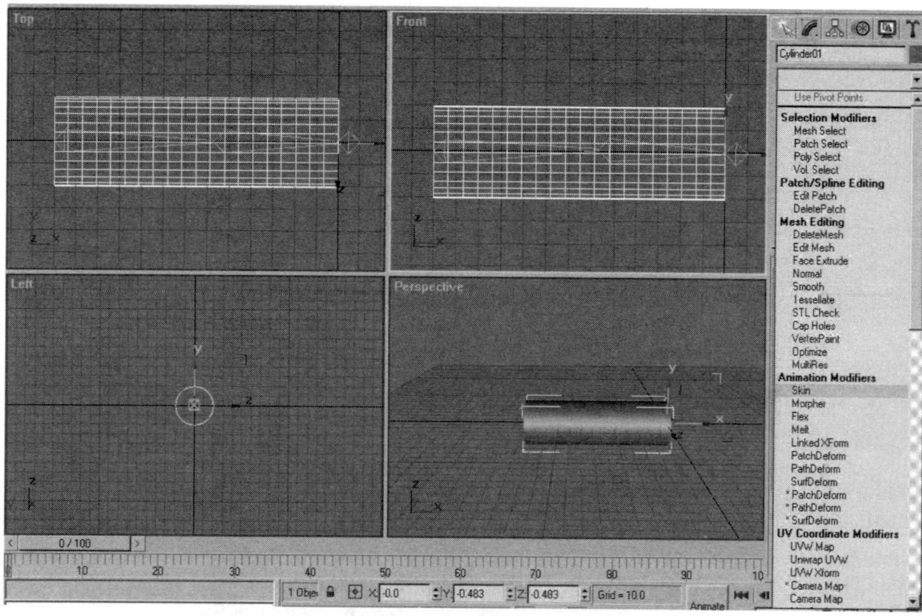

Figure 7.23: Choosing Skin from the Modifier List

10. On the Skin modifier's Parameters rollout, click **Add**. The names of the bones are now displayed in the list.

11. In the Front view port, select the **bone end effector** (IK Chain01), as shown in Figure 7.24, and move it around.

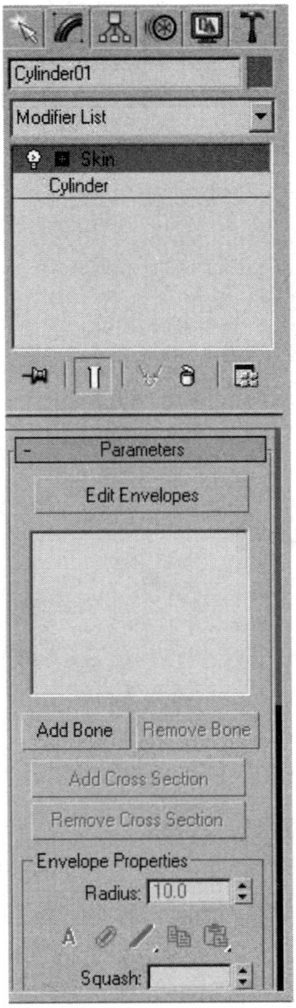

Figure 7.24: Selecting the Bone End Effector

When you click the **Add Bone** button, the Select Bones dialog box appears, as shown in Figure 7.25.

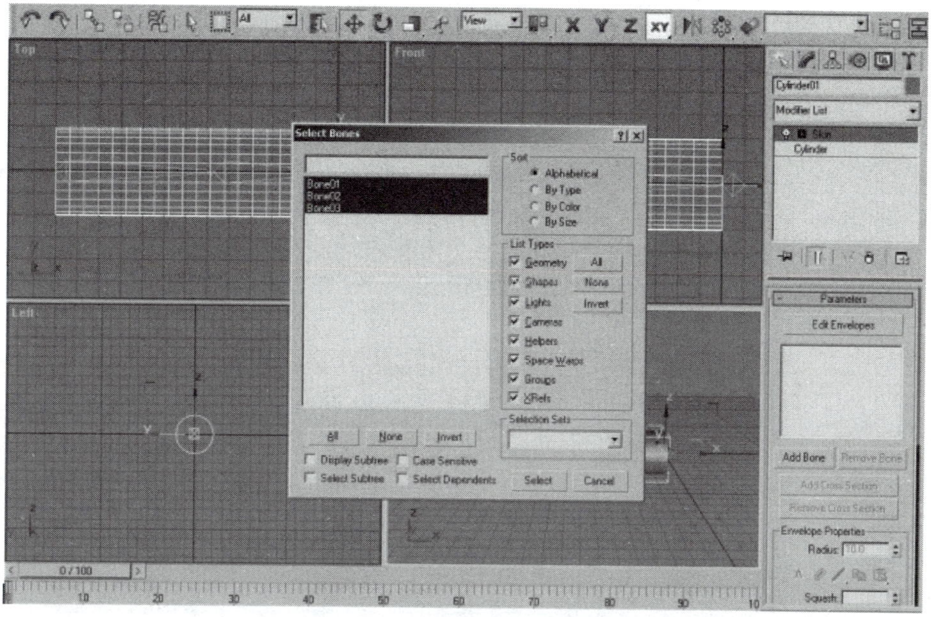

Figure 7.25: Select Bones Dialog Box

12. Save the file as **ch07_morphangle.max**.

The cylinder deforms to follow the bones. You may have to enlarge the envelopes to encompass the entire cylinder. To adjust envelopes to refine the surface deformation, choose the skin modifier's Envelope sub-object level, and use the Edit Envelopes controls to resize envelopes and change vertex weights.

Gizmos

Gizmos are controllers that show up in the view ports and provide an interactive way to transform objects. A gizmo is a spherical area around the selected vertices through which the vertices can be deformed. Controls in the Gizmos rollout enable you to deform the mesh according to the angle of the joint, and add gizmos to selected points on the object. The rollout consists of a list box containing all the gizmos for different modifiers, a drop-down list of the current types of gizmos, and four buttons (Add, Remove, Copy, and Paste).

To apply a gizmo, the first step is to select the vertices. To select vertices, enable the Vertices check box of the Parameters rollout and drag over the vertices. In the view port, select the vertices.

After adding the gizmo, click on the Edit Lattice button. To edit the lattices of the gizmo, select some lattices of the gizmo, and move them as required. The mesh will move according to the gizmo's lattice movement, so the mesh will be deformed as the shape of the gizmo changes. The changed shape of the gizmo is shown in Figure 7.26.

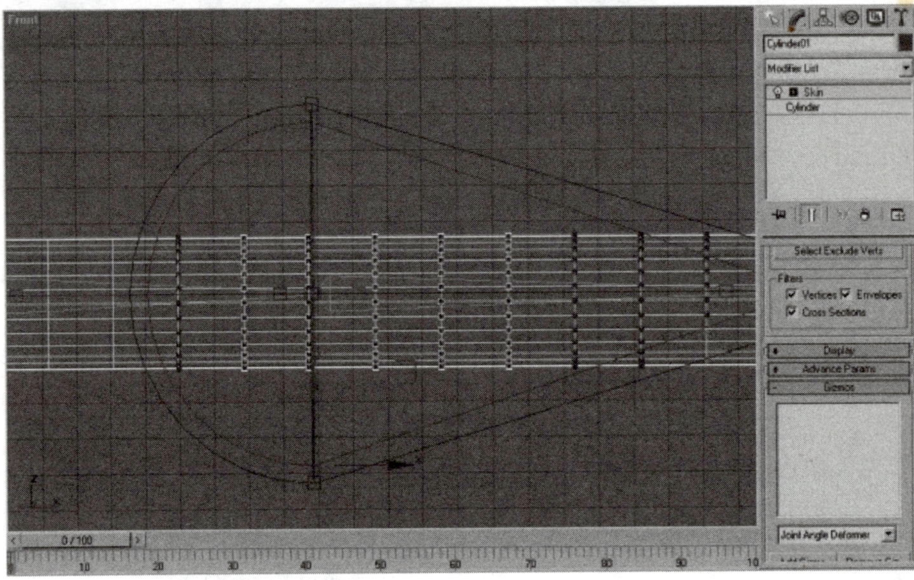

Figure 7.26: Changed Shape of the Gizmo

The workflow for adding a gizmo is to select the vertices that you want to affect, then select the bones that will drive the deformation, and click the Add button.

7.2.2 Deformers

Identify the types of deformers.

Deformers are controlling devices for a group of vertices, a single vertex, or an entire object. Deformers act like a bag. In this bag, a selected number of vertices can be collected and tied up inside. Whenever this bag is moved, the vertices collected inside the bag will also travel with it. Deformation controls allow you to scale, twist, teeter, bevel, or fit shapes along a path.

The three deformers available are:

- Joint Angle Deformer: This deformer deforms the vertices of a mesh object around the joint between two bones where the skin can bunch up and cause problems while deforming. For example, suppose we have created the model of a human hand and attached bones to it. When we bend the hand, the vertices of the elbow may distort. To overcome this problem, we can use a joint angle deformer, as an elbow is a point where two bones join. This deformer is required when you need to move vertices on both the parent and child bones.
- Bulge Angle Deformer: This deformer moves vertices of a mesh object away from the bone to simulate bulging muscles. For example, suppose we have created the model of a hand, attached bones to it, and added skins. When a human hand bends, the biceps muscles move, and it bulges. In the model, the parent bone contains the biceps mesh position of the hand. To make it realistic, you may use a bulge angle deformer. This deformer is required when you need to move only the parent bone.
- Morph Angle Deformer: This deformer can be used on vertices for both the parent and child bones to move the vertices to a morph position. This deformer is used when a shape is morphed into another shape. It provides smooth deformation between the two shapes.

You should keep these distinctions in mind when you select vertices to deform. For example, if you want to use the Joint Angle deformer, then select vertices close to the joint that will drive the deformation. If you want the parent bone vertices to deform like a biceps muscle, then select vertices that are only assigned to the parent bone before adding the Bulge Angle deformer. If all the vertices of the parent and child bone must be deformed, then select all of the vertices and add the Morph Angle deformer.

Morph Angle Deformer

Create the cylinder and bones from the procedure above before you continue with this procedure. To use the morph angle deformer, perform the following steps:

1. At frame 50, animate bone 2 so that bones 1 and 2 represent a 90-degree angle.
2. Ensure that the bones are at about a 180-degree angle at frame 0.
3. Move to frame 0.
4. Turn on Edit Envelopes in the Parameters rollout.
5. Select the child bone (bone 2) in the modifiers list of bones.
6. Turn on Vertices in the Filters area.
7. Select a portion of the vertices controlled by both bones in the view ports, region window.

8. Select the Morph Angle Deformer in the drop-down list in the Gizmos rollout.
9. Click **Add Gizmo.**
10. Scrub the Time Slider to frame 50.
11. Add an Edit Mesh modifier above the skin modifier in the modifier stack.
12. Turn on Vertex and Soft Selection in the Edit Mesh modifier.
13. Edit the mesh to the shape you want.
14. Go back down in the stack to the skin modifier. Click **Yes** if the topology warning dialog appears.
15. Click **Add from Stack** in the Deforms Parameters rollout.
16. Delete the Edit Mesh modifier from the stack. Bending the arm without the Morph Angle deformer causes the sleeve to crease, as shown in Figure 7.27.

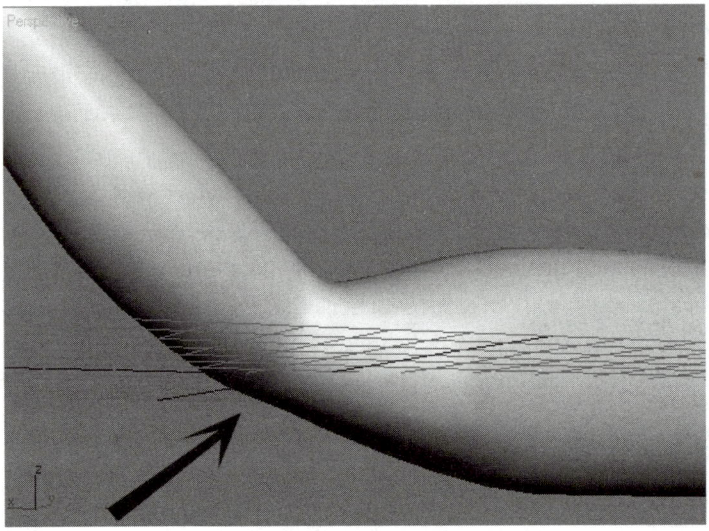

Figure 7.27: Bending the Arm

If you use the morph angle deformer, it creates a smooth bend in the sleeve, as shown in Figure 7.28.

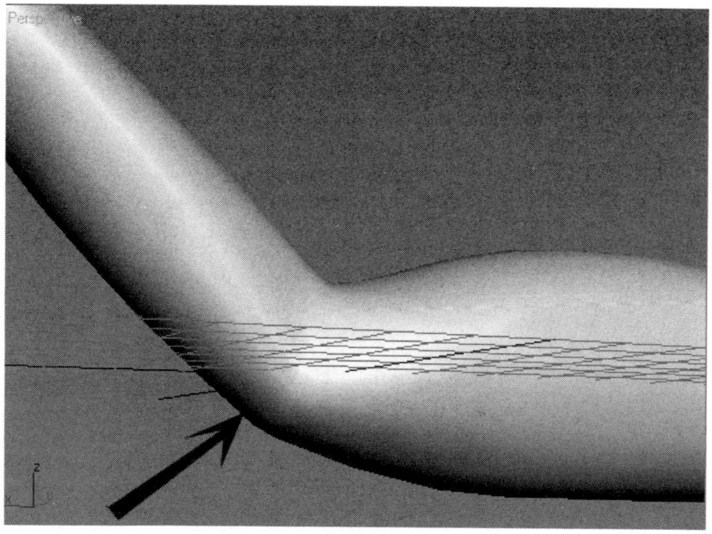

Figure 7.28: Morph Angle Deformer

To add a gizmo:

1. Select the child bone for the joint you want to deform.
2. Select the vertices that you want to deform.
3. Add a gizmo.

After a gizmo is added, a Deform Parameters rollout is displayed that contains gizmo parameters that you can adjust.

Figure 7.29 shows the Gizmo Parameter rollout.

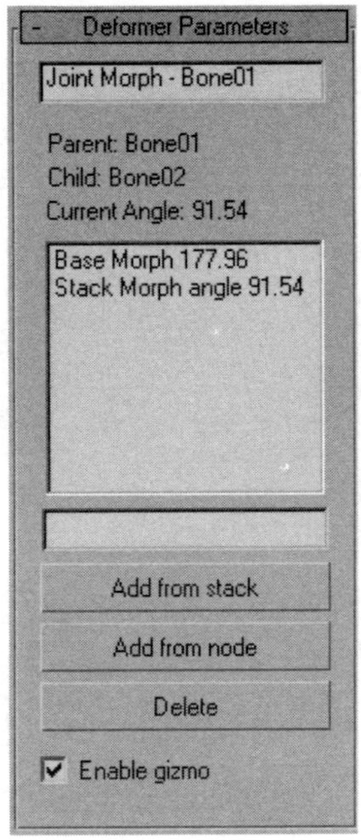

Figure 7.29: Gizmo Parameter Rollout

The Gizmo Parameter rollout consists of the following options:

- Remove Gizmo: Removes the selected gizmo from the list.
- Copy: Copies the selected gizmo.
- Paste: The Paste button pastes the current copy buffer into the currently selected gizmo. You can only paste to the same type of gizmos. For instance, you cannot paste from a bulge gizmo to a joint gizmo.
- Add from Stack: Uses the current state of the stack to get the morph target. When we go for a morph angle deformer, after skinning and applying morph angle deformers to it, we have to apply the Edit Mesh modifier to edit the mesh object. You can edit the mesh object in the modifier stack. You can see the modifiers that are cylinders, then skin, followed by edit mesh. When we come down to skin we lose the effect of modifications of the Edit Mesh modifier. By clicking the Add from Stack button, you will get the effect of an Edit Mesh modifier as the target of the morph.
- Add from Node: Uses another object as your morph target for this angle.

You can use Snap Shot on the main toolbar to create a new target for morphing.

The Joint Angle deformer and the Bulge Angle deformer are almost identical in the way they operate. The difference is that the Bulge Angle deformer only works on vertices of the parent bone, while the Joint Angle works on vertices on both the child and parent bone. Figure 7.30 shows the Joint Angle and Bulge Angle Parameters rollout.

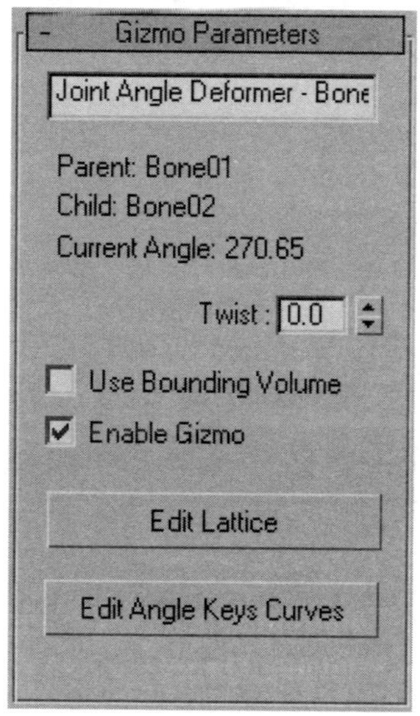

Figure 7.30: Joint Angle Parameters Rollout

The following parameters are for the Joint Angle and Bulge Angle deformer. These two deformers are similar in the way they operate.

The Joint Angle and Bulge Angle parameters rollout consists of:

- Name Field: Enables you to change the name of the deformer.
- Twist: Enables you to spin the gizmo around the mesh to place control points appropriately.
- Use Bounding Volume: Turn this option on if you want to change the geometry, such as increase the segments on a cylinder. If the geometry changes, the mesh will still deform inside the lattice if this is turned on.
- Enable Gizmo: Toggles the effect of the gizmo on and off.

- Edit Lattice: Enables you to move the lattice control points in the view ports.
- Edit Angle Keys Curves: Brings up a curve editor that lets you manipulate the shape of the lattice at a particular angle. This curve is mapped into a position versus angle relationship. The Y-axis is the position and the X-axis is the angle. The X-axis and Y-axis will show you the curves of the current selected points. The red curves are X, green curves are Y, and blue curves are Z. Figure 7.31 shows the Joint Graph.

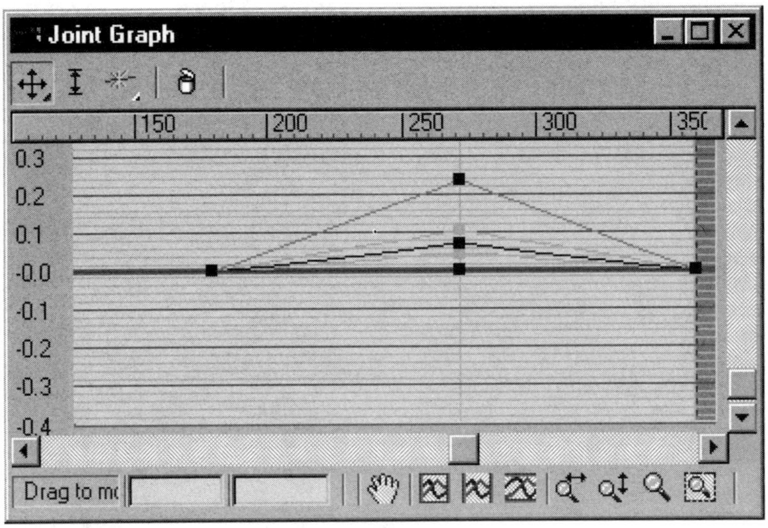

Figure 7.31: Joint Graph

To apply any of these deformers, first select the child link, then select vertices on the mesh, and then apply the deformers. Remember to turn on Vertices in the Filters group before trying to region-select vertices in the view ports.

Practice Questions

1. Explain deformation.
2. List the steps to apply the skin modifier and adjust the skin and/or bones without affecting the envelopes.
3. List the three deformers available and explain them.

Summary

- The skin modifier is useful for creating skin to surround a skeletal system. When a skin modifier is applied to an object, it gets a capsule-shaped envelope attached to it.
- An envelope is an area that surrounds the bone and defines which vertices of the skin object are to be moved with the bone.
- Any mesh, patch, or NURBS object can be made into a skin using the skin modifier.
- The different rollouts of the skin modifier rollout are:
  - Display
  - Mirror
  - Advanced
  - Gizmos
- Editing an envelope influences the skeleton by adding and removing bones to and from the skin.
- Envelopes assign weights to each vertex of the skin to define how strongly the envelope influences the vertex.
- A vertex weight can range from 0 to 1. Weight 0 means the bone does not affect the vertex. At 0.5, the vertex is affected partially by the bone, and partially by one or more other bones. At weight 1, only that bone influences the vertex.
- A weight table can be used for the skin modifier to change vertex weights for several vertices and bones at a time.
- Painting weights is a process where you can assign weight to individual vertices of your skin object.
- Deformation denotes any change in shape. The model of a character has a particular shape but when the character is animated, the shape changes.
- A lattice that supports the freeform deformation of a mesh object is called a freeform deformation lattice (FFD).

- The following steps need to be performed to apply the skin modifier and adjust the skin and/or bones without affecting the envelopes:
    - Select the object to which the skin modifier is applied.
    - In the Advanced Parameters rollout, turn off Always Deform.
    - Apply any necessary transforms to the mesh/patch object or bones objects.
    - Turn Always Deform back on.
- Gizmos are controllers that show up in the view ports and provide an interactive way to transform objects. A gizmo is a spherical area around the selected vertices through which the vertices can be deformed.
- Deformers are controlling devices for a group of vertices, a single vertex, or an entire object. Deformers act like a bag. In this bag, a selected number of vertices can be collected and tied up inside.
- The three deformers are:
    - Joint Angle Deformer
    - Bulge Angle Deformer
    - Morph Angle Deformer

References

- http://www.billysalisbury.com/tutorials_skinning.htm (February 10, 2004)
- http://www.vecpix.com/tutorials/3dstudio/sm004.php (February 10, 2004)
- http://www.geocities.com/my3dstudio/tutorials/animating/skin/singlepageskin.htm (February 10, 2004)
- http://www3.sympatico.ca/psykopat/tutorials/skin_modifier.htm (February 10, 2004)
- http://www.piggyson.com/gr/ (February 10, 2004)
- http://avl.etsu.edu/intranet/resources/CharacterAnimSite/Envelopes.htm (February 10, 2004)
- http://www.metasynth.com/AMPRODOCS/pages_picts/pages/animation.html (February 10, 2004)
- http://www.vecpix.com/tutorials/freehand/fh007.php (February 10, 2004)
- http://www.webreference.com/3d/lesson99/ (February 10, 2004)

Assignments

1. Research on the Internet and create a report detailing:
   a. Definition of skinning.
   b. Tasks that can be performed using this methodology.
   c. Uses of skinning in the modern animation development.
   d. Links to sample works of animation created using the skinning technique.
2. List the different options of the display rollout in the skin modifier rollout.
3. List the various options of the Mirror Parameters rollout and explain them.
4. Identify the different options of the Advanced Parameters rollout and explain them.
5. Identify the options of the Weight Parameters rollout and state their functions.
6. List the steps of applying the skin modifier to a cylinder with a bones skeleton.

Lab Exercises

Exercise 1

Objective

- Apply the skin modifier.

Problem Statement

Apply the skin modifier to a cylinder with a bone skeleton.

Procedure

1. Click **Cylinder** on the Create panel, under Standard Primitives.
2. Create a cylinder of radius 10 and height 120 in the Top viewport.
3. Set Height Segment to 20 on the Parameter rollout. This will give you a smooth deformation. Figure 7.32 shows the cylinder.

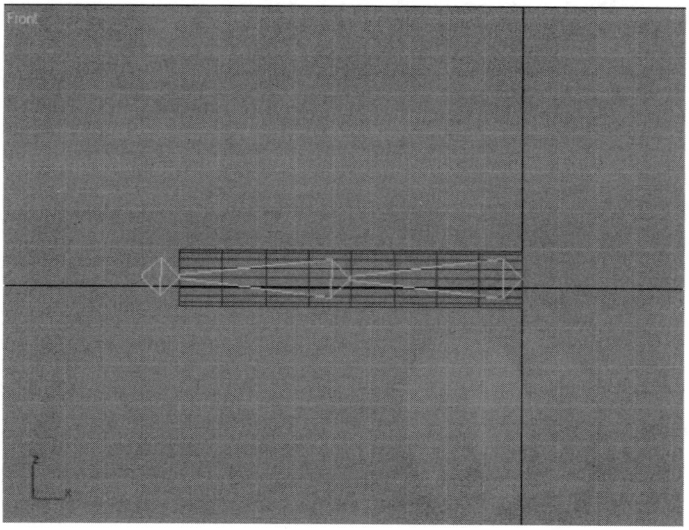

Figure 7.32: Cylinder

4. Click **Bones** from Create panel → Systems. Ensure that an IK Solver is selected from the IK Solver list. Check the Assign to Children and Assign to Root check boxes. Figure 7.33 shows the Bones Creation rollout.

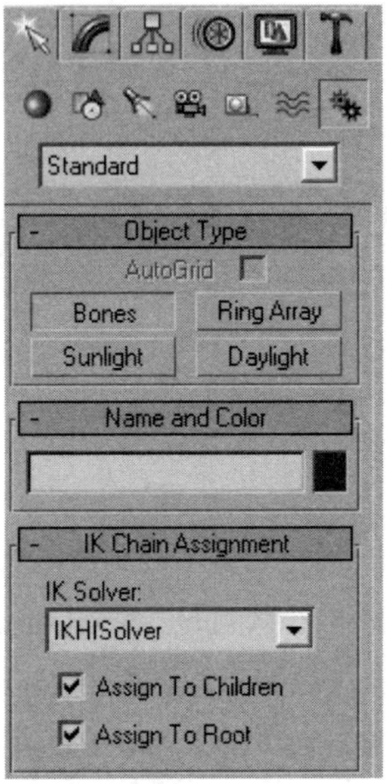

Figure 7.33: Bones Creation Rollout

5. In the Front viewport, click three times successively: below the cylinder, in the middle of the cylinder, and above the top of the cylinder. Figure 7.34 shows the bones with the cylinder.

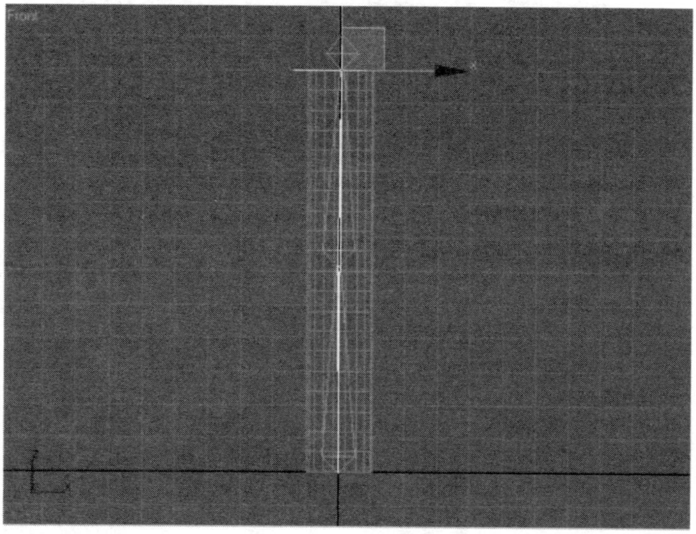

Figure 7.34: Bones with the Cylinder

6. Select the cylinder from the viewport.
7. Select the skin modifier from the Modify panel.

8. On the skin modifier's Parameters rollout, click **Add** and use the Select Bones dialog box to select the three bones. Figure 7.35 shows the Select Bones window.

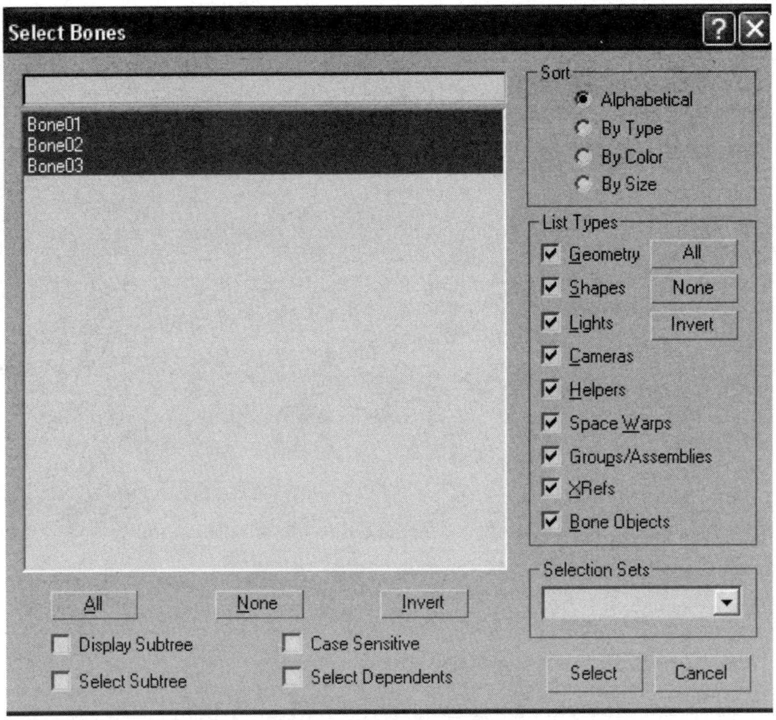

Figure 7.35: Select Bones Window

The names of the bones are now displayed in the list. In the Front viewport, select the bone end effector (IK Chain01) and move it around.

Lab Activity Checklist

S. No.	Tasks	Completed	
		Yes	No
1.	Created a cylinder of radius 10 and height 120 in the Top viewport		
2.	Set Height Segment to 20 on the Parameter rollout		
3.	IK solver was selected		
4.	Successfully applied the skin modifier		

Exercise 2

Objective

- Apply the skin modifier.

Problem Statement

Adjust the envelopes to refine the surface deformation.

Procedure

1. Choose the skin modifier's Envelope sub-object level, and use the Edit Envelopes option. Figure 7.36 shows the cylinder attached with the Skin modifier and the skin modifier Parameters rollout.

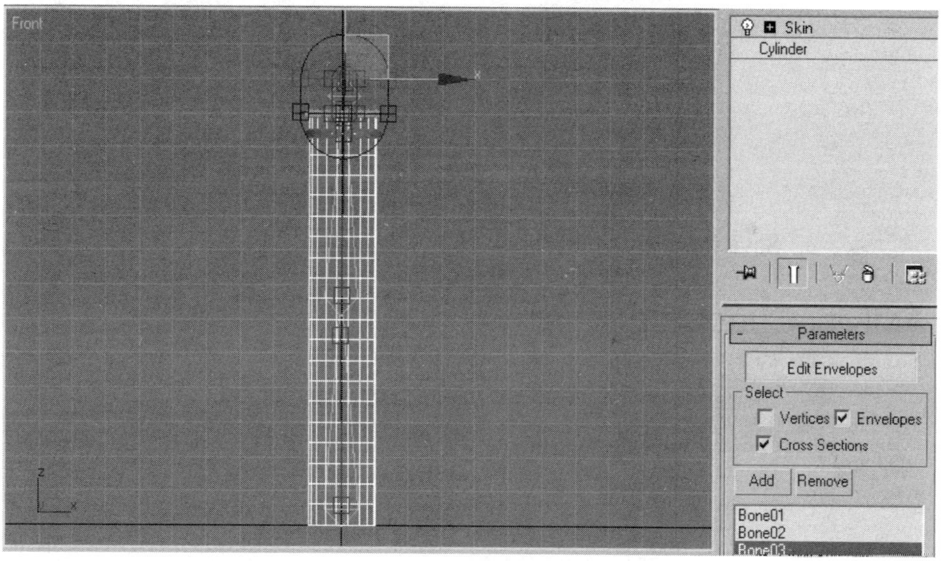

Figure 7.36: Skin Modifier Parameters Rollout

The cylinder deforms to follow the bones.

2. Enlarge the envelopes to encompass the entire cylinder. Figure 7.37 shows the influence vertices.

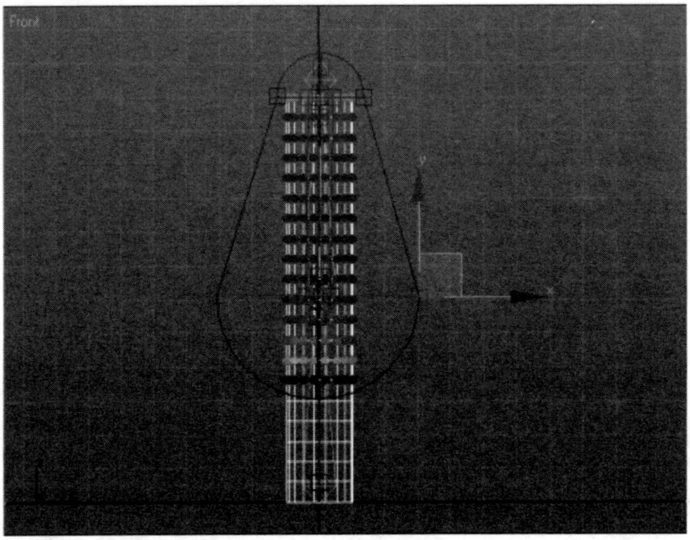

Figure 7.37: Influence Vertices

3. Save the file as **ch07_lab_ex2_sol.max**.

Lab Activity Checklist

S. No.	Tasks	Completed	
		Yes	No
1.	Selected the Edit Envelopes option		
2.	Successfully adjusted the envelopes to refine the surface deformation		
3.	Saved the files as ch07_lab_ex2_sol.max		

Exercise 3

Objective

- Apply the skin modifier.

Problem Statement

Modify the skin object without affecting the envelopes.

Procedure

To modify the skin object without affecting the envelopes, perform the following steps:

1. Open the file created in the previous scene, **ch07_lab_ex2_sol.max**.
2. Select the cylinder to which the Skin modifier is applied. By default, the Always Deform option is marked. Figure 7.38 shows the Advanced Parameters rollout.

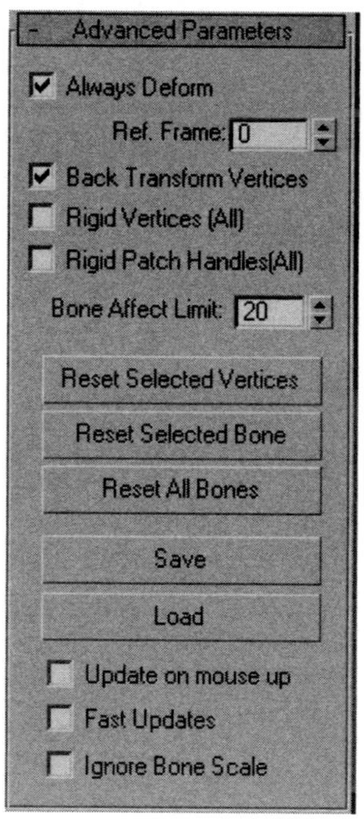

Figure 7.38: Advanced Parameters Rollout

3. Unmark the Always Deform option.

4. Apply any necessary transforms to the cylinder or bones objects.
5. Mark the Always Deform option.

Lab Activity Checklist

S. No.	Tasks	Completed	
		Yes	No
1.	Unmarked the Always Deform option		
2.	Marked the Always Deform option		
3.	Modified the Skin object without affecting the envelopes		

Project

Activities

- Attach the bone with the character model using the skin modifier. To do this, you need to perform the following tasks:
  - Align the mesh with the skeleton.
  - Assign the skin modifier to the objects and add thc bone to it.
  - Adjust the envelope of the arms.
  - Adjust the envelope of the legs.
  - Adjust the envelope of the torso section.
  - Assign the deformer at the elbow and the knee joints.

Animating Expressions

8

Character animation is incomplete if the characters fail to emote or exhibit various expressions. To bring out realism in a digital character, a character animator should be aware of the several components of character acting. This requires the general understanding of body language and facial expressions. 3ds max 6.0 provides some powerful constraints and modifiers to animate the expressions and the eyes of a character.

At the end of this chapter, you will be able to:

- Identify the characteristics of character motion and character acting.
- Identify the use of body language and facial expression in character animation.
- Use the Morpher modifier to get an overview of the lip synchronization process.

8.1 Characters in Motion

8.2 Animating the Eyes and Mouth

8.1 Characters in Motion

Applying motion to a computer graphic character is an intricate process. In this process, objects are not only embodied with movements but also with personality. The challenge of character animation lies in giving life-like motions to animate computer graphic characters. A good animator can make broomsticks dance with passion and can turn a simple table lamp into an emotional actor.

In this section, you will learn about various characteristics of moving characters that govern their motion and expressions.

8.1.1 Character Acting

Identify the features of character acting.

Character acting involves the movement of various body parts. These parts should also exhibit the emotional aspect so that they look realistic. The important features of character acting are:

- Head movement
- Eye movement
- Expression

Head Movement

In character animation, the position and the motion of a head is very crucial. Each human has a unique personality and a unique style of walking and running. The motion of the head becomes a key factor when a character is walking. For example, a head held straight or angled upwards at 5 to 10 degrees symbolizes an energetic and confident character. This is also reflected in the walking style.

Head movement, when reacting to some external force, also plays an important part in character animation. The speed of the head movement conveys a lot of information. For example, if the head turns back and forth really slowly, it may seem as if the character is stretching its neck. A bit faster, and it can be seen as saying "no". If it is really fast, then it may seem that the character is reacting to getting hit by a baseball bat. John Lasseter gave this famous example in his Siggraph paper. Further, the head movement of a male character is different from the head movement of a female character. A male character's upper body moves much more than that of a female.

Eye Movement

Eye movement is another indispensable aspect of character animation. It defines the intellect level of a character. The mindset, mental state, and mood of a character become evident from the movement of the eyes. It also gives a lot of information about the psychology of the character and its feelings. Viewers can anticipate a character's attitude through its eyes.

By implementing proper eye movement, you can bring out realism in an animation and make a binary character stand out in a crowd. Exaggeration is a principle of character animation that uses eyes as one of the major areas of action. For example, Walt Disney productions give a lot of importance to the eye movement of a character and that is why all Disney characters have been so popular for the last few decades. Proper eye movement and rotation increases the appeal of a character. Staging too depends a lot on proper eye motions. Earlier, when sound was not available in the movies, expressions traveled to the heart of spectators through the eyes and gestures of the character.

Expression

The expression feature combines all the other aspects and principles of character animation. It makes a digital character take the center stage. To put a proper expression into a digital character, the animator must be a good actor. Otherwise, it will be difficult for him to think from an actor's point of view. Expressions involve body language, gestures, and head and eye movements. Humans use expressions to express their feelings. Sometimes, dialogues are not sufficient and need external support.

To make a character more expressive, the following simple rules need to be followed:

- Hand and leg movement should be asymmetrical
- Strong use of overlapping
- Snapping of motion in case of hand movement generally indicates whether or not the character is angry
- Secondary motion should be included because it reflects the personality of the character

Snapping is directly related to animation timing. Snapping is the way of applying sudden changes in character pose within a very few frames. The ease in, ease out, and snapping elements make characters more appealing.

8.1.2 Character Expressions

- Identify the features of body language.
- Identify the various types of facial expressions.

There are a number of ways to bring out desired expressions in a digital character. The ability to do this depends largely on the technical and the acting capabilities of the animator.

The main difference between a lifeless object and an organic object is not just motion. A lifeless object can be moved by an external source. The difference lies in the fact whether the object is "moved" or is "moving." A character should seem to move as a result of its own apparent intentionality, not just because that is where the animator wants it to be. There has to be a reason behind what the character is doing. If it moves due to a specific reason, it is more likely to appear to be externalization than internal thinking process. This is very important and makes the difference between a character that has been "posed," and one that "strikes a pose."

All the motions of a character depend on its emotional state and basic expressions. These two are very closely related and vary from character to character.

The elements which affect a character's expression are body expressions and facial expressions.

Body Expressions

The body language of a character plays a crucial role in making the character look real. It is conveyed by the following body parts:

- Head
- Arms and legs
- Shoulders
- Chest

Each of these parts speaks a lot about the character itself. These are driven by emotional and psychological states of the mind. Imagine a person who has just won a raffle. The person's body expressions would convey happiness. For example, the person might be standing with the legs spread apart, with only a slight bend at the knees. The spine would be arched and the chest curved out while the arms would be away from the body. The person will appear to be full of energy.

Figure 8.1 shows some common emotions depicted by body expressions.

Figure 8.1: Different Body Expressions

Body parts can easily be animated by rotating the bones. The mental state of a character can easily be seen by the way the head is positioned and moved.

The head is the heaviest part of the body and a powerful bunch of muscles in the neck keep it straight and upright. However, sometimes the head seems to be a burden when the character is depressed. When the character is in a cheerful mood, the head seems to lead the way.

For example, two characters are having a conversation. If the head of one character is tilted slightly on one side, it would mean that the character is at ease with the other person and loves to keep the conversation going. If the head is absolutely vertical, then the chances are that the character is not much interested in the other or may want to avoid the latter. This is how body parts signal the psychological and emotional states.

The way a character's arms and legs move depicts the character's mood. A happy character moves his arms and legs in commanding motions, whereas a depressed character would hardly move his arms when walking. Similarly, a sad character would not take long strides.

The orientation of the shoulder and the chest is very important as part of the body language because it shows the interest level of the character in an action. A character would orient its upper body fully when doing something or watching something which interests it.

Facial Expressions

Facial expressions are often depicted using a combination of the following features:

- Eyebrows
- Eyes
- Lips
- Cheeks
- Teeth
- Nose
- Blinking of an eye

To convey happiness after winning a raffle, the character should be grinning and the teeth should be visible. The cheeks should bulge out, the eyebrows raised, and the eyes wide open. There are several emotions that can be conveyed through facial expressions. The most common emotions are shown in Figure 8.2.

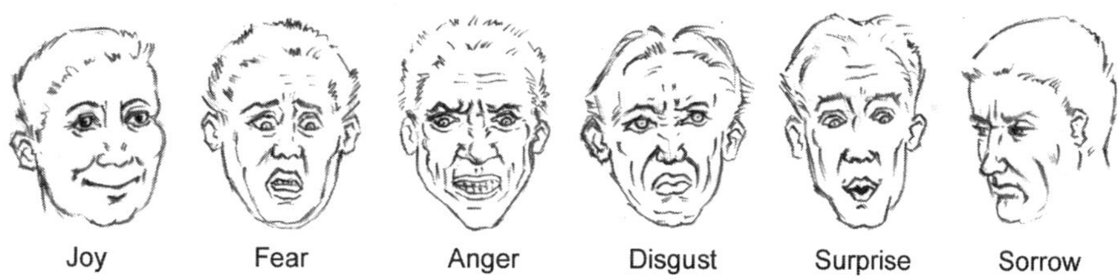

Figure 8.2: Common Facial Expressions

The eyebrow plays a crucial role in determining facial expressions and is certainly the first facial muscle to react to a situation followed by eyes and other parts.

Figure 8.3 shows how changing the eyebrow shape can display the various mind states of the character.

Figure 8.3: Common Eyebrow Movements

Eyes, lips, and cheeks are also important elements of facial expressions and are most extensively used by women in showing their emotional mindset and feelings to others.

Eyes are supremely expressive and a character can easily communicate with eyes alone.

The blinking of eyelids determines whether a character is normal or in a different mental state. For example, if the character does not blink, it might be excited.

There are around 26 muscles in the human face which play a role in various types of expressions. Out of these, eight muscles are very important while assigning proper facial animations to a digital character.

Figure 8.4 shows the location of the eight muscles in the face.

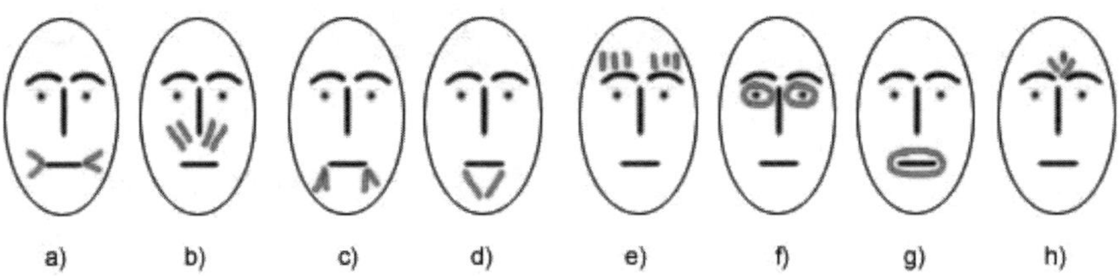

Figure 8.4: Muscle Groups That Take Part in Facial Animation

Table 8.1 shows the six main facial expressions and the muscles involved in each of the expressions. The "X" sign indicates that the muscle is involved in producing that particular expression.

	Joy	Anger	Surprise	Laugh	Fear	Sadness
Zyg Major	X			X		
Nasi		X	X		X	
Traingularis		X	X		X	X
Ment		X	X		X	X
Fronta			X			
Orb-Oclui	X	X		X		
Orb-Oris	X	X		X		
Corrugator		X				

Table 8.1: Muscles Involved in Facial Expressions

Practice Questions

1. State five principles of animation.
2. Why is a motion arc required in character animation?
3. Why is the head movement important in determining character acting?
4. What do you mean by body language?
5. What is the importance of the movement of arms and legs in the body language?
6. On which facial features do facial expressions depend?
7. What are the functions of the Metalis and Frontalis muscles of the face?

8.2 Animating the Eyes and Mouth

This section explains the various techniques of creating expressive eyes and how to use the LookAt constraint to animate the eye.

The important part of facial animation is lip synchronization which is vital in bringing out the liveliness of a character.

8.2.1 Animating Eyes

Identify the process to animate eyes using the LookAt constraint.

Animating eyes is another important part of character animation. The eye is a fast moving object in a character and never stops moving even for a single second.

Animating an eye involves the following critical considerations:

- Eyes are dynamic and keep moving for most part of the animation. So you need to rotate each eye a multiple number of times during the animation.
- Both eyes need to be rotated by exactly the same angle or else the model appears squint-eyed.

Manually animating eyes is a tedious process and can never be accurate. The LookAt constraint enables you to automate this process. Animating eyes using the LookAt constraint involves:

- Creating the target object
- Constraining eyes

Creating the Target Object

In this topic, you are going to implement LookAt constraint to automate the motion of the eyes. The .max file required to perform this exercise can be found in the student CD provided with the course material. You will find a character face complete with eyes in the above mentioned file. First you have to create a dummy object which will act as the target for both eyes. Then assign the LookAt constraint to both the eyes from the Motion Panel and select the dummy as the target. To implement the LookAt constraint to automate the motion of the eyes, perform the following steps:

1. Open the **ch08_eyeConstraint_Start.max** file from the CD. It contains a face model complete with the eye setup. Animate the eyes with the help of the constraint. Figure 8.5 shows the file opened in the viewport.

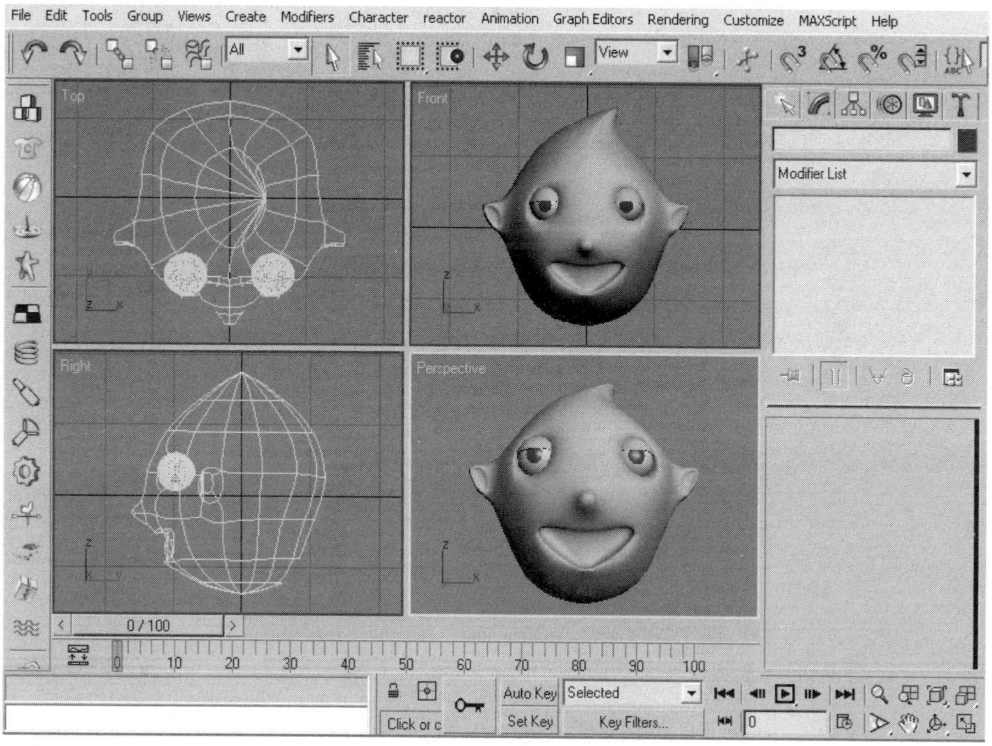

Figure 8.5: ch08_eyeConstraint_Start.max File Opened

2. Create a target object. Link both eyes to the target object, so that moving the targets would move both eyes.

Care should be taken while deciding the pivot of the eyes. A slight change in the pivot position will affect the rotation of the eyelid.

3. From the Helpers panel, create a dummy object in the top viewport exactly in the middle of the two eyes, as shown in Figure 8.6.

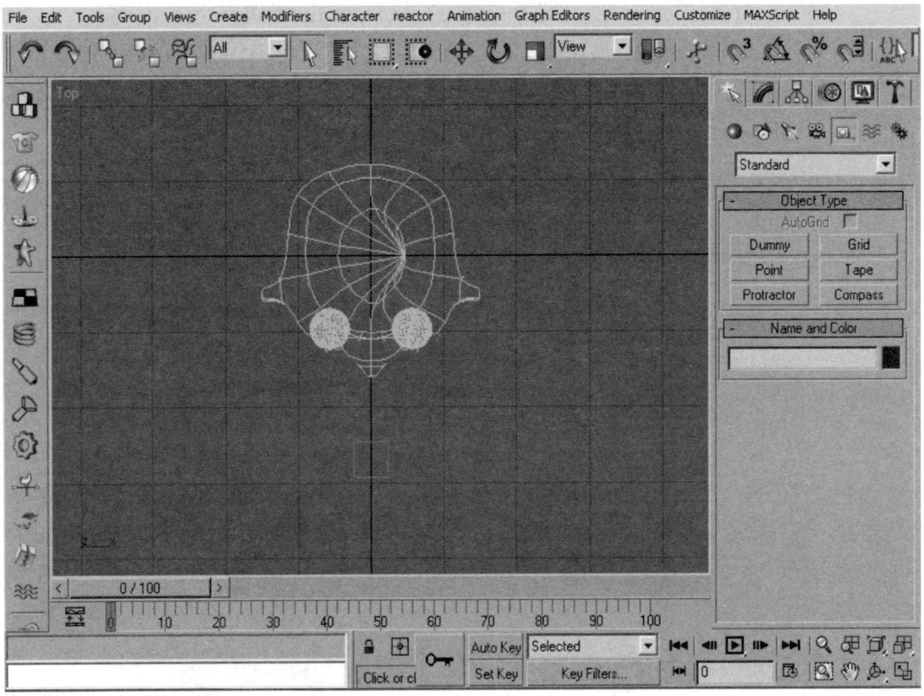

Figure 8.6: Dummy Object Is Created in the Top Viewport

4. A dummy is created so that it can be selected easily for animation, as shown in Figure 8.7.

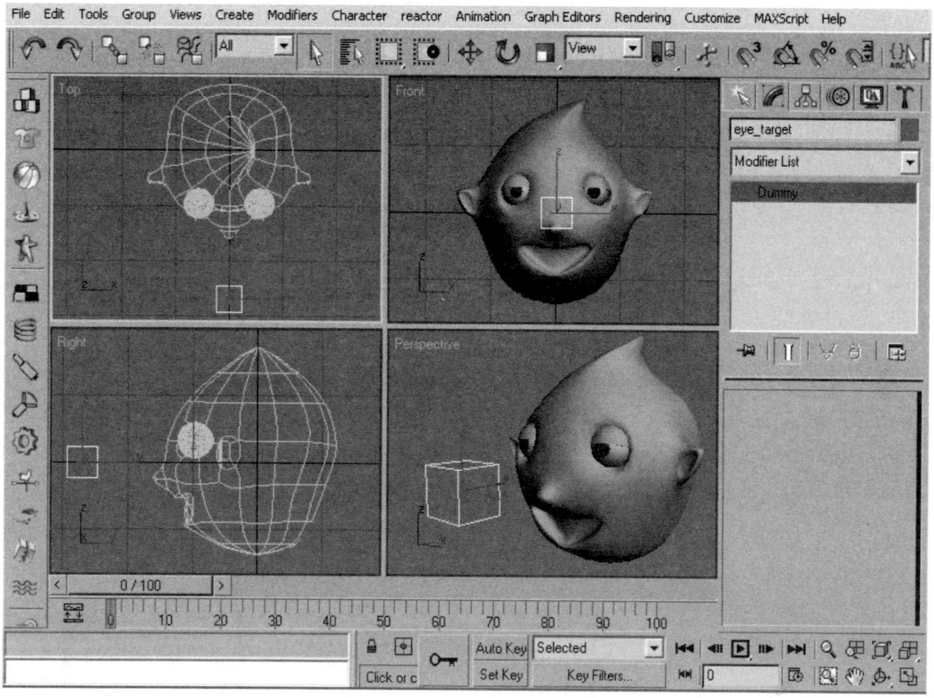

Figure 8.7: Dummy Object Is Renamed to eye_target

5. Rename the target object eye_target.

Constraining the Eyes

To constrain the eyes, perform the following steps:

1. Select the l_eye object from the scene and go to the Motion panel. Select Rotation Transform and click the Assign Controller icon.
2. From the Assign Rotation Controller panel, select the LookAt Constraint, as shown in Figure 8.8.

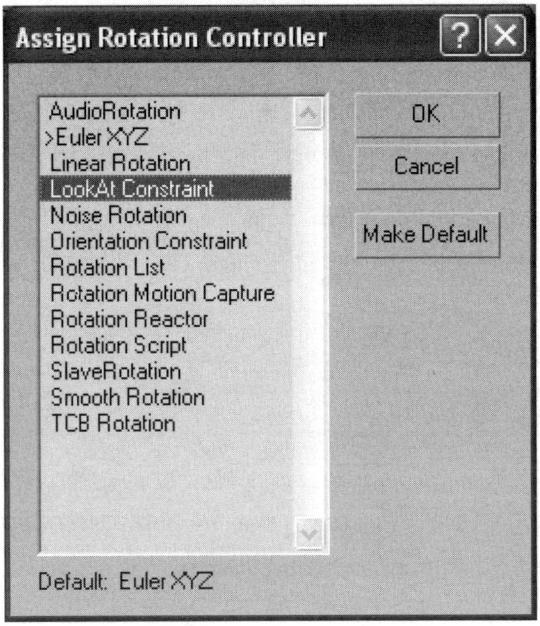

Figure 8.8: Assign Rotation Controller Dialog Options

3. In the LookAt Constraint rollout, click the Add LookAt Target and select the eye_target object.

   The target object is added to the target list with the default value of 50, as shown in Figure 8.9.

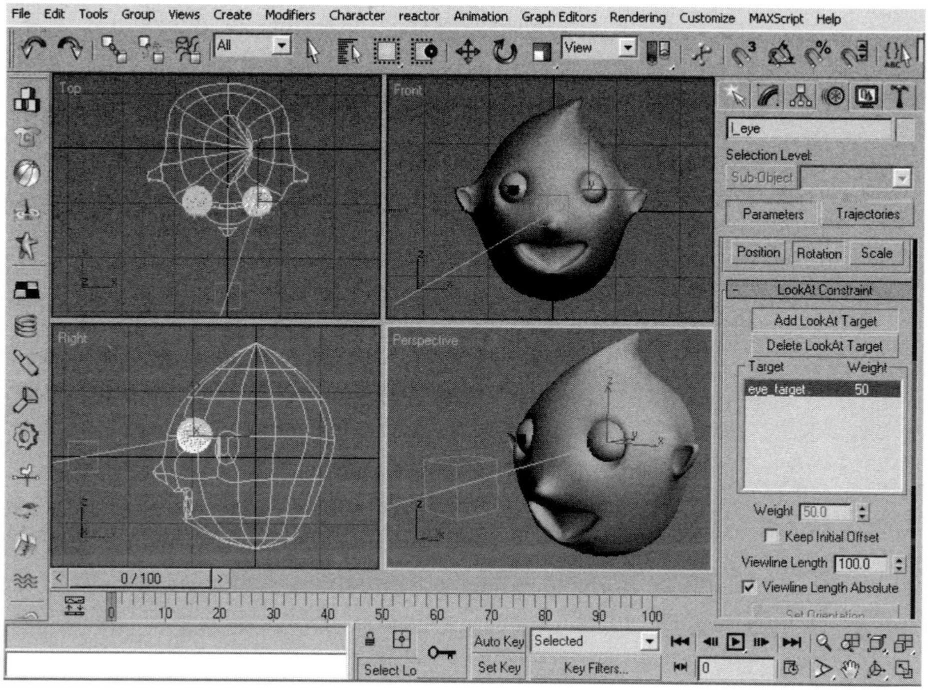

Figure 8.9: The eye_target Is Selected as LookAt Target Object

4. By default, when you use the LookAt constraint, the eye is aligned with the axis of the target object, and as a result, the orientation of the eye changes.

5. Select the Keep Initial Offset check box to prevent aligning the eye with the target object, as shown in Figure 8.10.

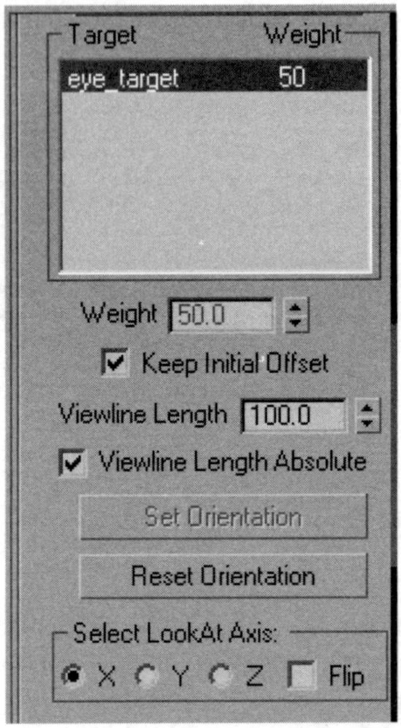

Figure 8.10: LookAt Constraint Options

6. Add the LookAt constraint to the eye_target object also and constrain the eye to the dummy.
7. Select and move the eye_target object to see how the eye is rotating, as shown in Figure 8.11.

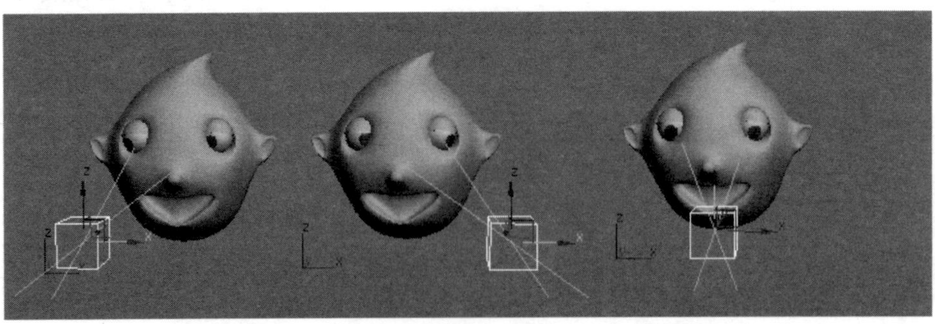

Figure 8.11: Different Orientation of the Eyes Object

8. Save the file using a different file name. Open the **ch08_eyeConstraint_end.max** file from the Student CD for the final file.

8.2.2 Morpher Modifier

Define the use of Morpher modifier in facial animation.

Morpher modifier is used to animate facial expression based on the target object. You need to create different facial expressions that are required for the animation; these are known as target poses. The target poses are created using modifiers, such as FFD, Xform, or Edit Mesh on the base object. The Morpher modifier is then applied to the model's head, and the target poses are assigned to the morph channels of the Morpher modifier. After that the different channel spinner is adjusted to activate or deactivate some channels and provides a complex blending of different poses. So a good number of expressions can be created using only three to four target poses.

To apply the Morpher modifier, you need to complete the following tasks:

- Creating target poses
- Assigning target poses
- Morphing target poses to create the animation

Creating Target Poses

All facial expressions that will be depicted by the character in the animation should be created as target poses before animating the facial expressions. For example, if the animation requires you to depict a character smiling before hearing some sad news and crying, you need to create target poses for both happy and sad expressions. In this procedure, you will create two target poses, happy and sad.

For creating the two target poses, you will copy the model's face twice. You need to copy the face and create the target poses because the Morpher modifier morphs the objects based on the placement and number of vertices. Therefore, the number of vertices of the model's face and the target poses should be the same, or the morphing will not function. After creating two copies of the model's face, you will deform the copies using the FFD (box) modifier for creating the different expressions.

To create target poses, perform the following steps:

1. Launch 3ds max 6 and open the **ch08_morpher_Start.max** file in the viewport, as shown in Figure 8.12.

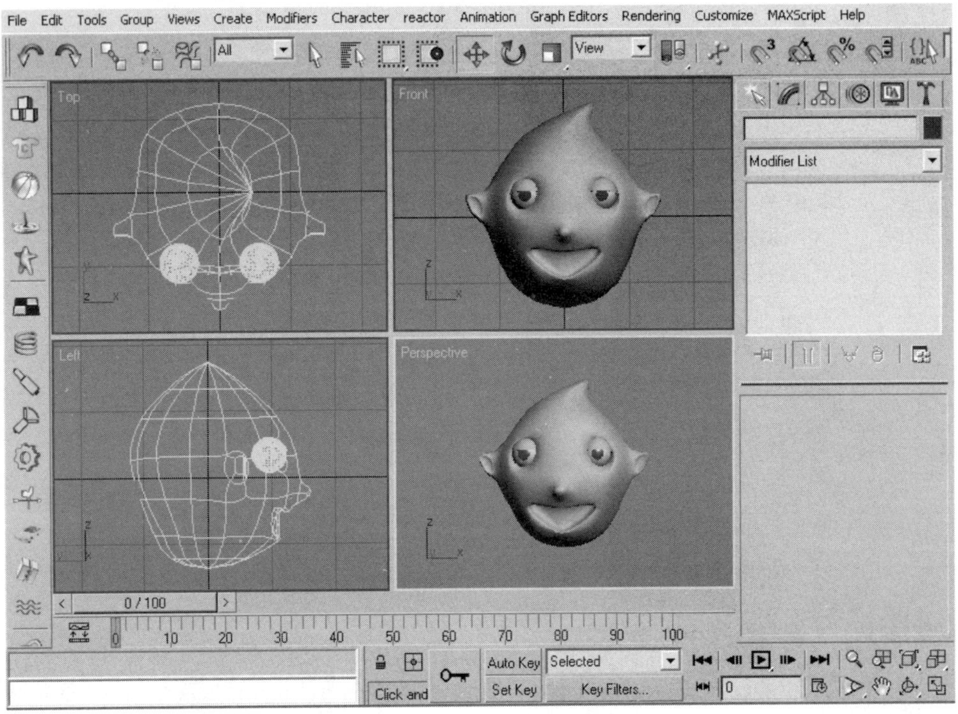

Figure 8.12: ch08_morpher_Start.max File Opened from the CD

2. Select all the objects from the Perspective viewport, including the eyes and eyelids and keeping the Shift key pressed, drag the mouse along the x-axis to create a copy clone.

This creates two face objects including all the other depended objects like eyes and eyelids. These two faces will be used as two poses by the Morpher modifier. The first pose is already depicting a happy face. So you have to change the second object into a sad pose.

3. Select the face01 object, go to the modifier stack and apply the FFD (box) modifier below the MeshSmooth level. Set the Number of Points to 2, 7 and 8 to increase the lattice resolution, as shown in Figure 8.13.

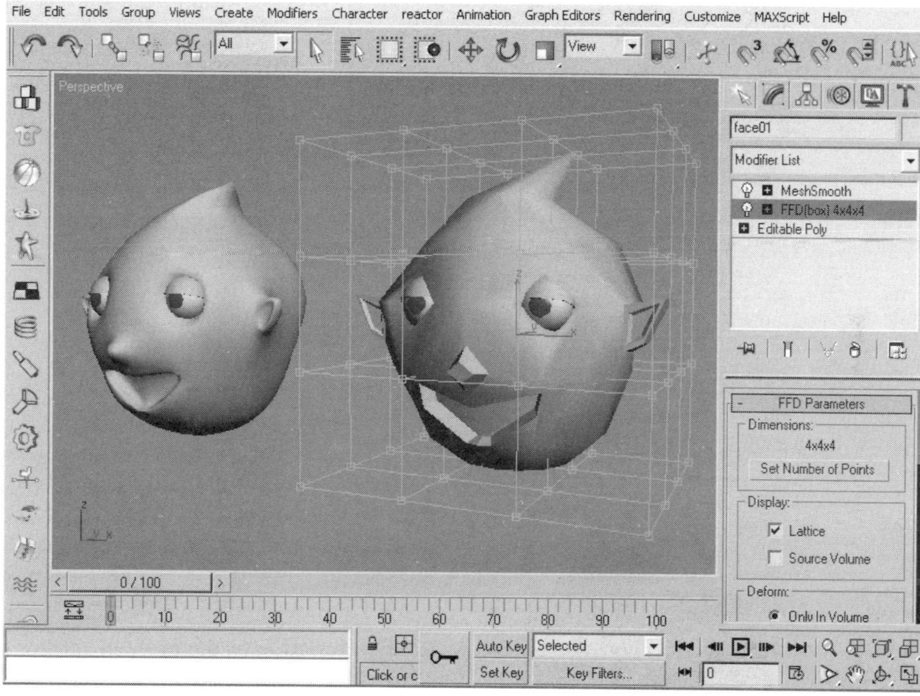

Figure 8.13: FFD Modifier Assigned to the Target Pose for Modification

4. Select the four vertices, as shown in Figure 8.14.

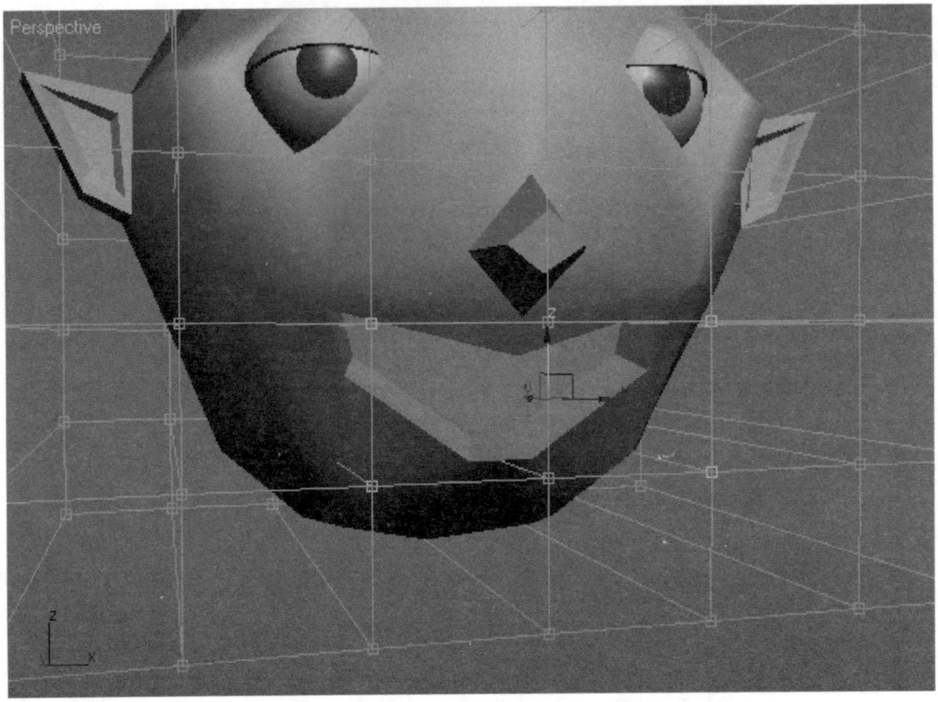

Figure 8.14: Four Vertices Selected from the Front of the Lattice

5. Drag the vertices downward –5.0 unit along the z-axis, as shown in Figure 8.15.

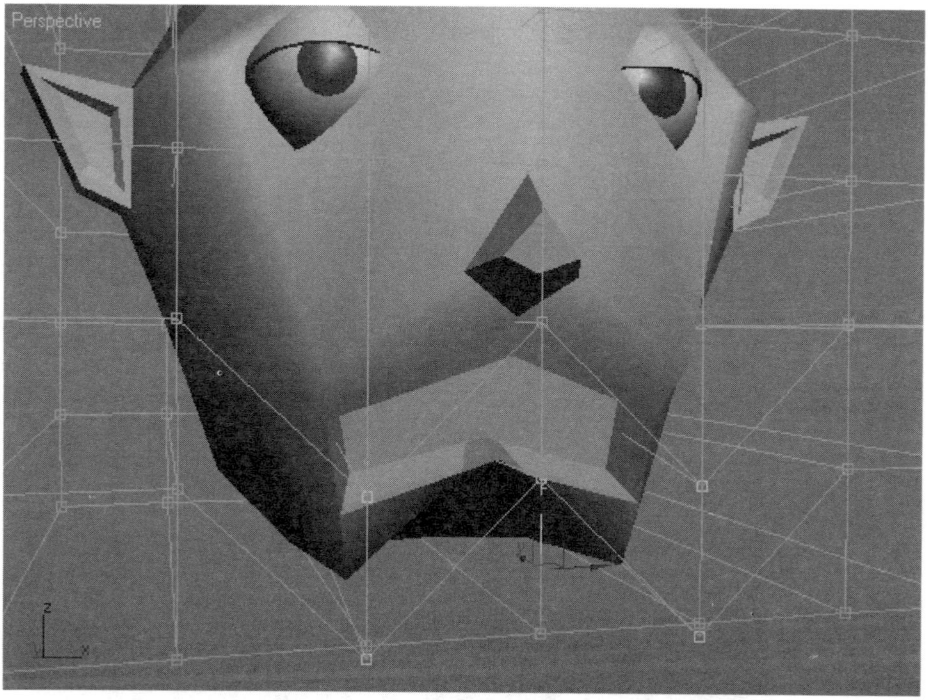

Figure 8.15: Selected Vertices Are Pulled Along the z-axis

6. In the next step select the two vertices along the middle of the mouth, as shown in Figure 8.16.

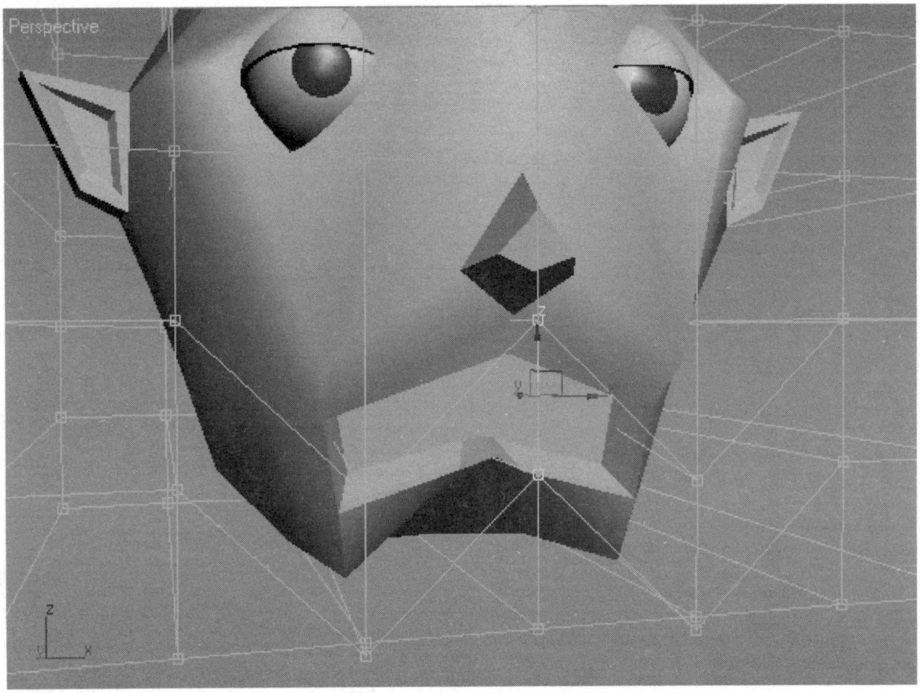

Figure 8.16: Two Vertices Selected from the Middle of the Mouth and Pulled Upward

7. Move the vertices 2.0 units along the z-axis. Refer to Figure 8.17 after the translation of the vertices.

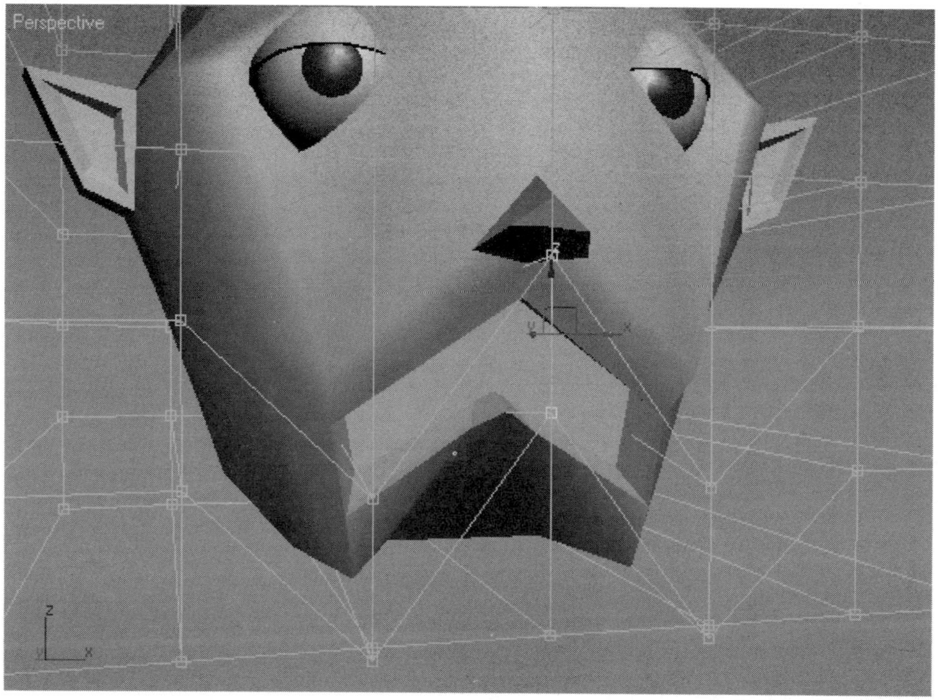

Figure 8.17: The Target Face with Sad Pose

The two target poses are created and in the next step you will assign the morpher modifier to the base object.

While selecting the control points to deform the face, be sure not to select the control points on the rear half of the head to prevent incorrect deformation of the face.

Assigning Target Poses

To assign the morpher modifier to the face object, perform the following steps:

1. Select the face object and from the modifier list apply Morpher modifier. Make sure the Morpher modifier is added below the MeshSmooth, as shown in Figure 8.18.

Figure 8.18: Morpher Modifier Added Below MeshSmooth

To apply Morpher below MeshSmooth, first select Editable Poly from the modifier stack menu and then assign the modifier. This will keep the new modifier just above the Editable Poly.

---

2. Delete MeshSmooth modifier from the face01 object. Select the face object and from the Morpher option panel click on the first empty channel. Go to the Channel Parameter rollout and click on the Pick Object from Scene and click on the face01.

3. The face01 object gets added to base object as a morph target. In the Channel List first channel is used, as shown in Figure 8.19.

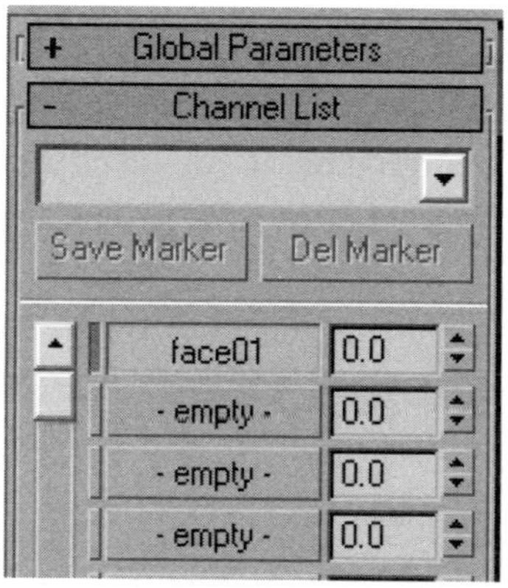

Figure 8.19: The First Morpher Channel

4. The label changes color to indicate that this channel contains morph data.
5. You can also rename channel default text in the Channel Parameter rollout. Rename the channel default text to Sad Face. Make sure Channel Active box is selected.
6. This way more target poses can be added in the other channels. 3ds max 6 provides 100 channels. In the next section you will animate the morph data.

Morphing Target Poses to Create the Animation

In this section you will animate the channel spinner to create an animated facial expression.

1. Hide the face01 object and its accessories and concentrate on the face object which contains the morph data. If you want you can delete the face01 since it won't be required anymore. Figure 8.20 shows the two target objects in the viewport.

Figure 8.20: Two Target Objects in the Viewport

2. In the first frame the value of sad face spinner is 0 meaning that channel has no effect in the object, as shown in Figure 8.21.

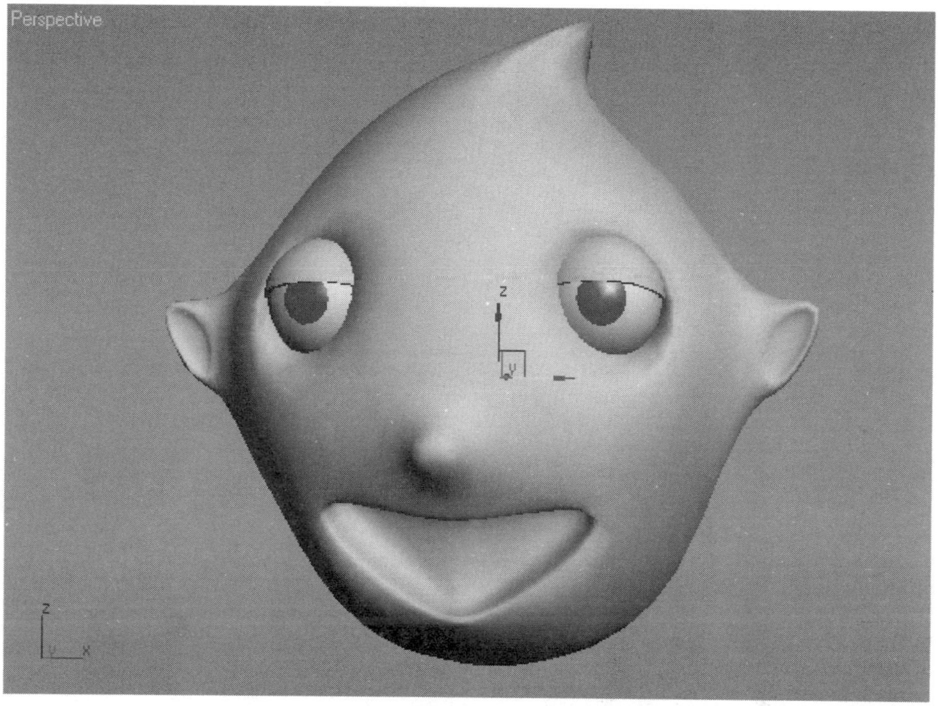

Figure 8.21: Face Depicts Happy Pose

A value of 100 means the channel is fully active.

3. Increase the spinner value to 100 to see how the expression changes, as shown in Figure 8.22.

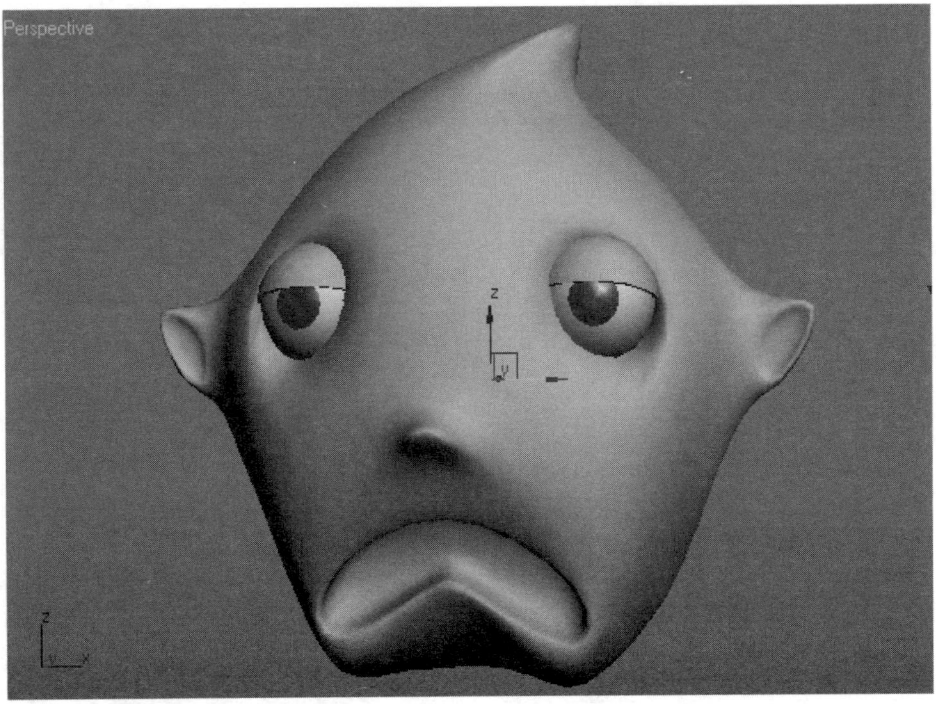

Figure 8.22: Expression Turned to Sad Pose

4. To animate the expression, click the Auto Key button. Go to frame 20 and scrub the spinner to 50. This sets a key at frame 20, as shown in Figure 8.23.

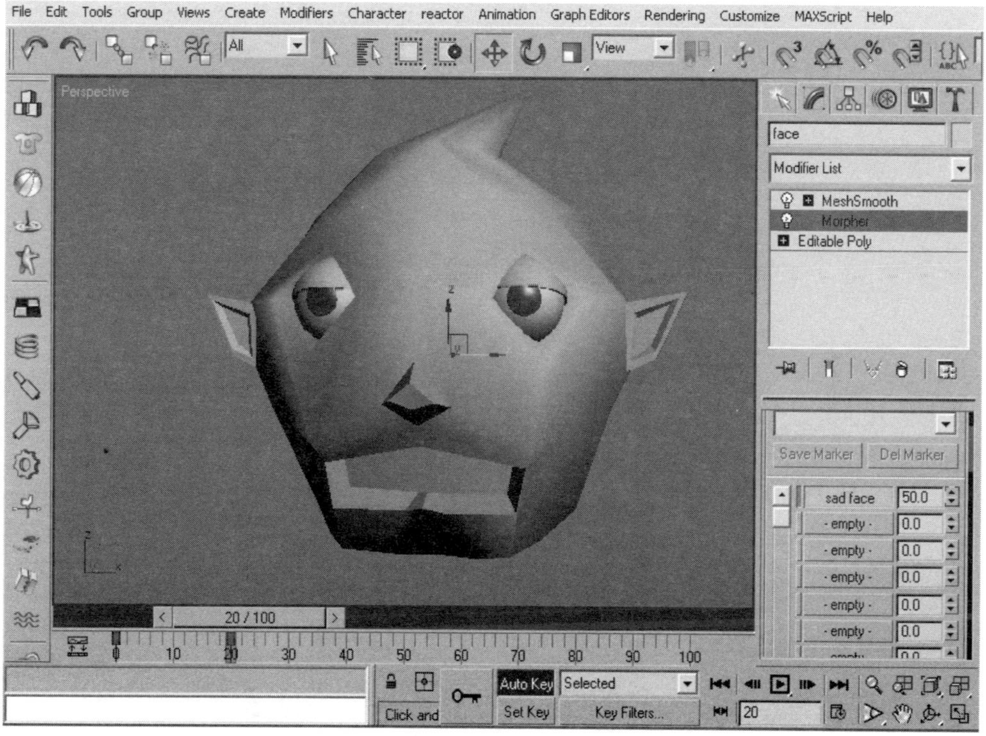

Figure 8.23: Morph Data Is Animated at Frame 20

5. Then again in frame 40 set the value to happy face by entering 0, as displayed in Figure 8.24.

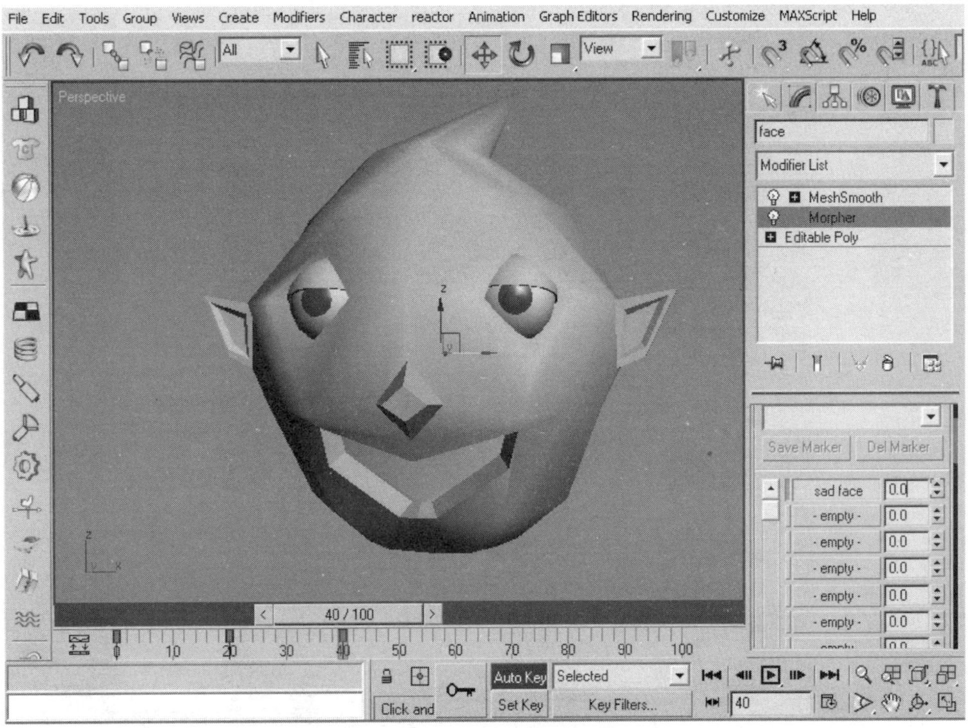

Figure 8.24: Face at Frame 40

6. In frame 65, increase the value to 100, as shown in Figure 8.25.

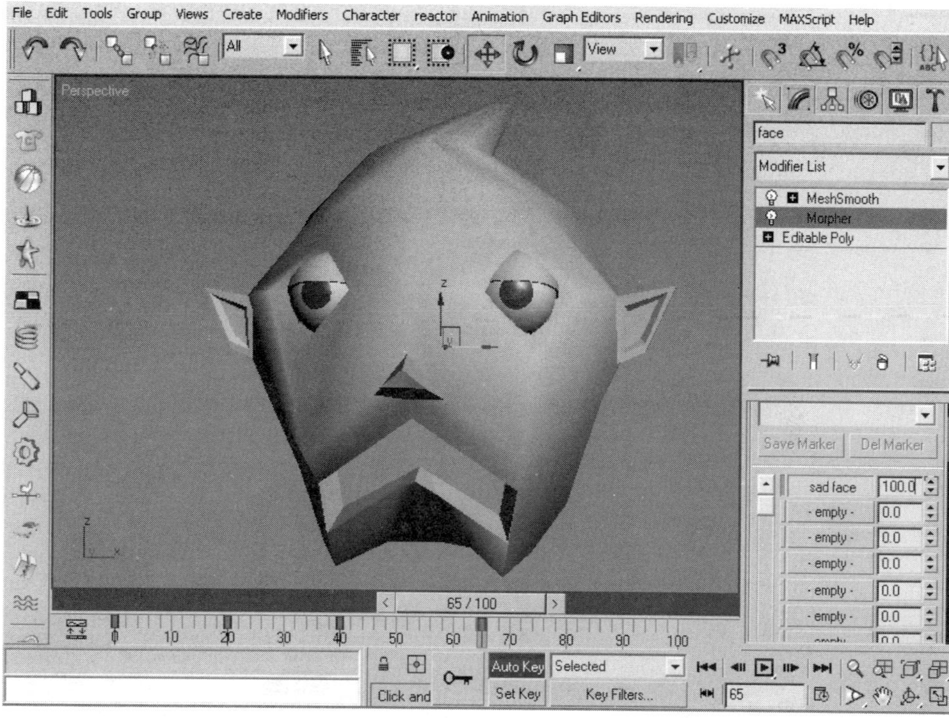

Figure 8.25: At Frame 65 the Pose Turned to Sad

7. Finally, bring the value to 0 at Frame 90. The keys are shown in Figure 8.26 in the track bar.

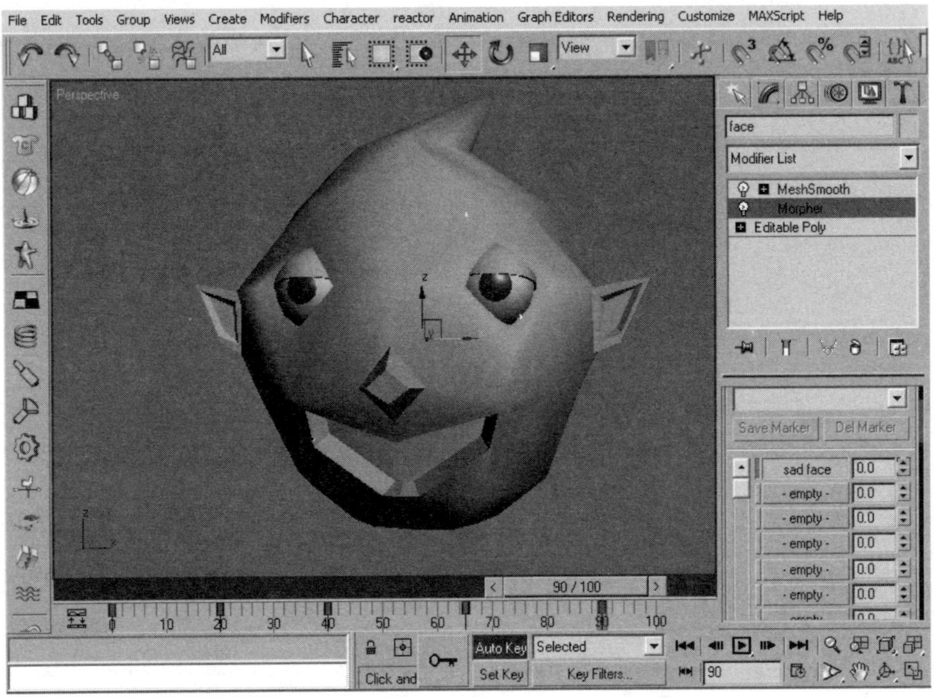

Figure 8.26: Face Is Animated and the Keys Are Shown at the Track Bar

8. Save the file using a different file name.

This is how a character face can be animated using the Morpher modifier to depict different facial expressions. Open the **ch08_morpher_end.max** to see the final model.

8.2.3 Lip-Sync

Identify the features of lip synchronization.

Use Lip-Sync features to make a character talk, sing, or communicate. The process of synchronizing the lip movements of a character with the dialog is called lip synchronization. Lip-sync is the art of making a character appear to speak a pre-recorded track of a dialogue.

These dialogs are recorded by voice-over artists and are stored as separate audio tracks, which are played simultaneously with animations. As in real life, when a character speaks, the lip movements of the character should match the dialog so that the audience believes that the words were spoken by the character and not by a voice-over artist. If the lip movements do not match the dialog, the audience loses interest in the animation.

Lip synchronization involves the following processes:

1. Basic mouth positions: Involve creating targets for the animation by cloning basic mouth shapes into multiple targets. The vertex and poly count of targets have to be the same for the tools to work.
2. Expression morphs: Used to add exaggeration. There are certain facial expressions that are not directly related to lip sync, but enhance the overall process. It mainly includes blinking of the eye, raising eyebrows, and wrinkling the forehead.
3. Speech morphs: Involve drawing various mouth shapes for a character on different frames. By animating mouth shapes timed to the dialogue, the character appears to speak. Each of these mouth shapes is usually referred to as a phoneme. Phoneme poses are mouth shapes created based on the phonetics of a particular language. Figures 8.27 and 8.28 show the different phonemes used according to letters in English.

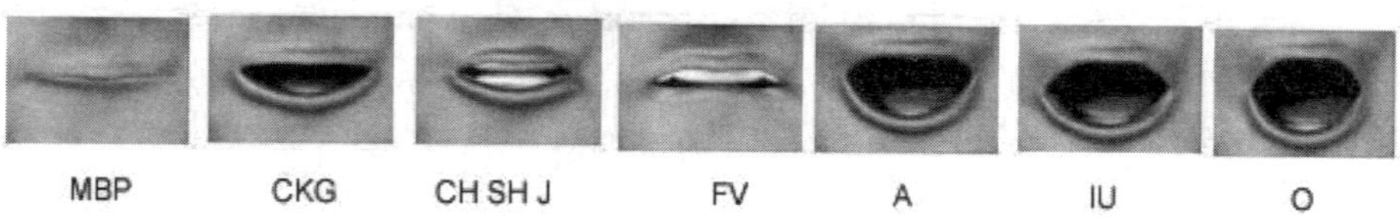

Figure 8.27: Phoneme Samples

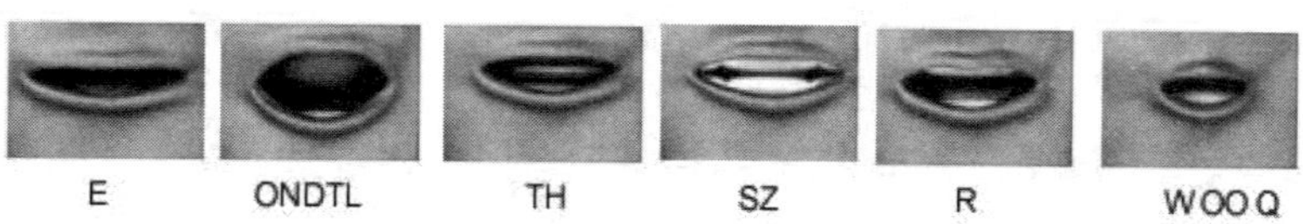

Figure 8.28: Phoneme Samples

4. Tracking the audio: Involves identifying the phoneme for a given dialog track by breaking the dialog track into individual phonemes. This process is also called track reading. Based on the phonemes that are identified, phoneme poses are created, as shown in Figures 8.27 and 8.28.

To understand the concept of phoneme poses, identify the phonemes for the dialog, "I am the best." This dialog can be broken down into phonemes, as shown in Table 8.2.

Letter	Phoneme
I	AA
A	A
M	M
The	A
B	B
Est	AA

Table 8.2: Phonemes for the Dialog "I Am the Best"

After breaking the dialog into phonemes, you need to create the required phoneme poses. After creating the phoneme poses, add the audio track to the animation so that the frames at which the phonemes occur can be identified.

Practice Questions

1. Why are LookAt constraints used to animate Eyes?
2. What are the processes involved in Lip Synchronization?
3. Identify the Basic Phoneme of the English Language.

Summary

- Character acting consists of the following features:
  - Head movement
  - Eye movement
  - Expressions
- Thc body language is conveyed using the following body parts:
  - Head
  - Arms and legs
  - Shoulder
  - Chest
- Facial expressions are conveyed using the following major face elements:
  - Eyebrows
  - Eyes
  - Lips
  - Cheeks
  - Teeth
  - Nose
  - Blinking of eyelids
- Using the LookAt constraint, you can constrain both eyes of the model to a target object so that the eyes can be rotated by moving the target. Because both eyes are assigned to the same target, the angle of rotation of the eyes remains the same.
- The Morpher modifier enables you to animate facial expressions of a character by using different target poses. These target poses are the extreme states of a particular expression.
- Animating facial expressions using the Morpher modifier involves:
  - Creating target poses
  - Assigning target poses
  - Morphing target poses to create the animation

- Lip synchronization is the process of synchronizing the lip movements of a character with a dialog track.
- Lip-sync is performed using phoneme poses. Phoneme poses are mouth shapes created based on the phonetics of a particular language.
- The procedure for lip synchronizing a character with an audio track involves:
  - Listening to the audio track
  - Identifying phonemes
  - Creating phoneme poses
  - Morphing phoneme poses

References

- http://www.mpi-sb.mpg.de/resources/FAM/ (February 10, 2004)
- http://research.microsoft.com/features/images.asp (February 10, 2004)
- http://www.filmandvideomagazine.com/2002/09_sep/features/facialanimation.htm (February 10, 2004)
- http://www.3dartist.com/3dao/s/30/kmshape.htm (February 10, 2004)
- http://www.di-o-matic.com/press/mom_cgi.html (February 10, 2004)
- http://www.massassi.net/tutorials/jo_uv_mapping/ (February 10, 2004)
- http://millimeter.com/ar/video_spongebob_squarepants/ (February 10, 2004)
- http://www.lifemi.com/lifestudio/head/faq/ (February 10, 2004)
- http://www.digimation.com/newsletters/display_archivearticle.asp?featureid=3 (February 10, 2004)
- http://www.photoimpactzone.com/tutorials/newyears.htm (February 10, 2004)
- http://www.scriptspot.com/bobo/rendfaq/RFAQ0116.HTM (February 10, 2004)
- http://www.jhaywood.com/croiProjectEyes00.htm (February 10, 2004)

Assignments

1. State whether the following statements are true or false:
    a. Objects are deformed while in motion due to Squash and Stretch.
    b. Phoneme uses facial muscles to create a particular shape.
    c. The LookAt controller can use multiple targets.
2. List the process involved in assigning lip synchronization to a character.
3. Follow the case study and answer the question: A dog came running and suddenly stopped in front of its food. The long hanging ears were still moving. What principle of character animation is this due to?
4. Name at least two muscles that are used in facial expressions.
5. What is the importance of anticipation in character animation?
6. Fill in the blanks:
    a. A Morpher modifier can store _____ morph data in channels.
    b. Phonemes are identified based on an ______.

Lab Exercise

Exercise 1

Objective

- Create the facial expression of a character watching a comedy scene.

Problem Statement

Create the facial expression of a character watching a comedy scene followed by a sad scene. Morph these facial expressions using the Morpher modifier. Use the skinned model from the ch08_lab_ex1_model.max file.

Lab Setup

3ds max 6.0

Procedure

To create the facial expression:

1. Open the **ch08_lab_ex1_model.max** file that contains the skinned model of the character.
2. Create two copies of the model's head. Rename the first copy **Happy_face**, and the second one **Sad_face**. You have a three face object in the scene.
3. Select **Happy_face**, and select the **FFD (box)** modifier from the Modifier List.
4. In the FFD Parameters rollout, click **Set Number of Points**.

   The Set FFD Dimensions dialog box appears.

5. Set the values of Length, Width, and Height as 4, 7, and 6, respectively, as shown in Figure 8.29, and click OK.

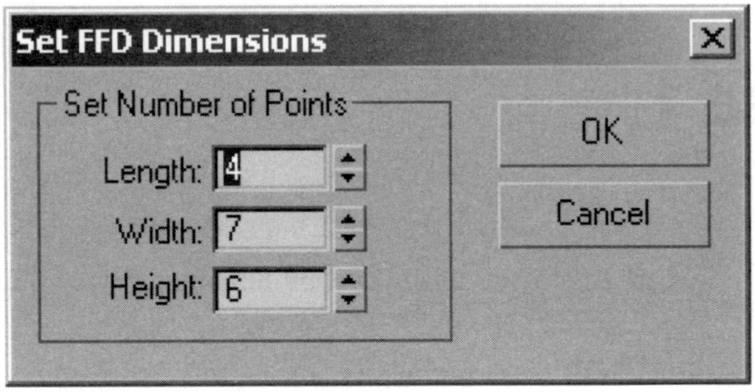

Figure 8.29: Number of Control Points Increased for Creating the Target Pose

6. Select the Control Point sub-object of the FFD (box) modifier.
7. Using the control points, deform Happy_face to obtain the face of a smiling person, as shown in Figure 8.30.

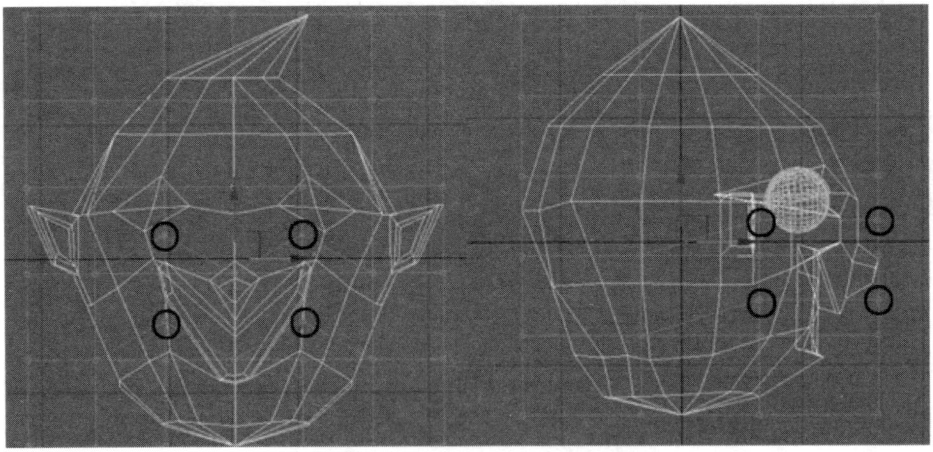

Figure 8.30: First Target Pose Deformed to Depict a Smile

8. Similarly, apply the FFD (box) modifier on the second target pose and deform it to obtain the face of a sad person, as shown in Figure 8.31.

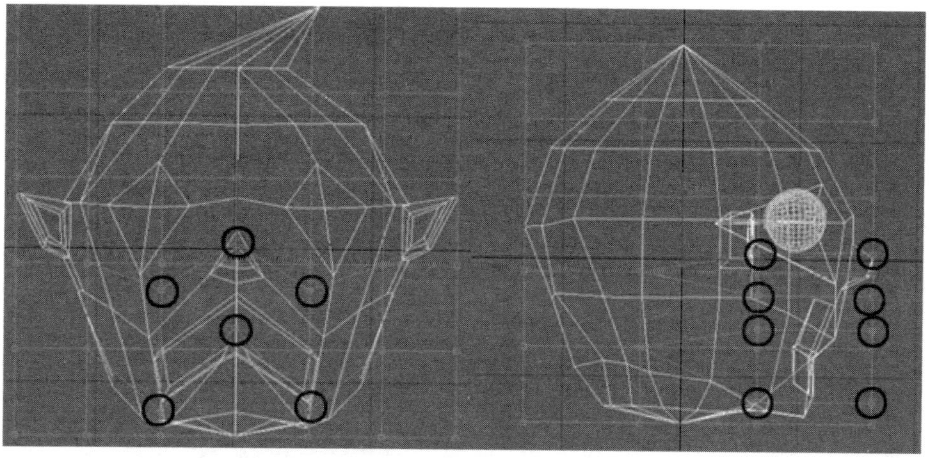

Figure 8.31: Second Target Pose Deformed to Depict a Sad Expression

9. Select the head of the base model and select the Morpher modifier from the Modifier list.

10. In the Channel List rollout of the Morpher modifier, right-click the first morph channel, and select Pick from Scene, as shown in Figure 8.32.

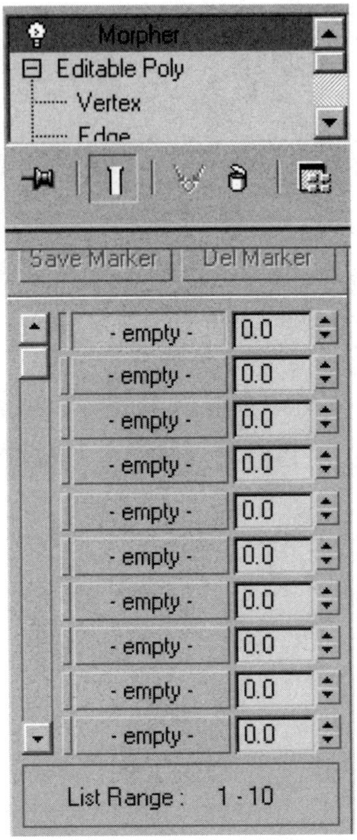

Figure 8.32: First Morph Channel Selected to Add a Target Pose

11. Click Happy_face to assign the target pose to the first morph channel, as shown in Figure 8.33. Also change the label of channel 1 from the default, -empty- to Happy_face.

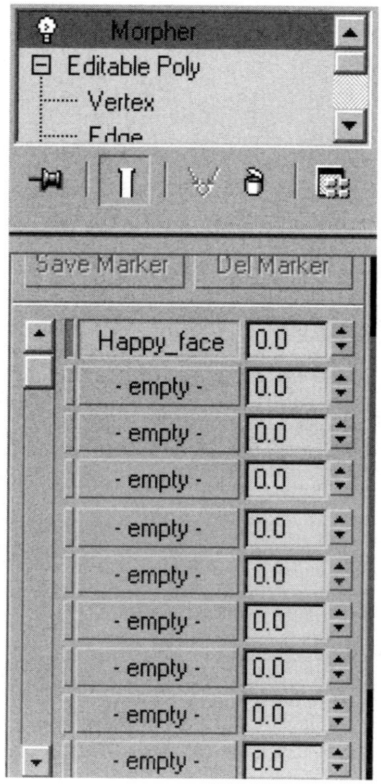

Figure 8.33: Target Pose Assigned to the First Morph Channel

12. Similarly, assign the Sad_face pose to the second morph channel and rename the label to Sad_face, as shown in Figure 8.34.

Figure 8.34: Both the Target Poses Assigned to the Morph Channel

13. Move the time slider to Frame 20 in the track bar.
14. Change the Happy_face morph channel value to 50 so that the character appears to be smiling.

15. Now you have a keyframe in Frame 0 and Frame 20. Press the shift key on the keyboard and copy the key at Frame 0 to Frame 10 so that the animation of the Happy_face morph channel starts from Frame 0. The track bar should appear as shown in Figure 8.35. The value of the Happy_face morph channel is 0 at Frame 0 and Frame 10 and 50 at Frame 20.

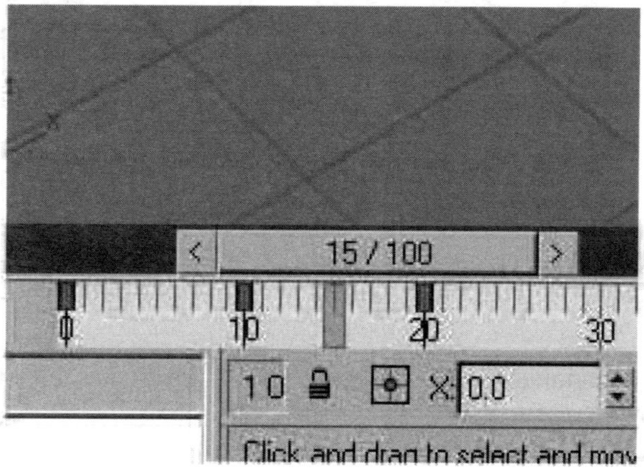

Figure 8.35: Keyframes at the Track Bar

16. Move the time slider to Frame 50, and copy the key on Frame 20 to Frame 50 to maintain the smile on the character's face between these frames. There is no animation in between Frame 20 and Frame 50.
17. Move the time slider to Frame 55 and change the Happy_face morph channel value to 100, so that the character appears to be smiling broadly at this stage. Refer to Figure 8.36 for the position of the keys in the Track bar.

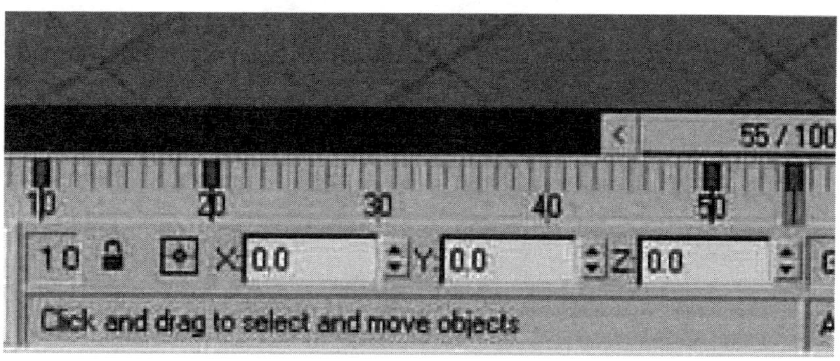

Figure 8.36: The Keyframes at the Track Bar at This Stage

18. To animate the smile, change the value of the Happy_face morph channel to 90 and 100 at Frames 60 and 65, respectively. Change the Happy_face morph channel value to 90 and 100 at Frames 70 and 75, respectively. Figure 8.37 shows the Track bar at this stage.

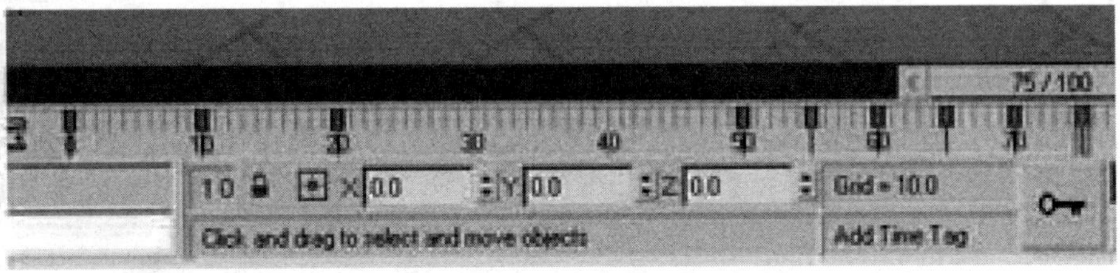

Figure 8.37: Keyframes at the Track Bar

19. Move to Frame 80, and set the value of the Happy_face morph channel to 0.
20. Create a key on Frame 85 by clicking the down arrow of the Sad_face morph channel as shown in Figure 8.38. This creates a key of value 0 for the Sad_face Morph Channel.

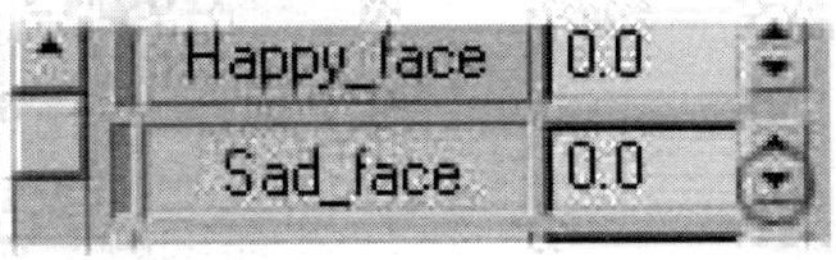

Figure 8.38: Down Arrow of the Morph Channel

21. Move to Frame 90, and increase the value of the Sad_face morph channel to 50 so that the face appears to be sad from Frame 85 to Frame 90.

22. Copy the key on Frame 90 to Frame 95 to maintain the same sad pose. Then, move to Frame 100, and increase the value of the Sad_face morph channel to 100, as shown in Figure 8.39.

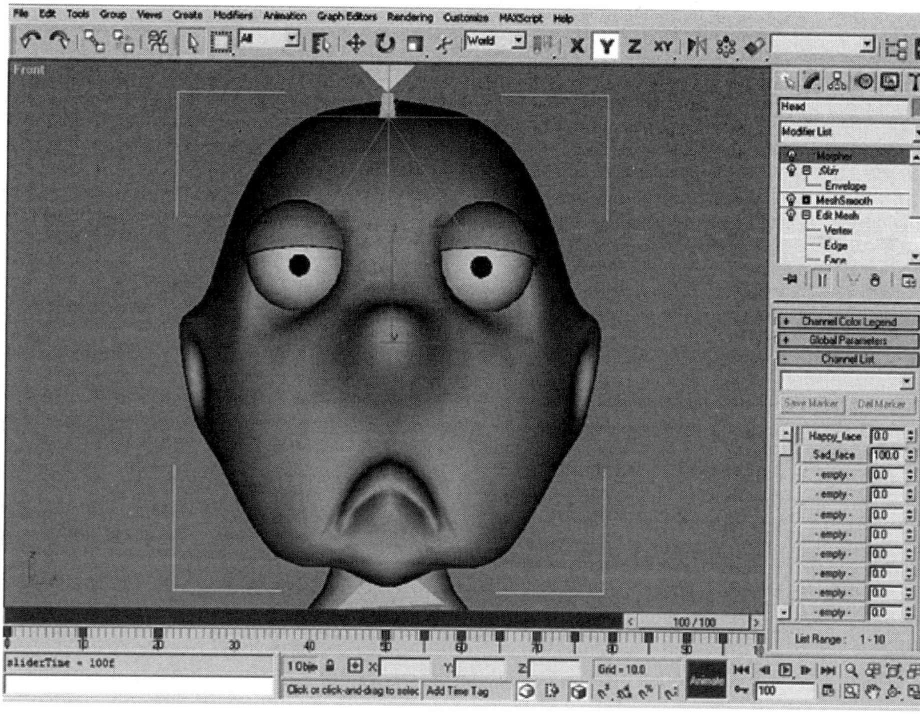

Figure 8.39: Keys Created on Different Frames to Morph the Happy and Sad Expressions

The final positions of the keys are shown in Figure 8.40.

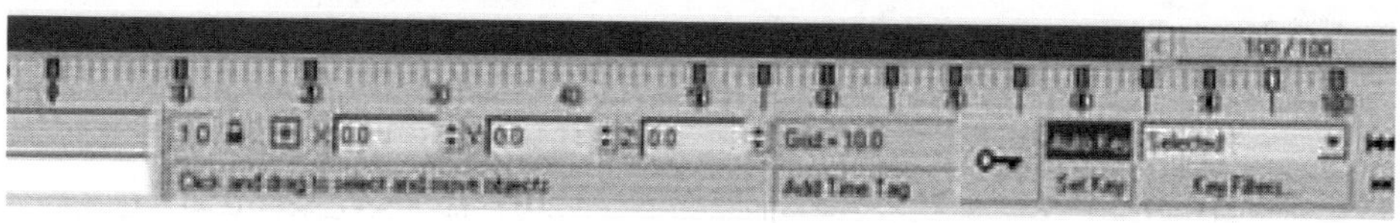

Figure 8.40: The Final Positions of the Keys at the Track Bar

23. Deactivate the Animate button.

24. Play the animation to view the character's facial expression while watching a comedy scene followed by a sad scene in a movie.

25. Save the file as **ch08_lab_ex1_sol.max**.

Lab Activity Checklist

S. No.	Tasks	Completed	
		Yes	No
1.	Created target poses showing a smiling face and a sad one		
2.	Assigned the target poses to a morph channel		
3.	The transition of expression on the character's face is believable		

Project

Activities

- Add facial animation and eye motion to the character you modeled in Chapter 5. For this, perform the following tasks:
  - Create the Look At constraint for the eye.
  - Test the eye motion.
  - Create several target poses for the facial expressions.
  - Break the dialog "Hi! It's me" into the phonemes.
  - Create mouth targets for the phonemes.
  - Animate the morpher to make the character speak.

Glossary

A

Add and Remove Bone buttons option: It enables you to add or remove the bones from an object.

Add and Remove Cross-Section buttons option: It enables you to add or remove a cross-section from the shape of the envelope in the viewports.

Advanced Parameters rollout: It is one of the four rollouts of the Skin modifier that enables you to manage bones, vertices, and envelopes by performing resetting, saving, and loading functions.

Amplify: This tool helps in making changes in the scaling factor for a minor axis and produces a multiplier in the same way as done by the Stretch tool.

Anatomy: Anatomy is the study of body structures involving the positioning of bones, muscles, and ligaments. The study of anatomy enables a character modeler to fashion the skeleton and other parts of the body.

Animation modifiers: Animation modifiers modify the shape of an object.

Animation: Animation is the illusion of movement that is created by playing a number of images of an object taken from different axes in sequenced order.

Ancestors: Ancestors are parent objects above a selected child object.

Anticipation: Anticipation is an element of character animation that occurs before an actual action. For example, before throwing an object, your hand draws behind the body to gather momentum.

Appeal: Appeal makes a character lively and popular on the stage. Character design, dress code, walking style, and communication style together add to the appeal of the character. A character's appeal can be enhanced by using other principles, such as exaggerating the design, avoiding symmetry, and overlapping action.

Asymmetrical: In the asymmetrical state, the hands or legs of a character translate at different times and spaces. This enhances the realism of a character animation. If the scene contains more than two or three characters, all the characters move in a manner that does not match with others.

B

Body Language: Body language refers to the non-verbal expression of emotions and feelings. These non-verbal expressions are conveyed by various gestures of the head, chest, arms, legs, spine, and shoulders.

Bone Affect Limit option: It limits the number of bones that can affect one vertex.

BoxGizmo: BoxGizmo creates a box-shaped gizmo in the scene.

C

Cel animation: Cel animation is a manual method where a cel is derived from celluloid, which is a piece of transparent plastic.

Child objects: In addition to root and parent objects, hierarchies comprise child objects. A parent object manages a child object. A child object can also be a parent to other child objects.

Cone Angle Manipulator: The Cone Angle manipulator is a control whose base can be adjusted by wiring its angle value to a parameter of another object. You can create a custom control in a scene with visual feedback using the Cone Angle manipulator.

Constraint: A constraint automates the movement of an object by linking it with one or more target objects. An object's position, rotation, and scale can be linked or bound through a relationship with another object. A constraint is also used to assign a restriction to the translation of the object.

Controllers: Controllers help specify the properties of the object to be animated, such as scale, rotate, and transform.

Coordinate: In a 3D space, a point is the smallest area that can be occupied. Points are defined by a set of three numbers, called coordinates.

Cross-Sections option: This option forces cross-sections to be drawn on top.

Curve Editor: Curve Editor displays an animation, created by a designer, as function curves.

Curve Editor interface: The Curve Editor interface consists of a menu bar, a toolbar, a Controller window, and a Key window. There is also a Time ruler, and navigation and status tools at the bottom of the interface.

CylGizmo: CylGizmo creates a cylinder-shaped gizmo in the scene.

D

Deformation: In 3ds max, deformation refers to bending or modifying a surface in relation to the joint of a hierarchy. When bones are attached to the mesh, it deforms the surface, because the bones are rotated along their pivots, providing motion to objects.

Descendants: All the child objects below a selected parent object are called descendants.

Display rollout: It is one of the four rollouts of the Skin modifier that enables you to define the components that are visible in the viewports.

Dope Sheet: Dope Sheet displays an animation as a spreadsheet of keys and ranges.

Draw on Top group option: It determines which elements will be drawn on top of all other objects in viewports.

Dummy: A dummy is a non-renderable object with a pivot point at its geometric center. It is a wireframe cube with no parameters and is generally used as an animation helper.

Dummy object: A Dummy object is designed as a wireframe cube with a pivot point at its center. It does not have any parameters.

E

Easy In and Easy Out: Easy In and Easy Out is used to gradually change the speed of an object's acceleration or deceleration. This makes the movement of an object more fluid and realistic and prevents it from appearing robotic or mechanical.

Edit Envelopes option: It enables you to edit an envelope or simply select the Envelope sub-object in the modifier stack.

End effector: End effector is the pivot point of the selected child object at the end of a kinematics chain.

Envelope Properties option: It enables you to define the properties of the envelope, such as the values of Radius and Squash and Icon to handle the visibility of an envelope.

Envelopes option: It forces envelopes to be drawn on top.

Exaggeration: Exaggeration is used to accent an action and make a movement appear more realistic. The key is to make the animation extreme in some cases to increase believability.

F

Facial Muscles: There are twenty-six muscles in the human face, which are used in various expressions. These muscles control the way you smile, yawn, and frown. Eight muscles are used to animate facial expressions and lip synchronization.

Fast Updates option: It turns off the viewport display of weighted deformation and gizmos and uses rigid deformation when not rendering.

FFD (box): The FFD (box) modifier assigns a lattice cage to an object. The points on the lattice function as magnets. Any changes in positions of the points translate to the surface below. This modifier is used to control a group of vertices in lip synchronization.

Filters option: It enables you to select the types of controls.

Fire effects: Fire effects are used to produce animated effects of smoke and fire. They are used to show the effect of sun, fireballs, clouds, and explosions.

FollowThrough: FollowThrough occurs at the end of a motion. An object does not stop its movement abruptly; instead it tends to move a bit further than the target point. For example, after throwing a ball, the hand continues its movement forward in the throwing direction.

Forward kinematics: Forward kinematics controls the default animation of a hierarchy. In forward kinematics, the inheritance feature passes on transformations from the parent object to its child objects based on their relationship in the hierarchy.

Frame Rate: The frame rate is the number of frames the software displays and renders for each second of real time.

G

Gizmos rollout: It is one of the four rollouts of the Skin modifier that enables you to apply three kinds of deformers to the vertices of an object.

Grid: The grid is a 2D parametric object that is used to adjust the total size and spacing of the grid.

H

Hierarchy: Hierarchy refers to the arrangement of objects that are linked as parent and child nodes in a structure.

History-Dependent (HD) IK solver: It is a smooth but slow process that is best for short animations because it takes more time and memory.

History-Independent (HI) IK solver: It is a fast process that looks at each frame independently and is best for long animations.

I

IK limb solver: It is a process that works on two bones or objects and is best when animating limbs.

IK methods: Using IK methods, you can animate and manipulate hierarchies without applying IK solvers.

Inverse kinematics: Inverse kinematics controls the hierarchy from the child to the parent. It is an animation method based on hierarchical links that requires all the pivot points to be properly positioned.

K

Key Steps: The Key Steps section enables you to determine the method through which the Key Mode button works.

Keyframe Animation: Keyframe animation is similar to Cel animation, but the keyframe animation method can also be used to create 3D animation.

Kinematics: Kinematics is a process for manipulating a hierarchy of objects.

L

Leaf: Leaf is the last object in a branch.

Links: Links define the relationship between the parent and the child object.

Lip Synchronization: Lip synchronization is the process of synchronizing the lip movements of a character with a dialog track.

Look At constraint: The Look At constraint is used to control the orientation of an object, for example, controlling eye movements, because both eyes point toward the same target.

M

Manipulator: Manipulator is a type of Helper in 3ds max.

Mirror: The Mirror tool is located in the tool bar of 3ds max. This tool is used to flip the orientation of objects on a given axis. The tool has powerful options that are used to create copy clones, instanced clones, and reference clones of an object.

Modifier: A modifier is a tool that is used to change the shape of an object. Modifiers in the 3ds max Object-Oriented System are objects that work with the local co-ordinate system of the object to which they are applied.

Morph Channel: The Morph Channel is a component of the Morph modifier. The Morph Channel stores the morph data of various target objects. The modifier translates the shape of the base object by interpolating various morph targets. 3ds max 6 supports the data of 100 morph targets in 100 channels.

Motion Arcs: Motion arc is the visual path taken by a moving object. Organic objects do not move in a straight path, but in an arc. Using motion arcs in character animation makes the animation smoother and realistic.

Motion Capture: Motion Capture is the process of capturing the movement of a real object and mapping it to a computer generated object.

Multiple-track controllers: Multiple-track controllers manage multiple tracks and multiple values.

O

Overlapping: Overlapping is closely related to secondary animation. No two objects or limbs of a character move in the same way and at the same speed. The various parts of a body move differently at different times. This adds realism to the animation.

P

Parameters rollout: It is one of the four rollouts of the Skin modifier that allows an animator to add or delete the position, rotation, and scale keys on the track bar.

Parametric: There are a few objects in 3ds max that can be reshaped and altered using defined sets of values in the Modifiers panel. For example, you can change a sphere's radius and segments using the respective spinner values located in the Modifier panel of the sphere. An object that can be modified in this way is called a parametric object. Parameters can be changed during creation or from the Modifier panel of the object.

Parent object: Parent objects in a hierarchy control one or more child objects and, sometimes, other parent objects.

Path Animation: Path animation is used to create 2D and 3D animation in which an object travels on pre-defined paths of straight lines, curves, or both.

Personality: Personality refers to combining character animation principles to create realistic digital characters. No two characters behave or perform actions similarly. The personality of each character is unique and distinct.

Phoneme: Phoneme poses are used in the process of lip synchronization. These are lip movements formed to produce specific sounds while forming words. The muscles of only the lips and the cheeks are used. A sound track is broken down to phonemes before creating various phoneme poses for the character.

Physiology: Physiology is the science of the structure of organic bodies and their functions.

Pivot: A pivot forms the center point of an object. It also functions as a connecting point between child and parent objects. A modifier uses this point to translate an object.

Plane Angle Manipulator: The Plane Angle manipulator looks like a lever or joystick. It enables you to create a custom control in a scene with visual feedback.

Point3 controllers: Point3 controllers manage the values of parameters or tracks.

Polygon: A polygon is a closed area in a 3D space that is defined using three or more edges connected by a surface. A polygon forms the basis of any object in 3D graphics software.

Poses: The Morpher modifier animates a base object by interpolating its targets. These targets are called poses, which store morph data.

Position controllers: Position controllers place the parameter or track on the x-, y-, or z- axis.

Primitives: Primitives are basic geometry shapes provided by 3D software. The modeling process generally involves editing and modifying a primitive object in combination with other objects and tools to create more complex geometry. For example, spheres, boxes, and cylinders are primitive objects.

R

Rendered Animation: Rendered animation is a sequential arrangement of graphics in motion that cannot be created in real time. Rendered animation is created in a program dedicated to animation.

Rendering: Rendering is a term used to define the process of creating bit-mapped images of objects from 3D views, similar to taking sequential pictures of a scene using a camera. While rendering, the software regathers information about an object's location in z depth, color, opacity, shininess, and light and uses this information to produce the final output.

Reset All Bones option: It resets all vertex weights back to the original weights calculated for all the bones' envelopes.

Reset Selected Bone option: It resets the associated vertex weights back to the original weights calculated for a selected bone's envelopes.

Reset Selected Vertices option: It resets the weight of selected vertices to the envelope defaults. Use this to reset weights, if necessary, after manually changing the vertex weight.

Rigging: Rigging is a process in which the character mesh is attached with the skeleton framework created with hierarchy of bone or bonelike linked object. This is a link between the character model and the skeleton hierarchy.

Rigid Patch Handles (All) option: On a patch model, it forces the patch handle weights to equal the knots weights.

Root object: The root object is located at the top of the hierarchy.

Rotation controllers: Rotation controllers manage the rotation angle of the object or parameter.

S

Scale controllers: Scale controllers manage the size of the object or parameter.

Scale origin slider: This can be moved during scale value operations as a reference point for scaling.

Secondary Action: A secondary action occurs as a result of another action. For example, when a beetle walks, its antennae sway rhythmically. Secondary action adds more realism to the overall scene, but overdoing it may work against the objective.

Show All Envelopes option: It displays all envelopes at the same time.

Show All Gizmos option: It displays all the gizmos in addition to the currently selected gizmo.

Show All Vertices option: It draws a small check at every vertex and draws all the handles on a patch surface.

Show Colored Faces option: It displays colored faces in viewports, according to their weights.

Show Colored Vertices option: It displays colored vertices in viewports, according to their weights.

Show No Envelopes option: It displays none of the envelopes even when an envelope is selected.

Single-track controllers: Single-track controllers control a single track and manage a single value.

Skeleton: A skeleton is a structure design used in character animation. It is created using several hierarchies of links objects or bones to support the model and provide motion.

Skin modifier: A skeletal deformation tool that is useful for creating skin to surround a bones system.

Slider Manipulator: The Slider manipulator is a graphic control that is used to create a custom control in a scene for a specific object with visual feedback.

SphereGizmo: SphereGizmo creates a sphere-shaped gizmo in the scene.

Spline IK solver: Spline IK solver is a process that uses splines to control the movements of bone hierarchies.

Sprite Animation: Sprite animation uses sprites, which are small files that control objects such as graphics, buttons, or text, and render them in real time.

Squash and Stretch: Squash and Stretch is used to deform an object in the course of a movement. The degree of rigidity of an object can be determined by the way it deforms while in motion. The most obvious use of Squash and Stretch in character animation is in muscles. A muscle squashes when it is contracted, and stretches when it is extended.

Squint-Eyed: When an eye turns abnormally from the line of sight of the other eye, it is called a squint-eye. To prevent this in facial animation, a single target is set to rotate both the eyes in the same direction.

Staging: Actions of characters are presented using staging. Viewers should be aware of events as they occur. For example, you may have a sad character hunched over with arms hanging at the sides. You can not add a grin to the character's face because it will not suit the rest of the pose.

Stop Frame: The stop frame is a technique in which static objects appear to move.

Storyboard: A storyboard is a pictorial outline that helps visualize animation by mapping the movement in each scene.

Subtree: Subtree represents all the objects below the selected parent object in a hierarchy.

T

Time ruler: This can be increased to measure the keys against time.

Time slide: It is a scrollable bar that is part of the Time controller.

Timing: Timing is perhaps the most important principle of character animation. The speed at which an object moves and travels gives a sense of what the object is and why it is moving. For example, the speed or frequency of a character blinking its eyes conveys the emotional and mental state of the character.

Track View: Track View can perform a variety of scene management and animation control tasks.

Transform controllers: Transform controllers manage multiple values such as position, rotation, or scale, in one step.

U

Update on mouse up option: It helps to keep the workflow moving quickly by avoiding unnecessary updates. When the mouse button is pressed, no updates take place. When the mouse button is released, updates occur.

UVW Coordinate: The UVW coordinate system is used by 3ds max while assigning textures to objects. Texture maps are 2D planes. The location and orientation of such maps is described using a UVW coordinate system. It parallels the relative direction X, Y, and Z coordinate system in 3D space. U is the equivalent of X representing the horizontal plane. V is the equivalent of Y representing the vertical plane. W is the equivalent of Z and is perpendicular to the UV plane, because Z is perpendicular to the XY plane.

V

Volume Fog: Volume Fog provides more control over the exact position of the fog.

W

Weight Properties option: It enables you to define and remove weight values from the vertices of the skin, which decide how closely to follow the movement of the bone.

Weights: It is a value that is used to set the relative influence of multiple follow objects or end effectors and their priority in solving an IK solution.

Bibliography

- http://www.maxhelp.com (February 10, 2004)
- http://www.hash.com (February 10, 2004)
- http://www.discreet.com/docs/products/3dsmax/3dsmax6_techspec.pdf (February 10, 2004)
- http://www.siggraph.org/education/materials/HyperGraph/animation/character_animation/principles/prin_trad_anim.htm (February 10, 2004)
- http://home.comcast.net/~harrymott/principles.html (February 10, 2004)
- http://www.miralab.unige.ch/5teaching/assdb/htmls/StudentFiles/Cours_3DSMax/A03_Trackview.pdf (February 10, 2004)
- http://www.worldof3d.com/resources/docs/Designer/anim_controller.htm (February 10, 2004)
- http://www.digimation.com/software/asp/product.asp?product_id=234&category_id=1 (February 10, 2004)
- http://www.3dcafe.com/asp/tutorials/maya/charactermodeling/charactermodeling.asp (February 10, 2004)
- http://asifa.net/israel/pixelsandlead-part2.html (February 10, 2004)
- http://www.webreference.com/3d/ (February 10, 2004)

Index

A

Active Option, 6.21
Adjust Pivot Rollout, 4.15, 6.4, 6.5, 6.61
Adjust Transform rollout, 6.5
Affect Hierarchy Only, 6.6, 6.7
Affect Object Only, 6.6, 6.7
Affect Pivot Only, 4.15, 6.5, 6.6, 6.7, 6.61
Align to Object, 6.7
Align to Pivot, 6.7
Align to World, 6.7
Alignment Group, 6.7, 6.61
Amplify, 2.48
Animation, 1.1, 1.3, 1.4, 1.6, 1.7, 1.8, 1.10, 1.11, 1.13, 1.18, 1.20, 1.21, 1.22, 1.23, 1.24, 1.25, 1.39, 1.50, 2.1, 2.11, 2.41, 3.1, 3.3, 3.7, 3.12, 3.15, 3.16, 3.20, 3.28, 3.30, 3.33, 3.34, 3.45, 3.47, 3.48, 3.51, 3.62, 3.67, 3.74, 3.84, 3.87, 3.88, 3.89, 4.1, 4.6, 4.9, 4.12, 4.25, 4.63, 4.75, 5.1, 5.5, 5.69, 6.17, 6.24, 6.30, 6.56, 6.62, 6.66, 8.8, 8.26
Anticipation, 1.13, 1.16
Appeal, 1.18, 1.19
Auto key, 1.48, 3.15, 3.16, 3.30

B

Basic Mouth Position, 8.33
Bezier, 2.28, 3.18, 3.47, 6.29
Bone, 4.9, 4.10, 4.12, 4.19, 4.70, 5.62, 5.63, 5.64, 5.65, 5.66, 6.13, 6.27, 6.46, 6.60, 7.9, 7.13, 7.14, 7.26, 7.27
Bulge Angle Deformer, 7.10, 7.29, 7.36

C

Center to Object, 4.16, 6.7
Center to Pivot, 6.7
Claymation, 1.5
Controller Window, 2.14, 2.16, 2.17, 2.24, 2.30, 2.35, 2.41, 2.42, 2.43, 2.57
Current, 1.20, 1.24, 1.25, 3.37, 3.71
Curve Editor, 2.1, 2.10, 2.11, 2.12, 2.13, 2.14, 2.15, 2.19, 2.20, 2.22, 2.32, 2.34, 2.35, 2.36, 2.37, 2.38, 2.39, 2.40, 2.41, 2.46, 2.48, 2.56, 2.63

D

Deformation, 7.21, 7.23, 7.28, 7.35
Display Rollout, 5.66, 7.5

E

Edges, 4.59, 5.17, 5.32, 5.80, 5.90
Edit Window, 2.14, 2.15, 2.16, 2.17, 2.19, 2.20, 2.22, 2.34, 2.35, 2.42
Element, 5.57
End Effector Display Group, 6.11
Envelopes Option, 7.43, 7.44
Exaggeration, 1.13, 1.14, 8.4
Expression, 8.3, 8.4, 8.28, 8.33, 8.41
Expression Morphs, 8.33
Eye Movement, 8.3, 8.4

F

Faces, 5.51, 5.85, 7.5

Facial Expression, 8.7, 8.35

Fins, 4.10, 5.64, 5.65, 5.67

Float Controllers, 3.3, 3.53

Follow Through, 1.16

Forward Kinematics, 4.5, 4.67, 6.1, 6.3, 6.7, 6.46, 6.49

Frame, 1.5, 1.20, 1.21, 1.22, 1.23, 1.24, 1.25, 1.41, 1.42, 1.43, 1.44, 1.45, 1.46, 2.6, 2.8, 2.26, 2.53, 3.60, 3.61, 3.84, 4.75, 6.36, 6.37, 6.38, 8.29, 8.30, 8.31, 8.32, 8.44, 8.45, 8.46, 8.47

From and To Spinners, 6.20, 6.21

G

Goal Display Group, 6.11

H

Head Movement, 8.3, 8.35

Hierarchy, 2.43, 4.3, 4.4, 4.7, 4.9, 4.13, 4.15, 4.16, 4.18, 4.19, 4.79, 4.80, 5.61, 6.4, 6.22, 6.33, 6.46, 6.56, 6.61

Hierarchy Panel, 4.7, 4.15, 4.18, 4.79, 6.61

High-res, 5.3, 5.68, 5.70

HSDS, 5.4

I

IK, 1.6, 1.9, 4.6, 4.7, 4.12, 4.25, 4.26, 4.27, 4.67, 4.77, 5.63, 5.65, 6.1, 6.3, 6.4, 6.8, 6.9, 6.10, 6.11, 6.12, 6.14, 6.21, 6.22, 6.23, 6.24, 6.25, 6.26, 6.27, 6.28, 6.29, 6.30, 6.32, 6.46, 6.47, 6.49, 6.58, 6.61, 6.62, 6.63, 6.69, 6.70, 7.23, 7.26, 7.40, 7.42

IK Goal, 6.9, 6.61, 6.63

IK Solver Display Group, 6.12

IK Solver Rollout, 6.9, 6.10, 6.21

Inverse Kinematics, 1.9, 1.31, 4.6, 4.67, 6.1, 6.3, 6.8, 6.23, 6.31, 6.46

J

Joint Angle Deformer, 7.10, 7.28, 7.36

K

Keyframe, 1.6, 1.7, 1.10, 1.31

L

Limited option, 6.21

Link Info, 4.18

Linked, 4.13, 4.17, 4.81, 6.69

Lip Synchronization, 8.34

Low-res, 5.3

M

Manipulator, 4.42, 4.43, 4.44, 4.45, 4.68, 6.10, 6.13, 6.46

Menu bar, 2.14

Modes, 2.15, 2.48, 3.23

Modifier, 3.27, 4.22, 5.11, 5.29, 5.46, 5.52, 5.54, 5.64, 5.74, 5.75, 5.76, 5.94, 5.97, 5.103, 7.1, 7.3, 7.4, 7.11, 7.14, 7.16, 7.25, 7.43, 8.17, 8.19, 8.24, 8.39, 8.41

Morph Channel, 8.42, 8.43, 8.44, 8.46

Morpher, 8.1, 8.17, 8.18, 8.24, 8.25, 8.32, 8.36, 8.38, 8.39, 8.41, 8.42

Motion Panel, 3.4, 3.5, 3.6, 3.12, 3.13, 3.15, 3.17, 3.18, 3.20, 3.21, 3.22, 3.30, 3.35, 3.45, 3.47, 3.53, 3.57, 3.58, 3.59, 3.61, 3.75, 3.77, 3.85, 6.12, 6.21, 6.24, 6.25, 8.14

Move, 1.26, 1.36, 1.37, 1.39, 1.41, 1.42, 1.43, 1.44, 1.45, 1.48, 2.7, 2.16, 2.25, 2.26, 2.31, 2.38, 2.54, 2.58, 3.15, 3.23, 3.24, 3.30, 3.51, 3.57, 3.59, 3.63, 3.88, 4.15, 4.18, 4.36, 4.65, 4.80, 4.81, 6.5, 6.6, 6.14, 6.29, 6.30, 6.34, 6.35, 6.36, 6.37, 6.38, 6.39, 6.41, 6.42, 6.43, 7.29, 8.23, 8.44, 8.45, 8.46

Move/Rotate/Scale Group, 6.6

MultiRes, 5.46, 5.54, 5.55, 5.57, 5.58, 5.59, 5.60, 5.68, 5.88, 5.89, 5.94, 5.95, 5.97, 5.99, 5.110

N

NURBS Modeling, 5.4

O

Overlapping, 1.13, 1.16

P

Parameter Wiring, 6.17, 6.19, 6.66, 6.67, 6.68

Parameters Rollout, 1.47, 3.8, 3.47, 3.57, 3.58, 3.59, 3.66, 3.67, 3.71, 3.74, 4.10, 4.31, 4.32, 4.33, 4.37, 4.40, 4.41, 4.43, 4.45, 4.51, 4.58, 4.59, 4.60, 4.61, 4.66, 4.70, 4.75, 5.49, 5.54, 6.17, 6.21, 6.25, 6.30, 6.65, 6.66, 7.4, 7.6, 7.8, 7.12, 7.16, 7.22, 7.23, 7.25, 7.27, 7.29, 7.30, 7.31, 7.33, 7.36, 7.38, 7.42, 7.43, 7.45, 8.39

Parent Space, 6.9

Patch Modeling, 5.68

Path, 1.6, 1.8, 1.9, 1.10, 1.31, 3.1, 3.12, 3.28, 3.34, 3.37, 3.38, 3.45, 3.46, 3.47, 3.48, 3.56, 3.63, 3.66, 3.67, 3.74, 3.75, 3.76, 3.85, 3.86, 3.87, 3.88, 3.89

Phoneme, 8.33, 8.34, 8.36, 8.38

Pick Target, 6.9

Pivot, 4.15, 4.16, 6.4, 6.5, 6.6, 6.7, 6.61

Pivot Group, 6.7

Playback, 1.20, 1.21, 1.22, 1.23, 1.24

Polygon, 5.12, 5.13, 5.14, 5.28, 5.29, 5.32, 5.34, 5.35, 5.38, 5.39, 5.40, 5.46, 5.68, 5.88, 5.92, 5.93, 5.94, 5.95, 5.99

Polygon Modeling, 5.68

Position Controllers, 3.3, 3.15, 3.53

Primitives, 7.23, 7.39

Principle, 1.14, 1.18, 8.4, 8.38

R

Rendering, 3.26, 4.11, 5.3, 7.9

Rigging, 5.61

Rotate, 1.9, 1.26, 1.27, 1.38, 1.39, 1.49, 3.60, 4.15, 4.38, 6.6

Rotation Controllers, 3.4, 3.53

S

Scale, 1.25, 1.26, 1.27, 1.28, 2.16, 2.48, 3.4, 3.7, 3.8, 3.14, 3.23, 3.24, 3.30, 3.31, 3.32, 3.53, 3.64, 4.12, 4.15, 5.43, 5.67, 5.106, 6.6

Scale Controllers, 3.4, 3.53

Seamless, 5.58, 5.59

Secondary Action, 1.17

Segmented, 5.58, 5.59

Select and Link Button, 4.8, 6.56, 6.57

Skeleton, 6.59, 7.11

Skin Modifier, 4.19, 4.22, 4.23, 4.67, 4.70, 7.25, 7.43, 7.45

Speech Morph, 8.33

Spring Back, 6.21

Spring Back (spinner), 6.21

Sprite, 1.10

Squash, 1.13, 1.28, 1.29, 1.47, 1.51, 2.63, 7.15

Staging, 1.18, 8.4

Start Joint, 6.9

Stop Frame, 1.3, 1.5, 1.31

Storyboarding, 1.1, 1.10

Stretch, 1.13, 1.28, 4.12, 5.67

Swivel Angle, 6.9, 6.10, 6.11

Swivel Angle Manipulator Group, 6.11

Symmetry, 5.31, 5.46, 5.52, 5.53, 5.68, 5.71, 5.72, 5.73, 5.74, 5.75, 5.76, 5.77, 5.88, 5.110

T

Target Poses, 8.17, 8.24, 8.26, 8.44

Three-dimensional, 1.31

Time, 1.20, 1.22, 1.23, 1.24, 1.31, 1.36, 2.6, 2.8, 2.10, 2.14, 2.18, 2.19, 2.35, 3.9, 3.11, 3.14, 3.15, 3.21, 3.22, 3.23, 3.24, 3.27, 3.30, 3.41, 4.75, 4.81, 6.34, 6.45, 7.29

Time Ruler, 2.18

Time Slider, 1.20, 4.81, 6.34, 6.45

Timing, 1.13, 1.17, 6.32

Track, 1.20, 1.21, 1.25, 2.1, 2.3, 2.10, 2.11, 2.13, 2.14, 2.15, 2.17, 2.20, 2.22, 2.32, 2.34, 2.35, 2.36, 2.38, 2.40, 2.46, 2.56, 2.62, 3.4, 3.21, 3.22, 3.23, 3.25, 3.26, 3.27, 3.28, 3.29, 3.30, 3.31, 3.32, 3.45, 3.47, 3.53, 3.54, 3.59, 3.64, 6.18, 6.62, 6.66, 8.32, 8.45, 8.46, 8.47

Track view, 3.45, 6.62, 6.66

Trajectories, 3.4, 3.12, 3.13, 3.53, 3.59

Transform Controllers, 3.4, 3.53

Two-dimensional, 1.31

V

Vertex, 4.65, 5.8, 5.9, 5.27, 5.32, 5.33, 5.36, 5.43, 5.44, 5.47, 5.48, 5.54, 5.55, 5.56, 5.103, 6.30, 7.5, 7.6, 7.7, 7.9, 7.16, 7.17, 7.27, 7.28, 7.35, 7.36, 8.33